DEPARTMENT OF ECONOMIC AND SOCIAL AFFAIRS
POPULATION DIVISION

World Population Policies 2009

United Nations
New York, 2010

DESA

The Department of Economic and Social Affairs of the United Nations Secretariat is a vital interface between global policies in the economic, social and environmental spheres and national action. The Department works in three main interlinked areas: (i) it compiles, generates and analyses a wide range of economic, social and environmental data and information on which States Members of the United Nations draw to review common problems and take stock of policy options; (ii) it facilitates the negotiations of Member States in many intergovernmental bodies on joint courses of action to address ongoing or emerging global challenges; and (iii) it advises interested Governments on the ways and means of translating policy frameworks developed in United Nations conferences and summits into programmes at the country level and, through technical assistance, helps build national capacities.

Note

ST/ESA/SER.A/293

UNITED NATIONS PUBLICATION
Sales No. E.09.XIII.14
ISBN 978-92-1-151467-4

PREFACE

This report delineates Governments' views and policies concerning population and development for 195 countries. In particular, it itemizes policies in the areas of population size and growth, population age structure, fertility and family planning, health and mortality, spatial distribution and internal migration, and international migration. Previous editions of *World Population Policies* were issued as *World Population Policies 2007* (Sales No. E.08.XIII.8), *World Population Policies 2005* (Sales No. E.06.XIII.5) and *World Population Policies 2003* (Sales No. E.04.XIII.3). Prior to 2003, the publication was issued as *National Population Policies 2001* (Sales No. E.02.XIII.12*)* and *National Population Policies 1998 (*Sales No. E.99.XIII.3). Before 1998, the data were published as the *Global Review and Inventory of Population Policies (GRIPP).*

All the United Nations international population conferences held since 1974 have emphasized monitoring the implementation of their goals and recommendations. In particular, the International Conference on Population and Development held at Cairo in 1994 recommended that actions be taken "to measure, assess, monitor and evaluate progress towards meeting the goals of its Programme of Action".[1]

The Population Division of the Department of Economic and Social Affairs of the United Nations Secretariat is responsible for providing the international community with up-to-date, accurate and scientifically objective information on population and development. The Population Division provides guidance to the United Nations General Assembly, the Economic and Social Council, and the Commission on Population and Development on population and development issues. In addition, the Division undertakes studies on population levels and trends, population estimates and projections, population policies, and population and development interrelationships. The monitoring of population policies at the international level began after the World Population Plan of Action[2] was adopted at the World Population Conference held at Bucharest in 1974. The Plan of Action, the first global intergovernmental instrument on population policy, called upon the United Nations to monitor national population policies.

Responsibility for *World Population Policies 2009* rests with the Population Division. Preparation of this publication was facilitated by the cooperation of Member States and non-member States of the United Nations, the regional commissions, and the agencies, funds and programmes of the United Nations system. The Population Division is particularly grateful to the Statistics Division of the Department of Economic and Social Affairs for its continuing cooperation.

The data presented in this publication are also being released in electronic form on a CD-ROM. An order form is included in this volume. This publication, as well as other population information, may be accessed on the Population Division website at: http://www.unpopulation.org.

Questions and comments concerning this publication may be addressed to the Office of the Director, Population Division, Department of Economic and Social Affairs, United Nations Secretariat, New York, NY 10017, fax number 212-963-2147.

---

[1] *Report of the International Conference on Population and Development, Cairo, 5-13 September 1994 (*United Nations publication, Sales No. E.95.XIII.18), chap. I, resolution 1, annex, para. 13.6.

[2] *Report of the United Nations World Population Conference, Bucharest, 19-30 August 1974* (United Nations publication, Sales No. E.75.XIII.3), chap. I.

CONTENTS

Page

TABLES

United Nations Department of Economic and Social Affairs/Population Division

Page

PART TWO. COUNTRY PROFILES

EXPLANATORY NOTES

World Population Policies 2009 provides information on 195 countries, including all 192 Member States and three non-member States (Cook Islands, Holy See and Niue) of the United Nations.

Countries and areas are grouped geographically into six major areas: Africa; Asia; Europe; Latin America and the Caribbean; Northern America; and Oceania. Those major areas are further divided geographically into 21 regions. In addition, the regions are classified as belonging, for statistical convenience, to either of two general groups: more developed and less developed regions. The less developed regions include all regions of Africa, Asia (excluding Japan), Latin America and the Caribbean, Melanesia, Micronesia and Polynesia. The more developed regions comprise Northern America and Europe and the following countries: Australia, Japan and New Zealand.

The group of least developed countries currently comprises 49 countries: Afghanistan, Angola, Bangladesh, Benin, Bhutan, Burkina Faso, Burundi, Cambodia, Central African Republic, Chad, Comoros, Democratic Republic of the Congo, Djibouti, Equatorial Guinea, Eritrea, Ethiopia, the Gambia, Guinea, Guinea-Bissau, Haiti, Kiribati, Lao People's Democratic Republic, Lesotho, Liberia, Madagascar, Malawi, Maldives, Mali, Mauritania, Mozambique, Myanmar, Nepal, Niger, Rwanda, Samoa, Sao Tome and Principe, Senegal, Sierra Leone, Solomon Islands, Somalia, Sudan, Timor-Leste, Togo, Tuvalu, Uganda, the United Republic of Tanzania, Vanuatu, Yemen and Zambia.

Symbols of United Nations documents are composed of capital letters combined with figures.

Various symbols have been used in the tables throughout this report, as follows:

Two dots (..) indicate that data are not available or are not separately reported.

A hyphen (-) indicates that the item is not applicable.

A minus sign (-) before a figure indicates a decrease.

A full stop (.) is used to indicate decimals.

Years given begin with 1 July.

Use of a hyphen (-) between years, for example, 2005-2010, signifies the full period involved, from 1 July of the beginning year to 1 July of the end year.

Percentages in tables and figures do not necessarily add to 100 per cent because of rounding.

World Population Policies 2009 uses estimates and projections of demographic indicators from the most recent *2008 Revision of World Population Prospects*. This may result in minor discrepancies from *World Population Policies 2007* that used the *2006 Revision of World Population Prospects*.

For any newly-formed States, Government views and policies are not available for previous time points, but estimates of population indicators are provided using the *2008 World Population Prospects*.

INTRODUCTION

All the United Nations international population conferences held since 1974 have emphasized the need to monitor the implementation of their goals and recommendations. Thus, the International Conference on Population and Development (ICPD) held at Cairo in 1994 recommended that actions be taken "to measure, assess, monitor and evaluate progress towards meeting the goals" of its Programme of Action.[1]

The overriding goal of the ICPD Programme of Action, to improve human welfare and promote sustainable development, is fully consistent with the internationally agreed development goals, including the Millennium Development Goals (MDGs) contained in the Millennium Declaration of 2000.[2] Some goals in the Programme of Action are identical to the MDGs, including those pertaining to the reduction of child mortality, the improvement of maternal health and the achievement of universal primary education (United Nations, 2005).

The Population Division of the United Nations Department of Economic and Social Affairs is responsible for global monitoring of the implementation of the Programme of Action adopted by the 1994 ICPD, as it was for that of the World Population Plan of Action of the 1974 World Population Conference. In carrying out this task, it adhered to the principles of objectivity and neutrality. Reports on advances made in the implementation of the Programme of Action have been descriptive and concise, focusing on analytical comparisons among countries and regions over time.

This report is part of the effort of the Population Division to disseminate the information resulting from its monitoring activities. It provides an overview of population policies and dynamics for the 195 countries for which data referring to the middle of the 1970s, 1980s and 1990s decades are available — that is, data relate approximately to the times in which the United Nations population conferences were convened at Bucharest, Mexico City and Cairo — as well as for 2009.

Successive monitoring reports have documented significant changes since 1974 in government views on population issues as well as in the formulation, implementation and evaluation of population policy. Monitoring itself contributes to such evolution by increasing global awareness of population and development issues and the need for appropriate and timely policy responses.

Types of population policy questions addressed

The basic information relative to the monitoring of population policies encompasses three basic components. They are listed below together with the types of questions used to elicit the views of Governments.

Government views on population size and growth, population age structure and spatial distribution, and on the demographic components — fertility, mortality and migration — that affect them: For each variable, the following questions were posed to Governments: Is the level or trend viewed as a significant policy issue? Is the prevailing level or rate of change considered too high, too low, acceptable or satisfactory in relation to other social and economic conditions?

Government objectives with respect to each variable: Is the objective of the Government to raise or to lower the level of the variable or to maintain its current level?

Government policies concerning interventions to influence each variable: Does the Government consider intervention to alter levels and trends as a legitimate exercise of its authority? Has the Government actively intervened to influence the variable?

---

[1] *Report of the International Conference on Population and Development, Cairo, 5-13 September 1994 (*United Nations publication, Sales No. E.95.XIII.18), chap. I, resolution 1, annex, para. 13.6.
[2] General Assembly Resolution, A/RES/55/2.

Major sources of information

In order to compile the requisite information for monitoring the implementation of the World Population Plan of Action and later the ICPD Programme of Action, the Population Division established the Population Policy Data Bank. The major sources of information contained in the Data Bank are of four broad types (see box 1).

The first type of information comprises official government responses to the *United Nations Inquiry among Governments on Population and Development*, of which there have been ten separate rounds since 1963. The first and second rounds of the Inquiry were conducted prior to the 1974 World Population Conference. The eighth Inquiry, the first directed towards the ICPD Programme of Action, was initiated in 1997. The Ninth Inquiry was sent to Governments in 2003. The Tenth Inquiry was sent to Governments in 2008. Each round of the Inquiry has consisted of a detailed request for information sent to all Member States and non-member States of the United Nations.

The second type of information consists of publications, documents, statements and other materials issued by Governments, including development plans, laws, regulations and proclamations. These materials are a particularly important source of data because they reflect the official positions taken by Governments.

The third category of information consists of materials provided by international organizations, such as regional commissions, funds, programmes and agencies of the United Nations system, as well as other regional intergovernmental organizations. Because countries collectively are the source of these materials, an official status is attached to them.

The fourth type of information consists of non-governmental materials, including clippings from the world press, articles in academic journals, proceedings of conferences and seminars, reports and studies prepared by research centres and non-governmental organizations, as well as correspondence and personal communications with experts.

Organization of the report

The report is divided into two parts. Part One provides a global perspective on the evolution of selected aspects of population policies between 1976 and 2009 with respect to each of the major population variables and is based on six major topics.

The first topic is government views and policies on population size and growth. The second topic covers government views and policies on the changing age distribution of population. The third topic is government views and policies on fertility, family planning and adolescent fertility. Government views and policies on health and mortality, including life expectancy at birth, child mortality and maternal mortality and the HIV/AIDS epidemic are included in the fourth topic. The fifth topic covers government views and policies on the spatial distribution of population and internal migration. The sixth and last topic reviews government views and policies on international migration, including permanent and temporary migration, family reunification and migration of skilled workers.

Special attention is given to the reduction of child mortality, improvement of maternal health and government responses to the HIV/AIDS epidemic due to their importance in achieving the health-related MDGs. This chapter also provides useful information for the forty-third session of the United Nations Commission on Population and Development (12 to 16 April 2010) whose special theme was "Health, morbidity, mortality and development" and to the High-level Plenary Meeting of the sixty-fifth session of the General Assembly (20-22 September 2010), which will focus on accelerating progress towards the achievement of the MDGs by 2015 (resolution A/64/L.36). The grounds on which induced abortion is permitted are also examined under the fourth topic. The views and policies of Governments on emigration and the return migration of citizens are also examined. Government views and policies on international migration are also a key focus of this report in order to document how Member States have reacted to the management of international migration when faced with the ongoing global economic and financial crises.

Part Two presents for each country the evolution from 1976 to 2009 of government views and policies with respect to population size and growth, population age structure, fertility and family planning, health and mortality, the spatial distribution of the population, internal migration, and international migration. Country profiles are presented for each of the 192 Member States and three non-member States (Cook Islands, Holy See and Niue) of the United Nations. The material is presented in the form of data sheets, containing population policy information for each country referring to 1976, 1986, 1996 and 2009 or dates close to those years, as well as population indicators for those years.

The data included in this report are based on information available as of December 2009.

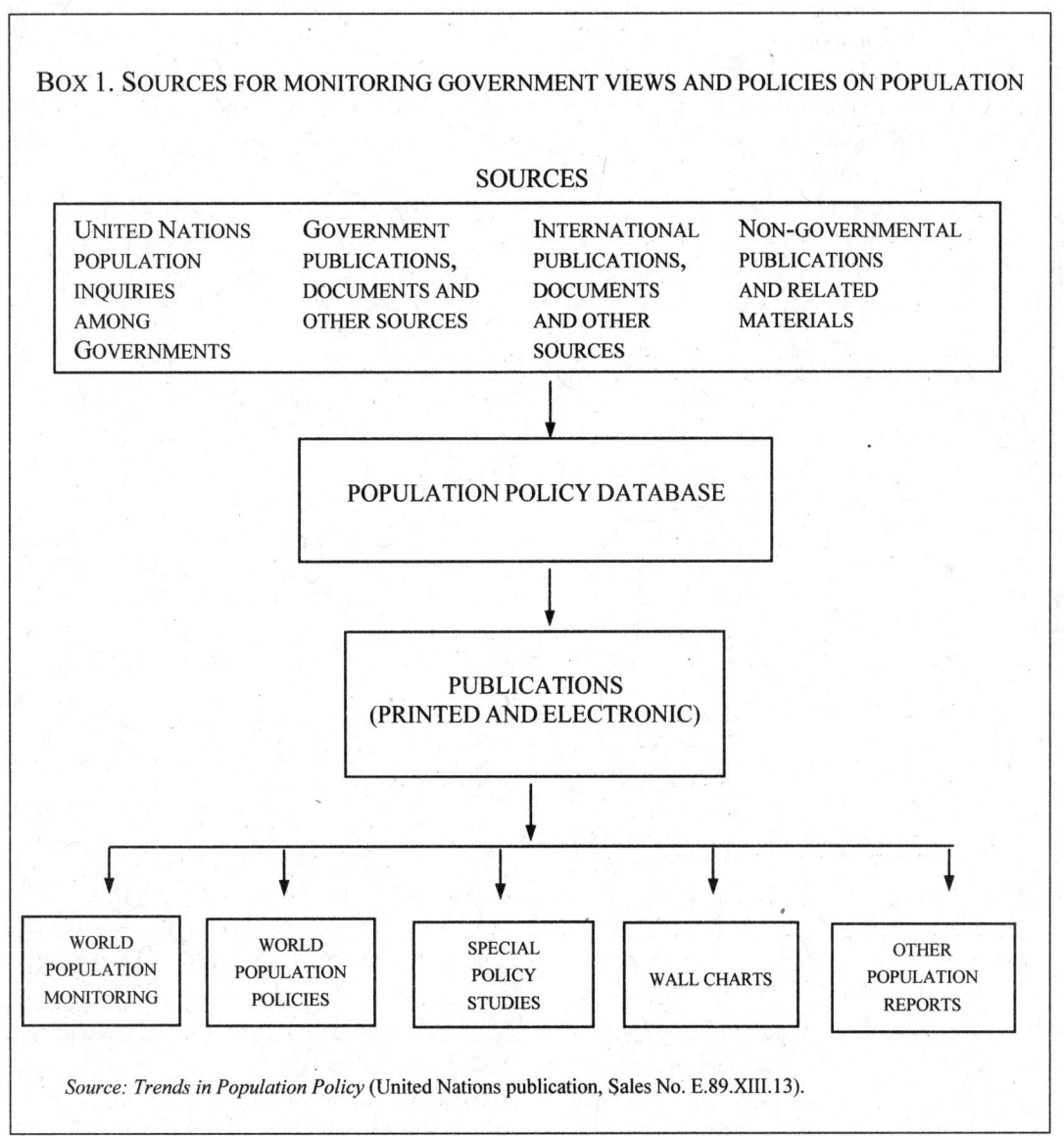

BOX 1. SOURCES FOR MONITORING GOVERNMENT VIEWS AND POLICIES ON POPULATION

SOURCES

| UNITED NATIONS POPULATION INQUIRIES AMONG GOVERNMENTS | GOVERNMENT PUBLICATIONS, DOCUMENTS AND OTHER SOURCES | INTERNATIONAL PUBLICATIONS, DOCUMENTS AND OTHER SOURCES | NON-GOVERNMENTAL PUBLICATIONS AND RELATED MATERIALS |

POPULATION POLICY DATABASE

PUBLICATIONS (PRINTED AND ELECTRONIC)

| WORLD POPULATION MONITORING | WORLD POPULATION POLICIES | SPECIAL POLICY STUDIES | WALL CHARTS | OTHER POPULATION REPORTS |

Source: Trends in Population Policy (United Nations publication, Sales No. E.89.XIII.13).

PART ONE

GOVERNMENT VIEWS AND POLICIES

I. MAJOR POPULATION CONCERNS

HIV/AIDS was the most common population concern of Governments in 2009, with 87 per cent considering it a major concern (box 2). Population ageing was the most common concern in developed countries, where 79 per cent of the Governments considered it a major concern in 2009. Other major population concerns in developed countries were HIV/AIDS, low fertility and a relatively small or declining number of persons of working age. In developing countries, 90 per cent of the Governments considered HIV/AIDS as a major concern. High infant and child mortality and high maternal mortality were the second and third most common concerns in developing countries after HIV/AIDS. Governments of developing countries were also concerned about their population of working age but mainly because they needed to create sufficient jobs for their growing working-age population.

BOX 2. MAJOR POPULATION CONCERNS OF GOVERNMENTS IN 2009:

ISSUES OF SIGNIFICANCE TO AT LEAST HALF OF ALL GOVERNMENTS IN 2009,
BY LEVEL OF DEVELOPMENT

Region and Issues	Percentage of Governments reporting it is significant
World	
HIV/AIDS	87
Infant and child mortality	70
Maternal mortality	66
Size of the population of working age	62
Adolescent fertility	57
Low life expectancy at birth	55
Population ageing	55
Pattern of spatial distribution	51
More developed regions	
Population ageing	79
HIV/AIDS	77
Low fertility	61
Size of the population of working age	59
Less developed regions	
IIIV/AIDS	90
Infant and child mortality	81
Maternal mortality	79
Adolescent fertility	65
Size of the population of working age	63
Low life expectancy at birth	62
Pattern of spatial distribution	58
High fertility	50

II. POPULATION SIZE AND GROWTH

High population growth remains a salient concern in the developing world. Many Governments in developing countries have realized the importance of reducing high rates of population growth in order to ease mounting pressure on renewable and non-renewable resources, combat climate change, prevent food shortages and provide decent employment and basic social services to all their inhabitants. Many of these Governments have also realized that effective implementation of population policy requires the creation of an institutional framework that ensures the integration of population variables into development planning with adequate mechanisms for monitoring and evaluation.

Although rates of population growth in developing countries continued to decline, from an average annual rate of 2.4 per cent in 1970-1975 to 1.4 per cent in 2005-2010 (United Nations, 2009a), nearly half of the Governments of developing countries still viewed their population growth as too high in 2009 (table 1). Among the least developed countries, the percentage of countries that viewed population growth as too high rose from 50 per cent in 1986 to 76 per cent in 2009.

Africa has the highest percentage of countries whose Governments consider their population growth as too high: 68 per cent of Governments in Africa did so in 2009, up from 35 per cent in 1976 (table 1). In Asia, where most countries have experienced substantial declines in fertility, 34 per cent of Governments view population growth as too high. Latin America and the Caribbean is the only region where the percentage of Governments that view population growth as too high has been decreasing steadily, from 48 per cent in 1986 to 21 per cent in 2009.

To a large extent, concerns about the detrimental consequences of high population growth have been translated into policy interventions. In 2009, 46 per cent of developing countries and 71 per cent of the least developed countries had policies aimed at reducing their population growth rate (table 2).

One of the most significant developments since the mid-1970s has been a continued rise in the number of Governments in Africa that reported having policies aimed at reducing the rapid growth of their respective populations: 64 per cent in 2009, up from 60 per cent in 1996, 39 per cent in 1986 and 25 per cent in 1976. Conversely, the percentage of Governments in Africa that did not intervene to influence population growth continued to decline, from 60 per cent in 1976 to 21 per cent in 2009.

In contrast to Africa, Latin America and the Caribbean has a rising percentage of Governments that did not intervene to influence the population growth rate: 52 per cent in 1996 and 61 per cent in 2009.

In developed countries, the persistence of low population growth has led to growing concerns about its consequences, such as shrinking labour force and growing proportions of the elderly. In 2009, 47 per cent of the Governments of developed countries considered their population growth to be too low, up from 18 per cent in 1986 (table 1), while the percentage of developed countries with policies aimed at raising the growth of their population climbed from 24 per cent in 1986 to 45 per cent in 2009 (table 2). All but one of the 23 developed countries whose Governments viewed their population growth as too low are in Europe. The percentage of Governments in Europe with policies aimed at raising their population growth rate increased from 28 per cent in 1986 to 48 per cent in 2009.

The changes in government views and policies described above have been matched by a slowdown in population growth in many countries. Whereas in 1970-1975, 35 countries had population growth rates of 3 per cent or more and 71 countries had growth rates ranging between 2 per cent and 3 per cent, the corresponding figures for 2000-2005 were 17 and 42, respectively (United Nations, 2009a). Nevertheless, six countries with population growth rates below 1 per cent in 2005-2010 still considered their growth rates as too high in 2009. Eight countries whose

Governments considered the rate of population growth as too high in 2009 did not have policies to influence it and seven countries whose Governments viewed population growth as too low also did not intervene. Among the 19 countries with negative population growth in 2005-2010, the Governments of 16 felt that the growth rate of their populations was too low in 2009 and 15 had implemented policies to raise it.

III. POPULATION AGE STRUCTURE

One of the inevitable consequences of the unprecedented transformation brought about by the transition from a regime of high mortality and high fertility to one of low mortality and low fertility has been population ageing. Many societies, particularly those in developed countries, have attained older population age structures than have ever existed in the past. In developed countries, 22 per cent of the population was aged 60 years or over in 2009 and in 2050, 33 per cent of the population is expected to be in that age range (United Nations, 2009b). The number of older persons in the more developed regions is already larger than the number of children under age 15, and in 2050, there will likely be two older persons for every child. Developing countries in the midst of the demographic transition have experienced rapid shifts in the proportions of children, the working age population and the population of older persons. In developing countries, the population of older persons is expected to climb from 8 per cent in 2009 to 20 per cent in 2050 (United Nations, 2009b).

In 2009, more than half of the Governments considered population ageing as a major concern (table 3, figure I). Among developed countries, 79 per cent of Governments identified population ageing as a major concern. Among developing countries, 46 per cent of Governments had a similar assessment of population ageing. In Latin America and the Caribbean, one of the major areas in the developing world where population ageing is most advanced, 70 per cent of Governments considered population ageing as a major concern (table 3).

Another important concern was the size of the working-age population, identified as such by 62 per cent of all reporting Governments (table 4). However, whereas developed countries were worried because their working age populations were small and growing slowly, if at all, developing countries were concerned about their large and rapidly growing labour force and about the challenge of providing decent jobs for all.

Figure I. Distribution of Governments according to their level of concern about population ageing, 2009

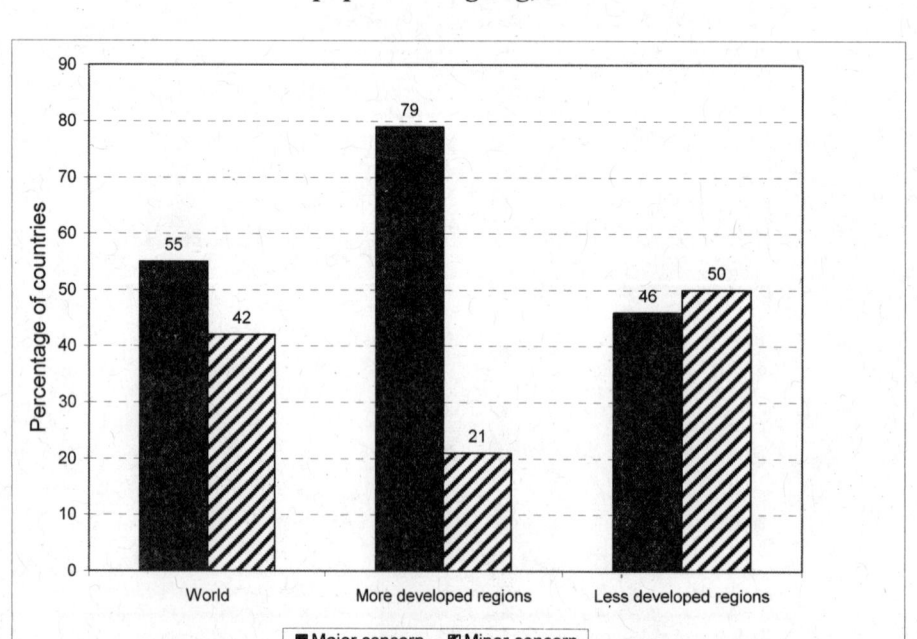

United Nations Department of Economic and Social Affairs/Population Division

Concerned by population ageing and the unsustainability of pension programmes, many Governments are modifying the parameters of those programmes, introducing mandatory fully-funded schemes, increasing the statutory retirement age, eliminating incentives for early retirement, reducing benefits and encouraging more women to enter the labour force. Thus, between 2002 and 2009, 43 countries out of the 165 having a statutory retirement age increased that age. As a result, men were eligible for full pension benefits at age 65 or over in 62 per cent of developed countries, while women were eligible for the same benefits at age 65 or over in 42 per cent of developed countries. In 24 developed countries, the statutory retirement age was higher for men than for women, although women are expected to live longer than men (United Nations, 2009c). In the European Union, half of the men in the labour force retired before age 61 and half of women before age 60 (EUROSTAT, 2007). The situation is similar in the United States of America, where more than half of working men and women opted for early retirement at an average age of 62 (Turner, 2007).

In addition, low-fertility countries have adopted family-friendly measures that support parents in combining work and parental roles. Countries with slowly growing labour force have also shown increasing willingness to rely on international migration, often of a temporary nature, to address unmet short-term labour demand.

Developing countries with high fertility are grappling with the challenge of providing decent work for their growing labour force. In 2009 there were 212 million unemployed persons, an increase of 21 per cent since 1999, and that number has continued to rise as a result of the recent economic crisis (ILO, 2010). The highest rates of unemployment and underemployment are found in the poorest countries. There is a general recognition that employment generation in developing countries requires employment-intensive economic growth combined with a coherent set of employment and human development policies.

IV. FERTILITY AND FAMILY PLANNING

The wealth of information collected on fertility trends provides evidence of the decline in fertility in most parts of the world. From 1975 to 2005, the number of countries with total fertility exceeding four children per woman decreased from 127 to 52. As a consequence, global total fertility declined from 4.3 children per woman in 1970-1975 to 2.7 children per woman in 2005-2010. For the period 2005-2010, fertility remains above five children per woman in 26 of the 150 developing countries. In contrast, fertility has reached below-replacement level in 26 developing countries (United Nations, 2009a).

Concerns of developing countries

Governments' views and policies concerning fertility have influenced the fertility decline in developing countries. In 1976, 47 per cent of Governments of the developing countries viewed their fertility as too high. This figure rose to 59 per cent in 1996. By 2009, fertility was viewed as too high in 50 per cent of developing countries, including most parts of Africa, South-central Asia and South-eastern Asia. Among the least developed countries, 86 per cent of Governments held the view that their fertility was too high in 2009 (table 5).

Figure II shows the evolution of government views on fertility in Africa. In 1976, just 38 per cent of the Governments of countries in Africa viewed fertility as too high but by 2009, 75 per cent of them did so (table 5).

While in the past Governments that considered fertility to be too high did not necessarily adopt policies to influence fertility levels, by 2009, almost all Governments of developing countries that viewed fertility as too high intervened to lower it. Governments have implemented a variety of measures to reduce fertility levels either directly or indirectly. These measures include integrating family planning and safe motherhood programmes into primary health care systems; providing access to reproductive health services; promoting the responsibility of men in sexual and reproductive health; raising the minimum legal age at marriage; improving female education and employment opportunities; discouraging son preference, and providing low-cost, safe and effective contraception.

In 1976, half of the Governments of developing countries did not intervene to modify the level of fertility and only 34 per cent intervened to lower fertility. In 2009, the percentage of developing countries lacking policies to influence fertility had fallen to 25 per cent and those having interventions to lower fertility amounted to 51 per cent (table 6, figure III).

One of the most significant developments in population policy in the wake of the 1994 International Conference on Population and Development was the increase in the number of Governments in Africa that reported having policies to reduce fertility. In 1976, 25 per cent of Governments in Africa had policies aimed at lowering fertility. By 2009, 70 per cent of Governments in the continent had interventions to promote lower fertility (table 6).

Concerns of developed countries

The persistence of low fertility was a concern for many developed countries. Fertility in developed countries as a group has been well below replacement level for some time and averaged 1.6 children per woman in 2005-2010. Whereas in 1976, only 21 per cent of Governments in developed countries felt that the fertility of their populations was too low, 61 per cent held that view in 2009 (table 5). The trend in the percentage of Governments that viewed fertility of their populations as too low was similar in Europe (figure IV).

Figure II. Governments in Africa according to their views on the level of fertility, 1976 and 2009

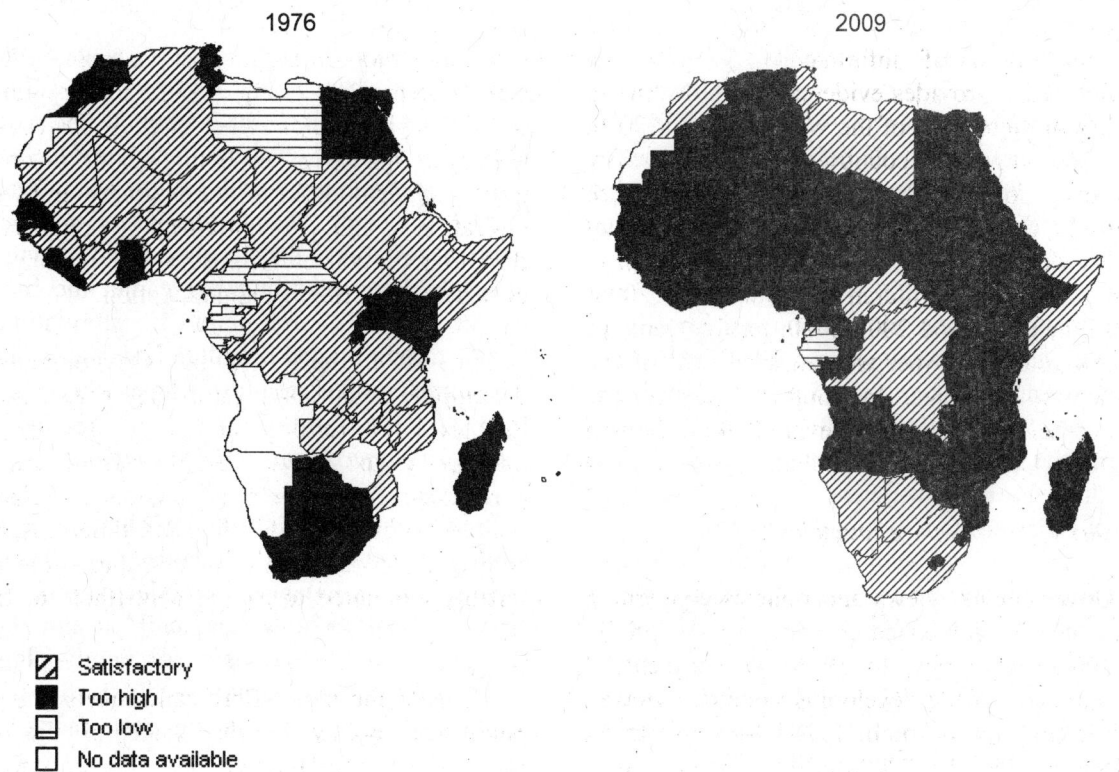

1976   2009

- ▨ Satisfactory
- ■ Too high
- ⊟ Too low
- □ No data available

Figure III. Government policies on the level of fertility, 1976, 1986, 1996 and 2009

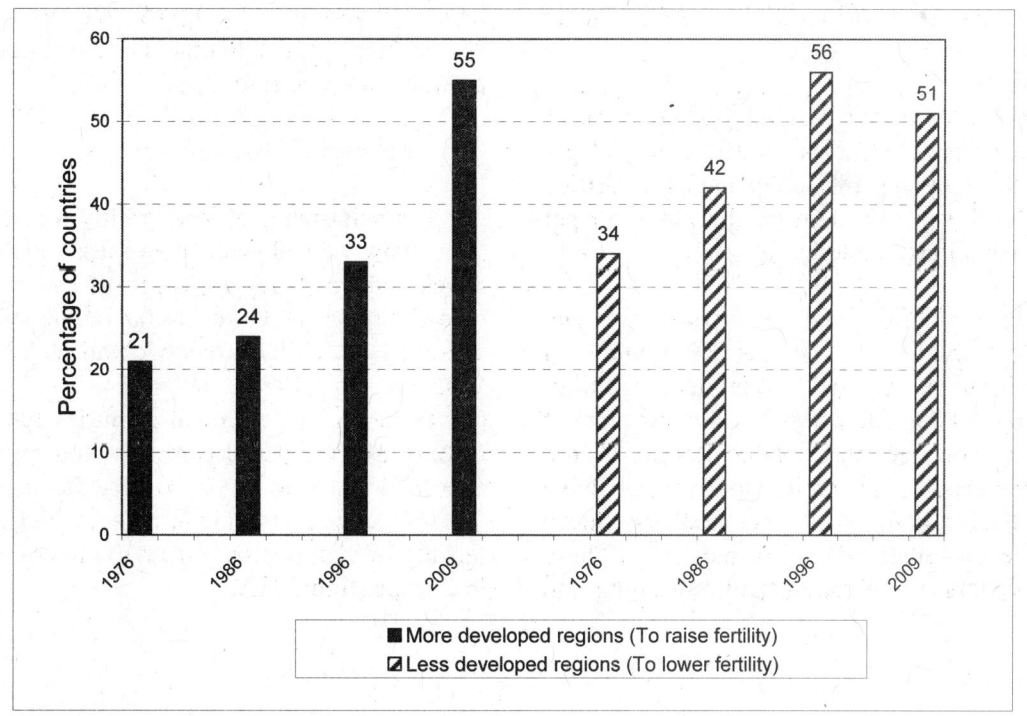

■ More developed regions (To raise fertility)
▨ Less developed regions (To lower fertility)

Among the 47 countries in the world that viewed fertility as too low in 2009, 85 per cent had policies to increase fertility. To raise fertility, Governments have used a number of measures including baby bonuses, family allowances, maternal and paternal leave, subsidized child care, tax incentives, subsidized housing, flexible work schedules, and campaigns to promote the sharing of parenting and household work between spouses.

Although a number of countries, mostly in Europe, that adopted such measures have experienced modest increases in fertility between 2000-2005 and 2005-2010 (United Nations 2009a), the evidence on the effectiveness of these measures is not sufficient to ascertain their impact. For instance, a public opinion poll conducted by the European Union's Eurobarometer in 2004 revealed that 84 per cent of the men surveyed either had not taken parental leave or did not intend to do so, even when informed of their rights (European Commission, 2004). A more recent Eurobarometer survey in

2006 confirmed that women still undertook most household work (European Commission, 2007).

In Eastern Europe, the profound economic and political changes that followed the end of the communist era were accompanied by a sharp decline in fertility, resulting in some of the lowest fertility levels in the world. Factors accounting for this trend include: "fear of the future" induced by political instability that resulted in a reluctance to have children; declining per capita income and living standards, and major transformations in family formation and dissolution (United Nations, Economic Commission for Europe, 2002).

Access to modern contraceptive methods

Government policies regarding access to modern contraceptive methods have been an important determinant of reproductive behaviour, as well as of maternal and child health. Direct support entails the provision of family planning services through Government-run facilities, such as hospitals, clinics, health posts and health

Figure IV. Governments in Europe according to their views on the level of fertility, 1976 and 2009

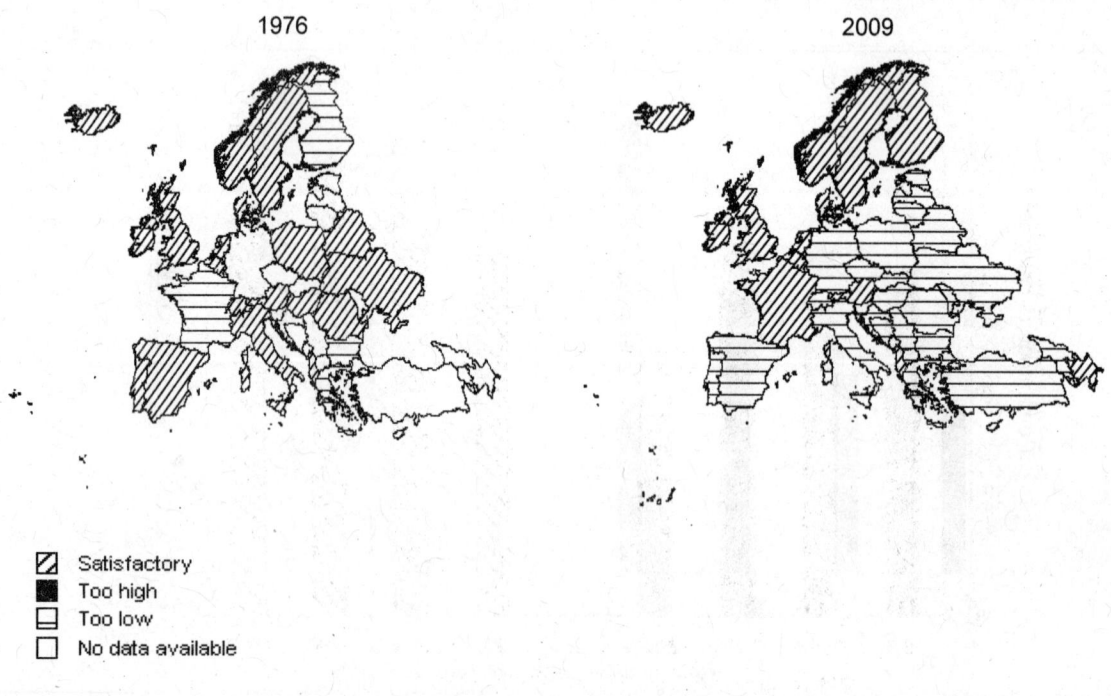

centres and through government fieldworkers. Government support for increased access to methods of contraception has steadily increased. In 2009, 91 per cent of countries supported contraceptive provision, either directly (75 per cent) or indirectly (16 per cent) by supporting non-governmental activities, such as those operated by family planning associations (table 7).

During the last three decades, most developing countries have strengthened their support for increasing access to contraceptive methods (table 7, figure V). In Africa, in 2009 only two countries did not provide support to increase access to contraceptive methods, down from 14 countries in 1976 (table 7, figure VI). Even previously pronatalist Governments, which in the past had wanted to maintain or even increase population growth, have gradually modified their stance and accepted family planning and contraception as integral components of maternal and child health programmes. Such countries include Cambodia,

Cameroon, Côte d'Ivoire, the Lao People's Democratic Republic, Oman and the United Arab Emirates.

Despite widespread government support for increasing access to contraceptives, there is evidence that demand outstrips supply, particularly in the least developed countries. Thus, an estimated 110 million women in developing countries, who are married or in union, lack ready access to safe and effective means of contraception (United Nations, 2009d).

More developed countries, particularly in Europe, have weakened their support for modern contraceptive methods, with only 39 per cent providing direct support in 2009, down from 62 per cent in 1976 (table 7, figure V). Such a change is likely a response to the low fertility levels of their populations or an acknowledgement that the private sector can meet the demand for contraception, making government subsidies less necessary.

Figure V. Percentage of Governments providing direct support to facilitate access to modern contraceptive methods, 1976, 1986, 1996 and 2009

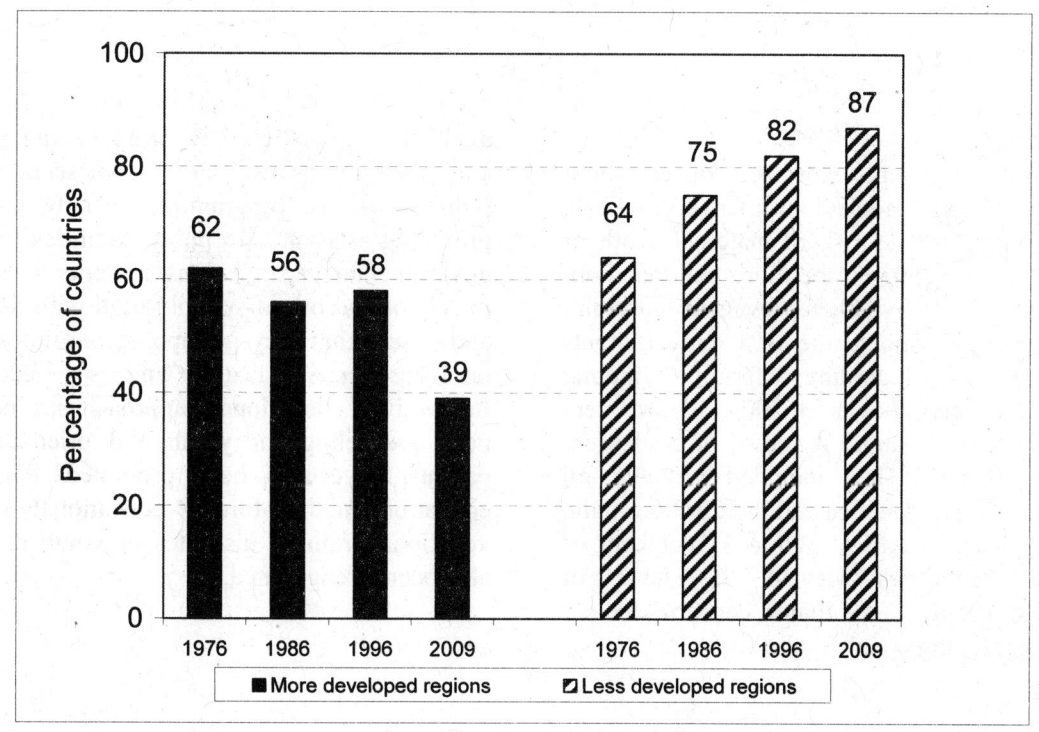

**Figure VI. Government policies on providing access to contraceptive methods,
Africa, 1976 and 2009**

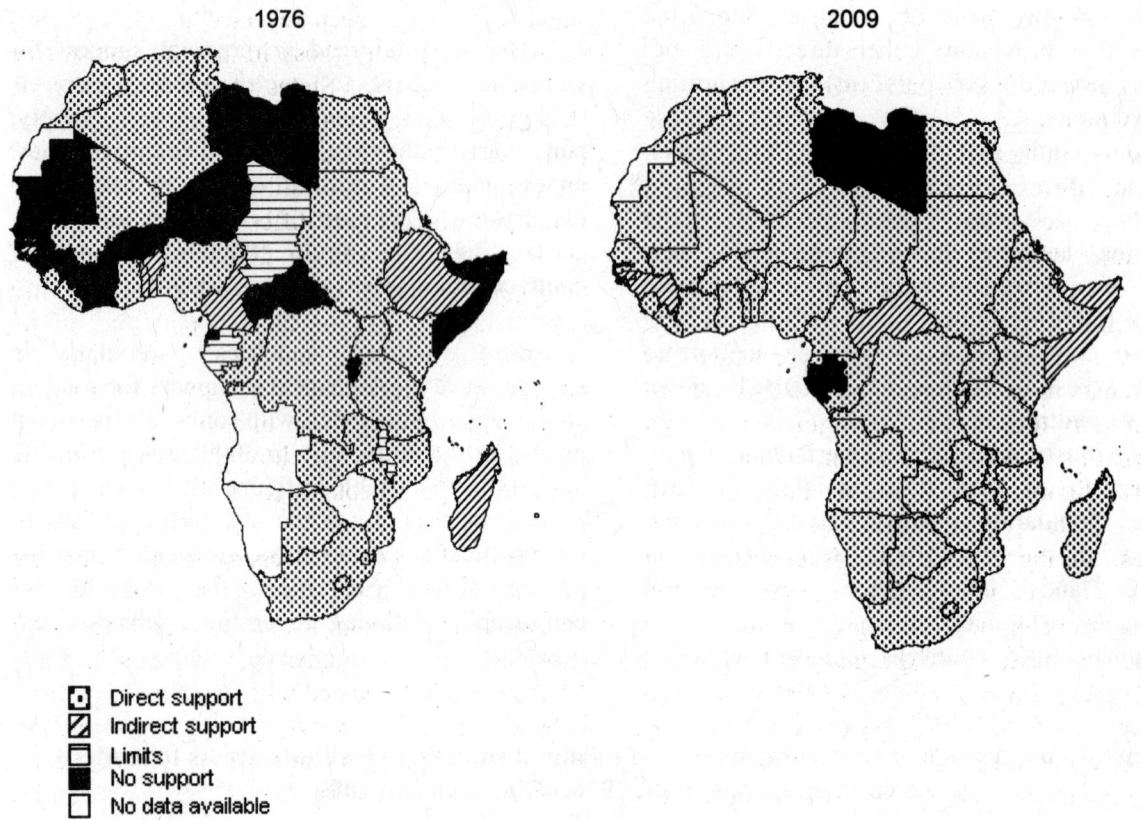

1976   2009

- ⊡ Direct support
- ▨ Indirect support
- ☐ Limits
- ■ No support
- ☐ No data available

Adolescent fertility

Many Governments expressed concern about high levels of adolescent fertility. Early childbearing increases risk of maternal death or physical impairment. Furthermore children born to young mothers have higher levels of morbidity and mortality. Among the 191 Governments whose views regarding fertility among adolescents were known in 2009, 87 per cent expressed concern about the level of adolescent fertility (table 8). They included virtually all countries in Latin America and the Caribbean and most countries in Africa. While 31 per cent of developed countries viewed the level of adolescent fertility as a major concern, 65 per cent of developing countries did so.

Of the 191 countries with information available, 82 per cent reported having policies and programmes to address adolescent fertility (table 9). These programmes usually focus on providing assistance to public facilities and non-governmental organizations in order to provide in-school and out-of-school youth with life skills and ensure that they get appropriate information on reproductive health and sex education. Innovative educational approaches, including peer counseling for youth and orientation for parents, have also been promoted. Population education in non-formal educational settings, vocational training institutes or youth clubs has also been strengthened.

V. HEALTH AND MORTALITY

Life expectancy at birth

The pursuit of health and longevity is not only a basic human desire but also one of the fundamental pillars of development. In most of the world, life expectancy at birth has increased markedly since 1950, particularly as focussed health interventions, increased education and economic development have led to significant reductions in infant and child mortality (Riley, 2001). Correspondingly, the percentage of Governments in developing countries that viewed their mortality level as acceptable increased from 24 per cent to 38 per cent between 1976 and 2009 (table 10, figure VII). However, there are still wide gaps between developed and developing countries. During 2005-2010, life expectancy at birth was 77 years in developed countries and 66 years in developing countries. In the least developed countries, life expectancy at birth was a low 56 years (United Nations, 2009a). Owing to the expansion of the HIV/AIDS epidemic, internal conflicts, economic crises and deficiencies in health systems, the transition to low mortality has

stagnated or even been reversed in a number of countries, especially those in sub-Saharan Africa and in the successor States of the former USSR (McMichael et al. 2004; Moser et al., 2005; Vallin and Meslé, 2004). Consequently, Governments' views regarding the mortality levels to which their populations are subject differ markedly according to development level. In 2009, 67 per cent of developed countries considered the level of life expectancy at birth of their populations to be acceptable, whereas only 38 per cent of developing countries had that view. Not a single Government among those of the least developed countries felt that the life expectancy of its population was acceptable (table 10).

While 111 countries, representing 53 per cent of the world's population, met the ICPD Programme of Action's goal of reaching a life expectancy at birth higher than 70 years in 2005, 24 countries had reached a life expectancy at birth between 65 and 70 years, and 61 countries still had a life expectancy at birth below 65 years. Among these countries, 45 had life expectancies

Figure VII. Developing countries that view their mortality level as acceptable, 1976, 1986, 1996 and 2009

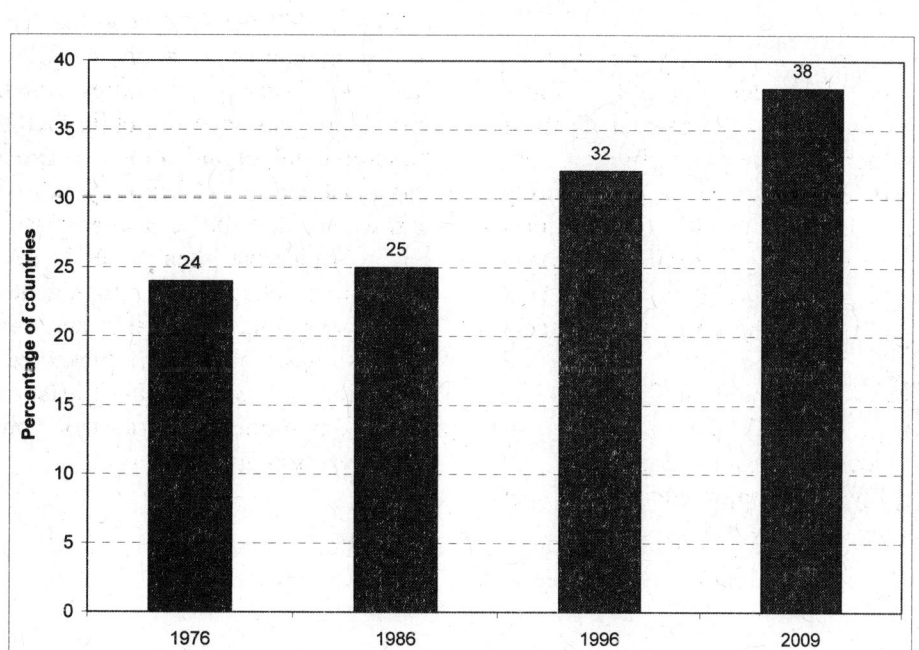

below 60 years and thus fell far short of the goal set in the Programme of Action. These countries account for 12 per cent of world population and are located mostly in sub-Saharan Africa. (United Nations, 2009b). Key factors responsible for the slow increases in life expectancy or the declines observed in a few cases include the expansion of the HIV/AIDS epidemic; the persistence of major infectious diseases, such as malaria and diarrhoea; the re-emergence of others, such as tuberculosis and cholera; military and political conflict; economic crises; socio-economic restructuring; and unhealthy lifestyles.

Low levels of health expenditure per capita are at the root of inadequate coverage of the population in developing countries by basic health services (WHO, 2008). In 2006, health expenditures per capita averaged US$ 113 among all developing countries and just US$20 in the least developed countries (World Bank, 2009). In many developing countries, the deficiencies in health coverage have been aggravated by the inability of health systems to absorb additional resources efficiently and by the shortages of health personnel exacerbated by inadequate salaries, poor working conditions and emigration (WHO, 2006; Connell et al., 2007).

Under-five mortality

At the world level, infant and child mortality and maternal mortality ranked as the second and third most commonly cited concerns of Governments after the HIV/AIDS epidemic. In 2009, an overwhelming majority of Governments of developing countries (81 per cent) cited the level of under-five mortality in their respective populations as unacceptable, whereas just 37 per cent of Governments of developed countries had that view. In developed countries, dissatisfaction among Governments with the level of infant and child mortality decreased between 1996 and 2009, dropping from 54 per cent to 37 per cent. In contrast, the proportion of Governments concerned over the level of infant and child mortality remained virtually unchanged in developing countries (table 11), mainly because the rapid reductions in child mortality recorded in developing countries prior to 1990 gave way to near stagnation during the 1990s in many developing countries.

Whereas under-five mortality has declined globally, the pace of progress has been uneven across regions and countries. In many countries, lack of basic sanitation, access to safe drinking water and adequate nutrition accounted for an important part of the high death toll among children. According to the MDGs, under-five mortality should be reduced by two thirds between 1990 and 2015. As of 2008, 44 developing countries had already reduced their under-five mortality by more than half since 1990 and another 65 countries had achieved reductions ranging from 30 per cent to 50 per cent. However, progress was slow in 41 countries, 73 per cent of which are located in Africa (United Nations, 2009b).

Globally, it is estimated that in 2008 the number of children dying before age five had fallen below 9 million per year, a marked improvement from the 12.5 million deaths of children under five estimated for 1990 (You et al., 2009). Despite these improvements, two thirds of child deaths are caused by preventable diseases, including acute respiratory infections, diarrhoea, measles and malaria (UNICEF, 2008).

Maternal mortality

Maternal mortality is a major concern for many developing countries. The inclusion of maternal mortality in the MDGs has heightened awareness among Governments about the need to provide reproductive health services to all women of reproductive age. The MDGs set a target of reducing maternal mortality by three quarters between 1990 and 2015 (United Nations 2005). Among the 195 countries considered, the Governments of 129, representing 66 per cent of the Governments of all countries, considered the level of maternal mortality in their populations as unacceptable (table 12). The Governments of 79 per cent of developing countries and of 94 per cent of the least developed countries were dissatisfied with the level of maternal mortality in their populations.

Each year, more than half a million women die from causes related to pregnancy and childbirth, 80 per cent of these causes are preventable. Almost all of those deaths occur in sub-Saharan Africa and in South-central Asia (UNICEF, 2008).

Among developed countries, health concerns revolve around the prevention and treatment of non-communicable diseases, especially cardiovascular disease, cancer, diabetes, respiratory disorders and Alzheimer's disease. Associated with such concerns are the prevalence of disability and the cost of providing health and long-term care for older persons. In some countries, concerns remain about communicable diseases, especially tuberculosis and HIV/AIDS. Concerns about ensuring the adequacy of health systems to address the increasing burden of non-communicable diseases are especially prevalent among countries with economies in transition (WHO, 2009; Organization for Economic Co-operation and Development, 2004 and 2009a).

HIV/AIDS

Controlling the HIV/AIDS epidemic and providing treatment for those who need it remain some of the major challenges confronting the international community in 2009. HIV/AIDS was the most often cited demographic concern by Governments of developing countries, 90 per cent of which viewed it as a major concern. Among Governments of developed countries, 77 per cent considered HIV/AIDS a major concern (box 2, table 13). These government views echo those of public opinion. In 2007, the Kaiser/Pew Global Health Survey, conducted in 47 countries, indicated that preventing and treating HIV/AIDS was a major concern among people in all countries, especially those in countries in sub-Saharan Africa and Asia (Kaiser Family Foundation and Pew Global Attitudes Project, 2007).

Although current estimates indicate that the epidemic peaked globally in 1996, the number of deaths due to AIDS only started to decline in 2004. Since the disease was first diagnosed in 1981, nearly 60 million people have been infected with HIV and 25 million people have died of HIV-related causes. In 2008, over 33 million people were living with HIV, an estimated 2.7 million new HIV infections occurred that year and 2 million persons died of AIDS-related illnesses (UNAIDS and WHO, 2009a and 2009b). Overall, the epidemic has erased decades of progress in reducing mortality in the most affected countries and has had a devastating impact on people and families in terms of increased morbidity and lost productivity and wages. Moreover, the epidemic has undermined households and families, enterprises and agriculture, and the education and health sectors in the most affected countries.

Although some Governments began formulating policies to address the spread of HIV and its consequences in the mid-to-late 1980s, these policies were often fragmented and had a narrow health focus. More recently, the epidemic has spawned an unprecedented array of global, regional and national responses. Governments have pursued a multi-pronged strategy to combat HIV/AIDS by focusing on the triad of prevention, care and treatment; ensuring protection from discrimination and stigmatization; developing multisectoral strategies; creating HIV/AIDS coordination bodies; and building of partnerships with civil society, including groups of people living with HIV/AIDS, community-based groups, non-governmental organizations and the private sector (United Nations, 2004a; UNAIDS and WHO, 2008).

Prevention is the foundation of measures to respond to the HIV/AIDS epidemic and most Governments have adopted prevention strategies at the same time they have worked to provide the needed care, support and treatment. Governments have raised public awareness about how to prevent HIV infection through information, education and communication (IEC) programmes using print media, theatre, radio, television and other means of transmitting key messages. The participation of non-governmental organizations, people living with HIV, religious institutions, and international and bilateral donors has been critical to the success of those efforts. However, much remains to be done to improve the effectiveness of government strategies to ensure the elimination of risky sexual behaviour, especially in the most affected countries.

In 2009, condom distribution was widespread: 86 per cent of Governments in both developed and developing countries promoted condom use to protect against sexual transmission of HIV (table 14, figure VIII). The lowest proportion of Governments supporting condom distribution is found in Oceania (69 per cent). Nevertheless, despite the stated support for programmes to distribute condoms, supply shortages and poor quality of the items distributed remain a concern. The global supply of condoms still falls short of what is needed to ensure adequate protection for the sexually active population (UNFPA, 2005 and 2009).

In 2009, 189 of the 195 Governments considered reported screening national blood

supplies and blood products for HIV. Little difference was seen between developed and developing countries regarding blood screening. In 2009, 98 per cent of the Governments in Africa had implemented such measures. The percentage of Governments having implemented blood screening measures was lowest in Oceania, at 81 per cent (table 14).

Antiretroviral therapy (ART) can significantly prolong life and alleviate suffering among people living with HIV. In 2009, 91 per cent of Governments — 98 per cent of developed-country Governments and 89 per cent of developing-country Governments — had programmes to provide ART. Despite most countries having policies aimed at the provision of ART, the MDG goal of achieving universal access to ART by 2010 for all those who need it remains elusive as ART coverage remains low in most developing countries. At the end of 2008,

Figure VIII. Distribution of countries according to the implementation of measures to respond to the HIV/AIDS epidemic, 2009

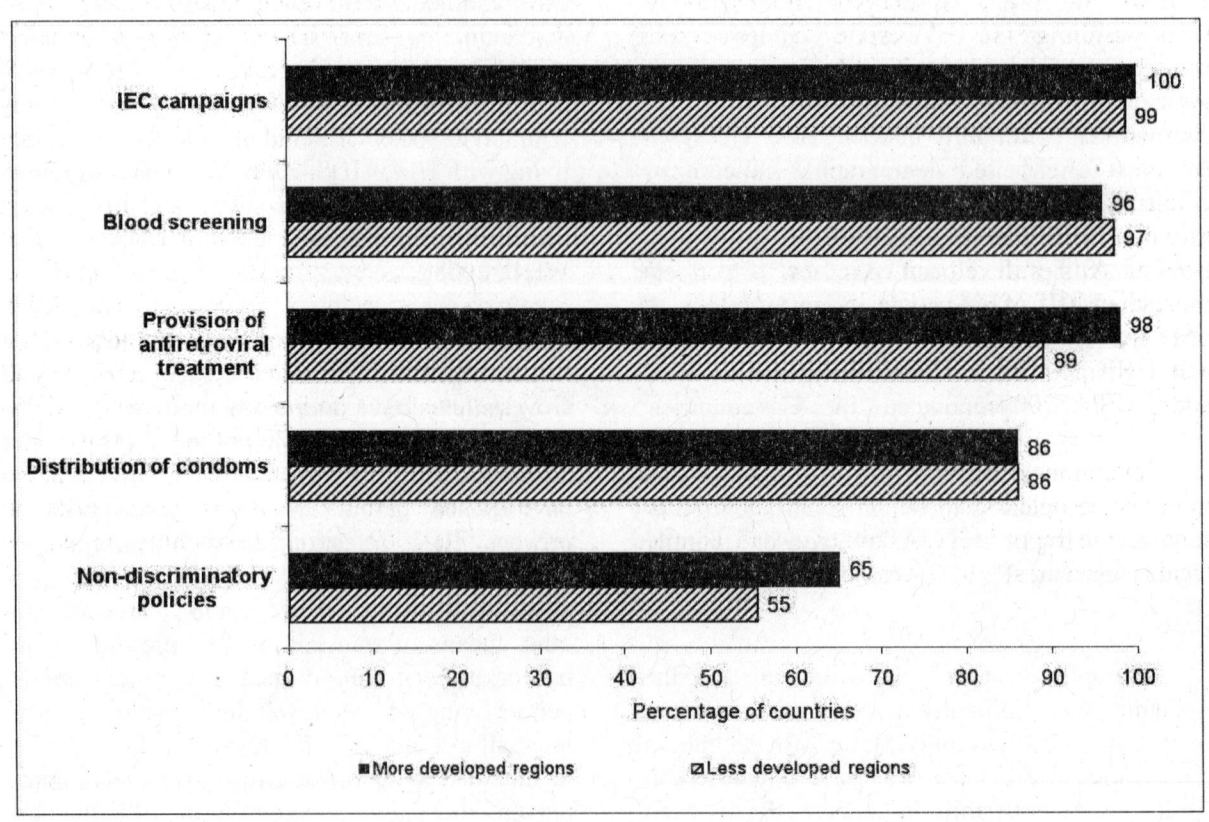

Figure IX. Countries with legal measures to prohibit AIDS-related discrimination, 2009

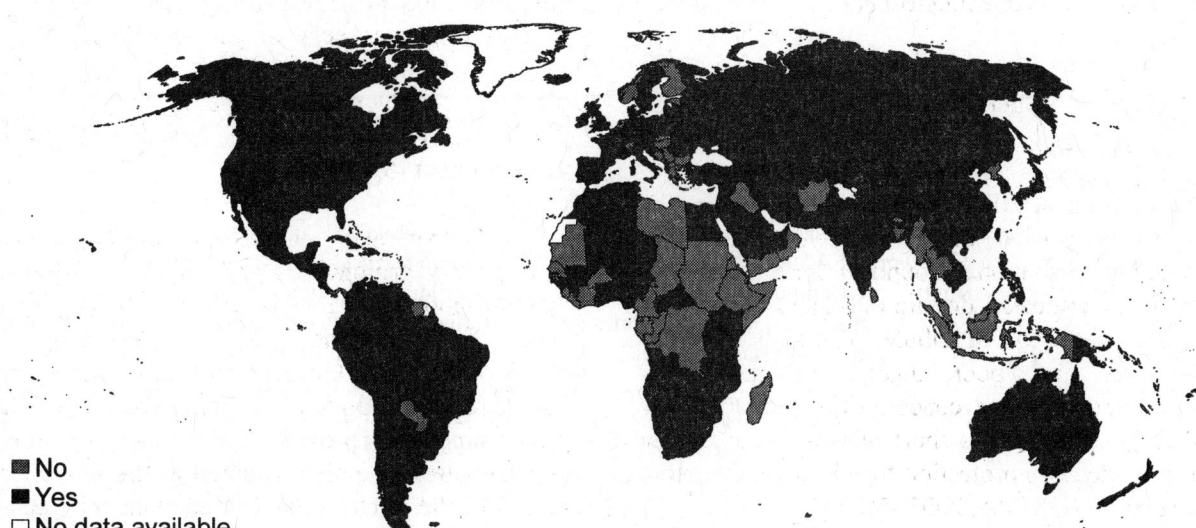

No
Yes
No data available

only 42 per cent of adults and children in need of treatment were receiving ART, and 45 per cent of pregnant women living with HIV got antiretroviral drugs to prevent mother-to-child transmission of HIV. Despite the remarkable progress made since the United Nations General Assembly Special Session on HIV/AIDS (UNGASS) in 2006 — the number of people receiving ART in low- and middle-income countries doubled from 2 million in 2006 to 4 million in late 2008 — more than 5 million people needing ART still did not have access to it, and more than half of all people living with HIV are unaware of their infection status (WHO, UNAIDS and UNICEF, 2009; UNICEF, UNAIDS, WHO and UNFPA, 2009).

Governments have increasingly enacted laws to protect people living with HIV. In 2009, 58 per cent of the reporting Governments had adopted legal measures to prohibit AIDS-related discrimination. The Governments of 65 per cent of developed countries had implemented such policies, whereas only 55 per cent of the Governments of developing countries had done so (table 14, figure VIII). In Africa, where the epidemic is most widespread, only 53 per cent of the Governments had adopted laws preventing discrimination on the basis of HIV status. Among the countries most affected by the epidemic in Eastern and Southern Africa, all except Cameroon, Gabon and Swaziland, had non-discriminatory policies (figure IX). Among the 52 countries experiencing a generalized HIV/AIDS epidemic, that is, those where adult HIV prevalence was at least 1 per cent in 2007, 23 still did not have legal provisions prohibiting AIDS-related discrimination in 2009 (box 3). Only three of those countries — Belize, the Central African Republic and Malawi — had adopted legislation during 2005-2009 barring discrimination on the basis of HIV status.

BOX 3. COUNTRIES WITH LEGAL MEASURES TO PROHIBIT AIDS-RELATED DISCRIMINATION IN 2009
BY RATE OF ADULT HIV PREVALENCE

Adult HIV prevalence rate (per cent) in 2007 (UNAIDS, 2008)	*Legal measures to prohibit AIDS-related discrimination in 2009*	
	No	*Yes*
Less than 1 per cent (n=69)	*17 countries*: Afghanistan, Bangladesh, Bhutan, the Democratic People's Republic of Korea, Gambia, Indonesia, Madagascar, Malaysia, Maldives, Mauritania, Myanmar, Panama, Paraguay, Senegal, Singapore, Somalia and Sri Lanka	*52 countries*: Algeria, Argentina, Armenia, Australia, Azerbaijan, Belarus, Bolivia (Plurinational State of), Brazil, Cambodia, Chile, China, Colombia, Comoros, Costa Rica, Cuba, Ecuador, Egypt, El Salvador, Fiji, Georgia, Guatemala, Honduras, India, Iran (Islamic Republic of), Israel, Japan, Kazakhstan, Kyrgyzstan, the Lao People's Democratic Republic, Latvia, Lebanon, Lithuania, Mexico, Mongolia, Morocco, Nepal, New Zealand, Nicaragua, Niger, Pakistan, Peru, Philippines, the Republic of Korea, the Republic of Moldova, Romania, Tajikistan, Tunisia, the United States of America, Uruguay, Uzbekistan, Venezuela (Bolivarian Republic of) and Viet Nam
1 to 5 per cent (n=37)	*20 countries*: Burkina Faso, Chad, Congo, Côte d'Ivoire, the Democratic Republic of the Congo, Djibouti, Equatorial Guinea, Eritrea, Estonia, Ethiopia, Guinea-Bissau, Haiti, Jamaica, Liberia, Mauritius, Sierra Leone, Sudan, Suriname, Thailand, and Trinidad and Tobago	*17 countries*: Angola, Bahamas, Barbados, Belize, Benin, Burundi, the Dominican Republic, Ghana, Guinea, Guyana, Mali, Nigeria, Papua New Guinea, the Russian Federation, Rwanda, Togo and Ukraine
5 to 10 per cent (n=6)	*2 countries*: Cameroon and Gabon	*4 countries*: The Central African Republic, Kenya, Uganda and the United Republic of Tanzania
10 to 20 per cent (n=6)	-	*6 countries*: Malawi, Mozambique, Namibia, South Africa, Zambia and Zimbabwe
20 per cent or more (n=3)	*1 country*: Swaziland	*2 countries*: Botswana and Lesotho

Induced abortion

In 2003, an estimated 42 million induced abortions occurred in the world, almost half of which were carried out using unsafe procedures (WHO, 2007; Sedgh et al., 2007a and 2007b; Singh et al., 2009). In 2009, almost all Governments, 96 per cent in developed countries and 97 per cent in developing countries, permitted abortion to save the woman's life (figure X). Only the Governments of Chile, the Dominican Republic, El Salvador, the Holy See, Malta and Nicaragua did not permit abortion under any circumstances.

Over the past three decades, since the United Nations began monitoring legal provisions regarding abortion (United Nations, 1982), the trend has been towards expanding the grounds on which abortion is permitted. Between 1980 and 2009, the percentage of Governments permitting abortion to save the woman's life increased from 85 per cent to 97 per cent. The percentage of Governments allowing abortion to preserve the physical health of a woman increased from 44 per cent to 67 per cent. The proportion of those allowing it in order to preserve the mental health of a woman rose from 21 per cent to 63 per cent. The proportion allowing abortion in cases of rape or incest increased from 17 per cent to 49 per cent, and the share of those permitting abortion in cases of foetal impairment rose from 23 per cent to 47 per cent. Abortion on the grounds of economic or social reasons became legal in 34 per cent of countries, up from 15 per cent in 1980, and 29 per cent of countries legalized abortion upon request, up from 10 per cent in 1980. Clearly, the conditions under which abortion may be performed legally varied considerably among countries.

Whereas in an increasing number of developed and developing countries the number of grounds on which abortion is allowed has been rising since the early 1980s, abortion laws and policies continue to be significantly more restrictive in developing countries on all grounds, except to save the woman's life (figure X). In 2009, 80 per cent of developed countries permitted abortion on economic or social grounds and in 69 per cent it was permitted upon request. In contrast, 19 per cent of developing countries permitted abortion on economic or social grounds and 16 per cent allowed abortion upon request.

As figure XI shows, many developing countries have restrictive laws and policies towards abortion, allowing it on the basis of very few grounds. Thus, 19 countries in Africa, 15 in Asia, 9 in Latin America and 7 in Oceania allow abortion only to save the woman's life, and another 38 developing countries allow abortion to preserve physical or mental health. Overall only 43 developing countries, located mostly in Eastern Asia, South-central Asia and Southern Africa, allow abortion on five grounds or more.

Between 1996 and 2009, 46 countries (18 in Africa, 10 in Latin America and the Caribbean, 8 in Asia, 6 in Europe and 4 in Oceania) increased the number of grounds for abortion, while 11 countries (6 in Latin America, 3 in Asia and 2 in Africa) restricted the number of grounds on which abortion is permitted. The Dominican Republic and Nicaragua that previously allowed abortion to save the woman's life no longer allow abortion on any grounds (box 4).

Figure X. Grounds on which abortion is permitted by level of development in 1980, 1996 and 2009

A. More developed countries

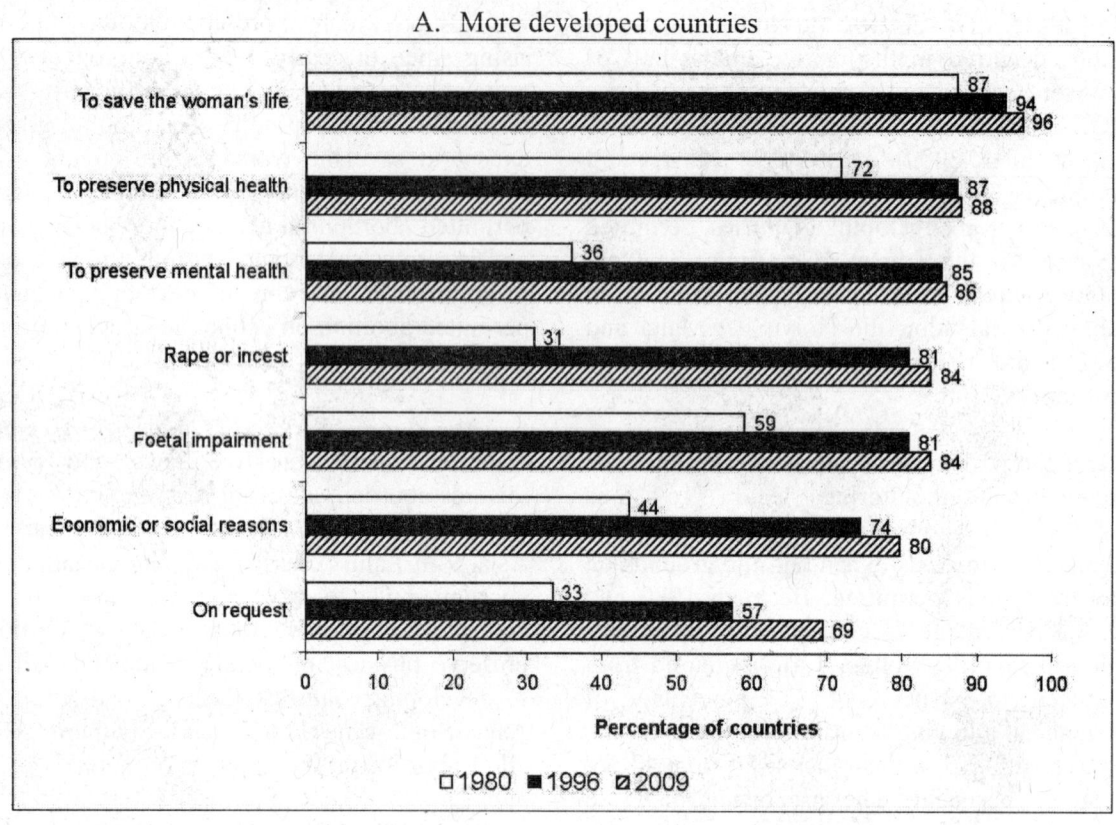

B. Less developed countries

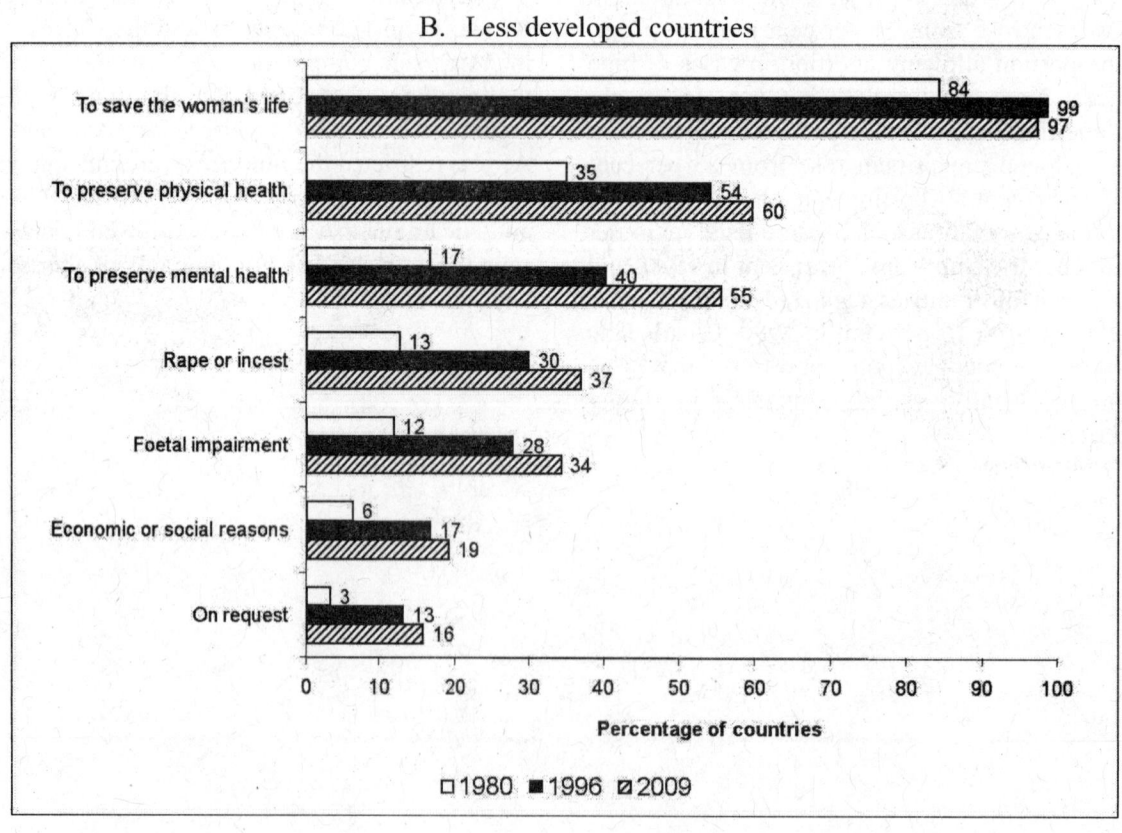

United Nations Department of Economic and Social Affairs/Population Division

Figure XI. Countries by grounds on which abortion is permitted, 2009

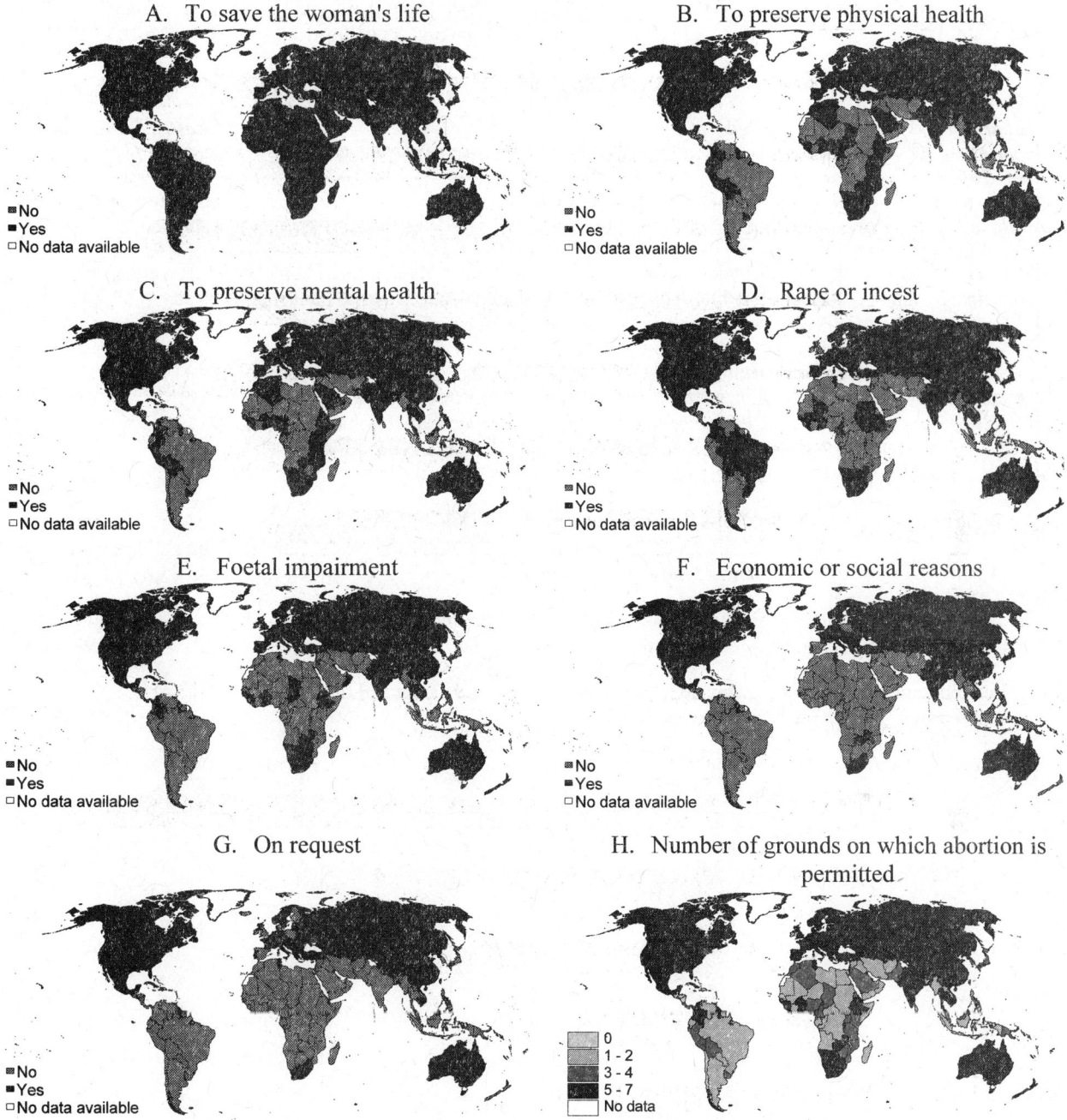

A. To save the woman's life

B. To preserve physical health

C. To preserve mental health

D. Rape or incest

E. Foetal impairment

F. Economic or social reasons

G. On request

H. Number of grounds on which abortion is permitted

BOX 4. COUNTRIES THAT LIBERALIZED OR RESTRICTED GROUNDS ON WHICH ABORTION IS PERMITTED BETWEEN 1996 AND 2009		
Grounds on which abortion is permitted	*Liberalized*	*Restricted*
a. To save the woman's life	Andorra , Timor-Leste	Dominican Republic, Nicaragua
b. To preserve physical health	Benin, Chad, Colombia, Equatorial Guinea, Kenya, Lao People's Dem. Republic, Mexico, Mozambique, Nepal, Nigeria, Panama, Swaziland, Togo	Argentina, Congo, Iraq, Qatar
c. To preserve mental health	Benin, Bhutan, Bolivia (Plurinational State of) , Burkina Faso, Burundi, Cameroon, Colombia, Comoros, Costa Rica, Equatorial Guinea, Ethiopia, Kenya, Mexico, Morocco, Mozambique, Nepal, Nigeria, Peru, Poland, Rwanda, Saudi Arabia, Swaziland, Thailand, Uruguay, Vanuatu	Iraq, Japan
d. Rape or incest	Bahrain, Benin, Bhutan, Burkina Faso, Colombia, Cook Islands, Ethiopia, Fiji, Guinea, Mali, Nepal, Saint Kitts and Nevis, Saint Lucia, Switzerland, Togo, Uruguay	Algeria, Belize, Ecuador, Iraq
e. Foetal impairment	Benin, Burkina Faso, Chad, Colombia, Ethiopia, Fiji, Guinea, Jordan, Mexico, Nepal, Oman, Swaziland, Switzerland, Togo	Iraq, Panama, Qatar
f. Economic or social reasons	Bahrain, Mexico, Nepal, Portugal, Saint Vincent and the Grenadines, Switzerland	-
g. On request	Australia, Bahrain, Belgium, Cape Verde, Italy, Mexico, Nepal, Portugal, Switzerland	-

VI. SPATIAL DISTRIBUTION AND INTERNAL MIGRATION

During the twentieth century, urbanization has been a major transforming force in most countries of the world. Between 1950 and 2009, the world's urban population more than quadrupled, growing from 732 million to 3.4 billion. Currently, there are just slightly more urban dwellers than rural dwellers and in 2050 the world population is expected to be 69 per cent urban, with 6.3 billion people living in urban areas. The projected 2.9 billion increase in the urban population will occur almost entirely in the less developed regions, particularly in Africa and Asia where currently the majority of people still live in rural areas. Despite the visibility of mega-cities, that is, cities with at least 10 million inhabitants such as Tokyo, São Paulo, Mexico City and New York in order of population size, the 21 mega-cities currently in existence account for only 9 per cent of the world's urban population. The majority of urban dwellers (52 per cent) live in small urban centres with fewer than half a million inhabitants (United Nations, 2010).

The change in the spatial distribution of the population is primarily due to economic growth and technological advances and has both positive and negative aspects. Generally, because of their economic dynamism and the economies of scale associated with higher population densities, urban centres can offer better economic and social prospects than rural areas. Cities often offer better access to health care, education and other services than rural areas and, within the city hierarchy, larger cities offer better access to social services than smaller ones. In both the more developed and less developed regions, countries with higher levels of urbanization have tended to have higher per capita incomes, more stable economies and stronger political institutions (OECD, 2007; UN-HABITAT, 2006).

Urbanization not only changes the spatial distribution of the population, it also modifies the distribution of poverty. Currently, the majority of the world's poor still reside in rural areas. However, the proportion of the population living in poverty is increasing faster in urban areas than in rural areas. Between 1993 and 2002, the number of urban poor is estimated to have increased by 50 million, while the number of rural poor declined by 150 million (Ravallion, Chen and Sangraula, 2007). Accompanying this growth is the expansion of slums in urban areas, which are characterized by precarious housing, inadequate sanitation and overcrowding.

In 2005, an estimated 37 per cent of the urban population in developing countries lived in slums (UN-HABITAT, 2008). Often, "peri-urban" areas or transitional zones between the countryside and already established cities bear the brunt of rapid urban population growth which, when urban planning is lacking and there is inadequate investment in infrastructure, contributes to rising poverty levels, the depletion of natural resources and pollution (UNFPA, 2007; Torres, Alves and De Oliveira, 2007).

Addressing the challenges posed by the spatial distribution of rapidly growing populations is key to reaching the MDGs. In many countries, rural areas have lagged behind urban areas in the achievement of various internationally agreed development goals. In order to halve by 2015 the proportion of people living in extreme poverty, Governments must improve the plight of the poor in urban areas.

Concerns about the spatial distribution of the population and policies to address them

Faced with the opportunities and challenges that growing urbanization brings, an increasing number of policymakers have focused on the population's spatial distribution. In 2009, 83 per cent of Governments expressed concern about their country's pattern of population distribution, a percentage comparable to those recorded in the 1970s and 1980s (table 15). The Governments of the least developed countries were particularly concerned, with 74 per cent considering that the spatial distribution of their respective populations needs a major change and 22 per cent calling for a minor change.

Among developed countries, the percentage of Governments dissatisfied with the spatial distribution of the population was lower, with 29 per cent and 43 per cent of Governments calling for a major or minor change, respectively (table 15).

Dissatisfaction with patterns of population distribution was highest in Africa and Asia, where 75 per cent and 57 per cent, respectively, of Governments desired major changes in their population distribution (table 15). This outcome is not surprising given that the most rapid urban population growth has occurred and will continue to occur in those two regions (United Nations, 2010). In Europe, Oceania, and Latin America and the Caribbean, where urban population growth has been slower, the proportion of Governments desiring major changes in the spatial distribution

of the population is lower at 30 per cent, 44 per cent and 36 per cent, respectively (figure XII).

In general, natural increase has accounted for 60 per cent or more of the population growth in urban areas (United Nations, 2008). However, net migration from rural to urban areas and the transformation of rural settlements into urban places are also important components of urban growth. According to current projections, it is likely that between 400 million and 600 million people in developing countries will become urban dwellers between 2009 and 2025 because of internal migration or re-classification of rural areas into urban areas. Aware of these trends, as of 2009, the majority of Governments had implemented measures to leverage the opportunities offered by urbanization and address the challenges it poses.

Figure XII. Government views on the spatial distribution of their population, 2009

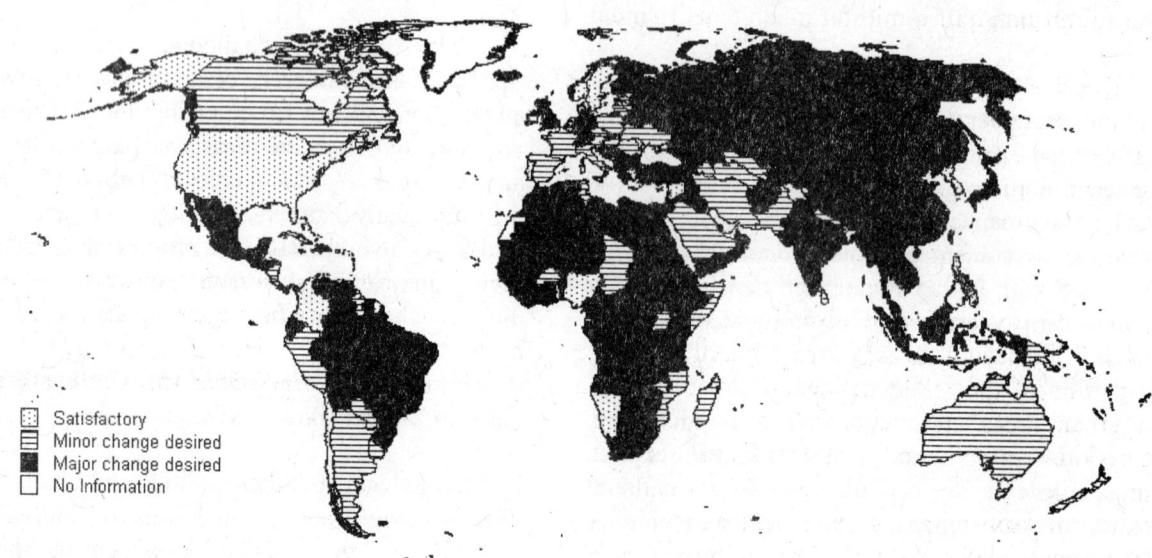

Satisfactory
Minor change desired
Major change desired
No Information

Rural to urban migration

At the global level, 67 per cent of the Governments with the required information for 2009 had implemented policies to reduce rural out-migration (table 16). Africa had the highest percentage of Governments seeking to stem migration from rural to urban areas (81 per cent) and Asia was the only region with a considerable percentage of Governments seeking to raise rural to urban migration (17 per cent).

Reducing or even reversing the flow of migrants from rural areas to cities has been the most common type of policy intervention pursued by Governments. Rural to urban migration can erode traditional lifestyles and accelerate the ageing of rural communities as younger people migrate to cities in search of employment. However, as noted earlier, migration to urban areas also has benefits. China, for example, seeks to raise rural to urban migration and improve the management of rural out-migration in order to reduce rural-urban inequities.

Historically, Governments have adopted different strategies in order to retain population in rural areas including establishing internal migration controls, undertaking land re-distribution and creating regional development zones.

In recent years, a new rural paradigm has emerged in developed countries, based on the recognition of the interdependence between rural and urban areas. This approach has led to the promotion of rural diversification and competitiveness; the mobilization of investment instead of subsidies; greater coherence and effectiveness of public expenditure; and improvements in the lives of rural dwellers. In more than one third of OECD countries, rural areas experienced the highest rate of employment creation (OECD, 2006a).

Migration to urban agglomerations

Another common type of policy has been to reduce the flow of internal migrants into large urban agglomerations. In many countries, especially those in the less developed regions, the inflow of large numbers of migrants to large cities has strained the ability of local governments to provide basic services, such as clean water, sanitation and public transportation. Between 1975 and 2009, the number of mega-cities climbed from 3 to 21. In 2025, there are expected to be 28 mega-cities. Nonetheless, 84 per cent of the world's urban population currently lives in cities with fewer than 5 million inhabitants. The concentration of urban dwellers in small and medium-sized cities is not expected to change much by 2025 (United Nations, 2010).

Since the 1970s, a growing proportion of Governments of developing countries have implemented policies aimed at reducing internal migration into large urban agglomerations, increasing from 44 per cent in 1976 to 72 per cent in 2009 (table 17). In contrast, the percentage of Governments of developed countries seeking to reduce flows into urban agglomerations declined from 55 per cent in 1976 to 26 per cent 2003, but has risen to 34 per cent since then.

In 2009, 62 per cent of Governments worldwide had implemented policies to reduce the inflow of migrants to large urban agglomerations. Among the Governments of the least developed countries, 76 per cent had adopted such policies. Oceania had the highest percentage of Governments seeking to stem migration to large urban agglomerations (83 per cent), followed by Africa (77 per cent), Latin America and the Caribbean (68 per cent) and Asia (66 per cent) (table 17).

Urban to urban migration

Only 15 per cent of Governments have implemented policies to encourage urban to urban migration, whereas another 15 per cent wish to maintain levels of urban to urban migration as they are and 66 per cent do not intervene to raise or lower urban to urban migration (table 18). Such policies usually promote movements from large urban agglomerations to small and medium-sized cities or to new settlements. The rationale for such interventions is that, while large urban agglomerations can foster innovation and entrepreneurship by attracting highly skilled workers and generating economies of scale, cities beyond a certain size become less efficient and productive (OECD, 2006b). The policy of encouraging urban dwellers to move from large urban settlements to smaller cities has been particularly common in countries where a large percentage of the urban population is concentrated in one or two large urban agglomerations. In 2009, the region with the highest percentage of Governments promoting urban to urban migration was Latin America and the Caribbean (29 per cent). In addition to promoting urban to urban migration, a number of countries have also attempted to foster internal migration by building new cities or relocating the capital.

Urban to rural migration

Other types of policies used to shape the spatial distribution of the population are less common. As of 2009, 33 per cent of Governments had adopted policies to promote out-migration from cities and large urban agglomerations into rural areas (table 19). These policies were intended to relieve population pressure on city infrastructure as well as to reduce urban unemployment, and to encourage the return of migrants to their communities of origin. As with measures aimed at reducing migration into large urban agglomerations, policies to promote urban to rural migration were more common in developing countries (38 per cent) than in developed countries (23 per cent). The regions with the highest percentage of countries that promoted urban to rural migration were Africa and Asia, with 48 per cent and 44 per cent of Governments in those regions, respectively, pursuing such policies.

A few developed countries have implemented measures to stem out-migration from cities and large urban agglomerations to rural areas. These types of interventions have tended to focus on the environmental costs of urban sprawl. Pollution, traffic congestion and commuting times are factors that Governments frequently consider when devising measures to limit the encroachment of urban settlements into the rural areas bordering large cities. In Asia, 9 per cent of Governments

have implemented policies to reduce migration from urban to rural areas.

Urbanization policies

In addition to policies aimed at influencing patterns of internal migration, Governments have also undertaken initiatives to improve the quality of life and the sustainability of cities. These policies are generally of two main types: regulatory and positivist (World Bank, 2005). Regulatory policies include controls on urban growth, regulations on zoning and land sub-division, and the adoption of building codes and standards. Positivist policies focus on public land acquisition and allocation, investment in public infrastructure and facilities, and public-private partnerships to undertake urban development projects. Most cities manage their development with various combinations of regulatory and positivist policies. An example of such a combined policy is *PlaNYC: A Greener, Greater New York* (City of New York, 2007). The plan for New York City proposes ambitious goals to create housing for an additional million people, increase access to parklands, update the water network, modernize power plants, and reduce water pollution and greenhouse gas emissions. The plan also included a proposal to introduce congestion pricing to reduce traffic in the central business district that has not been implemented. Such pricing schemes have been implemented in the cities of Bergen, London, Malta, Oslo, Singapore, Stockholm and Trondheim to reduce congestion.

In developing countries, where city dwellers often lack access to adequate infrastructure, including water and sanitation, transport, solid waste collection and disposal, safe housing and other basic services, many Governments have undertaken initiatives to improve the quality of life in poor urban areas. In India, for example, the Ministry of Urban Development and the Ministry of Housing and Poverty Alleviation designed a new programme for developing basic urban infrastructure and urban slum development in 63 cities in India. The Jawaharlal Nehru National Urban Renewal Mission was launched in 2005 and has as one of its objectives to provide services to the urban poor. Most of its funding (80 per cent) comes from national funds (Government of India, 2009). In Burkina Faso, with financial assistance from the French Agency for Development, the Government has undertaken initiatives to improve roadways and access to water and sanitation for the nearly one million inhabitants of Ouagadougou, the country's capital, 40 per cent of whom lived in peri-urban shantytowns.

For the urban poor, access to secure land tenure is of particular concern. With the costs of land and housing rising rapidly in many cities of the developing world, a growing proportion of people are forced to live in marginalized areas where lack of secure land tenure provides residents with little incentive to improve their housing. The threat of eviction and lack of public services results in the maintenance of poor physical conditions in such settlements and contributes to accelerate the environmental degradation of the lands available to the poor.

Public authorities are often reluctant to recognize the residents of informal urban settlements as legal occupants of the land they live in. Lack of legal tenure is often a barrier to access basic services such as water, sanitation, electricity and waste collection. Moreover, without a formal title, the poor are unable to use the property as collateral for loans to develop income-generating activities. In addition, lacking secure tenure and a right of ownership, the poor do not benefit from rising property prices as members of the middle-class often do.

VII. INTERNATIONAL MIGRATION

In 2010, the world is expected to have 214 million international migrants, i.e., people living in countries other than their country of birth, accounting for 3.1 per cent of the world population. Six of every 10 international migrants reside in developed countries and the majority of international migrants living in developed countries originate in developing countries (United Nations, 2009e).

International migration has become an increasingly important component of population growth in countries experiencing low fertility and rapid population ageing. In 2005-2010, net international migration in 11 countries or areas counterbalanced completely or in part the excess of deaths over births, and in another nine countries or areas it accounted for more than double the contribution of natural increase to population growth (United Nations, 2009f).

Over the next forty years, the major countries of destination for international migrants are projected to be the United States, Canada, the United Kingdom, Spain, Italy, Germany, Australia, and France, in order of significance. The major countries of origin are projected to be Mexico, China, India, the Philippines, Pakistan, Indonesia and Bangladesh, also in order of importance (United Nations 2009f).

In managing international migration flows, Governments focus on different types of international migrants, of which the most salient are migrant workers, refugees and asylum seekers, highly skilled migrants, and migrants in an irregular situation. Increasing attention is being paid to transnational communities or diasporas, because of their potential role in the development prospects of countries of origin. There is general agreement that the contribution of international migrants to both their countries of destination and their countries of origin depends crucially on safeguarding their human rights and ensuring that they are not subject to discrimination or xenophobia. The economic and financial crises of recent years have underscored the importance of these concerns and made more urgent the effective implementation of policies that maximize the benefits of international migration while minimizing its negative aspects.

International dialogue

Global attention to international migration has been rising. In 2006, the General Assembly of the United Nations conducted for the first time a High-level Dialogue on International Migration and Development and a second Dialogue will take place in 2013. An outcome of the first High-level Dialogue was the creation of a State-led, informal and non-decision-making Global Forum on Migration and Development, which has been meeting every year since 2007. The annual meetings of the Global Forum are organized and hosted by Governments on a voluntary basis. The Governments of Belgium, the Philippines and Greece hosted the first, second and third meetings of the Global Forum, respectively. In 2010, the Government of Mexico will host the fourth meeting of the Global Forum and the Governments of Spain and Morocco are expected to host meetings in 2011 and 2012.

The most recent meeting of the Global Forum, held in Athens, Greece, in November 2009, brought together representatives of about 140 countries and 35 international organizations. The meeting had as overarching theme "Integrating migration policies into development strategies for the benefit of all" and served to discuss how the linkages between international migration and development could be leveraged to accelerate the achievement of key MDGs, including the reduction of poverty. Other topics of discussion included the integration of international migrants in the host society, the reintegration of returning migrants in countries of origin, ways of engaging the diaspora in the development process of countries of origin, circulation as a type of migration allowing to maintain useful linkages between countries of origin and destination, an assessment of progress made in achieving coherence between development policy and international migration policy, and the role of partnerships between different migration actors.

Impact of the global economic and financial crises on international migration and policies in response

Because the majority of international migrants move in search of better economic opportunities, the economic crisis triggered by the unprecedented financial crisis that affected the world economy in 2008 is thought to have had a dampening effect on international migration flows. According to recent estimates and projections of the international migrant stock, the increase in the number of international migrants in developed countries declined in absolute terms between 2000-2005 and 2005-2010, from a 13 million net increase during the first period to 11 million during the second. The average annual growth rate of the number of international migrants in developed countries declined from 2.3 per cent in 2000-2005 to 1.7 per cent in 2005-2010. At the world level, however, the average annual growth rate of the international migrant stock remained unchanged between 2000-2005 and 2005-2010, at 1.8 per cent, largely because of the increase in the number of refugees during 2005-2010. Excluding refugees, the growth rate of the rest of the international migrants globally decreased from 2.2 per cent in 2000-2005 to 1.7 per cent in 2005-2010 (United Nations, 2009g).

In the United States, the country hosting one in every five international migrants, the total number of international migrants has remained nearly unchanged, at about 37 million, since early 2007. In addition, the number of migrants living in the United States and born in Mexico has also stabilized or even declined slightly. Estimates of unauthorized migration to the United States indicate that it started falling in 2007 and that the reduction accelerated in 2008 (Passel and Cohn, 2009). At the same time, the number of persons returning to Mexico has remained stable at about half a million per year. Overall, the number of Mexican migrants, both legal and unauthorized, immigrating annually to the United States is down by about 75 per cent from the peak reached in 2005 (Passel and Cohn, 2009). In the United States, unauthorized migration responds to economic cycles, with steep increases in the flow towards the end of an economic expansion and significant decreases during economic downturns.

In the European Union, newly available data indicate that, because of rising unemployment caused by the crisis, the number of unauthorized migrants working in the European Union has been decreasing and so has the number denied entry at the border. In addition, more unauthorized migrants have been leaving the European Union (Frontex, 2009).

There is also evidence of reductions in flows of legal migrants to key receiving countries. In Spain, for instance, the net number of admissions under the employer-nominated programme fell by about a third between 2007 and 2008. In Australia, employer applications for hiring foreign skilled migrants went down by 11 per cent between 2008 and 2009, and in the United Kingdom, worker registrations at the end of 2008 were down by 45 per cent compared to the end of 2007 (OECD, 2009b).

One expected consequence of the economic crisis was an increase in the number of international migrants returning to their countries of origin. However, the evidence available so far suggests that, except for a few cases in the European Union, increases in return migration have not materialized. One exception has been the return of Eastern European migrants, particularly Polish migrants, from Ireland and the United Kingdom to their countries of origin. The return of Polish workers was prompted both because of the recession in the countries of destination and better economic prospects in Poland.

Because most international migrants have emigrated years or decades ago and are well established in the countries of destination, they are expected to weather the crisis in the countries of destination. Furthermore, international migrants for whom returning to the country of origin deprives them of the right to re-enter the country of destination as migrants are usually less likely to return in response to deteriorating economic conditions. For that reason, the global number of international migrants is unlikely to decline as a result of the current crisis, particularly if the economic downturn is not prolonged.

Although the current economic crisis has likely dampened international migration flows to developed countries, it has not stopped or reversed them. Moreover, the major economic and demographic asymmetries that persist will remain powerful generators of international migration over the medium term. Reflecting the resilience of migration and its most immediate impact on countries of origin, estimates by the World Bank on the amount of remittances sent by migrants to developing countries during 2009 show only a modest decline with respect to 2008, amounting to between 5 per cent and 8 per cent (Ratha and Mohapatra, 2009).

Increases in unemployment in some of the major countries of destination are especially acute among international migrants because they are overrepresented in the sectors that have been most affected by the crisis, including construction, manufacturing and services. In Spain, for instance, 20 per cent of international migrants were unemployed in late 2008 when unemployment stood at 11.2 per cent among natives (OECD, 2009b).

Rising unemployment generally results in pressure on policymakers to limit inflows of foreign workers. In developed countries, policymakers have used some of the following mechanisms to adjust inflows to changing conditions: (a) modify numerical quotas; (b) adopt more stringent labour market tests; (c) limit the possibilities that migrants have to change status or renew work permits; (d) apply supplementary conditions to non-discretionary flows; and (e) promote return migration (OECD, 2009b). Spain, for instance, has reduced its quota for non-seasonal migrant workers, Italy reduced its quota for entries and Canada has maintained constant its migration quota. In addition, Canada has introduced more stringent advertising requirements for job openings before considering applications for the entry of temporary foreign workers. The Republic of Korea stopped recruitment of temporary migrant workers under its Employment Permit System in 2008. The United Kingdom introduced a stricter test for the admission of skilled migrants. In the United States, employers of persons with temporary worker visas are not allowed to apply for new migrant workers if they lay off similar workers

over a certain period, a condition that is likely to dampen migrant worker admissions in the future.

Some countries have been promoting voluntary return migration. The Czech Republic and Spain have offered incentives to promote the return of migrants to their home countries. Incentives include covering the return passage and lump sum payments to assist in the reestablishment of migrants in the home country (OECD, 2009b; ILO, 2009).

In most developed countries, international migration policy is complex and revolves around several categories of international migrants whose admission has become "non-discretionary" (for instance, migrants admitted under family reunification or commitments on the resettlement of refugees). OECD estimates that just 20 per cent of flows to developed countries are "discretionary" and therefore amenable to short-term modification in response to changed conditions (OECD, 2009b). Therefore, policymakers have relatively few tools to tailor migration to the changing economic situation. Furthermore, while the current crisis may justify restrictions on labour migration in the short term, over the medium and longer term, international migration is likely to be an important mechanism to address labour shortages in specific sectors and to counteract the effects of population ageing.

Government views and policies on immigration

In 2009, 78 per cent of Governments were satisfied with their immigration levels and 73 per cent wished to maintain their current levels of immigration or did not intervene to change them (tables 20 and 21). This level of satisfaction represented a major increase from the situation in 1996 when only 55 per cent of Governments wanted to maintain current immigration levels or did not intervene to change them and a further 41 per cent wished to lower immigration levels (table 21, figure XIII). In both Europe and Latin America and the Caribbean, 82 per cent of Governments wished to maintain current immigration levels in 2009 or did not intervene to change them. In Asia, just 55 per cent of Governments had those policies and a further 30 per cent wished to reduce their immigration levels. At the world level, the percentage of Governments wishing to raise immigration levels doubled from 4 per cent in 1996 to 8 per cent in 2009 (table 21, figure XIII).

The trend toward less restrictive immigration has been especially pronounced in developed countries, where the percentage of Governments having policies to lower immigration fell from 60 per cent in 1996 to 8 per cent in 2009 (table 21). In 2009, only four developed countries — Denmark, France, the Netherlands and the Russian Federation — wished to reduce immigration, whereas six developed countries — Australia, Canada, Estonia, Finland, New Zealand and Sweden — wished to increase immigration in line with their labour demands. Sweden introduced significant reforms in 2008 to ease the process of recruiting migrant workers abroad (OECD, 2009b).

The shift towards somewhat less restrictive immigration policies can be attributed to a number of factors including an improved understanding of the consequences of international migration; a growing recognition by Governments of the need to manage international migration better, rather than to limit it; the persistence of labour shortages in certain sectors of the economies of countries of

destination; a global economy that was expanding until 2008; and the acceleration of population ageing in many developed countries.

Permanent settlement

With the advent of less costly and more rapid forms of transport, countries have become more diverse with respect to immigration policies and, in particular, to the length of stay of international migrants. At the world level, 74 per cent of countries desired to maintain the current level of admissions of permanent settlers or did not intervene, while 19 per cent of countries wanted to lower it. In developed countries, 77 per cent of Governments wished to maintain their levels of settler migration or did not intervene and 13 per cent had policies to lower those levels (table 22).

Highly skilled migrants

Migration policies in countries of destination have become more selective, favouring the admission of international migrants with skills considered to be in short supply. In 2009, 27 per cent of Governments reported promoting the admission of highly skilled workers. Among developed countries, the Governments of 47 per cent wanted to increase the number of admissions

Figure XIII. Government policies on immigration, 1996 and 2009

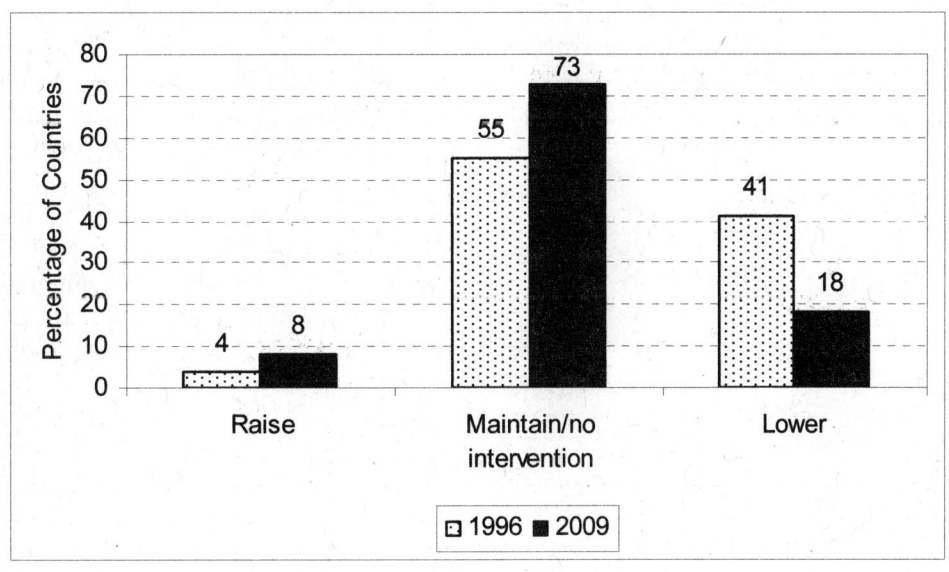

of highly skilled workers compared to only 19 per cent of those of developing countries (table 23, figure XIV).

Labour migration has become increasingly selective, with the skills of migrants determining to a large extent the likelihood of their being admitted into countries of destination. Many countries amended their laws in the late 1990s to facilitate the entry of skilled migrants and launched specific recruitment programmes to attract them. Yet, in 2009, seven countries — Australia, Serbia, Botswana, Bhutan, Jordan, the Philippines and Saudi Arabia — reported that they wished to reduce the number of highly skilled migrants admitted in order to improve the employment prospects of their citizens.

Temporary workers

Although countries of destination have focused mainly on attracting highly skilled migrants, population ageing and rising job expectations have produced labour shortages in low-skilled sectors of the economy, sectors such as agriculture, construction and domestic services. Demand for low-skilled workers has generally been filled by temporary migrant workers. Several countries of destination have established annual quotas and signed bilateral agreements with countries of origin to recruit such migrants. Those bilateral agreements usually cover seasonal workers, contract and project-linked workers, guest workers and cross-border workers. Many of those workers are admitted on the basis of temporary contracts for a fixed period without the expectation of ever obtaining permanent resident status.

In 2009, 71 per cent of Governments wished to maintain the number of temporary migrants already present in their countries or did not intervene in this regard (table 24). In Asia and Oceania, however, 33 per cent and 50 per cent, respectively, of Governments wished to reduce the number of temporary migrants in their countries.

Family reunification

Most countries of destination allow migration for family reunification under specific conditions. However, family reunification is not universally accepted as a right. Most migrant workers moving

Figure XIV. Government policies on the immigration of highly skilled workers, 2009

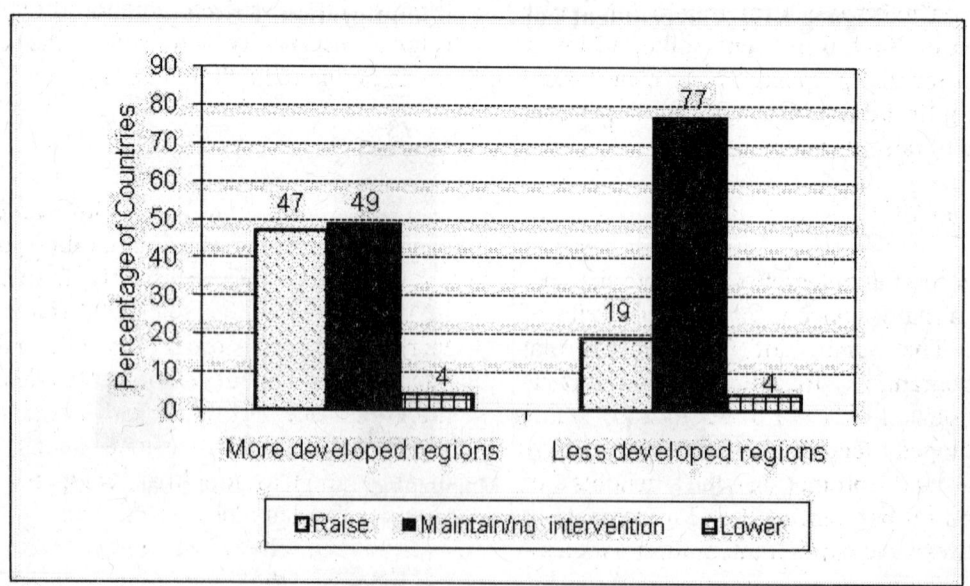

United Nations Department of Economic and Social Affairs/Population Division

Temporary workers

under temporary contracts are not allowed to be accompanied by family members. In a number of countries of destination, debate has focused on the cost of providing migrants' dependants with health and education services or welfare benefits.

Since the 1980s, family reunification has been the major basis for immigration in many countries, particularly in Europe. A majority of legal migrants to Canada, Denmark, France, Norway, Sweden and the United States have been admitted under family reunification. High levels of immigration for family reunification have been a contentious issue in a number of European countries. In recent years, several European countries have sought to limit admissions of family members, including Denmark, France, Ireland and Italy. While family reunification ensures the integrity of the family unit, it is a form of international migration that is open to potential abuse through fake marriages or adoptions. Such abuses have led some countries to tighten requirements for the immigration of spouses by, for instance, raising the minimum age required for spouses or granting permanent status to the migrant spouse only after a few years of stay and proof of successful integration.

Among the 153 countries having information on policies on international migration for family reunification in 2009, 6 per cent wished to lower immigration for that purpose, 87 per cent wished to maintain it or did not intervene, and 7 per cent had policies to raise it (table 25).

Integration policies

The successful integration of international migrants is a major concern for most countries of destination. The number of Governments that reported programmes to integrate non-citizens increased from 52 in 1996 to 82 in 2009 (table 26). Developed countries are increasingly recognizing and promoting the benefits of diversity and 89 per cent of the Governments of those countries have explicit integration policies.

Many countries have adopted non-discrimination provisions to protect religious freedom and the use of other languages in addition to those of host countries. Developed countries have undertaken initiatives to make it easier for international migrants to become a part of society, in particular through language training and by providing courses to inform immigrants about the life and culture of the host country. The aim of such programmes is to offer support during the integration process, while instituting stricter requirements for admission. The integration process has not always been smooth, particularly in countries where foreigners experience higher unemployment than citizens and are thus more dependent on welfare. To improve the access of international migrants to labour markets, many countries have expanded and improved education and employment training programmes for international migrants and their children.

In most countries, foreigners do not enjoy the same rights as citizens, especially with regard to political representation. Many countries have historically not regarded themselves as countries of immigration and thus have not encouraged foreigners to obtain permanent residence or to naturalize. In some countries, citizenship laws may disadvantage migrant women or women marrying foreigners (United Nations, 2004b). A growing number of countries — both of destination and origin — allow dual citizenship. By allowing naturalized citizens to maintain their original nationality, links with the country of origin are more likely to be maintained.

Emigration

The proportion of Governments that considered their level of emigration as too high has been increasing consistently, from 13 per cent in 1976 to 30 per cent in 2009 (table 27). This increase has been more pronounced in developing countries than in developed countries. In 2009, more than one-half of the Governments in Latin America and the Caribbean considered their level of emigration as too high, compared with less than one-third in other world regions.

Despite the increasing proportion of Governments considering their level of emigration as too high, the proportion of

Governments wishing to lower emigration has remained nearly constant, varying between 22 per cent and 23 per cent since the mid-1980s (table 28). While a number of developed and developing countries are concerned about the level of emigration, especially when it involves highly skilled workers, Governments of 10 developing countries, 7 of which are in Asia, have policies to increase emigration. These are countries with young populations, high unemployment, particularly among young people, and a tradition of emigration. Several countries, including Bangladesh, the Philippines, Thailand and Viet Nam, have established government units to manage emigration flows or entered into bilateral agreements with receiving States to protect the rights of their citizens while abroad.

The sharp rise in the emigration of skilled workers has prompted many countries to address the challenges posed by the brain drain, particularly through initiatives to encourage the return of skilled citizens living abroad. In 2009, 89 countries had policies and programmes to encourage their citizens to return (table 29), up from 59 countries in 1996. The Philippines has established an Expatriate Livelihood Support Fund to provide loans for returnees wishing to start businesses. In addition, the Department of

Labour of the Philippines has extensive programmes to assist returnees in finding employment (Awad, 2009).

Emigration generates both opportunities and challenges for developing countries. Concerns have often been raised about the loss of highly skilled workers whose absence may hinder the development process. The provision of medical care in Africa has been particularly affected by the emigration of significant numbers of health workers. The negative effects of such emigration are not being counterbalanced by the remittances sent back by emigrants, although such financial flows play an important role in supporting national and local economies in some countries.

A number of Governments have undertaken initiatives to facilitate remittance transfers and promote the investment of remittances in development projects. Furthermore, more Governments are working to leverage the potential of emigration for the transfer of know-how and technology to countries of origin as well as for the generation of trade and investment. Governments are offering incentives to encourage their citizens abroad to invest in the countries of origin and to participate in transnational knowledge networks.

REFERENCES

Awad, Ibrahim (2009). *The Global Economic Crisis and Migrant Workers: Impact and Response*. Geneva: International Labour Office.

City of New York (2007). *PlaNYC: A Greener, Greater New York*. The City of New York.

Connell, John et al. (2007). Sub-Saharan Africa: Beyond the health worker migration crisis? *Social Science and Medicine*, vol. 64, No. 9, pp. 1876-1891.

European Commission (2004). *Europeans' Attitudes to Parental Leave*. Special Eurobarometer 189/Wave 59.1.

European Commission (2007). *European Social Reality*. Special Eurobarometer 273/Wave 66.3.

EUROSTAT (2007). Statistics in Focus, *Population and Social Conditions*, 97/2007. Luxembourg.

Frontex (2009). *The Impact of the Global Economic Crisis on Illegal Migration to the EU*, Warsaw, Poland: Frontex.

Government of India (2009). *Jawahar Lal Nehru Urban Renewal Mission: Overview*. Ministry of Urban Development and Ministry of Urban Employment and Poverty Alleviation.

International Labour Organization (2009). GMG Fact-Sheet on the Impact of the Economic Crisis on Labour Migration and Migrant Employment. Geneva: International Labour Office.

_____ (2010). *Global Employment Trends, January 2010*. Geneva: International Labour Office.

Kaiser Family Foundation and Pew Global Attitudes Project (2007). *A Global Look at Public Perceptions of Health Problems, Priorities and Donors: the Kaiser/Pew Global Health Survey*. Menlo Park, CA: The Henry J. Kaiser Family Foundation.

McMichael, A. J. et al. (2004). Mortality trends and setbacks: Global convergence or divergence? *The Lancet*, vol. 363, No. 9415, pp. 1155-1159.

Moser, K., V. Shkolnikov and D. A. Leon (2005). World mortality 1950-2000: Divergence replaces convergence from the late 1980s. *Bulletin of the World Health Organization*, vol. 83, No. 3, pp. 202-209.

Organization for Economic Co-operation and Development (2004). *Towards High-Performing Health Systems*. Paris: OECD publications.

_____ (2006a). *The New Rural Paradigm: Policies and Governance*. Paris: OECD publications.

_____ (2006b). *Competitive Cities in the Global Economy*. Paris: OECD publications.

_____ (2007). *OECD Regions at a Glance: 2007 Edition*. Paris: OECD publications.

_____ (2009a). *Achieving Better Value for Money in Health Care*. Paris: OECD publications.

_____ (2009b). *International Migration Outlook, SOPEMI 2009: Managing Labour Migration Beyond the Crisis*. Paris: OECD publications.

Passel, Jeffrey S. and D'Vera Cohn (2009). *Mexican Immigrants: How Many Come? How Many Leave?* Washington, D.C.: Pew Hispanic Center.

Ravallion, Martin, Shaohua Chen and Prem Sangraula (2007). New evidence on the urbanization of global poverty. Policy Research Working Paper, No. 4199. Washington, D.C.: World Bank.

Ratha, Dilip and Sanket Mohapatra (2009). Migration Development Brief 9: Revised Outlook for Remittance Flows 2009-2011. Migration and Remittances Team Development Prospects Group. Washington, D.C.: World Bank.

Riley, James C. (2001). *Rising Life Expectancy: A Global History.* Cambridge, England: Cambridge University Press.

Sedgh Gilda et al. (2007a). Induced Abortion: Estimated Rates and Trends Worldwide. *The Lancet*, vol. 370, No. 9595, pp. 1338–1345.

Sedgh Gilda et al. (2007b). Legal Abortion Worldwide: Incidence and Recent Trends. *International Family Planning Perspectives*, vol. 33, No. 3, pp. 106-116.

Singh, S. et al. (2009). *Abortion Worldwide: A Decade of Uneven Progress.* New York: Guttmacher Institute. October 2009.

Torres, Haroldo, Humberto Alves and Maria Aparecida De Oliveira (2007). São Paulo Peri-Urban Dynamics: Some Social Causes and Environmental Consequences. *Environment and Urbanization*, vol. 19, No. 1, pp. 207-223.

Turner, A. John (2007). Promoting Work: Implications of Raising Social Security's Early Retirement Age. *Work Opportunities for Older Americans*, No. 12. Boston, MA: Center for Retirement Research at Boston College.

UNAIDS and WHO (2008). *Report on the Global AIDS Epidemic.* UNAIDS/08.25E/ JC1510E Geneva: UNAIDS.

_____ (2009a). *AIDS Epidemic Update: November 2009.* UNAIDS/09.36E/JC1700E. Geneva: UNAIDS.

_____ (2009b). Global facts and figures: December 2009. Geneva: UNAIDS and WHO.

UNFPA (2005). *Achieving the ICPD Goals: Reproductive Health Commodity Requirements 2000-2015.* New York; United Nations Population Fund.

_____ (2007). *State of World Population 2007: Unleashing the Potential of Urban Growth.* New York: United Nations Population Fund.

_____ (2009). *Donor Support for Contraceptives and Condoms for STI/HIV Prevention 2008.* New York: United Nations Population Fund.

UNICEF (2007). *The State of the World's Children 2008.* United Nations publication, Sales No. E.08.XX.1.

_____ (2008). *The State of the World's Children 2009.* United Nations publication, Sales No. E.09.XX.1.

_____ UNAIDS, WHO and UNFPA (2009). *Children and AIDS: Fourth Stocktaking Report, 2009.* United Nations publication, Sales No. E.09.XX.3.

United Nations (1982). *World Population Trends and Policies. 1981 Monitoring Report. Vol. II. Population Policies.* Population Studies, No. 79. ST/ESA/SER.A/79/Add.1, pp. 116-145.

_____ (2004a). *The Impact of AIDS.* United Nations publication, Sales No. E.04.XIII.7.

_____ (2004b). *2004 World Survey on the Role of Women in Development: Women and Migration.* United Nations publication, Sales No. E.04.IV.4.

_____ (2005). Population Challenges and Development Goals. United Nations publication, Sales No. E.05.XIII.8.

_____ (2006). *World Urbanization Prospects. The 2005 Revision.* Working Paper. ESA/P/WP/200. New York: United Nations Population Division.

_____ (2010). World Urbanization Prospects. The 2009 Revision. Highlights. New York: United Nations Population Division.

_____ (2009a). World Population Prospects. The 2008 Revision, vol. 1, Comprehensive Tables. United Nations publication, Sales No. E.10.XIII.2.

_____ (2009b). *World Population Prospects: The 2008 Revision. CD-ROM Edition — Extended Dataset in Excel and ASCII formats.* United Nations publication, Sales No. E.09.XII.6.

_____ (2009c). *World Population Ageing and Development 2009 Wall Chart,* United Nations publication, Sales No. E.09.XIII.10.

_____ (2009d) *World Contraceptive Use 2009 Wall Chart.* United Nations publication, Sales No. E.09.XIII.7.

_____ (2009e). *International Migration 2009 Wall Chart.* United Nations publication, Sales No. E.09.X111.8

_____ (2009f). *World Population Prospects 2008 Wall Chart.* United Nations publication, Sales No. E.09.X111.2

_____ (2009g). *Trends in International Migrant Stock: 2008 Revision.* United Nations database, POP/DB/MIG/Stock/Rev.2008.

_____, Economic Commission for Africa (2004). *ICPD+10 Anniversary: Africa Regional Review Report.* Addis Ababa, Ethiopia. ECA.SDD.CM.ICPD at 10/2/Rev.1.

_____, Economic Commission for Europe (2002). *Economic Survey of Europe, 2002, No. 1.* United Nations publication, Sales No. E.02.II.E.7.

UN-HABITAT (2006). *State of the World's Cities 2006/2007: The Millennium Development Goals and Urban Sustainability.* Sterling, VA.: UN-Habitat and Earthscan.

_____ (2008). *State of the World's Cities 2008/2009: Harmonious Cities.* Sterling, VA: UN-Habitat and Earthscan.

Vallin, Jacques and France Meslé (2004). Convergences and Divergences in Mortality: A New Approach of Health Transition. *Demographic Research Special Collection,* No. 2, pp. 11-44.

You, D., T. Wardlaw, P. Salama, and G. Jones. (2009). Levels and Trends in Under-5 Mortality, 1990-2008. *The Lancet,* vol. 375, No. 9709, pp. 100-103.

World Bank (2005). *The Dynamics of Global Urban Expansion.* Washington, D.C.:World Bank.

World Bank (2009). *World Development Indicators 2009.* Washington, D.C. Available from http://publications. worldbank.org/WDI/ (accessed 22 December 2009).

World Health Organization (2006). *The World Health Report 2006 — Working Together for Health.* Geneva: WHO.

_____ (2007). *Unsafe Abortion: Global and Regional Estimates of the Incidence of Unsafe Abortion and Associated Mortality in 2003*, Fifth edition. Geneva: WHO.

_____ (2008). *The World Health Report 2008: Primary Health Care Now More than Ever*. Geneva: WHO.

_____ (2009). *Global Health Risks: Mortality and Burden of Disease Attributable to Selected Major Risks*. Geneva: WHO.

_____, UNAIDS and UNICEF (2009). *Towards Universal Access: Scaling Up Priority HIV/AIDS Interventions in the Health Sector, Progress Report 2009*. Geneva: WHO, UNAIDS and UNICEF.

TABLES

1-29

TABLE 1. GOVERNMENT VIEWS ON THE RATE OF POPULATION GROWTH: 1976, 1986, 1996 AND 2009

	A. By level of development							
Year	(Number of countries)				(Percentage)			
	Too low	Satisfactory	Too high	Total	Too low	Satisfactory	Too high	Total
				World				
1976	34	67	49	150	23	45	33	100
1986	26	73	65	164	16	45	40	100
1996	31	83	79	193	16	43	41	100
2009	43	84	68	195	22	43	35	100
				More developed regions				
1976	11	22	1	34	32	65	3	100
1986	6	28	0	34	18	82	0	100
1996	13	34	1	48	27	71	2	100
2009	23	26	0	49	47	53	0	100
				Less developed regions				
1976	23	45	48	116	20	39	41	100
1986	20	45	65	130	15	35	50	100
1996	18	49	78	145	12	34	54	100
2009	20	58	68	146	14	40	47	100
				Least developed countries				
1976	6	25	11	42	14	60	26	100
1986	4	20	24	48	8	42	50	100
1996	2	11	36	49	4	22	73	100
2009	0	12	37	49	0	24	76	100

TABLE 1. (CONTINUED)

	(Number of countries)				(Percentage)			
Year	Too low	Satisfactory	Too high	Total	Too low	Satisfactory	Too high	Total

B. By major area

Africa

Year	Too low	Satisfactory	Too high	Total	Too low	Satisfactory	Too high	Total
1976	7	24	17	48	15	50	35	100
1986	3	18	30	51	6	35	59	100
1996	1	13	39	53	2	25	74	100
2009	2	15	36	53	4	28	68	100

Asia

Year	Too low	Satisfactory	Too high	Total	Too low	Satisfactory	Too high	Total
1976	11	12	14	37	30	32	38	100
1986	13	13	12	38	34	34	32	100
1996	11	16	19	46	24	35	41	100
2009	14	17	16	47	30	36	34	100

Europe

Year	Too low	Satisfactory	Too high	Total	Too low	Satisfactory	Too high	Total
1976	11	18	0	29	38	62	0	100
1986	6	23	0	29	21	79	0	100
1996	13	29	1	43	30	67	2	100
2009	22	22	0	44	50	50	0	100

Latin America and the Caribbean

Year	Too low	Satisfactory	Too high	Total	Too low	Satisfactory	Too high	Total
1976	4	10	13	27	15	37	48	100
1986	3	14	16	33	9	42	48	100
1996	2	18	13	33	6	55	39	100
2009	1	25	7	33	3	76	21	100

Northern America

Year	Too low	Satisfactory	Too high	Total	Too low	Satisfactory	Too high	Total
1976	0	2	0	2	0	100	0	100
1986	0	2	0	2	0	100	0	100
1996	0	2	0	2	0	100	0	100
2009	0	2	0	2	0	100	0	100

Oceania

Year	Too low	Satisfactory	Too high	Total	Too low	Satisfactory	Too high	Total
1976	1	1	5	7	14	14	71	100
1986	1	3	7	11	9	27	64	100
1996	4	5	7	16	25	31	44	100
2009	4	3	9	16	25	19	56	100

TABLE 2. GOVERNMENT POLICIES ON THE RATE OF POPULATION GROWTH: 1976, 1986, 1996 AND 2009

	A. By level of development									
Year	*(Number of countries)*					*(Percentage)*				
	Raise	*Maintain*	*Lower*	*No intervention*	*Total*	*Raise*	*Maintain*	*Lower*	*No intervention*	*Total*
					World					
1976	28	0	39	83	150	19	0	26	55	100
1986	26	12	53	73	164	16	7	32	45	100
1996	25	16	71	81	193	13	8	37	42	100
2009	36	33	67	59	195	18	17	34	30	100
					More developed regions					
1976	8	0	0	26	34	24	0	0	76	100
1986	8	8	0	18	34	24	24	0	53	100
1996	11	6	1	30	48	23	12	2	62	100
2009	22	8	0	19	49	45	16	0	39	100
					Less developed regions					
1976	20	0	39	57	116	17	0	34	49	100
1986	18	4	53	55	130	14	3	41	42	100
1996	14	10	70	51	145	10	7	48	35	100
2009	14	25	67	40	146	10	17	46	27	100
					Least developed countries					
1976	5	0	6	31	42	12	0	14	74	100
1986	4	3	14	27	48	8	6	29	56	100
1996	1	1	27	20	49	2	2	55	41	100
2009	0	3	35	11	49	0	6	71	23	100

United Nations Department of Economic and Social Affairs/Population Division

TABLE 2. (CONTINUED)

	(Number of countries)					(Percentage)				
Year	Raise	Maintain	Lower	No intervention	Total	Raise	Maintain	Lower	No intervention	Total

Africa

Year	Raise	Maintain	Lower	No intervention	Total	Raise	Maintain	Lower	No intervention	Total
1976	7	0	12	29	48	15	0	25	60	100
1986	4	3	20	24	51	8	6	39	47	100
1996	2	2	32	17	53	4	4	60	32	100
2009	2	6	34	11	53	4	11	64	21	100

Asia

Year	Raise	Maintain	Lower	No intervention	Total	Raise	Maintain	Lower	No intervention	Total
1976	9	0	14	14	37	24	0	38	38	100
1986	13	1	12	12	38	34	3	32	32	100
1996	8	5	18	15	46	17	11	39	33	100
2009	11	12	18	6	47	23	26	38	13	100

Europe

Year	Raise	Maintain	Lower	No intervention	Total	Raise	Maintain	Lower	No intervention	Total
1976	8	0	0	21	29	28	0	0	72	100
1986	8	6	0	15	29	28	21	0	52	100
1996	11	6	1	25	43	26	14	2	58	100
2009	21	8	0	15	44	48	18	0	34	100

Latin America and the Caribbean

Year	Raise	Maintain	Lower	No intervention	Total	Raise	Maintain	Lower	No intervention	Total
1976	3	0	9	15	27	11	0	33	56	100
1986	0	0	15	18	33	0	0	45	55	100
1996	1	2	13	17	33	3	6	39	52	100
2009	0	6	7	20	33	0	18	21	61	100

Northern America

Year	Raise	Maintain	Lower	No intervention	Total	Raise	Maintain	Lower	No intervention	Total
1976	0	0	0	2	2	0	0	0	100	100
1986	0	1	0	1	2	0	50	0	50	100
1996	0	0	0	2	2	0	0	0	100	100
2009	0	0	0	2	2	0	0	0	100	100

Oceania

Year	Raise	Maintain	Lower	No intervention	Total	Raise	Maintain	Lower	No intervention	Total
1976	1	0	4	2	7	14	0	57	29	100
1986	1	1	6	3	11	9	9	55	27	100
1996	3	1	7	5	16	19	6	44	31	100
2009	2	1	8	5	16	13	6	50	31	100

TABLE 3. GOVERNMENT LEVEL OF CONCERN ABOUT THE AGEING OF THE POPULATION, 2009

	(Number of countries)				*(Percentage)*		
Major concern	*Minor concern*	*Not a concern*	*Total*	*Major concern*	*Minor concern*	*Not a concern*	*Total*

A. By level of development

World

| 98 | 76 | 5 | 179 | 55 | 42 | 3 | 100 |

More developed regions

| 38 | 10 | 0 | 48 | 79 | 21 | 0 | 100 |

Less developed regions

| 60 | 66 | 5 | 131 | 46 | 50 | 4 | 100 |

Least developed countries

| 10 | 27 | 2 | 39 | 26 | 69 | 5 | 100 |

B. By major area

Africa

| 16 | 28 | 2 | 46 | 35 | 61 | 4 | 100 |

Asia

| 22 | 23 | 2 | 47 | 47 | 49 | 4 | 100 |

Europe

| 35 | 8 | 0 | 43 | 81 | 19 | 0 | 100 |

Latin America and the Caribbean

| 23 | 9 | 1 | 33 | 70 | 27 | 3 | 100 |

Northern America

| 2 | 0 | 0 | 2 | 100 | 0 | 0 | 100 |

Oceania

| 0 | 8 | 0 | 8 | 0 | 100 | 0 | 100 |

TABLE 4. GOVERNMENT LEVEL OF CONCERN ABOUT THE SIZE OF THE POPULATION
OF WORKING-AGE, 2009

(Number of countries)				(Percentage)			
Major concern	Minor concern	Not a concern	Total	Major concern	Minor concern	Not a concern	Total

A. By level of development

World

| 103 | 47 | 16 | 166 | 62 | 28 | 10 | 100 |

More developed regions

| 27 | 10 | 9 | 46 | 59 | 22 | 20 | 100 |

Less developed regions

| 76 | 37 | 7 | 120 | 63 | 31 | 6 | 100 |

Least developed countries

| 27 | 8 | 0 | 35 | 77 | 23 | 0 | 100 |

B. By major area

Africa

| 27 | 11 | 0 | 38 | 71 | 29 | 0 | 100 |

Asia

| 31 | 12 | 2 | 45 | 69 | 27 | 4 | 100 |

Europe

| 24 | 10 | 7 | 41 | 59 | 24 | 17 | 100 |

Latin America and the Caribbean

| 12 | 13 | 5 | 30 | 40 | 43 | 17 | 100 |

Northern America

| 2 | 0 | 0 | 2 | 100 | 0 | 0 | 100 |

Oceania

| 7 | 1 | 2 | 10 | 70 | 10 | 20 | 100 |

TABLE 5. GOVERNMENT VIEWS ON THE LEVEL OF FERTILITY: 1976, 1986, 1996 AND 2009

	A. By level of development							
Year	(Number of countries)				(Percentage)			
	Too low	Satisfactory	Too high	Total	Too low	Satisfactory	Too high	Total
				World				
1976	16	79	55	150	11	53	37	100
1986	22	75	67	164	13	46	41	100
1996	28	78	87	193	15	40	45	100
2009	47	75	73	195	24	38	37	100
				More developed regions				
1976	7	27	0	34	21	79	0	100
1986	9	25	0	34	26	74	0	100
1996	19	28	1	48	40	58	2	100
2009	30	19	0	49	61	39	0	100
				Less developed regions				
1976	9	52	55	116	8	45	47	100
1986	13	50	67	130	10	38	52	100
1996	9	50	86	145	6	34	59	100
2009	17	56	73	146	12	38	50	100
				Least developed countries				
1976	3	26	13	42	7	62	31	100
1986	2	20	26	48	4	42	54	100
1996	0	11	38	49	0	22	78	100
2009	0	7	42	49	0	14	86	100

TABLE 5. (CONTINUED)

Year	(Number of countries)				(Percentage)			
	Too low	Satisfactory	Too high	Total	Too low	Satisfactory	Too high	Total

B. By major area

Africa

Year	Too low	Satisfactory	Too high	Total	Too low	Satisfactory	Too high	Total
1976	5	25	18	48	10	52	38	100
1986	3	17	31	51	6	33	61	100
1996	1	11	41	53	2	21	77	100
2009	1	12	40	53	2	23	75	100

Asia

Year	Too low	Satisfactory	Too high	Total	Too low	Satisfactory	Too high	Total
1976	2	18	17	37	5	49	46	100
1986	7	17	14	38	18	45	37	100
1996	7	20	19	46	15	43	41	100
2009	13	19	15	47	28	40	32	100

Europe

Year	Too low	Satisfactory	Too high	Total	Too low	Satisfactory	Too high	Total
1976	7	22	0	29	24	76	0	100
1986	9	20	0	29	31	69	0	100
1996	18	24	1	43	42	56	2	100
2009	27	17	0	44	61	39	0	100

Latin America and the Caribbean

Year	Too low	Satisfactory	Too high	Total	Too low	Satisfactory	Too high	Total
1976	2	9	16	27	7	33	59	100
1986	3	15	15	33	9	45	45	100
1996	1	14	18	33	3	42	55	100
2009	1	22	10	33	3	67	30	100

Northern America

Year	Too low	Satisfactory	Too high	Total	Too low	Satisfactory	Too high	Total
1976	0	2	0	2	0	100	0	100
1986	0	2	0	2	0	100	0	100
1996	0	2	0	2	0	100	0	100
2009	1	1	0	2	50	50	0	100

Oceania

Year	Too low	Satisfactory	Too high	Total	Too low	Satisfactory	Too high	Total
1976	0	3	4	7	0	43	57	100
1986	0	4	7	11	0	36	64	100
1996	1	7	8	16	6	44	50	100
2009	4	4	8	16	25	25	50	100

TABLE 6. GOVERNMENT POLICIES ON THE LEVEL OF FERTILITY: 1976, 1986, 1996 AND 2009

Year	(Number of countries)					(Percentage)				
	Raise	Maintain	Lower	No intervention	Total	Raise	Maintain	Lower	No intervention	Total

A. By level of development

World

Year	Raise	Maintain	Lower	No intervention	Total	Raise	Maintain	Lower	No intervention	Total
1976	13	19	40	78	150	9	13	27	52	100
1986	19	16	54	75	164	12	10	33	46	100
1996	27	19	82	65	193	14	10	42	34	100
2009	43	28	74	50	195	22	14	38	26	100

More developed regions

1976	7	7	0	20	34	21	21	0	59	100
1986	8	6	0	20	34	24	18	0	59	100
1996	16	4	1	27	48	33	8	2	56	100
2009	27	8	0	14	49	55	16	0	29	100

Less developed regions

1976	6	12	40	58	116	5	10	34	50	100
1986	11	10	54	55	130	8	8	42	42	100
1996	11	15	81	38	145	8	10	56	26	100
2009	16	20	74	36	146	11	14	51	25	100

Least developed countries

1976	1	2	6	33	42	2	5	14	79	100
1986	2	4	15	27	48	4	8	31	56	100
1996	0	3	32	14	49	0	6	65	29	100
2009	0	3	37	9	49	0	6	76	18	100

TABLE 6. (CONTINUED)

Year	Raise	Maintain	Lower	No intervention	Total	Raise	Maintain	Lower	No intervention	Total
	B. By major area									
	(Number of countries)					*(Percentage)*				
	Africa									
1976	2	2	12	32	48	4	4	25	67	100
1986	3	3	21	24	51	6	6	41	47	100
1996	2	3	36	12	53	4	6	68	23	100
2009	1	5	37	10	53	2	9	70	19	100
	Asia									
1976	2	9	14	12	37	5	24	38	32	100
1986	8	6	13	11	38	21	16	34	29	100
1996	7	9	19	11	46	15	20	41	24	100
2009	13	8	18	8	47	28	17	38	17	100
	Europe									
1976	7	7	0	15	29	24	24	0	52	100
1986	8	6	0	15	29	28	21	0	52	100
1996	16	4	1	22	43	37	9	2	51	100
2009	25	7	0	12	44	57	16	0	27	100
	Latin America and the Caribbean									
1976	2	0	10	15	27	7	0	37	56	100
1986	0	0	15	18	33	0	0	45	55	100
1996	1	0	18	14	33	3	0	55	42	100
2009	1	5	10	17	33	3	15	30	52	100
	Northern America									
1976	0	0	0	2	2	0	0	0	100	100
1986	0	0	0	2	2	0	0	0	100	100
1996	0	0	0	2	2	0	0	0	100	100
2009	0	0	0	2	2	0	0	0	100	100
	Oceania									
1976	0	1	4	2	7	0	14	57	29	100
1986	0	1	5	5	11	0	9	45	45	100
1996	1	3	8	4	16	6	19	50	25	100
2009	3	3	9	1	16	19	19	56	6	100

TABLE 7. GOVERNMENT POLICIES ON PROVIDING ACCESS TO CONTRACEPTIVE METHODS:
1976, 1986, 1996 AND 2009

	A. By level of development									
Year	(Number of countries)					(Percentage)				
	Limits	No support	Indirect support	Direct support	Total	Limits	No support	Indirect support	Direct support	Total
World										
1976	10	28	17	95	150	7	19	11	63	100
1986	7	18	22	117	164	4	11	13	71	100
1996	2	26	18	143	189	1	14	10	76	100
2009	1	17	31	146	195	1	9	16	75	100
More developed regions										
1976	3	4	6	21	34	9	12	18	62	100
1986	3	4	8	19	34	9	12	24	56	100
1996	1	12	7	28	48	2	25	15	58	100
2009	1	12	17	19	49	2	24	35	39	100
Less developed regions										
1976	7	24	11	74	116	6	21	9	64	100
1986	4	14	14	98	130	3	11	11	75	100
1996	1	14	11	115	141	1	10	8	82	100
2009	0	5	14	127	146	0	3	10	87	100
Least developed countries										
1976	4	14	6	18	42	10	33	14	43	100
1986	2	4	7	35	48	4	8	15	73	100
1996	0	3	3	42	48	0	6	6	88	100
2009	0	0	5	44	49	0	0	10	90	100

TABLE 7. (CONTINUED)

Year	(Number of countries)					(Percentage)				
	Limits	No support	Indirect support	Direct support	Total	Limits	No support	Indirect support	Direct support	Total

B. By major area

Africa

Year	Limits	No support	Indirect support	Direct support	Total	Limits	No support	Indirect support	Direct support	Total
1976	3	14	7	24	48	6	29	15	50	100
1986	0	7	6	38	51	0	14	12	75	100
1996	0	4	5	43	52	0	8	10	83	100
2009	0	2	4	47	53	0	4	8	89	100

Asia

Year	Limits	No support	Indirect support	Direct support	Total	Limits	No support	Indirect support	Direct support	Total
1976	3	7	2	25	37	8	19	5	68	100
1986	4	5	4	25	38	11	13	11	66	100
1996	1	9	3	32	45	2	20	7	71	100
2009	0	3	5	39	47	0	6	11	83	100

Europe

Year	Limits	No support	Indirect support	Direct support	Total	Limits	No support	Indirect support	Direct support	Total
1976	3	4	5	17	29	10	14	17	59	100
1986	3	4	6	16	29	10	14	21	55	100
1996	1	12	6	24	43	2	28	14	56	100
2009	1	12	14	17	44	2	27	32	39	100

Latin America and the Caribbean

Year	Limits	No support	Indirect support	Direct support	Total	Limits	No support	Indirect support	Direct support	Total
1976	1	3	2	21	27	4	11	7	78	100
1986	0	2	4	27	33	0	6	12	82	100
1996	0	1	3	29	33	0	3	9	88	100
2009	0	0	3	30	33	0	0	9	91	100

Northern America

Year	Limits	No support	Indirect support	Direct support	Total	Limits	No support	Indirect support	Direct support	Total
1976	0	0	0	2	2	0	0	0	100	100
1986	0	0	0	2	2	0	0	0	100	100
1996	0	0	0	2	2	0	0	0	100	100
2009	0	0	1	1	2	0	0	50	50	100

Oceania

Year	Limits	No support	Indirect support	Direct support	Total	Limits	No support	Indirect support	Direct support	Total
1976	0	0	1	6	7	0	0	14	86	100
1986	0	0	2	9	11	0	0	18	82	100
1996	0	0	1	13	14	0	0	7	93	100
2009	0	0	4	12	16	0	0	25	75	100

TABLE 8. GOVERNMENT LEVEL OF CONCERN ABOUT ADOLESCENT FERTILITY, 1996 AND 2009

Year	(Number of countries)				(Percentage)			
	Major concern	Minor concern	Not a concern	Total	Major concern	Minor concern	Not a concern	Total

A. By level of development

World

| 1996 | 59 | 39 | 30 | 128 | 46 | 30 | 23 | 100 |
| 2009 | 108 | 59 | 24 | 191 | 57 | 31 | 13 | 100 |

More developed regions

| 1996 | 9 | 12 | 12 | 33 | 27 | 36 | 36 | 100 |
| 2009 | 15 | 21 | 12 | 48 | 31 | 44 | 25 | 100 |

Less developed regions

| 1996 | 50 | 27 | 18 | 95 | 53 | 28 | 19 | 100 |
| 2009 | 93 | 38 | 12 | 143 | 65 | 27 | 8 | 100 |

Least developed countries

| 1996 | 16 | 9 | 8 | 33 | 48 | 27 | 24 | 100 |
| 2009 | 32 | 13 | 2 | 47 | 68 | 28 | 4 | 100 |

B. By major area

Africa

| 1996 | 24 | 8 | 9 | 41 | 59 | 20 | 22 | 100 |
| 2009 | 33 | 16 | 3 | 52 | 63 | 31 | 6 | 100 |

Asia

| 1996 | 7 | 12 | 8 | 27 | 26 | 44 | 30 | 100 |
| 2009 | 21 | 15 | 10 | 46 | 46 | 33 | 22 | 100 |

Europe

| 1996 | 7 | 9 | 12 | 28 | 25 | 32 | 43 | 100 |
| 2009 | 13 | 19 | 11 | 43 | 30 | 44 | 26 | 100 |

Latin America and the Caribbean

| 1996 | 18 | 6 | 1 | 25 | 72 | 24 | 4 | 100 |
| 2009 | 31 | 2 | 0 | 33 | 94 | 6 | 0 | 100 |

Northern America

| 1996 | 1 | 1 | 0 | 2 | 50 | 50 | 0 | 100 |
| 2009 | 1 | 1 | 0 | 2 | 50 | 50 | 0 | 100 |

Oceania

| 1996 | 2 | 3 | 0 | 5 | 40 | 60 | 0 | 100 |
| 2009 | 9 | 6 | 0 | 15 | 60 | 40 | 0 | 100 |

TABLE 9. GOVERNMENT POLICIES AND PROGRAMMES ADDRESSING ADOLESCENT FERTILITY,
1996 AND 2009

Year	(Number of countries)			(Percentage)		
	Yes	No	Total	Yes	No	Total

A. By level of development

World

1996	76	51	127	60	40	100
2009	156	35	191	82	18	100

More developed regions

1996	16	15	31	52	48	100
2009	34	14	48	71	29	100

Less developed regions

1996	60	36	96	63	38	100
2009	122	21	143	85	15	100

Least developed countries

1996	18	12	30	60	40	100
2009	42	5	47	89	11	100

B. By major area

Africa

1996	24	14	38	63	37	100
2009	44	8	52	85	15	100

Asia

1996	16	13	29	55	45	100
2009	34	12	46	74	26	100

Europe

1996	13	15	28	46	54	100
2009	30	13	43	70	30	100

Latin America and the Caribbean

1996	18	6	24	75	25	100
2009	33	0	33	100	0	100

Northern America

1996	2	0	2	100	0	100
2009	2	0	2	100	0	100

Oceania

1996	3	3	6	50	50	100
2009	13	2	15	87	13	100

TABLE 10. GOVERNMENT VIEWS ON THE ACCEPTABILITY OF THE MORTALITY LEVEL:
1976, 1986, 1996 AND 2009

	A. By level of development					
Year	(Number of countries)			(Percentage)		
	Acceptable	Unacceptable	Total	Acceptable	Unacceptable	Total
World						
1976	55	95	150	37	63	100
1986	60	104	164	37	63	100
1996	77	116	193	40	60	100
2009	88	107	195	45	55	100
More developed regions						
1976	27	7	34	79	21	100
1986	27	7	34	79	21	100
1996	30	18	48	62	38	100
2009	33	16	49	67	33	100
Less developed regions						
1976	28	88	116	24	76	100
1986	33	97	130	25	75	100
1996	47	98	145	32	68	100
2009	55	91	146	38	62	100
Least developed countries						
1976	2	40	42	5	95	100
1986	3	45	48	6	94	100
1996	1	48	49	2	98	100
2009	0	49	49	0	100	100

TABLE 10. (CONTINUED)

	B. By major area					
Year	(Number of countries)			(Percentage)		
	Acceptable	*Unacceptable*	*Total*	*Acceptable*	*Unacceptable*	*Total*
			Africa			
1976	2	46	48	4	96	100
1986	4	47	51	8	92	100
1996	7	46	53	13	87	100
2009	6	47	53	11	89	100
			Asia			
1976	13	24	37	35	65	100
1986	15	23	38	39	61	100
1996	19	27	46	41	59	100
2009	23	24	47	49	51	100
			Europe			
1976	22	7	29	76	24	100
1986	22	7	29	76	24	100
1996	28	15	43	65	35	100
2009	29	15	44	66	34	100
			Latin America and the Caribbean			
1976	11	16	27	41	59	100
1986	13	20	33	39	61	100
1996	17	16	33	52	48	100
2009	21	12	33	64	36	100
			Northern America			
1976	2	0	2	100	0	100
1986	2	0	2	100	0	100
1996	1	1	2	50	50	100
2009	1	1	2	50	50	100
			Oceania			
1976	5	2	7	71	29	100
1986	4	7	11	36	64	100
1996	5	11	16	31	69	100
2009	8	8	16	50	50	100

TABLE 11. GOVERNMENT VIEWS ON THE ACCEPTABILITY OF THE LEVEL OF
UNDER-FIVE MORTALITY, 1996 AND 2009

Year	(Number of countries)			(Percentage)		
	Acceptable	Unacceptable	Total	Acceptable	Unacceptable	Total

A. By level of development

World

1996	26	87	113	23	77	100
2009	59	136	195	30	70	100

More developed regions

1996	13	15	28	46	54	100
2009	31	18	49	63	37	100

Less developed regions

1996	13	72	85	15	85	100
2009	28	118	146	19	81	100

Least developed countries

1996	0	34	34	0	100	100
2009	0	49	49	0	100	100

B. By major area

Africa

1996	2	39	41	5	95	100
2009	2	51	53	4	96	100

Asia

1996	8	17	25	32	68	100
2009	14	33	47	30	70	100

Europe

1996	13	11	24	54	46	100
2009	29	15	44	66	34	100

Latin America and the Caribbean

1996	3	16	19	16	84	100
2009	8	25	33	24	76	100

Northern America

1996	0	1	1	0	100	100
2009	1	1	2	50	50	100

Oceania

1996	0	3	3	0	100	100
2009	5	11	16	31	69	100

TABLE 12. GOVERNMENT VIEWS ON THE ACCEPTABILITY OF THE LEVEL OF
MATERNAL MORTALITY, 2009

(Number of countries)			(Percentage)		
Acceptable	*Unacceptable*	*Total*	*Acceptable*	*Unacceptable*	*Total*

A. By level of development

World

| 66 | 129 | 195 | 34 | 66 | 100 |

More developed regions

| 36 | 13 | 49 | 73 | 27 | 100 |

Less developed regions

| 30 | 116 | 146 | 21 | 79 | 100 |

Least developed countries

| 3 | 46 | 49 | 6 | 94 | 100 |

B. By major area

Africa

| 1 | 52 | 53 | 2 | 98 | 100 |

Asia

| 14 | 33 | 47 | 30 | 70 | 100 |

Europe

| 33 | 11 | 44 | 75 | 25 | 100 |

Latin America and the Caribbean

| 8 | 25 | 33 | 24 | 76 | 100 |

Northern America

| 1 | 1 | 2 | 50 | 50 | 100 |

Oceania

| 9 | 7 | 16 | 56 | 44 | 100 |

TABLE 13. GOVERNMENT LEVEL OF CONCERN ABOUT HIV/AIDS, 1996 AND 2009

Year	(Number of countries)				(Percentage)			
	Major concern	Minor concern	Not a concern	Total	Major concern	Minor concern	Not a concern	Total

A. By level of development

World

1996	89	34	2	125	71	27	2	100
2009	169	24	1	194	87	12	1	100

More developed regions

1996	21	12	0	33	64	36	0	100
2009	37	11	0	48	77	23	0	100

Less developed regions

1996	68	22	2	92	74	24	2	100
2009	132	13	1	146	90	9	1	100

Least developed countries

1996	26	8	0	34	76	24	0	100
2009	49	0	0	49	100	0	0	100

B. By major area

Africa

1996	34	7	0	41	83	17	0	100
2009	48	4	1	53	91	8	2	100

Asia

1996	17	7	2	26	65	27	8	100
2009	39	8	0	47	83	17	0	100

Europe

1996	17	11	0	28	61	39	0	100
2009	32	11	0	43	74	26	0	100

Latin America and the Caribbean

1996	16	8	0	24	67	33	0	100
2009	32	1	0	33	97	3	0	100

Northern America

1996	2	0	0	2	100	0	0	100
2009	2	0	0	2	100	0	0	100

Oceania

1996	3	1	0	4	75	25	0	100
2009	16	0	0	16	100	0	0	100

TABLE 14. GOVERNMENT MEASURES IMPLEMENTED IN RESPONSE TO THE HIV/AIDS EPIDEMIC, 2009

(Number of countries)					(Percentage)				
IEC campaigns	Blood Screening	Distribution of condoms	Access to antiretroviral treatment	Non discriminatory policies	IEC campaigns	Blood Screening	Distribution of condoms	Provision of antiretroviral treatment	Non discriminatory policies
A. By level of development									
World									
193	189	167	178	113	99	97	86	91	58
More developed regions									
49	47	42	48	32	100	96	86	98	65
Less developed regions									
144	142	125	130	81	99	97	86	89	55
Least developed countries									
48	47	42	42	19	98	96	85	85	39
B. By major area									
Africa									
52	52	46	50	28	98	98	87	94	53
Asia									
47	47	38	38	29	100	100	81	81	62
Europe									
44	42	37	43	27	100	95	84	98	61
Latin America and the Caribbean									
33	33	33	33	21	100	100	100	100	64
Northern America									
2	2	2	2	2	100	100	100	100	100
Oceania									
15	13	11	12	6	94	81	69	75	38

TABLE 15. GOVERNMENT VIEWS ON THE SPATIAL DISTRIBUTION OF THE POPULATION:
1976, 1986, 1996 AND 2009

	A. By level of development							
	(Number of countries)				(Percentage)			
Year	Major change desired	Minor change desired	Satisfactory	Total	Major change desired	Minor change desired	Satisfactory	Total
			World					
1976	78	55	17	150	52	37	11	100
1986	75	71	18	164	46	43	11	100
1996	80	57	55	192	42	30	29	100
2009	99	62	34	195	51	32	17	100
			More developed regions					
1976	4	19	11	34	12	56	32	100
1986	3	18	13	34	9	53	38	100
1996	11	15	22	48	23	31	46	100
2009	14	21	14	49	29	43	29	100
			Less developed regions					
1976	74	36	6	116	64	31	5	100
1986	72	53	5	130	55	41	4	100
1996	69	42	33	144	48	29	23	100
2009	85	41	20	146	58	28	14	100
			Least developed countries					
1976	27	15	0	42	64	36	0	100
1986	26	22	0	48	54	46	0	100
1996	30	12	6	48	63	25	13	100
2009	36	11	2	49	74	22	4	100

TABLE 15. (CONTINUED)

| | (Number of countries) | | | | (Percentage) | | | |
Year	Major change desired	Minor change desired	Satisfactory	Total	Major change desired	Minor change desired	Satisfactory	Total
	B. By major area							
	Africa							
1976	36	12	0	48	75	25	0	100
1986	34	17	0	51	67	33	0	100
1996	33	13	6	52	63	25	12	100
2009	40	11	2	53	75	21	4	100
	Asia							
1976	14	19	4	37	38	51	11	100
1986	11	24	3	38	29	63	8	100
1996	17	18	11	46	37	39	24	100
2009	27	11	9	47	57	23	19	100
	Europe							
1976	2	17	10	29	7	59	34	100
1986	2	15	12	29	7	52	41	100
1996	10	13	20	43	23	30	47	100
2009	13	18	13	44	30	41	30	100
	Latin America and the Caribbean							
1976	22	4	1	27	81	15	4	100
1986	24	8	1	33	73	24	3	100
1996	16	7	10	33	48	21	30	100
2009	12	15	6	33	36	45	18	100
	Northern America							
1976	0	1	1	2	0	50	50	100
1986	0	1	1	2	0	50	50	100
1996	0	0	2	2	0	0	100	100
2009	0	1	1	2	0	50	50	100
	Oceania							
1976	4	2	1	7	57	29	14	100
1986	4	6	1	11	36	55	9	100
1996	4	6	6	16	25	38	38	100
2009	7	6	3	16	44	38	19	100

TABLE 16. GOVERNMENT POLICIES ON INTERNAL MIGRATION FROM RURAL AREAS TO URBAN AREAS, 2009

	(Number of countries)				(Percentage)				
Raise	Maintain	Lower	No intervention	Total	Raise	Maintain	Lower	No intervention	Total

A. By level of development

World

| 10 | 2 | 116 | 45 | 173 | 6 | 1 | 67 | 26 | 100 |

More developed regions

| 2 | 0 | 23 | 19 | 44 | 5 | 0 | 52 | 43 | 100 |

Less developed regions

| 8 | 2 | 93 | 26 | 129 | 6 | 2 | 72 | 20 | 100 |

Least developed countries

| 2 | 2 | 32 | 7 | 43 | 5 | 5 | 74 | 16 | 100 |

B. By major area

Africa

| 0 | 0 | 39 | 9 | 48 | 0 | 0 | 81 | 19 | 100 |

Asia

| 7 | 2 | 27 | 6 | 42 | 17 | 5 | 64 | 14 | 100 |

Europe

| 2 | 0 | 21 | 16 | 39 | 5 | 0 | 54 | 41 | 100 |

Latin America and the Caribbean

| 0 | 0 | 20 | 10 | 30 | 0 | 0 | 67 | 33 | 100 |

Northern America

| 0 | 0 | 0 | 2 | 2 | 0 | 0 | 0 | 100 | 100 |

Oceania

| 1 | 0 | 9 | 2 | 12 | 8 | 0 | 75 | 17 | 100 |

TABLE 17. GOVERNMENT POLICIES ON INTERNAL MIGRATION INTO URBAN AGGLOMERATIONS:
1976, 1986, 1996 AND 2009

	A. By level of development									
Year	(Number of countries)					(Percentage)				
	Raise	Maintain	Lower	No intervention	Total	Raise	Maintain	Lower	No intervention	Total
				World						
1976	4	0	39	40	83	5	0	47	48	100
1986	2	1	50	41	94	2	1	53	44	100
1996	3	5	55	60	123	2	4	45	49	100
2009	6	7	109	53	175	3	4	62	30	100
				More developed regions						
1976	2	0	11	7	20	10	0	55	35	100
1986	1	1	8	9	19	5	5	42	47	100
1996	3	3	8	17	31	10	10	26	55	100
2009	2	3	15	24	44	5	7	34	55	100
				Less developed regions						
1976	2	0	28	33	63	3	0	44	52	100
1986	1	0	42	32	75	1	0	56	43	100
1996	0	2	47	43	92	0	2	51	47	100
2009	4	4	94	29	131	3	3	72	22	100
				Least developed countries						
1976	0	0	11	15	26	0	0	42	58	100
1986	0	0	7	19	26	0	0	27	73	100
1996	0	0	17	17	34	0	0	50	50	100
2009	0	1	32	9	42	0	2	76	22	100

TABLE 17. (CONTINUED)

Year	(Number of countries)					(Percentage)				
	Raise	Maintain	Lower	No intervention	Total	Raise	Maintain	Lower	No intervention	Total

Africa

Year	Raise	Maintain	Lower	No intervention	Total	Raise	Maintain	Lower	No intervention	Total
1976	0	0	18	19	37	0	0	49	51	100
1986	0	0	16	17	33	0	0	48	52	100
1996	0	1	22	18	41	0	2	54	44	100
2009	0	0	36	11	47	0	0	77	23	100

Asia

Year	Raise	Maintain	Lower	No intervention	Total	Raise	Maintain	Lower	No intervention	Total
1976	1	0	4	0	5	20	0	80	0	100
1986	1	0	12	6	19	5	0	63	32	100
1996	0	0	18	9	27	0	0	67	33	100
2009	4	4	29	7	44	9	9	66	16	100

Europe

Year	Raise	Maintain	Lower	No intervention	Total	Raise	Maintain	Lower	No intervention	Total
1976	2	0	11	6	19	11	0	58	32	100
1986	1	1	8	6	16	6	6	50	38	100
1996	3	3	7	13	26	12	12	27	50	100
2009	2	3	13	21	39	5	8	33	54	100

Latin America and the Caribbean

Year	Raise	Maintain	Lower	No intervention	Total	Raise	Maintain	Lower	No intervention	Total
1976	1	0	6	13	20	5	0	30	65	100
1986	0	0	13	6	19	0	0	68	32	100
1996	0	0	8	15	23	0	0	35	65	100
2009	0	0	21	10	31	0	0	68	32	100

Northern America

Year	Raise	Maintain	Lower	No intervention	Total	Raise	Maintain	Lower	No intervention	Total
1976	0	0	0	1	1	0	0	0	100	100
1986	0	0	0	2	2	0	0	0	100	100
1996	0	0	0	2	2	0	0	0	100	100
2009	0	0	0	2	2	0	0	0	100	100

Oceania

Year	Raise	Maintain	Lower	No intervention	Total	Raise	Maintain	Lower	No intervention	Total
1976	0	0	0	1	1	0	0	0	100	100
1986	0	0	1	4	5	0	0	20	80	100
1996	0	1	0	3	4	0	25	0	75	100
2009	0	0	10	2	12	0	0	83	17	100

TABLE 18. GOVERNMENT POLICIES ON INTERNAL MIGRATION FROM URBAN AREAS TO URBAN AREAS, 2009

	(Number of countries)					*(Percentage)*			
Raise	*Maintain*	*Lower*	*No intervention*	*Total*	*Raise*	*Maintain*	*Lower*	*No intervention*	*Total*

A. By level of development

World

| 19 | 19 | 5 | 85 | 128 | 15 | 15 | 4 | 66 | 100 |

More developed regions

| 2 | 2 | 1 | 31 | 36 | 6 | 6 | 3 | 86 | 100 |

Less developed regions

| 17 | 17 | 4 | 54 | 92 | 18 | 18 | 4 | 59 | 100 |

Least developed countries

| 5 | 5 | 1 | 15 | 26 | 19 | 19 | 4 | 58 | 100 |

B. By major area

Africa

| 5 | 5 | 2 | 19 | 31 | 16 | 16 | 6 | 61 | 100 |

Asia

| 4 | 11 | 2 | 18 | 35 | 11 | 31 | 6 | 51 | 100 |

Europe

| 2 | 2 | 1 | 26 | 31 | 6 | 6 | 3 | 84 | 100 |

Latin America and the Caribbean

| 7 | 1 | 0 | 16 | 24 | 29 | 4 | 0 | 67 | 100 |

Northern America

| 0 | 0 | 0 | 2 | 2 | 0 | 0 | 0 | 100 | 100 |

Oceania

| 1 | 0 | 0 | 4 | 5 | 20 | 0 | 0 | 80 | 100 |

TABLE 19. GOVERNMENT POLICIES ON INTERNAL MIGRATION FROM URBAN AREAS TO RURAL AREAS, 2009

| | *(Number of countries)* | | | | | *(Percentage)* | | | |
Raise	Maintain	Lower	No intervention	Total	Raise	Maintain	Lower	No intervention	Total
					A. By level of development				
				World					
39	9	5	66	119	33	8	4	55	100
				More developed regions					
9	2	2	26	39	23	5	5	67	100
				Less developed regions					
30	7	3	40	80	38	9	4	50	100
				Least developed countries					
9	1	1	11	22	41	5	5	50	100
				B. By major area					
				Africa					
13	1	0	13	27	48	4	0	48	100
				Asia					
14	3	3	12	32	44	9	9	38	100
				Europe					
8	2	2	22	34	24	6	6	65	100
				Latin America and the Caribbean					
4	2	0	13	19	21	11	0	68	100
				Northern America					
0	0	0	2	2	0	0	0	100	100
				Oceania					
0	1	0	4	5	0	20	0	80	100

TABLE 20. GOVERNMENT VIEWS ON THE LEVEL OF IMMIGRATION: 1976, 1986, 1996 AND 2009

A. By level of development

Year	(Number of countries)				(Percentage)			
	Too low	Satisfactory	Too high	Total	Too low	Satisfactory	Too high	Total
World								
1976	11	129	10	150	7	86	7	100
1986	6	125	33	164	4	76	20	100
1996	4	148	41	193	2	77	21	100
2009	9	152	34	195	5	78	17	100
More developed regions								
1976	1	27	6	34	3	79	18	100
1986	0	26	8	34	0	76	24	100
1996	1	31	16	48	2	65	33	100
2009	4	41	4	49	8	84	8	100
Less developed regions								
1976	10	102	4	116	9	88	3	100
1986	6	99	25	130	5	76	19	100
1996	3	117	25	145	2	81	17	100
2009	5	111	30	146	3	76	21	100
Least developed countries								
1976	2	39	1	42	5	93	2	100
1986	1	40	7	48	2	83	15	100
1996	0	41	8	49	0	84	16	100
2009	0	41	8	49	0	84	16	100

TABLE 20. (CONTINUED)

	B. By major area							
Year	(Number of countries)				(Percentage)			
	Too low	Satisfactory	Too high	Total	Too low	Satisfactory	Too high	Total
				Africa				
1976	5	41	2	48	10	85	4	100
1986	1	39	11	51	2	76	22	100
1996	0	46	7	53	0	87	13	100
2009	0	38	15	53	0	72	28	100
				Asia				
1976	4	32	1	37	11	86	3	100
1986	1	30	7	38	3	79	18	100
1996	1	35	10	46	2	76	22	100
2009	3	34	10	47	6	72	21	100
				Europe				
1976	0	24	5	29	0	83	17	100
1986	0	22	7	29	0	76	24	100
1996	0	27	16	43	0	63	37	100
2009	2	38	4	44	5	86	9	100
				Latin America and the Caribbean				
1976	1	25	1	27	4	93	4	100
1986	4	23	6	33	12	70	18	100
1996	2	26	5	33	6	79	15	100
2009	1	29	3	33	3	88	9	100
				Northern America				
1976	0	2	0	2	0	100	0	100
1986	0	1	1	2	0	50	50	100
1996	0	2	0	2	0	100	0	100
2009	1	1	0	2	50	50	0	100
				Oceania				
1976	1	5	1	7	14	71	14	100
1986	0	10	1	11	0	91	9	100
1996	1	12	3	16	6	75	19	100
2009	2	12	2	16	13	75	13	100

TABLE 21. GOVERNMENT POLICIES ON IMMIGRATION: 1976, 1986, 1996 AND 2009

	A. By level of development							
	(Number of countries)				(Percentage)			
Year	Raise	Maintain/No intervention	Lower	Total	Raise	Maintain/No intervention	Lower	Total
World								
1976	11	129	10	150	7	86	7	100
1986	6	125	33	164	4	76	20	100
1996	8	107	78	193	4	55	41	100
2009	16	143	36	195	8	73	18	100
More developed regions								
1976	1	27	6	34	3	79	18	100
1986	0	21	13	34	0	62	38	100
1996	1	18	29	48	2	38	60	100
2009	6	39	4	49	12	80	8	100
Less developed regions								
1976	10	102	4	116	9	88	3	100
1986	6	104	20	130	5	80	15	100
1996	7	89	49	145	5	61	34	100
2009	10	104	32	146	7	72	22	100
Least developed countries								
1976	2	39	1	42	5	93	2	100
1986	1	43	4	48	2	90	8	100
1996	1	35	13	49	2	71	27	100
2009	0	41	8	49	0	84	16	100

TABLE 21. (CONTINUED*)*

Year	(Number of countries)				(Percentage)			
	Raise	Maintain/No intervention	Lower	Total	Raise	Maintain/No intervention	Lower	Total

B. By major area

Africa

Year	Raise	Maintain/No intervention	Lower	Total	Raise	Maintain/No intervention	Lower	Total
1976	5	41	2	48	10	85	4	100
1986	1	41	9	51	2	80	18	100
1996	2	35	16	53	4	66	30	100
2009	0	41	12	53	0	77	23	100

Asia

Year	Raise	Maintain/No intervention	Lower	Total	Raise	Maintain/No intervention	Lower	Total
1976	4	32	1	37	11	86	3	100
1986	1	30	7	38	3	79	18	100
1996	2	23	21	46	4	50	46	100
2009	7	26	14	47	15	55	30	100

Europe

Year	Raise	Maintain/No intervention	Lower	Total	Raise	Maintain/No intervention	Lower	Total
1976	0	24	5	29	0	83	17	100
1986	0	16	13	29	0	55	45	100
1996	0	15	28	43	0	35	65	100
2009	4	36	4	44	9	82	9	100

Latin America and the Caribbean

Year	Raise	Maintain/No intervention	Lower	Total	Raise	Maintain/No intervention	Lower	Total
1976	1	25	1	27	4	93	4	100
1986	4	25	4	33	12	76	12	100
1996	3	20	10	33	9	61	30	100
2009	2	27	4	33	6	82	12	100

Northern America

Year	Raise	Maintain/No intervention	Lower	Total	Raise	Maintain/No intervention	Lower	Total
1976	0	2	0	2	0	100	0	100
1986	0	2	0	2	0	100	0	100
1996	0	1	1	2	0	50	50	100
2009	1	1	0	2	50	50	0	100

Oceania

Year	Raise	Maintain/No intervention	Lower	Total	Raise	Maintain/No intervention	Lower	Total
1976	1	5	1	7	14	71	14	100
1986	0	11	0	11	0	100	0	100
1996	1	13	2	16	6	81	13	100
2009	2	12	2	16	13	76	13	100

TABLE 22. GOVERNMENT POLICIES ON IMMIGRATION FOR PERMANENT SETTLEMENT, 2009

	(Number of countries)					*(Percentage)*			
Raise	*Maintain*	*Lower*	*No intervention*	*Total*	*Raise*	*Maintain*	*Lower*	*No intervention*	*Total*

A. By level of development

World

| 12 | 90 | 32 | 35 | 169 | 7 | 53 | 19 | 21 | 100 |

More developed regions

| 5 | 33 | 6 | 4 | 48 | 10 | 69 | 13 | 8 | 100 |

Less developed regions

| 7 | 57 | 26 | 31 | 121 | 6 | 47 | 21 | 26 | 100 |

Least developed countries

| 0 | 9 | 6 | 19 | 34 | 0 | 26 | 17 | 57 | 100 |

B. By major area

Africa

| 0 | 12 | 9 | 20 | 41 | 0 | 29 | 22 | 49 | 100 |

Asia

| 5 | 19 | 10 | 8 | 42 | 12 | 45 | 24 | 19 | 100 |

Europe

| 3 | 31 | 6 | 3 | 43 | 7 | 72 | 14 | 7 | 100 |

Latin America and the Caribbean

| 1 | 23 | 5 | 3 | 32 | 3 | 72 | 16 | 9 | 100 |

Northern America

| 1 | 1 | 0 | 0 | 2 | 50 | 50 | 0 | 0 | 100 |

Oceania

| 2 | 4 | 2 | 1 | 9 | 22 | 44 | 22 | 11 | 100 |

TABLE 23. GOVERNMENT POLICIES ON IMMIGRATION OF HIGHLY SKILLED WORKERS, 2009

	(Number of countries)					(Percentage)			
Raise	Maintain	Lower	No intervention	Total	Raise	Maintain	Lower	No intervention	Total

A. By level of development

World

42	83	6	27	158	27	53	4	17	100

More developed regions

21	16	2	6	45	47	36	4	13	100

Less developed regions

21	67	4	21	113	19	59	4	19	100

Least developed countries

3	11	1	13	28	11	39	4	46	100

B. By major area

Africa

5	10	1	17	33	15	30	3	52	100

Asia

11	26	3	2	42	26	62	7	5	100

Europe

17	16	1	6	40	43	40	3	15	100

Latin America and the Caribbean

5	26	0	1	32	16	81	0	3	100

Northern America

2	0	0	0	2	100	0	0	0	100

Oceania

2	5	1	1	9	22	56	11	11	100

TABLE 24. GOVERNMENT POLICIES ON IMMIGRATION OF TEMPORARY WORKERS, 2009

	(Number of countries)				(Percentage)				
Raise	*Maintain*	*Lower*	*No intervention*	*Total*	*Raise*	*Maintain*	*Lower*	*No intervention*	*Total*
				A. By level of development					
				World					
11	97	39	28	175	6	55	22	16	100
				More developed regions					
7	31	6	4	48	15	65	13	8	100
				Less developed regions					
4	66	33	24	127	3	52	26	19	100
				Least developed countries					
1	15	6	14	36	3	41	17	39	100
				B. By major area					
				Africa					
0	13	10	17	40	0	33	25	43	100
				Asia					
2	25	15	3	45	4	56	33	7	100
				Europe					
5	30	5	3	43	12	70	12	7	100
				Latin America and the Caribbean					
1	23	2	5	31	3	74	6	16	100
				Northern America					
1	1	0	0	2	50	50	0	0	100
				Oceania					
2	5	7	0	14	14	36	50	0	100

TABLE 25. GOVERNMENT POLICIES ON IMMIGRATION FOR FAMILY REUNIFICATION, 2009

	(Number of countries)					(Percentage)			
Raise	Maintain	Lower	No intervention	Total	Raise	Maintain	Lower	No intervention	Total

A. By level of development

World

| 11 | 98 | 9 | 35 | 153 | 7 | 64 | 6 | 23 | 100 |

More developed regions

| 5 | 34 | 3 | 4 | 46 | 11 | 74 | 7 | 9 | 100 |

Less developed regions

| 6 | 64 | 6 | 31 | 107 | 6 | 60 | 6 | 29 | 100 |

Least developed countries

| 1 | 9 | 0 | 18 | 28 | 4 | 32 | 0 | 64 | 100 |

B. By major area

Africa

| 1 | 12 | 2 | 20 | 35 | 3 | 34 | 6 | 57 | 100 |

Asia

| 4 | 25 | 2 | 7 | 38 | 11 | 66 | 5 | 18 | 100 |

Europe

| 3 | 32 | 3 | 3 | 41 | 7 | 78 | 7 | 7 | 100 |

Latin America and the Caribbean

| 1 | 23 | 2 | 4 | 30 | 3 | 77 | 7 | 13 | 100 |

Northern America

| 1 | 1 | 0 | 0 | 2 | 50 | 50 | 0 | 0 | 100 |

Oceania

| 1 | 5 | 0 | 1 | 7 | 14 | 71 | 0 | 14 | 100 |

TABLE 26. GOVERNMENT POLICIES ON INTEGRATION OF NON-CITIZENS, 2009

(Number of countries)			*(Percentage)*		
Yes	*No*	*Total*	*Yes*	*No*	*Total*

A. By level of development

World
| 82 | 49 | 131 | 63 | 37 | 100 |

More developed regions
| 39 | 5 | 44 | 89 | 11 | 100 |

Less developed regions
| 43 | 44 | 87 | 49 | 51 | 100 |

Least developed countries
| 5 | 16 | 21 | 24 | 76 | 100 |

B. By major area

Africa
| 11 | 16 | 27 | 41 | 59 | 100 |

Asia
| 18 | 18 | 36 | 50 | 50 | 100 |

Europe
| 35 | 4 | 39 | 90 | 10 | 100 |

Latin America and the Caribbean
| 12 | 11 | 23 | 52 | 48 | 100 |

Northern America
| 2 | 0 | 2 | 100 | 0 | 100 |

Oceania
| 4 | 0 | 4 | 100 | 0 | 100 |

TABLE 27. GOVERNMENT VIEWS ON THE LEVEL OF EMIGRATION: 1976, 1986, 1996 AND 2009

Year	(Number of countries)				(Percentage)			
	Too low	Satisfactory	Too high	Total	Too low	Satisfactory	Too high	Total

A. By level of development

World

1976	6	125	19	150	4	83	13	100
1986	9	124	31	164	5	76	19	100
1996	5	133	55	193	3	69	28	100
2009	7	130	58	195	4	67	30	100

More developed regions

1976	1	28	5	34	3	82	15	100
1986	2	29	3	34	6	85	9	100
1996	1	35	12	48	2	73	25	100
2009	0	39	10	49	0	80	20	100

Less developed regions

1976	5	97	14	116	4	84	12	100
1986	7	95	28	130	5	73	22	100
1996	4	98	43	145	3	68	30	100
2009	7	91	48	146	5	62	33	100

Least developed countries

1976	0	39	3	42	0	93	7	100
1986	1	39	8	48	2	81	17	100
1996	1	37	11	49	2	76	22	100
2009	2	38	9	49	4	78	18	100

TABLE 27. (CONTINUED)

Year	(Number of countries)				(Percentage)			
	Too low	Satisfactory	Too high	Total	Too low	Satisfactory	Too high	Total

B. By major area

Africa								
1976	1	44	3	48	2	92	6	100
1986	3	41	7	51	6	80	14	100
1996	2	40	11	53	4	75	21	100
2009	2	36	15	53	4	68	28	100
Asia								
1976	4	31	2	37	11	84	5	100
1986	3	28	7	38	8	74	18	100
1996	2	31	13	46	4	67	28	100
2009	4	32	11	47	9	68	23	100
Europe								
1976	1	23	5	29	3	79	17	100
1986	1	26	2	29	3	90	7	100
1996	1	31	11	43	2	72	26	100
2009	0	34	10	44	0	77	23	100
Latin America and the Caribbean								
1976	0	18	9	27	0	67	33	100
1986	2	17	14	33	6	52	42	100
1996	0	18	15	33	0	55	45	100
2009	0	16	17	33	0	48	52	100
Northern America								
1976	0	2	0	2	0	100	0	100
1986	0	2	0	2	0	100	0	100
1996	0	2	0	2	0	100	0	100
2009	0	2	0	2	0	100	0	100
Oceania								
1976	0	7	0	7	0	100	0	100
1986	0	10	1	11	0	91	9	100
1996	0	11	5	16	0	69	31	100
2009	1	10	5	16	6	63	31	100

TABLE 28. GOVERNMENT POLICIES ON EMIGRATION: 1976, 1986, 1996 AND 2009

Year	*(Number of countries)*				*(Percentage)*			
	Raise	*Maintain/ No intervention*	*Lower*	*Total*	*Raise*	*Maintain/ No intervention*	*Lower*	*Total*
World								
1976	6	125	19	150	4	83	13	100
1986	8	120	36	164	5	73	22	100
1996	6	142	45	193	3	74	23	100
2009	10	142	43	195	5	73	22	100
More developed regions								
1976	1	28	5	34	3	82	15	100
1986	2	28	4	34	6	82	12	100
1996	1	35	12	48	2	73	25	100
2009	0	40	9	49	0	81	18	100
Less developed regions								
1976	5	97	14	116	4	84	12	100
1986	6	92	32	130	5	71	25	100
1996	5	107	33	145	3	74	23	100
2009	10	102	34	146	7	70	23	100
Least developed countries								
1976	0	39	3	42	0	93	7	100
1986	0	39	9	48	0	81	19	100
1996	1	39	9	49	2	80	18	100
2009	4	37	8	49	8	76	16	100

A. By level of development

United Nations Department of Economic and Social Affairs/Population Division

TABLE 28. (CONTINUED)

	B. By major area							
	(Number of countries)				(Percentage)			
Year	Raise	Maintain/ No intervention	Lower	Total	Raise	Maintain/ No intervention	Lower	Total
				Africa				
1976	1	44	3	48	2	92	6	100
1986	2	41	8	51	4	80	16	100
1996	2	42	9	53	4	79	17	100
2009	1	39	13	53	2	73	25	100
				Asia				
1976	4	31	2	37	11	84	5	100
1986	5	25	8	38	13	66	21	100
1996	3	32	11	46	7	70	24	100
2009	7	31	9	47	15	66	19	100
				Europe				
1976	1	23	5	29	3	79	17	100
1986	1	24	4	29	3	83	14	100
1996	1	30	12	43	2	70	28	100
2009	0	35	9	44	0	80	20	100
				Latin America and the Caribbean				
1976	0	18	9	27	0	67	33	100
1986	0	18	15	33	0	55	45	100
1996	0	23	10	33	0	70	30	100
2009	1	24	8	33	3	73	24	100
				Northern America				
1976	0	2	0	2	0	100	0	100
1986	0	2	0	2	0	100	0	100
1996	0	2	0	2	0	100	0	100
2009	0	2	0	2	0	100	0	100
				Oceania				
1976	0	7	0	7	0	100	0	100
1986	0	10	1	11	0	91	9	100
1996	0	13	3	16	0	81	19	100
2009	1	11	4	16	6	69	25	100

TABLE 29. GOVERNMENT POLICIES ON ENCOURAGING THE RETURN OF CITIZENS, 2009

	(Number of countries)			*(Percentage)*	
Yes	*No*	*Total*	*Yes*	*No*	*Total*
A. By level of development					
World					
89	65	154	58	42	100
More developed regions					
21	24	45	47	53	100
Less developed regions					
68	41	109	62	38	100
Least developed countries					
18	11	29	62	38	100
B. By major area					
Africa					
20	15	35	57	43	100
Asia					
27	14	41	66	34	100
Europe					
20	20	40	50	50	100
Latin America and the Caribbean					
17	11	28	61	39	100
Northern America					
0	2	2	0	100	100
Oceania					
5	3	8	63	38	100

PART TWO

COUNTRY PROFILES

VIII. DEFINITIONS AND SOURCES

A. GLOSSARY

1. GOVERNMENT VIEWS AND POLICIES

Population size and growth

View on growth – Government views on the level of the total population's prevailing rate of growth

Too high	The Government has indicated that the rate of population growth is too high;
Satisfactory	The Government has indicated that the rate of population growth is acceptable or has not expressed a view;
Too low	The Government has indicated that the rate of population growth is too low.

Policy on growth – Government policies on the rate of population growth

Raise	The Government has policies in place to raise population growth;
Maintain	The Government has policies in place to maintain population growth;
Lower	The Government has policies in place to lower population growth;
No intervention	The Government does not intervene with regard to population growth.

Population age structure

Size of the working-age population – Government level of concern regarding the current size of the working age population in relation to the domestic labour market

Major concern	The Government has expressed serious concern that the working-age population is either too small or too large for the present labour market;
Minor concern	The Government has expressed some concern that the working-age population is either too small or too large for the present labour market;
Not a concern	The Government has indicated that the size of the working-age population is not a concern;
..	The Government's view on the working-age population is not known.

Ageing of the population – Government level of concern regarding the transformation of the age structure of the population, especially the growing proportion of the elderly population

Major concern	The Government has expressed serious concern about the ageing of the population or increased burden on health and welfare provisions due to the growing proportion of the elderly population;
Minor concern	The Government has expressed some concern about the ageing of the population or increased burden on health and welfare provisions due to the growing proportion of the elderly population;
Not a concern	The Government has indicated that population ageing is not a concern;
..	The Government's view on population ageing is not known.

Fertility and family planning

View on fertility level – Government views on the level of fertility

Too high	The Government has indicated that the fertility level is too high;
Satisfactory	The Government has indicated that the fertility level is acceptable or has not expressed a view;
Too low	The Government has indicated that the fertility level is too low.

Policy on fertility – Government policies on the level of fertility

Raise	The Government has policies in place to raise fertility levels;
Maintain	The Government has policies to maintain fertility levels;
Lower	The Government has policies in place to lower fertility levels;
No intervention	The Government does not intervene with regard to fertility levels.

Access to contraceptive methods – Government level of support for modern methods of contraception (e.g. the pill, IUD, injectables, hormonal implants, condoms and female barrier methods)

Direct support	The Government directly supports the dissemination of information, guidance and materials through Government facilities;
Indirect support	The Government indirectly supports provision of information, guidance and materials by non-governmental sources;
No support	The Government permits the provision of information, guidance and materials by non-governmental sources but provides no support to such organizations;
Limits	The Government prevents access to information, guidance and materials in respect to modern methods of contraception.

Adolescent fertility – Government level of concern regarding the fertility of women under 20 years of age

Major concern	The Government has expressed serious concern about the level of adolescent fertility;
Minor concern	The Government has expressed some concern about the level of adolescent fertility;
Not a concern	The Government has indicated that adolescent fertility is not a concern;
..	The Government's view on adolescent fertility is not known.

Policies and programmes addressing adolescent fertility – Government policies and programmes that support activities to lower fertility among women under 20 years of age

Yes	The Government has policies or programmes in place to lower adolescent fertility rates (e.g. counselling and family planning services, education programmes);
No	The Government has no policies or programmes in place to lower adolescent fertility rates;
..	It is not known whether the Government has policies or programmes in place to lower adolescent fertility rates.

Health and mortality

View on the level of expectation of life – Government views on the current level of life expectancy at birth

Acceptable   The Government considers the present life expectancy at birth as acceptable;
Unacceptable   The Government considers the present life expectancy at birth as unacceptable.

View on the level of under-five mortality – Government views on the current level of mortality of children under five years of age

Acceptable   The Government considers the present level of under-five mortality as acceptable;
Unacceptable   The Government considers the present level of under-five mortality as unacceptable.

View on the level of maternal mortality – Government views on the current level of maternal mortality

Acceptable   The Government considers the present maternal mortality level as acceptable;
Unacceptable   The Government considers the present maternal mortality level as unacceptable.

View on the level of HIV/AIDS – Government level of concern regarding the prevalence of HIV/AIDS

Major concern   The Government has expressed serious concern about the level of HIV/AIDS or the risk that it poses to the country;
Minor concern   The Government has expressed some concern about the level of HIV/AIDS or the risk that it poses to the country;
Not a concern   The Government has indicated that HIV/AIDS is not a concern;
..   The Government's view on HIV/AIDS is not known.

Measures implemented to control HIV/AIDS – Government policies on selected approaches to respond to the HIV/AIDS epidemic

1.   Blood screening
2.   Information, education and communication (IEC) campaigns
3.   Provision of antiretroviral treatment (ART)
4.   Non–discriminatory policies
5.   Distribution of condoms

Grounds on which abortion is permitted – <u>Legally</u> permissible grounds for granting an abortion

1.   To save the woman's life;
2.   To preserve the physical health of the woman;
3.   To preserve the mental health of the woman;
4.   Rape or incest;
5.   Foetal impairment;
6.   Economic or social reasons;
7.   On request.

Spatial distribution and internal migration

View on spatial distribution – Government views on modifying the spatial distribution of population

Major change desired	The Government has indicated a desire to significantly alter the spatial distribution of the population;
Minor change desired	The Government has indicated a desire to somewhat alter the spatial distribution of the population;
Satisfactory	The Government has indicated that the spatial distribution of the population is acceptable, or has not expressed a view.

Policy on internal migration from rural to urban areas – Government policies to alter internal migration from rural to urban areas

Raise	The Government has policies in place to raise internal migration from rural to urban areas;
Maintain	The Government has policies in place to maintain internal migration from rural to urban areas;
Lower	The Government has policies in place to lower internal migration from rural to urban areas;
No intervention	The Government does not intervene to alter internal migration from rural to urban areas;
..	It is not known whether the Government intervenes to alter internal migration from rural to urban areas.

Policy on internal migration from rural to rural areas – Government policies to alter internal migration from rural to rural areas

Raise	The Government has policies in place to raise internal migration from rural to rural areas;
Maintain	The Government has policies in place to maintain internal migration from rural to rural areas;
Lower	The Government has policies in place to lower internal migration from rural to rural areas;
No intervention	The Government does not intervene to alter internal migration from rural to rural areas;
..	It is not known whether the Government intervenes to alter internal migration from rural to rural areas;

Policy on internal migration from urban to rural areas – Government policies to alter internal migration from urban to rural areas

Raise	The Government has policies in place to raise internal migration from urban to rural areas;
Maintain	The Government has policies in place to maintain internal migration from urban to rural areas;
Lower	The Government has policies in place to lower internal migration from urban to rural areas;
No intervention	The Government does not intervene to alter internal migration from urban to rural areas;
..	It is not known whether the Government intervenes to alter internal migration from urban to rural areas.

Policy on internal migration from urban to urban areas – Government policies to alter internal migration from urban to urban areas

Raise	The Government has policies in place to raise internal migration from urban to urban areas;
Maintain	The Government has policies in place to maintain internal migration from urban to urban areas;
Lower	The Government has policies in place to lower internal migration from urban to urban areas;
No intervention	The Government does not intervene to alter internal migration from urban to urban areas;
..	It is not known whether the Government intervenes to alter internal migration from urban to urban areas.

Policy on internal migration into urban agglomerations

Raise	The Government has policies in place to raise internal migration into urban agglomerations;
Maintain	The Government has policies in place to maintain internal migration into urban agglomerations;
Lower	The Government has policies in place to lower internal migration into urban agglomerations;
No intervention	The Government does not intervene to alter internal migration into urban agglomerations;
..	It is not known whether the Government intervenes to alter internal migration into urban agglomerations.

International migration

View on immigration – Government views on the level of documented immigration into the country, including immigration for permanent settlement, temporary and highly skilled work and family reunification. Government views towards asylum-seekers, refugees and undocumented migrants are not reflected in this variable.

Too high	The Government has indicated that the level of immigration is too high;
Satisfactory	The Government has indicated that the level of immigration is satisfactory or has not expressed a view;
Too low	The Government has indicated that the level of immigration is too low.

Policy on immigration - Government policies regarding the overall level of immigration

Raise	The Government has policies in place to raise the overall level of immigration;
Maintain	The Government has policies in place to maintain the overall level of immigration;
Lower	The Government has policies in place to lower the overall level of immigration;
No intervention	The Government does not intervene with regard to the overall level of immigration.

Policy on permanent settlement – *Government* policies on immigration for the purpose of permanent settlement

Raise	The Government has policies in place to raise immigration for permanent settlement;
Maintain	The Government has policies in place to maintain immigration for permanent settlement;
Lower	The Government has policies in place to lower immigration for permanent settlement;
No intervention	The Government does not intervene with regard to immigration for permanent settlement;
..	It is not known whether the Government intervenes with regard to immigration for permanent settlement.

Policy on temporary workers – Government policies on immigration of temporary workers

Raise	The Government has policies in place to raise immigration of temporary workers;
Maintain	The Government has policies in place to maintain immigration of temporary workers;
Lower	The Government has policies in place to lower immigration of temporary workers;
No intervention	The Government does not intervene with regard to immigration of temporary workers;
..	It is not known whether the Government intervenes with regard to immigration of temporary workers.

Policy on highly skilled workers – Government policies on immigration of highly skilled workers

Raise	The Government has policies in place to raise immigration of highly skilled workers;
Maintain	The Government has policies in place to maintain immigration of highly skilled workers;
Lower	The Government has policies in place to lower immigration of highly skilled workers;
No intervention	The Government does not intervene with regard to immigration of highly skilled workers;
..	It is not known whether the Government intervenes with regard to immigration of highly skilled workers.

Policy on family reunification – Government policies concerning immigration for the purpose of family reunification

Raise	The Government has policies in place to raise immigration for family reunification;
Maintain	The Government has policies in place to maintain immigration for family reunification;
Lower	The Government has policies in place to lower immigration for family reunification;
No intervention	The Government does not intervene with regard to immigration for family reunification;
..	It is not known whether the Government intervenes with regard to immigration for family reunification.

Integration of non-citizens – Government policies or programmes to foster the integration of non-citizens into society

Yes	The Government has policies or programmes to foster the integration of non-citizens (e.g. language classes, provision of social services);
No	The Government has no policies or programmes to foster the integration of non-citizens;
..	It is not known whether the Government has a policy or programme to foster the integration of non-citizens.

View on emigration – Government views of the current level of emigration from the country

Too high	The Government has indicated that the level of emigration is too high;
Satisfactory	The Government has indicated that the level of emigration is satisfactory, or has not expressed a view;
Too low	The Government has indicated that the level of emigration is too low.

Policy on emigration – Government policies towards citizens leaving to establish residency outside of the country

Raise	The Government has policies in place to raise emigration;
Maintain	The Government has policies in place to maintain emigration;
Lower	The Government has policies in place to lower emigration;
No intervention	The Government does not intervene with regard to emigration.

Policy on encouraging the return of citizens – Government policies designed to encourage citizens to return to the country

Yes	The Government has policies to encourage citizens to return (e.g. tax incentives, financial inducements);
No	The Government has no policies to encourage citizens to return;
..	It is not known whether the Government has a policy to encourage citizens to return.

2. DEMOGRAPHIC INDICATORS

Annual population growth rate: The exponential average annual rate of population growth expressed as a percentage.

Total fertility: Average number of children that would be born per woman if all women lived to the end of their childbearing years and if a given set of age-specific fertility rates remained constant during their childbearing years.

Adolescent fertility rate: The number of births to women aged 15 to19 years over a year per 1,000 women in that age group during that year.

Percentage of married women using contraception: The percentage of women aged 15 to 49 years who are in a marital or consensual union and using a modern contraceptive method (sterilization, the pill, injectables, IUD, condom, vaginal barrier method or implant) or any method (modern contraceptive method, rhythm, withdrawal or other traditional methods).

Life expectancy at birth: The expected average number of years to be lived by a newly born baby if current age-specific mortality rates were to remain constant.

Infant mortality rate: The probability of dying before age 1 expressed per 1,000 live births.

Under-five mortality: The probability of dying before age 5 expressed per 1,000 live births.

Maternal mortality ratio: The annual number of deaths of women occurring during pregnancy or within 42 days of termination of pregnancy, regardless of the cause of death, per 100,000 live births in the reference year.

People living with HIV: The estimated number of people infected with HIV, alive at the end of 2007. For additional information, see *Report on the Global AIDS Epidemic, 2008.* Joint United Nations Programme on HIV/AIDS (UNAIDS), Geneva.

Adult HIV prevalence: The percentage of adults aged 15 to 49 years living with HIV at the end of 2007.

Urban population: The estimated population living in urban areas at mid-year as a percentage of the total mid-year population in a country.

Migrant stock: The estimated number of persons born outside the country at mid-year.

B. SOURCES

Population indicators. Sources: *World Population Prospects: The 2008 Revision, vol. I, Comprehensive Tables* (United Nations publication, Sales No. E.10.XIII.2); *World Population Prospects: The 2008 Revision, vol. II, Sex and Age Distribution of the World Population* (United Nations publication, Sales No. E.10.XIII.3); *World Population Prospects: The 2008 Revision. CD-ROM Edition - Extended Dataset in Excel and ASCII formats* (United Nations publication, Sales No. E.09.XII.6); and *World Urbanization Prospects: The 2007 Revision* (United Nations publication, ESA/P/WP/205); *World Urbanization Prospects: The 2007 Revision. CD-ROM Edition – Data in digital form* (POP/DB/WUP/Rev.2007). As regards demographic indicators, the period indicators, such as annual growth rate, total fertility and the infant mortality rate, the percentages of births to women under age 20 or those aged 35 or over, and life expectancy at birth are average values for the periods 1970-1975, 1980-1985, 1990-1995 and 2005-2010.

Contraceptive prevalence. Source: *World Contraceptive Use 2009* (United Nations Population Division, POP/DB/CP/Rev.2009). Annual indicators are given for 1975, 1985, 1995 and 2005, or the closest year.

Migrant stock. Source: *Database on Trends in Total Migrant Stock: The 2008 Revision* (United Nations Population Division, POP/DB/MIG/Stock/Rev.2008). Annual indicators are given for 1975, 1985, 1995 and 2005, or the closest year.

Maternal mortality ratio. Source: *Maternal Mortality in 2005: Estimates developed by WHO, UNICEF, UNFPA and the World Bank (2007).* World Health Organization. Geneva.

HIV/AIDS. Source: *Report on the Global AIDS Epidemic, 2008.* Joint United Nations Programme on HIV/AIDS (UNAIDS), Geneva. Aug. 2008. UNAIDS/08.25E/JC1510E. http://www.unaids.org /en/KnowledgeCentre/HIVData/GlobalReport/2008/2008_Global_report.asp. (accessed 28 December 2008).
See online table: "Adult (15-49) HIV prevalence percent by country, 1990-2007 (with 95% confidence intervals)", and; "Estimated number of people living with HIV by country, 1990-2007".
http://data.unaids.org/pub/GlobalReport/2008/20080813_gr08_prev1549_1990_2007_en.xls
http://data.unaids.org/pub/GlobalReport/2008/20080818_gr08_plwh_1990_2007_en.xls

C. Ordering the Data on CD-Rom

UNITED NATIONS

Department of Economic and Social Affairs
POPULATION DIVISION

World Population Policies 2009
Data in Digital Form

Date _____

Order form

World Population Policies 2009 (data formatted for Windows 95 or higher)	Unit price (in US$)	Quantity	Total price (in US$)
One CD-ROM disk	$100.00		

SHIP TO:

Name: ....

Institution: ....

Address: ....

Telephone: .... Fax No: ....

For overnight or express mail delivery, please provide a billing account number: ....

Notes

1. Data contained in the above data sets are copyrighted by the United Nations. No portion of the data files contained on disk can be reproduced, distributed or used to prepare derivative works or for commercial purposes without the express permission of the United Nations, to be obtained from the Secretary of the United Nations Publications Board. For further information, please contact the Director, Population Division, Department of Economic and Social Affairs, United Nations (Room DC2-1950), New York, NY 10017, United States of America; fax number (212) 963-2147.

2. The order form should be accompanied by a cheque or an international money order in **United States dollars drawn on a United States bank** for the correct amount, payable to the UNITED NATIONS POPULATION DIVISION, and mailed to: The Director, Population Division/DESA, United Nations, DC2-1950, New York, NY 10017, USA. **Credit cards are not accepted.**

IX. PROFILES OF NATIONAL POPULATION POLICIES

Government views and policies

Population policy variable	1976	1986	1996	2009
Population size and growth				
View on growth	Satisfactory	Too high	Too high	Satisfactory
Policy on growth	No intervention	No intervention	No intervention	No intervention
Population age structure				
Level of concern about				
Size of the working-age population	..	..	..	Minor concern
Ageing of the population	..	..	..	Minor concern
Fertility and family planning				
View on fertility level	Too high	Too high	Too high	Too high
Policy	No intervention	No intervention	No intervention	No intervention
Access to contraceptive methods	Direct support	Direct support	Direct support	Direct support
Adolescent fertility				
Level of concern	..	..	..	Major concern
Policies and programmes	..	..	..	Yes
Health and mortality				
View				
Life expectancy at birth	Unacceptable	Unacceptable	Unacceptable	Unacceptable
Under-five mortality	..	..	..	Unacceptable
Maternal mortality	..	..	..	Unacceptable
Level of concern about HIV/AIDS	..	..	..	Major concern
Measures to respond to HIV/AIDS*	..	..	..	1,2,5
Grounds on which abortion is permitted**	..	..	1	1
Spatial distribution and internal migration				
View on spatial distribution	Minor change desired	Minor change desired	Minor change desired	Major change desired
Policies on internal migration				
From rural to urban areas	..	..	..	Lower
From rural to rural areas	..	..	..	..
From urban to rural areas	..	..	..	..
From urban to urban areas	..	..	..	..
Into urban agglomerations	..	No intervention	..	Lower
International migration				
Immigration				
View	Satisfactory	Satisfactory	Satisfactory	Satisfactory
Policy	Maintain	Maintain	Maintain	Maintain
Permanent settlement	..	..	..	..
Temporary workers	..	..	..	Maintain
Highly skilled workers	..	..	..	..
Family reunification	..	..	..	..
Integration of non-citizens	..	..	..	..
Emigration				
View	Satisfactory	Too high	Too high	Satisfactory
Policy	Maintain	Lower	Lower	Maintain
Encouraging the return of citizens	Yes	..	..	Yes

* Measures implemented to respond to HIV/AIDS: (1) blood screening; (2) information/education campaigns; (3) antiretroviral treatment; (4) non-discriminatory policies; (5) distribution of condoms.
** Grounds on which abortion is permitted: (1) to save the woman's life; (2) to preserve physical health; (3) to preserve mental health; (4) rape or incest; (5) foetal impairment; (6) economic or social reasons; (7) on request.

Population indicators

Indicator	1975	1985	1995	2009
Population size and growth				
Population size (thousands)	13 329	12 293	18 084	28 150
Annual growth rate (percentage)*	..	-2.5	7.3	3.4
Population age structure				
Percentage of population under age 15	45	46	47	46
Percentage of population aged 60 or over	4	4	4	4
Fertility and family planning				
Total fertility (children per woman)*	7.7	7.8	8.0	6.6
Adolescent fertility rate (per 1,000 women, aged 15 - 19)*	..	..	150.0	121.0
Percentage of births to women under age 20*	..	..	9	9
Percentage of births to women aged 35 or over*	..	..	29	18
Percentage of married women using contraception				
Modern methods	2[a]	..	4[b]	16[c]
All methods	2[a]	..	5[b]	19[c]
Health and mortality				
Life expectancy at birth (years)*				
Males	36	40	42	44
Females	36	40	42	44
Both sexes combined	36	40	42	44
Infant mortality rate (per 1,000 live births)*	212	184	171	157
Under-five mortality (per 1,000 live births)*	..	275	256	235
Maternal mortality ratio (per 100,000 live births) (2005)	..	..	..	1 800
HIV/AIDS				
People living with HIV/AIDS (thousands)	..	..	..	..
Adult prevalence (percentage)	..	..	..	..
Spatial distribution				
Population density (per sq. km)	20	19	28	43
Urban population (percentage)	13	17	20	24
Annual urban population growth rate (percentage)	5.7	-0.4	5.4	5.3
Annual rural population growth rate (percentage)	1.3	-2.3	3.5	3.1
International migration				
Migrant stock				
Number of migrants (thousands)	57	56	70	91**
As percentage of total population	0.4	0.5	0.4	0.3**

* For the periods 1970-1975, 1980-1985, 1990-1995 and 2005-2010.
** For 2010.
[a] For 1973.
[b] For 2000.
[c] For 2006.

Government views and policies

Population policy variable	1976	1986	1996	2009
Population size and growth				
View on growth	Satisfactory	Satisfactory	Satisfactory	Satisfactory
Policy on growth	No intervention	Maintain	Maintain	Maintain
Population age structure				
Level of concern about				
Size of the working-age population	..	..	..	Minor concern
Ageing of the population	..	..	..	Minor concern
Fertility and family planning				
View on fertility level	Satisfactory	Satisfactory	Satisfactory	Satisfactory
Policy	Maintain	Maintain	Maintain	Maintain
Access to contraceptive methods	Direct support	Direct support	Direct support	Direct support
Adolescent fertility				
Level of concern	..	..	..	Minor concern
Policies and programmes	..	..	..	Yes
Health and mortality				
View				
Life expectancy at birth	Unacceptable	Unacceptable	Acceptable	Acceptable
Under-five mortality	..	..	..	Unacceptable
Maternal mortality	..	..	..	Unacceptable
Level of concern about HIV/AIDS	..	..	..	Major concern
Measures to respond to HIV/AIDS*	..	..	..	1,2,3,4,5
Grounds on which abortion is permitted**	..	..	1,2,3,4,5,6,7	1,2,3,4,5,6,7
Spatial distribution and internal migration				
View on spatial distribution	Minor change desired	Minor change desired	Satisfactory	Major change desired
Policies on internal migration				
From rural to urban areas	..	..	..	Lower
From rural to rural areas	..	..	..	..
From urban to rural areas	..	..	..	..
From urban to urban areas	..	..	..	..
Into urban agglomerations	..	..	..	Lower
International migration				
Immigration				
View	Satisfactory	Satisfactory	Satisfactory	Satisfactory
Policy	Maintain	Maintain	Maintain	Maintain
Permanent settlement	..	..	..	Maintain
Temporary workers	..	..	..	Maintain
Highly skilled workers	..	..	..	Maintain
Family reunification	..	..	..	Maintain
Integration of non-citizens	..	..	..	No
Emigration				
View	Satisfactory	Satisfactory	Satisfactory	Satisfactory
Policy	Maintain	Maintain	No intervention	Maintain
Encouraging the return of citizens	..	..	..	Yes

* Measures implemented to respond to HIV/AIDS: (1) blood screening; (2) information/education campaigns; (3) antiretroviral treatment; (4) non-discriminatory policies; (5) distribution of condoms.
** Grounds on which abortion is permitted: (1) to save the woman's life; (2) to preserve physical health; (3) to preserve mental health; (4) rape or incest; (5) foetal impairment; (6) economic or social reasons; (7) on request.

Population indicators

Indicator	1975	1985	1995	2009
Population size and growth				
Population size (thousands)	2 401	2 957	3 134	3 155
Annual growth rate (percentage)*	2.3	2.0	-1.0	0.4
Population age structure				
Percentage of population under age 15	40	35	32	24
Percentage of population aged 60 or over	7	7	9	13
Fertility and family planning				
Total fertility (children per woman)*	4.7	3.4	2.8	1.9
Adolescent fertility rate (per 1,000 women, aged 15 - 19)*	..	..	16.0	14.0
Percentage of births to women under age 20*	..	..	3	4
Percentage of births to women aged 35 or over*	..	..	13	10
Percentage of married women using contraception				
Modern methods	..	..	15[a]	22[b]
All methods	..	..	58[a]	60[b]
Health and mortality				
Life expectancy at birth (years)*				
Males	66	68	69	73
Females	70	73	75	80
Both sexes combined	68	70	72	76
Infant mortality rate (per 1,000 live births)*	58	45	31	16
Under-five mortality (per 1,000 live births)*	..	55	37	18
Maternal mortality ratio (per 100,000 live births) (2005)	..	..	..	92
HIV/AIDS				
People living with HIV/AIDS (thousands)	..	..	..	..
Adult prevalence (percentage)	..	..	..	..
Spatial distribution				
Population density (per sq. km)	84	103	109	110
Urban population (percentage)	33	35	39	47
Annual urban population growth rate (percentage)	2.8	3.3	0.5	1.9
Annual rural population growth rate (percentage)	1.9	2.1	-1.8	-0.6
International migration				
Migrant stock				
Number of migrants (thousands)	57	63	71	89**
As percentage of total population	2.4	2.1	2.3	2.8**

* For the periods 1970-1975, 1980-1985, 1990-1995 and 2005-2010.
** For 2010.
[a] For 2000.
[b] For 2005.

Government views and policies

Population policy variable	1976	1986	1996	2009
Population size and growth				
View on growth	Satisfactory	Too high	Too high	Too high
Policy on growth	No intervention	Lower	Lower	Lower
Population age structure				
Level of concern about				
Size of the working-age population	..	..	..	Major concern
Ageing of the population	..	..	..	Minor concern
Fertility and family planning				
View on fertility level	Satisfactory	Too high	Too high	Too high
Policy	No intervention	Lower	Lower	Lower
Access to contraceptive methods	Direct support	Direct support	Direct support	Direct support
Adolescent fertility				
Level of concern	..	..	Not a concern	Minor concern
Policies and programmes	..	..	No	No
Health and mortality				
View				
Life expectancy at birth	Unacceptable	Unacceptable	Unacceptable	Unacceptable
Under-five mortality	..	..	Unacceptable	Unacceptable
Maternal mortality	..	..	..	Unacceptable
Level of concern about HIV/AIDS	..	..	Major concern	Minor concern
Measures to respond to HIV/AIDS*	..	..	..	1,2,3,4,5
Grounds on which abortion is permitted**	..	..	1,2,3,4	1,2,3
Spatial distribution and internal migration				
View on spatial distribution	Major change desired	Major change desired	Major change desired	Major change desired
Policies on internal migration				
From rural to urban areas	..	..	..	Lower
From rural to rural areas	..	..	..	..
From urban to rural areas	..	..	..	..
From urban to urban areas	..	..	..	Raise
Into urban agglomerations	..	Lower	Lower	Lower
International migration				
Immigration				
View	Satisfactory	Satisfactory	Satisfactory	Too high
Policy	Maintain	Maintain	Maintain	Maintain
Permanent settlement	..	..	..	..
Temporary workers	..	..	..	Maintain
Highly skilled workers	..	..	..	..
Family reunification	..	..	..	Maintain
Integration of non-citizens	..	..	..	..
Emigration				
View	Too low	Satisfactory	Satisfactory	Too high
Policy	Raise	Lower	Lower	No intervention
Encouraging the return of citizens	..	..	Yes	Yes

* Measures implemented to respond to HIV/AIDS: (1) blood screening; (2) information/education campaigns; (3) antiretroviral treatment; (4) non-discriminatory policies; (5) distribution of condoms.
** Grounds on which abortion is permitted: (1) to save the woman's life; (2) to preserve physical health; (3) to preserve mental health; (4) rape or incest; (5) foetal impairment; (6) economic or social reasons; (7) on request.

Population indicators

Indicator	1975	1985	1995	2009
Population size and growth				
Population size (thousands)	16 018	22 097	28 265	34 895
Annual growth rate (percentage)*	3.1	3.2	2.2	1.5
Population age structure				
Percentage of population under age 15	48	45	40	27
Percentage of population aged 60 or over	6	5	6	7
Fertility and family planning				
Total fertility (children per woman)*	7.4	6.5	4.1	2.4
Adolescent fertility rate (per 1,000 women, aged 15 - 19)*	..	..	24.0	7.0
Percentage of births to women under age 20*	..	..	3	2
Percentage of births to women aged 35 or over*	..	..	31	26
Percentage of married women using contraception				
Modern methods	..	31[a]	49	52[b]
All methods	..	36[a]	57	61[b]
Health and mortality				
Life expectancy at birth (years)*				
Males	54	60	67	71
Females	56	63	69	74
Both sexes combined	55	61	68	72
Infant mortality rate (per 1,000 live births)*	131	84	54	31
Under-five mortality (per 1,000 live births)*	..	106	61	33
Maternal mortality ratio (per 100,000 live births) (2005)	..	..	..	180
HIV/AIDS				
People living with HIV/AIDS (thousands)	..	..	<1	21[c]
Adult prevalence (percentage)	..	..	..	0.1[c]
Spatial distribution				
Population density (per sq. km)	7	9	12	15
Urban population (percentage)	40	48	56	66
Annual urban population growth rate (percentage)	3.6	4.8	3.1	2.4
Annual rural population growth rate (percentage)	2.9	1.2	0.0	-0.3
International migration				
Migrant stock				
Number of migrants (thousands)	160	289	299	242**
As percentage of total population	1.0	1.3	1.1	0.7**

*. For the periods 1970-1975, 1980-1985, 1990-1995 and 2005-2010.
** For 2010.
[a] For 1986/1987.
[b] For 2006.
[c] For 2007.

Government views and policies

Population policy variable	1976	1986	1996	2009
Population size and growth				
View on growth	..	..	Satisfactory	Satisfactory
Policy on growth	..	..	Maintain	Maintain
Population age structure				
Level of concern about				
Size of the working-age population	..	..	..	Not a concern
Ageing of the population	..	..	..	Minor concern
Fertility and family planning				
View on fertility level	..	..	Satisfactory	Satisfactory
Policy	..	..	Maintain	Maintain
Access to contraceptive methods	..	..	No support	No support
Adolescent fertility				
Level of concern	..	..	..	Minor concern
Policies and programmes	..	..	..	Yes
Health and mortality				
View				
Life expectancy at birth	..	..	Acceptable	Acceptable
Under-five mortality	..	..	..	Acceptable
Maternal mortality	..	..	..	Acceptable
Level of concern about HIV/AIDS	..	..	..	Major concern
Measures to respond to HIV/AIDS*	..	..	..	2,3
Grounds on which abortion is permitted**	..	..	Not permitted	1
Spatial distribution and internal migration				
View on spatial distribution	..	..	Satisfactory	Satisfactory
Policies on internal migration				
From rural to urban areas	..	..	..	No intervention
From rural to rural areas	..	..	..	No intervention
From urban to rural areas	..	..	..	No intervention
From urban to urban areas	..	..	..	No intervention
Into urban agglomerations	..	..	..	No intervention
International migration				
Immigration				
View	..	..	Satisfactory	Satisfactory
Policy	..	..	Maintain	Maintain
Permanent settlement	..	..	Maintain	Maintain
Temporary workers	..	..	..	Maintain
Highly skilled workers	..	..	..	No intervention
Family reunification	..	..	..	Maintain
Integration of non-citizens	..	..	..	Yes
Emigration				
View	..	..	Satisfactory	Satisfactory
Policy	..	..	Maintain	Maintain
Encouraging the return of citizens	..	..	..	No

* Measures implemented to respond to HIV/AIDS: (1) blood screening; (2) information/education campaigns; (3) antiretroviral treatment; (4) non-discriminatory policies; (5) distribution of condoms.
** Grounds on which abortion is permitted: (1) to save the woman's life; (2) to preserve physical health; (3) to preserve mental health; (4) rape or incest; (5) foetal impairment; (6) economic or social reasons; (7) on request.

Population indicators

Indicator	1975	1985	1995	2009
Population size and growth				
Population size (thousands)	31	47	65	86
Annual growth rate (percentage)*	4.8	4.8	4.1	1.7
Population age structure				
Percentage of population under age 15	..	..	..	..
Percentage of population aged 60 or over	..	..	..	..
Fertility and family planning				
Total fertility (children per woman)*	..	..	..	..
Adolescent fertility rate (per 1,000 women, aged 15 - 19)*	..	..	..	..
Percentage of births to women under age 20*	..	..	..	..
Percentage of births to women aged 35 or over*	..	..	..	..
Percentage of married women using contraception				
Modern methods	..	..	..	..
All methods	..	..	..	..
Health and mortality				
Life expectancy at birth (years)*				
Males	..	..	..	..
Females	..	..	..	..
Both sexes combined	..	..	..	..
Infant mortality rate (per 1,000 live births)*	..	..	..	..
Under-five mortality (per 1,000 live births)*	..	..	..	..
Maternal mortality ratio (per 100,000 live births) (2005)	..	..	..	..
HIV/AIDS				
People living with HIV/AIDS (thousands)	..	..	..	..
Adult prevalence (percentage)	..	..	..	..
Spatial distribution				
Population density (per sq. km)	66	101	138	183
Urban population (percentage)	87	95	94	88
Annual urban population growth rate (percentage)	5.1	2.8	1.2	-0.4
Annual rural population growth rate (percentage)	-5.5	-0.9	5.2	3.7
International migration				
Migrant stock				
Number of migrants (thousands)	19	32	44	56**
As percentage of total population	60.1	68.1	68.3	64.4**

* For the periods 1970-1975, 1980-1985, 1990-1995 and 2005-2010.
** For 2010.

Government views and policies

Population policy variable	1976	1986	1996	2009
Population size and growth				
View on growth	..	Satisfactory	Satisfactory	Satisfactory
Policy on growth	..	No intervention	No intervention	Maintain
Population age structure				
Level of concern about				
Size of the working-age population	..	..	..	..
Ageing of the population	..	..	..	Minor concern
Fertility and family planning				
View on fertility level	..	Satisfactory	Too high	Too high
Policy	..	No intervention	No intervention	Maintain
Access to contraceptive methods	..	Direct support	Direct support	Direct support
Adolescent fertility				
Level of concern	..	..	Major concern	Major concern
Policies and programmes	..	..	Yes	Yes
Health and mortality				
View				
Life expectancy at birth	..	Unacceptable	Unacceptable	Unacceptable
Under-five mortality	..	..	Unacceptable	Unacceptable
Maternal mortality	..	..	..	Unacceptable
Level of concern about HIV/AIDS	..	..	Minor concern	Major concern
Measures to respond to HIV/AIDS*	..	..	..	1,2,3,4,5
Grounds on which abortion is permitted**	..	..	1	1
Spatial distribution and internal migration				
View on spatial distribution	..	Major change desired	Satisfactory	Major change desired
Policies on internal migration				
From rural to urban areas	..	..	..	No intervention
From rural to rural areas	..	..	..	..
From urban to rural areas	..	..	..	..
From urban to urban areas	..	..	..	..
Into urban agglomerations	..	..	No intervention	No intervention
International migration				
Immigration				
View	..	Satisfactory	Satisfactory	Satisfactory
Policy	..	Maintain	No intervention	No intervention
Permanent settlement	..	..	No intervention	..
Temporary workers	..	..	No intervention	..
Highly skilled workers	..	..	..	..
Family reunification	..	..	No intervention	..
Integration of non-citizens	..	..	Yes	..
Emigration				
View	..	Satisfactory	Satisfactory	Satisfactory
Policy	..	Maintain	No intervention	No intervention
Encouraging the return of citizens	..	..	No	No

* Measures implemented to respond to HIV/AIDS: (1) blood screening; (2) information/education campaigns; (3) antiretroviral treatment; (4) non-discriminatory policies; (5) distribution of condoms.
** Grounds on which abortion is permitted: (1) to save the woman's life; (2) to preserve physical health; (3) to preserve mental health; (4) rape or incest; (5) foetal impairment; (6) economic or social reasons; (7) on request.

Population indicators

Indicator	1975	1985	1995	2009
Population size and growth				
Population size (thousands)	6 815	9 331	12 539	18 498
Annual growth rate (percentage)*	2.3	3.4	3.2	2.7
Population age structure				
Percentage of population under age 15	46	47	48	45
Percentage of population aged 60 or over	5	4	4	4
Fertility and family planning				
Total fertility (children per woman)*	7.2	7.2	7.1	5.8
Adolescent fertility rate (per 1,000 women, aged 15 - 19)*	..	..	226.0	124.0
Percentage of births to women under age 20*	..	..	16	11
Percentage of births to women aged 35 or over*	..	..	20	23
Percentage of married women using contraception				
Modern methods	..	..	4[a]	5[b]
All methods	..	..	8[a]	6[b]
Health and mortality				
Life expectancy at birth (years)*				
Males	36	39	41	45
Females	40	43	44	49
Both sexes combined	38	41	42	47
Infant mortality rate (per 1,000 live births)*	173	154	145	117
Under-five mortality (per 1,000 live births)*	..	269	253	205
Maternal mortality ratio (per 100,000 live births) (2005)	..	..	..	1 400
HIV/AIDS				
People living with HIV/AIDS (thousands)	..	..	46	190[c]
Adult prevalence (percentage)	..	..	0.7	2.1[c]
Spatial distribution				
Population density (per sq. km)	5	7	10	15
Urban population (percentage)	19	30	44	58
Annual urban population growth rate (percentage)	7.4	6.9	4.9	4.3
Annual rural population growth rate (percentage)	1.3	0.8	0.8	0.7
International migration				
Migrant stock				
Number of migrants (thousands)	31	109	38	65**
As percentage of total population	0.5	1.2	0.3	0.3**

* For the periods 1970-1975, 1980-1985, 1990-1995 and 2005-2010.
** For 2010.
[a] For 1996.
[b] For 2001.
[c] For 2007.

Government views and policies

Population policy variable	1976	1986	1996	2009
Population size and growth				
View on growth	..	Too high	Satisfactory	Satisfactory
Policy on growth	..	Lower	Maintain	No intervention
Population age structure				
Level of concern about				
Size of the working-age population	..	..	..	..
Ageing of the population	..	..	..	Major concern
Fertility and family planning				
View on fertility level	..	Too high	Satisfactory	Satisfactory
Policy	..	Lower	No intervention	No intervention
Access to contraceptive methods	..	Direct support	Direct support	Indirect support
Adolescent fertility				
Level of concern	..	..	..	Minor concern
Policies and programmes	..	..	..	Yes
Health and mortality				
View				
Life expectancy at birth	..	Unacceptable	Acceptable	Acceptable
Under-five mortality	..	..	..	Acceptable
Maternal mortality	..	..	..	Acceptable
Level of concern about HIV/AIDS	..	..	..	Major concern
Measures to respond to HIV/AIDS*	..	..	..	1,2,3,5
Grounds on which abortion is permitted**	..	..	1	1
Spatial distribution and internal migration				
View on spatial distribution	..	Minor change desired	Major change desired	Satisfactory
Policies on internal migration				
From rural to urban areas	..	..	..	No intervention
From rural to rural areas	..	..	..	No intervention
From urban to rural areas	..	..	..	No intervention
From urban to urban areas	..	..	..	No intervention
Into urban agglomerations	..	..	..	No intervention
International migration				
Immigration				
View	..	Satisfactory	Satisfactory	Satisfactory
Policy	..	Maintain	Maintain	Maintain
Permanent settlement	..	..	..	Maintain
Temporary workers	..	..	..	Maintain
Highly skilled workers	..	..	..	Maintain
Family reunification	..	..	..	..
Integration of non-citizens	..	..	..	..
Emigration				
View	..	Satisfactory	Satisfactory	Too high
Policy	..	Maintain	Lower	No intervention
Encouraging the return of citizens	..	..	..	Yes

* Measures implemented to respond to HIV/AIDS: (1) blood screening; (2) information/education campaigns; (3) antiretroviral treatment; (4) non-discriminatory policies; (5) distribution of condoms.

** Grounds on which abortion is permitted: (1) to save the woman's life; (2) to preserve physical health; (3) to preserve mental health; (4) rape or incest; (5) foetal impairment; (6) economic or social reasons; (7) on request.

Population indicators

Indicator	1975	1985	1995	2009
Population size and growth				
Population size (thousands)	76	68	68	88
Annual growth rate (percentage)*	2.0	-1.3	1.9	1.2
Population age structure				
Percentage of population under age 15	..	..	..	..
Percentage of population aged 60 or over	..	..	..	..
Fertility and family planning				
Total fertility (children per woman)*	..	..	..	..
Adolescent fertility rate (per 1,000 women, aged 15 - 19)*	..	..	..	..
Percentage of births to women under age 20*	..	..	..	..
Percentage of births to women aged 35 or over*	..	..	..	..
Percentage of married women using contraception				
Modern methods	..	51[a]	..	..
All methods	..	53[a]	..	..
Health and mortality				
Life expectancy at birth (years)*				
Males	..	..	..	..
Females	..	..	..	..
Both sexes combined	..	..	..	..
Infant mortality rate (per 1,000 live births)*	..	..	..	..
Under-five mortality (per 1,000 live births)*	..	..	..	..
Maternal mortality ratio (per 100,000 live births) (2005)	..	..	..	..
HIV/AIDS				
People living with HIV/AIDS (thousands)	..	..	..	..
Adult prevalence (percentage)	..	..	..	..
Spatial distribution				
Population density (per sq. km)	173	153	154	198
Urban population (percentage)	34	35	34	30
Annual urban population growth rate (percentage)	0.2	-1.8	1.5	1.1
Annual rural population growth rate (percentage)	-0.2	-2.2	3.1	1.1
International migration				
Migrant stock				
Number of migrants (thousands)	8	10	14	21**
As percentage of total population	10.4	15.5	20.3	23.6**

* For the periods 1970-1975, 1980-1985, 1990-1995 and 2005-2010.
** For 2010.
[a] For 1988.

Government views and policies

Population policy variable	1976	1986	1996	2009
Population size and growth				
View on growth	Too low	Satisfactory	Satisfactory	Satisfactory
Policy on growth	Raise	No intervention	No intervention	No intervention
Population age structure				
Level of concern about				
Size of the working-age population	..	..	..	Not a concern
Ageing of the population	..	..	..	Not a concern
Fertility and family planning				
View on fertility level	Too low	Satisfactory	Satisfactory	Satisfactory
Policy	Raise	No intervention	No intervention	No intervention
Access to contraceptive methods	Limits	No support	No support	Direct support
Adolescent fertility				
Level of concern	..	..	Major concern	Major concern
Policies and programmes	..	..	Yes	Yes
Health and mortality				
View				
Life expectancy at birth	Unacceptable	Acceptable	Unacceptable	Acceptable
Under-five mortality	..	..	Unacceptable	Unacceptable
Maternal mortality	..	..	..	Unacceptable
Level of concern about HIV/AIDS	..	..	Minor concern	Minor concern
Measures to respond to HIV/AIDS*	..	..	..	1,2,3,4,5
Grounds on which abortion is permitted**	..	..	1,2	1
Spatial distribution and internal migration				
View on spatial distribution	Major change desired	Major change desired	Satisfactory	Minor change desired
Policies on internal migration				
From rural to urban areas	..	..	..	Lower
From rural to rural areas	..	..	..	No intervention
From urban to rural areas	..	..	..	Raise
From urban to urban areas	..	..	..	Raise
Into urban agglomerations	Lower	Lower	No intervention	Lower
International migration				
Immigration				
View	Too low	Satisfactory	Satisfactory	Satisfactory
Policy	Raise	Maintain	Maintain	Raise
Permanent settlement	..	..	Maintain	Maintain
Temporary workers	..	..	Maintain	Maintain
Highly skilled workers	..	..	..	Maintain
Family reunification	..	..	Lower	Maintain
Integration of non-citizens	..	..	Yes	Yes
Emigration				
View	Satisfactory	Too high	Satisfactory	Satisfactory
Policy	Maintain	Lower	No intervention	Lower
Encouraging the return of citizens	Yes	..	No	Yes

* Measures implemented to respond to HIV/AIDS: (1) blood screening; (2) information/education campaigns; (3) antiretroviral treatment; (4) non-discriminatory policies; (5) distribution of condoms.

** Grounds on which abortion is permitted: (1) to save the woman's life; (2) to preserve physical health; (3) to preserve mental health; (4) rape or incest; (5) foetal impairment; (6) economic or social reasons; (7) on request.

Population indicators

Indicator	1975	1985	1995	2009
Population size and growth				
Population size (thousands)	26 012	30 227	34 772	40 276
Annual growth rate (percentage)*	1.6	1.4	1.4	1.0
Population age structure				
Percentage of population under age 15	29	31	29	25
Percentage of population aged 60 or over	12	13	14	15
Fertility and family planning				
Total fertility (children per woman)*	3.1	3.2	2.9	2.3
Adolescent fertility rate (per 1,000 women, aged 15 - 19)*	..	..	73.0	57.0
Percentage of births to women under age 20*	..	..	13	13
Percentage of births to women aged 35 or over*	..	..	15	16
Percentage of married women using contraception				
Modern methods	..	..	..	64[a]
All methods	..	..	..	65[a]
Health and mortality				
Life expectancy at birth (years)*				
Males	64	67	69	72
Females	71	74	76	79
Both sexes combined	67	70	72	75
Infant mortality rate (per 1,000 live births)*	48	32	24	13
Under-five mortality (per 1,000 live births)*	..	38	28	16
Maternal mortality ratio (per 100,000 live births) (2005)	..	..	..	77
HIV/AIDS				
People living with HIV/AIDS (thousands)	..	..	68	120[b]
Adult prevalence (percentage)	..	..	0.4	0.5[b]
Spatial distribution				
Population density (per sq. km)	9	11	13	14
Urban population (percentage)	81	85	89	92
Annual urban population growth rate (percentage)	2.1	2.0	1.6	1.2
Annual rural population growth rate (percentage)	-0.5	-1.3	-1.5	-1.4
International migration				
Migrant stock				
Number of migrants (thousands)	2 064	1 780	1 588	1 449**
As percentage of total population	7.9	5.9	4.6	3.6**

* For the periods 1970-1975, 1980-1985, 1990-1995 and 2005-2010.
** For 2010.
[a] For 2001.
[b] For 2007.

Government views and policies

Population policy variable	1976	1986	1996	2009
Population size and growth				
View on growth	..	..	Satisfactory	Too low
Policy on growth	..	..	Maintain	Raise
Population age structure				
Level of concern about				
Size of the working-age population	..	..	..	Minor concern
Ageing of the population	..	..	..	Major concern
Fertility and family planning				
View on fertility level	..	..	Satisfactory	Too low
Policy	..	..	Raise	Raise
Access to contraceptive methods	..	..	Direct support	Indirect support
Adolescent fertility				
Level of concern	..	..	..	Minor concern
Policies and programmes	..	..	No	Yes
Health and mortality				
View				
Life expectancy at birth	..	..	Acceptable	Acceptable
Under-five mortality	..	..	..	Unacceptable
Maternal mortality	..	..	..	Unacceptable
Level of concern about HIV/AIDS	..	..	..	Major concern
Measures to respond to HIV/AIDS*	..	..	...	1,2,3,4,5
Grounds on which abortion is permitted**	..	..	1,2,3,4,5,6,7	1,2,3,4,5,6,7
Spatial distribution and internal migration				
View on spatial distribution	..	..	Major change desired	Major change desired
Policies on internal migration				
From rural to urban areas	..	..	..	Lower
From rural to rural areas	..	..	..	No intervention
From urban to rural areas	..	..	..	Raise
From urban to urban areas	..	..	..	No intervention
Into urban agglomerations	..	..	..	Maintain
International migration				
Immigration				
View	..	..	Satisfactory	Too low
Policy	..	..	No intervention	Raise
Permanent settlement	..	..	No intervention	Raise
Temporary workers	..	..	No intervention	Maintain
Highly skilled workers	..	..	..	Maintain
Family reunification	..	..	No intervention	No intervention
Integration of non-citizens	..	..	No	Yes
Emigration				
View	..	..	Too high	Too high
Policy	..	..	Lower	Lower
Encouraging the return of citizens	..	..	No	Yes

* Measures implemented to respond to HIV/AIDS: (1) blood screening; (2) information/education campaigns; (3) antiretroviral treatment; (4) non−discriminatory policies; (5) distribution of condoms.

** Grounds on which abortion is permitted: (1) to save the woman's life; (2) to preserve physical health; (3) to preserve mental health; (4) rape or incest; (5) foetal impairment; (6) economic or social reasons; (7) on request.

Population indicators

Indicator	1975	1985	1995	2009
Population size and growth				
Population size (thousands)	2 826	3 339	3 223	3 083
Annual growth rate (percentage)*	2.3	1.5	-1.9	0.2
Population age structure				
Percentage of population under age 15	34	30	29	20
Percentage of population aged 60 or over	8	8	13	14
Fertility and family planning				
Total fertility (children per woman)*	3.0	2.4	2.4	1.7
Adolescent fertility rate (per 1,000 women, aged 15 - 19)*	..	..	76.0	36.0
Percentage of births to women under age 20*	..	..	16	10
Percentage of births to women aged 35 or over*	..	..	6	6
Percentage of married women using contraception				
Modern methods	..	..	25[a]	19[b]
All methods	..	..	56[a]	53[b]
Health and mortality				
Life expectancy at birth (years)*				
Males	68	68	65	70
Females	74	74	72	77
Both sexes combined	71	71	68	74
Infant mortality rate (per 1,000 live births)*	63	53	44	25
Under-five mortality (per 1,000 live births)*	..	63	53	28
Maternal mortality ratio (per 100,000 live births) (2005)	..	..	..	76
HIV/AIDS				
People living with HIV/AIDS (thousands)	..	..	..	2.4[c]
Adult prevalence (percentage)	..	..	..	0.1[c]
Spatial distribution				
Population density (per sq. km)	95	112	108	103
Urban population (percentage)	64	67	66	64
Annual urban population growth rate (percentage)	2.9	2.0	-1.9	-0.2
Annual rural population growth rate (percentage)	0.3	1.1	-0.8	-0.1
International migration				
Migrant stock				
Number of migrants (thousands)	..	..	682	324**
As percentage of total population	0.0	0.0	21.1	10.5**

* For the periods 1970-1975, 1980-1985, 1990-1995 and 2005-2010.
** For 2010.
[a] For 1991.
[b] For 2005.
[c] For 2007.

Government views and policies

Population policy variable	1976	1986	1996	2009
Population size and growth				
View on growth	Satisfactory	Satisfactory	Satisfactory	Satisfactory
Policy on growth	No intervention	Maintain	No intervention	No intervention
Population age structure				
Level of concern about				
Size of the working-age population	..	..	..	Not a concern
Ageing of the population	..	..	..	Minor concern
Fertility and family planning				
View on fertility level	Satisfactory	Satisfactory	Satisfactory	Too low
Policy	No intervention	No intervention	No intervention	Raise
Access to contraceptive methods	Indirect support	Indirect support	Indirect support	Indirect support
Adolescent fertility				
Level of concern	..	..	Minor concern	Minor concern
Policies and programmes	..	..	..	Yes
Health and mortality				
View				
Life expectancy at birth	Acceptable	Acceptable	Unacceptable	Acceptable
Under-five mortality	..	..	Unacceptable	Acceptable
Maternal mortality	..	..	..	Acceptable
Level of concern about HIV/AIDS	..	..	Major concern	Major concern
Measures to respond to HIV/AIDS[*]	..	..	..	1,2,3,4,5
Grounds on which abortion is permitted[**]	..	..	1,2,3,4,5,6	1,2,3,4,5,6,7
Spatial distribution and internal migration				
View on spatial distribution	Major change desired	Major change desired	Minor change desired	Minor change desired
Policies on internal migration				
From rural to urban areas	..	..	..	Lower
From rural to rural areas	..	..	..	No intervention
From urban to rural areas	..	..	..	No intervention
From urban to urban areas	..	..	..	No intervention
Into urban agglomerations	..	..	No intervention	Lower
International migration				
Immigration				
View	Too low	Satisfactory	Satisfactory	Satisfactory
Policy	Raise	Maintain	Maintain	Maintain
Permanent settlement	..	..	Maintain	Maintain
Temporary workers	..	..	Maintain	Lower
Highly skilled workers	..	..	..	Lower
Family reunification	..	..	Maintain	Maintain
Integration of non-citizens	..	..	Yes	Yes
Emigration				
View	Satisfactory	Satisfactory	Satisfactory	Satisfactory
Policy	Maintain	Maintain	No intervention	No intervention
Encouraging the return of citizens	..	..	No	No

[*] Measures implemented to respond to HIV/AIDS: (1) blood screening; (2) information/education campaigns; (3) antiretroviral treatment; (4) non-discriminatory policies; (5) distribution of condoms.

[**] Grounds on which abortion is permitted: (1) to save the woman's life; (2) to preserve physical health; (3) to preserve mental health; (4) rape or incest; (5) foetal impairment; (6) economic or social reasons; (7) on request.

Population indicators

Indicator	1975	1985	1995	2009
Population size and growth				
Population size (thousands)	13 625	15 800	18 118	21 293
Annual growth rate (percentage)*	1.4	1.5	1.2	1.1
Population age structure				
Percentage of population under age 15	28	24	21	19
Percentage of population aged 60 or over	13	15	16	19
Fertility and family planning				
Total fertility (children per woman)*	2.5	1.9	1.9	1.8
Adolescent fertility rate (per 1,000 women, aged 15 - 19)*	..	..	21.0	15.0
Percentage of births to women under age 20*	..	..	6	4
Percentage of births to women aged 35 or over*	..	..	12	21
Percentage of married women using contraception				
Modern methods	..	72[a]	64	71[b]
All methods	..	76[a]	67	71[b]
Health and mortality				
Life expectancy at birth (years)*				
Males	68	72	75	79
Females	75	79	81	84
Both sexes combined	72	75	78	81
Infant mortality rate (per 1,000 live births)*	17	10	7	5
Under-five mortality (per 1,000 live births)*	..	12	8	6
Maternal mortality ratio (per 100,000 live births) (2005)	..	..	..	4
HIV/AIDS				
People living with HIV/AIDS (thousands)	..	..	8.6	18[c]
Adult prevalence (percentage)	..	..	0.1	0.2[c]
Spatial distribution				
Population density (per sq. km)	2	2	2	3
Urban population (percentage)	86	85	86	89
Annual urban population growth rate (percentage)	1.5	1.4	1.4	1.2
Annual rural population growth rate (percentage)	0.8	1.9	-0.1	-0.6
International migration				
Migrant stock				
Number of migrants (thousands)	2 659	3 143	3 854	4 711**
As percentage of total population	19.5	19.9	21.3	21.9**

* For the periods 1970-1975, 1980-1985, 1990-1995 and 2005-2010.
** For 2010.
[a] For 1986.
[b] For 2001/2002.
[c] For 2007.

Government views and policies

Population policy variable	1976	1986	1996	2009
Population size and growth				
View on growth	Satisfactory	Satisfactory	Satisfactory	Too low
Policy on growth	No intervention	No intervention	Maintain	Raise
Population age structure				
Level of concern about				
Size of the working-age population	..	..	..	Major concern
Ageing of the population	..	..	..	Major concern
Fertility and family planning				
View on fertility level	Satisfactory	Satisfactory	Satisfactory	Too low
Policy	No intervention	No intervention	No intervention	Raise
Access to contraceptive methods	Direct support	Direct support	Direct support	No support
Adolescent fertility				
Level of concern	..	..	Not a concern	Minor concern
Policies and programmes	..	..	No	No
Health and mortality				
View				
Life expectancy at birth	Acceptable	Acceptable	Acceptable	Acceptable
Under-five mortality	..	..	Acceptable	Acceptable
Maternal mortality	..	..	..	Acceptable
Level of concern about HIV/AIDS	..	..	Minor concern	Minor concern
Measures to respond to HIV/AIDS*	..	..	..	1,2,3,4,5
Grounds on which abortion is permitted**	..	..	1,2,3,4,5,6,7	1,2,3,4,5,6,7
Spatial distribution and internal migration				
View on spatial distribution	Minor change desired	Minor change desired	Minor change desired	Satisfactory
Policies on internal migration				
From rural to urban areas	..	..	..	Lower
From rural to rural areas	..	..	..	No intervention
From urban to rural areas	..	..	..	No intervention
From urban to urban areas	..	..	..	No intervention
Into urban agglomerations	Lower	..	..	No intervention
International migration				
Immigration				
View	Satisfactory	Satisfactory	Too high	Satisfactory
Policy	Maintain	Lower	Lower	Maintain
Permanent settlement	..	..	Lower	Maintain
Temporary workers	..	..	Lower	Lower
Highly skilled workers	..	..	..	Maintain
Family reunification	..	..	Lower	Maintain
Integration of non-citizens	..	..	Yes	Yes
Emigration				
View	Satisfactory	Satisfactory	Satisfactory	Satisfactory
Policy	Maintain	Maintain	No intervention	No intervention
Encouraging the return of citizens	No	..	..	Yes

* Measures implemented to respond to HIV/AIDS: (1) blood screening; (2) information/education campaigns; (3) antiretroviral treatment; (4) non-discriminatory policies; (5) distribution of condoms.
** Grounds on which abortion is permitted: (1) to save the woman's life; (2) to preserve physical health; (3) to preserve mental health; (4) rape or incest; (5) foetal impairment; (6) economic or social reasons; (7) on request.

Population indicators

Indicator	1975	1985	1995	2009
Population size and growth				
Population size (thousands)	7 578	7 560	7 936	8 364
Annual growth rate (percentage)*	0.3	0.0	0.7	0.4
Population age structure				
Percentage of population under age 15	23	18	18	15
Percentage of population aged 60 or over	20	20	20	23
Fertility and family planning				
Total fertility (children per woman)*	2.0	1.6	1.5	1.4
Adolescent fertility rate (per 1,000 women, aged 15 - 19)*	..	..	22.0	13.0
Percentage of births to women under age 20*	..	..	8	5
Percentage of births to women aged 35 or over*	..	..	9	14
Percentage of married women using contraception				
Modern methods	..	56[a]	47[b]	..
All methods	..	71[a]	51[b]	..
Health and mortality				
Life expectancy at birth (years)*				
Males	67	69	73	77
Females	74	77	79	83
Both sexes combined	71	73	76	80
Infant mortality rate (per 1,000 live births)*	24	13	7	4
Under-five mortality (per 1,000 live births)*	..	15	8	5
Maternal mortality ratio (per 100,000 live births) (2005)	..	..	..	4
HIV/AIDS				
People living with HIV/AIDS (thousands)	..	..	2.4	9.8[c]
Adult prevalence (percentage)	..	..	0.1	0.2[c]
Spatial distribution				
Population density (per sq. km)	90	90	95	100
Urban population (percentage)	65	66	66	67
Annual urban population growth rate (percentage)	0.0	0.3	0.4	0.6
Annual rural population growth rate (percentage)	0.0	0.1	0.4	-0.4
International migration				
Migrant stock				
Number of migrants (thousands)	721	728	989	1 310**
As percentage of total population	9.5	9.6	12.5	15.6**

* For the periods 1970-1975, 1980-1985, 1990-1995 and 2005-2010.
** For 2010.
[a] For 1982.
[b] For 1995/1996.
[c] For 2007.

Government views and policies

Population policy variable	1976	1986	1996	2009
Population size and growth				
View on growth	..	..	Too low	Satisfactory
Policy on growth	..	..	Maintain	Raise
Population age structure				
Level of concern about				
Size of the working-age population	..	..	..	Minor concern
Ageing of the population	..	..	..	Major concern
Fertility and family planning				
View on fertility level	..	..	Satisfactory	Satisfactory
Policy	..	..	Maintain	Raise
Access to contraceptive methods	..	..	Indirect support	Direct support
Adolescent fertility				
Level of concern	..	..	..	Major concern
Policies and programmes	..	..	No	Yes
Health and mortality				
View				
Life expectancy at birth	..	..	Unacceptable	Unacceptable
Under-five mortality	..	..	..	Unacceptable
Maternal mortality	..	..	..	Unacceptable
Level of concern about HIV/AIDS	..	..	..	Major concern
Measures to respond to HIV/AIDS*	..	..	..	1,2,4,5
Grounds on which abortion is permitted**	..	..	1,2,3,4,5,6,7	1,2,3,4,5,6,7
Spatial distribution and internal migration				
View on spatial distribution	..	..	Satisfactory	Minor change desired
Policies on internal migration				
From rural to urban areas	..	..	..	Lower
From rural to rural areas	..	..	..	..
From urban to rural areas	..	..	..	Maintain
From urban to urban areas	..	..	..	..
Into urban agglomerations	..	..	..	Lower
International migration				
Immigration				
View	..	..	Satisfactory	Satisfactory
Policy	..	..	Maintain	Raise
Permanent settlement	..	..	No intervention	Maintain
Temporary workers	..	..	..	Maintain
Highly skilled workers	..	..	..	Raise
Family reunification	..	..	..	Maintain
Integration of non-citizens	..	..	Yes	Yes
Emigration				
View	..	..	Satisfactory	Satisfactory
Policy	..	..	No intervention	Maintain
Encouraging the return of citizens	..	..	No	Yes

* Measures implemented to respond to HIV/AIDS: (1) blood screening; (2) information/education campaigns; (3) antiretroviral treatment; (4) non-discriminatory policies; (5) distribution of condoms.
** Grounds on which abortion is permitted: (1) to save the woman's life; (2) to preserve physical health; (3) to preserve mental health; (4) rape or incest; (5) foetal impairment; (6) economic or social reasons; (7) on request.

Population indicators

Indicator	1975	1985	1995	2009
Population size and growth				
Population size (thousands)	5 689	6 670	7 784	8 832
Annual growth rate (percentage)*	1.9	1.6	1.5	1.1
Population age structure				
Percentage of population under age 15	40	33	34	24
Percentage of population aged 60 or over	8	7	8	9
Fertility and family planning				
Total fertility (children per woman)*	4.3	3.0	2.9	2.2
Adolescent fertility rate (per 1,000 women, aged 15 - 19)*	..	..	54.0	34.0
Percentage of births to women under age 20*	..	..	9	8
Percentage of births to women aged 35 or over*	..	..	8	8
Percentage of married women using contraception				
Modern methods	..	..	12[a]	13[b]
All methods	..	..	55[a]	51[b]
Health and mortality				
Life expectancy at birth (years)*				
Males	62	61	61	68
Females	69	69	70	72
Both sexes combined	66	65	65	70
Infant mortality rate (per 1,000 live births)*	100	90	82	43
Under-five mortality (per 1,000 live births)*	..	113	97	53
Maternal mortality ratio (per 100,000 live births) (2005)	..	..	..	82
HIV/AIDS				
People living with HIV/AIDS (thousands)	..	..	..	7.8[c]
Adult prevalence (percentage)	..	..	..	0.2[c]
Spatial distribution				
Population density (per sq. km)	66	77	90	102
Urban population (percentage)	52	53	52	52
Annual urban population growth rate (percentage)	2.0	1.9	0.6	1.1
Annual rural population growth rate (percentage)	1.3	1.1	1.8	0.4
International migration				
Migrant stock				
Number of migrants (thousands)	..	..	525	264**
As percentage of total population	0.0	0.0	6.7	3.0**

* For the periods 1970-1975, 1980-1985, 1990-1995 and 2005-2010.
** For 2010.
[a] For 2001.
[b] For 2006.
[c] For 2007.

Government views and policies

Population policy variable	1976	1986	1996	2009
Population size and growth				
View on growth	Too low	Satisfactory	Satisfactory	Satisfactory
Policy on growth	Raise	No intervention	No intervention	Maintain
Population age structure				
Level of concern about				
Size of the working-age population	..	..	..	Minor concern
Ageing of the population	..	..	..	Major concern
Fertility and family planning				
View on fertility level	Satisfactory	Satisfactory	Satisfactory	Satisfactory
Policy	No intervention	No intervention	No intervention	No intervention
Access to contraceptive methods	Indirect support	Indirect support	Indirect support	Direct support
Adolescent fertility				
Level of concern	..	..	Minor concern	Major concern
Policies and programmes	..	..	..	Yes
Health and mortality				
View				
Life expectancy at birth	Unacceptable	Acceptable	Acceptable	Acceptable
Under-five mortality	..	..	..	Unacceptable
Maternal mortality	..	..	..	Unacceptable
Level of concern about HIV/AIDS	..	..	Major concern	Major concern
Measures to respond to HIV/AIDS*	..	..	..	1,2,3,4,5
Grounds on which abortion is permitted**	..	..	1,2,3	1,2,3
Spatial distribution and internal migration				
View on spatial distribution	Minor change desired	Major change desired	Satisfactory	Satisfactory
Policies on internal migration				
From rural to urban areas	..	..	..	No intervention
From rural to rural areas	..	..	..	No intervention
From urban to rural areas	..	..	..	No intervention
From urban to urban areas	..	..	..	No intervention
Into urban agglomerations	..	No intervention	No intervention	No intervention
International migration				
Immigration				
View	Satisfactory	Too high	Too high	Too high
Policy	Maintain	Maintain	Lower	Lower
Permanent settlement	..	..	Lower	Lower
Temporary workers	..	..	Lower	Maintain
Highly skilled workers	..	..	..	Maintain
Family reunification	..	..	Lower	Maintain
Integration of non-citizens	..	..	No	No
Emigration				
View	Satisfactory	Too low	Satisfactory	Satisfactory
Policy	Maintain	Maintain	No intervention	No intervention
Encouraging the return of citizens	..	..	No	Yes

* Measures implemented to respond to HIV/AIDS: (1) blood screening; (2) information/education campaigns; (3) antiretroviral treatment; (4) non-discriminatory policies; (5) distribution of condoms.
** Grounds on which abortion is permitted: (1) to save the woman's life; (2) to preserve physical health; (3) to preserve mental health; (4) rape or incest; (5) foetal impairment; (6) economic or social reasons; (7) on request.

Population indicators

Indicator	1975	1985	1995	2009
Population size and growth				
Population size (thousands)	189	234	281	342
Annual growth rate (percentage)*	2.1	2.1	1.9	1.2
Population age structure				
Percentage of population under age 15	41	36	31	26
Percentage of population aged 60 or over	6	6	7	10
Fertility and family planning				
Total fertility (children per woman)*	3.4	3.2	2.6	2.0
Adolescent fertility rate (per 1,000 women, aged 15 - 19)*	..	..	69.0	53.0
Percentage of births to women under age 20*	..	..	13	13
Percentage of births to women aged 35 or over*	..	..	14	13
Percentage of married women using contraception				
Modern methods	..	60[a]	..	..
All methods	..	62[a]	..	..
Health and mortality				
Life expectancy at birth (years)*				
Males	63	65	66	71
Females	70	72	73	76
Both sexes combined	67	68	70	73
Infant mortality rate (per 1,000 live births)*	38	19	17	9
Under-five mortality (per 1,000 live births)*	..	28	25	13
Maternal mortality ratio (per 100,000 live births) (2005)	..	..	..	16
HIV/AIDS				
People living with HIV/AIDS (thousands)	..	..	6.3	6.2[b]
Adult prevalence (percentage)	..	..	3.8	3.0[b]
Spatial distribution				
Population density (per sq. km)	14	17	20	25
Urban population (percentage)	70	77	81	84
Annual urban population growth rate (percentage)	3.0	2.7	2.0	1.4
Annual rural population growth rate (percentage)	-0.1	-1.1	0.6	-0.1
International migration				
Migrant stock				
Number of migrants (thousands)	27	25	28	33**
As percentage of total population	14.4	10.9	10.1	9.7**

* For the periods 1970-1975, 1980-1985, 1990-1995 and 2005-2010.
** For 2010.
[a] For 1988.
[b] For 2007.

Government views and policies

Population policy variable	1976	1986	1996	2009
Population size and growth				
View on growth	Satisfactory	Satisfactory	Satisfactory	Too high
Policy on growth	No intervention	No intervention	No intervention	Lower
Population age structure				
Level of concern about				
Size of the working-age population	..	..	..	Minor concern
Ageing of the population	..	..	..	Minor concern
Fertility and family planning				
View on fertility level	Too high	Satisfactory	Satisfactory	Too high
Policy	No intervention	No intervention	Lower	Lower
Access to contraceptive methods	Indirect support	Direct support	Direct support	Direct support
Adolescent fertility				
Level of concern	..	..	Not a concern	Not a concern
Policies and programmes	..	..	No	No
Health and mortality				
View				
Life expectancy at birth	Unacceptable	Acceptable	Acceptable	Acceptable
Under-five mortality	..	..	Unacceptable	Unacceptable
Maternal mortality	..	..	..	Acceptable
Level of concern about HIV/AIDS	..	..	..	Major concern
Measures to respond to HIV/AIDS*	..	..	..	1,2,3
Grounds on which abortion is permitted**	..	..	1,2,3,5	1,2,3,4,5,6,7
Spatial distribution and internal migration				
View on spatial distribution	Satisfactory	Satisfactory	Satisfactory	Satisfactory
Policies on internal migration				
From rural to urban areas	..	..	..	..
From rural to rural areas	..	..	..	..
From urban to rural areas	..	..	..	..
From urban to urban areas	..	..	..	..
Into urban agglomerations	..	Raise	No intervention	..
International migration				
Immigration				
View	Satisfactory	Too high	Satisfactory	Satisfactory
Policy	Maintain	Lower	No intervention	Maintain
Permanent settlement	..	..	No intervention	..
Temporary workers	..	..	No intervention	Lower
Highly skilled workers	..	..	..	..
Family reunification	..	..	No intervention	Maintain
Integration of non-citizens	..	..	..	..
Emigration				
View	Satisfactory	Satisfactory	Satisfactory	Satisfactory
Policy	Maintain	Maintain	No intervention	No intervention
Encouraging the return of citizens	..	..	No	..

* Measures implemented to respond to HIV/AIDS: (1) blood screening; (2) information/education campaigns; (3) antiretroviral treatment; (4) non-discriminatory policies; (5) distribution of condoms.

** Grounds on which abortion is permitted: (1) to save the woman's life; (2) to preserve physical health; (3) to preserve mental health; (4) rape or incest; (5) foetal impairment; (6) economic or social reasons; (7) on request.

Population indicators

Indicator	1975	1985	1995	2009
Population size and growth				
Population size (thousands)	272	413	578	791
Annual growth rate (percentage)*	4.3	3.5	3.2	2.1
Population age structure				
Percentage of population under age 15	43	32	30	26
Percentage of population aged 60 or over	4	4	4	4
Fertility and family planning				
Total fertility (children per woman)*	5.9	4.6	3.4	2.3
Adolescent fertility rate (per 1,000 women, aged 15 - 19)*	..	..	24.0	17.0
Percentage of births to women under age 20*	..	..	4	4
Percentage of births to women aged 35 or over*	..	..	28	30
Percentage of married women using contraception				
Modern methods	..	30[a]	31	..
All methods	..	54[a]	62	..
Health and mortality				
Life expectancy at birth (years)*				
Males	62	67	71	74
Females	65	71	75	77
Both sexes combined	63	69	73	76
Infant mortality rate (per 1,000 live births)*	50	21	15	10
Under-five mortality (per 1,000 live births)*	..	29	20	13
Maternal mortality ratio (per 100,000 live births) (2005)	..	..	..	32
HIV/AIDS				
People living with HIV/AIDS (thousands)	..	..	..	<1[b]
Adult prevalence (percentage)	..	..	..	..
Spatial distribution				
Population density (per sq. km)	392	596	832	1 140
Urban population (percentage)	85	87	88	89
Annual urban population growth rate (percentage)	5.3	3.7	2.6	1.7
Annual rural population growth rate (percentage)	3.5	1.9	2.6	1.2
International migration				
Migrant stock				
Number of migrants (thousands)	60	137	206	315**
As percentage of total population	22.1	33.1	35.7	39.1**

* For the periods 1970-1975, 1980-1985, 1990-1995 and 2005-2010.
** For 2010.
[a] For 1989.
[b] For 2007.

BANGLADESH

Government views and policies

Population policy variable	1976	1986	1996	2009
Population size and growth				
View on growth	Too high	Too high	Too high	Too high
Policy on growth	Lower	Lower	Lower	Lower
Population age structure				
Level of concern about				
Size of the working-age population	..	..	..	Major concern
Ageing of the population	..	..	..	Major concern
Fertility and family planning				
View on fertility level	Too high	Too high	Too high	Too high
Policy	Lower	Lower	Lower	Lower
Access to contraceptive methods	Direct support	Direct support	Direct support	Direct support
Adolescent fertility				
Level of concern	..	..	Minor concern	Major concern
Policies and programmes	..	..	Yes	Yes
Health and mortality				
View				
Life expectancy at birth	Unacceptable	Unacceptable	Unacceptable	Unacceptable
Under-five mortality	..	..	Unacceptable	Unacceptable
Maternal mortality	..	..	..	Unacceptable
Level of concern about HIV/AIDS	..	..	Minor concern	Major concern
Measures to respond to HIV/AIDS*	..	..	..	1,2,5
Grounds on which abortion is permitted**	..	..	1	1
Spatial distribution and internal migration				
View on spatial distribution	Minor change desired	Minor change desired	Major change desired	Satisfactory
Policies on internal migration				
From rural to urban areas	..	..	..	Lower
From rural to rural areas	..	..	..	..
From urban to rural areas	..	..	..	..
From urban to urban areas	..	..	..	Maintain
Into urban agglomerations	..	No intervention	No intervention	Lower
International migration				
Immigration				
View	Satisfactory	Satisfactory	Satisfactory	Satisfactory
Policy	Maintain	Maintain	Lower	Lower
Permanent settlement	..	..	No intervention	No intervention
Temporary workers	..	..	No intervention	Maintain
Highly skilled workers	..	..	..	..
Family reunification	..	..	No intervention	Maintain
Integration of non-citizens	..	..	No	No
Emigration				
View	Satisfactory	Satisfactory	Satisfactory	Too low
Policy	Maintain	Maintain	No intervention	Raise
Encouraging the return of citizens	..	..	No	No

* Measures implemented to respond to HIV/AIDS: (1) blood screening; (2) information/education campaigns; (3) antiretroviral treatment; (4) non-discriminatory policies; (5) distribution of condoms.
** Grounds on which abortion is permitted: (1) to save the woman's life; (2) to preserve physical health; (3) to preserve mental health; (4) rape or incest; (5) foetal impairment; (6) economic or social reasons; (7) on request.

United Nations Department of Economic and Social Affairs/Population Division

Population indicators

Indicator	1975	1985	1995	2009
Population size and growth				
Population size (thousands)	79 049	102 993	128 086	162 221
Annual growth rate (percentage)*	2.7	2.6	2.0	1.4
Population age structure				
Percentage of population under age 15	45	45	40	31
Percentage of population aged 60 or over	5	5	5	6
Fertility and family planning				
Total fertility (children per woman)*	6.9	5.9	4.0	2.4
Adolescent fertility rate (per 1,000 women, aged 15 - 19)*	..	..	140.0	72.0
Percentage of births to women under age 20*	..	..	18	15
Percentage of births to women aged 35 or over*	..	..	14	12
Percentage of married women using contraception				
Modern methods	5	18	42[a]	48[b]
All methods	8	25	49[a]	56[b]
Health and mortality				
Life expectancy at birth (years)*				
Males	44	49	55	65
Females	45	50	57	67
Both sexes combined	45	49	56	66
Infant mortality rate (per 1,000 live births)*	152	124	91	45
Under-five mortality (per 1,000 live births)*	..	183	129	57
Maternal mortality ratio (per 100,000 live births) (2005)	..	..	..	570
HIV/AIDS				
People living with HIV/AIDS (thousands)	..	..	..	12[b]
Adult prevalence (percentage)	..	..	..	..
Spatial distribution				
Population density (per sq. km)	549	715	890	1 127
Urban population (percentage)	10	17	22	28
Annual urban population growth rate (percentage)	10.8	4.9	3.8	3.4
Annual rural population growth rate (percentage)	1.4	1.9	1.6	0.9
International migration				
Migrant stock				
Number of migrants (thousands)	769	842	1 006	1 085**
As percentage of total population	1.0	0.8	0.8	0.7**

* For the periods 1970-1975, 1980-1985, 1990-1995 and 2005-2010.
** For 2010.
[a] For 1996/1997.
[b] For 2007.

Government views and policies

Population policy variable	1976	1986	1996	2009
Population size and growth				
View on growth	Too high	Too high	Satisfactory	Satisfactory
Policy on growth	Lower	Lower	No intervention	No intervention
Population age structure				
Level of concern about				
Size of the working-age population	..	..		Minor concern
Ageing of the population	..	..	..	Major concern
Fertility and family planning				
View on fertility level	Too high	Too high	Satisfactory	Too low
Policy	Lower	Lower	No intervention	Raise
Access to contraceptive methods	Direct support	Direct support	Direct support	Direct support
Adolescent fertility				
Level of concern	..	..	Minor concern	Major concern
Policies and programmes	..	..	Yes	Yes
Health and mortality				
View				
Life expectancy at birth	Acceptable	Acceptable	Acceptable	Acceptable
Under-five mortality	..	..	..	Acceptable
Maternal mortality	..	..	..	Unacceptable
Level of concern about HIV/AIDS	..	..	..	Major concern
Measures to respond to HIV/AIDS*	..	..	..	1,2,3,4,5
Grounds on which abortion is permitted**	..	..	1,2,3,4,5,6	1,2,3,4,5,6
Spatial distribution and internal migration				
View on spatial distribution	Satisfactory	Satisfactory	Satisfactory	Satisfactory
Policies on internal migration				
From rural to urban areas	..	..	..	No intervention
From rural to rural areas	..	..	..	No intervention
From urban to rural areas	..	..	..	No intervention
From urban to urban areas	..	..	..	No intervention
Into urban agglomerations	No intervention	..	..	No intervention
International migration				
Immigration				
View	Satisfactory	Satisfactory	Satisfactory	Satisfactory
Policy	Maintain	Maintain	Lower	Maintain
Permanent settlement	..	..	..	Lower
Temporary workers	..	..	..	Maintain
Highly skilled workers	..	..	..	Raise
Family reunification	..	..	..	Maintain
Integration of non-citizens	..	..	..	No
Emigration				
View	Satisfactory	Satisfactory	Satisfactory	Too high
Policy	Maintain	Maintain	No intervention	No intervention
Encouraging the return of citizens	No	..	No	Yes

* Measures implemented to respond to HIV/AIDS: (1) blood screening; (2) information/education campaigns; (3) antiretroviral treatment; (4) non-discriminatory policies; (5) distribution of condoms.
** Grounds on which abortion is permitted: (1) to save the woman's life; (2) to preserve physical health; (3) to preserve mental health; (4) rape or incest; (5) foetal impairment; (6) economic or social reasons; (7) on request.

Population indicators

Indicator	1975	1985	1995	2009
Population size and growth				
Population size (thousands)	246	254	258	256
Annual growth rate (percentage)*	0.6	0.4	-0.1	0.3
Population age structure				
Percentage of population under age 15	31	27	23	17
Percentage of population aged 60 or over	14	14	13	15
Fertility and family planning				
Total fertility (children per woman)*	2.7	1.9	1.6	1.5
Adolescent fertility rate (per 1,000 women, aged 15 - 19)*	..	..	47.0	43.0
Percentage of births to women under age 20*	..	..	15	14
Percentage of births to women aged 35 or over*	..	..	11	10
Percentage of married women using contraception				
Modern methods	..	53[a]	..	..
All methods	..	55[a]	..	..
Health and mortality				
Life expectancy at birth (years)*				
Males	67	70	72	74
Females	72	75	77	80
Both sexes combined	69	73	75	77
Infant mortality rate (per 1,000 live births)*	33	19	14	10
Under-five mortality (per 1,000 live births)*	..	24	16	11
Maternal mortality ratio (per 100,000 live births) (2005)	..	..	..	16
HIV/AIDS				
People living with HIV/AIDS (thousands)	..	..	2	2.2[b]
Adult prevalence (percentage)	..	..	1.2	1.2[b]
Spatial distribution				
Population density (per sq. km)	571	592	600	595
Urban population (percentage)	39	36	34	40
Annual urban population growth rate (percentage)	0.9	-1.1	1.6	1.5
Annual rural population growth rate (percentage)	0.0	2.0	0.0	-0.6
International migration				
Migrant stock				
Number of migrants (thousands)	16	20	23	28**
As percentage of total population	6.5	7.9	8.9	10.9**

* For the periods 1970-1975, 1980-1985, 1990-1995 and 2005-2010.
** For 2010.
[a] For 1988.
[b] For 2007.

Government views and policies

Population policy variable	1976	1986	1996	2009
Population size and growth				
View on growth	Too low	Satisfactory	Too low	Too low
Policy on growth	Raise	Maintain	Raise	Raise
Population age structure				
Level of concern about				
Size of the working-age population	..	..	..	Major concern
Ageing of the population	..	..	..	Major concern
Fertility and family planning				
View on fertility level	Satisfactory	Satisfactory	Satisfactory	Too low
Policy	Maintain	Maintain	Raise	Raise
Access to contraceptive methods	Direct support	Direct support	Direct support	Direct support
Adolescent fertility				
Level of concern	..	..	Major concern	Major concern
Policies and programmes	..	..	No	Yes
Health and mortality				
View				
Life expectancy at birth	Unacceptable	Unacceptable	Acceptable	Unacceptable
Under-five mortality	..	..	Unacceptable	Unacceptable
Maternal mortality	..	..	..	Acceptable
Level of concern about HIV/AIDS	..	..	Major concern	Major concern
Measures to respond to HIV/AIDS*	..	..	..	1,2,3,4,5
Grounds on which abortion is permitted**	..	..	1,2,3,4,5,6,7	1,2,3,4,5,6,7
Spatial distribution and internal migration				
View on spatial distribution	Minor change desired	Minor change desired	Satisfactory	Minor change desired
Policies on internal migration				
From rural to urban areas	..	..	..	Lower
From rural to rural areas	..	..	..	No intervention
From urban to rural areas	..	..	..	Raise
From urban to urban areas	..	..	..	No intervention
Into urban agglomerations	..	..	Maintain	Lower
International migration				
Immigration				
View	Satisfactory	Satisfactory	Satisfactory	Satisfactory
Policy	Maintain	Maintain	Maintain	Raise
Permanent settlement	..	..	Maintain	Raise
Temporary workers	..	..	Maintain	Raise
Highly skilled workers	..	..	Maintain	No intervention
Family reunification	..	..	..	Maintain
Integration of non-citizens	..	..	Maintain	Raise
			No	Yes
Emigration				
View	Satisfactory	Satisfactory	Satisfactory	Too high
Policy	Maintain	Maintain	Lower	Lower
Encouraging the return of citizens	..	..	Yes	Yes

* Measures implemented to respond to HIV/AIDS: (1) blood screening; (2) information/education campaigns; (3) antiretroviral treatment; (4) non-discriminatory policies; (5) distribution of condoms.
** Grounds on which abortion is permitted: (1) to save the woman's life; (2) to preserve physical health; (3) to preserve mental health; (4) rape or incest; (5) foetal impairment; (6) economic or social reasons; (7) on request.

Population indicators

Indicator	1975	1985	1995	2009
Population size and growth				
Population size (thousands)	9 367	9 999	10 270	9 634
Annual growth rate (percentage)*	0.7	0.7	0.0	-0.5
Population age structure				
Percentage of population under age 15	26	23	22	15
Percentage of population aged 60 or over	14	15	18	18
Fertility and family planning				
Total fertility (children per woman)*	2.3	2.1	1.7	1.3
Adolescent fertility rate (per 1,000 women, aged 15 - 19)*	..	..	44.0	21.0
Percentage of births to women under age 20*	..	..	13	8
Percentage of births to women aged 35 or over*	..	..	5	7
Percentage of married women using contraception				
Modern methods	..	..	42	56[a]
All methods	..	..	50	73[a]
Health and mortality				
Life expectancy at birth (years)*				
Males	67	66	64	63
Females	76	75	75	75
Both sexes combined	72	71	70	69
Infant mortality rate (per 1,000 live births)*	21	20	15	9
Under-five mortality (per 1,000 live births)*	..	24	18	12
Maternal mortality ratio (per 100,000 live births) (2005)	..	..	..	18
HIV/AIDS				
People living with HIV/AIDS (thousands)	..	..	4.2	13[b]
Adult prevalence (percentage)	..	..	0.1	0.2[b]
Spatial distribution				
Population density (per sq. km)	45	48	49	46
Urban population (percentage)	51	62	68	74
Annual urban population growth rate (percentage)	3.0	2.3	0.3	0.0
Annual rural population growth rate (percentage)	-1.9	-2.1	-1.5	-2.1
International migration				
Migrant stock				
Number of migrants (thousands)	..	..	1 185	1 090**
As percentage of total population	0.0	0.0	11.5	11.4**

* For the periods 1970-1975, 1980-1985, 1990-1995 and 2005-2010.
** For 2010.
[a] For 2005/2006.
[b] For 2007.

Government views and policies

Population policy variable	1976	1986	1996	2009
Population size and growth				
View on growth	Satisfactory	Satisfactory	Satisfactory	Satisfactory
Policy on growth	No intervention	Maintain	No intervention	No intervention
Population age structure				
Level of concern about				
Size of the working-age population	..	..	..	Major concern
Ageing of the population	..	..	..	Major concern
Fertility and family planning				
View on fertility level	Satisfactory	Satisfactory	Satisfactory	Satisfactory
Policy	No intervention	Maintain	No intervention	No intervention
Access to contraceptive methods	Indirect support	Indirect support	Indirect support	Direct support
Adolescent fertility				
Level of concern	..	..	Minor concern	Minor concern
Policies and programmes	..	..	..	Yes
Health and mortality				
View				
Life expectancy at birth	Acceptable	Acceptable	Acceptable	Acceptable
Under-five mortality	..	..	Acceptable	Acceptable
Maternal mortality	..	..	..	Acceptable
Level of concern about HIV/AIDS	..	..	Minor concern	Minor concern
Measures to respond to HIV/AIDS*	..	..		1,2,3,4,5
Grounds on which abortion is permitted**	..	..	1,2,3,4,5,6	1,2,3,4,5,6,7
Spatial distribution and internal migration				
View on spatial distribution	Satisfactory	Satisfactory	Satisfactory	Minor change desired
Policies on internal migration				
From rural to urban areas	..	..	..	No intervention
From rural to rural areas	..	..	..	No intervention
From urban to rural areas	..	..	..	No intervention
From urban to urban areas	..	..	..	No intervention
Into urban agglomerations	..	..	Raise	No intervention
International migration				
Immigration				
View	Satisfactory	Satisfactory	Too high	Satisfactory
Policy	Maintain	Maintain	Lower	Maintain
Permanent settlement	..	..	Lower	Maintain
Temporary workers	..	..	Lower	Maintain
Highly skilled workers	..	..	..	Maintain
Family reunification	..	..	Lower	Maintain
Integration of non-citizens	..	..	Yes	Yes
Emigration				
View	Satisfactory	Satisfactory	Satisfactory	Satisfactory
Policy	Maintain	Maintain	No intervention	No intervention
Encouraging the return of citizens	..	..	No	No

* Measures implemented to respond to HIV/AIDS: (1) blood screening; (2) information/education campaigns; (3) antiretroviral treatment; (4) non-discriminatory policies; (5) distribution of condoms.
** Grounds on which abortion is permitted: (1) to save the woman's life; (2) to preserve physical health; (3) to preserve mental health; (4) rape or incest; (5) foetal impairment; (6) economic or social reasons; (7) on request.

Population indicators

Indicator	1975	1985	1995	2009
Population size and growth				
Population size (thousands)	9 779	9 816	10 084	10 647
Annual growth rate (percentage)[*]	0.3	0.0	0.3	0.5
Population age structure				
Percentage of population under age 15	22	19	18	17
Percentage of population aged 60 or over	19	20	21	23
Fertility and family planning				
Total fertility (children per woman)[*]	2.0	1.6	1.6	1.8
Adolescent fertility rate (per 1,000 women, aged 15 - 19)[*]	..	..	11.0	8.0
Percentage of births to women under age 20[*]	..	..	3	2
Percentage of births to women aged 35 or over[*]	..	..	8	13
Percentage of married women using contraception				
Modern methods	47[a]	63[b]	74[c]	73[d]
All methods	87[a]	81[b]	78[c]	75[d]
Health and mortality				
Life expectancy at birth (years)[*]				
Males	68	71	73	77
Females	75	77	80	83
Both sexes combined	72	74	76	80
Infant mortality rate (per 1,000 live births)[*]	17	10	8	4
Under-five mortality (per 1,000 live births)[*]	..	13	9	5
Maternal mortality ratio (per 100,000 live births) (2005)	..	..	..	8
HIV/AIDS				
People living with HIV/AIDS (thousands)	..	..	9.7	15[e]
Adult prevalence (percentage)	..	..	0.2	0.2[e]
Spatial distribution				
Population density (per sq. km)	320	322	330	349
Urban population (percentage)	94	96	97	97
Annual urban population growth rate (percentage)	0.3	0.2	0.3	0.2
Annual rural population growth rate (percentage)	-2.0	-2.2	-2.1	-1.0
International migration				
Migrant stock				
Number of migrants (thousands)	820	872	916	975[**]
As percentage of total population	8.4	8.9	9.1	9.1[**]

[*] For the periods 1970-1975, 1980-1985, 1990-1995 and 2005-2010.
[**] For 2010.
[a] For 1976.
[b] For 1983.
[c] For 1991/1992.
[d] For 2004.
[e] For 2007.

Government views and policies

Population policy variable	1976	1986	1996	2009
Population size and growth				
View on growth	..	Satisfactory	Too low	Too high
Policy on growth	..	No intervention	No intervention	No intervention
Population age structure				
Level of concern about				
Size of the working-age population	..	..	..	Minor concern
Ageing of the population	..	..	..	Major concern
Fertility and family planning				
View on fertility level	..	Satisfactory	Too high	Too high
Policy	..	No intervention	No intervention	No intervention
Access to contraceptive methods	..	No support	Indirect support	Indirect support
Adolescent fertility				
Level of concern	..	..	Major concern	Major concern
Policies and programmes	..	..	Yes	Yes
Health and mortality				
View				
Life expectancy at birth	..	Acceptable	Acceptable	Acceptable
Under-five mortality	..	..	Unacceptable	Unacceptable
Maternal mortality	..	..	..	Unacceptable
Level of concern about HIV/AIDS	..	..	Major concern	Major concern
Measures to respond to HIV/AIDS*	..	..	..	1,2,3,4,5
Grounds on which abortion is permitted**	..	..	1,2,3,4,5,6	1,2,3,5,6
Spatial distribution and internal migration				
View on spatial distribution	..	Minor change desired	Minor change desired	Minor change desired
Policies on internal migration				
From rural to urban areas	..	..	..	No intervention
From rural to rural areas	..	..	..	No intervention
From urban to rural areas	..	..	..	No intervention
From urban to urban areas	..	..	..	No intervention
Into urban agglomerations	..	No intervention	No intervention	No intervention
International migration				
Immigration				
View	..	Satisfactory	Too high	Too high
Policy	..	Maintain	Lower	Lower
Permanent settlement	..	..	Lower	Lower
Temporary workers	..	..	Maintain	Lower
Highly skilled workers	..	..	..	Maintain
Family reunification	..	..	Maintain	Lower
Integration of non-citizens	..	..	Yes	No
Emigration				
View	..	Too high	Too high	Satisfactory
Policy	..	Lower	Lower	No intervention
Encouraging the return of citizens	..	..	No	No

* Measures implemented to respond to HIV/AIDS: (1) blood screening; (2) information/education campaigns; (3) antiretroviral treatment; (4) non-discriminatory policies; (5) distribution of condoms.

** Grounds on which abortion is permitted: (1) to save the woman's life; (2) to preserve physical health; (3) to preserve mental health; (4) rape or incest; (5) foetal impairment; (6) economic or social reasons; (7) on request.

Population indicators

Indicator	1975	1985	1995	2009
Population size and growth				
Population size (thousands)	134	165	220	307
Annual growth rate (percentage)*	1.7	2.8	3.0	2.1
Population age structure				
Percentage of population under age 15	47	45	43	35
Percentage of population aged 60 or over	7	6	6	6
Fertility and family planning				
Total fertility (children per woman)*	6.3	5.4	4.3	2.9
Adolescent fertility rate (per 1,000 women, aged 15 - 19)*	..	..	122.0	79.0
Percentage of births to women under age 20*	..	..	14	13
Percentage of births to women aged 35 or over*	..	..	15	13
Percentage of married women using contraception				
Modern methods	..	..	49[a]	31[b]
All methods	..	..	56[a]	34[b]
Health and mortality				
Life expectancy at birth (years)*				
Males	67	70	71	74
Females	68	73	74	78
Both sexes combined	68	71	72	76
Infant mortality rate (per 1,000 live births)*	52	34	30	17
Under-five mortality (per 1,000 live births)*	..	42	37	21
Maternal mortality ratio (per 100,000 live births) (2005)	..	..	..	52
HIV/AIDS				
People living with HIV/AIDS (thousands)	..	..	2.1	3.6[c]
Adult prevalence (percentage)	..	..	1.9	2.1[c]
Spatial distribution				
Population density (per sq. km)	6	7	10	13
Urban population (percentage)	50	48	47	52
Annual urban population growth rate (percentage)	1.0	2.2	2.9	2.9
Annual rural population growth rate (percentage)	1.7	2.9	2.7	0.9
International migration				
Migrant stock				
Number of migrants (thousands)	11	26	38	47**
As percentage of total population	8.2	15.6	17.5	15.0**

* For the periods 1970-1975, 1980-1985, 1990-1995 and 2005-2010.
** For 2010.
[a] For 1999.
[b] For 2006.
[c] For 2007.

Government views and policies

Population policy variable	1976	1986	1996	2009
Population size and growth				
View on growth	Satisfactory	Satisfactory	Satisfactory	Too high
Policy on growth	No intervention	No intervention	No intervention	Lower
Population age structure				
Level of concern about				
Size of the working-age population	..	..	..	Major concern
Ageing of the population	..	..	..	Minor concern
Fertility and family planning				
View on fertility level	Satisfactory	Satisfactory	Satisfactory	Too high
Policy	No intervention	No intervention	No intervention	Lower
Access to contraceptive methods	Indirect support	Indirect support	Direct support	Direct support
Adolescent fertility				
Level of concern	..	..	Minor concern	Major concern
Policies and programmes	..	..	No	Yes
Health and mortality				
View				
Life expectancy at birth	Unacceptable	Unacceptable	Unacceptable	Unacceptable
Under-five mortality	..	..	Unacceptable	Unacceptable
Maternal mortality	..	..	..	Unacceptable
Level of concern about HIV/AIDS	..	..	Major concern	Major concern
Measures to respond to HIV/AIDS*	..	..	..	1,2,3,4,5
Grounds on which abortion is permitted**	..	..	1	1,2,3,4,5
Spatial distribution and internal migration				
View on spatial distribution	Major change desired	Major change desired	Major change desired	Major change desired
Policies on internal migration				
From rural to urban areas	..	..	..	Lower
From rural to rural areas	..	..	..	Maintain
From urban to rural areas	..	..	..	Raise
From urban to urban areas	..	..	..	Maintain
Into urban agglomerations	No intervention	..	No intervention	Lower
International migration				
Immigration				
View	Satisfactory	Satisfactory	Satisfactory	Too high
Policy	Maintain	Maintain	No intervention	No intervention
Permanent settlement	..	..	No intervention	No intervention
Temporary workers	..	..	No intervention	No intervention
Highly skilled workers	..	..	..	No intervention
Family reunification	..	..	No intervention	No intervention
Integration of non-citizens	..	..	No	No
Emigration				
View	Satisfactory	Satisfactory	Satisfactory	Satisfactory
Policy	Maintain	Maintain	No intervention	Lower
Encouraging the return of citizens	..	..	Yes	No

* Measures implemented to respond to HIV/AIDS: (1) blood screening; (2) information/education campaigns; (3) antiretroviral treatment; (4) non-discriminatory policies; (5) distribution of condoms.

** Grounds on which abortion is permitted: (1) to save the woman's life; (2) to preserve physical health; (3) to preserve mental health; (4) rape or incest; (5) foetal impairment; (6) economic or social reasons; (7) on request.

Population indicators

Indicator	1975	1985	1995	2009
Population size and growth				
Population size (thousands)	3 109	4 122	5 723	8 935
Annual growth rate (percentage)*	2.4	2.9	3.5	3.2
Population age structure				
Percentage of population under age 15	44	45	45	43
Percentage of population aged 60 or over	7	6	5	5
Fertility and family planning				
Total fertility (children per woman)*	6.7	7.0	6.6	5.5
Adolescent fertility rate (per 1,000 women, aged 15 - 19)*	..	..	128.0	112.0
Percentage of births to women under age 20*	..	..	10	10
Percentage of births to women aged 35 or over*	..	..	26	22
Percentage of married women using contraception				
Modern methods	..	1[a]	3[b]	6[c]
All methods	..	9[a]	16[b]	17[c]
Health and mortality				
Life expectancy at birth (years)*				
Males	45	50	54	60
Females	48	53	56	62
Both sexes combined	47	51	55	61
Infant mortality rate (per 1,000 live births)*	146	126	111	85
Under-five mortality (per 1,000 live births)*	..	206	173	121
Maternal mortality ratio (per 100,000 live births) (2005)	..	..	..	840
HIV/AIDS				
People living with HIV/AIDS (thousands)	..	..	25	64[d]
Adult prevalence (percentage)	..	..	0.8	1.2[d]
Spatial distribution				
Population density (per sq. km)	28	37	51	79
Urban population (percentage)	22	31	37	42
Annual urban population growth rate (percentage)	7.9	5.6	4.0	4.0
Annual rural population growth rate (percentage)	1.2	2.2	2.7	2.2
International migration				
Migrant stock				
Number of migrants (thousands)	50	68	146	232**
As percentage of total population	1.6	1.6	2.6	2.5**

* For the periods 1970-1975, 1980-1985, 1990-1995 and 2005-2010.
** For 2010.
[a] For 1982.
[b] For 1996.
[c] For 2006.
[d] For 2007.

Government views and policies

Population policy variable	1976	1986	1996	2009
Population size and growth				
View on growth	Too low	Too low	Too low	Satisfactory
Policy on growth	No intervention	No intervention	No intervention	Lower
Population age structure				
Level of concern about				
Size of the working-age population	..	..	..	Major concern
Ageing of the population	..	..	..	Minor concern
Fertility and family planning				
View on fertility level	Satisfactory	Satisfactory	Satisfactory	Satisfactory
Policy	No intervention	No intervention	No intervention	Lower
Access to contraceptive methods	Direct support	Direct support	Direct support	Direct support
Adolescent fertility				
Level of concern	..	..	..	Major concern
Policies and programmes	..	..	..	Yes
Health and mortality				
View				
Life expectancy at birth	Unacceptable	Unacceptable	Unacceptable	Unacceptable
Under-five mortality	..	..	..	Unacceptable
Maternal mortality	..	..	..	Unacceptable
Level of concern about HIV/AIDS	..	..	..	Major concern
Measures to respond to HIV/AIDS*	..	..	..	1,2,3,5
Grounds on which abortion is permitted**	..	..	1	1,3,4
Spatial distribution and internal migration				
View on spatial distribution	Minor change desired	Minor change desired	Minor change desired	Major change desired
Policies on internal migration				
From rural to urban areas	..	..	..	Maintain
From rural to rural areas	..	..	..	No intervention
From urban to rural areas	..	..	..	No intervention
From urban to urban areas	..	..	..	Raise
Into urban agglomerations	..	..	..	Lower
International migration				
Immigration				
View	Satisfactory	Satisfactory	Too high	Too high
Policy	Maintain	Maintain	Lower	Lower
Permanent settlement	..	..	Lower	Lower
Temporary workers	..	..	..	Lower
Highly skilled workers	..	..	..	Lower
Family reunification	..	..	..	Maintain
Integration of non-citizens	..	..	..	No
Emigration				
View	Satisfactory	Satisfactory	Satisfactory	Satisfactory
Policy	Maintain	Maintain	Maintain	Lower
Encouraging the return of citizens	..	..	..	No

* Measures implemented to respond to HIV/AIDS: (1) blood screening; (2) information/education campaigns; (3) antiretroviral treatment; (4) non-discriminatory policies; (5) distribution of condoms.

** Grounds on which abortion is permitted: (1) to save the woman's life; (2) to preserve physical health; (3) to preserve mental health; (4) rape or incest; (5) foetal impairment; (6) economic or social reasons; (7) on request.

Population indicators

Indicator	1975	1985	1995	2009
Population size and growth				
Population size (thousands)	358	481	509	697
Annual growth rate (percentage)*	3.7	2.6	-1.5	1.7
Population age structure				
Percentage of population under age 15	41	43	44	31
Percentage of population aged 60 or over	5	5	6	7
Fertility and family planning				
Total fertility (children per woman)*	6.7	6.5	5.4	2.7
Adolescent fertility rate (per 1,000 women, aged 15 - 19)*	..	..	110.0	38.0
Percentage of births to women under age 20*	..	..	10	7
Percentage of births to women aged 35 or over*	..	..	26	20
Percentage of married women using contraception				
Modern methods	..	..	19[a]	31[b]
All methods	..	..	19[a]	31[b]
Health and mortality				
Life expectancy at birth (years)*				
Males	41	47	53	64
Females	43	49	56	68
Both sexes combined	42	48	54	66
Infant mortality rate (per 1,000 live births)*	149	117	88	44
Under-five mortality (per 1,000 live births)*	..	194	140	64
Maternal mortality ratio (per 100,000 live births) (2005)	..	..	..	440
HIV/AIDS				
People living with HIV/AIDS (thousands)	..	..	..	<0.5[c]
Adult prevalence (percentage)	..	..	..	0.1[c]
Spatial distribution				
Population density (per sq. km)	8	10	11	15
Urban population (percentage)	8	13	21	36
Annual urban population growth rate (percentage)	8.7	8.0	4.8	4.5
Annual rural population growth rate (percentage)	3.1	2.5	-0.8	-0.5
International migration				
Migrant stock				
Number of migrants (thousands)	15	20	28	40**
As percentage of total population	4.2	4.3	5.4	5.7**

* For the periods 1970-1975, 1980-1985, 1990-1995 and 2005-2010.
** For 2010.
[a] For 1994.
[b] For 2000.
[c] For 2007.

Government views and policies

Population policy variable	1976	1986	1996	2009
Population size and growth				
View on growth	Satisfactory	Too low	Satisfactory	Satisfactory
Policy on growth	No intervention	No intervention	No intervention	No intervention
Population age structure				
Level of concern about				
Size of the working-age population	..	..	..	Not a concern
Ageing of the population	..	..	..	Major concern
Fertility and family planning				
View on fertility level	Satisfactory	Too low	Satisfactory	Satisfactory
Policy	No intervention	No intervention	No intervention	No intervention
Access to contraceptive methods	Direct support	Indirect support	Direct support	Direct support
Adolescent fertility				
Level of concern	..	..	Minor concern	Major concern
Policies and programmes	..	..	Yes	Yes
Health and mortality				
View				
Life expectancy at birth	Unacceptable	Unacceptable	Unacceptable	Unacceptable
Under-five mortality	..	..	Unacceptable	Unacceptable
Maternal mortality	..	..	..	Unacceptable
Level of concern about HIV/AIDS	..	..	Minor concern	Major concern
Measures to respond to HIV/AIDS[*]	..	..	..	1,2,3,4,5
Grounds on which abortion is permitted[**]	..	..	1,2,4	1,2,3,4
Spatial distribution and internal migration				
View on spatial distribution	Major change desired	Major change desired	Satisfactory	Major change desired
Policies on internal migration				
From rural to urban areas	..	..	..	Lower
From rural to rural areas	..	..	..	..
From urban to rural areas	..	..	..	..
From urban to urban areas	..	..	..	..
Into urban agglomerations	..	Lower	No intervention	Lower
International migration				
Immigration				
View	Satisfactory	Too low	Satisfactory	Satisfactory
Policy	Maintain	Raise	No intervention	Maintain
Permanent settlement	..	..	No intervention	Maintain
Temporary workers	..	..	No intervention	No intervention
Highly skilled workers	..	..	..	Maintain
Family reunification	..	..	No intervention	Maintain
Integration of non-citizens	..	..	No	No
Emigration				
View	Satisfactory	Too high	Satisfactory	Too high
Policy	Maintain	Lower	No intervention	No intervention
Encouraging the return of citizens	..	..	No	..

[*] Measures implemented to respond to HIV/AIDS: (1) blood screening; (2) information/education campaigns; (3) antiretroviral treatment; (4) non-discriminatory policies; (5) distribution of condoms.

[**] Grounds on which abortion is permitted: (1) to save the woman's life; (2) to preserve physical health; (3) to preserve mental health; (4) rape or incest; (5) foetal impairment; (6) economic or social reasons; (7) on request.

Population indicators

Indicator	1975	1985	1995	2009
Population size and growth				
Population size (thousands)	4 759	5 966	7 484	9 863
Annual growth rate (percentage)*	2.4	2.2	2.3	1.8
Population age structure				
Percentage of population under age 15	43	42	41	36
Percentage of population aged 60 or over	6	6	6	7
Fertility and family planning				
Total fertility (children per woman)*	6.5	5.3	4.8	3.5
Adolescent fertility rate (per 1,000 women, aged 15 - 19)*	..	..	89.0	78.0
Percentage of births to women under age 20*	..	..	9	11
Percentage of births to women aged 35 or over*	..	..	24	21
Percentage of married women using contraception				
Modern methods	..	12[a]	18[b]	34[c]
All methods	..	26[a]	45[b]	61[c]
Health and mortality				
Life expectancy at birth (years)*				
Males	45	52	58	63
Females	49	56	62	68
Both sexes combined	47	54	60	66
Infant mortality rate (per 1,000 live births)*	151	109	75	46
Under-five mortality (per 1,000 live births)*	..	165	100	61
Maternal mortality ratio (per 100,000 live births) (2005)	..	..	..	290
HIV/AIDS				
People living with HIV/AIDS (thousands)	..	..	2.9	8.1[d]
Adult prevalence (percentage)	..	..	0.1	0.2[d]
Spatial distribution				
Population density (per sq. km)	4	5	7	9
Urban population (percentage)	41	51	59	66
Annual urban population growth rate (percentage)	3.2	4.2	3.0	2.4
Annual rural population growth rate (percentage)	1.9	0.1	1.0	0.3
International migration				
Migrant stock				
Number of migrants (thousands)	57	59	70	146**
As percentage of total population	1.2	1.0	0.9	1.5**

* For the periods 1970-1975, 1980-1985, 1990-1995 and 2005-2010.
** For 2010.
[a] For 1983.
[b] For 1993/1994.
[c] For 2008.
[d] For 2007.

Government views and policies

Population policy variable	1976	1986	1996	2009
Population size and growth				
View on growth	..	..	Too low	Too low
Policy on growth	..	..	No intervention	No intervention
Population age structure				
Level of concern about				
Size of the working-age population	..	..	..	Major concern
Ageing of the population	..	..	..	Major concern
Fertility and family planning				
View on fertility level	..	..	Too low	Too low
Policy	..	..	No intervention	No intervention
Access to contraceptive methods	..	..	Indirect support	Indirect support
Adolescent fertility				
Level of concern	..	..	..	Minor concern
Policies and programmes	..	..	..	No
Health and mortality				
View				
Life expectancy at birth	..	..	Unacceptable	Unacceptable
Under-five mortality	..	..	..	Unacceptable
Maternal mortality	..	..	..	Unacceptable
Level of concern about HIV/AIDS	..	..	..	Major concern
Measures to respond to HIV/AIDS*	..	..	..	1,2,3
Grounds on which abortion is permitted**	..	..	1,2,3,4,5,6,7	1,2,3,4,5,6,7
Spatial distribution and internal migration				
View on spatial distribution	..	..	Major change desired	Major change desired
Policies on internal migration				
From rural to urban areas	..	..	..	Lower
From rural to rural areas	..	..	..	..
From urban to rural areas	..	..	..	Raise
From urban to urban areas	..	..	..	..
Into urban agglomerations	..	..	..	Lower
International migration				
Immigration				
View	..	..	Satisfactory	Satisfactory
Policy	..	..	No intervention	Maintain
Permanent settlement	..	..	..	Maintain
Temporary workers	..	..	..	Maintain
Highly skilled workers	..	..	..	..
Family reunification	..	..	..	Maintain
Integration of non-citizens	..	..	..	..
Emigration				
View	..	..	Too high	Too high
Policy	..	..	Lower	Lower
Encouraging the return of citizens	..	..	Yes	Yes

* Measures implemented to respond to HIV/AIDS: (1) blood screening; (2) information/education campaigns; (3) antiretroviral treatment; (4) non-discriminatory policies; (5) distribution of condoms.

** Grounds on which abortion is permitted: (1) to save the woman's life; (2) to preserve physical health; (3) to preserve mental health; (4) rape or incest; (5) foetal impairment; (6) economic or social reasons; (7) on request.

Population indicators

Indicator	1975	1985	1995	2009
Population size and growth				
Population size (thousands)	3 747	4 122	3 332	3 767
Annual growth rate (percentage)*	1.0	1.0	-5.1	-0.1
Population age structure				
Percentage of population under age 15	31	25	22	15
Percentage of population aged 60 or over	8	9	13	19
Fertility and family planning				
Total fertility (children per woman)*	2.6	2.0	1.5	1.2
Adolescent fertility rate (per 1,000 women, aged 15 - 19)*	..	..	33.0	16.0
Percentage of births to women under age 20*	..	..	11	7
Percentage of births to women aged 35 or over*	..	..	7	9
Percentage of married women using contraception				
Modern methods	..	..	16[a]	11[b]
All methods	..	..	48[a]	36[b]
Health and mortality				
Life expectancy at birth (years)*				
Males	65	68	56	72
Females	70	73	73	78
Both sexes combined	67	71	64	75
Infant mortality rate (per 1,000 live births)*	51	27	22	13
Under-five mortality (per 1,000 live births)*	..	30	24	15
Maternal mortality ratio (per 100,000 live births) (2005)	..	..	..	3
HIV/AIDS				
People living with HIV/AIDS (thousands)	..	..	..	<0.5[c]
Adult prevalence (percentage)	..	..	..	<0.1[c]
Spatial distribution				
Population density (per sq. km)	73	81	65	74
Urban population (percentage)	31	38	41	48
Annual urban population growth rate (percentage)	3.5	2.6	0.4	1.2
Annual rural population growth rate (percentage)	-0.3	1.2	-1.3	-1.2
International migration				
Migrant stock				
Number of migrants (thousands)	..	..	73	28**
As percentage of total population	0.0	0.0	2.2	0.7**

* For the periods 1970-1975, 1980-1985, 1990-1995 and 2005-2010.
** For 2010.
[a] For 2000.
[b] For 2005/2006.
[c] For 2007.

Government views and policies

Population policy variable	1976	1986	1996	2009
Population size and growth				
View on growth	Too high	Too high	Too high	Too low
Policy on growth	Lower	Lower	Lower	Raise
Population age structure				
Level of concern about				
Size of the working-age population	..	..	..	..
Ageing of the population	..	..	..	Minor concern
Fertility and family planning				
View on fertility level	Too high	Too high	Too high	Satisfactory
Policy	Lower	Lower	Lower	Maintain
Access to contraceptive methods	Direct support	Direct support	Direct support	Direct support
Adolescent fertility				
Level of concern	..	..	Major concern	Major concern
Policies and programmes	..	..	No	Yes
Health and mortality				
View				
Life expectancy at birth	Unacceptable	Unacceptable	Unacceptable	Unacceptable
Under-five mortality	..	..	Unacceptable	Unacceptable
Maternal mortality	..	..	..	Unacceptable
Level of concern about HIV/AIDS	..	..	Major concern	Major concern
Measures to respond to HIV/AIDS*	..	..	..	1,2,3,4,5
Grounds on which abortion is permitted**	..	..	1,2,3,4,5	1,2,3,4,5
Spatial distribution and internal migration				
View on spatial distribution	Major change desired	Major change desired	Major change desired	Major change desired
Policies on internal migration				
From rural to urban areas	..	..	..	Lower
From rural to rural areas	..	..	..	..
From urban to rural areas	..	..	..	..
From urban to urban areas	..	..	..	..
Into urban agglomerations	Lower	No intervention	Lower	Lower
International migration				
Immigration				
View	Satisfactory	Satisfactory	Satisfactory	Too high
Policy	Maintain	Maintain	No intervention	Lower
Permanent settlement	..	..	No intervention	No intervention
Temporary workers	..	..	No intervention	Lower
Highly skilled workers	..	..	..	Lower
Family reunification	..	..	No intervention	No intervention
Integration of non-citizens	..	..	No	Yes
Emigration				
View	Too high	Satisfactory	Satisfactory	Satisfactory
Policy	Lower	Lower	No intervention	No intervention
Encouraging the return of citizens	No	..	No	No

* Measures implemented to respond to HIV/AIDS: (1) blood screening; (2) information/education campaigns; (3) antiretroviral treatment; (4) non-discriminatory policies; (5) distribution of condoms.
** Grounds on which abortion is permitted: (1) to save the woman's life; (2) to preserve physical health; (3) to preserve mental health; (4) rape or incest; (5) foetal impairment; (6) economic or social reasons; (7) on request.

Population indicators

Indicator	1975	1985	1995	2009
Population size and growth				
Population size (thousands)	817	1 161	1 550	1 950
Annual growth rate (percentage)*	3.3	3.3	2.7	1.5
Population age structure				
Percentage of population under age 15	47	47	42	33
Percentage of population aged 60 or over	4	4	4	6
Fertility and family planning				
Total fertility (children per woman)*	6.5	6.0	4.3	2.9
Adolescent fertility rate (per 1,000 women, aged 15 - 19)*	..	..	87.0	52.0
Percentage of births to women under age 20*	..	..	10	9
Percentage of births to women aged 35 or over*	..	..	27	23
Percentage of married women using contraception				
Modern methods	..	32[a]	..	42[b]
All methods	..	33[a]	48[c]	44[b]
Health and mortality				
Life expectancy at birth (years)*				
Males	54	59	61	55
Females	58	63	65	55
Both sexes combined	56	61	63	55
Infant mortality rate (per 1,000 live births)*	90	64	52	36
Under-five mortality (per 1,000 live births)*	..	91	71	54
Maternal mortality ratio (per 100,000 live births) (2005)	..	..	..	380
HIV/AIDS				
People living with HIV/AIDS (thousands)	..	..	160	300[d]
Adult prevalence (percentage)	..	..	19.0	23.9[d]
Spatial distribution				
Population density (per sq. km)	1	2	3	3
Urban population (percentage)	12	27	49	60
Annual urban population growth rate (percentage)	10.4	13.0	4.0	2.4
Annual rural population growth rate (percentage)	2.7	-0.7	0.6	-0.7
International migration				
Migrant stock				
Number of migrants (thousands)	13	20	39	115**
As percentage of total population	1.5	1.7	2.5	5.8**

* For the periods 1970-1975, 1980-1985, 1990-1995 and 2005-2010.
** For 2010.
[a] For 1988.
[b] For 2000.
[c] For 1996.
[d] For 2007.

Government views and policies

Population policy variable	1976	1986	1996	2009
Population size and growth				
View on growth	Satisfactory	Satisfactory	Satisfactory	Satisfactory
Policy on growth	No intervention	No intervention	No intervention	No intervention
Population age structure				
Level of concern about				
Size of the working-age population	..	..	..	Minor concern
Ageing of the population	..	..	..	Major concern
Fertility and family planning				
View on fertility level	Satisfactory	Satisfactory	Satisfactory	Satisfactory
Policy	No intervention	No intervention	No intervention	No intervention
Access to contraceptive methods	Indirect support	Direct support	Direct support	Direct support
Adolescent fertility				
Level of concern	..	..	Major concern	Major concern
Policies and programmes	..	..	Yes	Yes
Health and mortality				
View				
Life expectancy at birth	Unacceptable	Unacceptable	Unacceptable	Unacceptable
Under-five mortality	..	..	Unacceptable	Unacceptable
Maternal mortality	..	..	..	Unacceptable
Level of concern about HIV/AIDS	..	..	Major concern	Major concern
Measures to respond to HIV/AIDS*	..	..	..	1,2,3,4,5
Grounds on which abortion is permitted**	..	..	1,4	1,4
Spatial distribution and internal migration				
View on spatial distribution	Minor change desired	Minor change desired	Minor change desired	Major change desired
Policies on internal migration				
From rural to urban areas	..	..	..	Lower
From rural to rural areas	..	..	..	Raise
From urban to rural areas	..	..	..	Raise
From urban to urban areas	..	..	..	No intervention
Into urban agglomerations	Raise	..	Lower	Lower
International migration				
Immigration				
View	Satisfactory	Satisfactory	Satisfactory	Satisfactory
Policy	Maintain	Maintain	Maintain	Maintain
Permanent settlement	..	..	Maintain	Maintain
Temporary workers	..	..	Maintain	Maintain
Highly skilled workers	..	..	..	Maintain
Family reunification	..	..	Maintain	Maintain
Integration of non-citizens	..	..	No	Yes
Emigration				
View	Satisfactory	Satisfactory	Too high	Satisfactory
Policy	Maintain	Maintain	No intervention	No intervention
Encouraging the return of citizens	No	..	No	No

* Measures implemented to respond to HIV/AIDS: (1) blood screening; (2) information/education campaigns; (3) antiretroviral treatment;
(4) non−discriminatory policies; (5) distribution of condoms.
** Grounds on which abortion is permitted: (1) to save the woman's life; (2) to preserve physical health; (3) to preserve mental health; (4) rape or incest;
(5) foetal impairment; (6) economic or social reasons; (7) on request.

Population indicators

Indicator	1975	1985	1995	2009
Population size and growth				
Population size (thousands)	108 127	136 149	161 692	193 734
Annual growth rate (percentage)[*]	2.4	2.3	1.6	1.0
Population age structure				
Percentage of population under age 15	40	37	32	26
Percentage of population aged 60 or over	6	6	7	10
Fertility and family planning				
Total fertility (children per woman)[*]	4.7	3.8	2.6	1.9
Adolescent fertility rate (per 1,000 women, aged 15 - 19)[*]	..	..	84.0	76.0
Percentage of births to women under age 20[*]	..	..	16	20
Percentage of births to women aged 35 or over[*]	..	..	13	11
Percentage of married women using contraception				
Modern methods	..	57[a]	70[b]	..
All methods	..	66[a]	77[b]	..
Health and mortality				
Life expectancy at birth (years)[*]				
Males	57	60	64	69
Females	62	67	71	76
Both sexes combined	60	63	67	72
Infant mortality rate (per 1,000 live births)[*]	91	63	43	23
Under-five mortality (per 1,000 live births)[*]	..	79	55	29
Maternal mortality ratio (per 100,000 live births) (2005)	..	..	..	110
HIV/AIDS				
People living with HIV/AIDS (thousands)	..	..	530	730[c]
Adult prevalence (percentage)	..	..	0.6	0.6[c]
Spatial distribution				
Population density (per sq. km)	13	16	19	23
Urban population (percentage)	62	71	78	86
Annual urban population growth rate (percentage)	4.2	3.1	2.2	1.7
Annual rural population growth rate (percentage)	-0.7	-0.5	-1.0	-1.8
International migration				
Migrant stock				
Number of migrants (thousands)	1 171	945	731	688[**]
As percentage of total population	1.1	0.7	0.5	0.4[**]

[*] For the periods 1970-1975, 1980-1985, 1990-1995 and 2005-2010.
[**] For 2010.
[a] For 1986.
[b] For 1996.
[c] For 2007.

Government views and policies

Population policy variable	1976	1986	1996	2009
Population size and growth				
View on growth	..	Satisfactory	Satisfactory	Too low
Policy on growth	..	No intervention	No intervention	No intervention
Population age structure				
Level of concern about				
Size of the working-age population	..	..	..	Minor concern
Ageing of the population	..	..	..	Minor concern
Fertility and family planning				
View on fertility level	..	Satisfactory	Satisfactory	Too low
Policy	..	No intervention	No intervention	No intervention
Access to contraceptive methods	..	No support	No support	No support
Adolescent fertility				
Level of concern	..	..	Not a concern	Not a concern
Policies and programmes	..	..	No	No
Health and mortality				
View				
Life expectancy at birth	..	Acceptable	Acceptable	Acceptable
Under-five mortality	..	..	Acceptable	Acceptable
Maternal mortality	..	..	..	Acceptable
Level of concern about HIV/AIDS	..	..	Minor concern	Major concern
Measures to respond to HIV/AIDS*	..	..	..	1,2,3
Grounds on which abortion is permitted**	..	..	1	1
Spatial distribution and internal migration				
View on spatial distribution	..	Minor change desired	Minor change desired	Minor change desired
Policies on internal migration				
From rural to urban areas	..	..	..	..
From rural to rural areas	..	..	..	..
From urban to rural areas	..	..	..	..
From urban to urban areas	..	..	..	..
Into urban agglomerations	..	..	No intervention	..
International migration				
Immigration				
View	..	Satisfactory	Satisfactory	Satisfactory
Policy	..	Maintain	Lower	Maintain
Permanent settlement	..	..	Lower	Maintain
Temporary workers	..	..	Maintain	Maintain
Highly skilled workers	..	..	..	Raise
Family reunification	..	..	Lower	No intervention
Integration of non-citizens	..	..	No	No
Emigration				
View	..	Satisfactory	Satisfactory	Satisfactory
Policy	..	Maintain	No intervention	No intervention
Encouraging the return of citizens	..	..	No	No

* Measures implemented to respond to HIV/AIDS: (1) blood screening; (2) information/education campaigns; (3) antiretroviral treatment; (4) non−discriminatory policies; (5) distribution of condoms.
** Grounds on which abortion is permitted: (1) to save the woman's life; (2) to preserve physical health; (3) to preserve mental health; (4) rape or incest; (5) foetal impairment; (6) economic or social reasons; (7) on request.

Population indicators

Indicator	1975	1985	1995	2009
Population size and growth				
Population size (thousands)	161	223	295	400
Annual growth rate (percentage)*	4.3	2.9	2.8	1.9
Population age structure				
Percentage of population under age 15	40	38	33	27
Percentage of population aged 60 or over	6	4	4	6
Fertility and family planning				
Total fertility (children per woman)*	5.4	3.8	3.1	2.1
Adolescent fertility rate (per 1,000 women, aged 15 - 19)*	..	..	39.0	25.0
Percentage of births to women under age 20*	..	..	6	6
Percentage of births to women aged 35 or over*	..	..	22	20
Percentage of married women using contraception				
Modern methods	..	..	..	..
All methods	..	..	..	..
Health and mortality				
Life expectancy at birth (years)*				
Males	67	70	72	75
Females	70	74	77	80
Both sexes combined	68	72	74	77
Infant mortality rate (per 1,000 live births)*	54	14	8	6
Under-five mortality (per 1,000 live births)*	..	16	9	7
Maternal mortality ratio (per 100,000 live births) (2005)	..	..	..	13
HIV/AIDS				
People living with HIV/AIDS (thousands)	..	..	..	..
Adult prevalence (percentage)	..	..	..	..
Spatial distribution				
Population density (per sq. km)	28	39	51	69
Urban population (percentage)	62	62	69	75
Annual urban population growth rate (percentage)	3.3	4.0	3.3	2.5
Annual rural population growth rate (percentage)	5.0	0.9	0.9	0.3
International migration				
Migrant stock				
Number of migrants (thousands)	41	61	87	148**
As percentage of total population	25.5	27.5	29.6	36.4**

* For the periods 1970-1975, 1980-1985, 1990-1995 and 2005-2010.
** For 2010.

Government views and policies

Population policy variable	1976	1986	1996	2009
Population size and growth				
View on growth	Too low	Too low	Too low	Too low
Policy on growth	Raise	Raise	No intervention	Raise
Population age structure				
Level of concern about				
Size of the working-age population	..	..	..	Major concern
Ageing of the population	..	..	..	Major concern
Fertility and family planning				
View on fertility level	Too low	Too low	Too low	Too low
Policy	Raise	Raise	Raise	Raise
Access to contraceptive methods	Direct support	Direct support	No support	Indirect support
Adolescent fertility				
Level of concern	..	..	Not a concern	Major concern
Policies and programmes	..	..	No	No
Health and mortality				
View				
Life expectancy at birth	Acceptable	Acceptable	Unacceptable	Unacceptable
Under-five mortality	..	..	Unacceptable	Unacceptable
Maternal mortality	..	..	..	Unacceptable
Level of concern about HIV/AIDS	..	..	Minor concern	Major concern
Measures to respond to HIV/AIDS*	..	..	..	1,2,3,5
Grounds on which abortion is permitted**	..	..	1,2,3,4,5,6,7	1,2,3,4,5,6,7
Spatial distribution and internal migration				
View on spatial distribution	Minor change desired	Minor change desired	Major change desired	Minor change desired
Policies on internal migration				
From rural to urban areas	..	..	..	Lower
From rural to rural areas	..	..	..	Maintain
From urban to rural areas	..	..	..	Raise
From urban to urban areas	..	..	..	Maintain
Into urban agglomerations	Lower	Lower	No intervention	Maintain
International migration				
Immigration				
View	Satisfactory	Satisfactory	Too high	Satisfactory
Policy	Maintain	Maintain	Maintain	Maintain
Permanent settlement	..	..	Maintain	No intervention
Temporary workers	..	..	Maintain	Maintain
Highly skilled workers	..	..	..	Maintain
Family reunification	..	..	Maintain	Maintain
Integration of non-citizens	..	..	No	Yes
Emigration				
View	Satisfactory	Satisfactory	Too high	Too high
Policy	Maintain	Maintain	Lower	Lower
Encouraging the return of citizens	..	..	No	Yes

* Measures implemented to respond to HIV/AIDS: (1) blood screening; (2) information/education campaigns; (3) antiretroviral treatment; (4) non–discriminatory policies; (5) distribution of condoms.
** Grounds on which abortion is permitted: (1) to save the woman's life; (2) to preserve physical health; (3) to preserve mental health; (4) rape or incest; (5) foetal impairment; (6) economic or social reasons; (7) on request.

Population indicators

Indicator	1975	1985	1995	2009
Population size and growth				
Population size (thousands)	8 721	8 960	8 357	7 545
Annual growth rate (percentage)*	0.5	0.2	-1.1	-0.6
Population age structure				
Percentage of population under age 15	22	21	18	13
Percentage of population aged 60 or over	16	17	21	24
Fertility and family planning				
Total fertility (children per woman)*	2.2	2.0	1.5	1.4
Adolescent fertility rate (per 1,000 women, aged 15 - 19)*	..	..	62.0	42.0
Percentage of births to women under age 20*	..	..	21	15
Percentage of births to women aged 35 or over*	..	..	4	7
Percentage of married women using contraception				
Modern methods	8[a]	..	46	..
All methods	76[a]	..	86	..
Health and mortality				
Life expectancy at birth (years)*				
Males	69	68	68	70
Females	73	74	75	77
Both sexes combined	71	71	71	73
Infant mortality rate (per 1,000 live births)*	26	18	16	12
Under-five mortality (per 1,000 live births)*	..	22	20	15
Maternal mortality ratio (per 100,000 live births) (2005)	..	..	..	11
HIV/AIDS				
People living with HIV/AIDS (thousands)	..	..	..	..
Adult prevalence (percentage)	..	..	..	..
Spatial distribution				
Population density (per sq. km)	79	81	75	68
Urban population (percentage)	58	65	68	71
Annual urban population growth rate (percentage)	2.1	0.6	-0.7	-0.3
Annual rural population growth rate (percentage)	-1.9	-1.2	-1.7	-1.8
International migration				
Migrant stock				
Number of migrants (thousands)	22	22	47	107**
As percentage of total population	0.2	0.2	0.6	1.4**

* For the periods 1970-1975, 1980-1985, 1990-1995 and 2005-2010.
** For 2010.
[a] For 1976.

Government views and policies

Population policy variable	1976	1986	1996	2009
Population size and growth				
View on growth	Satisfactory	Satisfactory	Too high	Too high
Policy on growth	No intervention	No intervention	No intervention	Lower
Population age structure				
Level of concern about				
Size of the working-age population	..	..	..	Minor concern
Ageing of the population	..	..	..	Minor concern
Fertility and family planning				
View on fertility level	Satisfactory	Satisfactory	Too high	Too high
Policy	No intervention	No intervention	Lower	Lower
Access to contraceptive methods	No support	Indirect support	Direct support	Direct support
Adolescent fertility				
Level of concern	..	..	Major concern	Major concern
Policies and programmes	..	..	Yes	Yes
Health and mortality				
View				
Life expectancy at birth	Unacceptable	Unacceptable	Unacceptable	Unacceptable
Under-five mortality	..	..	Unacceptable	Unacceptable
Maternal mortality	..	..	..	Unacceptable
Level of concern about HIV/AIDS	..	..	Major concern	Major concern
Measures to respond to HIV/AIDS*	..	..	..	1,2,3,5
Grounds on which abortion is permitted**	..	..	1,2	1,2,3,4,5
Spatial distribution and internal migration				
View on spatial distribution	Major change desired	Major change desired	Major change desired	Minor change desired
Policies on internal migration				
From rural to urban areas	..	..	..	Lower
From rural to rural areas	..	..	..	Lower
From urban to rural areas	..	..	..	Maintain
From urban to urban areas	..	..	..	No intervention
Into urban agglomerations	No intervention	No intervention	Lower	Lower
International migration				
Immigration				
View	Satisfactory	Satisfactory	Satisfactory	Satisfactory
Policy	Maintain	Maintain	No intervention	No intervention
Permanent settlement	..	..	No intervention	No intervention
Temporary workers	..	..	No intervention	No intervention
Highly skilled workers	..	..	..	No intervention
Family reunification	..	..	No intervention	No intervention
Integration of non-citizens	..	..	No	No
Emigration				
View	Too high	Satisfactory	Too high	Too high
Policy	Lower	Maintain	Lower	No intervention
Encouraging the return of citizens	No	..	No	Yes

* Measures implemented to respond to HIV/AIDS: (1) blood screening; (2) information/education campaigns; (3) antiretroviral treatment; (4) non–discriminatory policies; (5) distribution of condoms.
** Grounds on which abortion is permitted: (1) to save the woman's life; (2) to preserve physical health; (3) to preserve mental health; (4) rape or incest; (5) foetal impairment; (6) economic or social reasons; (7) on request.

Population indicators

Indicator	1975	1985	1995	2009
Population size and growth				
Population size (thousands)	6 173	7 704	10 127	15 757
Annual growth rate (percentage)*	1.9	2.3	2.8	3.4
Population age structure				
Percentage of population under age 15	45	47	47	46
Percentage of population aged 60 or over	5	5	4	3
Fertility and family planning				
Total fertility (children per woman)*	6.7	7.1	6.7	5.9
Adolescent fertility rate (per 1,000 women, aged 15 - 19)*	..	..	142.0	131.0
Percentage of births to women under age 20*	..	..	11	11
Percentage of births to women aged 35 or over*	..	..	27	9
Percentage of married women using contraception				
Modern methods	..	..	4[a]	13[b]
All methods	..	..	8[a]	17[b]
Health and mortality				
Life expectancy at birth (years)*				
Males	42	45	47	52
Females	43	46	49	54
Both sexes combined	42	46	48	53
Infant mortality rate (per 1,000 live births)*	147	121	102	80
Under-five mortality (per 1,000 live births)*	..	225	202	157
Maternal mortality ratio (per 100,000 live births) (2005)	..	..	..	700
HIV/AIDS				
People living with HIV/AIDS (thousands)	..	..	97	130[c]
Adult prevalence (percentage)	..	..	1.8	1.6[c]
Spatial distribution				
Population density (per sq. km)	23	28	37	58
Urban population (percentage)	6	12	15	20
Annual urban population growth rate (percentage)	7.2	6.6	4.7	5.0
Annual rural population growth rate (percentage)	1.9	2.1	2.5	2.3
International migration				
Migrant stock				
Number of migrants (thousands)	106	273	464	1 043**
As percentage of total population	1.7	3.5	4.6	6.4**

* For the periods 1970-1975, 1980-1985, 1990-1995 and 2005-2010.
** For 2010.
[a] For 1992/1993.
[b] For 2006.
[c] For 2007.

Government views and policies

Population policy variable	1976	1986	1996	2009
Population size and growth				
View on growth	Satisfactory	Too high	Too high	Too high
Policy on growth	No intervention	Lower	Lower	Lower
Population age structure				
Level of concern about				
Size of the working-age population	..	..	..	..
Ageing of the population	..	..	..	Minor concern
Fertility and family planning				
View on fertility level	Satisfactory	Too high	Too high	Too high
Policy	No intervention	Lower	Lower	Lower
Access to contraceptive methods	No support	Direct support	Direct support	Direct support
Adolescent fertility				
Level of concern	..	..	Not a concern	Not a concern
Policies and programmes	..	..	No	No
Health and mortality				
View				
Life expectancy at birth	Unacceptable	Unacceptable	Unacceptable	Unacceptable
Under-five mortality	..	..	Unacceptable	Unacceptable
Maternal mortality	..	..	..	Unacceptable
Level of concern about HIV/AIDS	..	..	Major concern	Major concern
Measures to respond to HIV/AIDS*	..	..	..	1,2,3,4,5
Grounds on which abortion is permitted**	..	..	1,2	1,2,3
Spatial distribution and internal migration				
View on spatial distribution	Minor change desired	Minor change desired	Minor change desired	Major change desired
Policies on internal migration				
From rural to urban areas	..	..	..	Lower
From rural to rural areas	..	..	..	Raise
From urban to rural areas	..	..	..	..
From urban to urban areas	..	..	..	..
Into urban agglomerations	No intervention	..	Lower	Lower
International migration				
Immigration				
View	Satisfactory	Satisfactory	Satisfactory	Satisfactory
Policy	Maintain	Maintain	No intervention	No intervention
Permanent settlement	..	..	No intervention	No intervention
Temporary workers	..	..	..	..
Highly skilled workers	..	..	..	..
Family reunification	..	..	..	..
Integration of non-citizens	..	..	No	..
Emigration				
View	Satisfactory	Satisfactory	Satisfactory	Satisfactory
Policy	Maintain	Maintain	No intervention	No intervention
Encouraging the return of citizens	No	..	Yes	..

* Measures implemented to respond to HIV/AIDS: (1) blood screening; (2) information/education campaigns; (3) antiretroviral treatment; (4) non-discriminatory policies; (5) distribution of condoms.
** Grounds on which abortion is permitted: (1) to save the woman's life; (2) to preserve physical health; (3) to preserve mental health; (4) rape or incest; (5) foetal impairment; (6) economic or social reasons; (7) on request.

Population indicators

Indicator	1975	1985	1995	2009
Population size and growth				
Population size (thousands)	3 680	4 885	6 167	8 303
Annual growth rate (percentage)*	0.9	3.4	1.6	2.9
Population age structure				
Percentage of population under age 15	45	44	47	38
Percentage of population aged 60 or over	6	5	4	4
Fertility and family planning				
Total fertility (children per woman)*	6.8	6.8	6.5	4.7
Adolescent fertility rate (per 1,000 women, aged 15 - 19)*	..	..	43.0	19.0
Percentage of births to women under age 20*	..	..	3	2
Percentage of births to women aged 35 or over*	..	..	33	30
Percentage of married women using contraception				
Modern methods	..	1[a]	..	9[b]
All methods	..	9[a]	..	20[b]
Health and mortality				
Life expectancy at birth (years)*				
Males	42	46	43	49
Females	46	49	46	52
Both sexes combined	44	47	45	50
Infant mortality rate (per 1,000 live births)*	137	119	129	98
Under-five mortality (per 1,000 live births)*	..	206	217	166
Maternal mortality ratio (per 100,000 live births) (2005)	..	..	..	1 100
HIV/AIDS				
People living with HIV/AIDS (thousands)	..	..	170	110[c]
Adult prevalence (percentage)	..	..	5.2	2.0[c]
Spatial distribution				
Population density (per sq. km)	132	175	222	298
Urban population (percentage)	3	5	7	11
Annual urban population growth rate (percentage)	8.1	7.1	3.9	6.6
Annual rural population growth rate (percentage)	1.4	3.2	0.9	3.3
International migration				
Migrant stock				
Number of migrants (thousands)	140	343	295	61**
As percentage of total population	3.8	7.0	4.8	0.7**

* For the periods 1970-1975, 1980-1985, 1990-1995 and 2005-2010.
** For 2010.
[a] For 1987.
[b] For 2002.
[c] For 2007.

Government views and policies

Population policy variable	1976	1986	1996	2009
Population size and growth				
View on growth	Too low	Too low	Too high	Too high
Policy on growth	Raise	Raise	Lower	Lower
Population age structure				
Level of concern about				
Size of the working-age population	..	..	..	Major concern
Ageing of the population	..	..	..	Major concern
Fertility and family planning				
View on fertility level	Too low	Too low	Too high	Too high
Policy	Raise	Raise	Lower	Lower
Access to contraceptive methods	Limits	Limits	Direct support	Direct support
Adolescent fertility				
Level of concern	..	..	..	Minor concern
Policies and programmes	..	..	..	Yes
Health and mortality				
View				
Life expectancy at birth	Unacceptable	Unacceptable	Unacceptable	Unacceptable
Under-five mortality	..	..	..	Unacceptable
Maternal mortality	..	..	..	Unacceptable
Level of concern about HIV/AIDS	..	..	..	Major concern
Measures to respond to HIV/AIDS*	..	..	..	1,2,3,4,5
Grounds on which abortion is permitted**	..	..	1,2,3,4,5,6,7	1,2,3,4,5,6,7
Spatial distribution and internal migration				
View on spatial distribution	Major change desired	Major change desired	Major change desired	Major change desired
Policies on internal migration				
From rural to urban areas	..	..	..	Lower
From rural to rural areas	..	..	..	Maintain
From urban to rural areas	..	..	..	Raise
From urban to urban areas	..	..	..	No intervention
Into urban agglomerations	..	..	..	Lower
International migration				
Immigration				
View	Satisfactory	Satisfactory	Satisfactory	Satisfactory
Policy	Maintain	Maintain	Maintain	Maintain
Permanent settlement	..	..	Maintain	No intervention
Temporary workers	..	..	..	Maintain
Highly skilled workers	..	..	..	Maintain
Family reunification	..	..	..	No intervention
Integration of non-citizens	..	..	..	No
Emigration				
View	Satisfactory	Too high	Too high	Satisfactory
Policy	Maintain	Lower	Lower	Maintain
Encouraging the return of citizens	..	..	Yes	Yes

* Measures implemented to respond to HIV/AIDS: (1) blood screening; (2) information/education campaigns; (3) antiretroviral treatment; (4) non-discriminatory policies; (5) distribution of condoms.
** Grounds on which abortion is permitted: (1) to save the woman's life; (2) to preserve physical health; (3) to preserve mental health; (4) rape or incest; (5) foetal impairment; (6) economic or social reasons; (7) on request.

Population indicators

Indicator	1975	1985	1995	2009
Population size and growth				
Population size (thousands)	7 098	8 099	11 380	14 805
Annual growth rate (percentage)*	0.5	3.7	3.2	1.6
Population age structure				
Percentage of population under age 15	42	43	46	33
Percentage of population aged 60 or over	5	5	4	6
Fertility and family planning				
Total fertility (children per woman)*	5.5	6.6	5.5	3.0
Adolescent fertility rate (per 1,000 women, aged 15 - 19)*	..	..	87.0	39.0
Percentage of births to women under age 20*	..	..	8	7
Percentage of births to women aged 35 or over*	..	..	27	19
Percentage of married women using contraception				
Modern methods	..	..	7	27[a]
All methods	..	..	13	40[a]
Health and mortality				
Life expectancy at birth (years)*				
Males	39	49	54	59
Females	42	52	57	63
Both sexes combined	40	51	56	61
Infant mortality rate (per 1,000 live births)*	181	116	90	62
Under-five mortality (per 1,000 live births)*	..	181	132	89
Maternal mortality ratio (per 100,000 live births) (2005)	..	..	..	540
HIV/AIDS				
People living with HIV/AIDS (thousands)	..	..	100	75[b]
Adult prevalence (percentage)	..	..	1.2	0.8[b]
Spatial distribution				
Population density (per sq. km)	39	45	63	82
Urban population (percentage)	4	13	14	22
Annual urban population growth rate (percentage)	-1.3	3.9	5.6	4.6
Annual rural population growth rate (percentage)	-1.2	3.9	2.1	0.9
International migration				
Migrant stock				
Number of migrants (thousands)	15	13	116	336**
As percentage of total population	0.2	0.2	1.0	2.2**

* For the periods 1970-1975, 1980-1985, 1990-1995 and 2005-2010.
** For 2010.
[a] For 2005
[b] For 2007.

Government views and policies

Population policy variable	1976	1986	1996	2009
Population size and growth				
View on growth	Too low	Too high	Too high	Too high
Policy on growth	Raise	No intervention	Lower	No intervention
Population age structure				
Level of concern about				
Size of the working-age population	..	..	..	Minor concern
Ageing of the population	..	..	..	Not a concern
Fertility and family planning				
View on fertility level	Too low	Too high	Too high	Too high
Policy	No intervention	No intervention	Lower	No intervention
Access to contraceptive methods	Indirect support	Direct support	Indirect support	Direct support
Adolescent fertility				
Level of concern	..	..	Major concern	Major concern
Policies and programmes	..	..	Yes	Yes
Health and mortality				
View				
Life expectancy at birth	Unacceptable	Unacceptable	Unacceptable	Unacceptable
Under-five mortality	..	..	Unacceptable	Unacceptable
Maternal mortality	..	..	..	Unacceptable
Level of concern about HIV/AIDS	..	..	Major concern	Major concern
Measures to respond to HIV/AIDS*	..	..	..	1,2,3,5
Grounds on which abortion is permitted**	..	..	1,2,4	1,2,3,4
Spatial distribution and internal migration				
View on spatial distribution	Major change desired	Minor change desired	Major change desired	Major change desired
Policies on internal migration				
From rural to urban areas	..	..	..	Lower
From rural to rural areas	..	..	..	Maintain
From urban to rural areas	..	..	..	Raise
From urban to urban areas	..	..	..	Maintain
Into urban agglomerations	Lower	Lower	Lower	Lower
International migration				
Immigration				
View	Satisfactory	Satisfactory	Satisfactory	Too high
Policy	Maintain	Maintain	Lower	Maintain
Permanent settlement	..	..	Lower	Maintain
Temporary workers	..	..	Lower	Maintain
Highly skilled workers	..	..	..	Raise
Family reunification	..	..	Maintain	Maintain
Integration of non-citizens	..	..	Yes	No
Emigration				
View	Satisfactory	Satisfactory	Satisfactory	Too high
Policy	Maintain	Maintain	No intervention	Lower
Encouraging the return of citizens	Yes	..	No	Yes

* Measures implemented to respond to HIV/AIDS: (1) blood screening; (2) information/education campaigns; (3) antiretroviral treatment; (4) non-discriminatory policies; (5) distribution of condoms.
** Grounds on which abortion is permitted: (1) to save the woman's life; (2) to preserve physical health; (3) to preserve mental health; (4) rape or incest; (5) foetal impairment; (6) economic or social reasons; (7) on request.

Population indicators

Indicator	1975	1985	1995	2009
Population size and growth				
Population size (thousands)	7 826	10 509	14 054	19 522
Annual growth rate (percentage)[*]	2.7	2.9	2.8	2.3
Population age structure				
Percentage of population under age 15	44	45	45	41
Percentage of population aged 60 or over	6	6	5	5
Fertility and family planning				
Total fertility (children per woman)[*]	6.3	6.4	5.7	4.7
Adolescent fertility rate (per 1,000 women, aged 15 - 19)[*]	..	..	163.0	128.0
Percentage of births to women under age 20[*]	..	..	14	14
Percentage of births to women aged 35 or over[*]	..	..	21	18
Percentage of married women using contraception				
Modern methods	1[a]	..	7[b]	12[c]
All methods	2[a]	..	19[b]	29[c]
Health and mortality				
Life expectancy at birth (years)[*]				
Males	46	51	53	50
Females	48	54	56	52
Both sexes combined	47	53	54	51
Infant mortality rate (per 1,000 live births)[*]	121	93	87	87
Under-five mortality (per 1,000 live births)[*]	..	160	142	144
Maternal mortality ratio (per 100,000 live births) (2005)	..	..	..	1 000
HIV/AIDS				
People living with HIV/AIDS (thousands)	..	..	320	540[d]
Adult prevalence (percentage)	..	..	4.7	5.1[d]
Spatial distribution				
Population density (per sq. km)	16	22	30	41
Urban population (percentage)	27	36	45	58
Annual urban population growth rate (percentage)	7.9	5.5	4.6	3.3
Annual rural population growth rate (percentage)	1.0	1.6	0.8	0.0
International migration				
Migrant stock				
Number of migrants (thousands)	216	248	246	197[**]
As percentage of total population	2.8	2.4	1.8	1.0[**]

[*] For the periods 1970-1975, 1980-1985, 1990-1995 and 2005-2010.
[**] For 2010.
[a] For 1978.
[b] For 1998.
[c] For 2006.
[d] For 2007.

Government views and policies

Population policy variable	1976	1986	1996	2009
Population size and growth				
View on growth	Satisfactory	Satisfactory	Satisfactory	Satisfactory
Policy on growth	No intervention	Maintain	No intervention	No intervention
Population age structure				
Level of concern about				
Size of the working-age population	..	..	..	Major concern
Ageing of the population	..	..	..	Major concern
Fertility and family planning				
View on fertility level	Satisfactory	Satisfactory	Satisfactory	Too low
Policy	No intervention	No intervention	No intervention	No intervention
Access to contraceptive methods	Direct support	Direct support	Direct support	Indirect support
Adolescent fertility				
Level of concern	..	..	Minor concern	Minor concern
Policies and programmes	..	..	Yes	Yes
Health and mortality				
View				
Life expectancy at birth	Acceptable	Acceptable	Acceptable	Acceptable
Under-five mortality	..	..	..	Acceptable
Maternal mortality	..	..	..	Acceptable
Level of concern about HIV/AIDS	..	..	Major concern	Major concern
Measures to respond to HIV/AIDS[*]	..	..	..	1,2,3,4,5
Grounds on which abortion is permitted[**]	..	..	1,2,3,4,5,6,7	1,2,3,4,5,6,7
Spatial distribution and internal migration				
View on spatial distribution	Minor change desired	Minor change desired	Satisfactory	Minor change desired
Policies on internal migration				
From rural to urban areas	..	..	..	No intervention
From rural to rural areas	..	..	..	No intervention
From urban to rural areas	..	..	..	No intervention
From urban to urban areas	..	..	..	No intervention
Into urban agglomerations	No intervention	No intervention	No intervention	No intervention
International migration				
Immigration				
View	Satisfactory	Satisfactory	Satisfactory	Too low
Policy	Maintain	Maintain	Lower	Raise
Permanent settlement	..	..	Lower	Raise
Temporary workers	..	..	Maintain	Raise
Highly skilled workers	..	..	..	Raise
Family reunification	..	..	Lower	Raise
Integration of non-citizens	..	..	Yes	Yes
Emigration				
View	Satisfactory	Satisfactory	Satisfactory	Satisfactory
Policy	Maintain	Maintain	No intervention	No intervention
Encouraging the return of citizens	No	..	No	No

[*] Measures implemented to respond to HIV/AIDS: (1) blood screening; (2) information/education campaigns; (3) antiretroviral treatment; (4) non-discriminatory policies; (5) distribution of condoms.

[**] Grounds on which abortion is permitted: (1) to save the woman's life; (2) to preserve physical health; (3) to preserve mental health; (4) rape or incest; (5) foetal impairment; (6) economic or social reasons; (7) on request.

Population indicators

Indicator	1975	1985	1995	2009
Population size and growth				
Population size (thousands)	23 142	25 843	29 302	33 573
Annual growth rate (percentage)*	1.3	1.1	1.1	1.0
Population age structure				
Percentage of population under age 15	26	21	20	17
Percentage of population aged 60 or over	12	15	16	20
Fertility and family planning				
Total fertility (children per woman)*	2.0	1.6	1.7	1.6
Adolescent fertility rate (per 1,000 women, aged 15 - 19)*	..	..	22.0	13.0
Percentage of births to women under age 20*	..	..	6	4
Percentage of births to women aged 35 or over*	..	..	12	16
Percentage of married women using contraception				
Modern methods	..	70[a]	73	72[b]
All methods	..	73[a]	75	74[b]
Health and mortality				
Life expectancy at birth (years)*				
Males	70	73	75	78
Females	77	80	81	83
Both sexes combined	73	76	78	81
Infant mortality rate (per 1,000 live births)*	16	9	6	5
Under-five mortality (per 1,000 live births)*	..	11	8	6
Maternal mortality ratio (per 100,000 live births) (2005)	..	..	..	7
HIV/AIDS				
People living with HIV/AIDS (thousands)	..	..	38	73[c]
Adult prevalence (percentage)	..	..	0.2	0.4[c]
Spatial distribution				
Population density (per sq. km)	2	3	3	3
Urban population (percentage)	76	76	78	80
Annual urban population growth rate (percentage)	1.0	1.5	1.3	1.0
Annual rural population growth rate (percentage)	1.6	0.7	-0.3	0.3
International migration				
Migrant stock				
Number of migrants (thousands)	3 518	3 901	5 047	7 202**
As percentage of total population	15.2	15.1	17.2	21.3**

* For the periods 1970-1975, 1980-1985, 1990-1995 and 2005-2010.
** For 2010.
[a] For 1984.
[b] For 2002.
[c] For 2007.

Government views and policies

Population policy variable	1976	1986	1996	2009
Population size and growth				
View on growth	Satisfactory	Satisfactory	Too high	Satisfactory
Policy on growth	No intervention	No intervention	Lower	Maintain
Population age structure				
Level of concern about				
Size of the working-age population	..	..	..	Major concern
Ageing of the population	..	..	..	Major concern
Fertility and family planning				
View on fertility level	Satisfactory	Satisfactory	Too high	Too high
Policy	No intervention	No intervention	Lower	Lower
Access to contraceptive methods	Direct support	Direct support	Direct support	Direct support
Adolescent fertility				
Level of concern	..	..	..	Major concern
Policies and programmes	..	..	No	Yes
Health and mortality				
View				
Life expectancy at birth	Unacceptable	Unacceptable	Unacceptable	Unacceptable
Under-five mortality	..	..	..	Unacceptable
Maternal mortality	..	..	..	Unacceptable
Level of concern about HIV/AIDS	..	..	..	Minor concern
Measures to respond to HIV/AIDS*	..	..	..	1,2,3,4
Grounds on which abortion is permitted**	..	..	1,2,3,4,5,6	1,2,3,4,5,6,7
Spatial distribution and internal migration				
View on spatial distribution	Major change desired	Major change desired	Major change desired	Major change desired
Policies on internal migration				
From rural to urban areas	..	..	..	Lower
From rural to rural areas	..	..	..	..
From urban to rural areas	..	..	..	..
From urban to urban areas	..	..	..	..
Into urban agglomerations	No intervention	..	..	Lower
International migration				
Immigration				
View	Satisfactory	Satisfactory	Satisfactory	Satisfactory
Policy	Maintain	Maintain	No intervention	No intervention
Permanent settlement	..	..	No intervention	No intervention
Temporary workers	..	..	..	No intervention
Highly skilled workers	..	..	..	No intervention
Family reunification	..	..	..	No intervention
Integration of non-citizens	..	..	..	No
Emigration				
View	Satisfactory	Satisfactory	Too low	Satisfactory
Policy	Maintain	Maintain	Maintain	Maintain
Encouraging the return of citizens	No	..	..	Yes

* Measures implemented to respond to HIV/AIDS: (1) blood screening; (2) information/education campaigns; (3) antiretroviral treatment; (4) non-discriminatory policies; (5) distribution of condoms.

** Grounds on which abortion is permitted: (1) to save the woman's life; (2) to preserve physical health; (3) to preserve mental health; (4) rape or incest; (5) foetal impairment; (6) economic or social reasons; (7) on request.

Population indicators

Indicator	1975	1985	1995	2009
Population size and growth				
Population size (thousands)	278	318	398	506
Annual growth rate (percentage)*	0.8	1.9	2.3	1.4
Population age structure				
Percentage of population under age 15	47	46	46	36
Percentage of population aged 60 or over	8	7	7	5
Fertility and family planning				
Total fertility (children per woman)*	7.0	6.1	4.9	2.8
Adolescent fertility rate (per 1,000 women, aged 15 - 19)*	..	..	111.0	95.0
Percentage of births to women under age 20*	..	..	11	17
Percentage of births to women aged 35 or over*	..	..	23	19
Percentage of married women using contraception				
Modern methods	..	..	46[a]	..
All methods	..	..	53[a]	61[b]
Health and mortality				
Life expectancy at birth (years)*				
Males	56	61	64	68
Females	59	65	69	74
Both sexes combined	57	63	67	71
Infant mortality rate (per 1,000 live births)*	83	58	42	26
Under-five mortality (per 1,000 live births)*	..	78	53	31
Maternal mortality ratio (per 100,000 live births) (2005)	..	..	..	210
HIV/AIDS				
People living with HIV/AIDS (thousands)	..	..	..	..
Adult prevalence (percentage)	..	..	..	..
Spatial distribution				
Population density (per sq. km)	69	79	99	125
Urban population (percentage)	21	32	49	60
Annual urban population growth rate (percentage)	2.3	9.4	4.3	3.3
Annual rural population growth rate (percentage)	0.0	-1.4	0.5	0.4
International migration				
Migrant stock				
Number of migrants (thousands)	8	8	10	12**
As percentage of total population	2.8	2.7	2.4	2.4**

* For the periods 1970-1975, 1980-1985, 1990-1995 and 2005-2010.
** For 2010.
[a] For 1998.
[b] For 2005.

Government views and policies

Population policy variable	1976	1986	1996	2009
Population size and growth				
View on growth	Too low	Too high	Too high	Satisfactory
Policy on growth	Raise	No intervention	No intervention	No intervention
Population age structure				
Level of concern about				
Size of the working-age population	..	..	..	Major concern
Ageing of the population	..	..	..	..
Fertility and family planning				
View on fertility level	Too low	Too high	Too high	Satisfactory
Policy	No intervention	No intervention	No intervention	No intervention
Access to contraceptive methods	No support	Direct support	Direct support	Indirect support
Adolescent fertility				
Level of concern	..	..	Not a concern	Minor concern
Policies and programmes	..	..	..	Yes
Health and mortality				
View				
Life expectancy at birth	Unacceptable	Unacceptable	Unacceptable	Unacceptable
Under-five mortality	..	..	Unacceptable	Unacceptable
Maternal mortality	..	..	..	Unacceptable
Level of concern about HIV/AIDS	..	..	Major concern	Major concern
Measures to respond to HIV/AIDS*	..	..	..	1,2,3,4
Grounds on which abortion is permitted**	..	..	1	1
Spatial distribution and internal migration				
View on spatial distribution	Major change desired	Minor change desired	Minor change desired	Major change desired
Policies on internal migration				
From rural to urban areas	..	..	..	Lower
From rural to rural areas	..	..	..	..
From urban to rural areas	..	..	..	..
From urban to urban areas	..	..	..	..
Into urban agglomerations	Lower	Lower	No intervention	Lower
International migration				
Immigration				
View	Satisfactory	Satisfactory	Satisfactory	Satisfactory
Policy	Maintain	Maintain	No intervention	No intervention
Permanent settlement	..	..	No intervention	No intervention
Temporary workers	..	..	No intervention	..
Highly skilled workers	..	..	..	..
Family reunification	..	..	No intervention	..
Integration of non-citizens	..	..	No	..
Emigration				
View	Satisfactory	Satisfactory	Too high	Too high
Policy	Maintain	Maintain	No intervention	No intervention
Encouraging the return of citizens	No	..	No	..

* Measures implemented to respond to HIV/AIDS: (1) blood screening; (2) information/education campaigns; (3) antiretroviral treatment; (4) non-discriminatory policies; (5) distribution of condoms.
** Grounds on which abortion is permitted: (1) to save the woman's life; (2) to preserve physical health; (3) to preserve mental health; (4) rape or incest; (5) foetal impairment; (6) economic or social reasons; (7) on request.

Population indicators

Indicator	1975	1985	1995	2009
Population size and growth				
Population size (thousands)	2 016	2 620	3 335	4 422
Annual growth rate (percentage)*	2.0	2.9	2.6	1.9
Population age structure				
Percentage of population under age 15	42	42	42	41
Percentage of population aged 60 or over	7	6	6	6
Fertility and family planning				
Total fertility (children per woman)*	6.0	6.0	5.7	4.8
Adolescent fertility rate (per 1,000 women, aged 15 - 19)*	..	..	143.0	107.0
Percentage of births to women under age 20*	..	..	13	11
Percentage of births to women aged 35 or over*	..	..	26	30
Percentage of married women using contraception				
Modern methods	..	..	3	9[a]
All methods	..	..	15	19[a]
Health and mortality				
Life expectancy at birth (years)*				
Males	42	47	46	45
Females	46	52	51	48
Both sexes combined	44	49	49	47
Infant mortality rate (per 1,000 live births)*	138	109	110	105
Under-five mortality (per 1,000 live births)*	..	190	187	180
Maternal mortality ratio (per 100,000 live births) (2005)	..	..	..	980
HIV/AIDS				
People living with HIV/AIDS (thousands)	..	..	84	160[b]
Adult prevalence (percentage)	..	..	4.9	6.3[b]
Spatial distribution				
Population density (per sq. km)	3	4	5	7
Urban population (percentage)	32	36	37	39
Annual urban population growth rate (percentage)	4.1	3.4	2.7	2.4
Annual rural population growth rate (percentage)	1.3	1.9	2.4	1.5
International migration				
Migrant stock				
Number of migrants (thousands)	52	59	67	80**
As percentage of total population	2.6	2.2	2.0	1.8**

* For the periods 1970-1975, 1980-1985, 1990-1995 and 2005-2010.
** For 2010.
[a] For 2006.
[b] For 2007.

Government views and policies

Population policy variable	1976	1986	1996	2009
Population size and growth				
View on growth	Satisfactory	Satisfactory	Too high	Too high
Policy on growth	No intervention	No intervention	Lower	Lower
Population age structure				
Level of concern about				
Size of the working-age population	..	..	..	..
Ageing of the population	..	..	..	..
Fertility and family planning				
View on fertility level	Satisfactory	Satisfactory	Satisfactory	Too high
Policy	No intervention	No intervention	No intervention	No intervention
Access to contraceptive methods	Limits	No support	Indirect support	Direct support
Adolescent fertility				
Level of concern	..	..	..	Minor concern
Policies and programmes	..	..	..	Yes
Health and mortality				
View				
Life expectancy at birth	Unacceptable	Unacceptable	Unacceptable	Unacceptable
Under-five mortality	..	..	..	Unacceptable
Maternal mortality	..	..	..	Unacceptable
Level of concern about HIV/AIDS	..	..	..	Major concern
Measures to respond to HIV/AIDS*	..	..	..	1,2,3,5
Grounds on which abortion is permitted**	..	..	1	1,2,5
Spatial distribution and internal migration				
View on spatial distribution	Minor change desired	Minor change desired	Minor change desired	Minor change desired
Policies on internal migration				
From rural to urban areas	..	..	..	No intervention
From rural to rural areas	..	..	..	No intervention
From urban to rural areas	..	..	..	No intervention
From urban to urban areas	..	..	..	No intervention
Into urban agglomerations	No intervention	..	..	No intervention
International migration				
Immigration				
View	Satisfactory	Satisfactory	Satisfactory	Satisfactory
Policy	Maintain	Maintain	Maintain	Maintain
Permanent settlement	..	..	Maintain	Maintain
Temporary workers	..	..	..	..
Highly skilled workers	..	..	..	..
Family reunification	..	..	..	..
Integration of non-citizens	..	..	..	..
Emigration				
View	Satisfactory	Satisfactory	Satisfactory	Satisfactory
Policy	Maintain	Maintain	Maintain	Maintain
Encouraging the return of citizens	No	..	..	..

* Measures implemented to respond to HIV/AIDS: (1) blood screening; (2) information/education campaigns; (3) antiretroviral treatment; (4) non-discriminatory policies; (5) distribution of condoms.

** Grounds on which abortion is permitted: (1) to save the woman's life; (2) to preserve physical health; (3) to preserve mental health; (4) rape or incest; (5) foetal impairment; (6) economic or social reasons; (7) on request.

Population indicators

Indicator	1975	1985	1995	2009
Population size and growth				
Population size (thousands)	4 155	5 222	7 128	11 206
Annual growth rate (percentage)*	2.4	2.5	3.1	2.8
Population age structure				
Percentage of population under age 15	43	45	46	46
Percentage of population aged 60 or over	6	6	5	4
Fertility and family planning				
Total fertility (children per woman)*	6.6	6.8	6.6	6.2
Adolescent fertility rate (per 1,000 women, aged 15 - 19)*	..	..	196.0	164.0
Percentage of births to women under age 20*	..	..	15	13
Percentage of births to women aged 35 or over*	..	..	20	18
Percentage of married women using contraception				
Modern methods	..	..	1[a]	2[b]
All methods	..	..	4[a]	3[b]
Health and mortality				
Life expectancy at birth (years)*				
Males	44	48	49	47
Females	48	51	53	50
Both sexes combined	46	49	51	49
Infant mortality rate (per 1,000 live births)*	152	134	127	130
Under-five mortality (per 1,000 live births)*	..	223	205	211
Maternal mortality ratio (per 100,000 live births) (2005)	..	..	..	1 500
HIV/AIDS				
People living with HIV/AIDS (thousands)	..	..	68	200[c]
Adult prevalence (percentage)	..	..	2.0	3.5[c]
Spatial distribution				
Population density (per sq. km)	3	4	6	9
Urban population (percentage)	16	20	22	27
Annual urban population growth rate (percentage)	7.8	4.0	4.4	4.6
Annual rural population growth rate (percentage)	1.1	2.7	2.9	2.0
International migration				
Migrant stock				
Number of migrants (thousands)	64	71	78	388**
As percentage of total population	1.5	1.4	1.1	3.4**

* For the periods 1970-1975, 1980-1985, 1990-1995 and 2005-2010.
** For 2010.
[a] For 1996/1997.
[b] For 2004.
[c] For 2007.

Government views and policies

Population policy variable	1976	1986	1996	2009
Population size and growth				
View on growth	Satisfactory	Too low	Satisfactory	Satisfactory
Policy on growth	No intervention	No intervention	No intervention	No intervention
Population age structure				
Level of concern about				
Size of the working-age population	..	..	..	Minor concern
Ageing of the population	..	..	..	Major concern
Fertility and family planning				
View on fertility level	Too high	Too low	Satisfactory	Satisfactory
Policy	No intervention	No intervention	No intervention	No intervention
Access to contraceptive methods	Direct support	Direct support	Direct support	Direct support
Adolescent fertility				
Level of concern	..	..	Major concern	Major concern
Policies and programmes	..	..	Yes	Yes
Health and mortality				
View				
Life expectancy at birth	Acceptable	Acceptable	Acceptable	Acceptable
Under-five mortality	..	..	Acceptable	Unacceptable
Maternal mortality	..	..	..	Acceptable
Level of concern about HIV/AIDS	..	..	Minor concern	Major concern
Measures to respond to HIV/AIDS*	..	..	..	1,2,3,4,5
Grounds on which abortion is permitted**	..	..	Not permitted	Not permitted
Spatial distribution and internal migration				
View on spatial distribution	Major change desired	Major change desired	Minor change desired	Satisfactory
Policies on internal migration				
From rural to urban areas	..	..	..	No intervention
From rural to rural areas	..	..	..	No intervention
From urban to rural areas	..	..	..	No intervention
From urban to urban areas	..	..	..	No intervention
Into urban agglomerations	No intervention	..	Lower	No intervention
International migration				
Immigration				
View	Satisfactory	Satisfactory	Satisfactory	Satisfactory
Policy	Maintain	Maintain	Maintain	Maintain
Permanent settlement	..	..	No intervention	Maintain
Temporary workers	..	..	Lower	Maintain
Highly skilled workers	..	..	..	Maintain
Family reunification	..	..	..	Raise
Integration of non-citizens	..	..	Yes	Yes
Emigration				
View	Satisfactory	Satisfactory	Satisfactory	Satisfactory
Policy	Maintain	Maintain	No intervention	Maintain
Encouraging the return of citizens	..	..	Yes	No

* Measures implemented to respond to HIV/AIDS: (1) blood screening; (2) information/education campaigns; (3) antiretroviral treatment; (4) non-discriminatory policies; (5) distribution of condoms.
** Grounds on which abortion is permitted: (1) to save the woman's life; (2) to preserve physical health; (3) to preserve mental health; (4) rape or incest; (5) foetal impairment; (6) economic or social reasons; (7) on request.

Population indicators

Indicator	1975	1985	1995	2009
Population size and growth				
Population size (thousands)	10 419	12 111	14 410	16 970
Annual growth rate (percentage)*	1.7	1.6	1.8	1.0
Population age structure				
Percentage of population under age 15	37	31	30	23
Percentage of population aged 60 or over	8	9	10	13
Fertility and family planning				
Total fertility (children per woman)*	3.6	2.7	2.6	1.9
Adolescent fertility rate (per 1,000 women, aged 15 - 19)*	..	..	68.0	60.0
Percentage of births to women under age 20*	..	..	13	15
Percentage of births to women aged 35 or over*	..	..	14	16
Percentage of married women using contraception				
Modern methods	..	..	..	..
All methods	..	..	..	64[a]
Health and mortality				
Life expectancy at birth (years)*				
Males	60	67	71	76
Females	67	74	77	82
Both sexes combined	64	71	74	78
Infant mortality rate (per 1,000 live births)*	69	24	14	7
Under-five mortality (per 1,000 live births)*	..	28	17	9
Maternal mortality ratio (per 100,000 live births) (2005)	..	..	..	16
HIV/AIDS				
People living with HIV/AIDS (thousands)	..	..	12	31[b]
Adult prevalence (percentage)	..	..	0.2	0.3[b]
Spatial distribution				
Population density (per sq. km)	14	16	19	22
Urban population (percentage)	78	83	84	89
Annual urban population growth rate (percentage)	2.2	1.8	1.8	1.2
Annual rural population growth rate (percentage)	-1.3	0.9	-0.2	-1.3
International migration				
Migrant stock				
Number of migrants (thousands)	86	90	136	320**
As percentage of total population	0.8	0.7	0.9	1.9**

* For the periods 1970-1975, 1980-1985, 1990-1995 and 2005-2010.
** For 2010.
[a] For 2006.
[b] For 2007.

Government views and policies

Population policy variable	1976	1986	1996	2009
Population size and growth				
View on growth	Too high	Too high	Satisfactory	Satisfactory
Policy on growth	Lower	Lower	Lower	Maintain
Population age structure				
Level of concern about				
Size of the working-age population	..	..	..	Major concern
Ageing of the population	..	..	..	Major concern
Fertility and family planning				
View on fertility level	Too high	Too high	Satisfactory	Satisfactory
Policy	Lower	Lower	Lower	Maintain
Access to contraceptive methods	Direct support	Direct support	Direct support	Direct support
Adolescent fertility				
Level of concern	..	..	Major concern	Not a concern
Policies and programmes	..	..	Yes	No
Health and mortality				
View				
Life expectancy at birth	Unacceptable	Unacceptable	Acceptable	Acceptable
Under-five mortality	..	..	Acceptable	Acceptable
Maternal mortality	..	..	..	Acceptable
Level of concern about HIV/AIDS	..	..	Major concern	Minor concern
Measures to respond to HIV/AIDS*	..	..	..	1,2,3,4,5
Grounds on which abortion is permitted**	..	..	1,2,3,4,5,6,7	1,2,3,4,5,6,7
Spatial distribution and internal migration				
View on spatial distribution	Minor change desired	Minor change desired	Minor change desired	Major change desired
Policies on internal migration				
From rural to urban areas	..	..	..	Raise
From rural to rural areas	..	..	..	No intervention
From urban to rural areas	..	..	..	No intervention
From urban to urban areas	..	..	..	No intervention
Into urban agglomerations	..	..	Lower	Raise
International migration				
Immigration				
View	Satisfactory	Satisfactory	Satisfactory	Satisfactory
Policy	Maintain	Maintain	Maintain	Raise
Permanent settlement	..	..	Maintain	Raise
Temporary workers	..	..	Maintain	Maintain
Highly skilled workers	..	..	..	Maintain
Family reunification	..	..	Maintain	Raise
Integration of non-citizens	..	..	..	Yes
Emigration				
View	Satisfactory	Satisfactory	Satisfactory	Satisfactory
Policy	Maintain	Maintain	Maintain	No intervention
Encouraging the return of citizens	..	..	No	Yes

* Measures implemented to respond to HIV/AIDS: (1) blood screening; (2) information/education campaigns; (3) antiretroviral treatment; (4) non-discriminatory policies; (5) distribution of condoms.
** Grounds on which abortion is permitted: (1) to save the woman's life; (2) to preserve physical health; (3) to preserve mental health; (4) rape or incest; (5) foetal impairment; (6) economic or social reasons; (7) on request.

Population indicators

Indicator	1975	1985	1995	2009
Population size and growth				
Population size (thousands)	911 167	1 053 219	1 210 969	1 345 751
Annual growth rate (percentage)*	2.2	1.4	1.2	0.6
Population age structure				
Percentage of population under age 15	39	31	28	20
Percentage of population aged 60 or over	7	8	9	12
Fertility and family planning				
Total fertility (children per woman)*	4.8	2.6	2.0	1.8
Adolescent fertility rate (per 1,000 women, aged 15 - 19)*	..	..	5.0	10.0
Percentage of births to women under age 20*	..	..	1	3
Percentage of births to women aged 35 or over*	..	..	4	7
Percentage of married women using contraception				
Modern methods	..	68[a]	83[b]	86[c]
All methods	..	71[a]	84[b]	87[c]
Health and mortality				
Life expectancy at birth (years)*				
Males	63	65	67	71
Females	64	68	70	75
Both sexes combined	63	66	69	73
Infant mortality rate (per 1,000 live births)*	61	40	30	23
Under-five mortality (per 1,000 live births)*	..	62	40	29
Maternal mortality ratio (per 100,000 live births) (2005)	..	..	..	45
HIV/AIDS				
People living with HIV/AIDS (thousands)	..	..	130	700[d]
Adult prevalence (percentage)	..	..	..	0.1[d]
Spatial distribution				
Population density (per sq. km)	95	110	126	140
Urban population (percentage)	17	23	31	44
Annual urban population growth rate (percentage)	4.2	5.1	3.6	2.6
Annual rural population growth rate (percentage)	1.2	0.4	-0.2	-1.0
International migration				
Migrant stock				
Number of migrants (thousands)	298	324	437	686**
As percentage of total population	0.0	0.0	0.0	0.1**

* For the periods 1970-1975, 1980-1985, 1990-1995 and 2005-2010.
** For 2010.
[a] For 1982.
[b] For 1997.
[c] For 2001.
[d] For 2007.

Government views and policies

Population policy variable	1976	1986	1996	2009
Population size and growth				
View on growth	Too high	Satisfactory	Satisfactory	Satisfactory
Policy on growth	Lower	No intervention	No intervention	No intervention
Population age structure				
Level of concern about				
Size of the working-age population	..	..	..	..
Ageing of the population	..	..	..	Major concern
Fertility and family planning				
View on fertility level	Too high	Satisfactory	Satisfactory	Too high
Policy	Lower	No intervention	No intervention	Lower
Access to contraceptive methods	Direct support	Direct support	Indirect support	Direct support
Adolescent fertility				
Level of concern	..	..	Not a concern	Major concern
Policies and programmes	..	..	No	Yes
Health and mortality				
View				
Life expectancy at birth	Unacceptable	Unacceptable	Acceptable	Acceptable
Under-five mortality	..	..	..	Unacceptable
Maternal mortality	..	..	..	Unacceptable
Level of concern about HIV/AIDS	..	..	Major concern	Major concern
Measures to respond to HIV/AIDS*	..	..	..	1,2,3,4,5
Grounds on which abortion is permitted**	..	..	1	1,2,3,4,5
Spatial distribution and internal migration				
View on spatial distribution	Major change desired	Major change desired	Satisfactory	Satisfactory
Policies on internal migration				
From rural to urban areas	..	..	..	No intervention
From rural to rural areas	..	..	..	No intervention
From urban to rural areas	..	..	..	No intervention
From urban to urban areas	..	..	..	No intervention
Into urban agglomerations	Lower	Lower	No intervention	No intervention
International migration				
Immigration				
View	Satisfactory	Satisfactory	Satisfactory	Satisfactory
Policy	Maintain	Maintain	No intervention	Maintain
Permanent settlement	..	..	No intervention	Lower
Temporary workers	..	..	No intervention	Raise
Highly skilled workers	..	..	..	Raise
Family reunification	..	..	No intervention	Maintain
Integration of non-citizens	..	..	No	Yes
Emigration				
View	Satisfactory	Too high	Too high	Too high
Policy	Maintain	Lower	Lower	Lower
Encouraging the return of citizens	No	..	Yes	Yes

* Measures implemented to respond to HIV/AIDS: (1) blood screening; (2) information/education campaigns; (3) antiretroviral treatment; (4) non-discriminatory policies; (5) distribution of condoms.

** Grounds on which abortion is permitted: (1) to save the woman's life; (2) to preserve physical health; (3) to preserve mental health; (4) rape or incest; (5) foetal impairment; (6) economic or social reasons; (7) on request.

Population indicators

Indicator	1975	1985	1995	2009
Population size and growth				
Population size (thousands)	23 969	29 997	36 459	45 660
Annual growth rate (percentage)[*]	2.3	2.2	1.9	1.5
Population age structure				
Percentage of population under age 15	44	38	35	29
Percentage of population aged 60 or over	6	6	7	8
Fertility and family planning				
Total fertility (children per woman)[*]	5.0	3.7	3.0	2.5
Adolescent fertility rate (per 1,000 women, aged 15 - 19)[*]	..	..	87.0	74.0
Percentage of births to women under age 20[*]	..	..	15	15
Percentage of births to women aged 35 or over[*]	..	..	16	14
Percentage of married women using contraception				
Modern methods	30[a]	53[b]	59	68[c]
All methods	43[a]	65[b]	72	78[c]
Health and mortality				
Life expectancy at birth (years)[*]				
Males	60	64	65	69
Females	64	70	73	77
Both sexes combined	62	67	69	73
Infant mortality rate (per 1,000 live births)[*]	73	43	28	19
Under-five mortality (per 1,000 live births)[*]	..	59	37	26
Maternal mortality ratio (per 100,000 live births) (2005)	..	..	..	130
HIV/AIDS				
People living with HIV/AIDS (thousands)	..	..	67	170[d]
Adult prevalence (percentage)	..	..	0.3	0.6[d]
Spatial distribution				
Population density (per sq. km)	21	26	32	40
Urban population (percentage)	59	66	71	75
Annual urban population growth rate (percentage)	3.5	2.9	2.2	1.6
Annual rural population growth rate (percentage)	0.5	0.4	0.7	0.0
International migration				
Migrant stock				
Number of migrants (thousands)	85	97	109	110[**]
As percentage of total population	0.4	0.3	0.3	0.2[**]

[*] For the periods 1970-1975, 1980-1985, 1990-1995 and 2005-2010.
[**] For 2010.
[a] For 1976.
[b] For 1986.
[c] For 2004/2005.
[d] For 2007.

Government views and policies

Population policy variable	1976	1986	1996	2009
Population size and growth				
View on growth	Too high	Too high	Too high	Too high
Policy on growth	No intervention	Lower	Lower	Lower
Population age structure				
Level of concern about				
Size of the working-age population	..	..	..	Major concern
Ageing of the population	..	..	..	..
Fertility and family planning				
View on fertility level	Too high	Too high	Too high	Too high
Policy	No intervention	Lower	Lower	Lower
Access to contraceptive methods	No support	Direct support	Direct support	Direct support
Adolescent fertility				
Level of concern	..	..	Major concern	Major concern
Policies and programmes	..	..	No	Yes
Health and mortality				
View				
Life expectancy at birth	Unacceptable	Unacceptable	Unacceptable	Unacceptable
Under-five mortality	..	..	Unacceptable	Unacceptable
Maternal mortality	..	..	..	Unacceptable
Level of concern about HIV/AIDS	..	..	Major concern	Major concern
Measures to respond to HIV/AIDS*	..	..	..	1,2,4,5
Grounds on which abortion is permitted**	..	..	1,2	1,2,3
Spatial distribution and internal migration				
View on spatial distribution	Minor change desired	Minor change desired	Satisfactory	Major change desired
Policies on internal migration				
From rural to urban areas	..	..	..	..
From rural to rural areas	..	..	..	..
From urban to rural areas	..	..	..	..
From urban to urban areas	..	..	..	..
Into urban agglomerations	..	No intervention	No intervention	..
International migration				
Immigration				
View	Satisfactory	Too high	Satisfactory	Satisfactory
Policy	Maintain	Maintain	No intervention	No intervention
Permanent settlement	..	..	No intervention	No intervention
Temporary workers	..	..	..	..
Highly skilled workers	..	..	..	..
Family reunification	..	..	..	..
Integration of non-citizens	..	..	No	..
Emigration				
View	Satisfactory	Satisfactory	Satisfactory	Satisfactory
Policy	Maintain	Maintain	No intervention	No intervention
Encouraging the return of citizens	No	..	No	..

* Measures implemented to respond to HIV/AIDS: (1) blood screening; (2) information/education campaigns; (3) antiretroviral treatment; (4) non-discriminatory policies; (5) distribution of condoms.
** Grounds on which abortion is permitted: (1) to save the woman's life; (2) to preserve physical health; (3) to preserve mental health; (4) rape or incest; (5) foetal impairment; (6) economic or social reasons; (7) on request.

Population indicators

Indicator	1975	1985	1995	2009
Population size and growth				
Population size (thousands)	270	386	493	676
Annual growth rate (percentage)*	2.6	3.2	2.4	2.3
Population age structure				
Percentage of population under age 15	46	47	43	38
Percentage of population aged 60 or over	5	5	5	5
Fertility and family planning				
Total fertility (children per woman)*	7.1	7.1	5.1	4.0
Adolescent fertility rate (per 1,000 women, aged 15 - 19)*	..	..	66.0	46.0
Percentage of births to women under age 20*	..	..	6	6
Percentage of births to women aged 35 or over*	..	..	27	20
Percentage of married women using contraception				
Modern methods	..	..	11[a]	19[b]
All methods	..	..	21[a]	26[b]
Health and mortality				
Life expectancy at birth (years)*				
Males	47	51	56	63
Females	51	55	60	67
Both sexes combined	49	53	58	65
Infant mortality rate (per 1,000 live births)*	127	106	80	48
Under-five mortality (per 1,000 live births)*	..	153	113	63
Maternal mortality ratio (per 100,000 live births) (2005)	..	..	..	400
HIV/AIDS				
People living with HIV/AIDS (thousands)	..	..	..	<0.2[c]
Adult prevalence (percentage)	..	..	<0.1	<0.1[c]
Spatial distribution				
Population density (per sq. km)	145	207	265	363
Urban population (percentage)	21	25	28	28
Annual urban population growth rate (percentage)	5.5	4.8	2.7	2.8
Annual rural population growth rate (percentage)	3.3	2.4	2.9	2.2
International migration				
Migrant stock				
Number of migrants (thousands)	7	14	14	14**
As percentage of total population	2.6	3.7	2.8	2.0**

* For the periods 1970-1975, 1980-1985, 1990-1995 and 2005-2010.
** For 2010.
[a] For 1996.
[b] For 2000.
[c] For 2007.

United Nations Department of Economic and Social Affairs/Population Division

Government views and policies

Population policy variable	1976	1986	1996	2009
Population size and growth				
View on growth	Satisfactory	Too low	Too high	Too high
Policy on growth	No intervention	No intervention	Lower	Lower
Population age structure				
Level of concern about				
Size of the working-age population	..	..	..	Minor concern
Ageing of the population	..	..	..	Minor concern
Fertility and family planning				
View on fertility level	Satisfactory	Too low	Too high	Too high
Policy	No intervention	No intervention	Lower	Lower
Access to contraceptive methods	Direct support	Direct support	Direct support	Direct support
Adolescent fertility				
Level of concern	..	..	Major concern	Major concern
Policies and programmes	..	..	Yes	Yes
Health and mortality				
View				
Life expectancy at birth	Unacceptable	Unacceptable	Unacceptable	Unacceptable
Under-five mortality	..	..	Unacceptable	Unacceptable
Maternal mortality	..	..	..	Unacceptable
Level of concern about HIV/AIDS	..	..	Major concern	Major concern
Measures to respond to HIV/AIDS*	..	..	..	1,2,3,5
Grounds on which abortion is permitted**	..	..	1,2	1
Spatial distribution and internal migration				
View on spatial distribution	Major change desired	Major change desired	Major change desired	Major change desired
Policies on internal migration				
From rural to urban areas	..	..	..	Lower
From rural to rural areas	..	..	..	..
From urban to rural areas	..	..	..	..
From urban to urban areas	..	..	..	..
Into urban agglomerations	No intervention	Lower	Lower	Lower
International migration				
Immigration				
View	Satisfactory	Satisfactory	Satisfactory	Satisfactory
Policy	Maintain	Maintain	Lower	No intervention
Permanent settlement	..	..	Maintain	..
Temporary workers	..	..	Lower	..
Highly skilled workers	..	..	..	..
Family reunification	..	..	Maintain	..
Integration of non-citizens	..	..	Yes	..
Emigration				
View	Satisfactory	Satisfactory	Satisfactory	Satisfactory
Policy	Maintain	Maintain	No intervention	No intervention
Encouraging the return of citizens	No	..	No	..

* Measures implemented to respond to HIV/AIDS: (1) blood screening; (2) information/education campaigns; (3) antiretroviral treatment; (4) non-discriminatory policies; (5) distribution of condoms.
** Grounds on which abortion is permitted: (1) to save the woman's life; (2) to preserve physical health; (3) to preserve mental health; (4) rape or incest; (5) foetal impairment; (6) economic or social reasons; (7) on request.

Population indicators

Indicator	1975	1985	1995	2009
Population size and growth				
Population size (thousands)	1 551	2 117	2 782	3 683
Annual growth rate (percentage)*	3.0	3.1	2.6	1.9
Population age structure				
Percentage of population under age 15	45	45	43	40
Percentage of population aged 60 or over	6	6	6	6
Fertility and family planning				
Total fertility (children per woman)*	6.3	6.0	5.2	4.4
Adolescent fertility rate (per 1,000 women, aged 15 - 19)*	..	..	130.0	113.0
Percentage of births to women under age 20*	..	..	13	13
Percentage of births to women aged 35 or over*	..	..	24	22
Percentage of married women using contraception				
Modern methods	..	..	..	13[a]
All methods	..	..	..	44[a]
Health and mortality				
Life expectancy at birth (years)*				
Males	54	59	56	53
Females	58	62	60	55
Both sexes combined	56	60	58	54
Infant mortality rate (per 1,000 live births)*	82	63	66	79
Under-five mortality (per 1,000 live births)*	..	103	106	128
Maternal mortality ratio (per 100,000 live births) (2005)	..	..	..	740
HIV/AIDS				
People living with HIV/AIDS (thousands)	..	..	88	79[b]
Adult prevalence (percentage)	..	..	5.8	3.5[b]
Spatial distribution				
Population density (per sq. km)	5	6	8	11
Urban population (percentage)	43	52	56	62
Annual urban population growth rate (percentage)	5.2	3.7	3.5	2.7
Annual rural population growth rate (percentage)	1.5	2.0	1.9	1.1
International migration				
Migrant stock				
Number of migrants (thousands)	58	99	131	143**
As percentage of total population	3.8	4.7	4.7	3.8**

* For the periods 1970-1975, 1980-1985, 1990-1995 and 2005-2010.
** For 2010.
[a] For 2005.
[b] For 2007.

Government views and policies

Population policy variable[.]	1976	1986	1996	2009
Population size and growth				
View on growth	..	..	Too low	Too low
Policy on growth	..	..	Raise	Raise
Population age structure				
Level of concern about				
Size of the working-age population	..	..	..	Major concern
Ageing of the population	..	..	..	Minor concern
Fertility and family planning				
View on fertility level	..	..	Satisfactory	Too low
Policy	..	..	Maintain	Raise
Access to contraceptive methods	..	..	Direct support	Direct support
Adolescent fertility				
Level of concern	..	..	Minor concern	Major concern
Policies and programmes	..	..	Yes	Yes
Health and mortality				
View				
Life expectancy at birth	..	..	Acceptable	Acceptable
Under-five mortality	..	..	..	Acceptable
Maternal mortality	..	..	..	Acceptable
Level of concern about HIV/AIDS	..	..	..	Major concern
Measures to respond to HIV/AIDS[*]	..	..	..	1,2,3,4,5
Grounds on which abortion is permitted[**]	..	..	1,2,3	1,2,3,4
Spatial distribution and internal migration				
View on spatial distribution	..	..	Satisfactory	Satisfactory
Policies on internal migration				
From rural to urban areas	..	..	..	Raise
From rural to rural areas	..	..	..	No intervention
From urban to rural areas	..	..	..	No intervention
From urban to urban areas	..	..	..	No intervention
Into urban agglomerations	..	..	..	Lower
International migration				
Immigration				
View	..	..	Satisfactory	Satisfactory
Policy	..	..	No intervention	Lower
Permanent settlement	..	..	..	Lower
Temporary workers	..	..	..	Lower
Highly skilled workers	..	..	..	No intervention
Family reunification	..	..	..	No intervention
Integration of non-citizens	..	..	..	Yes
Emigration				
View	..	..	Too high	Too high
Policy	..	..	Lower	Lower
Encouraging the return of citizens	..	..	..	Yes

[*] Measures implemented to respond to HIV/AIDS: (1) blood screening; (2) information/education campaigns; (3) antiretroviral treatment; (4) non-discriminatory policies; (5) distribution of condoms.

[**] Grounds on which abortion is permitted: (1) to save the woman's life; (2) to preserve physical health; (3) to preserve mental health; (4) rape or incest; (5) foetal impairment; (6) economic or social reasons; (7) on request.

Population indicators

Indicator	1975	1985	1995	2009
Population size and growth				
Population size (thousands)	20	18	19	20
Annual growth rate (percentage)*	-0.9	0.1	0.8	0.9
Population age structure				
Percentage of population under age 15	..	..	..	..
Percentage of population aged 60 or over	..	..	..	..
Fertility and family planning				
Total fertility (children per woman)*	..	..	..	..
Adolescent fertility rate (per 1,000 women, aged 15 - 19)*	..	..	..	..
Percentage of births to women under age 20*	..	..	..	..
Percentage of births to women aged 35 or over*	..	..	..	..
Percentage of married women using contraception				
Modern methods	..	..	60[a]	..
All methods	..	..	63[a]	..
Health and mortality				
Life expectancy at birth (years)*				
Males	..	..	..	..
Females	..	..	..	..
Both sexes combined	..	..	..	..
Infant mortality rate (per 1,000 live births)*	..	..	..	..
Under-five mortality (per 1,000 live births)*	..	..	..	..
Maternal mortality ratio (per 100,000 live births) (2005)	..	..	..	..
HIV/AIDS				
People living with HIV/AIDS (thousands)	..	..	..	..
Adult prevalence (percentage)	..	..	..	..
Spatial distribution				
Population density (per sq. km)	87	76	78	84
Urban population (percentage)	54	53	59	75
Annual urban population growth rate (percentage)	-2.5	-0.3	-1.3	-0.6
Annual rural population growth rate (percentage)	-2.8	0.5	-1.5	-6.2
International migration				
Migrant stock				
Number of migrants (thousands)	2	2	3	3**
As percentage of total population	7.5	13.7	14.8	14.1**

* For the periods 1970-1975, 1980-1985, 1990-1995 and 2005-2010.
** For 2010.
[a] For 1996.

Government views and policies

Population policy variable	1976	1986	1996	2009
Population size and growth				
View on growth	Too high	Satisfactory	Too high	Satisfactory
Policy on growth	No intervention	No intervention	Lower	No intervention
Population age structure				
Level of concern about				
Size of the working-age population	..	..	..	Minor concern
Ageing of the population	..	..	..	Major concern
Fertility and family planning				
View on fertility level	Too high	Satisfactory	Too high	Satisfactory
Policy	No intervention	No intervention	Lower	Lower
Access to contraceptive methods	Direct support	Direct support	Direct support	Direct support
Adolescent fertility				
Level of concern	..	..	..	Major concern
Policies and programmes	..	..	..	Yes
Health and mortality				
View				
Life expectancy at birth	Acceptable	Acceptable	Acceptable	Acceptable
Under-five mortality	..	..	..	Acceptable
Maternal mortality	..	..	..	Unacceptable
Level of concern about HIV/AIDS	..	..	..	Major concern
Measures to respond to HIV/AIDS*	..	..	..	1,2,3,4,5
Grounds on which abortion is permitted**	..	..	1,2	1,2,3
Spatial distribution and internal migration				
View on spatial distribution	Major change desired	Major change desired	Major change desired	Minor change desired
Policies on internal migration				
From rural to urban areas	..	..	..	Lower
From rural to rural areas	..	..	..	..
From urban to rural areas	..	..	..	..
From urban to urban areas	..	..	..	Raise
Into urban agglomerations	No intervention	Lower	..	Lower
International migration				
Immigration				
View	Satisfactory	Too high	Too high	Satisfactory
Policy	Maintain	Lower	Lower	Maintain
Permanent settlement	..	..	Lower	Maintain
Temporary workers	..	..	Maintain	Maintain
Highly skilled workers	..	..	..	Maintain
Family reunification	..	..	Maintain	Maintain
Integration of non-citizens	..	..	..	Yes
Emigration				
View	Satisfactory	Too low	Satisfactory	Satisfactory
Policy	Maintain	Maintain	No intervention	No intervention
Encouraging the return of citizens	Yes	..	Yes	No

* Measures implemented to respond to HIV/AIDS: (1) blood screening; (2) information/education campaigns; (3) antiretroviral treatment; (4) non-discriminatory policies; (5) distribution of condoms.

** Grounds on which abortion is permitted: (1) to save the woman's life; (2) to preserve physical health; (3) to preserve mental health; (4) rape or incest; (5) foetal impairment; (6) economic or social reasons; (7) on request.

Population indicators

Indicator	1975	1985	1995	2009
Population size and growth				
Population size (thousands)	2 052	2 699	3 479	4 579
Annual growth rate (percentage)*	2.4	2.8	2.4	1.4
Population age structure				
Percentage of population under age 15	41	36	34	26
Percentage of population aged 60 or over	7	7	7	9
Fertility and family planning				
Total fertility (children per woman)*	4.3	3.5	2.9	2.0
Adolescent fertility rate (per 1,000 women, aged 15 - 19)*	..	..	94.0	67.0
Percentage of births to women under age 20*	..	..	16	17
Percentage of births to women aged 35 or over*	..	..	15	12
Percentage of married women using contraception				
Modern methods	54[a]	58[b]	72[c]	..
All methods	64[a]	70[b]	80[c]	..
Health and mortality				
Life expectancy at birth (years)*				
Males	66	72	74	76
Females	70	76	79	81
Both sexes combined	68	74	76	79
Infant mortality rate (per 1,000 live births)*	53	19	15	10
Under-five mortality (per 1,000 live births)*	..	24	17	11
Maternal mortality ratio (per 100,000 live births) (2005)	..	..	..	30
HIV/AIDS				
People living with HIV/AIDS (thousands)	..	..	<1	9.7[d]
Adult prevalence (percentage)	..	..	<0.1	0.4[d]
Spatial distribution				
Population density (per sq. km)	40	53	68	90
Urban population (percentage)	41	46	56	64
Annual urban population growth rate (percentage)	3.4	4.9	4.3	2.2
Annual rural population growth rate (percentage)	2.0	0.8	0.2	0.0
International migration				
Migrant stock				
Number of migrants (thousands)	29	117	228	489**
As percentage of total population	1.4	4.3	6.6	10.5**

* For the periods 1970-1975, 1980-1985, 1990-1995 and 2005-2010.
** For 2010.
[a] For 1976.
[b] For 1986.
[c] For 1999.
[d] For 2007.

Government views and policies

Population policy variable	1976	1986	1996	2009
Population size and growth				
View on growth	Too low	Satisfactory	Satisfactory	Too high
Policy on growth	Raise	Raise	Raise	Lower
Population age structure				
Level of concern about				
Size of the working-age population	..	..	..	Minor concern
Ageing of the population	..	..	..	Major concern
Fertility and family planning				
View on fertility level	Satisfactory	Satisfactory	Satisfactory	Too high
Policy	Maintain	Raise	Raise	Lower
Access to contraceptive methods	No support	No support	Indirect support	Direct support
Adolescent fertility				
Level of concern	..	..	..	Major concern
Policies and programmes	..	..	..	Yes
Health and mortality				
View				
Life expectancy at birth	Unacceptable	Acceptable	Acceptable	Unacceptable
Under-five mortality	..	..	..	Unacceptable
Maternal mortality	..	..	..	Unacceptable
Level of concern about HIV/AIDS	..	..	..	Major concern
Measures to respond to HIV/AIDS*	..	..	..	1,2,3,5
Grounds on which abortion is permitted**	..	..	1	1
Spatial distribution and internal migration				
View on spatial distribution	Major change desired	Major change desired	Major change desired	Major change desired
Policies on internal migration				
From rural to urban areas	..	..	..	Lower
From rural to rural areas	..	..	..	Maintain
From urban to rural areas	..	..	..	Raise
From urban to urban areas	..	..	..	Maintain
Into urban agglomerations	Lower	Lower	..	Lower
International migration				
Immigration				
View	Too high	Too high	Too high	Too high
Policy	Lower	Lower	Lower	Lower
Permanent settlement	..	..	Lower	Lower
Temporary workers	..	..	Lower	Lower
Highly skilled workers	..	..	..	Maintain
Family reunification	..	..	Lower	Lower
Integration of non-citizens	..	..	No	No
Emigration				
View	Satisfactory	Satisfactory	Satisfactory	Satisfactory
Policy	Maintain	Maintain	Maintain	No intervention
Encouraging the return of citizens	No	..	..	No

* Measures implemented to respond to HIV/AIDS: (1) blood screening; (2) information/education campaigns; (3) antiretroviral treatment;
(4) non−discriminatory policies; (5) distribution of condoms.
** Grounds on which abortion is permitted: (1) to save the woman's life; (2) to preserve physical health; (3) to preserve mental health; (4) rape or incest;
(5) foetal impairment; (6) economic or social reasons; (7) on request.

Population indicators

Indicator	1975	1985	1995	2009
Population size and growth				
Population size (thousands)	6 621	10 476	14 981	21 075
Annual growth rate (percentage)*	4.7	4.4	3.4	2.3
Population age structure				
Percentage of population under age 15	45	46	43	41
Percentage of population aged 60 or over	4	4	5	6
Fertility and family planning				
Total fertility (children per woman)*	7.9	7.3	5.9	4.6
Adolescent fertility rate (per 1,000 women, aged 15 - 19)*	..	..	150.0	130.0
Percentage of births to women under age 20*	..	..	13	14
Percentage of births to women aged 35 or over*	..	..	26	22
Percentage of married women using contraception				
Modern methods	..	1[a]	7[b]	8[c]
All methods	..	3[a]	15[b]	13[c]
Health and mortality				
Life expectancy at birth (years)*				
Males	48	55	56	56
Females	51	58	60	59
Both sexes combined	50	56	57	57
Infant mortality rate (per 1,000 live births)*	133	106	100	87
Under-five mortality (per 1,000 live births)*	..	162	148	123
Maternal mortality ratio (per 100,000 live births) (2005)	..	..	..	810
HIV/AIDS				
People living with HIV/AIDS (thousands)	..	..	430	480[d]
Adult prevalence (percentage)	..	..	5.8	3.9[d]
Spatial distribution				
Population density (per sq. km)	21	32	46	65
Urban population (percentage)	32	38	41	49
Annual urban population growth rate (percentage)	8.8	4.9	3.7	3.2
Annual rural population growth rate (percentage)	2.6	3.8	2.3	0.6
International migration				
Migrant stock				
Number of migrants (thousands)	1 391	1 662	1 985	2 407**
As percentage of total population	21.0	15.9	13.3	11.2**

* For the periods 1970-1975, 1980-1985, 1990-1995 and 2005-2010.
** For 2010.
[a] For 1981.
[b] For 1998/1999.
[c] For 2006.
[d] For 2007.

Government views and policies

Population policy variable	1976	1986	1996	2009
Population size and growth				
View on growth	..	..	Satisfactory	Too low
Policy on growth	..	..	Raise	Raise
Population age structure				
Level of concern about				
Size of the working-age population	..	..	..	Major concern
Ageing of the population	..	..	..	Major concern
Fertility and family planning				
View on fertility level	..	..	Too low	Too low
Policy	..	..	Raise	Raise
Access to contraceptive methods	..	..	Direct support	Direct support
Adolescent fertility				
Level of concern	..	..	Not a concern	Minor concern
Policies and programmes	..	..	..	Yes
Health and mortality				
View				
Life expectancy at birth	..	..	Acceptable	Acceptable
Under-five mortality	..	..	..	Unacceptable
Maternal mortality	..	..	..	Acceptable
Level of concern about HIV/AIDS	..	..	Major concern	Major concern
Measures to respond to HIV/AIDS*	..	..	..	1,2,3,4,5
Grounds on which abortion is permitted**	..	..	1,2,3,4,5,6,7	1,2,3,4,5,6,7
Spatial distribution and internal migration				
View on spatial distribution	..	..	Major change desired	Major change desired
Policies on internal migration				
From rural to urban areas	..	..	..	Lower
From rural to rural areas	..	..	..	No intervention
From urban to rural areas	..	..	..	Maintain
From urban to urban areas	..	..	..	No intervention
Into urban agglomerations	..	..	No intervention	No intervention
International migration				
Immigration				
View	..	..	Satisfactory	Satisfactory
Policy	..	..	No intervention	Maintain
Permanent settlement	..	..	No intervention	Lower
Temporary workers	..	..	No intervention	Raise
Highly skilled workers	..	..	..	Raise
Family reunification	..	..	No intervention	Maintain
Integration of non-citizens	..	..	..	Yes
Emigration				
View	..	..	Too high	Too high
Policy	..	..	Lower	Lower
Encouraging the return of citizens	..	..	Yes	Yes

* Measures implemented to respond to HIV/AIDS: (1) blood screening; (2) information/education campaigns; (3) antiretroviral treatment; (4) non-discriminatory policies; (5) distribution of condoms.
** Grounds on which abortion is permitted: (1) to save the woman's life; (2) to preserve physical health; (3) to preserve mental health; (4) rape or incest; (5) foetal impairment; (6) economic or social reasons; (7) on request.

Population indicators

Indicator	1975	1985	1995	2009
Population size and growth				
Population size (thousands)	4 263	4 471	4 669	4 416
Annual growth rate (percentage)*	0.4	0.4	0.7	-0.2
Population age structure				
Percentage of population under age 15	21	21	19	15
Percentage of population aged 60 or over	16	16	20	23
Fertility and family planning				
Total fertility (children per woman)*	2.0	2.0	1.5	1.4
Adolescent fertility rate (per 1,000 women, aged 15 - 19)*	..	..	18.0	14.0
Percentage of births to women under age 20*	..	..	6	5
Percentage of births to women aged 35 or over*	..	..	10	12
Percentage of married women using contraception				
Modern methods	..	..	..	..
All methods	..	..	..	..
Health and mortality				
Life expectancy at birth (years)*				
Males	66	66	68	73
Females	73	75	77	80
Both sexes combined	70	70	73	76
Infant mortality rate (per 1,000 live births)*	27	18	11	6
Under-five mortality (per 1,000 live births)*	..	20	12	8
Maternal mortality ratio (per 100,000 live births) (2005)	..	..	..	7
HIV/AIDS				
People living with HIV/AIDS (thousands)	..	..	..	<0.5[a]
Adult prevalence (percentage)	..	..	..	<0.1[a]
Spatial distribution				
Population density (per sq. km)	75	79	83	78
Urban population (percentage)	45	52	55	57
Annual urban population growth rate (percentage)	2.7	0.9	-0.1	0.3
Annual rural population growth rate (percentage)	-1.3	-0.5	-0.6	-0.9
International migration				
Migrant stock				
Number of migrants (thousands)	..	..	721	700**
As percentage of total population	0.0	0.0	15.4	15.9**

* For the periods 1970-1975, 1980-1985, 1990-1995 and 2005-2010.
** For 2010.
[a] For 2007.

Government views and policies

Population policy variable	1976	1986	1996	2009
Population size and growth				
View on growth	Satisfactory	Satisfactory	Satisfactory	Satisfactory
Policy on growth	No intervention	No intervention	No intervention	No intervention
Population age structure				
Level of concern about				
Size of the working-age population	..	..	..	Minor concern
Ageing of the population	..	..	..	Major concern
Fertility and family planning				
View on fertility level	Satisfactory	Satisfactory	Satisfactory	Satisfactory
Policy	No intervention	No intervention	No intervention	No intervention
Access to contraceptive methods	Direct support	Direct support	Direct support	Direct support
Adolescent fertility				
Level of concern	..	..	Major concern	Major concern
Policies and programmes	..	..	Yes	Yes
Health and mortality				
View				
Life expectancy at birth	Acceptable	Acceptable	Acceptable	Acceptable
Under-five mortality	..	..	Acceptable	Acceptable
Maternal mortality	..	..	..	Acceptable
Level of concern about HIV/AIDS	..	..	Major concern	Major concern
Measures to respond to HIV/AIDS*	..	..	..	1,2,3,4,5
Grounds on which abortion is permitted**	..	..	1,2,3,4,5,6,7	1,2,3,4,5,6,7
Spatial distribution and internal migration				
View on spatial distribution	Minor change desired	Minor change desired	Minor change desired	Minor change desired
Policies on internal migration				
From rural to urban areas	..	..	..	Lower
From rural to rural areas	..	..	..	No intervention
From urban to rural areas	..	..	..	No intervention
From urban to urban areas	..	..	..	No intervention
Into urban agglomerations	..	No intervention	Lower	Lower
International migration				
Immigration				
View	Satisfactory	Satisfactory	Satisfactory	Satisfactory
Policy	Maintain	Maintain	Maintain	Maintain
Permanent settlement	..	..	Maintain	Maintain
Temporary workers	..	..	Maintain	Maintain
Highly skilled workers	..	..	..	Maintain
Family reunification	..	..	Maintain	Maintain
Integration of non-citizens	..	..	No	No
Emigration				
View	Satisfactory	Satisfactory	Satisfactory	Satisfactory
Policy	Maintain	Lower	Maintain	Maintain
Encouraging the return of citizens	..	..	No	No

* Measures implemented to respond to HIV/AIDS: (1) blood screening; (2) information/education campaigns; (3) antiretroviral treatment; (4) non–discriminatory policies; (5) distribution of condoms.
** Grounds on which abortion is permitted: (1) to save the woman's life; (2) to preserve physical health; (3) to preserve mental health; (4) rape or incest; (5) foetal impairment; (6) economic or social reasons; (7) on request.

Population indicators

Indicator	1975	1985	1995	2009
Population size and growth				
Population size (thousands)	9 439	10 084	10 910	11 204
Annual growth rate (percentage)*	1.6	0.5	0.6	0.0
Population age structure				
Percentage of population under age 15	37	26	22	18
Percentage of population aged 60 or over	10	11	13	17
Fertility and family planning				
Total fertility (children per woman)*	3.6	1.8	1.7	1.5
Adolescent fertility rate (per 1,000 women, aged 15 - 19)*	..	..	69.0	45.0
Percentage of births to women under age 20*	..	..	21	15
Percentage of births to women aged 35 or over*	..	..	6	9
Percentage of married women using contraception				
Modern methods	..	67[a]	..	72[b]
All methods	..	70[a]	..	73[b]
Health and mortality				
Life expectancy at birth (years)*				
Males	69	73	73	77
Females	73	76	77	81
Both sexes combined	71	74	75	79
Infant mortality rate (per 1,000 live births)*	38	17	15	5
Under-five mortality (per 1,000 live births)*	..	21	19	8
Maternal mortality ratio (per 100,000 live births) (2005)	..	..	..	45
HIV/AIDS				
People living with HIV/AIDS (thousands)	..	..	..	6.2[c]
Adult prevalence (percentage)	..	..	..	0.1[c]
Spatial distribution				
Population density (per sq. km)	85	91	98	101
Urban population (percentage)	64	71	74	76
Annual urban population growth rate (percentage)	2.3	1.6	0.7	0.0
Annual rural population growth rate (percentage)	-1.1	-0.8	-0.1	-0.3
International migration				
Migrant stock				
Number of migrants (thousands)	93	48	25	15**
As percentage of total population	1.0	0.5	0.2	0.1**

* For the periods 1970-1975, 1980-1985, 1990-1995 and 2005-2010.
** For 2010.
[a] For 1987.
[b] For 2006.
[c] For 2007.

Government views and policies

Population policy variable	1976	1986	1996	2009
Population size and growth				
View on growth	Satisfactory	Too low	Too low	Too low
Policy on growth	No intervention	Raise	Raise	Raise
Population age structure				
Level of concern about				
Size of the working-age population	..	..	..	Major concern
Ageing of the population	..	..	..	Major concern
Fertility and family planning				
View on fertility level	Satisfactory	Too low	Too low	Too low
Policy	No intervention	Raise	Raise	Raise
Access to contraceptive methods	No support	Direct support	Indirect support	Direct support
Adolescent fertility				
Level of concern	..	..	Minor concern	Minor concern
Policies and programmes	..	..	No	Yes
Health and mortality				
View				
Life expectancy at birth	Acceptable	Acceptable	Acceptable	Acceptable
Under-five mortality	..	..	Acceptable	Acceptable
Maternal mortality	..	..	..	Acceptable
Level of concern about HIV/AIDS	..	..	Major concern	Major concern
Measures to respond to HIV/AIDS*	..	..	..	1,2,3,4,5
Grounds on which abortion is permitted**	..	..	1,2,3,4,5	1,2,3,4,5
Spatial distribution and internal migration				
View on spatial distribution	Minor change desired	Major change desired	Major change desired	Major change desired
Policies on internal migration				
From rural to urban areas	..	..	..	Lower
From rural to rural areas	..	..	..	Maintain
From urban to rural areas	..	..	..	Raise
From urban to urban areas	..	..	..	Maintain
Into urban agglomerations	Raise	No intervention	..	Lower
International migration				
Immigration				
View	Satisfactory	Satisfactory	Satisfactory	Satisfactory
Policy	Maintain	Maintain	Lower	Lower
Permanent settlement	..	..	Lower	Maintain
Temporary workers	..	..	Lower	Lower
Highly skilled workers	..	..	..	Raise
Family reunification	..	..	No intervention	Maintain
Integration of non-citizens	..	..	No	Yes
Emigration				
View	Too high	Satisfactory	Satisfactory	Satisfactory
Policy	Lower	Maintain	Lower	Maintain
Encouraging the return of citizens	Yes	..	Yes	Yes

* Measures implemented to respond to HIV/AIDS: (1) blood screening; (2) information/education campaigns; (3) antiretroviral treatment; (4) non−discriminatory policies; (5) distribution of condoms.
** Grounds on which abortion is permitted: (1) to save the woman's life; (2) to preserve physical health; (3) to preserve mental health; (4) rape or incest; (5) foetal impairment; (6) economic or social reasons; (7) on request.

Population indicators

Indicator	1975	1985	1995	2009
Population size and growth				
Population size (thousands)	609	647	731	871
Annual growth rate (percentage)*	-0.2	1.2	1.4	1.0
Population age structure				
Percentage of population under age 15	26	25	25	18
Percentage of population aged 60 or over	14	14	15	18
Fertility and family planning				
Total fertility (children per woman)*	2.5	2.4	2.4	1.5
Adolescent fertility rate (per 1,000 women, aged 15 - 19)*	..	..	16.0	6.0
Percentage of births to women under age 20*	..	..	3	2
Percentage of births to women aged 35 or over*	..	..	11	15
Percentage of married women using contraception				
Modern methods	..	..	..	..
All methods	..	..	..	..
Health and mortality				
Life expectancy at birth (years)*				
Males	70	73	75	77
Females	73	78	79	82
Both sexes combined	71	75	77	80
Infant mortality rate (per 1,000 live births)*	29	16	7	5
Under-five mortality (per 1,000 live births)*	..	17	8	7
Maternal mortality ratio (per 100,000 live births) (2005)	..	..	..	10
HIV/AIDS				
People living with HIV/AIDS (thousands)	..	..	..	<0.5[a]
Adult prevalence (percentage)	..	..	..	..
Spatial distribution				
Population density (per sq. km)	66	70	79	94
Urban population (percentage)	47	65	68	70
Annual urban population growth rate (percentage)	4.5	1.7	1.7	1.3
Annual rural population growth rate (percentage)	-4.7	-0.2	1.1	0.3
International migration				
Migrant stock				
Number of migrants (thousands)	37	41	55	154**
As percentage of total population	6.0	6.4	7.5	17.5**

* For the periods 1970-1975, 1980-1985, 1990-1995 and 2005-2010.
** For 2010.
[a] For 2007.

Government views and policies

Population policy variable	1976	1986	1996	2009
Population size and growth				
View on growth	..	..	Satisfactory	Too low
Policy on growth	..	..	No intervention	Raise
Population age structure				
Level of concern about				
Size of the working-age population	..	..	..	Major concern
Ageing of the population	..	..	..	Major concern
Fertility and family planning				
View on fertility level	..	..	Satisfactory	Too low
Policy	..	..	No intervention	Raise
Access to contraceptive methods	..	..	Indirect support	Indirect support
Adolescent fertility				
Level of concern	..	..	..	Not a concern
Policies and programmes	..	..	..	No
Health and mortality				
View				
Life expectancy at birth	..	..	Unacceptable	Acceptable
Under-five mortality	..	..	..	Acceptable
Maternal mortality	..	..	..	Acceptable
Level of concern about HIV/AIDS	..	..	..	Major concern
Measures to respond to HIV/AIDS[*]	..	..	..	1,2,3,4,5
Grounds on which abortion is permitted[**]	..	..	1,2,3,4,5,6,7	1,2,3,4,5,6,7
Spatial distribution and internal migration				
View on spatial distribution	..	..	Minor change desired	Minor change desired
Policies on internal migration				
From rural to urban areas	..	..	..	No intervention
From rural to rural areas	..	..	..	No intervention
From urban to rural areas	..	..	..	No intervention
From urban to urban areas	..	..	..	No intervention
Into urban agglomerations	..	..	..	No intervention
International migration				
Immigration				
View	..	..	Satisfactory	Satisfactory
Policy	..	..	Maintain	Maintain
Permanent settlement	..	..	Maintain	Maintain
Temporary workers	..	..	Maintain	Maintain
Highly skilled workers	..	..	..	Raise
Family reunification	..	..	Maintain	Maintain
Integration of non-citizens	..	..	Yes	Yes
Emigration				
View	..	..	Satisfactory	Satisfactory
Policy	..	..	No intervention	No intervention
Encouraging the return of citizens	..	..	..	No

[*] Measures implemented to respond to HIV/AIDS: (1) blood screening; (2) information/education campaigns; (3) antiretroviral treatment; (4) non-discriminatory policies; (5) distribution of condoms.

[**] Grounds on which abortion is permitted: (1) to save the woman's life; (2) to preserve physical health; (3) to preserve mental health; (4) rape or incest; (5) foetal impairment; (6) economic or social reasons; (7) on request.

Population indicators

Indicator	1975	1985	1995	2009
Population size and growth				
Population size (thousands)	10 034	10 310	10 319	10 369
Annual growth rate (percentage)*	0.5	0.1	0.0	0.4
Population age structure				
Percentage of population under age 15	22	23	19	14
Percentage of population aged 60 or over	19	17	18	22
Fertility and family planning				
Total fertility (children per woman)*	2.2	2.0	1.7	1.4
Adolescent fertility rate (per 1,000 women, aged 15 - 19)*	..	..	41.0	11.0
Percentage of births to women under age 20*	..	..	13	4
Percentage of births to women aged 35 or over*	..	..	4	12
Percentage of married women using contraception				
Modern methods	49[a]	..	63[b]	..
All methods	95[a]	..	72[b]	..
Health and mortality				
Life expectancy at birth (years)*				
Males	67	67	69	73
Females	74	74	76	80
Both sexes combined	70	71	73	76
Infant mortality rate (per 1,000 live births)*	21	15	8	4
Under-five mortality (per 1,000 live births)*	..	17	10	5
Maternal mortality ratio (per 100,000 live births) (2005)	..	..	..	4
HIV/AIDS				
People living with HIV/AIDS (thousands)	..	..	<1	1.5[c]
Adult prevalence (percentage)	..	..	..	..
Spatial distribution				
Population density (per sq. km)	127	131	131	131
Urban population (percentage)	70	75	75	73
Annual urban population growth rate (percentage)	2.1	-0.1	-0.3	0.0
Annual rural population growth rate (percentage)	-3.2	0.1	0.4	-0.2
International migration				
Migrant stock				
Number of migrants (thousands)	..	..	454	453**
As percentage of total population	0.0	0.0	4.4	4.4**

* For the periods 1970-1975, 1980-1985, 1990-1995 and 2005-2010.
** For 2010.
[a] For 1977.
[b] For 1997.
[c] For 2007.

Government views and policies

Population policy variable	1976	1986	1996	2009
Population size and growth				
View on growth	Too low	Too low	Satisfactory	Too low
Policy on growth	Raise	Raise	No intervention	Maintain
Population age structure				
Level of concern about				
Size of the working-age population	..	..	..	Not a concern
Ageing of the population	..	..	..	Minor concern
Fertility and family planning				
View on fertility level	Satisfactory	Satisfactory	Satisfactory	Too low
Policy	Maintain	Maintain	Maintain	No intervention
Access to contraceptive methods	Direct support	Direct support	Direct support	Direct support
Adolescent fertility				
Level of concern	..	..	..	Not a concern
Policies and programmes	..	..	..	No
Health and mortality				
View				
Life expectancy at birth	Unacceptable	Unacceptable	Acceptable	Unacceptable
Under-five mortality	..	..	..	Unacceptable
Maternal mortality	..	..	..	Unacceptable
Level of concern about HIV/AIDS	..	..	..	Minor concern
Measures to respond to HIV/AIDS*	..	..		1,2,5
Grounds on which abortion is permitted**	..	..	1,2,3,4,5,6,7	1,2,3,4,5,6,7
Spatial distribution and internal migration				
View on spatial distribution	Minor change desired	Minor change desired	Minor change desired	Satisfactory
Policies on internal migration				
From rural to urban areas	..	..	..	Lower
From rural to rural areas	..	..	..	Maintain
From urban to rural areas	..	..	..	Raise
From urban to urban areas	..	..	..	Maintain
Into urban agglomerations	..	..	..	Maintain
International migration				
Immigration				
View	Satisfactory	Satisfactory	Satisfactory	Satisfactory
Policy	Maintain	Maintain	Maintain	Maintain
Permanent settlement	..	..	..	Lower
Temporary workers	..	..	..	Lower
Highly skilled workers	..	..	..	Maintain
Family reunification	..	..	..	Raise
Integration of non-citizens	..	..	..	No
Emigration				
View	Satisfactory	Satisfactory	Satisfactory	Satisfactory
Policy	Maintain	Maintain	Maintain	Maintain
Encouraging the return of citizens	..	..	No	..

* Measures implemented to respond to HIV/AIDS: (1) blood screening; (2) information/education campaigns; (3) antiretroviral treatment; (4) non-discriminatory policies; (5) distribution of condoms.
** Grounds on which abortion is permitted: (1) to save the woman's life; (2) to preserve physical health; (3) to preserve mental health; (4) rape or incest; (5) foetal impairment; (6) economic or social reasons; (7) on request.

Population indicators

Indicator	1975	1985	1995	2009
Population size and growth				
Population size (thousands)	16 072	18 721	21 717	23 906
Annual growth rate (percentage)*	2.4	1.6	1.5	0.4
Population age structure				
Percentage of population under age 15	38	30	27	22
Percentage of population aged 60 or over	3	6	10	14
Fertility and family planning				
Total fertility (children per woman)*	3.7	2.9	2.4	1.9
Adolescent fertility rate (per 1,000 women, aged 15 - 19)*	..	..	0.0	0.0
Percentage of births to women under age 20*	..	..	0	0
Percentage of births to women aged 35 or over*	..	..	9	9
Percentage of married women using contraception				
Modern methods	..	..	56[a]	58[b]
All methods	..	..	67[a]	69[b]
Health and mortality				
Life expectancy at birth (years)*				
Males	61	65	66	65
Females	66	72	74	69
Both sexes combined	64	69	70	67
Infant mortality rate (per 1,000 live births)*	44	30	42	48
Under-five mortality (per 1,000 live births)*	..	37	55	63
Maternal mortality ratio (per 100,000 live births) (2005)	..	..	..	370
HIV/AIDS				
People living with HIV/AIDS (thousands)	..	..	..	..
Adult prevalence (percentage)	..	..	..	..
Spatial distribution				
Population density (per sq. km)	133	155	180	198
Urban population (percentage)	57	58	59	63
Annual urban population growth rate (percentage)	1.7	1.8	1.6	0.9
Annual rural population growth rate (percentage)	1.6	1.2	0.9	-0.7
International migration				
Migrant stock				
Number of migrants (thousands)	30	33	35	37**
As percentage of total population	0.2	0.2	0.2	0.2**

* For the periods 1970-1975, 1980-1985, 1990-1995 and 2005-2010.
** For 2010.
[a] For 1997.
[b] For 2002.

Government views and policies

Population policy variable	1976	1986	1996	2009
Population size and growth				
View on growth	Satisfactory	Satisfactory	Satisfactory	Satisfactory
Policy on growth	No intervention	No intervention	No intervention	No intervention
Population age structure				
Level of concern about				
Size of the working-age population	..	..	..	..
Ageing of the population	..	..	..	Minor concern
Fertility and family planning				
View on fertility level	Satisfactory	Satisfactory	Satisfactory	Satisfactory
Policy	No intervention	No intervention	No intervention	No intervention
Access to contraceptive methods	Direct support	Indirect support	Direct support	Direct support
Adolescent fertility				
Level of concern	..	..	Minor concern	Minor concern
Policies and programmes	..	..	Yes	Yes
Health and mortality				
View				
Life expectancy at birth	Unacceptable	Unacceptable	Unacceptable	Unacceptable
Under-five mortality	..	..	Unacceptable	Unacceptable
Maternal mortality	..	..	..	Unacceptable
Level of concern about HIV/AIDS	..	..	Major concern	Major concern
Measures to respond to HIV/AIDS*	..	..	..	1,2,3,5
Grounds on which abortion is permitted**	..	..	1	1
Spatial distribution and internal migration				
View on spatial distribution	Major change desired	Major change desired	Major change desired	Major change desired
Policies on internal migration				
From rural to urban areas	..	..	..	..
From rural to rural areas	..	..	..	..
From urban to rural areas	..	..	..	..
From urban to urban areas	..	..	..	..
Into urban agglomerations	Lower	Lower	No intervention	..
International migration				
Immigration				
View	Satisfactory	Satisfactory	Satisfactory	Satisfactory
Policy	Maintain	Maintain	Lower	Lower
Permanent settlement	..	..	No intervention	..
Temporary workers	..	..	Lower	..
Highly skilled workers	..	..	..	..
Family reunification	..	..	No intervention	..
Integration of non-citizens	..	..	Yes	..
Emigration				
View	Satisfactory	Satisfactory	Satisfactory	Too high
Policy	Maintain	Maintain	No intervention	No intervention
Encouraging the return of citizens	No	..	No	..

* Measures implemented to respond to HIV/AIDS: (1) blood screening; (2) information/education campaigns; (3) antiretroviral treatment; (4) non-discriminatory policies; (5) distribution of condoms.
** Grounds on which abortion is permitted: (1) to save the woman's life; (2) to preserve physical health; (3) to preserve mental health; (4) rape or incest; (5) foetal impairment; (6) economic or social reasons; (7) on request.

Population indicators

Indicator	1975	1985	1995	2009
Population size and growth				
Population size (thousands)	23 433	31 402	44 921	66 020
Annual growth rate (percentage)*	2.9	2.9	3.9	2.8
Population age structure				
Percentage of population under age 15	45	46	48	47
Percentage of population aged 60 or over	5	5	4	4
Fertility and family planning				
Total fertility (children per woman)*	6.3	6.7	7.1	6.1
Adolescent fertility rate (per 1,000 women, aged 15 - 19)*	..	..	245.0	201.0
Percentage of births to women under age 20*	..	..	17	17
Percentage of births to women aged 35 or over*	..	..	21	21
Percentage of married women using contraception				
Modern methods	..	..	2[a]	6[b]
All methods	..	..	8[a]	21[b]
Health and mortality				
Life expectancy at birth (years)*				
Males	43	46	46	46
Females	46	49	49	49
Both sexes combined	45	47	48	47
Infant mortality rate (per 1,000 live births)*	135	120	113	117
Under-five mortality (per 1,000 live births)*	..	208	198	198
Maternal mortality ratio (per 100,000 live births) (2005)	..	..	..	1 100
HIV/AIDS				
People living with HIV/AIDS (thousands)	..	..	..	..
Adult prevalence (percentage)	..	..	..	..
Spatial distribution				
Population density (per sq. km)	10	13	19	28
Urban population (percentage)	30	28	28	35
Annual urban population growth rate (percentage)	2.6	2.6	3.3	5.1
Annual rural population growth rate (percentage)	3.4	3.1	2.2	2.2
International migration				
Migrant stock				
Number of migrants (thousands)	1 218	725	1 919	445**
As percentage of total population	5.2	2.3	4.3	0.7**

* For the periods 1970-1975, 1980-1985, 1990-1995 and 2005-2010.
** For 2010.
[a] For 1991.
[b] For 2007.

Government views and policies

Population policy variable	1976	1986	1996	2009
Population size and growth				
View on growth	Satisfactory	Satisfactory	Satisfactory	Satisfactory
Policy on growth	No intervention	No intervention	No intervention	No intervention
Population age structure				
Level of concern about				
Size of the working-age population	..	..	..	Major concern
Ageing of the population	..	..	..	Major concern
Fertility and family planning				
View on fertility level	Satisfactory	Satisfactory	Satisfactory	Satisfactory
Policy	No intervention	No intervention	No intervention	No intervention
Access to contraceptive methods	Direct support	Direct support	Direct support	Indirect support
Adolescent fertility				
Level of concern	..	..	Minor concern	Minor concern
Policies and programmes	..	..	Yes	Yes
Health and mortality				
View				
Life expectancy at birth	Acceptable	Acceptable	Acceptable	Acceptable
Under-five mortality	..	..	Acceptable	Acceptable
Maternal mortality	..	..	..	Acceptable
Level of concern about HIV/AIDS	..	..	Major concern	Minor concern
Measures to respond to HIV/AIDS*	..	..	..	1,2,3,4,5
Grounds on which abortion is permitted**	..	..	1,2,3,4,5,6,7	1,2,3,4,5,6,7
Spatial distribution and internal migration				
View on spatial distribution	Satisfactory	Satisfactory	Satisfactory	Satisfactory
Policies on internal migration				
From rural to urban areas	..	..	..	No intervention
From rural to rural areas	..	..	..	No intervention
From urban to rural areas	..	..	..	No intervention
From urban to urban areas	..	..	..	No intervention
Into urban agglomerations	Raise	..	No intervention	No intervention
International migration				
Immigration				
View	Satisfactory	Satisfactory	Too high	Too high
Policy	Maintain	Maintain	Lower	Lower
Permanent settlement	..	..	Lower	Lower
Temporary workers	..	..	Lower	Maintain
Highly skilled workers	..	..	..	Raise
Family reunification	..	..	Lower	Lower
Integration of non-citizens	..	..	Yes	Yes
Emigration				
View	Satisfactory	Satisfactory	Satisfactory	Satisfactory
Policy	Maintain	Maintain	No intervention	No intervention
Encouraging the return of citizens	No	..	No	No

* Measures implemented to respond to HIV/AIDS: (1) blood screening; (2) information/education campaigns; (3) antiretroviral treatment; (4) non-discriminatory policies; (5) distribution of condoms.
** Grounds on which abortion is permitted: (1) to save the woman's life; (2) to preserve physical health; (3) to preserve mental health; (4) rape or incest; (5) foetal impairment; (6) economic or social reasons; (7) on request.

Population indicators

Indicator	1975	1985	1995	2009
Population size and growth				
Population size (thousands)	5 060	5 114	5 228	5 470
Annual growth rate (percentage)*	0.5	0.0	0.3	0.2
Population age structure				
Percentage of population under age 15	23	18	17	18
Percentage of population aged 60 or over	19	20	20	23
Fertility and family planning				
Total fertility (children per woman)*	2.0	1.4	1.7	1.8
Adolescent fertility rate (per 1,000 women, aged 15 - 19)*	..	..	8.0	6.0
Percentage of births to women under age 20*	..	..	2	2
Percentage of births to women aged 35 or over*	..	..	13	17
Percentage of married women using contraception				
Modern methods	60	72[a]	..	..
All methods	63	78[a]	..	..
Health and mortality				
Life expectancy at birth (years)*				
Males	71	72	73	76
Females	76	78	78	81
Both sexes combined	74	75	75	78
Infant mortality rate (per 1,000 live births)*	12	8	7	4
Under-five mortality (per 1,000 live births)*	..	10	8	6
Maternal mortality ratio (per 100,000 live births) (2005)	..	..	..	3
HIV/AIDS				
People living with HIV/AIDS (thousands)	..	..	2.4	4.8[b]
Adult prevalence (percentage)	..	..	0.1	0.2[b]
Spatial distribution				
Population density (per sq. km)	117	119	121	127
Urban population (percentage)	82	84	85	87
Annual urban population growth rate (percentage)	0.9	0.1	0.4	0.5
Annual rural population growth rate (percentage)	-2.2	-0.7	0.2	-1.8
International migration				
Migrant stock				
Number of migrants (thousands)	139	196	297	484**
As percentage of total population	2.7	3.8	5.7	8.8**

* For the periods 1970-1975, 1980-1985, 1990-1995 and 2005-2010.
** For 2010.
[a] For 1988.
[b] For 2007.

Government views and policies

Population policy variable	1976	1986	1996	2009
Population size and growth				
View on growth	..	Satisfactory	Satisfactory	Too high
Policy on growth	..	No intervention	No intervention	Lower
Population age structure				
Level of concern about				
Size of the working-age population	..	..	..	Major concern
Ageing of the population	..	..	..	Not a concern
Fertility and family planning				
View on fertility level	..	Satisfactory	Satisfactory	Too high
Policy	..	No intervention	No intervention	No intervention
Access to contraceptive methods	..	No support	No support	Direct support
Adolescent fertility				
Level of concern	..	..	Not a concern	Minor concern
Policies and programmes	..	..	..	No
Health and mortality				
View				
Life expectancy at birth	..	Unacceptable	Unacceptable	Unacceptable
Under-five mortality	..	..	Unacceptable	Unacceptable
Maternal mortality	..	..	..	Unacceptable
Level of concern about HIV/AIDS	..	..	Minor concern	Major concern
Measures to respond to HIV/AIDS*	..	..	..	1,2,3,5
Grounds on which abortion is permitted**	..	..	1	1
Spatial distribution and internal migration				
View on spatial distribution	..	Minor change desired	Minor change desired	Major change desired
Policies on internal migration				
From rural to urban areas	..	..	..	Lower
From rural to rural areas	..	..	..	..
From urban to rural areas	..	..	..	..
From urban to urban areas	..	..	..	..
Into urban agglomerations	..	No intervention	No intervention	Lower
International migration				
Immigration				
View	..	Too high	Too high	Too high
Policy	..	Maintain	Lower	Lower
Permanent settlement	..	..	Lower	Lower
Temporary workers	..	..	Maintain	Lower
Highly skilled workers	..	..	..	Maintain
Family reunification	..	..	Maintain	Maintain
Integration of non-citizens	..	..	No	No
Emigration				
View	..	Satisfactory	Satisfactory	Satisfactory
Policy	..	Maintain	No intervention	No intervention
Encouraging the return of citizens	..	..	No	No

* Measures implemented to respond to HIV/AIDS: (1) blood screening; (2) information/education campaigns; (3) antiretroviral treatment; (4) non-discriminatory policies; (5) distribution of condoms.
** Grounds on which abortion is permitted: (1) to save the woman's life; (2) to preserve physical health; (3) to preserve mental health; (4) rape or incest; (5) foetal impairment; (6) economic or social reasons; (7) on request.

Population indicators

Indicator	1975	1985	1995	2009
Population size and growth				
Population size (thousands)	224	402	624	864
Annual growth rate (percentage)*	6.5	3.4	2.1	1.8
Population age structure				
Percentage of population under age 15	46	45	43	36
Percentage of population aged 60 or over	4	4	4	5
Fertility and family planning				
Total fertility (children per woman)*	7.2	6.6	5.9	3.9
Adolescent fertility rate (per 1,000 women, aged 15 - 19)*	..	..	68.0	23.0
Percentage of births to women under age 20*	..	..	6	3
Percentage of births to women aged 35 or over*	..	..	29	36
Percentage of married women using contraception				
Modern methods	..	..	..	17[a]
All methods	..	..	..	18[a]
Health and mortality				
Life expectancy at birth (years)*				
Males	43	47	50	54
Females	46	50	53	57
Both sexes combined	44	49	52	55
Infant mortality rate (per 1,000 live births)*	154	127	112	85
Under-five mortality (per 1,000 live births)*	..	196	167	125
Maternal mortality ratio (per 100,000 live births) (2005)	..	..	..	650
HIV/AIDS				
People living with HIV/AIDS (thousands)	..	..	4.9	16[b]
Adult prevalence (percentage)	..	..	1.5	3.1[b]
Spatial distribution				
Population density (per sq. km)	10	17	27	37
Urban population (percentage)	67	75	80	88
Annual urban population growth rate (percentage)	10.6	6.6	3.8	2.1
Annual rural population growth rate (percentage)	5.9	6.1	-1.1	-1.2
International migration				
Migrant stock				
Number of migrants (thousands)	29	67	105	114**
As percentage of total population	12.9	16.7	16.9	13.0**

* For the periods 1970-1975, 1980-1985, 1990-1995 and 2005-2010.
** For 2010.
[a] For 2006.
[b] For 2007.

Government views and policies

Population policy variable	1976	1986	1996	2009
Population size and growth				
View on growth	..	Too high	Too high	Satisfactory
Policy on growth	..	Lower	Lower	No intervention
Population age structure				
Level of concern about				
Size of the working-age population	..	..	..	Major concern
Ageing of the population	..	..	..	Major concern
Fertility and family planning				
View on fertility level	..	Too high	Too high	Satisfactory
Policy	..	Lower	Lower	No intervention
Access to contraceptive methods	..	Direct support	Direct support	Direct support
Adolescent fertility				
Level of concern	..	..	..	Major concern
Policies and programmes	..	..	..	Yes
Health and mortality				
View				
Life expectancy at birth	..	Unacceptable	Unacceptable	Acceptable
Under-five mortality	..	..	..	Acceptable
Maternal mortality	..	..	..	Acceptable
Level of concern about HIV/AIDS	..	..	..	Major concern
Measures to respond to HIV/AIDS*	..	..	..	1,2,3,5
Grounds on which abortion is permitted**	..	..	1	1
Spatial distribution and internal migration				
View on spatial distribution	..	Minor change desired	Minor change desired	Satisfactory
Policies on internal migration				
From rural to urban areas	..	..	..	No intervention
From rural to rural areas	..	..	..	No intervention
From urban to rural areas	..	..	..	No intervention
From urban to urban areas	..	..	..	No intervention
Into urban agglomerations	..	..	..	No intervention
International migration				
Immigration				
View	..	Satisfactory	Satisfactory	Satisfactory
Policy	..	Maintain	Maintain	Maintain
Permanent settlement	..	..	Maintain	Maintain
Temporary workers	..	..	..	Maintain
Highly skilled workers	..	..	..	Maintain
Family reunification	..	..	..	Maintain
Integration of non-citizens	..	..	..	Yes
Emigration				
View	..	Too high	Too high	Satisfactory
Policy	..	Maintain	Maintain	No intervention
Encouraging the return of citizens	..	..	..	Yes

* Measures implemented to respond to HIV/AIDS: (1) blood screening; (2) information/education campaigns; (3) antiretroviral treatment; (4) non−discriminatory policies; (5) distribution of condoms.
** Grounds on which abortion is permitted: (1) to save the woman's life; (2) to preserve physical health; (3) to preserve mental health; (4) rape or incest; (5) foetal impairment; (6) economic or social reasons; (7) on request.

Population indicators

Indicator	1975	1985	1995	2009
Population size and growth				
Population size (thousands)	68	72	69	67
Annual growth rate (percentage)*	1.0	-0.4	0.0	-0.3
Population age structure				
Percentage of population under age 15	..	..	..	..
Percentage of population aged 60 or over	..	..	..	..
Fertility and family planning				
Total fertility (children per woman)*	..	..	..	..
Adolescent fertility rate (per 1,000 women, aged 15 - 19)*	..	..	..	..
Percentage of births to women under age 20*	..	..	..	..
Percentage of births to women aged 35 or over*	..	..	..	..
Percentage of married women using contraception				
Modern methods	..	48[a]	..	..
All methods	..	50[a]	..	..
Health and mortality				
Life expectancy at birth (years)*				
Males	..	..	..	..
Females	..	..	..	..
Both sexes combined	..	..	..	..
Infant mortality rate (per 1,000 live births)*	..	..	..	..
Under-five mortality (per 1,000 live births)*	..	..	..	..
Maternal mortality ratio (per 100,000 live births) (2005)	..	..	..	..
HIV/AIDS				
People living with HIV/AIDS (thousands)	..	..	..	..
Adult prevalence (percentage)	..	..	..	..
Spatial distribution				
Population density (per sq. km)	90	95	91	89
Urban population (percentage)	55	66	69	74
Annual urban population growth rate (percentage)	4.5	-0.3	0.5	0.3
Annual rural population growth rate (percentage)	-2.2	-1.9	-1.1	-1.6
International migration				
Migrant stock				
Number of migrants (thousands)	2	2	3	6**
As percentage of total population	2.8	2.9	4.5	8.3**

* For the periods 1970-1975, 1980-1985, 1990-1995 and 2005-2010.
** For 2010.
[a] For 1987.

Government views and policies

Population policy variable	1976	1986	1996	2009
Population size and growth				
View on growth	Too high	Too high	Too high	Too high
Policy on growth	Lower	Lower	Lower	Lower
Population age structure				
Level of concern about				
Size of the working-age population	..	..	..	Major concern
Ageing of the population	..	..	..	Major concern
Fertility and family planning				
View on fertility level	Too high	Too high	Too high	Too high
Policy	Lower	Lower	Lower	Lower
Access to contraceptive methods	Direct support	Direct support	Direct support	Direct support
Adolescent fertility				
Level of concern	..	..	Major concern	Major concern
Policies and programmes	..	..	No	Yes
Health and mortality				
View				
Life expectancy at birth	Unacceptable	Unacceptable	Unacceptable	Unacceptable
Under-five mortality	..	..	Unacceptable	Unacceptable
Maternal mortality	..	..	..	Unacceptable
Level of concern about HIV/AIDS	..	..	Minor concern	Major concern
Measures to respond to HIV/AIDS*	..	..	..	1,2,3,4,5
Grounds on which abortion is permitted**	..	..	1	Not permitted
Spatial distribution and internal migration				
View on spatial distribution	Major change desired	Major change desired	Satisfactory	Major change desired
Policies on internal migration				
From rural to urban areas	..	..	..	Lower
From rural to rural areas	..	..	..	..
From urban to rural areas	..	..	..	..
From urban to urban areas	..	..	..	..
Into urban agglomerations	No intervention	Lower	No intervention	Lower
International migration				
Immigration				
View	Satisfactory	Too high	Too high	Satisfactory
Policy	Maintain	Lower	Lower	Maintain
Permanent settlement	..	..	No intervention	Maintain
Temporary workers	..	..	No intervention	Maintain
Highly skilled workers	..	..	..	Maintain
Family reunification	..	..	No intervention	Maintain
Integration of non-citizens	..	..	No	No
Emigration				
View	Satisfactory	Too high	Too high	Satisfactory
Policy	Maintain	Lower	No intervention	No intervention
Encouraging the return of citizens	No	..	No	Yes

* Measures implemented to respond to HIV/AIDS: (1) blood screening; (2) information/education campaigns; (3) antiretroviral treatment; (4) non-discriminatory policies; (5) distribution of condoms.
** Grounds on which abortion is permitted: (1) to save the woman's life; (2) to preserve physical health; (3) to preserve mental health; (4) rape or incest; (5) foetal impairment; (6) economic or social reasons; (7) on request.

Population indicators

Indicator	1975	1985	1995	2009
Population size and growth				
Population size (thousands)	5 261	6 637	8 124	10 090
Annual growth rate (percentage)*	2.7	2.3	1.9	1.4
Population age structure				
Percentage of population under age 15	46	40	37	31
Percentage of population aged 60 or over	4	5	7	9
Fertility and family planning				
Total fertility (children per woman)*	5.7	4.2	3.3	2.7
Adolescent fertility rate (per 1,000 women, aged 15 - 19)*	..	..	114.0	109.0
Percentage of births to women under age 20*	..	..	17	20
Percentage of births to women aged 35 or over*	..	..	11	9
Percentage of married women using contraception				
Modern methods	26	47[a]	59[b]	70[c]
All methods	32	50[a]	64[b]	73[c]
Health and mortality				
Life expectancy at birth (years)*				
Males	58	62	66	70
Females	62	66	71	75
Both sexes combined	60	64	69	72
Infant mortality rate (per 1,000 live births)*	96	75	48	30
Under-five mortality (per 1,000 live births)*	..	89	56	33
Maternal mortality ratio (per 100,000 live births) (2005)	..	..	..	150
HIV/AIDS				
People living with HIV/AIDS (thousands)	..	..	53	62[c]
Adult prevalence (percentage)	..	..	1.2	1.1[c]
Spatial distribution				
Population density (per sq. km)	108	137	167	208
Urban population (percentage)	46	54	58	70
Annual urban population growth rate (percentage)	4.9	2.5	3.4	2.4
Annual rural population growth rate (percentage)	0.4	1.4	-0.5	-0.9
International migration				
Migrant stock				
Number of migrants (thousands)	216	263	322	434**
As percentage of total population	4.1	4.0	4.0	4.2**

* For the periods 1970-1975, 1980-1985, 1990-1995 and 2005-2010.
** For 2010.
[a] For 1986.
[b] For 1996.
[c] For 2007.

Government views and policies

Population policy variable	1976	1986	1996	2009
Population size and growth				
View on growth	Too high	Satisfactory	Satisfactory	Satisfactory
Policy on growth	No intervention	No intervention	No intervention	No intervention
Population age structure				
Level of concern about				
Size of the working-age population	..	..	..	Not a concern
Ageing of the population	..	..	..	Minor concern
Fertility and family planning				
View on fertility level	Too high	Satisfactory	Too high	Satisfactory
Policy	No intervention	No intervention	Lower	No intervention
Access to contraceptive methods	Direct support	Direct support	Direct support	Direct support
Adolescent fertility				
Level of concern	..	..	Major concern	Major concern
Policies and programmes	..	..	Yes	Yes
Health and mortality				
View				
Life expectancy at birth	Acceptable	Unacceptable	Unacceptable	Unacceptable
Under-five mortality	..	..	Unacceptable	Unacceptable
Maternal mortality	..	..	..	Unacceptable
Level of concern about HIV/AIDS	..	..	Minor concern	Major concern
Measures to respond to HIV/AIDS*	..	..	..	1,2,3,4,5
Grounds on which abortion is permitted**	..	..	1,2,4	1,2
Spatial distribution and internal migration				
View on spatial distribution	Major change desired	Major change desired	Major change desired	Major change desired
Policies on internal migration				
From rural to urban areas	..	..	..	No intervention
From rural to rural areas	..	..	..	No intervention
From urban to rural areas	..	..	..	No intervention
From urban to urban areas	..	..	..	No intervention
Into urban agglomerations	No intervention	Lower	Lower	No intervention
International migration				
Immigration				
View	Satisfactory	Too high	Satisfactory	Too high
Policy	Maintain	Maintain	Lower	Lower
Permanent settlement	..	..	No intervention	No intervention
Temporary workers	..	..	Lower	No intervention
Highly skilled workers	..	..	..	No intervention
Family reunification	..	..	Lower	No intervention
Integration of non-citizens	..	..	No	Yes
Emigration				
View	Satisfactory	Satisfactory	Satisfactory	Too high
Policy	Maintain	Maintain	No intervention	Lower
Encouraging the return of citizens	Yes	..	No	Yes

* Measures implemented to respond to HIV/AIDS: (1) blood screening; (2) information/education campaigns; (3) antiretroviral treatment; (4) non-discriminatory policies; (5) distribution of condoms.
** Grounds on which abortion is permitted: (1) to save the woman's life; (2) to preserve physical health; (3) to preserve mental health; (4) rape or incest; (5) foetal impairment; (6) economic or social reasons; (7) on request.

Population indicators

Indicator	1975	1985	1995	2009
Population size and growth				
Population size (thousands)	6 910	9 103	11 407	13 625
Annual growth rate (percentage)[*]	2.9	2.7	2.1	1.1
Population age structure				
Percentage of population under age 15	44	41	36	31
Percentage of population aged 60 or over	6	6	7	9
Fertility and family planning				
Total fertility (children per woman)[*]	6.0	4.7	3.4	2.6
Adolescent fertility rate (per 1,000 women, aged 15 - 19)[*]	..	..	84.0	83.0
Percentage of births to women under age 20[*]	..	..	12	16
Percentage of births to women aged 35 or over[*]	..	..	19	16
Percentage of married women using contraception				
Modern methods	26[a]	36[b]	46[c]	58[d]
All methods	34[a]	44[b]	57[c]	73[d]
Health and mortality				
Life expectancy at birth (years)[*]				
Males	57	62	68	72
Females	60	67	73	78
Both sexes combined	59	65	70	75
Infant mortality rate (per 1,000 live births)[*]	95	68	44	21
Under-five mortality (per 1,000 live births)[*]	..	95	57	26
Maternal mortality ratio (per 100,000 live births) (2005)	..	..	..	210
HIV/AIDS				
People living with HIV/AIDS (thousands)	..	..	10	26[e]
Adult prevalence (percentage)	..	..	0.2	0.3[e]
Spatial distribution				
Population density (per sq. km)	24	32	40	48
Urban population (percentage)	42	51	58	66
Annual urban population growth rate (percentage)	5.0	4.0	2.6	2.1
Annual rural population growth rate (percentage)	1.3	0.9	0.5	-0.8
International migration				
Migrant stock				
Number of migrants (thousands)	59	77	88	394[**]
As percentage of total population	0.9	0.8	0.8	2.9[**]

[*] For the periods 1970-1975, 1980-1985, 1990-1995 and 2005-2010.
[**] For 2010.
[a] For 1979.
[b] For 1987.
[c] For 1994.
[d] For 2004.
[e] For 2007.

Government views and policies

Population policy variable	1976	1986	1996	2009
Population size and growth				
View on growth	Too high	Too high	Too high	Too high
Policy on growth	Lower	Lower	Lower	Lower
Population age structure				
Level of concern about				
Size of the working-age population	..	..	..	Major concern
Ageing of the population	..	..	..	Minor concern
Fertility and family planning				
View on fertility level	Too high	Too high	Too high	Too high
Policy	Lower	Lower	Lower	Lower
Access to contraceptive methods	Direct support	Direct support	Direct support	Direct support
Adolescent fertility				
Level of concern	..	..	Major concern	Minor concern
Policies and programmes	..	..	No	Yes
Health and mortality				
View				
Life expectancy at birth	Unacceptable	Unacceptable	Acceptable	Acceptable
Under-five mortality	..	..	Acceptable	Unacceptable
Maternal mortality	..	..	..	Unacceptable
Level of concern about HIV/AIDS	..	..	Minor concern	Minor concern
Measures to respond to HIV/AIDS*	..	..	..	1,2,3,4,5
Grounds on which abortion is permitted**	..	..	1	1
Spatial distribution and internal migration				
View on spatial distribution	Major change desired	Major change desired	Major change desired	Major change desired
Policies on internal migration				
From rural to urban areas	..	..	..	Lower
From rural to rural areas	..	..	..	No intervention
From urban to rural areas	..	..	..	No intervention
From urban to urban areas	..	..	..	Raise
Into urban agglomerations	Lower	Lower	No intervention	Lower
International migration				
Immigration				
View	Satisfactory	Satisfactory	Satisfactory	Too high
Policy	Maintain	Maintain	Lower	Lower
Permanent settlement	..	..	Lower	Lower
Temporary workers	..	..	Maintain	Lower
Highly skilled workers	..	..	..	Maintain
Family reunification	..	..	Lower	Maintain
Integration of non-citizens	..	..	No	Yes
Emigration				
View	Satisfactory	Satisfactory	Too low	Too low
Policy	Maintain	Maintain	Raise	Maintain
Encouraging the return of citizens	No	..	No	Yes

* Measures implemented to respond to HIV/AIDS: (1) blood screening; (2) information/education campaigns; (3) antiretroviral treatment; (4) non−discriminatory policies; (5) distribution of condoms.
** Grounds on which abortion is permitted: (1) to save the woman's life; (2) to preserve physical health; (3) to preserve mental health; (4) rape or incest; (5) foetal impairment; (6) economic or social reasons; (7) on request.

Population indicators

Indicator	1975	1985	1995	2009
Population size and growth				
Population size (thousands)	39 599	50 655	63 858	82 999
Annual growth rate (percentage)*	2.1	2.6	2.0	1.8
Population age structure				
Percentage of population under age 15	42	42	40	32
Percentage of population aged 60 or over	6	6	6	7
Fertility and family planning				
Total fertility (children per woman)*	5.7	5.5	3.9	2.9
Adolescent fertility rate (per 1,000 women, aged 15 - 19)*	..	..	69.0	39.0
Percentage of births to women under age 20*	..	..	9	7
Percentage of births to women aged 35 or over*	..	..	16	12
Percentage of married women using contraception				
Modern methods	22	29[a]	46	58[b]
All methods	25	30[a]	48	60[b]
Health and mortality				
Life expectancy at birth (years)*				
Males	51	57	63	68
Females	53	60	66	72
Both sexes combined	52	58	64	70
Infant mortality rate (per 1,000 live births)*	138	97	64	35
Under-five mortality (per 1,000 live births)*	..	128	79	41
Maternal mortality ratio (per 100,000 live births) (2005)	..	..	..	130
HIV/AIDS				
People living with HIV/AIDS (thousands)	..	..	2.5	9.2[c]
Adult prevalence (percentage)	..	..	..	..
Spatial distribution				
Population density (per sq. km)	40	51	64	83
Urban population (percentage)	43	44	43	43
Annual urban population growth rate (percentage)	2.7	2.4	1.5	1.9
Annual rural population growth rate (percentage)	1.7	2.4	2.1	1.6
International migration				
Migrant stock				
Number of migrants (thousands)	196	183	174	245**
As percentage of total population	0.5	0.4	0.3	0.3**

* For the periods 1970-1975, 1980-1985, 1990-1995 and 2005-2010.
** For 2010.
[a] For 1984.
[b] For 2008.
[c] For 2007.

Government views and policies

Population policy variable	1976	1986	1996	2009
Population size and growth				
View on growth	Too high	Too high	Too high	Satisfactory
Policy on growth	Lower	Lower	Lower	No intervention
Population age structure				
Level of concern about				
Size of the working-age population	..	..	..	Not a concern
Ageing of the population	..	..	..	Minor concern
Fertility and family planning				
View on fertility level	Too high	Too high	Too high	Satisfactory
Policy	Lower	Lower	Lower	No intervention
Access to contraceptive methods	Direct support	Direct support	Direct support	Direct support
Adolescent fertility				
Level of concern	..	..	Minor concern	Major concern
Policies and programmes	..	..	No	Yes
Health and mortality				
View				
Life expectancy at birth	Unacceptable	Unacceptable	Unacceptable	Unacceptable
Under-five mortality	..	..	Unacceptable	Unacceptable
Maternal mortality	..	..	..	Unacceptable
Level of concern about HIV/AIDS	..	..	Major concern	Major concern
Measures to respond to HIV/AIDS*	..	..	..	1,2,3,4,5
Grounds on which abortion is permitted**	..	..	Not permitted	Not permitted
Spatial distribution and internal migration				
View on spatial distribution	Major change desired	Major change desired	Major change desired	Major change desired
Policies on internal migration				
From rural to urban areas	..	..	..	Lower
From rural to rural areas	..	..	..	No intervention
From urban to rural areas	..	..	..	No intervention
From urban to urban areas	..	..	..	No intervention
Into urban agglomerations	No intervention	No intervention	No intervention	Lower
International migration				
Immigration				
View	Satisfactory	Satisfactory	Satisfactory	Satisfactory
Policy	Maintain	Maintain	No intervention	No intervention
Permanent settlement	..	..	No intervention	No intervention
Temporary workers	..	..	No intervention	No intervention
Highly skilled workers	..	..	..	Maintain
Family reunification	..	..	No intervention	Maintain
Integration of non-citizens	..	..	Yes	No
Emigration				
View	Satisfactory	Too high	Satisfactory	Too high
Policy	Maintain	Lower	No intervention	Lower
Encouraging the return of citizens	No	..	No	Yes

* Measures implemented to respond to HIV/AIDS: (1) blood screening; (2) information/education campaigns; (3) antiretroviral treatment; (4) non-discriminatory policies; (5) distribution of condoms.
** Grounds on which abortion is permitted: (1) to save the woman's life; (2) to preserve physical health; (3) to preserve mental health; (4) rape or incest; (5) foetal impairment; (6) economic or social reasons; (7) on request.

Population indicators

Indicator	1975	1985	1995	2009
Population size and growth				
Population size (thousands)	4 235	4 999	5 728	6 163
Annual growth rate (percentage)*	2.5	1.4	1.4	0.4
Population age structure				
Percentage of population under age 15	45	44	39	32
Percentage of population aged 60 or over	6	6	7	10
Fertility and family planning				
Total fertility (children per woman)*	5.9	4.8	3.7	2.3
Adolescent fertility rate (per 1,000 women, aged 15 - 19)*	..	..	117.0	83.0
Percentage of births to women under age 20*	..	..	16	18
Percentage of births to women aged 35 or over*	..	..	17	14
Percentage of married women using contraception				
Modern methods	18	46	54[a]	66[b]
All methods	19	48	60[a]	73[b]
Health and mortality				
Life expectancy at birth (years)*				
Males	53	51	63	67
Females	61	64	73	76
Both sexes combined	57	57	68	71
Infant mortality rate (per 1,000 live births)*	105	77	40	22
Under-five mortality (per 1,000 live births)*	..	118	49	26
Maternal mortality ratio (per 100,000 live births) (2005)	..	..	..	170
HIV/AIDS				
People living with HIV/AIDS (thousands)	..	..	13	35[c]
Adult prevalence (percentage)	..	..	0.4	0.8[c]
Spatial distribution				
Population density (per sq. km)	201	238	272	293
Urban population (percentage)	42	47	54	61
Annual urban population growth rate (percentage)	3.7	2.1	4.4	1.9
Annual rural population growth rate (percentage)	1.6	0.1	-0.8	0.5
International migration				
Migrant stock				
Number of migrants (thousands)	31	28	28	40**
As percentage of total population	0.7	0.6	0.5	0.7**

* For the periods 1970-1975, 1980-1985, 1990-1995 and 2005-2010.
** For 2010.
[a] For 1998.
[b] For 2008.
[c] For 2007.

Government views and policies

Population policy variable	1976	1986	1996	2009
Population size and growth				
View on growth	Too low	Too low	Satisfactory	Satisfactory
Policy on growth	Raise	Raise	Maintain	Maintain
Population age structure				
Level of concern about				
Size of the working-age population	..	..	..	..
Ageing of the population	..	..	..	Major concern
Fertility and family planning				
View on fertility level	Too low	Too low	Satisfactory	Satisfactory
Policy	No intervention	Raise	Maintain	Maintain
Access to contraceptive methods	No support	No support	No support	Direct support
Adolescent fertility				
Level of concern	..	..	..	Major concern
Policies and programmes	..	..	..	Yes
Health and mortality				
View				
Life expectancy at birth	Unacceptable	Unacceptable	Unacceptable	Unacceptable
Under-five mortality	..	..	Unacceptable	Unacceptable
Maternal mortality	..	..	..	Unacceptable
Level of concern about HIV/AIDS	..	..	Major concern	Major concern
Measures to respond to HIV/AIDS*	..	..	..	1,2,3,5
Grounds on which abortion is permitted**	..	..	1	1,2,3
Spatial distribution and internal migration				
View on spatial distribution	Major change desired	Major change desired	Satisfactory	Minor change desired
Policies on internal migration				
From rural to urban areas	..	..	..	Lower
From rural to rural areas	..	..	..	..
From urban to rural areas	..	..	..	..
From urban to urban areas	..	..	..	..
Into urban agglomerations	Lower	..	No intervention	Lower
International migration				
Immigration				
View	Too low	Too low	Satisfactory	Satisfactory
Policy	Raise	Raise	No intervention	Maintain
Permanent settlement	..	..	No intervention	Maintain
Temporary workers	..	..	..	Maintain
Highly skilled workers	..	..	..	Maintain
Family reunification	..	..	..	..
Integration of non-citizens	..	..	No	..
Emigration				
View	Satisfactory	Satisfactory	Satisfactory	Satisfactory
Policy	Maintain	Maintain	No intervention	Lower
Encouraging the return of citizens	Yes	..	Yes	..

* Measures implemented to respond to HIV/AIDS: (1) blood screening; (2) information/education campaigns; (3) antiretroviral treatment; (4) non-discriminatory policies; (5) distribution of condoms.
** Grounds on which abortion is permitted: (1) to save the woman's life; (2) to preserve physical health; (3) to preserve mental health; (4) rape or incest; (5) foetal impairment; (6) economic or social reasons; (7) on request.

Population indicators

Indicator	1975	1985	1995	2009
Population size and growth				
Population size (thousands)	238	314	452	676
Annual growth rate (percentage)*	-4.0	7.1	3.5	2.6
Population age structure				
Percentage of population under age 15	45	35	43	41
Percentage of population aged 60 or over	8	7	6	4
Fertility and family planning				
Total fertility (children per woman)*	5.7	5.8	5.9	5.4
Adolescent fertility rate (per 1,000 women, aged 15 - 19)*	..	..	134.0	123.0
Percentage of births to women under age 20*	..	..	11	11
Percentage of births to women aged 35 or over*	..	..	28	26
Percentage of married women using contraception				
Modern methods	..	..	6[a]	..
All methods	..	..	10[a]	..
Health and mortality				
Life expectancy at birth (years)*				
Males	39	42	46	49
Females	42	45	49	51
Both sexes combined	41	44	48	50
Infant mortality rate (per 1,000 live births)*	157	138	118	100
Under-five mortality (per 1,000 live births)*	..	241	205	168
Maternal mortality ratio (per 100,000 live births) (2005)	..	..	..	680
HIV/AIDS				
People living with HIV/AIDS (thousands)	..	..	5.3	11[b]
Adult prevalence (percentage)	..	..	2.5	3.4[b]
Spatial distribution				
Population density (per sq. km)	8	11	16	24
Urban population (percentage)	27	30	39	39
Annual urban population growth rate (percentage)	-4.2	6.9	2.4	2.9
Annual rural population growth rate (percentage)	-4.6	2.5	2.4	2.1
International migration				
Migrant stock				
Number of migrants (thousands)	7	4	4	7**
As percentage of total population	3.1	1.2	0.8	1.1**

* For the periods 1970-1975, 1980-1985, 1990-1995 and 2005-2010.
** For 2010.
[a] For 2000.
[b] For 2007.

Government views and policies

Population policy variable	1976	1986	1996	2009
Population size and growth				
View on growth	..	..	Too high	Too high
Policy on growth	..	..	Lower	Lower
Population age structure				
Level of concern about				
Size of the working-age population	..	..	..	..
Ageing of the population	..	..	..	Minor concern
Fertility and family planning				
View on fertility level	..	..	Too high	Too high
Policy	..	..	Lower	Lower
Access to contraceptive methods	..	..	..	Direct support
Adolescent fertility				
Level of concern	..	..	..	Minor concern
Policies and programmes	..	..	..	Yes
Health and mortality				
View				
Life expectancy at birth	..	..	Unacceptable	Unacceptable
Under-five mortality	..	..	..	Unacceptable
Maternal mortality	..	..	..	Unacceptable
Level of concern about HIV/AIDS	..	..	..	Major concern
Measures to respond to HIV/AIDS*	..	..	..	1,2,3,5
Grounds on which abortion is permitted**	..	..	1,2,3	1,2,3
Spatial distribution and internal migration				
View on spatial distribution	..	..	..	Major change desired
Policies on internal migration				
From rural to urban areas	..	..	..	No intervention
From rural to rural areas	..	..	..	No intervention
From urban to rural areas	..	..	..	No intervention
From urban to urban areas	..	..	..	No intervention
Into urban agglomerations	..	..	..	No intervention
International migration				
Immigration				
View	..	..	Satisfactory	Satisfactory
Policy	..	..	No intervention	No intervention
Permanent settlement	..	..	..	..
Temporary workers	..	..	..	..
Highly skilled workers	..	..	..	..
Family reunification	..	..	..	..
Integration of non-citizens	..	..	..	..
Emigration				
View	..	..	Satisfactory	Satisfactory
Policy	..	..	No intervention	No intervention
Encouraging the return of citizens	..	..	Yes	Yes

* Measures implemented to respond to HIV/AIDS: (1) blood screening; (2) information/education campaigns; (3) antiretroviral treatment; (4) non-discriminatory policies; (5) distribution of condoms.
** Grounds on which abortion is permitted: (1) to save the woman's life; (2) to preserve physical health; (3) to preserve mental health; (4) rape or incest; (5) foetal impairment; (6) economic or social reasons; (7) on request.

Population indicators

Indicator	1975	1985	1995	2009
Population size and growth				
Population size (thousands)	2 115	2 807	3 206	5 073
Annual growth rate (percentage)*	2.7	2.6	0.3	3.1
Population age structure				
Percentage of population under age 15	45	48	47	42
Percentage of population aged 60 or over	4	5	4	4
Fertility and family planning				
Total fertility (children per woman)*	6.5	6.5	6.1	4.7
Adolescent fertility rate (per 1,000 women, aged 15 - 19)*	..	..	113.0	67.0
Percentage of births to women under age 20*	..	..	9	7
Percentage of births to women aged 35 or over*	..	..	30	30
Percentage of married women using contraception				
Modern methods	..	..	4	5[a]
All methods	..	..	8	8[a]
Health and mortality				
Life expectancy at birth (years)*				
Males	42	42	48	57
Females	46	46	52	62
Both sexes combined	44	44	50	59
Infant mortality rate (per 1,000 live births)*	133	116	90	54
Under-five mortality (per 1,000 live births)*	..	175	134	75
Maternal mortality ratio (per 100,000 live births) (2005)	..	..	..	450
HIV/AIDS				
People living with HIV/AIDS (thousands)	..	..	17	38[b]
Adult prevalence (percentage)	..	..	0.9	1.3[b]
Spatial distribution				
Population density (per sq. km)	18	24	27	43
Urban population (percentage)	13	15	17	21
Annual urban population growth rate (percentage)	4.4	3.5	2.8	5.3
Annual rural population growth rate (percentage)	2.9	2.6	1.4	2.5
International migration				
Migrant stock				
Number of migrants (thousands)	10	11	12	16**
As percentage of total population	0.5	0.4	0.4	0.3**

* For the periods 1970-1975, 1980-1985, 1990-1995 and 2005-2010.
** For 2010.
[a] For 2002.
[b] For 2007.

Government views and policies

Population policy variable	1976	1986	1996	2009
Population size and growth				
View on growth	..	..	Satisfactory	Satisfactory
Policy on growth	..	..	No intervention	Raise
Population age structure				
Level of concern about				
Size of the working-age population	..	..	..	Not a concern
Ageing of the population	..	..	..	Major concern
Fertility and family planning				
View on fertility level	..	..	Too low	Too low
Policy	..	..	Raise	Raise
Access to contraceptive methods	..	..	No support	Indirect support
Adolescent fertility				
Level of concern	..	..	Not a concern	Not a concern
Policies and programmes	..	..	No	No
Health and mortality				
View				
Life expectancy at birth	..	..	Acceptable	Unacceptable
Under-five mortality	..	..	..	Acceptable
Maternal mortality	..	..	..	Acceptable
Level of concern about HIV/AIDS	..	..	Minor concern	Major concern
Measures to respond to HIV/AIDS*	..	..	..	1,2,3,5
Grounds on which abortion is permitted**	..	..	1,2,3,4,5,6,7	1,2,3,4,5,6,7
Spatial distribution and internal migration				
View on spatial distribution	..	..	Satisfactory	Minor change desired
Policies on internal migration				
From rural to urban areas	..	..	..	No intervention
From rural to rural areas	..	..	..	No intervention
From urban to rural areas	..	..	..	No intervention
From urban to urban areas	..	..	..	No intervention
Into urban agglomerations	..	..	No intervention	No intervention
International migration				
Immigration				
View	..	..	Too high	Satisfactory
Policy	..	..	Lower	Maintain
Permanent settlement	..	..	Lower	No intervention
Temporary workers	..	..	No intervention	No intervention
Highly skilled workers	..	..	..	Raise
Family reunification	..	..	Lower	Maintain
Integration of non-citizens	..	..	Yes	Yes
Emigration				
View	..	..	Satisfactory	Satisfactory
Policy	..	..	Maintain	No intervention
Encouraging the return of citizens	..	..	No	Yes

* Measures implemented to respond to HIV/AIDS: (1) blood screening; (2) information/education campaigns; (3) antiretroviral treatment; (4) non-discriminatory policies; (5) distribution of condoms.

** Grounds on which abortion is permitted: (1) to save the woman's life; (2) to preserve physical health; (3) to preserve mental health; (4) rape or incest; (5) foetal impairment; (6) economic or social reasons; (7) on request.

Population indicators

Indicator	1975	1985	1995	2009
Population size and growth				
Population size (thousands)	1 432	1 525	1 439	1 340
Annual growth rate (percentage)*	1.0	0.7	-1.7	-0.1
Population age structure				
Percentage of population under age 15	22	22	21	15
Percentage of population aged 60 or over	17	16	19	22
Fertility and family planning				
Total fertility (children per woman)*	2.2	2.1	1.6	1.6
Adolescent fertility rate (per 1,000 women, aged 15 - 19)*	..	..	47.0	21.0
Percentage of births to women under age 20*	..	..	15	7
Percentage of births to women aged 35 or over*	..	..	6	13
Percentage of married women using contraception				
Modern methods	..	..	56[a]	..
All methods	..	..	70[a]	..
Health and mortality				
Life expectancy at birth (years)*				
Males	66	64	63	68
Females	75	74	74	78
Both sexes combined	71	70	68	73
Infant mortality rate (per 1,000 live births)*	21	16	14	8
Under-five mortality (per 1,000 live births)*	..	21	18	10
Maternal mortality ratio (per 100,000 live births) (2005)	..	..	..	25
HIV/AIDS				
People living with HIV/AIDS (thousands)	..	..	..	9.9[b]
Adult prevalence (percentage)	..	..	..	1.3[b]
Spatial distribution				
Population density (per sq. km)	32	34	32	30
Urban population (percentage)	68	71	70	69
Annual urban population growth rate (percentage)	1.4	1.2	-1.6	-0.3
Annual rural population growth rate (percentage)	-0.9	0.2	-1.1	-0.5
International migration				
Migrant stock				
Number of migrants (thousands)	..	..	309	182**
As percentage of total population	0.0	0.0	21.4	13.6**

* For the periods 1970-1975, 1980-1985, 1990-1995 and 2005-2010.
** For 2010.
[a] For 1994.
[b] For 2007.

Government views and policies

Population policy variable	1976	1986	1996	2009
Population size and growth				
View on growth	Satisfactory	Too high	Too high	Too high
Policy on growth	No intervention	No intervention	No intervention	Lower
Population age structure				
Level of concern about				
Size of the working-age population	..	..	..	Major concern
Ageing of the population	..	..	..	Minor concern
Fertility and family planning				
View on fertility level	Satisfactory	Too high	Too high	Too high
Policy	No intervention	No intervention	Lower	Lower
Access to contraceptive methods	Indirect support	Direct support	Direct support	Direct support
Adolescent fertility				
Level of concern	..	..	Major concern	Major concern
Policies and programmes	..	..	Yes	No
Health and mortality				
View				
Life expectancy at birth	Unacceptable	Unacceptable	Unacceptable	Unacceptable
Under-five mortality	..	..	Unacceptable	Unacceptable
Maternal mortality	..	..	..	Unacceptable
Level of concern about HIV/AIDS	..	..	Major concern	Major concern
Measures to respond to HIV/AIDS*	..	..	..	1,2,3,5
Grounds on which abortion is permitted**	..	..	1,2	1,2,3,4,5
Spatial distribution and internal migration				
View on spatial distribution	Major change desired	Minor change desired	Major change desired	Major change desired
Policies on internal migration				
From rural to urban areas	..	..	..	Lower
From rural to rural areas	..	..	..	No intervention
From urban to rural areas	..	..	..	Raise
From urban to urban areas	..	..	..	No intervention
Into urban agglomerations	No intervention	No intervention	No intervention	Lower
International migration				
Immigration				
View	Satisfactory	Satisfactory	Satisfactory	Satisfactory
Policy	Maintain	Maintain	No intervention	No intervention
Permanent settlement	..	..	..	No intervention
Temporary workers	..	..	..	No intervention
Highly skilled workers	..	..	..	No intervention
Family reunification	..	..	..	No intervention
Integration of non-citizens	..	..	..	No
Emigration				
View	Satisfactory	Satisfactory	Satisfactory	Satisfactory
Policy	Maintain	Maintain	No intervention	No intervention
Encouraging the return of citizens	..	..	..	Yes

* Measures implemented to respond to HIV/AIDS: (1) blood screening; (2) information/education campaigns; (3) antiretroviral treatment; (4) non-discriminatory policies; (5) distribution of condoms.
** Grounds on which abortion is permitted: (1) to save the woman's life; (2) to preserve physical health; (3) to preserve mental health; (4) rape or incest; (5) foetal impairment; (6) economic or social reasons; (7) on request.

Population indicators

Indicator	1975	1985	1995	2009
Population size and growth				
Population size (thousands)	32 945	41 049	56 983	82 825
Annual growth rate (percentage)[*]	2.6	3.0	3.3	2.6
Population age structure				
Percentage of population under age 15	45	45	46	44
Percentage of population aged 60 or over	5	5	5	5
Fertility and family planning				
Total fertility (children per woman)[*]	6.8	6.9	7.0	5.4
Adolescent fertility rate (per 1,000 women, aged 15 - 19)[*]	..	..	116.0	104.0
Percentage of births to women under age 20[*]	..	..	8	10
Percentage of births to women aged 35 or over[*]	..	..	29	24
Percentage of married women using contraception				
Modern methods	..	..	3[a]	14[b]
All methods	..	..	3[a]	15[b]
Health and mortality				
Life expectancy at birth (years)[*]				
Males	42	42	47	54
Females	45	45	50	56
Both sexes combined	44	43	48	55
Infant mortality rate (per 1,000 live births)[*]	140	140	115	79
Under-five mortality (per 1,000 live births)[*]	..	240	200	131
Maternal mortality ratio (per 100,000 live births) (2005)	..	..	..	720
HIV/AIDS				
People living with HIV/AIDS (thousands)	..	..	730	980[c]
Adult prevalence (percentage)	..	..	2.4	2.1[c]
Spatial distribution				
Population density (per sq. km)	30	37	52	75
Urban population (percentage)	9	11	14	17
Annual urban population growth rate (percentage)	3.7	5.2	4.4	4.3
Annual rural population growth rate (percentage)	1.6	3.0	2.8	2.1
International migration				
Migrant stock				
Number of migrants (thousands)	392	584	795	548[**]
As percentage of total population	1.2	1.4	1.4	0.6[**]

[*] For the periods 1970-1975, 1980-1985, 1990-1995 and 2005-2010.
[**] For 2010.
[a] For 1997.
[b] For 2005.
[c] For 2007.

Government views and policies

Population policy variable	1976	1986	1996	2009
Population size and growth				
View on growth	Too high	Too high	Satisfactory	Satisfactory
Policy on growth	Lower	Lower	Maintain	Maintain
Population age structure				
Level of concern about				
Size of the working-age population	..	..	..	Major concern
Ageing of the population	..	..	..	Minor concern
Fertility and family planning				
View on fertility level	Too high	Too high	Too high	Satisfactory
Policy	Lower	Lower	Lower	Lower
Access to contraceptive methods	Direct support	Direct support	Direct support	Direct support
Adolescent fertility				
Level of concern	..	..	..	Minor concern
Policies and programmes	..	..	..	Yes
Health and mortality				
View				
Life expectancy at birth	Acceptable	Acceptable	Acceptable	Acceptable
Under-five mortality	..	..	..	Acceptable
Maternal mortality	..	..	..	Acceptable
Level of concern about HIV/AIDS	..	..	..	Major concern
Measures to respond to HIV/AIDS*	..	..	..	1,2,3,4,5
Grounds on which abortion is permitted**	..	..	1,2,3	1,2,3,4,5
Spatial distribution and internal migration				
View on spatial distribution	Major change desired	Major change desired	Minor change desired	Major change desired
Policies on internal migration				
From rural to urban areas	..	..	..	Lower
From rural to rural areas	..	..	..	..
From urban to rural areas	..	..	..	..
From urban to urban areas	..	..	..	..
Into urban agglomerations	No intervention	Lower	..	Lower
International migration				
Immigration				
View	Satisfactory	Satisfactory	Satisfactory	Satisfactory
Policy	Maintain	Maintain	Maintain	Maintain
Permanent settlement	..	..	Maintain	Maintain
Temporary workers	..	..	..	Maintain
Highly skilled workers	..	..	..	Maintain
Family reunification	..	..	..	Maintain
Integration of non-citizens	..	..	..	..
Emigration				
View	Satisfactory	Satisfactory	Satisfactory	Too high
Policy	Maintain	Lower	No intervention	Lower
Encouraging the return of citizens	No	..	..	No

* Measures implemented to respond to HIV/AIDS: (1) blood screening; (2) information/education campaigns; (3) antiretroviral treatment; (4) non−discriminatory policies; (5) distribution of condoms.
** Grounds on which abortion is permitted: (1) to save the woman's life; (2) to preserve physical health; (3) to preserve mental health; (4) rape or incest; (5) foetal impairment; (6) economic or social reasons; (7) on request.

Population indicators

Indicator	1975	1985	1995	2009
Population size and growth				
Population size (thousands)	576	709	768	849
Annual growth rate (percentage)*	2.0	2.2	1.2	0.6
Population age structure				
Percentage of population under age 15	40	39	36	31
Percentage of population aged 60 or over	4	5	5	8
Fertility and family planning				
Total fertility (children per woman)*	4.2	3.8	3.4	2.8
Adolescent fertility rate (per 1,000 women, aged 15 - 19)*	..	..	55.0	32.0
Percentage of births to women under age 20*	..	..	8	6
Percentage of births to women aged 35 or over*	..	..	14	16
Percentage of married women using contraception				
Modern methods	35[a]	..	..	..
All methods	41[a]	..	..	..
Health and mortality				
Life expectancy at birth (years)*				
Males	59	63	65	67
Females	63	67	69	71
Both sexes combined	61	65	67	69
Infant mortality rate (per 1,000 live births)*	52	40	35	20
Under-five mortality (per 1,000 live births)*	..	51	44	24
Maternal mortality ratio (per 100,000 live births) (2005)	..	..	..	210
HIV/AIDS				
People living with HIV/AIDS (thousands)	..	..	..	..
Adult prevalence (percentage)	..	..	<0.1	0.1[b]
Spatial distribution				
Population density (per sq. km)	32	39	42	46
Urban population (percentage)	37	39	45	53
Annual urban population growth rate (percentage)	2.9	1.3	2.8	1.6
Annual rural population growth rate (percentage)	1.2	0.7	-0.4	-0.5
International migration				
Migrant stock				
Number of migrants (thousands)	15	13	15	19**
As percentage of total population	2.6	1.8	1.9	2.2**

* For the periods 1970-1975, 1980-1985, 1990-1995 and 2005-2010.
** For 2010.
[a] For 1974.
[b] For 2007.

FINLAND

World Population Policies 2009

Government views and policies

Population policy variable	1976	1986	1996	2009
Population size and growth				
View on growth	Too low	Satisfactory	Satisfactory	Satisfactory
Policy on growth	No intervention	No intervention	No intervention	No intervention
Population age structure				
Level of concern about				
Size of the working-age population	..	..	..	Major concern
Ageing of the population	..	..	..	Major concern
Fertility and family planning				
View on fertility level	Too low	Satisfactory	Satisfactory	Satisfactory
Policy	Raise	No intervention	Raise	Maintain
Access to contraceptive methods	Direct support	Direct support	Direct support	Direct support
Adolescent fertility				
Level of concern	..	..	Minor concern	Minor concern
Policies and programmes	..	..	No	Yes
Health and mortality				
View				
Life expectancy at birth	Unacceptable	Acceptable	Acceptable	Unacceptable
Under-five mortality	..	..	Acceptable	Acceptable
Maternal mortality	..	..	..	Acceptable
Level of concern about HIV/AIDS	..	..	Major concern	Major concern
Measures to respond to HIV/AIDS*	..	..	..	1,2,3,5
Grounds on which abortion is permitted**	..	..	1,2,3,4,5,6	1,2,3,4,5,6
Spatial distribution and internal migration				
View on spatial distribution	Minor change desired	Satisfactory	Minor change desired	Major change desired
Policies on internal migration				
From rural to urban areas	..	..	..	Lower
From rural to rural areas	..	..	..	Maintain
From urban to rural areas	..	..	..	Raise
From urban to urban areas	..	..	..	Maintain
Into urban agglomerations	Lower	Lower	Maintain	Lower
International migration				
Immigration				
View	Satisfactory	Satisfactory	Satisfactory	Too low
Policy	Maintain	Maintain	Lower	Raise
Permanent settlement	..	..	Lower	Maintain
Temporary workers	..	..	Lower	Raise
Highly skilled workers	..	..	..	Raise
Family reunification	..	..	No intervention	Raise
Integration of non-citizens	..	..	Yes	Yes
Emigration				
View	Too high	Satisfactory	Satisfactory	Satisfactory
Policy	Lower	Maintain	Maintain	No intervention
Encouraging the return of citizens	Yes	..	Yes	Yes

* Measures implemented to respond to HIV/AIDS: (1) blood screening; (2) information/education campaigns; (3) antiretroviral treatment; (4) non-discriminatory policies; (5) distribution of condoms.

** Grounds on which abortion is permitted: (1) to save the woman's life; (2) to preserve physical health; (3) to preserve mental health; (4) rape or incest; (5) foetal impairment; (6) economic or social reasons; (7) on request.

United Nations Department of Economic and Social Affairs/Population Division

Population indicators

Indicator	1975	1985	1995	2009
Population size and growth				
Population size (thousands)	4 711	4 902	5 108	5 326
Annual growth rate (percentage)*	0.5	0.5	0.5	0.4
Population age structure				
Percentage of population under age 15	22	19	19	17
Percentage of population aged 60 or over	16	17	19	24
Fertility and family planning				
Total fertility (children per woman)*	1.6	1.7	1.8	1.8
Adolescent fertility rate (per 1,000 women, aged 15 - 19)*	..	..	10.0	11.0
Percentage of births to women under age 20*	..	..	3	3
Percentage of births to women aged 35 or over*	..	..	15	18
Percentage of married women using contraception				
Modern methods	78[a]	75[b]	..	..
All methods	80[a]	77[b]	..	..
Health and mortality				
Life expectancy at birth (years)*				
Males	67	70	72	76
Females	75	78	80	83
Both sexes combined	71	74	76	80
Infant mortality rate (per 1,000 live births)*	12	6	5	3
Under-five mortality (per 1,000 live births)*	..	8	6	4
Maternal mortality ratio (per 100,000 live births) (2005)	..	..	..	7
HIV/AIDS				
People living with HIV/AIDS (thousands)	..	..	..	2.4[c]
Adult prevalence (percentage)	..	..	..	0.1[c]
Spatial distribution				
Population density (per sq. km)	14	14	15	16
Urban population (percentage)	58	60	61	64
Annual urban population growth rate (percentage)	1.5	0.7	0.3	0.8
Annual rural population growth rate (percentage)	-1.3	-0.1	0.5	-0.6
International migration				
Migrant stock				
Number of migrants (thousands)	35	49	103	226**
As percentage of total population	0.8	1.0	2.0	4.2**

* For the periods 1970-1975, 1980-1985, 1990-1995 and 2005-2010.
** For 2010.
[a] For 1977.
[b] For 1989.
[c] For 2007.

Government views and policies

Population policy variable	1976	1986	1996	2009
Population size and growth				
View on growth	Too low	Too low	Satisfactory	Satisfactory
Policy on growth	Raise	Raise	Raise	Maintain
Population age structure				
Level of concern about				
Size of the working-age population	..	..	..	Major concern
Ageing of the population	..	..	..	Major concern
Fertility and family planning				
View on fertility level	Too low	Too low	Too low	Satisfactory
Policy	Raise	Raise	Raise	Raise
Access to contraceptive methods	Direct support	Indirect support	No support	Indirect support
Adolescent fertility				
Level of concern	..	..	Major concern	Minor concern
Policies and programmes	..	..	Yes	Yes
Health and mortality				
View				
Life expectancy at birth	Unacceptable	Acceptable	Acceptable	Acceptable
Under-five mortality	..	..	Acceptable	Acceptable
Maternal mortality	..	..	..	Unacceptable
Level of concern about HIV/AIDS	..	..	Major concern	Major concern
Measures to respond to HIV/AIDS*	..	..	..	1,2,3,4,5
Grounds on which abortion is permitted**	..	..	1,2,3,4,5,6,7	1,2,3,4,5,6,7
Spatial distribution and internal migration				
View on spatial distribution	Major change desired	Minor change desired	Minor change desired	Minor change desired
Policies on internal migration				
From rural to urban areas	..	..	..	Lower
From rural to rural areas	..	..	..	No intervention
From urban to rural areas	..	..	..	No intervention
From urban to urban areas	..	..	..	No intervention
Into urban agglomerations	Lower	Lower	Lower	Lower
International migration				
Immigration				
View	Satisfactory	Too high	Too high	Too high
Policy	Maintain	Lower	Lower	Lower
Permanent settlement	..	..	Lower	Lower
Temporary workers	..	..	Lower	Lower
Highly skilled workers	..	..	..	Raise
Family reunification	..	..	Maintain	Lower
Integration of non-citizens	..	..	Yes	Yes
Emigration				
View	Satisfactory	Satisfactory	Satisfactory	Satisfactory
Policy	Maintain	Maintain	Maintain	No intervention
Encouraging the return of citizens	No	..	No	No

* Measures implemented to respond to HIV/AIDS: (1) blood screening; (2) information/education campaigns; (3) antiretroviral treatment; (4) non-discriminatory policies; (5) distribution of condoms.
** Grounds on which abortion is permitted: (1) to save the woman's life; (2) to preserve physical health; (3) to preserve mental health; (4) rape or incest; (5) foetal impairment; (6) economic or social reasons; (7) on request.

Population indicators

Indicator	1975	1985	1995	2009
Population size and growth				
Population size (thousands)	52 729	55 393	57 999	62 343
Annual growth rate (percentage)*	0.8	0.5	0.4	0.5
Population age structure				
Percentage of population under age 15	24	21	20	18
Percentage of population aged 60 or over	18	18	20	23
Fertility and family planning				
Total fertility (children per woman)*	2.3	1.9	1.7	1.9
Adolescent fertility rate (per 1,000 women, aged 15 - 19)*	..	..	8.0	7.0
Percentage of births to women under age 20*	..	..	2	2
Percentage of births to women aged 35 or over*	..	..	13	18
Percentage of married women using contraception				
Modern methods	21[a]	67[b]	69[c]	..
All methods	64[a]	81[b]	75[c]	71[d]
Health and mortality				
Life expectancy at birth (years)*				
Males	69	71	73	78
Females	76	79	81	85
Both sexes combined	72	75	77	81
Infant mortality rate (per 1,000 live births)*	16	9	7	4
Under-five mortality (per 1,000 live births)*	..	11	8	5
Maternal mortality ratio (per 100,000 live births) (2005)	..	..	..	8
HIV/AIDS				
People living with HIV/AIDS (thousands)	..	..	78	140[e]
Adult prevalence (percentage)	..	..	0.3	0.4[e]
Spatial distribution				
Population density (per sq. km)	96	100	105	113
Urban population (percentage)	73	74	75	78
Annual urban population growth rate (percentage)	0.6	0.6	0.6	0.7
Annual rural population growth rate (percentage)	0.3	0.2	-0.3	-0.6
International migration				
Migrant stock				
Number of migrants (thousands)	5 572	5 953	6 085	6 685**
As percentage of total population	10.6	10.7	10.5	10.7**

* For the periods 1970-1975, 1980-1985, 1990-1995 and 2005-2010.
** For 2010.
[a] For 1972.
[b] For 1988.
[c] For 1994.
[d] For 2004/2005.
[e] For 2007.

Government views and policies

Population policy variable	1976	1986	1996	2009
Population size and growth				
View on growth	Too low	Too low	Too low	Too low
Policy on growth	Raise	Raise	Raise	Raise
Population age structure				
Level of concern about				
Size of the working-age population	..	..	..	..
Ageing of the population	..	..	..	Major concern
Fertility and family planning				
View on fertility level	Too low	Too low	Too low	Too low
Policy	Raise	Raise	Raise	Raise
Access to contraceptive methods	Limits	No support	No support	No support
Adolescent fertility				
Level of concern	..	..	..	Minor concern
Policies and programmes	..	..	..	Yes
Health and mortality				
View				
Life expectancy at birth	Unacceptable	Unacceptable	Unacceptable	Unacceptable
Under-five mortality	..	..	..	Unacceptable
Maternal mortality	..	..	..	Unacceptable
Level of concern about HIV/AIDS	..	..	..	Major concern
Measures to respond to HIV/AIDS*	..	..	..	1,2,3,5
Grounds on which abortion is permitted**	..	..	1	1
Spatial distribution and internal migration				
View on spatial distribution	Major change desired	Major change desired	Major change desired	Major change desired
Policies on internal migration				
From rural to urban areas	..	..	..	Lower
From rural to rural areas	..	..	..	..
From urban to rural areas	..	..	..	..
From urban to urban areas	..	..	..	..
Into urban agglomerations	Lower	Lower	..	Lower
International migration				
Immigration				
View	Too low	Too high	Too high	Too high
Policy	Raise	Lower	Lower	Lower
Permanent settlement	..	..	Lower	Lower
Temporary workers	..	..	Lower	Lower
Highly skilled workers	..	..	..	..
Family reunification	..	..	..	Lower
Integration of non-citizens	..	..	..	..
Emigration				
View	Satisfactory	Too high	Too high	Too high
Policy	Maintain	Lower	Lower	Lower
Encouraging the return of citizens	No	..	..	No

* Measures implemented to respond to HIV/AIDS: (1) blood screening; (2) information/education campaigns; (3) antiretroviral treatment; (4) non-discriminatory policies; (5) distribution of condoms.
** Grounds on which abortion is permitted: (1) to save the woman's life; (2) to preserve physical health; (3) to preserve mental health; (4) rape or incest; (5) foetal impairment; (6) economic or social reasons; (7) on request.

Population indicators

Indicator	1975	1985	1995	2009
Population size and growth				
Population size (thousands)	595	792	1 084	1 475
Annual growth rate (percentage)*	2.3	3.0	3.2	1.8
Population age structure				
Percentage of population under age 15	35	40	42	36
Percentage of population aged 60 or over	10	9	7	6
Fertility and family planning				
Total fertility (children per woman)*	4.9	5.2	5.1	3.4
Adolescent fertility rate (per 1,000 women, aged 15 - 19)*	..	..	152.0	90.0
Percentage of births to women under age 20*	..	..	15	13
Percentage of births to women aged 35 or over*	..	..	20	18
Percentage of married women using contraception				
Modern methods	..	..	..	12[a]
All methods	..	..	..	33[a]
Health and mortality				
Life expectancy at birth (years)*				
Males	47	55	59	59
Females	50	58	63	62
Both sexes combined	49	57	61	60
Infant mortality rate (per 1,000 live births)*	114	78	59	51
Under-five mortality (per 1,000 live births)*	..	130	93	80
Maternal mortality ratio (per 100,000 live births) (2005)	..	..	..	520
HIV/AIDS				
People living with HIV/AIDS (thousands)	..	..	16	49[b]
Adult prevalence (percentage)	..	..	3.0	5.9[b]
Spatial distribution				
Population density (per sq. km)	2	3	4	6
Urban population (percentage)	43	62	75	86
Annual urban population growth rate (percentage)	7.9	5.1	3.9	1.9
Annual rural population growth rate (percentage)	-1.5	-0.5	-2.0	-1.5
International migration				
Migrant stock				
Number of migrants (thousands)	62	110	164	284**
As percentage of total population	10.4	13.9	15.1	18.9**

* For the periods 1970-1975, 1980-1985, 1990-1995 and 2005-2010.
** For 2010.
[a] For 2000.
[b] For 2007.

Government views and policies

Population policy variable	1976	1986	1996	2009
Population size and growth				
View on growth	Satisfactory	Too high	Too high	Too high
Policy on growth	No intervention	Lower	Lower	Lower
Population age structure				
Level of concern about				
Size of the working-age population	..	..	..	Major concern
Ageing of the population	..	..	..	Minor concern
Fertility and family planning				
View on fertility level	Satisfactory	Too high	Too high	Too high
Policy	No intervention	Lower	Lower	Lower
Access to contraceptive methods	Indirect support	Direct support	Direct support	Direct support
Adolescent fertility				
Level of concern	..	..	Minor concern	Major concern
Policies and programmes	..	..	Yes	Yes
Health and mortality				
View				
Life expectancy at birth	Unacceptable	Unacceptable	Unacceptable	Unacceptable
Under-five mortality	..	..	Unacceptable	Unacceptable
Maternal mortality	..	..	..	Unacceptable
Level of concern about HIV/AIDS	..	..	Major concern	Major concern
Measures to respond to HIV/AIDS*	..	..	..	1,2,3,5
Grounds on which abortion is permitted**	..	..	1,2,3	1,2,3
Spatial distribution and internal migration				
View on spatial distribution	Minor change desired	Major change desired	Major change desired	Major change desired
Policies on internal migration				
From rural to urban areas	..	..	..	Lower
From rural to rural areas	..	..	..	No intervention
From urban to rural areas	..	..	..	Raise
From urban to urban areas	..	..	..	Lower
Into urban agglomerations	Lower	No intervention	Lower	Lower
International migration				
Immigration				
View	Satisfactory	Too high	Too high	Too high
Policy	Maintain	Lower	Lower	Lower
Permanent settlement	..	..	Lower	Lower
Temporary workers	..	..	Lower	Lower
Highly skilled workers	..	..	..	No intervention
Family reunification	..	..	Lower	No intervention
Integration of non-citizens	..	..	No	..
Emigration				
View	Satisfactory	Satisfactory	Satisfactory	Satisfactory
Policy	Maintain	Maintain	No intervention	No intervention
Encouraging the return of citizens	No	..	Yes	No

* Measures implemented to respond to HIV/AIDS: (1) blood screening; (2) information/education campaigns; (3) antiretroviral treatment; (4) non-discriminatory policies; (5) distribution of condoms.
** Grounds on which abortion is permitted: (1) to save the woman's life; (2) to preserve physical health; (3) to preserve mental health; (4) rape or incest; (5) foetal impairment; (6) economic or social reasons; (7) on request.

Population indicators

Indicator	1975	1985	1995	2009
Population size and growth				
Population size (thousands)	517	735	1 085	1 705
Annual growth rate (percentage)*	3.7	3.5	3.8	2.7
Population age structure				
Percentage of population under age 15	41	43	43	42
Percentage of population aged 60 or over	5	5	5	5
Fertility and family planning				
Total fertility (children per woman)*	6.2	6.3	6.0	5.1
Adolescent fertility rate (per 1,000 women, aged 15 - 19)*	..	..	150.0	88.0
Percentage of births to women under age 20*	..	..	12	9
Percentage of births to women aged 35 or over*	..	..	22	23
Percentage of married women using contraception				
Modern methods	..	..	7[a]	13[b]
All methods	..	..	12[a]	18[b]
Health and mortality				
Life expectancy at birth (years)*				
Males	41	47	51	54
Females	43	49	53	57
Both sexes combined	42	48	52	56
Infant mortality rate (per 1,000 live births)*	167	132	106	77
Under-five mortality (per 1,000 live births)*	..	207	158	116
Maternal mortality ratio (per 100,000 live births) (2005)	..	..	..	690
HIV/AIDS				
People living with HIV/AIDS (thousands)	..	..	1.6	8.2[c]
Adult prevalence (percentage)	..	..	0.3	0.9[c]
Spatial distribution				
Population density (per sq. km)	46	65	96	151
Urban population (percentage)	24	33	44	57
Annual urban population growth rate (percentage)	6.4	6.8	6.1	3.9
Annual rural population growth rate (percentage)	2.3	2.2	1.7	0.6
International migration				
Migrant stock				
Number of migrants (thousands)	60	94	148	290**
As percentage of total population	11.6	12.8	13.6	16.6**

* For the periods 1970-1975, 1980-1985, 1990-1995 and 2005-2010.
** For 2010.
[a] For 1990.
[b] For 2001.
[c] For 2007.

Government views and policies

Population policy variable	1976	1986	1996	2009
Population size and growth				
View on growth	..	..	Too low	Too low
Policy on growth	..	..	No intervention	Raise
Population age structure				
Level of concern about				
Size of the working-age population	..	..	..	..
Ageing of the population	..	..	..	Major concern
Fertility and family planning				
View on fertility level	..	..	Too low	Too low
Policy	..	..	Raise	Raise
Access to contraceptive methods	..	..	No support	Direct support
Adolescent fertility				
Level of concern	..	..	Minor concern	Minor concern
Policies and programmes	..	..	No	Yes
Health and mortality				
View				
Life expectancy at birth	..	..	Acceptable	Unacceptable
Under-five mortality	..	..	Unacceptable	Unacceptable
Maternal mortality	..	..	..	Unacceptable
Level of concern about HIV/AIDS	..	..	Not a concern	Major concern
Measures to respond to HIV/AIDS*	..	..	..	1,2,3,4,5
Grounds on which abortion is permitted**	..	..	1,2,3,4,5,6,7	1,2,3,4,5,6,7
Spatial distribution and internal migration				
View on spatial distribution	..	..	Minor change desired	Major change desired
Policies on internal migration				
From rural to urban areas	..	..	..	Lower
From rural to rural areas	..	..	..	..
From urban to rural areas	..	..	..	..
From urban to urban areas	..	..	..	..
Into urban agglomerations	..	..	Lower	Lower
International migration				
Immigration				
View	..	..	Satisfactory	Satisfactory
Policy	..	..	No intervention	Maintain
Permanent settlement	..	..	No intervention	Maintain
Temporary workers	..	..	No intervention	Maintain
Highly skilled workers	..	..	..	Maintain
Family reunification	..	..	No intervention	Maintain
Integration of non-citizens	..	..	No	No
Emigration				
View	..	..	Too high	Too high
Policy	..	..	No intervention	Lower
Encouraging the return of citizens	..	..	No	Yes

* Measures implemented to respond to HIV/AIDS: (1) blood screening; (2) information/education campaigns; (3) antiretroviral treatment; (4) non-discriminatory policies; (5) distribution of condoms.

** Grounds on which abortion is permitted: (1) to save the woman's life; (2) to preserve physical health; (3) to preserve mental health; (4) rape or incest; (5) foetal impairment; (6) economic or social reasons; (7) on request.

Population indicators

Indicator	1975	1985	1995	2009
Population size and growth				
Population size (thousands)	4 908	5 287	5 069	4 260
Annual growth rate (percentage)*	0.8	0.8	-1.5	-1.1
Population age structure				
Percentage of population under age 15	28	25	24	17
Percentage of population aged 60 or over	12	13	16	19
Fertility and family planning				
Total fertility (children per woman)*	2.6	2.3	2.1	1.6
Adolescent fertility rate (per 1,000 women, aged 15 - 19)*	..	..	69.0	45.0
Percentage of births to women under age 20*	..	..	17	14
Percentage of births to women aged 35 or over*	..	..	7	9
Percentage of married women using contraception				
Modern methods	..	..	20[a]	27[b]
All methods	..	..	41[a]	47[b]
Health and mortality				
Life expectancy at birth (years)*				
Males	64	66	67	68
Females	72	73	74	75
Both sexes combined	68	70	71	72
Infant mortality rate (per 1,000 live births)*	52	47	40	35
Under-five mortality (per 1,000 live births)*	..	49	43	36
Maternal mortality ratio (per 100,000 live births) (2005)	..	..	..	66
HIV/AIDS				
People living with HIV/AIDS (thousands)	..	..	..	2.7[c]
Adult prevalence (percentage)	..	..	..	0.1[c]
Spatial distribution				
Population density (per sq. km)	70	76	73	61
Urban population (percentage)	50	54	54	53
Annual urban population growth rate (percentage)	1.5	1.8	-2.0	-0.4
Annual rural population growth rate (percentage)	-0.1	0.1	-1.1	-1.0
International migration				
Migrant stock				
Number of migrants (thousands)	..	..	250	167**
As percentage of total population	0.0	0.0	4.9	4.0**

* For the periods 1970-1975, 1980-1985, 1990-1995 and 2005-2010.
** For 2010.
[a] For 1999/2000.
[b] For 2005.
[c] For 2007.

Government views and policies

Population policy variable	1976	1986	1996	2009
Population size and growth				
View on growth	..	..	Satisfactory	Too low
Policy on growth	..	..	No intervention	Raise
Population age structure				
Level of concern about				
Size of the working-age population	..	..	..	Major concern
Ageing of the population	..	..	..	Major concern
Fertility and family planning				
View on fertility level	..	..	Too low	Too low
Policy	..	..	No intervention	Raise
Access to contraceptive methods	..	..	No support	No support
Adolescent fertility				
Level of concern	..	..	Not a concern	Major concern
Policies and programmes	..	..	No	Yes
Health and mortality				
View				
Life expectancy at birth	..	..	Acceptable	Acceptable
Under-five mortality	..	..	Acceptable	Acceptable
Maternal mortality	..	..	..	Acceptable
Level of concern about HIV/AIDS	..	..	Major concern	Major concern
Measures to respond to HIV/AIDS*	..	..		1,2,3,4,5
Grounds on which abortion is permitted**	..	..	1,2,3,4,5,6,7	1,2,3,4,5,6,7
Spatial distribution and internal migration				
View on spatial distribution	..	..	Satisfactory	Major change desired
Policies on internal migration				
From rural to urban areas	..	..	..	Lower
From rural to rural areas	..	..	..	No intervention
From urban to rural areas	..	..	..	Lower
From urban to urban areas	..	..	..	No intervention
Into urban agglomerations	..	..	No intervention	No intervention
International migration				
Immigration				
View	..	..	Too high	Satisfactory
Policy	..	..	Lower	Maintain
Permanent settlement	..	..	Lower	Lower
Temporary workers	..	..	Lower	Maintain
Highly skilled workers	..	..	..	Raise
Family reunification	..	..	Lower	Maintain
Integration of non-citizens	..	..	Yes	Yes
Emigration				
View	..	..	Satisfactory	Satisfactory
Policy	..	..	No intervention	No intervention
Encouraging the return of citizens	..	..	No	No

* Measures implemented to respond to HIV/AIDS: (1) blood screening; (2) information/education campaigns; (3) antiretroviral treatment; (4) non-discriminatory policies; (5) distribution of condoms.

** Grounds on which abortion is permitted: (1) to save the woman's life; (2) to preserve physical health; (3) to preserve mental health; (4) rape or incest; (5) foetal impairment; (6) economic or social reasons; (7) on request.

Population indicators

Indicator	1975	1985	1995	2009
Population size and growth				
Population size (thousands)	78 674	77 685	81 622	82 167
Annual growth rate (percentage)*	0.1	-0.2	0.5	-0.1
Population age structure				
Percentage of population under age 15	22	16	16	14
Percentage of population aged 60 or over	20	20	21	26
Fertility and family planning				
Total fertility (children per woman)*	1.6	1.5	1.3	1.3
Adolescent fertility rate (per 1,000 women, aged 15 - 19)*	..	..	12.0	8.0
Percentage of births to women under age 20*	..	..	5	3
Percentage of births to women aged 35 or over*	..	..	11	19
Percentage of married women using contraception				
Modern methods	..	68	66[a]	..
All methods	..	78	70[a]	..
Health and mortality				
Life expectancy at birth (years)*				
Males	68	70	73	77
Females	74	77	79	82
Both sexes combined	71	74	76	80
Infant mortality rate (per 1,000 live births)*	21	11	6	4
Under-five mortality (per 1,000 live births)*	..	12	7	5
Maternal mortality ratio (per 100,000 live births) (2005)	..	..	..	4
HIV/AIDS				
People living with HIV/AIDS (thousands)	..	..	31	53[b]
Adult prevalence (percentage)	..	..	0.1	0.1[b]
Spatial distribution				
Population density (per sq. km)	220	218	229	230
Urban population (percentage)	73	73	73	74
Annual urban population growth rate (percentage)	0.0	0.1	0.2	0.1
Annual rural population growth rate (percentage)	-0.2	0.6	0.5	-0.6
International migration				
Migrant stock				
Number of migrants (thousands)	..	..	8 992	10 758**
As percentage of total population	..	..	11.0	13.1**

* For the periods 1970-1975, 1980-1985, 1990-1995 and 2005-2010.
** For 2010.
[a] For 1992.
[b] For 2007.

Government views and policies

Population policy variable	1976	1986	1996	2009
Population size and growth				
View on growth	Too high	Too high	Too high	Too high
Policy on growth	Lower	Lower	Lower	Lower
Population age structure				
Level of concern about				
Size of the working-age population	..	..	..	Major concern
Ageing of the population	..	..	..	Major concern
Fertility and family planning				
View on fertility level	Too high	Too high	Too high	Too high
Policy	Lower	Lower	Lower	Lower
Access to contraceptive methods	Direct support	Direct support	Direct support	Direct support
Adolescent fertility				
Level of concern	..	..	Major concern	Major concern
Policies and programmes	..	..	Yes	Yes
Health and mortality				
View				
Life expectancy at birth	Unacceptable	Unacceptable	Unacceptable	Unacceptable
Under-five mortality	..	..	Unacceptable	Unacceptable
Maternal mortality	..	..	..	Unacceptable
Level of concern about HIV/AIDS	..	..	Major concern	Major concern
Measures to respond to HIV/AIDS*	..	..	..	1,2,3,4,5
Grounds on which abortion is permitted**	..	..	1,2,3,4,5	1,2,3,4,5
Spatial distribution and internal migration				
View on spatial distribution	Major change desired	Major change desired	Minor change desired	Major change desired
Policies on internal migration				
From rural to urban areas	..	..	..	Lower
From rural to rural areas	..	..	..	No intervention
From urban to rural areas	..	..	..	Raise
From urban to urban areas	..	..	..	No intervention
Into urban agglomerations	Lower	..	Lower	Lower
International migration				
Immigration				
View	Too high	Too high	Satisfactory	Too high
Policy	Lower	Lower	No intervention	Lower
Permanent settlement	..	..	No intervention	Lower
Temporary workers	..	..	No intervention	Lower
Highly skilled workers	..	..	..	No intervention
Family reunification	..	..	No intervention	Maintain
Integration of non-citizens	..	..	No	No
Emigration				
View	Satisfactory	Satisfactory	Too high	Too high
Policy	Maintain	Maintain	Lower	Lower
Encouraging the return of citizens	No	..	No	Yes

* Measures implemented to respond to HIV/AIDS: (1) blood screening; (2) information/education campaigns; (3) antiretroviral treatment; (4) non-discriminatory policies; (5) distribution of condoms.
** Grounds on which abortion is permitted: (1) to save the woman's life; (2) to preserve physical health; (3) to preserve mental health; (4) rape or incest; (5) foetal impairment; (6) economic or social reasons; (7) on request.

Population indicators

Indicator	1975	1985	1995	2009
Population size and growth				
Population size (thousands)	10 001	13 006	17 245	23 837
Annual growth rate (percentage)*	2.7	3.3	2.8	2.1
Population age structure				
Percentage of population under age 15	46	45	43	38
Percentage of population aged 60 or over	5	5	5	6
Fertility and family planning				
Total fertility (children per woman)*	6.9	6.3	5.3	4.3
Adolescent fertility rate (per 1,000 women, aged 15 - 19)*	..	..	106.0	64.0
Percentage of births to women under age 20*	..	..	10	7
Percentage of births to women aged 35 or over*	..	..	27	27
Percentage of married women using contraception				
Modern methods	6[a]	5[b]	13[c]	17[d]
All methods	10[a]	13[b]	22[c]	24[d]
Health and mortality				
Life expectancy at birth (years)*				
Males	49	53	58	56
Females	51	55	60	57
Both sexes combined	50	54	59	57
Infant mortality rate (per 1,000 live births)*	107	90	67	73
Under-five mortality (per 1,000 live births)*	..	145	112	117
Maternal mortality ratio (per 100,000 live births) (2005)	..	..	..	560
HIV/AIDS				
People living with HIV/AIDS (thousands)	..	..	160	260[e]
Adult prevalence (percentage)	..	..	1.8	1.9[e]
Spatial distribution				
Population density (per sq. km)	42	55	72	100
Urban population (percentage)	30	33	40	51
Annual urban population growth rate (percentage)	2.7	5.2	4.4	3.4
Annual rural population growth rate (percentage)	1.7	2.1	1.2	0.4
International migration				
Migrant stock				
Number of migrants (thousands)	385	494	1 038	1 852**
As percentage of total population	3.8	3.8	6.0	7.6**

* For the periods 1970-1975, 1980-1985, 1990-1995 and 2005-2010.
** For 2010.
[a] For 1979.
[b] For 1988.
[c] For 1998/1999.
[d] For 2008.
[e] For 2007.

Government views and policies

Population policy variable	1976	1986	1996	2009
Population size and growth				
View on growth	Too low	Too low	Too low	Too low
Policy on growth	Raise	Raise	Raise	Raise
Population age structure				
Level of concern about				
Size of the working-age population	..	..	..	Major concern
Ageing of the population	..	..	..	Major concern
Fertility and family planning				
View on fertility level	Too low	Too low	Too low	Too low
Policy	Raise	Raise	Raise	Raise
Access to contraceptive methods	Limits	No support	No support	No support
Adolescent fertility				
Level of concern	..	..	..	Major concern
Policies and programmes	..	..	..	Yes
Health and mortality				
View				
Life expectancy at birth	Acceptable	Unacceptable	Unacceptable	Acceptable
Under-five mortality	..	..	..	Acceptable
Maternal mortality	..	..	..	Acceptable
Level of concern about HIV/AIDS	..	..	..	Major concern
Measures to respond to HIV/AIDS*	..	..	..	1,2,3
Grounds on which abortion is permitted**	..	..	1,2,3,4,5,6,7	1,2,3,4,5,6,7
Spatial distribution and internal migration				
View on spatial distribution	Minor change desired	Major change desired	Major change desired	Minor change desired
Policies on internal migration				
From rural to urban areas	..	..	..	Lower
From rural to rural areas	..	..	..	No intervention
From urban to rural areas	..	..	..	Raise
From urban to urban areas	..	..	..	No intervention
Into urban agglomerations	Lower	Lower	..	Lower
International migration				
Immigration				
View	Satisfactory	Too high	Too high	Satisfactory
Policy	Maintain	Lower	Lower	Maintain
Permanent settlement	..	..	Lower	Maintain
Temporary workers	..	..	..	Maintain
Highly skilled workers	..	..	..	Raise
Family reunification	..	..	..	Maintain
Integration of non-citizens	..	..	..	Yes
Emigration				
View	Too high	Satisfactory	Satisfactory	Satisfactory
Policy	Lower	Lower	Lower	No intervention
Encouraging the return of citizens	Yes	..	Yes	Yes

* Measures implemented to respond to HIV/AIDS: (1) blood screening; (2) information/education campaigns; (3) antiretroviral treatment; (4) non-discriminatory policies; (5) distribution of condoms.
** Grounds on which abortion is permitted: (1) to save the woman's life; (2) to preserve physical health; (3) to preserve mental health; (4) rape or incest; (5) foetal impairment; (6) economic or social reasons; (7) on request.

Population indicators

Indicator	1975	1985	1995	2009
Population size and growth				
Population size (thousands)	9 047	9 934	10 672	11 161
Annual growth rate (percentage)*	0.6	0.6	1.0	0.2
Population age structure				
Percentage of population under age 15	24	21	17	14
Percentage of population aged 60 or over	17	18	21	24
Fertility and family planning				
Total fertility (children per woman)*	2.3	2.0	1.4	1.4
Adolescent fertility rate (per 1,000 women, aged 15 - 19)*	..	..	16.0	9.0
Percentage of births to women under age 20*	..	..	6	3
Percentage of births to women aged 35 or over*	..	..	10	15
Percentage of married women using contraception				
Modern methods	..	..	34[a]	46[b]
All methods	..	..	61[a]	76[b]
Health and mortality				
Life expectancy at birth (years)*				
Males	71	73	75	77
Females	74	78	80	81
Both sexes combined	72	75	77	79
Infant mortality rate (per 1,000 live births)*	34	15	9	4
Under-five mortality (per 1,000 live births)*	..	16	10	4
Maternal mortality ratio (per 100,000 live births) (2005)	..	..	..	3
HIV/AIDS				
People living with HIV/AIDS (thousands)	..	..	5	11[c]
Adult prevalence (percentage)	..	..	0.1	0.2[c]
Spatial distribution				
Population density (per sq. km)	69	75	81	85
Urban population (percentage)	55	58	59	61
Annual urban population growth rate (percentage)	2.0	0.5	0.9	0 6
Annual rural population growth rate (percentage)	0.0	0.2	0.6	-0.5
International migration				
Migrant stock				
Number of migrants (thousands)	123	309	549	1 133**
As percentage of total population	1.4	3.1	5.1	10.1**

* For the periods 1970-1975, 1980-1985, 1990-1995 and 2005-2010.
** For 2010.
[a] For 1999.
[b] For 2001.
[c] For 2007.

Government views and policies

Population policy variable	1976	1986	1996	2009
Population size and growth				
View on growth	Too high	Too high	Satisfactory	Satisfactory
Policy on growth	Lower	Lower	Maintain	No intervention
Population age structure				
Level of concern about				
Size of the working-age population	..	..	..	..
Ageing of the population	..	..	..	Minor concern
Fertility and family planning				
View on fertility level	Too high	Too high	Too high	Satisfactory
Policy	Lower	Lower	Lower	No intervention
Access to contraceptive methods	Direct support	Direct support	Direct support	Direct support
Adolescent fertility				
Level of concern	..	..	Major concern	Major concern
Policies and programmes	..	..	Yes	Yes
Health and mortality				
View				
Life expectancy at birth	Unacceptable	Unacceptable	Unacceptable	Acceptable
Under-five mortality	..	..	Unacceptable	Acceptable
Maternal mortality	..	..	..	Acceptable
Level of concern about HIV/AIDS	..	..	Major concern	Major concern
Measures to respond to HIV/AIDS*	..	..	..	1,2,3,5
Grounds on which abortion is permitted**	..	..	1,2,3	1,2,3
Spatial distribution and internal migration				
View on spatial distribution	Major change desired	Major change desired	Satisfactory	Minor change desired
Policies on internal migration				
From rural to urban areas	..	..	..	..
From rural to rural areas	..	..	..	..
From urban to rural areas	..	..	..	..
From urban to urban areas	..	..	..	..
Into urban agglomerations	Lower	..	No intervention	..
International migration				
Immigration				
View	Satisfactory	Satisfactory	Satisfactory	Satisfactory
Policy	Maintain	Maintain	Maintain	Maintain
Permanent settlement	..	..	..	Maintain
Temporary workers	..	..	..	Maintain
Highly skilled workers	..	..	..	Maintain
Family reunification	..	..	..	Maintain
Integration of non-citizens	..	..	..	..
Emigration				
View	Satisfactory	Satisfactory	Too high	Too high
Policy	Maintain	Maintain	Lower	Lower
Encouraging the return of citizens	No	..	Yes	Yes

* Measures implemented to respond to HIV/AIDS: (1) blood screening; (2) information/education campaigns; (3) antiretroviral treatment; (4) non-discriminatory policies; (5) distribution of condoms.
** Grounds on which abortion is permitted: (1) to save the woman's life; (2) to preserve physical health; (3) to preserve mental health; (4) rape or incest; (5) foetal impairment; (6) economic or social reasons; (7) on request.

Population indicators

Indicator	1975	1985	1995	2009
Population size and growth				
Population size (thousands)	92	100	100	104
Annual growth rate (percentage)*	-0.4	2.3	0.8	0.4
Population age structure				
Percentage of population under age 15	43	38	38	28
Percentage of population aged 60 or over	9	8	10	9
Fertility and family planning				
Total fertility (children per woman)*	4.6	4.2	3.5	2.3
Adolescent fertility rate (per 1,000 women, aged 15 - 19)*	..	..	83.0	42.0
Percentage of births to women under age 20*	..	..	12	9
Percentage of births to women aged 35 or over*	..	..	19	17
Percentage of married women using contraception				
Modern methods	..	27	52[a]	..
All methods	..	31	54[a]	..
Health and mortality				
Life expectancy at birth (years)*				
Males	62	63	69	74
Females	67	67	72	77
Both sexes combined	65	66	71	75
Infant mortality rate (per 1,000 live births)*	52	47	26	13
Under-five mortality (per 1,000 live births)*	..	61	32	15
Maternal mortality ratio (per 100,000 live births) (2005)	..	..	..	..
HIV/AIDS				
People living with HIV/AIDS (thousands)	..	..	..	..
Adult prevalence (percentage)	..	..	..	..
Spatial distribution				
Population density (per sq. km)	269	290	291	302
Urban population (percentage)	33	33	32	31
Annual urban population growth rate (percentage)	-0.9	0.0	0.0	0.4
Annual rural population growth rate (percentage)	-1.2	0.4	0.6	-0.3
International migration				
Migrant stock				
Number of migrants (thousands)	3	3	6	13**
As percentage of total population	3.0	3.1	5.8	12.1**

* For the periods 1970-1975, 1980-1985, 1990-1995 and 2005-2010.
** For 2010.
[a] For 1990.

Government views and policies

Population policy variable	1976	1986	1996	2009
Population size and growth				
View on growth	Too high	Too high	Satisfactory	Too high
Policy on growth	No intervention	No intervention	No intervention	Lower
Population age structure				
Level of concern about				
Size of the working-age population	..	..	..	Major concern
Ageing of the population	..	..	..	Minor concern
Fertility and family planning				
View on fertility level	Too high	Satisfactory	Too high	Too high
Policy	No intervention	No intervention	Lower	Lower
Access to contraceptive methods	Direct support	Direct support	Direct support	Direct support
Adolescent fertility				
Level of concern	..	..	Minor concern	Major concern
Policies and programmes	..	..	No	Yes
Health and mortality				
View				
Life expectancy at birth	Unacceptable	Unacceptable	Unacceptable	Unacceptable
Under-five mortality	..	..	..	Unacceptable
Maternal mortality	..	..	..	Unacceptable
Level of concern about HIV/AIDS	..	..	..	Major concern
Measures to respond to HIV/AIDS*	..	..	..	1,2,3,4,5
Grounds on which abortion is permitted**	..	..	1	1
Spatial distribution and internal migration				
View on spatial distribution	Major change desired	Major change desired	Major change desired	Major change desired
Policies on internal migration				
From rural to urban areas	..	..	..	Lower
From rural to rural areas	..	..	..	Maintain
From urban to rural areas	..	..	..	Raise
From urban to urban areas	..	..	..	Maintain
Into urban agglomerations	No intervention	..	..	Lower
International migration				
Immigration				
View	Satisfactory	Satisfactory	Satisfactory	Satisfactory
Policy	Maintain	Maintain	No intervention	No intervention
Permanent settlement	..	..	No intervention	No intervention
Temporary workers	..	..	..	No intervention
Highly skilled workers	..	..	..	Maintain
Family reunification	..	..	..	No intervention
Integration of non-citizens	..	..	..	Yes
Emigration				
View	Satisfactory	Satisfactory	Too high	Satisfactory
Policy	Maintain	Maintain	No intervention	No intervention
Encouraging the return of citizens	..	..	..	No

* Measures implemented to respond to HIV/AIDS: (1) blood screening; (2) information/education campaigns; (3) antiretroviral treatment; (4) non-discriminatory policies; (5) distribution of condoms.
** Grounds on which abortion is permitted: (1) to save the woman's life; (2) to preserve physical health; (3) to preserve mental health; (4) rape or incest; (5) foetal impairment; (6) economic or social reasons; (7) on request.

Population indicators

Indicator	1975	1985	1995	2009
Population size and growth				
Population size (thousands)	6 206	7 937	10 007	14 027
Annual growth rate (percentage)*	2.7	2.5	2.3	2.5
Population age structure				
Percentage of population under age 15	45	46	45	42
Percentage of population aged 60 or over	5	5	6	6
Fertility and family planning				
Total fertility (children per woman)*	6.2	6.1	5.5	4.2
Adolescent fertility rate (per 1,000 women, aged 15 - 19)*	..	..	128.0	107.0
Percentage of births to women under age 20*	..	..	12	13
Percentage of births to women aged 35 or over*	..	..	20	18
Percentage of married women using contraception				
Modern methods	15[a]	19[b]	27	34[c]
All methods	18[a]	23[b]	31	43[c]
Health and mortality				
Life expectancy at birth (years)*				
Males	52	56	61	67
Females	55	61	67	74
Both sexes combined	54	58	64	70
Infant mortality rate (per 1,000 live births)*	102	79	55	30
Under-five mortality (per 1,000 live births)*	..	119	74	39
Maternal mortality ratio (per 100,000 live births) (2005)	..	..	..	290
HIV/AIDS				
People living with HIV/AIDS (thousands)	..	..	15	59[d]
Adult prevalence (percentage)	..	..	0.3	0.8[d]
Spatial distribution				
Population density (per sq. km)	57	73	92	129
Urban population (percentage)	37	39	43	49
Annual urban population growth rate (percentage)	2.9	3.4	3.2	3.4
Annual rural population growth rate (percentage)	2.3	1.7	1.6	1.5
International migration				
Migrant stock				
Number of migrants (thousands)	38	82	46	59**
As percentage of total population	0.6	1.0	0.5	0.4**

* For the periods 1970-1975, 1980-1985, 1990-1995 and 2005-2010.
** For 2010.
[a] For 1978.
[b] For 1987.
[c] For 2002.
[d] For 2007.

Government views and policies

Population policy variable	1976	1986	1996	2009
Population size and growth				
View on growth	Satisfactory	Satisfactory	Too high	Too high
Policy on growth	No intervention	No intervention	Lower	Lower
Population age structure				
Level of concern about				
Size of the working-age population	..	..	..	Minor concern
Ageing of the population	..	..	..	Minor concern
Fertility and family planning				
View on fertility level	Satisfactory	Too high	Too high	Too high
Policy	No intervention	No intervention	Lower	Lower
Access to contraceptive methods	No support	Direct support	Direct support	Indirect support
Adolescent fertility				
Level of concern	..	..	Major concern	Minor concern
Policies and programmes	..	..	No	No
Health and mortality				
View				
Life expectancy at birth	Unacceptable	Unacceptable	Unacceptable	Unacceptable
Under-five mortality	..	..	Unacceptable	Unacceptable
Maternal mortality	..	..	..	Unacceptable
Level of concern about HIV/AIDS	..	..	Major concern	Major concern
Measures to respond to HIV/AIDS*	..	..	..	2,3,4,5
Grounds on which abortion is permitted**	..	..	1,2,3	1,2,3,4,5
Spatial distribution and internal migration				
View on spatial distribution	Minor change desired	Minor change desired	Major change desired	Major change desired
Policies on internal migration				
From rural to urban areas	..	..	..	Lower
From rural to rural areas	..	..	..	No intervention
From urban to rural areas	..	..	..	Raise
From urban to urban areas	..	..	..	Maintain
Into urban agglomerations	..	..	Lower	Lower
International migration				
Immigration				
View	Satisfactory	Satisfactory	Satisfactory	Satisfactory
Policy	Maintain	Maintain	Lower	No intervention
Permanent settlement	..	..	No intervention	No intervention
Temporary workers	..	..	Lower	No intervention
Highly skilled workers	..	..	..	No intervention
Family reunification	..	..	No intervention	No intervention
Integration of non-citizens	..	..	No	No
Emigration				
View	Too high	Too high	Satisfactory	Satisfactory
Policy	Lower	Lower	No intervention	No intervention
Encouraging the return of citizens	..	..	Yes	No

* Measures implemented to respond to HIV/AIDS: (1) blood screening; (2) information/education campaigns; (3) antiretroviral treatment; (4) non−discriminatory policies; (5) distribution of condoms.

** Grounds on which abortion is permitted: (1) to save the woman's life; (2) to preserve physical health; (3) to preserve mental health; (4) rape or incest; (5) foetal impairment; (6) economic or social reasons; (7) on request.

Population indicators

Indicator	1975	1985	1995	2009
Population size and growth				
Population size (thousands)	4 037	5 267	7 478	10 069
Annual growth rate (percentage)*	1.0	2.6	3.9	2.3
Population age structure				
Percentage of population under age 15	43	44	45	43
Percentage of population aged 60 or over	5	5	5	5
Fertility and family planning				
Total fertility (children per woman)*	6.8	6.9	6.6	5.5
Adolescent fertility rate (per 1,000 women, aged 15 - 19)*	..	..	183.0	152.0
Percentage of births to women under age 20*	..	..	14	14
Percentage of births to women aged 35 or over*	..	..	25	22
Percentage of married women using contraception				
Modern methods	..	..	4[a]	4[b]
All methods	..	..	6[a]	9[b]
Health and mortality				
Life expectancy at birth (years)*				
Males	39	44	48	56
Females	41	46	51	60
Both sexes combined	40	45	50	58
Infant mortality rate (per 1,000 live births)*	177	154	132	98
Under-five mortality (per 1,000 live births)*	..	266	219	148
Maternal mortality ratio (per 100,000 live births) (2005)	..	..	..	910
HIV/AIDS				
People living with HIV/AIDS (thousands)	..	..	21	87[c]
Adult prevalence (percentage)	..	..	0.6	1.6[c]
Spatial distribution				
Population density (per sq. km)	16	21	30	41
Urban population (percentage)	20	27	29	35
Annual urban population growth rate (percentage)	6.0	3.7	3.8	3.8
Annual rural population growth rate (percentage)	1.1	2.3	2.4	1.6
International migration				
Migrant stock				
Number of migrants (thousands)	21	31	814	395**
As percentage of total population	0.5	0.6	10.9	3.8**

* For the periods 1970-1975, 1980-1985, 1990-1995 and 2005-2010.
** For 2010.
[a] For 1999.
[b] For 2005.
[c] For 2007.

Government views and policies

Population policy variable	1976	1986	1996	2009
Population size and growth				
View on growth	Satisfactory	Satisfactory	Satisfactory	Satisfactory
Policy on growth	No intervention	No intervention	No intervention	No intervention
Population age structure				
Level of concern about				
Size of the working-age population	..	..	..	Minor concern
Ageing of the population	..	..	..	Minor concern
Fertility and family planning				
View on fertility level	Satisfactory	Satisfactory	Too high	Too high
Policy	No intervention	No intervention	No intervention	No intervention
Access to contraceptive methods	Indirect support	Direct support	Direct support	Indirect support
Adolescent fertility				
Level of concern	..	..	Major concern	Major concern
Policies and programmes	..	..	Yes	Yes
Health and mortality				
View				
Life expectancy at birth	Unacceptable	Unacceptable	Unacceptable	Unacceptable
Under-five mortality	..	..	Unacceptable	Unacceptable
Maternal mortality	..	..	..	Unacceptable
Level of concern about HIV/AIDS	..	..	Major concern	Major concern
Measures to respond to HIV/AIDS*	..	..	..	1,2,3
Grounds on which abortion is permitted**	..	..	1	1
Spatial distribution and internal migration				
View on spatial distribution	Major change desired	Minor change desired	Major change desired	Major change desired
Policies on internal migration				
From rural to urban areas	..	..	..	No intervention
From rural to rural areas	..	..	..	No intervention
From urban to rural areas	..	..	..	No intervention
From urban to urban areas	..	..	..	No intervention
Into urban agglomerations	Lower	Lower	Lower	No intervention
International migration				
Immigration				
View	Satisfactory	Satisfactory	Satisfactory	Satisfactory
Policy	Maintain	Maintain	No intervention	No intervention
Permanent settlement	..	..	No intervention	No intervention
Temporary workers	..	..	No intervention	No intervention
Highly skilled workers	..	..	..	No intervention
Family reunification	..	..	No intervention	No intervention
Integration of non-citizens	..	..	Yes	..
Emigration				
View	Satisfactory	Satisfactory	Too high	Too high
Policy	Maintain	Maintain	Lower	Lower
Encouraging the return of citizens	Yes	..	Yes	..

* Measures implemented to respond to HIV/AIDS: (1) blood screening; (2) information/education campaigns; (3) antiretroviral treatment; (4) non-discriminatory policies; (5) distribution of condoms.

** Grounds on which abortion is permitted: (1) to save the woman's life; (2) to preserve physical health; (3) to preserve mental health; (4) rape or incest; (5) foetal impairment; (6) economic or social reasons; (7) on request.

Population indicators

Indicator	1975	1985	1995	2009
Population size and growth				
Population size (thousands)	695	919	1 166	1 611
Annual growth rate (percentage)*	2.8	1.9	2.6	2.2
Population age structure				
Percentage of population under age 15	41	44	41	43
Percentage of population aged 60 or over	6	6	6	5
Fertility and family planning				
Total fertility (children per woman)*	7.3	5.7	5.9	5.7
Adolescent fertility rate (per 1,000 women, aged 15 - 19)*	..	..	125.0	129.0
Percentage of births to women under age 20*	..	..	11	11
Percentage of births to women aged 35 or over*	..	..	23	25
Percentage of married women using contraception				
Modern methods	..	..	4[a]	6[b]
All methods	..	..	8[a]	10[b]
Health and mortality				
Life expectancy at birth (years)*				
Males	37	40	43	46
Females	39	43	46	49
Both sexes combined	38	41	44	48
Infant mortality rate (per 1,000 live births)*	174	153	136	114
Under-five mortality (per 1,000 live births)*	..	254	236	196
Maternal mortality ratio (per 100,000 live births) (2005)	..	..	..	1 100
HIV/AIDS				
People living with HIV/AIDS (thousands)	..	..	4.4	16[c]
Adult prevalence (percentage)	..	..	0.8	1.8[c]
Spatial distribution				
Population density (per sq. km)	19	25	32	45
Urban population (percentage)	16	22	30	30
Annual urban population growth rate (percentage)	4.8	7.0	2.8	3.4
Annual rural population growth rate (percentage)	3.6	1.0	2.9	2.8
International migration				
Migrant stock				
Number of migrants (thousands)	13	13	32	19**
As percentage of total population	1.8	1.4	2.7	1.2**

* For the periods 1970-1975, 1980-1985, 1990-1995 and 2005-2010.
** For 2010.
[a] For 2000.
[b] For 2006.
[c] For 2007.

Government views and policies

Population policy variable	1976	1986	1996	2009
Population size and growth				
View on growth	Satisfactory	Satisfactory	Satisfactory	Satisfactory
Policy on growth	No intervention	No intervention	No intervention	No intervention
Population age structure				
Level of concern about				
Size of the working-age population	..	..	..	Major concern
Ageing of the population	..	..	..	Major concern
Fertility and family planning				
View on fertility level	Satisfactory	Satisfactory	Satisfactory	Satisfactory
Policy	No intervention	No intervention	No intervention	No intervention
Access to contraceptive methods	No support	Direct support	Direct support	Direct support
Adolescent fertility				
Level of concern	..	..	..	Major concern
Policies and programmes	..	..	..	Yes
Health and mortality				
View				
Life expectancy at birth	Unacceptable	Acceptable	Unacceptable	Unacceptable
Under-five mortality	..	..	..	Unacceptable
Maternal mortality	..	..	..	Unacceptable
Level of concern about HIV/AIDS	..	..	..	Major concern
Measures to respond to HIV/AIDS*	..	..	..	1,2,3,4,5
Grounds on which abortion is permitted**	..	..	1,2,3,4,5,6,7	1,2,3,4,5,6,7
Spatial distribution and internal migration				
View on spatial distribution	Major change desired	Major change desired	Minor change desired	Minor change desired
Policies on internal migration				
From rural to urban areas	..	..	..	Lower
From rural to rural areas	..	..	..	..
From urban to rural areas	..	..	..	..
From urban to urban areas	..	..	..	..
Into urban agglomerations	No intervention	..	..	Lower
International migration				
Immigration				
View	Satisfactory	Too low	Satisfactory	Satisfactory
Policy	Maintain	Raise	Raise	Maintain
Permanent settlement	..	..	Raise	Maintain
Temporary workers	..	..	..	..
Highly skilled workers	..	..	..	Maintain
Family reunification	..	..	..	Maintain
Integration of non-citizens	..	..	..	..
Emigration				
View	Too high	Too high	Too high	Too high
Policy	Lower	Lower	No intervention	Lower
Encouraging the return of citizens	Yes	..	..	..

* Measures implemented to respond to HIV/AIDS: (1) blood screening; (2) information/education campaigns; (3) antiretroviral treatment; (4) non-discriminatory policies; (5) distribution of condoms.
** Grounds on which abortion is permitted: (1) to save the woman's life; (2) to preserve physical health; (3) to preserve mental health; (4) rape or incest; (5) foetal impairment; (6) economic or social reasons; (7) on request.

Population indicators

Indicator	1975	1985	1995	2009
Population size and growth				
Population size (thousands)	734	771	759	762
Annual growth rate (percentage)*	0.7	-0.1	0.3	-0.1
Population age structure				
Percentage of population under age 15	44	39	33	30
Percentage of population aged 60 or over	5	6	7	9
Fertility and family planning				
Total fertility (children per woman)*	4.9	3.3	2.6	2.3
Adolescent fertility rate (per 1,000 women, aged 15 - 19)*	..	..	86.0	63.0
Percentage of births to women under age 20*	..	..	17	13
Percentage of births to women aged 35 or over*	..	..	11	11
Percentage of married women using contraception				
Modern methods	28	..	37ᵃ	33ᵇ
All methods	31	..	38ᵃ	34ᵇ
Health and mortality				
Life expectancy at birth (years)*				
Males	58	58	59	64
Females	62	64	66	70
Both sexes combined	60	61	62	67
Infant mortality rate (per 1,000 live births)*	79	70	63	42
Under-five mortality (per 1,000 live births)*	..	98	87	56
Maternal mortality ratio (per 100,000 live births) (2005)	..	..	..	470
HIV/AIDS				
People living with HIV/AIDS (thousands)	..	..	16	13ᶜ
Adult prevalence (percentage)	..	..	3.6	2.5ᶜ
Spatial distribution				
Population density (per sq. km)	3	4	4	4
Urban population (percentage)	30	30	29	28
Annual urban population growth rate (percentage)	1.1	-1.0	-0.3	0.0
Annual rural population growth rate (percentage)	0.6	-0.5	0.1	-0.5
International migration				
Migrant stock				
Number of migrants (thousands)	9	5	5	12**
As percentage of total population	1.2	0.7	0.7	1.5**

* For the periods 1970-1975, 1980-1985, 1990-1995 and 2005-2010.
** For 2010.
ᵃ For 1991/1992.
ᵇ For 2006/2007.
ᶜ For 2007.

Government views and policies

Population policy variable	1976	1986	1996	2009
Population size and growth				
View on growth	Too high	Too high	Too high	Too high
Policy on growth	Lower	Lower	Lower	Lower
Population age structure				
Level of concern about				
Size of the working-age population	..	..	..	Minor concern
Ageing of the population	..	..	..	Minor concern
Fertility and family planning				
View on fertility level	Too high	Too high	Too high	Too high
Policy	Lower	Lower	Lower	Lower
Access to contraceptive methods	Direct support	Direct support	Direct support	Direct support
Adolescent fertility				
Level of concern	..	..	..	Major concern
Policies and programmes	..	..		Yes
Health and mortality				
View				
Life expectancy at birth	Unacceptable	Unacceptable	Unacceptable	Unacceptable
Under-five mortality	..	..	..	Unacceptable
Maternal mortality	..	..	..	Unacceptable
Level of concern about HIV/AIDS	..	..	..	Major concern
Measures to respond to HIV/AIDS*	..	..	..	1,2,3,5
Grounds on which abortion is permitted**	..	..	1	1
Spatial distribution and internal migration				
View on spatial distribution	Major change desired	Major change desired	Major change desired	Major change desired
Policies on internal migration				
From rural to urban areas	..	..	..	Lower
From rural to rural areas	..	..	..	No intervention
From urban to rural areas	..	..	..	No intervention
From urban to urban areas	..	..	..	No intervention
Into urban agglomerations	Lower	Lower	..	Lower
International migration				
Immigration				
View	Satisfactory	Satisfactory	Satisfactory	Satisfactory
Policy	Maintain	Maintain	Maintain	Maintain
Permanent settlement	..	..	..	..
Temporary workers	..	..	..	..
Highly skilled workers	..	..	..	..
Family reunification	..	..	..	..
Integration of non-citizens	..	..	..	..
Emigration				
View	Too high	Too high	Too high	Satisfactory
Policy	Lower	Lower	Lower	Maintain
Encouraging the return of citizens	Yes	..	..	Yes

* Measures implemented to respond to HIV/AIDS: (1) blood screening; (2) information/education campaigns; (3) antiretroviral treatment; (4) non-discriminatory policies; (5) distribution of condoms.
** Grounds on which abortion is permitted: (1) to save the woman's life; (2) to preserve physical health; (3) to preserve mental health; (4) rape or incest; (5) foetal impairment; (6) economic or social reasons; (7) on request.

Population indicators

Indicator	1975	1985	1995	2009
Population size and growth				
Population size (thousands)	5 144	6 385	7 861	10 033
Annual growth rate (percentage)*	1.8	2.3	2.0	1.6
Population age structure				
Percentage of population under age 15	41	42	43	36
Percentage of population aged 60 or over	6	6	6	6
Fertility and family planning				
Total fertility (children per woman)*	5.6	6.2	5.2	3.5
Adolescent fertility rate (per 1,000 women, aged 15 - 19)*	..	..	70.0	46.0
Percentage of births to women under age 20*	..	..	7	7
Percentage of births to women aged 35 or over*	..	..	31	27
Percentage of married women using contraception				
Modern methods	5[a]	4[b]	13	24[c]
All methods	19[a]	7[b]	18	32[c]
Health and mortality				
Life expectancy at birth (years)*				
Males	47	50	55	59
Females	49	53	58	63
Both sexes combined	48	51	56	61
Infant mortality rate (per 1,000 live births)*	135	121	92	62
Under-five mortality (per 1,000 live births)*	..	175	130	85
Maternal mortality ratio (per 100,000 live births) (2005)	..	..	..	670
HIV/AIDS				
People living with HIV/AIDS (thousands)	..	..	79	120[d]
Adult prevalence (percentage)	..	..	2.1	2.2[d]
Spatial distribution				
Population density (per sq. km)	185	230	283	362
Urban population (percentage)	20	23	33	48
Annual urban population growth rate (percentage)	2.0	6.4	3.7	4.2
Annual rural population growth rate (percentage)	1.8	0.9	1.0	-1.0
International migration				
Migrant stock				
Number of migrants (thousands)	12	16	22	35**
As percentage of total population	0.2	0.3	0.3	0.3**

* For the periods 1970-1975, 1980-1985, 1990-1995 and 2005-2010.
** For 2010.
[a] For 1977.
[b] For 1983.
[c] For 2005/2006.
[d] For 2007.

Government views and policies

Population policy variable	1976	1986	1996	2009
Population size and growth				
View on growth	Too low	Satisfactory	Satisfactory	Satisfactory
Policy on growth	No intervention	No intervention	No intervention	No intervention
Population age structure				
Level of concern about				
Size of the working-age population	..	..		..
Ageing of the population	..	..		
Fertility and family planning				
View on fertility level	Satisfactory	Satisfactory	Satisfactory	Satisfactory
Policy	No intervention	No intervention	No intervention	No intervention
Access to contraceptive methods	Limits	Limits	Limits	Limits
Adolescent fertility				
Level of concern	..	..	..	..
Policies and programmes	..	..	..	..
Health and mortality				
View				
Life expectancy at birth	Acceptable	Acceptable	Acceptable	Acceptable
Under-five mortality	..	..	..	Acceptable
Maternal mortality	..	..	..	Acceptable
Level of concern about HIV/AIDS	..	..	..	..
Measures to respond to HIV/AIDS*	..	..	..	2,3,4
Grounds on which abortion is permitted**	..	..	Not permitted	Not permitted
Spatial distribution and internal migration				
View on spatial distribution	Satisfactory	Satisfactory	Satisfactory	Satisfactory
Policies on internal migration				
From rural to urban areas	..	..	..	..
From rural to rural areas	..	..	..	..
From urban to rural areas	..	..	..	..
From urban to urban areas	..	..	..	..
Into urban agglomerations	No intervention	..	..	..
International migration				
Immigration				
View	Satisfactory	Satisfactory	Satisfactory	Satisfactory
Policy	Maintain	Maintain	Maintain	Maintain
Permanent settlement	..	..	..	..
Temporary workers	..	..	..	..
Highly skilled workers	..	..	..	..
Family reunification	..	..	..	..
Integration of non-citizens	..	..	..	..
Emigration				
View	Satisfactory	Satisfactory	Satisfactory	Satisfactory
Policy	Maintain	Maintain	Maintain	Maintain
Encouraging the return of citizens	No	..	..	..

* Measures implemented to respond to HIV/AIDS: (1) blood screening; (2) information/education campaigns; (3) antiretroviral treatment; (4) non-discriminatory policies; (5) distribution of condoms.
** Grounds on which abortion is permitted: (1) to save the woman's life; (2) to preserve physical health; (3) to preserve mental health; (4) rape or incest; (5) foetal impairment; (6) economic or social reasons; (7) on request.

Population indicators

Indicator	1975	1985	1995	2009
Population size and growth				
Population size (thousands)	1	1	1	1
Annual growth rate (percentage)*	2.4	0.6	0.3	0.1
Population age structure				
Percentage of population under age 15	..	..	..	..
Percentage of population aged 60 or over	..	..	..	..
Fertility and family planning				
Total fertility (children per woman)*	..	..	..	..
Adolescent fertility rate (per 1,000 women, aged 15 - 19)*	..	..	..	..
Percentage of births to women under age 20*	..	..	..	..
Percentage of births to women aged 35 or over*	..	..	..	..
Percentage of married women using contraception				
Modern methods	..	..	..	..
All methods	..	..	..	..
Health and mortality				
Life expectancy at birth (years)*				
Males	..	..	..	..
Females	..	..	..	..
Both sexes combined	..	..	..	..
Infant mortality rate (per 1,000 live births)*	..	..	..	..
Under-five mortality (per 1,000 live births)*	..	..	..	..
Maternal mortality ratio (per 100,000 live births) (2005)	..	..	..	..
HIV/AIDS				
People living with HIV/AIDS (thousands)	..	..	..	..
Adult prevalence (percentage)	..	..	..	..
Spatial distribution				
Population density (per sq. km)	1 657	1 698	1 775	1 782
Urban population (percentage)	100	100	100	100
Annual urban population growth rate (percentage)	1.1	0.7	0.1	0.1
Annual rural population growth rate (percentage)	0.0	0.0	0.0	0.0
International migration				
Migrant stock				
Number of migrants (thousands)	1	1	1	1**
As percentage of total population	100.0	100.0	100.0	100.0**

* For the periods 1970-1975, 1980-1985, 1990-1995 and 2005-2010.
** For 2010.

Government views and policies

Population policy variable	1976	1986	1996	2009
Population size and growth				
View on growth	Satisfactory	Too high	Satisfactory	Satisfactory
Policy on growth	No intervention	Lower	No intervention	No intervention
Population age structure				
Level of concern about				
Size of the working-age population	..	..	..	Major concern
Ageing of the population	..	..	..	Major concern
Fertility and family planning				
View on fertility level	Too high	Too high	Too high	Too high
Policy	Lower	Lower	Lower	Lower
Access to contraceptive methods	Direct support	Direct support	Direct support	Direct support
Adolescent fertility				
Level of concern	..	..	Minor concern	Major concern
Policies and programmes	..	..	Yes	Yes
Health and mortality				
View				
Life expectancy at birth	Acceptable	Unacceptable	Unacceptable	Unacceptable
Under-five mortality	..	..	Unacceptable	Unacceptable
Maternal mortality	..	..	..	Unacceptable
Level of concern about HIV/AIDS	..	..	Major concern	Major concern
Measures to respond to HIV/AIDS*	..	..	..	1,2,3,4,5
Grounds on which abortion is permitted**	..	..	1	1
Spatial distribution and internal migration				
View on spatial distribution	Major change desired	Major change desired	Major change desired	Major change desired
Policies on internal migration				
From rural to urban areas	..	..	..	Lower
From rural to rural areas	..	..	..	Lower
From urban to rural areas	..	..	..	..
From urban to urban areas	..	..	..	Raise
Into urban agglomerations	No intervention	Lower	No intervention	Lower
International migration				
Immigration				
View	Satisfactory	Too high	Satisfactory	Satisfactory
Policy	Maintain	Lower	Lower	Maintain
Permanent settlement	..	..	Lower	Maintain
Temporary workers	..	..	No intervention	Maintain
Highly skilled workers	..	..	..	Maintain
Family reunification	..	..	No intervention	Maintain
Integration of non-citizens	..	..	No	..
Emigration				
View	Too high	Too high	Satisfactory	Satisfactory
Policy	Lower	Lower	No intervention	Raise
Encouraging the return of citizens	No	..	No	..

* Measures implemented to respond to HIV/AIDS: (1) blood screening; (2) information/education campaigns; (3) antiretroviral treatment; (4) non-discriminatory policies; (5) distribution of condoms.
** Grounds on which abortion is permitted: (1) to save the woman's life; (2) to preserve physical health; (3) to preserve mental health; (4) rape or incest; (5) foetal impairment; (6) economic or social reasons; (7) on request.

Population indicators

Indicator	1975	1985	1995	2009
Population size and growth				
Population size (thousands)	3 107	4 236	5 588	7 466
Annual growth rate (percentage)*	2.9	3.1	2.6	2.0
Population age structure				
Percentage of population under age 15	48	46	44	37
Percentage of population aged 60 or over	5	5	5	6
Fertility and family planning				
Total fertility (children per woman)*	7.1	6.0	4.9	3.3
Adolescent fertility rate (per 1,000 women, aged 15 - 19)*	..	..	127.0	93.0
Percentage of births to women under age 20*	..	..	13	14
Percentage of births to women aged 35 or over*	..	..	21	19
Percentage of married women using contraception				
Modern methods	..	30[a]	41*[b]	56[c]
All methods	..	35[a]	50[b]	65[c]
Health and mortality				
Life expectancy at birth (years)*				
Males	52	59	65	70
Females	56	64	70	75
Both sexes combined	54	61	67	72
Infant mortality rate (per 1,000 live births)*	104	65	43	28
Under-five mortality (per 1,000 live births)*	..	102	60	39
Maternal mortality ratio (per 100,000 live births) (2005)	..	..	..	280
HIV/AIDS				
People living with HIV/AIDS (thousands)	..	..	36	28[d]
Adult prevalence (percentage)	..	..	1.3	0.7[d]
Spatial distribution				
Population density (per sq. km)	28	38	50	67
Urban population (percentage)	32	38	42	48
Annual urban population growth rate (percentage)	4.8	4.5	3.3	3.0
Annual rural population growth rate (percentage)	2.3	2.0	1.6	1.0
International migration				
Migrant stock				
Number of migrants (thousands)	14	83	31	24**
As percentage of total population	0.5	2.0	0.6	0.3**

* For the periods 1970-1975, 1980-1985, 1990-1995 and 2005-2010.
** For 2010.
[a] For 1984.
[b] For 1996.
[c] For 2005/2006.
[d] For 2007.

Government views and policies

Population policy variable	1976	1986	1996	2009
Population size and growth				
View on growth	Satisfactory	Too low	Too low	Too low
Policy on growth	No intervention	Raise	Raise	Raise
Population age structure				
Level of concern about				
Size of the working-age population	..	..	..	Minor concern
Ageing of the population	..	..	..	Major concern
Fertility and family planning				
View on fertility level	Satisfactory	Too low	Too low	Too low
Policy	Maintain	Raise	Raise	Raise
Access to contraceptive methods	Direct support	Direct support	Direct support	Indirect support
Adolescent fertility				
Level of concern	..	..	Not a concern	Minor concern
Policies and programmes	..	..	No	Yes
Health and mortality				
View				
Life expectancy at birth	Acceptable	Acceptable	Unacceptable	Unacceptable
Under-five mortality	..	..	Acceptable	Acceptable
Maternal mortality	..	..		Acceptable
Level of concern about HIV/AIDS	..	..	Minor concern	Minor concern
Measures to respond to HIV/AIDS*	..	..	..	1,2,3,5
Grounds on which abortion is permitted**	..	..	1,2,3,4,5,6,7	1,2,3,4,5,6,7
Spatial distribution and internal migration				
View on spatial distribution	Satisfactory	Satisfactory	Satisfactory	Minor change desired
Policies on internal migration				
From rural to urban areas	..	..	..	..
From rural to rural areas	..	..	..	..
From urban to rural areas	..	..	..	..
From urban to urban areas	..	..	..	..
Into urban agglomerations	No intervention	No intervention	No intervention	Lower
International migration				
Immigration				
View	Satisfactory	Satisfactory	Satisfactory	Satisfactory
Policy	Maintain	Maintain	Lower	Maintain
Permanent settlement	..	..	Lower	Maintain
Temporary workers	..	..	Lower	Maintain
Highly skilled workers	..	..	..	No intervention
Family reunification	..	..	No intervention	Maintain
Integration of non-citizens	..	..	No	Yes
Emigration				
View	Satisfactory	Satisfactory	Satisfactory	Satisfactory
Policy	Maintain	Maintain	No intervention	No intervention
Encouraging the return of citizens	No	..	Yes	No

* Measures implemented to respond to HIV/AIDS: (1) blood screening; (2) information/education campaigns; (3) antiretroviral treatment; (4) non-discriminatory policies; (5) distribution of condoms.

** Grounds on which abortion is permitted: (1) to save the woman's life; (2) to preserve physical health; (3) to preserve mental health; (4) rape or incest; (5) foetal impairment; (6) economic or social reasons; (7) on request.

Population indicators

Indicator	1975	1985	1995	2009
Population size and growth				
Population size (thousands)	10 532	10 579	10 332	9 993
Annual growth rate (percentage)*	0.4	-0.2	-0.1	-0.2
Population age structure				
Percentage of population under age 15	20	21	18	15
Percentage of population aged 60 or over	18	18	20	22
Fertility and family planning				
Total fertility (children per woman)*	2.1	1.8	1.7	1.4
Adolescent fertility rate (per 1,000 women, aged 15 - 19)*	..	..	37.0	20.0
Percentage of births to women under age 20*	..	..	11	7
Percentage of births to women aged 35 or over*	..	..	2	5
Percentage of married women using contraception				
Modern methods	44[a]	62[b]	71[c]	..
All methods	74[a]	73[b]	81[c]	..
Health and mortality				
Life expectancy at birth (years)*				
Males	66	65	65	69
Females	72	73	74	77
Both sexes combined	69	69	70	73
Infant mortality rate (per 1,000 live births)*	34	20	13	7
Under-five mortality (per 1,000 live births)*	..	23	15	8
Maternal mortality ratio (per 100,000 live births) (2005)	..	..	..	6
HIV/AIDS				
People living with HIV/AIDS (thousands)	..	..	1.5	3.3[d]
Adult prevalence (percentage)	..	..	<0.1	0.1[d]
Spatial distribution				
Population density (per sq. km)	113	114	111	107
Urban population (percentage)	62	65	65	68
Annual urban population growth rate (percentage)	1.1	-0.2	-0.3	0.3
Annual rural population growth rate (percentage)	-0.7	-0.9	0.2	-1.6
International migration				
Migrant stock				
Number of migrants (thousands)	402	339	293	368**
As percentage of total population	3.8	3.2	2.8	3.7**

* For the periods 1970-1975, 1980-1985, 1990-1995 and 2005-2010.
** For 2010.
[a] For 1974.
[b] For 1986.
[c] For 1992/1993.
[d] For 2007.

Government views and policies

Population policy variable	1976	1986	1996	2009
Population size and growth				
View on growth	Satisfactory	Satisfactory	Satisfactory	Satisfactory
Policy on growth	No intervention	No intervention	No intervention	Maintain
Population age structure				
Level of concern about				
Size of the working-age population	..	..	..	Not a concern
Ageing of the population	..	..	..	Minor concern
Fertility and family planning				
View on fertility level	Satisfactory	Satisfactory	Satisfactory	Satisfactory
Policy	No intervention	No intervention	No intervention	Maintain
Access to contraceptive methods	Direct support	Direct support	Direct support	Direct support
Adolescent fertility				
Level of concern	..	..	..	Minor concern
Policies and programmes	..	..	..	Yes
Health and mortality				
View				
Life expectancy at birth	Acceptable	Acceptable	Acceptable	Acceptable
Under-five mortality	..	..	..	Acceptable
Maternal mortality	..	..	..	Acceptable
Level of concern about HIV/AIDS	..	..	..	Minor concern
Measures to respond to HIV/AIDS*	..	..	..	1,2,3,4,5
Grounds on which abortion is permitted**	..	..	1,2,3,4,5,6	1,2,3,4,5,6
Spatial distribution and internal migration				
View on spatial distribution	Minor change desired	Minor change desired	Minor change desired	Major change desired
Policies on internal migration				
From rural to urban areas	..	..	..	Lower
From rural to rural areas	..	..	..	No intervention
From urban to rural areas	..	..	..	No intervention
From urban to urban areas	..	..	..	No intervention
Into urban agglomerations	No intervention	..	..	No intervention
International migration				
Immigration				
View	Satisfactory	Satisfactory	Satisfactory	Satisfactory
Policy	Maintain	Maintain	Maintain	Maintain
Permanent settlement	..	..	..	Maintain
Temporary workers	..	..	..	Maintain
Highly skilled workers	..	..	..	No intervention
Family reunification	..	..	..	Maintain
Integration of non-citizens	..	..	..	Yes
Emigration				
View	Satisfactory	Satisfactory	Satisfactory	Satisfactory
Policy	Maintain	Maintain	Maintain	No intervention
Encouraging the return of citizens	No	..	..	No

* Measures implemented to respond to HIV/AIDS: (1) blood screening; (2) information/education campaigns; (3) antiretroviral treatment; (4) non-discriminatory policies; (5) distribution of condoms.
** Grounds on which abortion is permitted: (1) to save the woman's life; (2) to preserve physical health; (3) to preserve mental health; (4) rape or incest; (5) foetal impairment; (6) economic or social reasons; (7) on request.

Population indicators

Indicator	1975	1985	1995	2009
Population size and growth				
Population size (thousands)	218	241	267	323
Annual growth rate (percentage)[*]	1.3	1.1	1.0	2.1
Population age structure				
Percentage of population under age 15	30	26	24	21
Percentage of population aged 60 or over	13	14	15	16
Fertility and family planning				
Total fertility (children per woman)[*]	2.8	2.2	2.2	2.1
Adolescent fertility rate (per 1,000 women, aged 15 - 19)[*]	..	..	25.0	15.0
Percentage of births to women under age 20[*]	..	..	6	4
Percentage of births to women aged 35 or over[*]	..	..	15	17
Percentage of married women using contraception				
Modern methods	..	..	..	..
All methods	..	..	..	..
Health and mortality				
Life expectancy at birth (years)[*]				
Males	71	74	76	80
Females	77	80	81	83
Both sexes combined	74	77	79	82
Infant mortality rate (per 1,000 live births)[*]	12	6	5	3
Under-five mortality (per 1,000 live births)[*]	..	8	6	4
Maternal mortality ratio (per 100,000 live births) (2005)	..	..	..	4
HIV/AIDS				
People living with HIV/AIDS (thousands)	..	..	<0.2	<0.5[a]
Adult prevalence (percentage)	..	..	0.1	0.2[a]
Spatial distribution				
Population density (per sq. km)	2	2	3	3
Urban population (percentage)	87	90	92	92
Annual urban population growth rate (percentage)	1.4	1.4	1.2	0.8
Annual rural population growth rate (percentage)	-1.5	-1.3	-1.0	0.6
International migration				
Migrant stock				
Number of migrants (thousands)	5	7	11	37[**]
As percentage of total population	2.4	2.9	4.0	11.3[**]

[*] For the periods 1970-1975, 1980-1985, 1990-1995 and 2005-2010.
[**] For 2010.
[a] For 2007.

Government views and policies

Population policy variable	1976	1986	1996	2009
Population size and growth				
View on growth	Too high	Too high	Too high	Too high
Policy on growth	Lower	Lower	Lower	Lower
Population age structure				
Level of concern about				
Size of the working-age population	..	..	..	Major concern
Ageing of the population	..	..		Major concern
Fertility and family planning				
View on fertility level	Too high	Too high	Too high	Too high
Policy	Lower	Lower	Lower	Lower
Access to contraceptive methods	Direct support	Direct support	Direct support	Direct support
Adolescent fertility				
Level of concern	..	..	Major concern	Major concern
Policies and programmes	..	..	Yes	Yes
Health and mortality				
View				
Life expectancy at birth	Unacceptable	Unacceptable	Unacceptable	Unacceptable
Under-five mortality	..	..	Unacceptable	Unacceptable
Maternal mortality	..	..	..	Unacceptable
Level of concern about HIV/AIDS	..	..	Major concern	Major concern
Measures to respond to HIV/AIDS*	..	..	..	1,2,3,4,5
Grounds on which abortion is permitted**	..	..	1,2,3,4,5,6	1,2,3,4,5,6
Spatial distribution and internal migration				
View on spatial distribution	Major change desired	Minor change desired	Major change desired	Major change desired
Policies on internal migration				
From rural to urban areas	..	..	..	Lower
From rural to rural areas	..	..	..	Maintain
From urban to rural areas	..	..	..	Raise
From urban to urban areas	..	..	..	Maintain
Into urban agglomerations	Lower	..	Lower	Lower
International migration				
Immigration				
View	Satisfactory	Satisfactory	Satisfactory	Satisfactory
Policy	Maintain	Maintain	Maintain	Maintain
Permanent settlement	..	..	..	..
Temporary workers	..	..	..	..
Highly skilled workers	..	..	..	Maintain
Family reunification	..	..	..	..
Integration of non-citizens	..	..	..	..
Emigration				
View	Satisfactory	Satisfactory	Satisfactory	Satisfactory
Policy	Maintain	Maintain	Maintain	Maintain
Encouraging the return of citizens	No	..	Yes	..

* Measures implemented to respond to HIV/AIDS: (1) blood screening; (2) information/education campaigns; (3) antiretroviral treatment; (4) non-discriminatory policies; (5) distribution of condoms.
** Grounds on which abortion is permitted: (1) to save the woman's life; (2) to preserve physical health; (3) to preserve mental health; (4) rape or incest; (5) foetal impairment; (6) economic or social reasons; (7) on request.

Population indicators

Indicator	1975	1985	1995	2009
Population size and growth				
Population size (thousands)	617 432	774 775	953 148	1 198 003
Annual growth rate (percentage)*	2.2	2.2	2.0	1.4
Population age structure				
Percentage of population under age 15	40	39	37	31
Percentage of population aged 60 or over	6	6	6	7
Fertility and family planning				
Total fertility (children per woman)*	5.3	4.5	3.9	2.8
Adolescent fertility rate (per 1,000 women, aged 15 - 19)*	..	..	115.0	68.0
Percentage of births to women under age 20*	..	..	15	12
Percentage of births to women aged 35 or over*	..	..	11	8
Percentage of married women using contraception				
Modern methods	10[a]	40[b]	43[c]	49[d]
All methods	14[a]	45[b]	48[c]	56[d]
Health and mortality				
Life expectancy at birth (years)*				
Males	51	56	58	62
Females	50	56	59	65
Both sexes combined	50	56	59	63
Infant mortality rate (per 1,000 live births)*	120	98	78	55
Under-five mortality (per 1,000 live births)*	..	138	111	81
Maternal mortality ratio (per 100,000 live births) (2005)	..	..	..	450
HIV/AIDS				
People living with HIV/AIDS (thousands)	..	..	1 200	2 400[e]
Adult prevalence (percentage)	..	..	0.2	0.3[e]
Spatial distribution				
Population density (per sq. km)	188	236	290	364
Urban population (percentage)	21	24	27	30
Annual urban population growth rate (percentage)	3.9	3.2	2.7	2.4
Annual rural population growth rate (percentage)	1.8	1.9	1.7	1.0
International migration				
Migrant stock				
Number of migrants (thousands)	9 011	8 131	7 022	5 436**
As percentage of total population	1.5	1.0	0.7	0.4**

* For the periods 1970-1975, 1980-1985, 1990-1995 and 2005-2010.
** For 2010.
[a] For 1970.
[b] For 1988.
[c] For 1998/1999.
[d] For 2005/2006.
[e] For 2007.

Government views and policies

Population policy variable	1976	1986	1996	2009
Population size and growth				
View on growth	Too high	Too high	Too high	Too high
Policy on growth	Lower	Lower	Lower	Lower
Population age structure				
Level of concern about				
Size of the working-age population	..	..	..	Major concern
Ageing of the population	..	..	..	Minor concern
Fertility and family planning				
View on fertility level	Too high	Too high	Too high	Too high
Policy	Lower	Lower	Lower	Lower
Access to contraceptive methods	Direct support	Direct support	Direct support	Direct support
Adolescent fertility				
Level of concern	..	..	Major concern	Major concern
Policies and programmes	..	..	Yes	Yes
Health and mortality				
View				
Life expectancy at birth	Unacceptable	Unacceptable	Unacceptable	Unacceptable
Under-five mortality	..	..	Unacceptable	Unacceptable
Maternal mortality	..	..	..	Unacceptable
Level of concern about HIV/AIDS	..	..	Major concern	Major concern
Measures to respond to HIV/AIDS*	..	..	..	1,2,3,5
Grounds on which abortion is permitted**	..	..	1	1
Spatial distribution and internal migration				
View on spatial distribution	Major change desired	Major change desired	Major change desired	Major change desired
Policies on internal migration				
From rural to urban areas	..	..	..	Lower
From rural to rural areas	..	..	..	No intervention
From urban to rural areas	..	..	..	No intervention
From urban to urban areas	..	..	..	No intervention
Into urban agglomerations	..	..	Lower	Lower
International migration				
Immigration				
View	Satisfactory	Satisfactory	Too high	Satisfactory
Policy	Maintain	Maintain	Lower	No intervention
Permanent settlement	..	..	Lower	No intervention
Temporary workers	..	..	..	No intervention
Highly skilled workers	..	..	..	No intervention
Family reunification	..	..	..	No intervention
Integration of non-citizens	..	..	..	No
Emigration				
View	Satisfactory	Satisfactory	Satisfactory	Too low
Policy	Maintain	Maintain	No intervention	Raise
Encouraging the return of citizens	..	..	..	No

* Measures implemented to respond to HIV/AIDS: (1) blood screening; (2) information/education campaigns; (3) antiretroviral treatment; (4) non-discriminatory policies; (5) distribution of condoms.
** Grounds on which abortion is permitted: (1) to save the woman's life; (2) to preserve physical health; (3) to preserve mental health; (4) rape or incest; (5) foetal impairment; (6) economic or social reasons; (7) on request.

Population indicators

Indicator	1975	1985	1995	2009
Population size and growth				
Population size (thousands)	131 329	162 348	191 501	229 965
Annual growth rate (percentage)*	2.3	2.0	1.5	1.2
Population age structure				
Percentage of population under age 15	42	38	33	27
Percentage of population aged 60 or over	5	6	7	9
Fertility and family planning				
Total fertility (children per woman)*	5.3	4.1	2.9	2.2
Adolescent fertility rate (per 1,000 women, aged 15 - 19)*	..	..	61.0	40.0
Percentage of births to women under age 20*	..	..	11	9
Percentage of births to women aged 35 or over*	..	..	17	17
Percentage of married women using contraception				
Modern methods	17[a]	37	53	57[b]
All methods	18[a]	39	54	61[b]
Health and mortality				
Life expectancy at birth (years)*				
Males	48	55	61	69
Females	51	58	65	73
Both sexes combined	49	56	63	71
Infant mortality rate (per 1,000 live births)*	126	89	58	27
Under-five mortality (per 1,000 live births)*	..	126	78	32
Maternal mortality ratio (per 100,000 live births) (2005)	..	..	..	420
HIV/AIDS				
People living with HIV/AIDS (thousands)	..	..	..	270[b]
Adult prevalence (percentage)	..	..	..	0.2[b]
Spatial distribution				
Population density (per sq. km)	69	85	101	121
Urban population (percentage)	19	26	36	53
Annual urban population growth rate (percentage)	5.0	5.1	4.9	3.1
Annual rural population growth rate (percentage)	1.6	0.7	-0.5	-1.2
International migration				
Migrant stock				
Number of migrants (thousands)	928	593	219	123**
As percentage of total population	0.7	0.4	0.1	0.1**

* For the periods 1970-1975, 1980-1985, 1990-1995 and 2005-2010.
** For 2010.
[a] For 1976.
[b] For 2007.

Government views and policies

Population policy variable	1976	1986	1996	2009
Population size and growth				
View on growth	Too high	Satisfactory	Too high	Too high
Policy on growth	Lower	No intervention	Lower	Lower
Population age structure				
Level of concern about				
Size of the working-age population	..	..	..	Major concern
Ageing of the population	..	..	..	Major concern
Fertility and family planning				
View on fertility level	Too high	Satisfactory	Too high	Too high
Policy	Lower	No intervention	Lower	Lower
Access to contraceptive methods	Direct support	Indirect support	Direct support	Direct support
Adolescent fertility				
Level of concern	..	..	Major concern	Major concern
Policies and programmes	..	..	Yes	Yes
Health and mortality				
View				
Life expectancy at birth	Unacceptable	Unacceptable	Unacceptable	Unacceptable
Under-five mortality	..	..	Unacceptable	Unacceptable
Maternal mortality	..	..	..	Unacceptable
Level of concern about HIV/AIDS	..	..	Major concern	Major concern
Measures to respond to HIV/AIDS*	..	..	..	1,2,3,4,5
Grounds on which abortion is permitted**	..	..	1	1
Spatial distribution and internal migration				
View on spatial distribution	Major change desired	Minor change desired	Major change desired	Minor change desired
Policies on internal migration				
From rural to urban areas	..	..	..	Lower
From rural to rural areas	..	..	..	Maintain
From urban to rural areas	..	..	..	..
From urban to urban areas	..	..	..	..
Into urban agglomerations	..	Lower	Lower	Lower
International migration				
Immigration				
View	Too low	Too high	Too high	Too high
Policy	Raise	Lower	Lower	Lower
Permanent settlement	..	..	Lower	Maintain
Temporary workers	..	..	No intervention	Maintain
Highly skilled workers	..	..	..	Maintain
Family reunification	..	..	No intervention	..
Integration of non-citizens	..	..	No	..
Emigration				
View	Satisfactory	Too high	Satisfactory	Satisfactory
Policy	Maintain	Lower	Lower	Lower
Encouraging the return of citizens	..	..	Yes	Yes

* Measures implemented to respond to HIV/AIDS: (1) blood screening; (2) information/education campaigns; (3) antiretroviral treatment; (4) non-discriminatory policies; (5) distribution of condoms.

** Grounds on which abortion is permitted: (1) to save the woman's life; (2) to preserve physical health; (3) to preserve mental health; (4) rape or incest; (5) foetal impairment; (6) economic or social reasons; (7) on request.

Population indicators

Indicator	1975	1985	1995	2009
Population size and growth				
Population size (thousands)	33 344	48 418	62 205	74 196
Annual growth rate (percentage)*	2.9	4.2	1.8	1.2
Population age structure				
Percentage of population under age 15	44	45	40	24
Percentage of population aged 60 or over	5	6	6	7
Fertility and family planning				
Total fertility (children per woman)*	6.4	6.6	4.0	1.8
Adolescent fertility rate (per 1,000 women, aged 15 - 19)*	..	..	83.0	18.0
Percentage of births to women under age 20*	..	..	10	5
Percentage of births to women aged 35 or over*	..	..	23	11
Percentage of married women using contraception				
Modern methods	..	28[a]	56[b]	59[c]
All methods	36[d]	49[a]	73[b]	73[c]
Health and mortality				
Life expectancy at birth (years)*				
Males	55	59	65	70
Females	55	61	67	73
Both sexes combined	55	60	66	71
Infant mortality rate (per 1,000 live births)*	115	88	55	29
Under-five mortality (per 1,000 live births)*	..	116	67	34
Maternal mortality ratio (per 100,000 live births) (2005)	..	..	..	140
HIV/AIDS				
People living with HIV/AIDS (thousands)	..	..	7	86[e]
Adult prevalence (percentage)	..	..	..	0.2[e]
Spatial distribution				
Population density (per sq. km)	20	29	38	45
Urban population (percentage)	46	53	60	69
Annual urban population growth rate (percentage)	5.0	5.0	2.8	2.1
Annual rural population growth rate (percentage)	1.3	2.1	-0.8	-0.2
International migration				
Migrant stock				
Number of migrants (thousands)	157	2 855	3 016	2 129**
As percentage of total population	0.5	5.9	4.8	2.8**

* For the periods 1970-1975, 1980-1985, 1990-1995 and 2005-2010.
** For 2010.
[a] For 1989.
[b] For 1997.
[c] For 2002.
[d] For 1977.
[e] For 2007.

Government views and policies

Population policy variable	1976	1986	1996	2009
Population size and growth				
View on growth	Satisfactory	Too low	Too low	Satisfactory
Policy on growth	No intervention	Raise	Raise	Maintain
Population age structure				
Level of concern about				
Size of the working-age population	..	..	..	Major concern
Ageing of the population	..	..	..	Major concern
Fertility and family planning				
View on fertility level	Satisfactory	Too low	Too low	Satisfactory
Policy	Maintain	Raise	Raise	No intervention
Access to contraceptive methods	Direct support	Limits	No support	Direct support
Adolescent fertility				
Level of concern	..	..	..	Minor concern
Policies and programmes	..	..	..	No
Health and mortality				
View				
Life expectancy at birth	Acceptable	Acceptable	Unacceptable	Unacceptable
Under-five mortality	..	..	..	Unacceptable
Maternal mortality	..	..	..	Unacceptable
Level of concern about HIV/AIDS	..	..	..	Minor concern
Measures to respond to HIV/AIDS*	..	..	..	1,2,3
Grounds on which abortion is permitted**	..	..	1,2,3,4,5	1
Spatial distribution and internal migration				
View on spatial distribution	Minor change desired	Minor change desired	Minor change desired	Major change desired
Policies on internal migration				
From rural to urban areas	..	..	..	..
From rural to rural areas	..	..	..	..
From urban to rural areas	..	..	..	..
From urban to urban areas	..	..	..	..
Into urban agglomerations	..	Lower	..	Lower
International migration				
Immigration				
View	Too low	Satisfactory	Satisfactory	Satisfactory
Policy	Raise	Maintain	Maintain	Maintain
Permanent settlement	..	..	Maintain	Maintain
Temporary workers	..	..	..	Maintain
Highly skilled workers	..	..	..	Maintain
Family reunification	..	..	..	..
Integration of non-citizens	..	..	..	Yes
Emigration				
View	Satisfactory	Satisfactory	Satisfactory	Too high
Policy	Maintain	Maintain	Maintain	Lower
Encouraging the return of citizens	..	..	..	..

* Measures implemented to respond to HIV/AIDS: (1) blood screening; (2) information/education campaigns; (3) antiretroviral treatment; (4) non-discriminatory policies; (5) distribution of condoms.
** Grounds on which abortion is permitted: (1) to save the woman's life; (2) to preserve physical health; (3) to preserve mental health; (4) rape or incest; (5) foetal impairment; (6) economic or social reasons; (7) on request.

Population indicators

Indicator	1975	1985	1995	2009
Population size and growth				
Population size (thousands)	12 016	16 093	20 971	30 747
Annual growth rate (percentage)*	3.3	2.8	3.0	2.2
Population age structure				
Percentage of population under age 15	46	46	44	41
Percentage of population aged 60 or over	6	5	5	5
Fertility and family planning				
Total fertility (children per woman)*	7.2	6.4	5.8	4.1
Adolescent fertility rate (per 1,000 women, aged 15 - 19)*	..	..	53.0	86.0
Percentage of births to women under age 20*	..	..	5	10
Percentage of births to women aged 35 or over*	..	..	31	20
Percentage of married women using contraception				
Modern methods	13[a]	10[b]	..	33[c]
All methods	15[a]	14[b]	..	50[c]
Health and mortality				
Life expectancy at birth (years)*				
Males	59	59	60	63
Females	59	65	73	72
Both sexes combined	59	62	66	67
Infant mortality rate (per 1,000 live births)*	74	52	48	33
Under-five mortality (per 1,000 live births)*	..	69	63	41
Maternal mortality ratio (per 100,000 live births) (2005)	..	..	..	300
HIV/AIDS				
People living with HIV/AIDS (thousands)	..	..	..	..
Adult prevalence (percentage)	..	..	..	..
Spatial distribution				
Population density (per sq. km)	27	37	48	70
Urban population (percentage)	61	69	69	66
Annual urban population growth rate (percentage)	5.0	3.5	2.8	2.0
Annual rural population growth rate (percentage)	0.7	0.5	3.7	2.3
International migration				
Migrant stock				
Number of migrants (thousands)	71	112	134	83**
As percentage of total population	0.6	0.7	0.6	0.3**

* For the periods 1970-1975, 1980-1985, 1990-1995 and 2005-2010.
** For 2010.
[a] For 1974.
[b] For 1989.
[c] For 2006.

Government views and policies

Population policy variable	1976	1986	1996	2009
Population size and growth				
View on growth	Too low	Satisfactory	Satisfactory	Satisfactory
Policy on growth	No intervention	Maintain	No intervention	No intervention
Population age structure				
Level of concern about				
Size of the working-age population	..	..	..	Not a concern
Ageing of the population	..	..	..	Major concern
Fertility and family planning				
View on fertility level	Satisfactory	Satisfactory	Satisfactory	Satisfactory
Policy	Maintain	Maintain	Maintain	No intervention
Access to contraceptive methods	No support	Limits	Direct support	Direct support
Adolescent fertility				
Level of concern	..	..	..	Major concern
Policies and programmes	..	..	Yes	Yes
Health and mortality				
View				
Life expectancy at birth	Acceptable	Acceptable	Acceptable	Acceptable
Under-five mortality	..	..	..	Acceptable
Maternal mortality	..	..	..	Acceptable
Level of concern about HIV/AIDS	..	..	Major concern	Minor concern
Measures to respond to HIV/AIDS*	..	..	..	1,2,3,4,5
Grounds on which abortion is permitted**	..	..	1	1
Spatial distribution and internal migration				
View on spatial distribution	Minor change desired	Minor change desired	Minor change desired	Minor change desired
Policies on internal migration				
From rural to urban areas	..	..	..	No intervention
From rural to rural areas	..	..	..	No intervention
From urban to rural areas	..	..	..	Raise
From urban to urban areas	..	..	..	No intervention
Into urban agglomerations	Lower	..	..	Lower
International migration				
Immigration				
View	Satisfactory	Satisfactory	Satisfactory	Satisfactory
Policy	Maintain	Maintain	Maintain	Maintain
Permanent settlement	..	..	Maintain	Raise
Temporary workers	..	..	..	Maintain
Highly skilled workers	..	..	..	Raise
Family reunification	..	..	..	Maintain
Integration of non-citizens	..	..	..	Yes
Emigration				
View	Too high	Too high	Too high	Satisfactory
Policy	Lower	Lower	Lower	No intervention
Encouraging the return of citizens	No	..	..	Yes

* Measures implemented to respond to HIV/AIDS: (1) blood screening; (2) information/education campaigns; (3) antiretroviral treatment; (4) non−discriminatory policies; (5) distribution of condoms.
** Grounds on which abortion is permitted: (1) to save the woman's life; (2) to preserve physical health; (3) to preserve mental health; (4) rape or incest; (5) foetal impairment; (6) economic or social reasons; (7) on request.

Population indicators

Indicator	1975	1985	1995	2009
Population size and growth				
Population size (thousands)	3 177	3 539	3 609	4 515
Annual growth rate (percentage)*	1.5	0.8	0.5	1.8
Population age structure				
Percentage of population under age 15	31	30	24	21
Percentage of population aged 60 or over	15	14	15	16
Fertility and family planning				
Total fertility (children per woman)*	3.8	2.9	2.0	2.0
Adolescent fertility rate (per 1,000 women, aged 15 - 19)*	..	..	18.0	16.0
Percentage of births to women under age 20*	..	..	5	4
Percentage of births to women aged 35 or over*	..	..	21	23
Percentage of married women using contraception				
Modern methods	..	..	68[a]	89[b]
All methods	..	..	77[a]	89[b]
Health and mortality				
Life expectancy at birth (years)*				
Males	69	70	73	78
Females	74	76	78	82
Both sexes combined	71	73	75	80
Infant mortality rate (per 1,000 live births)*	18	10	7	4
Under-five mortality (per 1,000 live births)*	..	12	8	6
Maternal mortality ratio (per 100,000 live births) (2005)	..	..	..	1
HIV/AIDS				
People living with HIV/AIDS (thousands)	..	..	2	5.5[c]
Adult prevalence (percentage)	..	..	0.1	0.2[c]
Spatial distribution				
Population density (per sq. km)	45	50	51	64
Urban population (percentage)	54	56	58	62
Annual urban population growth rate (percentage)	2.1	0.3	1.2	2.1
Annual rural population growth rate (percentage)	0.8	-0.3	0.3	0.8
International migration				
Migrant stock				
Number of migrants (thousands)	171	225	264	899**
As percentage of total population	5.4	6.4	7.3	19.6**

* For the periods 1970-1975, 1980-1985, 1990-1995 and 2005-2010.
** For 2010.
[a] For 1998.
[b] For 2003/2004.
[c] For 2007.

Government views and policies

Population policy variable	1976	1986	1996	2009
Population size and growth				
View on growth	Too low	Too low	Too low	Too low
Policy on growth	Raise	Raise	Raise	Raise
Population age structure				
Level of concern about				
Size of the working-age population	..	..	..	Major concern
Ageing of the population	..	..	..	Major concern
Fertility and family planning				
View on fertility level	Too low	Too low	Too low	Too low
Policy	Raise	Raise	Raise	Raise
Access to contraceptive methods	Direct support	Direct support	Direct support	Indirect support
Adolescent fertility				
Level of concern	..	..	..	Not a concern
Policies and programmes	..	..	..	Yes
Health and mortality				
View				
Life expectancy at birth	Acceptable	Acceptable	Acceptable	Acceptable
Under-five mortality	..	..	..	Acceptable
Maternal mortality	..	..	..	Acceptable
Level of concern about HIV/AIDS	..	..	..	Major concern
Measures to respond to HIV/AIDS*	..	..	..	1,2,3,4,5
Grounds on which abortion is permitted**	..	..	1,2,3,4,5	1,2,3,4,5
Spatial distribution and internal migration				
View on spatial distribution	Minor change desired	Minor change desired	Minor change desired	Minor change desired
Policies on internal migration				
From rural to urban areas	..	..	..	No intervention
From rural to rural areas	..	..	..	No intervention
From urban to rural areas	..	..	..	Lower
From urban to urban areas	..	..	..	No intervention
Into urban agglomerations	..	..	..	No intervention
International migration				
Immigration				
View	Too low	Too low	Too low	Too low
Policy	Raise	Raise	Raise	Raise
Permanent settlement	..	..	Raise	Raise
Temporary workers	..	..	..	Lower
Highly skilled workers	..	..	..	Maintain
Family reunification	..	..	..	Maintain
Integration of non-citizens	..	..	Yes	Yes
Emigration				
View	Satisfactory	Too high	Too high	Too high
Policy	Maintain	Lower	Lower	Lower
Encouraging the return of citizens	..	..	Yes	Yes

* Measures implemented to respond to HIV/AIDS: (1) blood screening; (2) information/education campaigns; (3) antiretroviral treatment; (4) non-discriminatory policies; (5) distribution of condoms.
** Grounds on which abortion is permitted: (1) to save the woman's life; (2) to preserve physical health; (3) to preserve mental health; (4) rape or incest; (5) foetal impairment; (6) economic or social reasons; (7) on request.

Population indicators

Indicator	1975	1985	1995	2009
Population size and growth				
Population size (thousands)	3 358	4 103	5 374	7 170
Annual growth rate (percentage)*	2.9	1.7	3.5	1.7
Population age structure				
Percentage of population under age 15	33	33	29	28
Percentage of population aged 60 or over	12	12	13	14
Fertility and family planning				
Total fertility (children per woman)*	3.8	3.1	2.9	2.8
Adolescent fertility rate (per 1,000 women, aged 15 - 19)*	..	..	18.0	14.0
Percentage of births to women under age 20*	..	..	3	3
Percentage of births to women aged 35 or over*	..	..	17	20
Percentage of married women using contraception				
Modern methods	..	52[a]	..	..
All methods	..	68[a]	..	..
Health and mortality				
Life expectancy at birth (years)*				
Males	70	73	75	79
Females	73	76	79	83
Both sexes combined	72	74	77	81
Infant mortality rate (per 1,000 live births)*	22	14	9	5
Under-five mortality (per 1,000 live births)*	..	16	10	6
Maternal mortality ratio (per 100,000 live births) (2005)	..	..	..	4
HIV/AIDS				
People living with HIV/AIDS (thousands)	..	..	2	5.1[b]
Adult prevalence (percentage)	..	..	0.1	0.1[b]
Spatial distribution				
Population density (per sq. km)	152	185	243	324
Urban population (percentage)	87	90	91	92
Annual urban population growth rate (percentage)	3.1	1.7	3.1	1.6
Annual rural population growth rate (percentage)	-0.5	0.5	1.7	1.2
International migration				
Migrant stock				
Number of migrants (thousands)	1 446	1 523	1 919	2 940**
As percentage of total population	43.1	37.1	35.7	40.4**

* For the periods 1970-1975, 1980-1985, 1990-1995 and 2005-2010.
** For 2010.
[a] For 1987/1988.
[b] For 2007.

Government views and policies

Population policy variable	1976	1986	1996	2009
Population size and growth				
View on growth	Satisfactory	Satisfactory	Satisfactory	Too low
Policy on growth	No intervention	No intervention	No intervention	Raise
Population age structure				
Level of concern about				
Size of the working-age population	..	..	..	Major concern
Ageing of the population	..	..	..	Major concern
Fertility and family planning				
View on fertility level	Satisfactory	Satisfactory	Satisfactory	Too low
Policy	No intervention	No intervention	No intervention	Raise
Access to contraceptive methods	Indirect support	Direct support	Direct support	Indirect support
Adolescent fertility				
Level of concern	..	..	Not a concern	Not a concern
Policies and programmes	..	..	No	No
Health and mortality				
View				
Life expectancy at birth	Unacceptable	Unacceptable	Acceptable	Acceptable
Under-five mortality	..	..	Acceptable	Acceptable
Maternal mortality	..	..	..	Acceptable
Level of concern about HIV/AIDS	..	..	Major concern	Major concern
Measures to respond to HIV/AIDS*	..	..	..	1,2,3,4
Grounds on which abortion is permitted**	..	..	1,2,3,4,5,6	1,2,3,4,5,6,7
Spatial distribution and internal migration				
View on spatial distribution	Minor change desired	Minor change desired	Satisfactory	Minor change desired
Policies on internal migration				
From rural to urban areas	..	..	..	Lower
From rural to rural areas	..	..	..	No intervention
From urban to rural areas	..	..	..	No intervention
From urban to urban areas	..	..	..	No intervention
Into urban agglomerations	Lower	No intervention	No intervention	No intervention
International migration				
Immigration				
View	Satisfactory	Too high	Satisfactory	Satisfactory
Policy	Maintain	Lower	Lower	Maintain
Permanent settlement	..	..	Lower	Maintain
Temporary workers	..	..	Lower	Maintain
Highly skilled workers	..	..	..	No intervention
Family reunification	..	..	Maintain	Maintain
Integration of non-citizens	..	..	Yes	Yes
Emigration				
View	Too high	Satisfactory	Satisfactory	Satisfactory
Policy	Lower	Lower	No intervention	No intervention
Encouraging the return of citizens	No	..	No	No

* Measures implemented to respond to HIV/AIDS: (1) blood screening; (2) information/education campaigns; (3) antiretroviral treatment; (4) non-discriminatory policies; (5) distribution of condoms.
** Grounds on which abortion is permitted: (1) to save the woman's life; (2) to preserve physical health; (3) to preserve mental health; (4) rape or incest; (5) foetal impairment; (6) economic or social reasons; (7) on request.

Population indicators

Indicator	1975	1985	1995	2009
Population size and growth				
Population size (thousands)	55 164	56 883	57 207	59 870
Annual growth rate (percentage)*	0.7	0.2	0.1	0.5
Population age structure				
Percentage of population under age 15	24	19	15	14
Percentage of population aged 60 or over	18	19	23	26
Fertility and family planning				
Total fertility (children per woman)*	2.4	1.5	1.3	1.4
Adolescent fertility rate (per 1,000 women, aged 15 - 19)*	..	..	8.0	5.0
Percentage of births to women under age 20*	..	..	3	2
Percentage of births to women aged 35 or over*	..	..	14	23
Percentage of married women using contraception				
Modern methods	32[a]	..	41[b]	..
All methods	78[a]	..	63[b]	..
Health and mortality				
Life expectancy at birth (years)*				
Males	69	71	74	78
Females	75	78	81	84
Both sexes combined	72	75	77	81
Infant mortality rate (per 1,000 live births)*	27	13	8	4
Under-five mortality (per 1,000 live births)*	..	15	9	5
Maternal mortality ratio (per 100,000 live births) (2005)	..	..	..	3
HIV/AIDS				
People living with HIV/AIDS (thousands)	..	..	130	150[c]
Adult prevalence (percentage)	..	..	0.4	0.4[c]
Spatial distribution				
Population density (per sq. km)	183	189	190	199
Urban population (percentage)	66	67	67	68
Annual urban population growth rate (percentage)	0.8	0.0	0.2	0.3
Annual rural population growth rate (percentage)	-0.1	0.1	0.0	-0.5
International migration				
Migrant stock				
Number of migrants (thousands)	1 006	1 253	1 723	4 463**
As percentage of total population	1.8	2.2	3.0	7.4**

* For the periods 1970-1975, 1980-1985, 1990-1995 and 2005-2010.
** For 2010.
[a] For 1979.
[b] For 1995/1996.
[c] For 2007.

Government views and policies

Population policy variable	1976	1986	1996	2009
Population size and growth				
View on growth	Too high	Too high	Too high	Too high
Policy on growth	Lower	Lower	Lower	Lower
Population age structure				
Level of concern about				
Size of the working-age population	..	..	..	Minor concern
Ageing of the population	..	..	..	Major concern
Fertility and family planning				
View on fertility level	Too high	Too high	Too high	Too high
Policy	Lower	Lower	Lower	Lower
Access to contraceptive methods	Direct support	Direct support	Direct support	Direct support
Adolescent fertility				
Level of concern	..	..	Major concern	Major concern
Policies and programmes	..	..	Yes	Yes
Health and mortality				
View				
Life expectancy at birth	Acceptable	Unacceptable	Acceptable	Acceptable
Under-five mortality	..	..	Unacceptable	Unacceptable
Maternal mortality	..	..	..	Unacceptable
Level of concern about HIV/AIDS	..	..	Major concern	Major concern
Measures to respond to HIV/AIDS*	..	..	..	1,2,3,5
Grounds on which abortion is permitted**	..	..	1,2,3	1,2,3
Spatial distribution and internal migration				
View on spatial distribution	Major change desired	Major change desired	Major change desired	Major change desired
Policies on internal migration				
From rural to urban areas	..	..	..	No intervention
From rural to rural areas	..	..	..	No intervention
From urban to rural areas	..	..	..	No intervention
From urban to urban areas	..	..	..	No intervention
Into urban agglomerations	Lower	No intervention	Lower	No intervention
International migration				
Immigration				
View	Satisfactory	Satisfactory	Satisfactory	Satisfactory
Policy	Maintain	Maintain	Maintain	No intervention
Permanent settlement	..	..	..	Maintain
Temporary workers	..	..	..	Maintain
Highly skilled workers	..	..	..	Raise
Family reunification	..	..	..	Maintain
Integration of non-citizens	..	..	Yes	No
Emigration				
View	Too high	Satisfactory	Too high	Too high
Policy	Lower	Maintain	Lower	No intervention
Encouraging the return of citizens	Yes	..	Yes	Yes

* Measures implemented to respond to HIV/AIDS: (1) blood screening; (2) information/education campaigns; (3) antiretroviral treatment; (4) non-discriminatory policies; (5) distribution of condoms.

** Grounds on which abortion is permitted: (1) to save the woman's life; (2) to preserve physical health; (3) to preserve mental health; (4) rape or incest; (5) foetal impairment; (6) economic or social reasons; (7) on request.

Population indicators

Indicator	1975	1985	1995	2009
Population size and growth				
Population size (thousands)	2 013	2 296	2 466	2 719
Annual growth rate (percentage)*	1.5	1.5	0.8	0.5
Population age structure				
Percentage of population under age 15	45	37	34	29
Percentage of population aged 60 or over	8	9	10	11
Fertility and family planning				
Total fertility (children per woman)*	5.0	3.6	2.8	2.4
Adolescent fertility rate (per 1,000 women, aged 15 - 19)*	..	..	103.0	77.0
Percentage of births to women under age 20*	..	..	18	16
Percentage of births to women aged 35 or over*	..	..	15	12
Percentage of married women using contraception				
Modern methods	36[a]	48[b]	63[c]	66[d]
All methods	38[a]	51[b]	66[c]	69[d]
Health and mortality				
Life expectancy at birth (years)*				
Males	67	68	69	68
Females	71	73	74	75
Both sexes combined	69	71	71	72
Infant mortality rate (per 1,000 live births)*	45	34	27	23
Under-five mortality (per 1,000 live births)*	..	42	33	28
Maternal mortality ratio (per 100,000 live births) (2005)	..	..	..	170
HIV/AIDS				
People living with HIV/AIDS (thousands)	..	..	12	27[e]
Adult prevalence (percentage)	..	..	0.9	1.6[e]
Spatial distribution				
Population density (per sq. km)	183	209	224	247
Urban population (percentage)	44	48	51	53
Annual urban population growth rate (percentage)	2.4	1.3	1.4	1.0
Annual rural population growth rate (percentage)	0.3	0.5	0.4	0.0
International migration				
Migrant stock				
Number of migrants (thousands)	25	22	22	30**
As percentage of total population	1.2	1.0	0.9	1.1**

* For the periods 1970-1975, 1980-1985, 1990-1995 and 2005-2010.
** For 2010.
[a] For 1976.
[b] For 1983.
[c] For 1997.
[d] For 2002/2003.
[e] For 2007.

Government views and policies

Population policy variable	1976	1986	1996	2009
Population size and growth				
View on growth	Satisfactory	Satisfactory	Satisfactory	Too low
Policy on growth	No intervention	No intervention	No intervention	Raise
Population age structure				
Level of concern about				
Size of the working-age population	..	..	..	Major concern
Ageing of the population	..	..	..	Major concern
Fertility and family planning				
View on fertility level	Satisfactory	Satisfactory	Too low	Too low
Policy	No intervention	No intervention	No intervention	Raise
Access to contraceptive methods	Direct support	Direct support	Direct support	Indirect support
Adolescent fertility				
Level of concern	..	..	Minor concern	Not a concern
Policies and programmes	..	..	..	No
Health and mortality				
View				
Life expectancy at birth	Acceptable	Acceptable	Acceptable	Acceptable
Under-five mortality	..	..	Unacceptable	Unacceptable
Maternal mortality	..	..	..	Unacceptable
Level of concern about HIV/AIDS	..	..	Major concern	Major concern
Measures to respond to HIV/AIDS*	..	..	..	1,2,3,4,5
Grounds on which abortion is permitted**	..	..	1,2,3,4,6	1,2,4,6
Spatial distribution and internal migration				
View on spatial distribution	Major change desired	Minor change desired	Major change desired	Major change desired
Policies on internal migration				
From rural to urban areas	..	..	..	Lower
From rural to rural areas	..	..	..	No intervention
From urban to rural areas	..	..	..	Raise
From urban to urban areas	..	..	..	No intervention
Into urban agglomerations	..	..	Lower	Lower
International migration				
Immigration				
View	Satisfactory	Satisfactory	Satisfactory	Satisfactory
Policy	Maintain	Maintain	Maintain	No intervention
Permanent settlement	..	..	Maintain	No intervention
Temporary workers	..	..	Raise	No intervention
Highly skilled workers	..	..	..	Raise
Family reunification	..	..	Maintain	No intervention
Integration of non-citizens	..	..	No	No
Emigration				
View	Satisfactory	Too low	Satisfactory	Satisfactory
Policy	Maintain	Raise	No intervention	No intervention
Encouraging the return of citizens	..	..	..	No

* Measures implemented to respond to HIV/AIDS: (1) blood screening; (2) information/education campaigns; (3) antiretroviral treatment; (4) non-discriminatory policies; (5) distribution of condoms.

** Grounds on which abortion is permitted: (1) to save the woman's life; (2) to preserve physical health; (3) to preserve mental health; (4) rape or incest; (5) foetal impairment; (6) economic or social reasons; (7) on request.

Population indicators

Indicator	1975	1985	1995	2009
Population size and growth				
Population size (thousands)	111 619	120 908	125 442	127 156
Annual growth rate (percentage)*	1.3	0.7	0.4	-0.1
Population age structure				
Percentage of population under age 15	24	22	16	13
Percentage of population aged 60 or over	12	15	20	30
Fertility and family planning				
Total fertility (children per woman)*	2.1	1.8	1.5	1.3
Adolescent fertility rate (per 1,000 women, aged 15 - 19)*	..	..	4.0	5.0
Percentage of births to women under age 20*	..	..	1	2
Percentage of births to women aged 35 or over*	..	..	8	15
Percentage of married women using contraception				
Modern methods	59	60[a]	51[b]	44[c]
All methods	61	63[a]	57[b]	54[c]
Health and mortality				
Life expectancy at birth (years)*				
Males	70	74	76	79
Females	76	80	83	86
Both sexes combined	73	77	79	83
Infant mortality rate (per 1,000 live births)*	12	7	4	3
Under-five mortality (per 1,000 live births)*	..	9	6	4
Maternal mortality ratio (per 100,000 live births) (2005)	..	..	..	6
HIV/AIDS				
People living with HIV/AIDS (thousands)	..	..	5.6	9.6[d]
Adult prevalence (percentage)	..	..	..	..
Spatial distribution				
Population density (per sq. km)	295	320	332	337
Urban population (percentage)	57	61	65	67
Annual urban population growth rate (percentage)	2.1	1.3	0.5	0.2
Annual rural population growth rate (percentage)	-0.3	-0.6	-0.2	-0.7
International migration				
Migrant stock				
Number of migrants (thousands)	770	851	1 363	2 176**
As percentage of total population	0.7	0.7	1.1	1.7**

* For the periods 1970-1975, 1980-1985, 1990-1995 and 2005-2010.
** For 2010.
[a] For 1986.
[b] For 1996.
[c] For 2005.
[d] For 2007.

Government views and policies

Population policy variable	1976	1986	1996	2009
Population size and growth				
View on growth	Satisfactory	Satisfactory	Too high	Too high
Policy on growth	No intervention	No intervention	Lower	Lower
Population age structure				
Level of concern about				
Size of the working-age population	..	..	..	Major concern
Ageing of the population	..	..	..	Minor concern
Fertility and family planning				
View on fertility level	Too high	Satisfactory	Too high	Too high
Policy	No intervention	No intervention	Lower	Lower
Access to contraceptive methods	Direct support	Indirect support	Direct support	Direct support
Adolescent fertility				
Level of concern	..	..	Not a concern	Not a concern
Policies and programmes	..	..	No	No
Health and mortality				
View				
Life expectancy at birth	Acceptable	Unacceptable	Acceptable	Acceptable
Under-five mortality	..	..	Acceptable	Unacceptable
Maternal mortality	..	..	..	Unacceptable
Level of concern about HIV/AIDS	..	..	Major concern	Major concern
Measures to respond to HIV/AIDS*	..	..	..	1,2,3,4,5
Grounds on which abortion is permitted**	..	..	1,2,3	1,2,3,5
Spatial distribution and internal migration				
View on spatial distribution	Major change desired	Minor change desired	Satisfactory	Major change desired
Policies on internal migration				
From rural to urban areas	..	..	..	Lower
From rural to rural areas	..	..	..	No intervention
From urban to rural areas	..	..	..	Raise
From urban to urban areas	..	..	..	No intervention
Into urban agglomerations	..	Lower	No intervention	Lower
International migration				
Immigration				
View	Satisfactory	Satisfactory	Satisfactory	Too high
Policy	Maintain	Maintain	Lower	Lower
Permanent settlement	..	..	Lower	Lower
Temporary workers	..	..	No intervention	Lower
Highly skilled workers	..	..	..	Lower
Family reunification	..	..	Lower	Maintain
Integration of non-citizens	..	..	No	No
Emigration				
View	Too high	Too high	Satisfactory	Too low
Policy	Lower	Lower	No intervention	Raise
Encouraging the return of citizens	..	..	No	No

* Measures implemented to respond to HIV/AIDS: (1) blood screening; (2) information/education campaigns; (3) antiretroviral treatment; (4) non-discriminatory policies; (5) distribution of condoms.
** Grounds on which abortion is permitted: (1) to save the woman's life; (2) to preserve physical health; (3) to preserve mental health; (4) rape or incest; (5) foetal impairment; (6) economic or social reasons; (7) on request.

Population indicators

Indicator	1975	1985	1995	2009
Population size and growth				
Population size (thousands)	1 937	2 706	4 304	6 316
Annual growth rate (percentage)*	3.5	3.9	5.6	3.0
Population age structure				
Percentage of population under age 15	47	47	41	34
Percentage of population aged 60 or over	4	5	4	6
Fertility and family planning				
Total fertility (children per woman)*	7.8	6.8	5.1	3.1
Adolescent fertility rate (per 1,000 women, aged 15 - 19)*	..	..	47.0	25.0
Percentage of births to women under age 20*	..	..	5	4
Percentage of births to women aged 35 or over*	..	..	23	21
Percentage of married women using contraception				
Modern methods	17[a]	22	38[b]	41[c]
All methods	25[a]	27	53[b]	57[c]
Health and mortality				
Life expectancy at birth (years)*				
Males	55	62	66	71
Females	58	66	70	74
Both sexes combined	57	64	68	73
Infant mortality rate (per 1,000 live births)*	82	52	33	19
Under-five mortality (per 1,000 live births)*	..	61	38	22
Maternal mortality ratio (per 100,000 live births) (2005)	..	..	..	62
HIV/AIDS				
People living with HIV/AIDS (thousands)	..	..	..	<1[c]
Adult prevalence (percentage)	..	..	..	..
Spatial distribution				
Population density (per sq. km)	22	30	48	71
Urban population (percentage)	58	66	78	78
Annual urban population growth rate (percentage)	3.2	5.2	3.1	2.5
Annual rural population growth rate (percentage)	1.9	-0.3	3.1	2.1
International migration				
Migrant stock				
Number of migrants (thousands)	676	943	1 608	2 973**
As percentage of total population	34.9	34.8	37.4	45.9**

* For the periods 1970-1975, 1980-1985, 1990-1995 and 2005-2010.
** For 2010.
[a] For 1976.
[b] For 1997.
[c] For 2007.

Government views and policies

Population policy variable	1976	1986	1996	2009
Population size and growth				
View on growth	..	..	Too low	Too low
Policy on growth	..	..	Raise	Raise
Population age structure				
Level of concern about				
Size of the working-age population	..	..	..	Major concern
Ageing of the population	..	..	..	Major concern
Fertility and family planning				
View on fertility level	..	..	Too low	Too low
Policy	..	..	Raise	Raise
Access to contraceptive methods	..	..	Direct support	Indirect support
Adolescent fertility				
Level of concern	..	..	..	Major concern
Policies and programmes	..	..	Yes	Yes
Health and mortality				
View				
Life expectancy at birth	..	..	Unacceptable	Unacceptable
Under-five mortality	..	..	..	Unacceptable
Maternal mortality	..	..	..	Unacceptable
Level of concern about HIV/AIDS	..	..	..	Major concern
Measures to respond to HIV/AIDS*	..	..	..	1,2,3,4
Grounds on which abortion is permitted**	..	..	1,2,3,4,5,6,7	1,2,3,4,5,6,7
Spatial distribution and internal migration				
View on spatial distribution	..	..	Satisfactory	Major change desired
Policies on internal migration				
From rural to urban areas	..	..	..	Raise
From rural to rural areas	..	..	..	Raise
From urban to rural areas	..	..	..	No intervention
From urban to urban areas	..	..	..	Raise
Into urban agglomerations	..	..	No intervention	Raise
International migration				
Immigration				
View	..	..	Satisfactory	Satisfactory
Policy	..	..	Maintain	Maintain
Permanent settlement	..	..	..	Maintain
Temporary workers	..	..	..	Maintain
Highly skilled workers	..	..	..	Raise
Family reunification	..	..	..	Maintain
Integration of non-citizens	..	..	..	Yes
Emigration				
View	..	..	Too high	Satisfactory
Policy	..	..	Lower	Maintain
Encouraging the return of citizens	..	..	Yes	Yes

* Measures implemented to respond to HIV/AIDS: (1) blood screening; (2) information/education campaigns; (3) antiretroviral treatment; (4) non-discriminatory policies; (5) distribution of condoms.
** Grounds on which abortion is permitted: (1) to save the woman's life; (2) to preserve physical health; (3) to preserve mental health; (4) rape or incest; (5) foetal impairment; (6) economic or social reasons; (7) on request.

Population indicators

Indicator	1975	1985	1995	2009
Population size and growth				
Population size (thousands)	14 136	15 780	15 926	15 637
Annual growth rate (percentage)*	1.5	1.1	-0.7	0.7
Population age structure				
Percentage of population under age 15	35	32	30	24
Percentage of population aged 60 or over	9	8	10	10
Fertility and family planning				
Total fertility (children per woman)*	3.5	3.0	2.6	2.3
Adolescent fertility rate (per 1,000 women, aged 15 - 19)*	..	..	53.0	31.0
Percentage of births to women under age 20*	..	..	10	7
Percentage of births to women aged 35 or over*	..	..	10	10
Percentage of married women using contraception				
Modern methods	..	..	46	49[a]
All methods	..	..	59	51[a]
Health and mortality				
Life expectancy at birth (years)*				
Males	58	60	61	59
Females	68	71	70	71
Both sexes combined	63	66	65	65
Infant mortality rate (per 1,000 live births)*	77	60	51	26
Under-five mortality (per 1,000 live births)*	..	72	61	30
Maternal mortality ratio (per 100,000 live births) (2005)	..	..	..	140
HIV/AIDS				
People living with HIV/AIDS (thousands)	..	..	<0.5	12[b]
Adult prevalence (percentage)	..	..	..	0.1[b]
Spatial distribution				
Population density (per sq. km)	5	6	6	6
Urban population (percentage)	53	56	56	58
Annual urban population growth rate (percentage)	1.7	1.4	-1.3	1.3
Annual rural population growth rate (percentage)	0.6	1.0	-1.4	-0.1
International migration				
Migrant stock				
Number of migrants (thousands)	..	..	3 295	3 079**
As percentage of total population	0.0	0.0	20.7	19.5**

* For the periods 1970-1975, 1980-1985, 1990-1995 and 2005-2010.
** For 2010.
[a] For 2006.
[b] For 2007.

Government views and policies

Population policy variable	1976	1986	1996	2009
Population size and growth				
View on growth	Too high	Too high	Too high	Too high
Policy on growth	Lower	Lower	Lower	Lower
Population age structure				
Level of concern about				
Size of the working-age population	..	..	..	Major concern
Ageing of the population	..	..	..	Major concern
Fertility and family planning				
View on fertility level	Too high	Too high	Too high	Too high
Policy	Lower	Lower	Lower	Lower
Access to contraceptive methods	Direct support	Direct support	Direct support	Direct support
Adolescent fertility				
Level of concern	..	..	Major concern	Major concern
Policies and programmes	..	..	Yes	Yes
Health and mortality				
View				
Life expectancy at birth	Unacceptable	Unacceptable	Unacceptable	Unacceptable
Under-five mortality	..	..	Unacceptable	Unacceptable
Maternal mortality	..	..	..	Unacceptable
Level of concern about HIV/AIDS	..	..	Major concern	Major concern
Measures to respond to HIV/AIDS*	..	..	..	1,2,3,4,5
Grounds on which abortion is permitted**	..	..	1	1,2,3
Spatial distribution and internal migration				
View on spatial distribution	Major change desired	Major change desired	Minor change desired	Major change desired
Policies on internal migration				
From rural to urban areas	..	..	..	Lower
From rural to rural areas	..	..	..	No intervention
From urban to rural areas	..	..	..	Raise
From urban to urban areas	..	..	..	No intervention
Into urban agglomerations	No intervention	..	Lower	Lower
International migration				
Immigration				
View	Satisfactory	Satisfactory	Satisfactory	Satisfactory
Policy	Maintain	Maintain	Maintain	No intervention
Permanent settlement	..	..	..	Lower
Temporary workers	..	..	..	No intervention
Highly skilled workers	..	..	..	No intervention
Family reunification	..	..	..	No intervention
Integration of non-citizens	..	..	No	No
Emigration				
View	Satisfactory	Satisfactory	Satisfactory	Satisfactory
Policy	Maintain	Maintain	No intervention	No intervention
Encouraging the return of citizens	No	..	No	No

* Measures implemented to respond to HIV/AIDS: (1) blood screening; (2) information/education campaigns; (3) antiretroviral treatment; (4) non-discriminatory policies; (5) distribution of condoms.
** Grounds on which abortion is permitted: (1) to save the woman's life; (2) to preserve physical health; (3) to preserve mental health; (4) rape or incest; (5) foetal impairment; (6) economic or social reasons; (7) on request.

Population indicators

Indicator	1975	1985	1995	2009
Population size and growth				
Population size (thousands)	13 481	19 648	27 492	39 802
Annual growth rate (percentage)*	3.6	3.8	3.2	2.6
Population age structure				
Percentage of population under age 15	50	50	46	43
Percentage of population aged 60 or over	5	4	4	4
Fertility and family planning				
Total fertility (children per woman)*	8.0	7.2	5.6	5.0
Adolescent fertility rate (per 1,000 women, aged 15 - 19)*	..	..	114.0	104.0
Percentage of births to women under age 20*	..	..	10	10
Percentage of births to women aged 35 or over*	..	..	25	23
Percentage of married women using contraception				
Modern methods	4[a]	10[b]	32[c]	32[d]
All methods	7[a]	17[b]	39[c]	39[d]
Health and mortality				
Life expectancy at birth (years)*				
Males	52	57	58	54
Females	56	61	61	55
Both sexes combined	54	59	59	54
Infant mortality rate (per 1,000 live births)*	92	69	65	64
Under-five mortality (per 1,000 live births)*	..	112	105	104
Maternal mortality ratio (per 100,000 live births) (2005)	..	..	..	560
HIV/AIDS				
People living with HIV/AIDS (thousands)	..	..	..	..
Adult prevalence (percentage)	..	..	..	..
Spatial distribution				
Population density (per sq. km)	23	34	47	69
Urban population (percentage)	13	17	19	22
Annual urban population growth rate (percentage)	8.1	5.2	3.6	4.1
Annual rural population growth rate (percentage)	3.0	3.3	2.6	2.2
International migration				
Migrant stock				
Number of migrants (thousands)	161	152	528	818**
As percentage of total population	1.2	0.8	1.9	2.0**

* For the periods 1970-1975, 1980-1985, 1990-1995 and 2005-2010.
** For 2010.
[a] For 1978.
[b] For 1984.
[c] For 1998.
[d] For 2003.

Government views and policies

Population policy variable	1976	1986	1996	2009
Population size and growth				
View on growth	..	Too high	Too high	Too high
Policy on growth	..	Lower	Lower	Lower
Population age structure				
Level of concern about				
Size of the working-age population	..	..	..	Major concern
Ageing of the population	..	..	..	..
Fertility and family planning				
View on fertility level	..	Too high	Too high	Too high
Policy	..	Lower	Lower	Lower
Access to contraceptive methods	..	Direct support	Direct support	Direct support
Adolescent fertility				
Level of concern	..	..	..	Minor concern
Policies and programmes	..	..	..	Yes
Health and mortality				
View				
Life expectancy at birth	..	Unacceptable	Unacceptable	Unacceptable
Under-five mortality	..	..	..	Unacceptable
Maternal mortality	..	..	..	Unacceptable
Level of concern about HIV/AIDS	..	..	..	Major concern
Measures to respond to HIV/AIDS*	..	..	..	1,2,3
Grounds on which abortion is permitted**	..	..	1	1
Spatial distribution and internal migration				
View on spatial distribution	..	Major change desired	Major change desired	Major change desired
Policies on internal migration				
From rural to urban areas	..	..	..	Lower
From rural to rural areas	..	..	..	..
From urban to rural areas	..	..	..	..
From urban to urban areas	..	..	..	..
Into urban agglomerations	..	No intervention	..	Lower
International migration				
Immigration				
View	..	Satisfactory	Satisfactory	Satisfactory
Policy	..	Maintain	Maintain	Maintain
Permanent settlement	..	..	..	..
Temporary workers	..	..	..	..
Highly skilled workers	..	..	..	..
Family reunification	..	..	..	..
Integration of non-citizens	..	..	..	..
Emigration				
View	..	Satisfactory	Satisfactory	Satisfactory
Policy	..	Maintain	Maintain	Maintain
Encouraging the return of citizens	..	..	..	..

* Measures implemented to respond to HIV/AIDS: (1) blood screening; (2) information/education campaigns; (3) antiretroviral treatment; (4) non-discriminatory policies; (5) distribution of condoms.
** Grounds on which abortion is permitted: (1) to save the woman's life; (2) to preserve physical health; (3) to preserve mental health; (4) rape or incest; (5) foetal impairment; (6) economic or social reasons; (7) on request.

Population indicators

Indicator	1975	1985	1995	2009
Population size and growth				
Population size (thousands)	48	63	77	98
Annual growth rate (percentage)*	2.0	2.7	1.5	1.6
Population age structure				
Percentage of population under age 15	..	..	..	..
Percentage of population aged 60 or over	..	..	..	..
Fertility and family planning				
Total fertility (children per woman)*	..	..	..	..
Adolescent fertility rate (per 1,000 women, aged 15 - 19)*	..	..	..	..
Percentage of births to women under age 20*	..	..	..	..
Percentage of births to women aged 35 or over*	..	..	..	..
Percentage of married women using contraception				
Modern methods	..	..	31[a]	..
All methods	..	..	36[a]	..
Health and mortality				
Life expectancy at birth (years)*				
Males	..	..	..	..
Females	..	..	..	..
Both sexes combined	..	..	..	..
Infant mortality rate (per 1,000 live births)*	..	..	..	..
Under-five mortality (per 1,000 live births)*	..	..	..	..
Maternal mortality ratio (per 100,000 live births) (2005)	..	..	..	
HIV/AIDS				
People living with HIV/AIDS (thousands)	..	..	..	..
Adult prevalence (percentage)	..	..	..	..
Spatial distribution				
Population density (per sq. km)	67	86	106	135
Urban population (percentage)	30	34	36	44
Annual urban population growth rate (percentage)	4.4	3.8	4.2	1.9
Annual rural population growth rate (percentage)	1.3	2.5	0.0	1.3
International migration				
Migrant stock				
Number of migrants (thousands)	1	2	2	2**
As percentage of total population	1.6	3.3	2.6	2.0**

* For the periods 1970-1975, 1980-1985, 1990-1995 and 2005-2010.
** For 2010.
[a] For 2000.

Government views and policies

Population policy variable	1976	1986	1996	2009
Population size and growth				
View on growth	Too low	Too low	Satisfactory	Too low
Policy on growth	No intervention	Raise	Maintain	Maintain
Population age structure				
Level of concern about				
Size of the working-age population	..	..	..	Minor concern
Ageing of the population	..	..	..	Minor concern
Fertility and family planning				
View on fertility level	Satisfactory	Too low	Satisfactory	Too low
Policy	Maintain	Raise	Maintain	Raise
Access to contraceptive methods	No support	No support	No support	Direct support
Adolescent fertility				
Level of concern	..	..	Not a concern	Minor concern
Policies and programmes	..	..	No	Yes
Health and mortality				
View				
Life expectancy at birth	Acceptable	Acceptable	Acceptable	Acceptable
Under-five mortality	..	..	Acceptable	Acceptable
Maternal mortality	..	..	..	Acceptable
Level of concern about HIV/AIDS	..	..	Major concern	Minor concern
Measures to respond to HIV/AIDS*	..	..	..	1,2,3,4,5
Grounds on which abortion is permitted**	..	..	1,2,3,5	1,2,3,5
Spatial distribution and internal migration				
View on spatial distribution	Satisfactory	Minor change desired	Satisfactory	Satisfactory
Policies on internal migration				
From rural to urban areas	..	..	..	No intervention
From rural to rural areas	..	..	..	No intervention
From urban to rural areas	..	..	..	No intervention
From urban to urban areas	..	..	..	No intervention
Into urban agglomerations	..	No intervention	Lower	No intervention
International migration				
Immigration				
View	Satisfactory	Too high	Satisfactory	Too high
Policy	Maintain	Lower	Lower	Lower
Permanent settlement	..	..	Lower	Lower
Temporary workers	..	..	Lower	Lower
Highly skilled workers	..	..	..	Maintain
Family reunification	..	..	Lower	Maintain
Integration of non-citizens	..	..	No	Yes
Emigration				
View	Satisfactory	Satisfactory	Satisfactory	Satisfactory
Policy	Maintain	Maintain	No intervention	No intervention
Encouraging the return of citizens	..	..	No	No

* Measures implemented to respond to HIV/AIDS: (1) blood screening; (2) information/education campaigns; (3) antiretroviral treatment; (4) non-discriminatory policies; (5) distribution of condoms.
** Grounds on which abortion is permitted: (1) to save the woman's life; (2) to preserve physical health; (3) to preserve mental health; (4) rape or incest; (5) foetal impairment; (6) economic or social reasons; (7) on request.

Population indicators

Indicator	1975	1985	1995	2009
Population size and growth				
Population size (thousands)	1 007	1 720	1 725	2 985
Annual growth rate (percentage)*	6.0	4.5	-4.3	2.4
Population age structure				
Percentage of population under age 15	44	37	29	23
Percentage of population aged 60 or over	3	2	2	4
Fertility and family planning				
Total fertility (children per woman)*	6.9	4.9	3.2	2.2
Adolescent fertility rate (per 1,000 women, aged 15 - 19)*	..	..	26.0	13.0
Percentage of births to women under age 20*	..	..	4	3
Percentage of births to women aged 35 or over*	..	..	19	18
Percentage of married women using contraception				
Modern methods	..	32[a]	41[b]	..
All methods	..	35[a]	50[b]	..
Health and mortality				
Life expectancy at birth (years)*				
Males	66	70	74	76
Females	70	74	77	80
Both sexes combined	68	71	75	78
Infant mortality rate (per 1,000 live births)*	41	24	13	9
Under-five mortality (per 1,000 live births)*	..	27	15	10
Maternal mortality ratio (per 100,000 live births) (2005)	..	..	..	4
HIV/AIDS				
People living with HIV/AIDS (thousands)	..	..	..	<1[c]
Adult prevalence (percentage)	..	..	..	..
Spatial distribution				
Population density (per sq. km)	56	97	97	168
Urban population (percentage)	89	98	98	98
Annual urban population growth rate (percentage)	8.0	5.8	1.6	2.2
Annual rural population growth rate (percentage)	-7.3	4.8	0.6	1.1
International migration				
Migrant stock				
Number of migrants (thousands)	664	1 241	1 090	2 098**
As percentage of total population	66.0	72.1	63.2	68.8**

* For the periods 1970-1975, 1980-1985, 1990-1995 and 2005-2010.
** For 2010.
[a] For 1987.
[b] For 1996.
[c] For 2007.

Government views and policies

Population policy variable	1976	1986	1996	2009
Population size and growth				
View on growth	..	..	Satisfactory	Satisfactory
Policy on growth	..	..	No intervention	Maintain
Population age structure				
Level of concern about				
Size of the working-age population	..	..	..	Minor concern
Ageing of the population	..	..	..	Minor concern
Fertility and family planning				
View on fertility level	..	..	Satisfactory	Satisfactory
Policy	..	..	No intervention	Maintain
Access to contraceptive methods	..	..	..	Direct support
Adolescent fertility				
Level of concern	..	..	..	Major concern
Policies and programmes	..	..	..	Yes
Health and mortality				
View				
Life expectancy at birth	..	..	Unacceptable	Unacceptable
Under-five mortality	..	..	..	Unacceptable
Maternal mortality	..	..	..	Unacceptable
Level of concern about HIV/AIDS	..	..	..	Major concern
Measures to respond to HIV/AIDS*	..	..	..	1,2,3,4,5
Grounds on which abortion is permitted**	..	..	1,2,3,4,5,6,7	1,2,3,4,5,6,7
Spatial distribution and internal migration				
View on spatial distribution	..	..	Minor change desired	Major change desired
Policies on internal migration				
From rural to urban areas	..	..	..	Lower
From rural to rural areas	..	..	..	Maintain
From urban to rural areas	..	..	..	Raise
From urban to urban areas	..	..	..	Maintain
Into urban agglomerations	..	..	..	Lower
International migration				
Immigration				
View	..	..	Satisfactory	Satisfactory
Policy	..	..	No intervention	Maintain
Permanent settlement	..	..	..	Maintain
Temporary workers	..	..	..	Maintain
Highly skilled workers	..	..	..	Maintain
Family reunification	..	..	..	Maintain
Integration of non-citizens	..	..	..	Yes
Emigration				
View	..	..	Too high	Satisfactory
Policy	..	..	Lower	Maintain
Encouraging the return of citizens	..	..	..	Yes

* Measures implemented to respond to HIV/AIDS: (1) blood screening; (2) information/education campaigns; (3) antiretroviral treatment; (4) non-discriminatory policies; (5) distribution of condoms.

** Grounds on which abortion is permitted: (1) to save the woman's life; (2) to preserve physical health; (3) to preserve mental health; (4) rape or incest; (5) foetal impairment; (6) economic or social reasons; (7) on request.

Population indicators

Indicator	1975	1985	1995	2009
Population size and growth				
Population size (thousands)	3 299	4 013	4 592	5 482
Annual growth rate (percentage)[*]	2.1	2.0	0.9	1.2
Population age structure				
Percentage of population under age 15	40	37	38	29
Percentage of population aged 60 or over	8	8	8	7
Fertility and family planning				
Total fertility (children per woman)[*]	4.7	4.1	3.6	2.6
Adolescent fertility rate (per 1,000 women, aged 15 - 19)[*]	..	..	46.0	32.0
Percentage of births to women under age 20[*]	..	..	6	6
Percentage of births to women aged 35 or over[*]	..	..	12	12
Percentage of married women using contraception				
Modern methods	..	..	49[a]	46[b]
All methods	..	..	60[a]	48[b]
Health and mortality				
Life expectancy at birth (years)[*]				
Males	57	60	62	64
Females	65	68	70	72
Both sexes combined	61	64	66	68
Infant mortality rate (per 1,000 live births)[*]	100	80	60	37
Under-five mortality (per 1,000 live births)[*]	..	96	72	46
Maternal mortality ratio (per 100,000 live births) (2005)	..	..	..	150
HIV/AIDS				
People living with HIV/AIDS (thousands)	..	..	..	4.2[c]
Adult prevalence (percentage)	..	..	..	0.1[c]
Spatial distribution				
Population density (per sq. km)	17	20	23	27
Urban population (percentage)	38	38	36	36
Annual urban population growth rate (percentage)	2.3	1.9	0.5	1.7
Annual rural population growth rate (percentage)	1.7	2.1	1.8	0.8
International migration				
Migrant stock				
Number of migrants (thousands)	..	..	482	223[**]
As percentage of total population	0.0	0.0	10.5	4.0[**]

[*] For the periods 1970-1975, 1980-1985, 1990-1995 and 2005-2010.
[**] For 2010.
[a] For 1997.
[b] For 2005/2006.
[c] For 2007.

Government views and policies

Population policy variable	1976	1986	1996	2009
Population size and growth				
View on growth	Too low	Too low	Too low	Too high
Policy on growth	Raise	Raise	Raise	Lower
Population age structure				
Level of concern about				
Size of the working-age population	..	..	..	Major concern
Ageing of the population	..	..	..	Minor concern
Fertility and family planning				
View on fertility level	Satisfactory	Satisfactory	Satisfactory	Too high
Policy	Maintain	Maintain	Maintain	Lower
Access to contraceptive methods	Limits	Limits	No support	Direct support
Adolescent fertility				
Level of concern	..	..	..	Minor concern
Policies and programmes	..	..	..	Yes
Health and mortality				
View				
Life expectancy at birth	Unacceptable	Acceptable	Unacceptable	Unacceptable
Under-five mortality	..	..	..	Unacceptable
Maternal mortality	..	..	..	Unacceptable
Level of concern about HIV/AIDS	..	..	..	Major concern
Measures to respond to HIV/AIDS*	..	..	..	1,2,3,4,5
Grounds on which abortion is permitted**	..	..	1	1,2
Spatial distribution and internal migration				
View on spatial distribution	Major change desired	Major change desired	Major change desired	Major change desired
Policies on internal migration				
From rural to urban areas	..	..	..	Lower
From rural to rural areas	..	..	..	No intervention
From urban to rural areas	..	..	..	Raise
From urban to urban areas	..	..	..	No intervention
Into urban agglomerations	..	..	..	Lower
International migration				
Immigration				
View	Satisfactory	Satisfactory	Satisfactory	Satisfactory
Policy	Maintain	Maintain	Maintain	Maintain
Permanent settlement	..	..	..	Lower
Temporary workers	..	..	..	Raise
Highly skilled workers	..	..	..	Raise
Family reunification	..	..	..	Maintain
Integration of non-citizens	..	..	..	..
Emigration				
View	Satisfactory	Satisfactory	Too high	Too high
Policy	Maintain	Maintain	Lower	Maintain
Encouraging the return of citizens	..	..	..	Yes

* Measures implemented to respond to HIV/AIDS: (1) blood screening; (2) information/education campaigns; (3) antiretroviral treatment;
(4) non-discriminatory policies; (5) distribution of condoms.
** Grounds on which abortion is permitted: (1) to save the woman's life; (2) to preserve physical health; (3) to preserve mental health; (4) rape or incest;
(5) foetal impairment; (6) economic or social reasons; (7) on request.

Population indicators

Indicator	1975	1985	1995	2009
Population size and growth				
Population size (thousands)	3 050	3 655	4 809	6 320
Annual growth rate (percentage)[*]	2.5	2.4	2.7	1.8
Population age structure				
Percentage of population under age 15	42	44	44	38
Percentage of population aged 60 or over	5	6	5	5
Fertility and family planning				
Total fertility (children per woman)[*]	6.0	6.3	5.8	3.5
Adolescent fertility rate (per 1,000 women, aged 15 - 19)[*]	..	..	70.0	37.0
Percentage of births to women under age 20[*]	..	..	6	5
Percentage of births to women aged 35 or over[*]	..	..	28	21
Percentage of married women using contraception				
Modern methods	..	..	15[a]	29[b]
All methods	..	..	19[a]	32[b]
Health and mortality				
Life expectancy at birth (years)[*]				
Males	45	49	55	63
Females	48	51	58	66
Both sexes combined	47	50	56	65
Infant mortality rate (per 1,000 live births)[*]	141	123	88	50
Under-five mortality (per 1,000 live births)[*]	..	181	125	65
Maternal mortality ratio (per 100,000 live births) (2005)	..	..	..	660
HIV/AIDS				
People living with HIV/AIDS (thousands)	..	..	<0.2	5.5[c]
Adult prevalence (percentage)	..	..	<0.1	0.2[c]
Spatial distribution				
Population density (per sq. km)	13	15	20	27
Urban population (percentage)	11	14	17	32
Annual urban population growth rate (percentage)	3.8	5.1	7.2	5.3
Annual rural population growth rate (percentage)	1.3	2.5	1.4	0.0
International migration				
Migrant stock				
Number of migrants (thousands)	21	23	23	19[**]
As percentage of total population	0.7	0.6	0.5	0.3[**]

[*] For the periods 1970-1975, 1980-1985, 1990-1995 and 2005-2010.
[**] For 2010.
[a] For 1993.
[b] For 2000.
[c] For 2007.

Government views and policies

Population policy variable	1976	1986	1996	2009
Population size and growth				
View on growth	..	..	Too low	Too low
Policy on growth	..	..	No intervention	Raise
Population age structure				
Level of concern about				
Size of the working-age population	..	..	..	Minor concern
Ageing of the population	..	..	..	Major concern
Fertility and family planning				
View on fertility level	..	..	Too low	Too low
Policy	..	..	Raise	Raise
Access to contraceptive methods	..	..	Direct support	No support
Adolescent fertility				
Level of concern	..	..	Minor concern	Major concern
Policies and programmes	..	..	No	Yes
Health and mortality				
View				
Life expectancy at birth	..	..	Unacceptable	Unacceptable
Under-five mortality	..	..	Unacceptable	Unacceptable
Maternal mortality	..	..	..	Unacceptable
Level of concern about HIV/AIDS	..	..	Minor concern	Major concern
Measures to respond to HIV/AIDS*	..	..	..	1,2,3,4,5
Grounds on which abortion is permitted**	..	..	1,2,3,4,5,6,7	1,2,3,4,5,6,7
Spatial distribution and internal migration				
View on spatial distribution	..	..	Major change desired	Minor change desired
Policies on internal migration				
From rural to urban areas	..	..	..	No intervention
From rural to rural areas	..	..	..	No intervention
From urban to rural areas	..	..	..	No intervention
From urban to urban areas	..	..	..	No intervention
Into urban agglomerations	..	..	Lower	No intervention
International migration				
Immigration				
View	..	..	Too high	Satisfactory
Policy	..	..	Lower	Maintain
Permanent settlement	..	..	Lower	Maintain
Temporary workers	..	..	Lower	Maintain
Highly skilled workers	..	..	..	Maintain
Family reunification	..	..	Lower	Maintain
Integration of non-citizens	..	..	Yes	Yes
Emigration				
View	..	..	Too low	Satisfactory
Policy	..	..	Raise	No intervention
Encouraging the return of citizens	..	..	Yes	Yes

* Measures implemented to respond to HIV/AIDS: (1) blood screening; (2) information/education campaigns; (3) antiretroviral treatment; (4) non-discriminatory policies; (5) distribution of condoms.

** Grounds on which abortion is permitted: (1) to save the woman's life; (2) to preserve physical health; (3) to preserve mental health; (4) rape or incest; (5) foetal impairment; (6) economic or social reasons; (7) on request.

Population indicators

Indicator	1975	1985	1995	2009
Population size and growth				
Population size (thousands)	2 456	2 579	2 492	2 249
Annual growth rate (percentage)*	0.8	0.5	-1.3	-0.5
Population age structure				
Percentage of population under age 15	21	21	21	14
Percentage of population aged 60 or over	18	17	19	22
Fertility and family planning				
Total fertility (children per woman)*	2.0	2.0	1.6	1.4
Adolescent fertility rate (per 1,000 women, aged 15 - 19)*	..	..	42.0	15.0
Percentage of births to women under age 20*	..	..	13	5
Percentage of births to women aged 35 or over*	..	..	7	13
Percentage of married women using contraception				
Modern methods	..	..	56	..
All methods	..	..	68	..
Health and mortality				
Life expectancy at birth (years)*				
Males	65	65	62	67
Females	75	74	74	77
Both sexes combined	70	69	68	72
Infant mortality rate (per 1,000 live births)*	21	18	15	9
Under-five mortality (per 1,000 live births)*	..	22	18	11
Maternal mortality ratio (per 100,000 live births) (2005)	..	..	..	10
HIV/AIDS				
People living with HIV/AIDS (thousands)	..	..	<0.1	10[a]
Adult prevalence (percentage)	..	..	..	0.8[a]
Spatial distribution				
Population density (per sq. km)	38	40	39	35
Urban population (percentage)	64	69	69	68
Annual urban population growth rate (percentage)	1.6	1.2	-1.4	-0.4
Annual rural population growth rate (percentage)	-1.3	0.2	-0.9	-0.7
International migration				
Migrant stock				
Number of migrants (thousands)	..	..	527	335**
As percentage of total population	0.0	0.0	21.2	15.0**

* For the periods 1970-1975, 1980-1985, 1990-1995 and 2005-2010.
** For 2010.
[a] For 2007.

Government views and policies

Population policy variable	1976	1986	1996	2009
Population size and growth				
View on growth	Satisfactory	Satisfactory	Satisfactory	Satisfactory
Policy on growth	No intervention	No intervention	No intervention	No intervention
Population age structure				
Level of concern about				
Size of the working-age population	..	..	..	Minor concern
Ageing of the population	..	..	..	Major concern
Fertility and family planning				
View on fertility level	Satisfactory	Satisfactory	Satisfactory	Satisfactory
Policy	No intervention	No intervention	No intervention	No intervention
Access to contraceptive methods	Indirect support	Indirect support	Indirect support	Direct support
Adolescent fertility				
Level of concern	..	..	..	Minor concern
Policies and programmes	..	..	..	Yes
Health and mortality				
View				
Life expectancy at birth	Unacceptable	Unacceptable	Unacceptable	Acceptable
Under-five mortality	..	..	..	Unacceptable
Maternal mortality	..	..	..	Unacceptable
Level of concern about HIV/AIDS	..	..	..	Minor concern
Measures to respond to HIV/AIDS*	..	..	..	1,2,3,4,5
Grounds on which abortion is permitted**	..	..	1	1
Spatial distribution and internal migration				
View on spatial distribution	Minor change desired	Minor change desired	Major change desired	Major change desired
Policies on internal migration				
From rural to urban areas	..	..	..	Lower
From rural to rural areas	..	..	..	No intervention
From urban to rural areas	..	..	..	No intervention
From urban to urban areas	..	..	..	No intervention
Into urban agglomerations	..	..	..	Lower
International migration				
Immigration				
View	Satisfactory	Satisfactory	Too high	Satisfactory
Policy	Maintain	Maintain	Lower	Maintain
Permanent settlement	..	..	..	Maintain
Temporary workers	..	..	..	Maintain
Highly skilled workers	..	..	..	Maintain
Family reunification	..	..	..	Maintain
Integration of non-citizens	..	..	..	No
Emigration				
View	Satisfactory	Satisfactory	Too high	Too high
Policy	Maintain	Maintain	Lower	No intervention
Encouraging the return of citizens	..	..	Yes	Yes

* Measures implemented to respond to HIV/AIDS: (1) blood screening; (2) information/education campaigns; (3) antiretroviral treatment; (4) non–discriminatory policies; (5) distribution of condoms.
** Grounds on which abortion is permitted: (1) to save the woman's life; (2) to preserve physical health; (3) to preserve mental health; (4) rape or incest; (5) foetal impairment; (6) economic or social reasons; (7) on request.

Population indicators

Indicator	1975	1985	1995	2009
Population size and growth				
Population size (thousands)	2 737	2 891	3 491	4 224
Annual growth rate (percentage)*	2.3	0.8	3.2	0.8
Population age structure				
Percentage of population under age 15	40	37	32	25
Percentage of population aged 60 or over	7	7	9	10
Fertility and family planning				
Total fertility (children per woman)*	4.8	3.9	3.0	1.9
Adolescent fertility rate (per 1,000 women, aged 15 - 19)*	..	..	34.0	16.0
Percentage of births to women under age 20*	..	..	6	4
Percentage of births to women aged 35 or over*	..	..	22	16
Percentage of married women using contraception				
Modern methods	23[a]	..	37[b]	34[c]
All methods	53[a]	..	61[b]	58[c]
Health and mortality				
Life expectancy at birth (years)*				
Males	63	65	67	70
Females	68	70	72	74
Both sexes combined	65	67	69	72
Infant mortality rate (per 1,000 live births)*	47	41	31	22
Under-five mortality (per 1,000 live births)*	..	51	38	26
Maternal mortality ratio (per 100,000 live births) (2005)	..	..	..	150
HIV/AIDS				
People living with HIV/AIDS (thousands)	..	..	1.3	3[d]
Adult prevalence (percentage)	..	..	0.1	0.1[d]
Spatial distribution				
Population density (per sq. km)	263	278	336	406
Urban population (percentage)	67	79	85	87
Annual urban population growth rate (percentage)	3.0	1.5	2.6	1.2
Annual rural population growth rate (percentage)	-3.4	-4.9	0.1	0.0
International migration				
Migrant stock				
Number of migrants (thousands)	209	348	656	758**
As percentage of total population	7.6	12.0	18.8	17.8**

* For the periods 1970-1975, 1980-1985, 1990-1995 and 2005-2010.
** For 2010.
[a] For 1971.
[b] For 1996.
[c] For 2004.
[d] For 2007.

Government views and policies

Population policy variable	1976	1986	1996	2009
Population size and growth				
View on growth	Too high	Too high	Too high	Satisfactory
Policy on growth	Lower	Lower	Lower	No intervention
Population age structure				
Level of concern about				
Size of the working-age population	..	..	..	Major concern
Ageing of the population	..	..	..	Minor concern
Fertility and family planning				
View on fertility level	Too high	Too high	Too high	Too high
Policy	Lower	Lower	Lower	Lower
Access to contraceptive methods	Direct support	Direct support	Direct support	Direct support
Adolescent fertility				
Level of concern	..	..	Major concern	Major concern
Policies and programmes	..	..	Yes	Yes
Health and mortality				
View				
Life expectancy at birth	Unacceptable	Unacceptable	Unacceptable	Unacceptable
Under-five mortality	..	..	Unacceptable	Unacceptable
Maternal mortality	..	..	..	Unacceptable
Level of concern about HIV/AIDS	..	..	Major concern	Major concern
Measures to respond to HIV/AIDS*	..	..	..	1,2,3,4,5
Grounds on which abortion is permitted**	..	..	1	1
Spatial distribution and internal migration				
View on spatial distribution	Minor change desired	Minor change desired	Minor change desired	Major change desired
Policies on internal migration				
From rural to urban areas	..	..	..	Lower
From rural to rural areas	..	..	..	No intervention
From urban to rural areas	..	..	..	No intervention
From urban to urban areas	..	..	..	No intervention
Into urban agglomerations	No intervention	No intervention	No intervention	No intervention
International migration				
Immigration				
View	Satisfactory	Satisfactory	Satisfactory	Satisfactory
Policy	Maintain	Maintain	No intervention	No intervention
Permanent settlement	..	..	No intervention	No intervention
Temporary workers	..	..	No intervention	No intervention
Highly skilled workers	..	..	..	No intervention
Family reunification	..	..	No intervention	No intervention
Integration of non-citizens	..	..	No	..
Emigration				
View	Satisfactory	Too high	Satisfactory	Satisfactory
Policy	Maintain	Lower	No intervention	No intervention
Encouraging the return of citizens	No	..	Yes	Yes

* Measures implemented to respond to HIV/AIDS: (1) blood screening; (2) information/education campaigns; (3) antiretroviral treatment; (4) non−discriminatory policies; (5) distribution of condoms.

** Grounds on which abortion is permitted: (1) to save the woman's life; (2) to preserve physical health; (3) to preserve mental health; (4) rape or incest; (5) foetal impairment; (6) economic or social reasons; (7) on request.

Population indicators

Indicator	1975	1985	1995	2009
Population size and growth				
Population size (thousands)	1 150	1 473	1 726	2 067
Annual growth rate (percentage)*	2.1	2.6	1.5	0.9
Population age structure				
Percentage of population under age 15	45	45	44	39
Percentage of population aged 60 or over	6	6	7	7
Fertility and family planning				
Total fertility (children per woman)*	5.8	5.5	4.7	3.4
Adolescent fertility rate (per 1,000 women, aged 15 - 19)*	..	..	86.0	73.0
Percentage of births to women under age 20*	..	..	9	11
Percentage of births to women aged 35 or over*	..	..	25	21
Percentage of married women using contraception				
Modern methods	2[a]	..	19[b]	35[c]
All methods	5[a]	..	23[b]	37[c]
Health and mortality				
Life expectancy at birth (years)*				
Males	48	53	58	44
Females	51	57	62	46
Both sexes combined	50	55	60	45
Infant mortality rate (per 1,000 live births)*	123	94	67	70
Under-five mortality (per 1,000 live births)*	..	134	98	104
Maternal mortality ratio (per 100,000 live births) (2005)	..	..	..	960
HIV/AIDS				
People living with HIV/AIDS (thousands)	..	..	130	270[d]
Adult prevalence (percentage)	..	..	14.2	23.2[d]
Spatial distribution				
Population density (per sq. km)	38	49	57	68
Urban population (percentage)	11	12	17	26
Annual urban population growth rate (percentage)	5.8	3.3	5.5	3.4
Annual rural population growth rate (percentage)	1.8	1.8	1.0	-0.4
International migration				
Migrant stock				
Number of migrants (thousands)	5	18	6	6**
As percentage of total population	0.4	1.2	0.4	0.3**

* For the periods 1970-1975, 1980-1985, 1990-1995 and 2005-2010.
** For 2010.
[a] For 1977.
[b] For 1991/1992.
[c] For 2004.
[d] For 2007.

Government views and policies

Population policy variable	1976	1986	1996	2009
Population size and growth				
View on growth	Too high	Too high	Too high	Too high
Policy on growth	No intervention	No intervention	Lower	Lower
Population age structure				
Level of concern about				
Size of the working-age population	..	..	..	Major concern
Ageing of the population	..	..	..	..
Fertility and family planning				
View on fertility level	Too high	Too high	Too high	Too high
Policy	No intervention	No intervention	Lower	Lower
Access to contraceptive methods	Direct support	Indirect support	Direct support	Direct support
Adolescent fertility				
Level of concern	..	..	Major concern	Major concern
Policies and programmes	..	..	Yes	Yes
Health and mortality				
View				
Life expectancy at birth	Unacceptable	Unacceptable	Unacceptable	Unacceptable
Under-five mortality	..	..	Unacceptable	Unacceptable
Maternal mortality	..	..	..	Unacceptable
Level of concern about HIV/AIDS	..	..	Major concern	Major concern
Measures to respond to HIV/AIDS*	..	..	..	1
Grounds on which abortion is permitted**	..	..	1,2,3,4,5	1,2,3,4,5
Spatial distribution and internal migration				
View on spatial distribution	Major change desired	Minor change desired	Major change desired	Major change desired
Policies on internal migration				
From rural to urban areas	..	..	..	..
From rural to rural areas	..	..	..	..
From urban to rural areas	..	..	..	..
From urban to urban areas	..	..	..	..
Into urban agglomerations	No intervention	..	Lower	..
International migration				
Immigration				
View	Satisfactory	Satisfactory	Satisfactory	Satisfactory
Policy	Maintain	Maintain	Maintain	Maintain
Permanent settlement	..	..	Maintain	Maintain
Temporary workers	..	..	Maintain	Maintain
Highly skilled workers	..	..	..	..
Family reunification	..	..	Maintain	..
Integration of non-citizens	..	..	Yes	Yes
Emigration				
View	Satisfactory	Satisfactory	Too high	Satisfactory
Policy	Maintain	Maintain	No intervention	No intervention
Encouraging the return of citizens	No	..	Yes	Yes

* Measures implemented to respond to HIV/AIDS: (1) blood screening; (2) information/education campaigns; (3) antiretroviral treatment; (4) non–discriminatory policies; (5) distribution of condoms.
** Grounds on which abortion is permitted: (1) to save the woman's life; (2) to preserve physical health; (3) to preserve mental health; (4) rape or incest; (5) foetal impairment; (6) economic or social reasons; (7) on request.

Population indicators

Indicator	1975	1985	1995	2009
Population size and growth				
Population size (thousands)	1 635	2 215	1 945	3 955
Annual growth rate (percentage)*	2.7	3.0	-2.2	4.1
Population age structure				
Percentage of population under age 15	45	44	45	43
Percentage of population aged 60 or over	5	5	5	5
Fertility and family planning				
Total fertility (children per woman)*	6.4	6.6	6.4	5.1
Adolescent fertility rate (per 1,000 women, aged 15 - 19)*	..	..	164.0	142.0
Percentage of births to women under age 20*	..	..	13	14
Percentage of births to women aged 35 or over*	..	..	28	23
Percentage of married women using contraception				
Modern methods	..	6[a]	..	10[b]
All methods	..	6[a]	..	11[b]
Health and mortality				
Life expectancy at birth (years)*				
Males	44	46	48	57
Females	47	49	52	59
Both sexes combined	45	48	50	58
Infant mortality rate (per 1,000 live births)*	152	142	132	95
Under-five mortality (per 1,000 live births)*	..	239	217	140
Maternal mortality ratio (per 100,000 live births) (2005)	..	..	..	1 200
HIV/AIDS				
People living with HIV/AIDS (thousands)	..	..	14	35[b]
Adult prevalence (percentage)	..	..	1.2	1.7[b]
Spatial distribution				
Population density (per sq. km)	15	20	17	36
Urban population (percentage)	30	40	50	61
Annual urban population growth rate (percentage)	6.0	3.3	8.0	5.3
Annual rural population growth rate (percentage)	1.6	-0.9	4.5	2.5
International migration				
Migrant stock				
Number of migrants (thousands)	64	83	199	96**
As percentage of total population	3.9	3.7	10.2	2.3**

* For the periods 1970-1975, 1980-1985, 1990-1995 and 2005-2010.
** For 2010.
[a] For 1986.
[b] For 2007.

Government views and policies

Population policy variable	1976	1986	1996	2009
Population size and growth				
View on growth	Too low	Satisfactory	Satisfactory	Satisfactory
Policy on growth	Raise	No intervention	No intervention	No intervention
Population age structure				
Level of concern about				
Size of the working-age population	..	..	..	..
Ageing of the population	..	..	..	Minor concern
Fertility and family planning				
View on fertility level	Too low	Satisfactory	Satisfactory	Satisfactory
Policy	Raise	No intervention	No intervention	No intervention
Access to contraceptive methods	No support	No support	No support	No support
Adolescent fertility				
Level of concern	..	..	..	Minor concern
Policies and programmes	..	..	..	Yes
Health and mortality				
View				
Life expectancy at birth	Unacceptable	Acceptable	Acceptable	Acceptable
Under-five mortality	..	..	..	Unacceptable
Maternal mortality	..	..	..	Unacceptable
Level of concern about HIV/AIDS	..	..	..	Not a concern
Measures to respond to HIV/AIDS*	..	..	..	1,2,3
Grounds on which abortion is permitted**	..	..	1	1
Spatial distribution and internal migration				
View on spatial distribution	Minor change desired	Major change desired	Major change desired	Major change desired
Policies on internal migration				
From rural to urban areas	..	..	..	Lower
From rural to rural areas	..	..	..	No intervention
From urban to rural areas	..	..	..	No intervention
From urban to urban areas	..	..	..	No intervention
Into urban agglomerations	Lower	Lower	..	Lower
International migration				
Immigration				
View	Too low	Too high	Too high	Too high
Policy	Raise	Lower	Lower	Lower
Permanent settlement	..	..	..	..
Temporary workers	..	..	..	Lower
Highly skilled workers	..	..	..	Maintain
Family reunification	..	..	..	..
Integration of non-citizens	..	..	..	..
Emigration				
View	Satisfactory	Satisfactory	Satisfactory	Satisfactory
Policy	Maintain	Maintain	Maintain	Maintain
Encouraging the return of citizens	No	..	..	No

* Measures implemented to respond to HIV/AIDS: (1) blood screening; (2) information/education campaigns; (3) antiretroviral treatment;
(4) non−discriminatory policies; (5) distribution of condoms.
** Grounds on which abortion is permitted: (1) to save the woman's life; (2) to preserve physical health; (3) to preserve mental health; (4) rape or incest;
(5) foetal impairment; (6) economic or social reasons; (7) on request.

Population indicators

Indicator	1975	1985	1995	2009
Population size and growth				
Population size (thousands)	2 466	3 850	4 834	6 420
Annual growth rate (percentage)*	4.2	4.6	2.0	2.0
Population age structure				
Percentage of population under age 15	46	47	38	30
Percentage of population aged 60 or over	4	4	5	7
Fertility and family planning				
Total fertility (children per woman)*	7.6	7.2	4.1	2.7
Adolescent fertility rate (per 1,000 women, aged 15 - 19)*	..	..	7.0	3.0
Percentage of births to women under age 20*	..	..	1	1
Percentage of births to women aged 35 or over*	..	..	40	32
Percentage of married women using contraception				
Modern methods	..	..	26	..
All methods	..	..	45	..
Health and mortality				
Life expectancy at birth (years)*				
Males	51	61	67	72
Females	55	64	72	77
Both sexes combined	53	62	69	74
Infant mortality rate (per 1,000 live births)*	105	50	31	18
Under-five mortality (per 1,000 live births)*	..	58	35	20
Maternal mortality ratio (per 100,000 live births) (2005)	..	..	..	97
HIV/AIDS				
People living with HIV/AIDS (thousands)	..	..	..	..
Adult prevalence (percentage)	..	..	..	..
Spatial distribution				
Population density (per sq. km)	1	2	3	4
Urban population (percentage)	63	75	76	78
Annual urban population growth rate (percentage)	6.6	3.3	2.1	2.2
Annual rural population growth rate (percentage)	0.0	3.0	1.8	1.0
International migration				
Migrant stock				
Number of migrants (thousands)	223	414	506	682**
As percentage of total population	9.1	10.8	10.5	10.4**

* For the periods 1970-1975, 1980-1985, 1990-1995 and 2005-2010.
** For 2010.

Government views and policies

Population policy variable	1976	1986	1996	2009
Population size and growth				
View on growth	Too low	Too low	Satisfactory	Too low
Policy on growth	Raise	Raise	No intervention	No intervention
Population age structure				
Level of concern about				
Size of the working-age population	..	..	..	Not a concern
Ageing of the population	..	..	..	Minor concern
Fertility and family planning				
View on fertility level	Too low	Too low	Satisfactory	Too low
Policy	Raise	Raise	No intervention	No intervention
Access to contraceptive methods	No support	No support	No support	No support
Adolescent fertility				
Level of concern	..	..	Not a concern	Not a concern
Policies and programmes	..	..	No	Yes
Health and mortality				
View				
Life expectancy at birth	Acceptable	Acceptable	Acceptable	Acceptable
Under-five mortality	..	..	..	Acceptable
Maternal mortality	..	..	..	Acceptable
Level of concern about HIV/AIDS	..	..	Minor concern	Minor concern
Measures to respond to HIV/AIDS*	..	..	..	1,2,3,5
Grounds on which abortion is permitted**	..	..	1,2,3	1,2,3
Spatial distribution and internal migration				
View on spatial distribution	Satisfactory	Satisfactory	Satisfactory	Satisfactory
Policies on internal migration				
From rural to urban areas	..	..	..	No intervention
From rural to rural areas	..	..	..	No intervention
From urban to rural areas	..	..	..	No intervention
From urban to urban areas	..	..	..	No intervention
Into urban agglomerations	..	..	No intervention	No intervention
International migration				
Immigration				
View	Satisfactory	Satisfactory	Satisfactory	Satisfactory
Policy	Maintain	Lower	Lower	Maintain
Permanent settlement	..	..	Lower	Maintain
Temporary workers	..	..	Maintain	Maintain
Highly skilled workers	..	..	..	Maintain
Family reunification	..	..	Maintain	Maintain
Integration of non-citizens	..	..	No	Yes
Emigration				
View	Satisfactory	Satisfactory	Satisfactory	Satisfactory
Policy	Maintain	Maintain	No intervention	No intervention
Encouraging the return of citizens	..	..	No	No

* Measures implemented to respond to HIV/AIDS: (1) blood screening; (2) information/education campaigns; (3) antiretroviral treatment; (4) non-discriminatory policies; (5) distribution of condoms.
** Grounds on which abortion is permitted: (1) to save the woman's life; (2) to preserve physical health; (3) to preserve mental health; (4) rape or incest; (5) foetal impairment; (6) economic or social reasons; (7) on request.

Population indicators

Indicator	1975	1985	1995	2009
Population size and growth				
Population size (thousands)	23	27	31	36
Annual growth rate (percentage)*	1.7	1.5	1.3	0.8
Population age structure				
Percentage of population under age 15	..	..	..	..
Percentage of population aged 60 or over	..	..	..	..
Fertility and family planning				
Total fertility (children per woman)*	..	..	..	..
Adolescent fertility rate (per 1,000 women, aged 15 - 19)*	..	..	..	..
Percentage of births to women under age 20*	..	..	..	..
Percentage of births to women aged 35 or over*	..	..	..	..
Percentage of married women using contraception				
Modern methods	..	..	..	..
All methods	..	..	..	..
Health and mortality				
Life expectancy at birth (years)*				
Males	..	..	..	..
Females	..	..	..	..
Both sexes combined	..	..	..	..
Infant mortality rate (per 1,000 live births)*	..	..	..	..
Under-five mortality (per 1,000 live births)*	..	..	..	..
Maternal mortality ratio (per 100,000 live births) (2005)	..	..	..	..
HIV/AIDS				
People living with HIV/AIDS (thousands)	..	..	..	..
Adult prevalence (percentage)	..	..	..	..
Spatial distribution				
Population density (per sq. km)	146	170	193	224
Urban population (percentage)	18	18	16	14
Annual urban population growth rate (percentage)	1.6	0.6	0.1	0.7
Annual rural population growth rate (percentage)	1.6	1.5	1.5	0.9
International migration				
Migrant stock				
Number of migrants (thousands)	8	10	12	13**
As percentage of total population	34.7	36.4	38.5	34.6**

* For the periods 1970-1975, 1980-1985, 1990-1995 and 2005-2010.
** For 2010.

Government views and policies

Population policy variable	1976	1986	1996	2009
Population size and growth				
View on growth	..	..	Satisfactory	Too low
Policy on growth	..	..	Raise	Raise
Population age structure				
Level of concern about				
Size of the working-age population	..	..	..	Major concern
Ageing of the population	..	..	..	Major concern
Fertility and family planning				
View on fertility level	..	..	Satisfactory	Too low
Policy	..	..	Raise	Raise
Access to contraceptive methods	..	..	Direct support	Indirect support
Adolescent fertility				
Level of concern	..	..	Not a concern	Major concern
Policies and programmes	..	..	No	Yes
Health and mortality				
View				
Life expectancy at birth	..	..	Acceptable	Acceptable
Under-five mortality	..	..	Acceptable	Acceptable
Maternal mortality	..	..	..	Acceptable
Level of concern about HIV/AIDS	..	..	Major concern	Major concern
Measures to respond to HIV/AIDS*	..	..	..	1,2,3,4,5
Grounds on which abortion is permitted**	..	..	1,2,3,4,5,6,7	1,2,3,4,5,6,7
Spatial distribution and internal migration				
View on spatial distribution	..	..	Satisfactory	Minor change desired
Policies on internal migration				
From rural to urban areas	..	..	..	Lower
From rural to rural areas	..	..	..	..
From urban to rural areas	..	..	..	..
From urban to urban areas	..	..	..	..
Into urban agglomerations	..	..	Lower	Lower
International migration				
Immigration				
View	..	..	Satisfactory	Satisfactory
Policy	..	..	Lower	Maintain
Permanent settlement	..	..	Lower	Maintain
Temporary workers	..	..	No intervention	Maintain
Highly skilled workers	..	..	..	Raise
Family reunification	..	..	No intervention	Maintain
Integration of non-citizens	..	..	Yes	Yes
Emigration				
View	..	..	Satisfactory	Satisfactory
Policy	..	..	Maintain	No intervention
Encouraging the return of citizens	..	..	Yes	Yes

* Measures implemented to respond to HIV/AIDS: (1) blood screening; (2) information/education campaigns; (3) antiretroviral treatment; (4) non-discriminatory policies; (5) distribution of condoms.
** Grounds on which abortion is permitted: (1) to save the woman's life; (2) to preserve physical health; (3) to preserve mental health; (4) rape or incest; (5) foetal impairment; (6) economic or social reasons; (7) on request.

Population indicators

Indicator	1975	1985	1995	2009
Population size and growth				
Population size (thousands)	3 302	3 545	3 630	3 287
Annual growth rate (percentage)*	1.0	0.8	-0.4	-1.0
Population age structure				
Percentage of population under age 15	25	23	22	15
Percentage of population aged 60 or over	15	15	18	21
Fertility and family planning				
Total fertility (children per woman)*	2.3	2.0	1.8	1.3
Adolescent fertility rate (per 1,000 women, aged 15 - 19)*	..	..	44.0	22.0
Percentage of births to women under age 20*	..	..	12	8
Percentage of births to women aged 35 or over*	..	..	7	11
Percentage of married women using contraception				
Modern methods	..	..	33	..
All methods	..	..	51	..
Health and mortality				
Life expectancy at birth (years)*				
Males	67	66	64	66
Females	75	76	76	78
Both sexes combined	71	71	70	72
Infant mortality rate (per 1,000 live births)*	22	18	14	9
Under-five mortality (per 1,000 live births)*	..	22	17	12
Maternal mortality ratio (per 100,000 live births) (2005)	..	..	..	11
HIV/AIDS				
People living with HIV/AIDS (thousands)	..	..	<0.2	2.2[a]
Adult prevalence (percentage)	..	..	..	0.1[a]
Spatial distribution				
Population density (per sq. km)	51	54	56	50
Urban population (percentage)	56	65	67	67
Annual urban population growth rate (percentage)	2.9	2.1	-0.8	-0.3
Annual rural population growth rate (percentage)	-2.1	-1.2	-0.5	-0.9
International migration				
Migrant stock				
Number of migrants (thousands)	..	..	272	129**
As percentage of total population	0.0	0.0	7.5	4.0**

* For the periods 1970-1975, 1980-1985, 1990-1995 and 2005-2010.
** For 2010.
[a] For 2007.

Government views and policies

Population policy variable	1976	1986	1996	2009
Population size and growth				
View on growth	Too low	Satisfactory	Satisfactory	Satisfactory
Policy on growth	Raise	Raise	Maintain	Maintain
Population age structure				
Level of concern about				
Size of the working-age population	..	..	..	Minor concern
Ageing of the population	..	..	..	Minor concern
Fertility and family planning				
View on fertility level	Too low	Too low	Too low	Satisfactory
Policy	Raise	Raise	Raise	Maintain
Access to contraceptive methods	Indirect support	Indirect support	Indirect support	Indirect support
Adolescent fertility				
Level of concern	..	..	..	Not a concern
Policies and programmes	..	..	..	No
Health and mortality				
View				
Life expectancy at birth	Acceptable	Acceptable	Acceptable	Acceptable
Under-five mortality	..	..	..	Acceptable
Maternal mortality	..	..	..	Acceptable
Level of concern about HIV/AIDS	..	..	..	Major concern
Measures to respond to HIV/AIDS*	..	..	..	1,2,3,4,5
Grounds on which abortion is permitted**	..	..	1,2,3,4,5,6	1,2,3,4,5,6
Spatial distribution and internal migration				
View on spatial distribution	Satisfactory	Minor change desired	Major change desired	Satisfactory
Policies on internal migration				
From rural to urban areas	..	..	..	..
From rural to rural areas	..	..	..	..
From urban to rural areas	..	..	..	..
From urban to urban areas	..	..	..	..
Into urban agglomerations	No intervention	..	..	..
International migration				
Immigration				
View	Satisfactory	Too high	Too high	Satisfactory
Policy	Maintain	Lower	Lower	Maintain
Permanent settlement	..	..	..	Maintain
Temporary workers	..	..	..	Maintain
Highly skilled workers	..	..	..	Maintain
Family reunification	..	..	..	Maintain
Integration of non-citizens	..	..	..	Yes
Emigration				
View	Satisfactory	Satisfactory	Satisfactory	Satisfactory
Policy	Maintain	Maintain	No intervention	No intervention
Encouraging the return of citizens	No	..	..	..

* Measures implemented to respond to HIV/AIDS: (1) blood screening; (2) information/education campaigns; (3) antiretroviral treatment;
(4) non−discriminatory policies; (5) distribution of condoms.
** Grounds on which abortion is permitted: (1) to save the woman's life; (2) to preserve physical health; (3) to preserve mental health; (4) rape or incest;
(5) foetal impairment; (6) economic or social reasons; (7) on request.

Population indicators

Indicator	1975	1985	1995	2009
Population size and growth				
Population size (thousands)	359	367	409	486
Annual growth rate (percentage)*	1.1	0.1	1.4	1.2
Population age structure				
Percentage of population under age 15	20	17	18	18
Percentage of population aged 60 or over	18	18	19	19
Fertility and family planning				
Total fertility (children per woman)*	1.7	1.5	1.7	1.7
Adolescent fertility rate (per 1,000 women, aged 15 - 19)*	..	..	12.0	12.0
Percentage of births to women under age 20*	..	..	4	4
Percentage of births to women aged 35 or over*	..	..	11	17
Percentage of married women using contraception				
Modern methods	..	..	..	..
All methods	..	..	..	..
Health and mortality				
Life expectancy at birth (years)*				
Males	67	70	72	77
Females	74	77	79	82
Both sexes combined	71	73	76	79
Infant mortality rate (per 1,000 live births)*	17	12	6	4
Under-five mortality (per 1,000 live births)*	..	18	8	6
Maternal mortality ratio (per 100,000 live births) (2005)	..	..	..	12
HIV/AIDS				
People living with HIV/AIDS (thousands)	..	..	<0.5	..
Adult prevalence (percentage)	..	..	0.2	0.2[a]
Spatial distribution				
Population density (per sq. km)	139	142	158	188
Urban population (percentage)	77	81	83	82
Annual urban population growth rate (percentage)	1.4	0.6	1.4	1.0
Annual rural population growth rate (percentage)	-1.9	0.2	1.8	1.6
International migration				
Migrant stock				
Number of migrants (thousands)	70	98	127	173**
As percentage of total population	19.5	26.8	31.1	35.2**

* For the periods 1970-1975, 1980-1985, 1990-1995 and 2005-2010.
** For 2010.
[a] For 2007.

Government views and policies

Population policy variable	1976	1986	1996	2009
Population size and growth				
View on growth	Too high	Too high	Too high	Too high
Policy on growth	No intervention	No intervention	Lower	Lower
Population age structure				
Level of concern about				
Size of the working-age population	..	..	..	..
Ageing of the population	..	..	..	Major concern
Fertility and family planning				
View on fertility level	Too high	Too high	Too high	Too high
Policy	No intervention	No intervention	Lower	Lower
Access to contraceptive methods	Indirect support	Direct support	Direct support	Direct support
Adolescent fertility				
Level of concern	..	..	Major concern	Major concern
Policies and programmes	..	..	Yes	Yes
Health and mortality				
View				
Life expectancy at birth	Unacceptable	Unacceptable	Unacceptable	Unacceptable
Under-five mortality	..	..	Unacceptable	Unacceptable
Maternal mortality	..	..	..	Unacceptable
Level of concern about HIV/AIDS	..	..	Minor concern	Major concern
Measures to respond to HIV/AIDS*	..	..	..	1,2,3,5
Grounds on which abortion is permitted**	..	..	1	1
Spatial distribution and internal migration				
View on spatial distribution	Major change desired	Minor change desired	Major change desired	Minor change desired
Policies on internal migration				
From rural to urban areas	..	..	..	No intervention
From rural to rural areas	..	..	..	..
From urban to rural areas	..	..	..	..
From urban to urban areas	..	..	..	..
Into urban agglomerations	..	No intervention	Lower	No intervention
International migration				
Immigration				
View	Satisfactory	Satisfactory	Satisfactory	Satisfactory
Policy	Maintain	Maintain	No intervention	No intervention
Permanent settlement	..	..	No intervention	No intervention
Temporary workers	..	..	No intervention	No intervention
Highly skilled workers	..	..	..	No intervention
Family reunification	..	..	No intervention	No intervention
Integration of non-citizens	..	..	No	No
Emigration				
View	Satisfactory	Satisfactory	Satisfactory	Satisfactory
Policy	Maintain	Maintain	No intervention	No intervention
Encouraging the return of citizens	Yes	..	No	No

* Measures implemented to respond to HIV/AIDS: (1) blood screening; (2) information/education campaigns; (3) antiretroviral treatment; (4) non−discriminatory policies; (5) distribution of condoms.

** Grounds on which abortion is permitted: (1) to save the woman's life; (2) to preserve physical health; (3) to preserve mental health; (4) rape or incest; (5) foetal impairment; (6) economic or social reasons; (7) on request.

Population indicators

Indicator	1975	1985	1995	2009
Population size and growth				
Population size (thousands)	7 498	9 778	13 121	19 625
Annual growth rate (percentage)*	2.7	2.6	3.0	2.7
Population age structure				
Percentage of population under age 15	46	45	45	43
Percentage of population aged 60 or over	6	5	5	5
Fertility and family planning				
Total fertility (children per woman)*	7.3	6.1	6.1	4.8
Adolescent fertility rate (per 1,000 women, aged 15 - 19)*	..	..	150.0	133.0
Percentage of births to women under age 20*	..	..	12	14
Percentage of births to women aged 35 or over*	..	..	25	20
Percentage of married women using contraception				
Modern methods	..	..	10[a]	17[b]
All methods	..	..	19[a]	27[b]
Health and mortality				
Life expectancy at birth (years)*				
Males	44	48	51	59
Females	46	50	54	62
Both sexes combined	45	49	53	60
Infant mortality rate (per 1,000 live births)*	133	111	96	65
Under-five mortality (per 1,000 live births)*	..	183	155	100
Maternal mortality ratio (per 100,000 live births) (2005)	..	..	..	510
HIV/AIDS				
People living with HIV/AIDS (thousands)	..	..	1.1	14[c]
Adult prevalence (percentage)	..	..	..	0.1[c]
Spatial distribution				
Population density (per sq. km)	13	17	22	33
Urban population (percentage)	16	21	26	30
Annual urban population growth rate (percentage)	5.2	5.2	4.0	3.8
Annual rural population growth rate (percentage)	2.2	2.2	2.6	2.1
International migration				
Migrant stock				
Number of migrants (thousands)	54	48	44	38**
As percentage of total population	0.7	0.5	0.3	0.2**

* For the periods 1970-1975, 1980-1985, 1990-1995 and 2005-2010.
** For 2010.
[a] For 1997.
[b] For 2003/2004.
[c] For 2007.

Government views and policies

Population policy variable	1976	1986	1996	2009
Population size and growth				
View on growth	Satisfactory	Too high	Too high	Too high
Policy on growth	No intervention	No intervention	No intervention	Lower
Population age structure				
Level of concern about				
Size of the working-age population	..	..	..	Minor concern
Ageing of the population	..	..	..	Major concern
Fertility and family planning				
View on fertility level	Satisfactory	Too high	Too high	Too high
Policy	No intervention	No intervention	Lower	Lower
Access to contraceptive methods	Limits	Direct support	Direct support	Direct support
Adolescent fertility				
Level of concern	..	..	Major concern	Major concern
Policies and programmes	..	..	Yes	Yes
Health and mortality				
View				
Life expectancy at birth	Unacceptable	Unacceptable	Unacceptable	Unacceptable
Under-five mortality	..	..	Unacceptable	Unacceptable
Maternal mortality	..	..	..	Unacceptable
Level of concern about HIV/AIDS	..	..	Major concern	Major concern
Measures to respond to HIV/AIDS*	..	..	..	1,2,3,4,5
Grounds on which abortion is permitted**	..	..	1	1
Spatial distribution and internal migration				
View on spatial distribution	Minor change desired	Minor change desired	Minor change desired	Major change desired
Policies on internal migration				
From rural to urban areas	..	..	..	Lower
From rural to rural areas	..	..	..	No intervention
From urban to rural areas	..	..	..	Raise
From urban to urban areas	..	..	..	No intervention
Into urban agglomerations	..	..	Lower	Lower
International migration				
Immigration				
View	Satisfactory	Satisfactory	Too high	Too high
Policy	Maintain	Maintain	Lower	Lower
Permanent settlement	..	..	No intervention	Lower
Temporary workers	..	..	No intervention	Lower
Highly skilled workers	..	..	..	Maintain
Family reunification	..	..	No intervention	No intervention
Integration of non-citizens	..	..	No	Yes
Emigration				
View	Satisfactory	Satisfactory	Satisfactory	Too high
Policy	Maintain	Maintain	No intervention	Lower
Encouraging the return of citizens	..	..	No	Yes

* Measures implemented to respond to HIV/AIDS: (1) blood screening; (2) information/education campaigns; (3) antiretroviral treatment; (4) non-discriminatory policies; (5) distribution of condoms.
** Grounds on which abortion is permitted: (1) to save the woman's life; (2) to preserve physical health; (3) to preserve mental health; (4) rape or incest; (5) foetal impairment; (6) economic or social reasons; (7) on request.

Population indicators

Indicator	1975	1985	1995	2009
Population size and growth				
Population size (thousands)	5 276	7 267	10 144	15 263
Annual growth rate (percentage)*	3.1	3.1	1.4	2.8
Population age structure				
Percentage of population under age 15	47	48	45	46
Percentage of population aged 60 or over	4	4	5	5
Fertility and family planning				
Total fertility (children per woman)*	7.4	7.5	6.8	5.6
Adolescent fertility rate (per 1,000 women, aged 15 - 19)*	..	..	159.0	135.0
Percentage of births to women under age 20*	..	..	12	12
Percentage of births to women aged 35 or over*	..	..	27	22
Percentage of married women using contraception				
Modern methods	..	1[a]	14[b]	38[c]
All methods	..	7[a]	22[b]	41[c]
Health and mortality				
Life expectancy at birth (years)*				
Males	41	45	50	52
Females	43	47	52	54
Both sexes combined	42	46	51	53
Infant mortality rate (per 1,000 live births)*	185	150	127	84
Under-five mortality (per 1,000 live births)*	..	255	208	121
Maternal mortality ratio (per 100,000 live births) (2005)	..	..	..	1 100
HIV/AIDS				
People living with HIV/AIDS (thousands)	..	..	600	930[d]
Adult prevalence (percentage)	..	..	12.1	11.9[d]
Spatial distribution				
Population density (per sq. km)	45	61	86	129
Urban population (percentage)	8	10	13	19
Annual urban population growth rate (percentage)	8.0	7.7	4.9	5.2
Annual rural population growth rate (percentage)	2.9	5.1	1.8	1.9
International migration				
Migrant stock				
Number of migrants (thousands)	290	285	325	276**
As percentage of total population	5.5	3.9	3.2	1.8**

* For the periods 1970-1975, 1980-1985, 1990-1995 and 2005-2010.
** For 2010.
[a] For 1984.
[b] For 1996.
[c] For 2006.
[d] For 2007.

Government views and policies

Population policy variable	1976	1986	1996	2009
Population size and growth				
View on growth	Too high	Satisfactory	Too high	Too high
Policy on growth	Lower	Maintain	Lower	No intervention
Population age structure				
Level of concern about				
Size of the working-age population	..	..	..	Minor concern
Ageing of the population	..	..	..	Minor concern
Fertility and family planning				
View on fertility level	Too high	Satisfactory	Too high	Satisfactory
Policy	Lower	Maintain	Lower	No intervention
Access to contraceptive methods	Direct support	Direct support	Direct support	Direct support
Adolescent fertility				
Level of concern	..	..	Minor concern	Major concern
Policies and programmes	..	..	Yes	Yes
Health and mortality				
View				
Life expectancy at birth	Acceptable	Unacceptable	Acceptable	Acceptable
Under-five mortality	..	..	Acceptable	Acceptable
Maternal mortality	..	..	..	Acceptable
Level of concern about HIV/AIDS	..	..	Major concern	Major concern
Measures to respond to HIV/AIDS*	..	..	..	1,2,3,5
Grounds on which abortion is permitted**	..	..	1,2,3	1,2,3
Spatial distribution and internal migration				
View on spatial distribution	Minor change desired	Minor change desired	Minor change desired	Major change desired
Policies on internal migration				
From rural to urban areas	..	..	..	Lower
From rural to rural areas	..	..	..	No intervention
From urban to rural areas	..	..	..	Maintain
From urban to urban areas	..	..	..	No intervention
Into urban agglomerations	..	Lower	Lower	Lower
International migration				
Immigration				
View	Satisfactory	Satisfactory	Too high	Satisfactory
Policy	Maintain	Maintain	Lower	Maintain
Permanent settlement	..	..	Lower	Lower
Temporary workers	..	..	Maintain	Maintain
Highly skilled workers	..	..	..	Maintain
Family reunification	..	..	No intervention	Maintain
Integration of non-citizens	..	..	Yes	Yes
Emigration				
View	Too low	Satisfactory	Satisfactory	Satisfactory
Policy	Raise	Maintain	No intervention	No intervention
Encouraging the return of citizens	..	..	No	Yes

* Measures implemented to respond to HIV/AIDS: (1) blood screening; (2) information/education campaigns; (3) antiretroviral treatment;
(4) non−discriminatory policies; (5) distribution of condoms.
** Grounds on which abortion is permitted: (1) to save the woman's life; (2) to preserve physical health; (3) to preserve mental health; (4) rape or incest;
(5) foetal impairment; (6) economic or social reasons; (7) on request.

Population indicators

Indicator	1975	1985	1995	2009
Population size and growth				
Population size (thousands)	12 258	15 677	20 594	27 468
Annual growth rate (percentage)*	2.4	2.6	2.6	1.7
Population age structure				
Percentage of population under age 15	42	39	36	29
Percentage of population aged 60 or over	6	6	6	8
Fertility and family planning				
Total fertility (children per woman)*	5.2	4.2	3.5	2.6
Adolescent fertility rate (per 1,000 women, aged 15 - 19)*	..	..	28.0	13.0
Percentage of births to women under age 20*	..	..	4	2
Percentage of births to women aged 35 or over*	..	..	20	19
Percentage of married women using contraception				
Modern methods	23[a]	30[b]	30[c]	..
All methods	33[a]	51[b]	55[c]	..
Health and mortality				
Life expectancy at birth (years)*				
Males	61	66	69	72
Females	65	70	73	77
Both sexes combined	63	68	71	74
Infant mortality rate (per 1,000 live births)*	42	28	15	9
Under-five mortality (per 1,000 live births)*	..	37	20	11
Maternal mortality ratio (per 100,000 live births) (2005)	..	..	..	62
HIV/AIDS				
People living with HIV/AIDS (thousands)	..	..	9.2	80[d]
Adult prevalence (percentage)	..	..	0.1	0.5[d]
Spatial distribution				
Population density (per sq. km)	37	48	62	83
Urban population (percentage)	38	46	56	71
Annual urban population growth rate (percentage)	4.6	4.5	4.8	2.8
Annual rural population growth rate (percentage)	0.9	1.4	-0.4	-1.3
International migration				
Migrant stock				
Number of migrants (thousands)	718	908	1 193	2 358**
As percentage of total population	5.9	5.8	5.8	8.4**

* For the periods 1970-1975, 1980-1985, 1990-1995 and 2005-2010.
** For 2010.
[a] For 1974.
[b] For 1984.
[c] For 1994.
[d] For 2007.

Government views and policies

Population policy variable	1976	1986	1996	2009
Population size and growth				
View on growth	Satisfactory	Satisfactory	Too high	Satisfactory
Policy on growth	No intervention	No intervention	Lower	Lower
Population age structure				
Level of concern about				
Size of the working-age population	..	..	..	Major concern
Ageing of the population	..	..	..	Minor concern
Fertility and family planning				
View on fertility level	Satisfactory	Satisfactory	Too high	Satisfactory
Policy	No intervention	No intervention	Lower	Lower
Access to contraceptive methods	No support	Direct support	Direct support	Direct support
Adolescent fertility				
Level of concern	..	..	Minor concern	Major concern
Policies and programmes	..	..	Yes	Yes
Health and mortality				
View				
Life expectancy at birth	Unacceptable	Unacceptable	Unacceptable	Unacceptable
Under-five mortality	..	..	Unacceptable	Unacceptable
Maternal mortality	..	..	..	Acceptable
Level of concern about HIV/AIDS	..	..	Major concern	Major concern
Measures to respond to HIV/AIDS*	..	..	..	1,2,3,5
Grounds on which abortion is permitted**	..	..	1,2	1,2
Spatial distribution and internal migration				
View on spatial distribution	Minor change desired	Major change desired	Major change desired	Major change desired
Policies on internal migration				
From rural to urban areas	..	..	..	Raise
From rural to rural areas	..	..	..	Lower
From urban to rural areas	..	..	..	Lower
From urban to urban areas	..	..	..	Raise
Into urban agglomerations	Lower	..	Lower	Lower
International migration				
Immigration				
View	Satisfactory	Satisfactory	Satisfactory	Satisfactory
Policy	Maintain	Maintain	Lower	Maintain
Permanent settlement	..	..	Lower	..
Temporary workers	..	..	Lower	Maintain
Highly skilled workers	..	..	..	Raise
Family reunification	..	..	Lower	Maintain
Integration of non-citizens	..	..	No	No
Emigration				
View	Satisfactory	Satisfactory	Satisfactory	Satisfactory
Policy	Maintain	Maintain	No intervention	No intervention
Encouraging the return of citizens	..	..	No	No

* Measures implemented to respond to HIV/AIDS: (1) blood screening; (2) information/education campaigns; (3) antiretroviral treatment; (4) non-discriminatory policies; (5) distribution of condoms.

** Grounds on which abortion is permitted: (1) to save the woman's life; (2) to preserve physical health; (3) to preserve mental health; (4) rape or incest; (5) foetal impairment; (6) economic or social reasons; (7) on request.

Population indicators

Indicator	1975	1985	1995	2009
Population size and growth				
Population size (thousands)	137	184	248	309
Annual growth rate (percentage)*	2.5	3.0	2.8	1.4
Population age structure				
Percentage of population under age 15	42	46	46	28
Percentage of population aged 60 or over	7	5	5	6
Fertility and family planning				
Total fertility (children per woman)*	7.0	6.8	5.3	2.1
Adolescent fertility rate (per 1,000 women, aged 15 - 19)*	..	..	79.0	13.0
Percentage of births to women under age 20*	..	..	7	3
Percentage of births to women aged 35 or over*	..	..	25	22
Percentage of married women using contraception				
Modern methods	..	..	33[a]	34[b]
All methods	..	..	42[a]	39[b]
Health and mortality				
Life expectancy at birth (years)*				
Males	53	58	61	70
Females	50	56	61	73
Both sexes combined	51	57	61	71
Infant mortality rate (per 1,000 live births)*	121	94	66	24
Under-five mortality (per 1,000 live births)*	..	128	90	28
Maternal mortality ratio (per 100,000 live births) (2005)	..	..	..	120
HIV/AIDS				
People living with HIV/AIDS (thousands)	..	..	..	..
Adult prevalence (percentage)	..	..	..	..
Spatial distribution				
Population density (per sq. km)	461	616	832	1 038
Urban population (percentage)	17	25	26	39
Annual urban population growth rate (percentage)	9.9	3.5	3.7	5.0
Annual rural population growth rate (percentage)	1.1	3.1	1.7	-0.3
International migration				
Migrant stock				
Number of migrants (thousands)	2	2	3	3**
As percentage of total population	1.5	1.3	1.2	1.0**

* For the periods 1970-1975, 1980-1985, 1990-1995 and 2005-2010.
** For 2010.
[a] For 1999.
[b] For 2004.

Government views and policies

Population policy variable	1976	1986	1996	2009
Population size and growth				
View on growth	Satisfactory	Satisfactory	Too high	Too high
Policy on growth	No intervention	Maintain	Lower	Lower
Population age structure				
Level of concern about				
Size of the working-age population	..	..	..	Major concern
Ageing of the population	..	..	..	Minor concern
Fertility and family planning				
View on fertility level	Satisfactory	Satisfactory	Too high	Too high
Policy	No intervention	Maintain	Lower	Lower
Access to contraceptive methods	Direct support	Direct support	Direct support	Direct support
Adolescent fertility				
Level of concern	..	..	Minor concern	Major concern
Policies and programmes	..	..	Yes	Yes
Health and mortality				
View				
Life expectancy at birth	Unacceptable	Unacceptable	Unacceptable	Unacceptable
Under-five mortality	..	..	Unacceptable	Unacceptable
Maternal mortality	..	..	..	Unacceptable
Level of concern about HIV/AIDS	..	..	Minor concern	Major concern
Measures to respond to HIV/AIDS*	..	..	..	1,2,3,4,5
Grounds on which abortion is permitted**	..	..	1	1,4
Spatial distribution and internal migration				
View on spatial distribution	Major change desired	Major change desired	Major change desired	Major change desired
Policies on internal migration				
From rural to urban areas	..	..	..	Lower
From rural to rural areas	..	..	..	Maintain
From urban to rural areas	..	..	..	Raise
From urban to urban areas	..	..	..	No intervention
Into urban agglomerations	..	Lower	Lower	Lower
International migration				
Immigration				
View	Satisfactory	Satisfactory	Satisfactory	Too high
Policy	Maintain	Maintain	Maintain	No intervention
Permanent settlement	..	..	Maintain	No intervention
Temporary workers	..	..	Lower	No intervention
Highly skilled workers	..	..	..	No intervention
Family reunification	..	..	Maintain	No intervention
Integration of non-citizens	..	..	No	No
Emigration				
View	Satisfactory	Satisfactory	Satisfactory	Too high
Policy	Maintain	Maintain	Maintain	Lower
Encouraging the return of citizens	..	..	Yes	Yes

* Measures implemented to respond to HIV/AIDS: (1) blood screening; (2) information/education campaigns; (3) antiretroviral treatment; (4) non-discriminatory policies; (5) distribution of condoms.
** Grounds on which abortion is permitted: (1) to save the woman's life; (2) to preserve physical health; (3) to preserve mental health; (4) rape or incest; (5) foetal impairment; (6) economic or social reasons; (7) on request.

Population indicators

Indicator	1975	1985	1995	2009
Population size and growth				
Population size (thousands)	6 598	7 858	9 549	13 010
Annual growth rate (percentage)*	1.8	1.8	2.0	2.4
Population age structure				
Percentage of population under age 15	43	44	46	44
Percentage of population aged 60 or over	5	5	4	4
Fertility and family planning				
Total fertility (children per woman)*	6.6	6.6	6.3	5.5
Adolescent fertility rate (per 1,000 women, aged 15 - 19)*	..	..	175.0	163.0
Percentage of births to women under age 20*	..	..	14	15
Percentage of births to women aged 35 or over*	..	..	25	23
Percentage of married women using contraception				
Modern methods	..	1[a]	5	6[b]
All methods	..	5[a]	7	8[b]
Health and mortality				
Life expectancy at birth (years)*				
Males	38	40	43	48
Females	39	41	44	49
Both sexes combined	38	41	44	48
Infant mortality rate (per 1,000 live births)*	158	143	128	106
Under-five mortality (per 1,000 live births)*	..	283	244	191
Maternal mortality ratio (per 100,000 live births) (2005)	..	..	..	970
HIV/AIDS				
People living with HIV/AIDS (thousands)	..	..	34	100[c]
Adult prevalence (percentage)	..	..	0.8	1.5[c]
Spatial distribution				
Population density (per sq. km)	5	6	8	10
Urban population (percentage)	16	21	26	33
Annual urban population growth rate (percentage)	4.7	4.9	4.4	4.8
Annual rural population growth rate (percentage)	1.7	1.7	2.0	2.1
International migration				
Migrant stock				
Number of migrants (thousands)	163	160	174	163**
As percentage of total population	2.5	2.0	1.8	1.2**

* For the periods 1970-1975, 1980-1985, 1990-1995 and 2005-2010.
** For 2010.
[a] For 1987.
[b] For 2006.
[c] For 2007.

Government views and policies

Population policy variable	1976	1986	1996	2009
Population size and growth				
View on growth	Satisfactory	Satisfactory	Satisfactory	Satisfactory
Policy on growth	No intervention	No intervention	No intervention	Maintain
Population age structure				
Level of concern about				
Size of the working-age population	..	..	..	Minor concern
Ageing of the population	..	..	..	Major concern
Fertility and family planning				
View on fertility level	Satisfactory	Satisfactory	Satisfactory	Too low
Policy	No intervention	No intervention	No intervention	No intervention
Access to contraceptive methods	No support	No support	No support	No support
Adolescent fertility				
Level of concern	..	..	..	Minor concern
Policies and programmes	..	..	..	Yes
Health and mortality				
View				
Life expectancy at birth	Acceptable	Acceptable	Acceptable	Acceptable
Under-five mortality	..	..	..	Acceptable
Maternal mortality	..	..	..	Acceptable
Level of concern about HIV/AIDS	..	..	..	Minor concern
Measures to respond to HIV/AIDS*	..	..	..	1,2,3,4,5
Grounds on which abortion is permitted**	..	..	Not permitted	Not permitted
Spatial distribution and internal migration				
View on spatial distribution	Satisfactory	Satisfactory	Satisfactory	Minor change desired
Policies on internal migration				
From rural to urban areas	..	..	..	No intervention
From rural to rural areas	..	..	..	No intervention
From urban to rural areas	..	..	..	No intervention
From urban to urban areas	..	..	..	Lower
Into urban agglomerations	..	No intervention	..	No intervention
International migration				
Immigration				
View	Satisfactory	Satisfactory	Satisfactory	Satisfactory
Policy	Maintain	Maintain	Maintain	Maintain
Permanent settlement	..	..	..	Maintain
Temporary workers	..	..	..	Maintain
Highly skilled workers	..	..	..	Maintain
Family reunification	..	..	..	Maintain
Integration of non-citizens	..	..	..	No
Emigration				
View	Satisfactory	Satisfactory	Satisfactory	Satisfactory
Policy	Maintain	Maintain	No intervention	No intervention
Encouraging the return of citizens	..	..	..	No

* Measures implemented to respond to HIV/AIDS: (1) blood screening; (2) information/education campaigns; (3) antiretroviral treatment;
(4) non-discriminatory policies; (5) distribution of condoms.
** Grounds on which abortion is permitted: (1) to save the woman's life; (2) to preserve physical health; (3) to preserve mental health; (4) rape or incest;
(5) foetal impairment; (6) economic or social reasons; (7) on request.

Population indicators

Indicator	1975	1985	1995	2009
Population size and growth				
Population size (thousands)	304	344	378	409
Annual growth rate (percentage)*	0.1	1.2	1.0	0.4
Population age structure				
Percentage of population under age 15	25	24	22	16
Percentage of population aged 60 or over	13	14	16	21
Fertility and family planning				
Total fertility (children per woman)*	2.1	2.0	2.0	1.3
Adolescent fertility rate (per 1,000 women, aged 15 - 19)*	..	..	18.0	11.0
Percentage of births to women under age 20*	..	..	4	5
Percentage of births to women aged 35 or over*	..	..	13	13
Percentage of married women using contraception				
Modern methods	..	..	43[a]	..
All methods	..	..	86[a]	..
Health and mortality				
Life expectancy at birth (years)*				
Males	69	71	74	78
Females	73	76	78	81
Both sexes combined	71	74	76	80
Infant mortality rate (per 1,000 live births)*	22	13	9	6
Under-five mortality (per 1,000 live births)*	..	15	11	7
Maternal mortality ratio (per 100,000 live births) (2005)	..	..	..	8
HIV/AIDS				
People living with HIV/AIDS (thousands)	..	..	<0.1	<0.5[b]
Adult prevalence (percentage)	..	..	<0.1	0.1[b]
Spatial distribution				
Population density (per sq. km)	963	1 090	1 196	1 293
Urban population (percentage)	90	90	91	94
Annual urban population growth rate (percentage)	0.9	1.1	0.9	0.6
Annual rural population growth rate (percentage)	0.8	0.2	-1.9	2.9
International migration				
Migrant stock				
Number of migrants (thousands)	8	5	7	15**
As percentage of total population	2.7	1.4	1.9	3.8**

* For the periods 1970-1975, 1980-1985, 1990-1995 and 2005-2010.
** For 2010.
[a] For 1993.
[b] For 2007.

Government views and policies

Population policy variable	1976	1986	1996	2009
Population size and growth				
View on growth	..	..	Too high	Too high
Policy on growth	..	..	Lower	Lower
Population age structure				
Level of concern about				
Size of the working-age population	..	..	..	Major concern
Ageing of the population	..	..	..	..
Fertility and family planning				
View on fertility level	..	..	Too high	Too high
Policy	..	..	Lower	Lower
Access to contraceptive methods	..	..	Direct support	Direct support
Adolescent fertility				
Level of concern	..	..	Major concern	Major concern
Policies and programmes	..	..	Yes	Yes
Health and mortality				
View				
Life expectancy at birth	..	..	Unacceptable	Acceptable
Under-five mortality	..	..	Unacceptable	Acceptable
Maternal mortality	..	..	..	Acceptable
Level of concern about HIV/AIDS	..	..	Major concern	Major concern
Measures to respond to HIV/AIDS*	..	..	..	1,2,3,5
Grounds on which abortion is permitted**	..	..	1	1
Spatial distribution and internal migration				
View on spatial distribution	..	..	Major change desired	Major change desired
Policies on internal migration				
From rural to urban areas	..	..	..	Lower
From rural to rural areas	..	..	..	..
From urban to rural areas	..	..	..	Maintain
From urban to urban areas	..	..	..	Raise
Into urban agglomerations	..	..	No intervention	Lower
International migration				
Immigration				
View	..	..	Satisfactory	Satisfactory
Policy	..	..	Lower	Maintain
Permanent settlement	..	..	Lower	..
Temporary workers	..	..	Lower	..
Highly skilled workers	..	..	..	Lower
Family reunification	..	..	Lower	..
Integration of non-citizens	..	..	No	..
Emigration				
View	..	..	Satisfactory	Satisfactory
Policy	..	..	No intervention	Maintain
Encouraging the return of citizens	..	..	No	No

* Measures implemented to respond to HIV/AIDS: (1) blood screening; (2) information/education campaigns; (3) antiretroviral treatment; (4) non-discriminatory policies; (5) distribution of condoms.
** Grounds on which abortion is permitted: (1) to save the woman's life; (2) to preserve physical health; (3) to preserve mental health; (4) rape or incest; (5) foetal impairment; (6) economic or social reasons; (7) on request.

Population indicators

Indicator	1975	1985	1995	2009
Population size and growth				
Population size (thousands)	26	38	51	62
Annual growth rate (percentage)*	4.5	4.5	1.5	2.2
Population age structure				
Percentage of population under age 15	..	..	..	..
Percentage of population aged 60 or over	..	..	..	..
Fertility and family planning				
Total fertility (children per woman)*	..	..	..	..
Adolescent fertility rate (per 1,000 women, aged 15 - 19)*	..	..	..	..
Percentage of births to women under age 20*	..	..	..	..
Percentage of births to women aged 35 or over*	..	..	..	..
Percentage of married women using contraception				
Modern methods	..	..	..	..
All methods	..	..	..	..
Health and mortality				
Life expectancy at birth (years)*				
Males	..	..	..	..
Females	..	..	..	..
Both sexes combined	..	..	..	..
Infant mortality rate (per 1,000 live births)*	..	..	..	..
Under-five mortality (per 1,000 live births)*	..	..	..	..
Maternal mortality ratio (per 100,000 live births) (2005)	..	..	..	..
HIV/AIDS				
People living with HIV/AIDS (thousands)	..	..	..	..
Adult prevalence (percentage)	..	..	..	..
Spatial distribution				
Population density (per sq. km)	141	212	282	343
Urban population (percentage)	61	62	67	71
Annual urban population growth rate (percentage)	3.0	6.0	1.0	2.7
Annual rural population growth rate (percentage)	4.9	2.7	-0.5	0.9
International migration				
Migrant stock				
Number of migrants (thousands)	1	1	2	2**
As percentage of total population	4.5	3.7	3.1	2.7**

* For the periods 1970-1975, 1980-1985, 1990-1995 and 2005-2010.
** For 2010.

Government views and policies

Population policy variable	1976	1986	1996	2009
Population size and growth				
View on growth	Satisfactory	Satisfactory	Satisfactory	Too high
Policy on growth	No intervention	Raise	No intervention	Lower
Population age structure				
Level of concern about				
Size of the working-age population	..	..	..	Minor concern
Ageing of the population	..	..	..	Minor concern
Fertility and family planning				
View on fertility level	Satisfactory	Satisfactory	Satisfactory	Too high
Policy	No intervention	No intervention	No intervention	Lower
Access to contraceptive methods	No support	No support	Direct support	Direct support
Adolescent fertility				
Level of concern	..	..	Not a concern	Minor concern
Policies and programmes	..	..	No	Yes
Health and mortality				
View				
Life expectancy at birth	Unacceptable	Unacceptable	Unacceptable	Unacceptable
Under-five mortality	..	..	Unacceptable	Unacceptable
Maternal mortality	..	..	..	Unacceptable
Level of concern about HIV/AIDS	..	..	Minor concern	Major concern
Measures to respond to HIV/AIDS*	..	..	..	1,2,3
Grounds on which abortion is permitted**	..	..	1	1
Spatial distribution and internal migration				
View on spatial distribution	Major change desired	Major change desired	Major change desired	Major change desired
Policies on internal migration				
From rural to urban areas	..	..	..	Lower
From rural to rural areas	..	..	..	..
From urban to rural areas	..	..	..	..
From urban to urban areas	..	..	..	..
Into urban agglomerations	..	No intervention	Lower	Lower
International migration				
Immigration				
View	Satisfactory	Satisfactory	Satisfactory	Satisfactory
Policy	Maintain	Maintain	No intervention	No intervention
Permanent settlement	..	..	No intervention	No intervention
Temporary workers	..	..	No intervention	No intervention
Highly skilled workers	..	..	No intervention	No intervention
Family reunification	..	..	..	No intervention
Integration of non-citizens	..	..	No intervention	No intervention
Emigration				
View	Satisfactory	Too high	Satisfactory	Satisfactory
Policy	Maintain	Maintain	No intervention	No intervention
Encouraging the return of citizens	..	..	No	..

* Measures implemented to respond to HIV/AIDS: (1) blood screening; (2) information/education campaigns; (3) antiretroviral treatment; (4) non–discriminatory policies; (5) distribution of condoms.

** Grounds on which abortion is permitted: (1) to save the woman's life; (2) to preserve physical health; (3) to preserve mental health; (4) rape or incest; (5) foetal impairment; (6) economic or social reasons; (7) on request.

Population indicators

Indicator	1975	1985	1995	2009
Population size and growth				
Population size (thousands)	1 325	1 749	2 270	3 291
Annual growth rate (percentage)*	2.8	2.7	2.7	2.4
Population age structure				
Percentage of population under age 15	45	45	44	39
Percentage of population aged 60 or over	5	5	5	4
Fertility and family planning				
Total fertility (children per woman)*	6.7	6.3	5.7	4.5
Adolescent fertility rate (per 1,000 women, aged 15 - 19)*	..	..	104.0	90.0
Percentage of births to women under age 20*	..	..	9	10
Percentage of births to women aged 35 or over*	..	..	31	30
Percentage of married women using contraception				
Modern methods	..	0[a]	1[b]	8[c]
All methods	..	1[a]	4[b]	9[c]
Health and mortality				
Life expectancy at birth (years)*				
Males	47	52	54	55
Females	50	56	58	59
Both sexes combined	49	54	56	57
Infant mortality rate (per 1,000 live births)*	148	90	75	73
Under-five mortality (per 1,000 live births)*	..	150	127	120
Maternal mortality ratio (per 100,000 live births) (2005)	..	..	..	820
HIV/AIDS				
People living with HIV/AIDS (thousands)	..	..	<1	14[c]
Adult prevalence (percentage)	..	..	0.1	0.8[c]
Spatial distribution				
Population density (per sq. km)	1	2	2	3
Urban population (percentage)	21	35	40	41
Annual urban population growth rate (percentage)	9.3	7.1	2.9	3.0
Annual rural population growth rate (percentage)	0.9	0.0	2.7	2.0
International migration				
Migrant stock				
Number of migrants (thousands)	26	44	118	99**
As percentage of total population	2.0	2.5	5.2	2.9**

* For the periods 1970-1975, 1980-1985, 1990-1995 and 2005-2010.
** For 2010.
[a] For 1981.
[b] For 1991/1992.
[c] For 2007.

Government views and policies

Population policy variable	1976	1986	1996	2009
Population size and growth				
View on growth	Too high	Too high	Satisfactory	Satisfactory
Policy on growth	Lower	Lower	Maintain	Maintain
Population age structure				
Level of concern about				
Size of the working-age population	..	..	..	Minor concern
Ageing of the population	..	..	..	Major concern
Fertility and family planning				
View on fertility level	Too high	Too high	Satisfactory	Satisfactory
Policy	Lower	Lower	Maintain	Maintain
Access to contraceptive methods	Direct support	Direct support	Direct support	Direct support
Adolescent fertility				
Level of concern	..	..	Major concern	Major concern
Policies and programmes	..	..	Yes	Yes
Health and mortality				
View				
Life expectancy at birth	Acceptable	Unacceptable	Acceptable	Acceptable
Under-five mortality	..	..	Acceptable	Unacceptable
Maternal mortality	..	..	..	Unacceptable
Level of concern about HIV/AIDS	..	..	Major concern	Major concern
Measures to respond to HIV/AIDS*	..	..	..	1,2,3,5
Grounds on which abortion is permitted**	..	..	1	1
Spatial distribution and internal migration				
View on spatial distribution	Major change desired	Major change desired	Satisfactory	Satisfactory
Policies on internal migration				
From rural to urban areas	..	..	..	No intervention
From rural to rural areas	..	..	..	No intervention
From urban to rural areas	..	..	..	No intervention
From urban to urban areas	..	..	..	No intervention
Into urban agglomerations	No intervention	No intervention	No intervention	No intervention
International migration				
Immigration				
View	Satisfactory	Satisfactory	Satisfactory	Satisfactory
Policy	Maintain	Maintain	Lower	Maintain
Permanent settlement	..	..	Lower	Maintain
Temporary workers	..	..	Maintain	Maintain
Highly skilled workers	..	..	..	Maintain
Family reunification	..	..	Maintain	Maintain
Integration of non-citizens	..	..	Yes	Yes
Emigration				
View	Satisfactory	Too low	Satisfactory	Satisfactory
Policy	Maintain	Raise	Maintain	No intervention
Encouraging the return of citizens	No	..	Yes	No

* Measures implemented to respond to HIV/AIDS: (1) blood screening; (2) information/education campaigns; (3) antiretroviral treatment; (4) non-discriminatory policies; (5) distribution of condoms.
** Grounds on which abortion is permitted: (1) to save the woman's life; (2) to preserve physical health; (3) to preserve mental health; (4) rape or incest; (5) foetal impairment; (6) economic or social reasons; (7) on request.

Population indicators

Indicator	1975	1985	1995	2009
Population size and growth				
Population size (thousands)	892	1 016	1 129	1 288
Annual growth rate (percentage)*	1.5	1.0	1.3	0.7
Population age structure				
Percentage of population under age 15	40	32	27	23
Percentage of population aged 60 or over	5	7	8	11
Fertility and family planning				
Total fertility (children per woman)*	3.2	2.5	2.3	1.8
Adolescent fertility rate (per 1,000 women, aged 15 - 19)*	..	..	42.0	39.0
Percentage of births to women under age 20*	..	..	9	11
Percentage of births to women aged 35 or over*	..	..	10	10
Percentage of married women using contraception				
Modern methods	29	44	49[a]	39[b]
All methods	46	75	75[a]	76[b]
Health and mortality				
Life expectancy at birth (years)*				
Males	61	64	66	69
Females	65	69	73	76
Both sexes combined	63	67	70	72
Infant mortality rate (per 1,000 live births)*	55	28	20	15
Under-five mortality (per 1,000 live births)*	..	36	25	17
Maternal mortality ratio (per 100,000 live births) (2005)	..	..	..	15
HIV/AIDS				
People living with HIV/AIDS (thousands)	..	..	<0.2	13[c]
Adult prevalence (percentage)	..	..	<0.1	1.7[c]
Spatial distribution				
Population density (per sq. km)	437	498	553	631
Urban population (percentage)	43	42	43	42
Annual urban population growth rate (percentage)	1.1	1.5	0.9	1.0
Annual rural population growth rate (percentage)	2.0	0.2	1.4	0.5
International migration				
Migrant stock				
Number of migrants (thousands)	10	9	18	43**
As percentage of total population	1.1	0.9	1.6	3.3**

* For the periods 1970-1975, 1980-1985, 1990-1995 and 2005-2010.
** For 2010.
[a] For 1991.
[b] For 2002.
[c] For 2007.

Government views and policies

Population policy variable	1976	1986	1996	2009
Population size and growth				
View on growth	Too high	Too high	Too high	Satisfactory
Policy on growth	Lower	Lower	Lower	Maintain
Population age structure				
Level of concern about				
Size of the working-age population	..	..	..	Major concern
Ageing of the population	..	..	..	Major concern
Fertility and family planning				
View on fertility level	Too high	Too high	Too high	Satisfactory
Policy	Lower	Lower	Lower	Lower
Access to contraceptive methods	Direct support	Direct support	Direct support	Direct support
Adolescent fertility				
Level of concern	..	..	Major concern	Major concern
Policies and programmes	..	..	Yes	Yes
Health and mortality				
View				
Life expectancy at birth	Acceptable	Acceptable	Acceptable	Acceptable
Under-five mortality	..	..	Unacceptable	Unacceptable
Maternal mortality	..	..	..	Unacceptable
Level of concern about HIV/AIDS	..	..	Major concern	Major concern
Measures to respond to HIV/AIDS[*]	..	..	..	1,2,3,4,5
Grounds on which abortion is permitted[**]	..	..	1,4	1,2,3,4,5,6,7
Spatial distribution and internal migration				
View on spatial distribution	Major change desired	Major change desired	Major change desired	Major change desired
Policies on internal migration				
From rural to urban areas	..	..	..	Lower
From rural to rural areas	..	..	..	Raise
From urban to rural areas	..	..	..	Maintain
From urban to urban areas	..	..	..	Raise
Into urban agglomerations	No intervention	Lower	Lower	Lower
International migration				
Immigration				
View	Satisfactory	Satisfactory	Satisfactory	Satisfactory
Policy	Maintain	Maintain	Lower	Maintain
Permanent settlement	..	..	Lower	Maintain
Temporary workers	..	..	Maintain	Maintain
Highly skilled workers	..	..	..	Maintain
Family reunification	..	..	Lower	Raise
Integration of non-citizens	..	..	No	Maintain
Emigration				
View	Too high	Satisfactory	Too high	Yes
Policy	Lower	Maintain	Lower	Too high
Encouraging the return of citizens	No	..	Yes	Lower
				Yes

[*] Measures implemented to respond to HIV/AIDS: (1) blood screening; (2) information/education campaigns; (3) antiretroviral treatment; (4) non-discriminatory policies; (5) distribution of condoms.

[**] Grounds on which abortion is permitted: (1) to save the woman's life; (2) to preserve physical health; (3) to preserve mental health; (4) rape or incest; (5) foetal impairment; (6) economic or social reasons; (7) on request.

Population indicators

Indicator	1975	1985	1995	2009
Population size and growth				
Population size (thousands)	60 430	75 765	91 650	109 610
Annual growth rate (percentage)*	3.0	1.9	1.9	1.0
Population age structure				
Percentage of population under age 15	46	42	36	28
Percentage of population aged 60 or over	6	6	7	9
Fertility and family planning				
Total fertility (children per woman)*	6.5	4.3	3.2	2.2
Adolescent fertility rate (per 1,000 women, aged 15 - 19)*	..	..	78.0	65.0
Percentage of births to women under age 20*	..	..	12	15
Percentage of births to women aged 35 or over*	..	..	16	12
Percentage of married women using contraception				
Modern methods	23[a]	45[b]	58	67[c]
All methods	30[a]	53[b]	67	71[c]
Health and mortality				
Life expectancy at birth (years)*				
Males	60	64	69	74
Females	65	71	75	79
Both sexes combined	63	68	72	76
Infant mortality rate (per 1,000 live births)*	69	47	33	17
Under-five mortality (per 1,000 live births)*	..	57	40	20
Maternal mortality ratio (per 100,000 live births) (2005)	..	..	..	60
HIV/AIDS				
People living with HIV/AIDS (thousands)	..	..	130	200[d]
Adult prevalence (percentage)	..	..	0.3	0.3[d]
Spatial distribution				
Population density (per sq. km)	31	39	47	56
Urban population (percentage)	63	69	73	78
Annual urban population growth rate (percentage)	4.0	2.6	2.2	1.5
Annual rural population growth rate (percentage)	0.9	0.2	0.7	-0.2
International migration				
Migrant stock				
Number of migrants (thousands)	230	479	458	726**
As percentage of total population	0.4	0.6	0.5	0.7**

* For the periods 1970-1975, 1980-1985, 1990-1995 and 2005-2010.
** For 2010.
[a] For 1976.
[b] For 1987.
[c] For 2006.
[d] For 2007.

Government views and policies

Population policy variable	1976	1986	1996	2009
Population size and growth				
View on growth	..	..	Too high	Too high
Policy on growth	..	..	Lower	Lower
Population age structure				
Level of concern about				
Size of the working-age population	..	..	..	..
Ageing of the population	..	..	..	..
Fertility and family planning				
View on fertility level	..	..	Too high	Too high
Policy	..	..	Lower	Lower
Access to contraceptive methods	..	..	Direct support	Direct support
Adolescent fertility				
Level of concern	..	..	..	Major concern
Policies and programmes	..	..	..	Yes
Health and mortality				
View				
Life expectancy at birth	..	..	Unacceptable	Unacceptable
Under-five mortality	..	..	..	Unacceptable
Maternal mortality	..	..	..	Unacceptable
Level of concern about HIV/AIDS	..	..	..	Major concern
Measures to respond to HIV/AIDS*	..	..	..	1,2,3
Grounds on which abortion is permitted**	..	..	..	1
Spatial distribution and internal migration				
View on spatial distribution	..	..	Satisfactory	Major change desired
Policies on internal migration				
From rural to urban areas	..	..	..	..
From rural to rural areas	..	..	..	..
From urban to rural areas	..	..	..	..
From urban to urban areas	..	..	..	..
Into urban agglomerations	..	..	..	..
International migration				
Immigration				
View	..	..	Too high	Too high
Policy	..	..	Lower	Lower
Permanent settlement	..	..	Lower	Lower
Temporary workers	..	..	Lower	Lower
Highly skilled workers	..	..	..	Maintain
Family reunification	..	..	..	Maintain
Integration of non-citizens	..	..	..	..
Emigration				
View	..	..	Too high	Too high
Policy	..	..	Lower	No intervention
Encouraging the return of citizens	..	..	Yes	..

* Measures implemented to respond to HIV/AIDS: (1) blood screening; (2) information/education campaigns; (3) antiretroviral treatment; (4) non-discriminatory policies; (5) distribution of condoms.
** Grounds on which abortion is permitted: (1) to save the woman's life; (2) to preserve physical health; (3) to preserve mental health; (4) rape or incest; (5) foetal impairment; (6) economic or social reasons; (7) on request.

Population indicators

Indicator	1975	1985	1995	2009
Population size and growth				
Population size (thousands)	63	86	107	111
Annual growth rate (percentage)*	0.6	3.2	2.1	0.3
Population age structure				
Percentage of population under age 15	47	46	43	37
Percentage of population aged 60 or over	7	5	6	6
Fertility and family planning				
Total fertility (children per woman)*	6.9	6.0	4.8	3.6
Adolescent fertility rate (per 1,000 women, aged 15 - 19)*	..	..	56.0	25.0
Percentage of births to women under age 20*	..	..	6	4
Percentage of births to women aged 35 or over*	..	..	30	24
Percentage of married women using contraception				
Modern methods	..	..	..	..
All methods	..	..	..	..
Health and mortality				
Life expectancy at birth (years)*				
Males	62	65	66	68
Females	63	66	67	69
Both sexes combined	63	65	66	69
Infant mortality rate (per 1,000 live births)*	58	47	42	34
Under-five mortality (per 1,000 live births)*	..	61	54	42
Maternal mortality ratio (per 100,000 live births) (2005)	..	..	..	..
HIV/AIDS				
People living with HIV/AIDS (thousands)	..	..	..	..
Adult prevalence (percentage)	..	..	..	..
Spatial distribution				
Population density (per sq. km)	90	122	153	158
Urban population (percentage)	26	26	25	23
Annual urban population growth rate (percentage)	2.4	2.4	-1.8	1.0
Annual rural population growth rate (percentage)	1.8	2.7	1.4	0.3
International migration				
Migrant stock				
Number of migrants (thousands)	5	4	3	3**
As percentage of total population	8.0	4.8	3.1	2.4**

* For the periods 1970-1975, 1980-1985, 1990-1995 and 2005-2010.
** For 2010.

Government views and policies

Population policy variable	1976	1986	1996	2009
Population size and growth				
View on growth	Too low	Too low	Too low	Satisfactory
Policy on growth	Raise	Raise	Raise	No intervention
Population age structure				
Level of concern about				
Size of the working-age population	..	..	..	
Ageing of the population	..	..	..	Minor concern
Fertility and family planning				
View on fertility level	Too low	Too low	Too low	Satisfactory
Policy	Raise	Raise	Raise	Maintain
Access to contraceptive methods	Direct support	Direct support	No support	No support
Adolescent fertility				
Level of concern	..	..	..	Not a concern
Policies and programmes	..	..	..	No
Health and mortality				
View				
Life expectancy at birth	Acceptable	Acceptable	Acceptable	Acceptable
Under-five mortality	..	..	..	Acceptable
Maternal mortality	..	..	..	Acceptable
Level of concern about HIV/AIDS	..	..	..	Minor concern
Measures to respond to HIV/AIDS*	..	..	..	1,2,5
Grounds on which abortion is permitted**	..	..	1	1
Spatial distribution and internal migration				
View on spatial distribution	Satisfactory	Satisfactory	Satisfactory	Satisfactory
Policies on internal migration				
From rural to urban areas	..	..	..	No intervention
From rural to rural areas	..	..	..	No intervention
From urban to rural areas	..	..	..	No intervention
From urban to urban areas	..	..	..	No intervention
Into urban agglomerations	..	..	..	No intervention
International migration				
Immigration				
View	Satisfactory	Satisfactory	Satisfactory	Satisfactory
Policy	Maintain	Lower	Lower	Maintain
Permanent settlement	..	..	..	Maintain
Temporary workers	..	..	..	Maintain
Highly skilled workers	..	..	..	..
Family reunification	..	..	..	..
Integration of non-citizens	..	..	..	..
Emigration				
View	Satisfactory	Satisfactory	Satisfactory	Satisfactory
Policy	Maintain	Maintain	Maintain	Maintain
Encouraging the return of citizens	..	..	..	..

* Measures implemented to respond to HIV/AIDS: (1) blood screening; (2) information/education campaigns; (3) antiretroviral treatment; (4) non−discriminatory policies; (5) distribution of condoms.

** Grounds on which abortion is permitted: (1) to save the woman's life; (2) to preserve physical health; (3) to preserve mental health; (4) rape or incest; (5) foetal impairment; (6) economic or social reasons; (7) on request.

Population indicators

Indicator	1975	1985	1995	2009
Population size and growth				
Population size (thousands)	25	28	31	33
Annual growth rate (percentage)*	1.2	1.3	0.9	0.3
Population age structure				
Percentage of population under age 15	..	..	..	..
Percentage of population aged 60 or over	..	..	..	..
Fertility and family planning				
Total fertility (children per woman)*	..	..	..	..
Adolescent fertility rate (per 1,000 women, aged 15 - 19)*	..	..	..	..
Percentage of births to women under age 20*	..	..	..	..
Percentage of births to women aged 35 or over*	..	..	..	..
Percentage of married women using contraception				
Modern methods	..	..	..	..
All methods	..	..	..	..
Health and mortality				
Life expectancy at birth (years)*				
Males	..	..	..	..
Females	..	..	..	..
Both sexes combined	..	..	..	..
Infant mortality rate (per 1,000 live births)*	..	..	..	..
Under-five mortality (per 1,000 live births)*	..	..	..	..
Maternal mortality ratio (per 100,000 live births) (2005)	..	..	..	..
HIV/AIDS				
People living with HIV/AIDS (thousands)	..	..	..	..
Adult prevalence (percentage)	..	..	..	..
Spatial distribution				
Population density (per sq. km)	16 881	18 683	20 547	22 021
Urban population (percentage)	100	100	100	100
Annual urban population growth rate (percentage)	0.8	1.4	0.5	0.4
Annual rural population growth rate (percentage)	0.0	0.0	0.0	0.0
International migration				
Migrant stock				
Number of migrants (thousands)	16	19	21	24**
As percentage of total population	64.8	67.2	68.2	71.6**

* For the periods 1970-1975, 1980-1985, 1990-1995 and 2005-2010.
** For 2010.

Government views and policies

Population policy variable	1976	1986	1996	2009
Population size and growth				
View on growth	Too low	Too low	Satisfactory	Too low
Policy on growth	Raise	Raise	Maintain	Raise
Population age structure				
Level of concern about				
Size of the working-age population	..	..	..	Major concern
Ageing of the population	..	..	..	Minor concern
Fertility and family planning				
View on fertility level	Satisfactory	Too low	Satisfactory	Too low
Policy	Maintain	Raise	Maintain	Raise
Access to contraceptive methods	Direct support	Direct support	Direct support	Direct support
Adolescent fertility				
Level of concern	..	..	Minor concern	Major concern
Policies and programmes	..	..	..	Yes
Health and mortality				
View				
Life expectancy at birth	Unacceptable	Unacceptable	Unacceptable	Unacceptable
Under-five mortality	..	..	..	Unacceptable
Maternal mortality	..	..	..	Unacceptable
Level of concern about HIV/AIDS	..	..	Major concern	Major concern
Measures to respond to HIV/AIDS*	..	..	..	1,2,4,5
Grounds on which abortion is permitted**	..	..	1,2,3,4,5,6,7	1,2,3,4,5,6,7
Spatial distribution and internal migration				
View on spatial distribution	Minor change desired	Minor change desired	Major change desired	Major change desired
Policies on internal migration				
From rural to urban areas	..	..	..	Lower
From rural to rural areas	..	..	..	Maintain
From urban to rural areas	..	..	..	Raise
From urban to urban areas	..	..	..	Maintain
Into urban agglomerations	..	..	Lower	Lower
International migration				
Immigration				
View	Satisfactory	Satisfactory	Satisfactory	Satisfactory
Policy	Maintain	Maintain	Maintain	Maintain
Permanent settlement	..	..	Maintain	Maintain
Temporary workers	..	..	Lower	Maintain
Highly skilled workers	..	..	..	Raise
Family reunification	..	..	Raise	Maintain
Integration of non-citizens	..	..	No	No
Emigration				
View	Satisfactory	Satisfactory	Satisfactory	Too high
Policy	Maintain	Maintain	No intervention	Maintain
Encouraging the return of citizens	..	..	Yes	Yes

* Measures implemented to respond to HIV/AIDS: (1) blood screening; (2) information/education campaigns; (3) antiretroviral treatment; (4) non-discriminatory policies; (5) distribution of condoms.

** Grounds on which abortion is permitted: (1) to save the woman's life; (2) to preserve physical health; (3) to preserve mental health; (4) rape or incest; (5) foetal impairment; (6) economic or social reasons; (7) on request.

Population indicators

Indicator	1975	1985	1995	2009
Population size and growth				
Population size (thousands)	1 447	1 909	2 270	2 671
Annual growth rate (percentage)*	2.8	2.8	0.5	1.2
Population age structure				
Percentage of population under age 15	44	42	39	26
Percentage of population aged 60 or over	5	5	6	6
Fertility and family planning				
Total fertility (children per woman)*	7.3	5.7	3.5	2.0
Adolescent fertility rate (per 1,000 women, aged 15 - 19)*	..	..	16.0	17.0
Percentage of births to women under age 20*	..	..	2	4
Percentage of births to women aged 35 or over*	..	..	14	16
Percentage of married women using contraception				
Modern methods	..	..	41[a]	61[b]
All methods	..	..	57[a]	66[b]
Health and mortality				
Life expectancy at birth (years)*				
Males	53	56	59	63
Females	55	59	63	70
Both sexes combined	54	57	61	66
Infant mortality rate (per 1,000 live births)*	98	78	68	42
Under-five mortality (per 1,000 live births)*	..	80	70	44
Maternal mortality ratio (per 100,000 live births) (2005)	..	..	..	46
HIV/AIDS				
People living with HIV/AIDS (thousands)	..	..	..	<1[c]
Adult prevalence (percentage)	..	..	..	0.1[c]
Spatial distribution				
Population density (per sq. km)	1	1	1	2
Urban population (percentage)	49	55	57	57
Annual urban population growth rate (percentage)	4.3	4.2	0.8	1.4
Annual rural population growth rate (percentage)	1.4	1.8	0.9	0.6
International migration				
Migrant stock				
Number of migrants (thousands)	5	6	7	10**
As percentage of total population	0.3	0.3	0.3	0.4**

* For the periods 1970-1975, 1980-1985, 1990-1995 and 2005-2010.
** For 2010.
[a] For 1994.
[b] For 2005.
[c] For 2007.

Government views and policies

Population policy variable	1976	1986	1996	2009
Population size and growth				
View on growth	..	..	..	Satisfactory
Policy on growth	..	..	..	Maintain
Population age structure				
Level of concern about				
Size of the working-age population	..	..	..	Minor concern
Ageing of the population	..	..	..	Major concern
Fertility and family planning				
View on fertility level	..	..	..	Too low
Policy	..	..	..	Raise
Access to contraceptive methods	..	..	..	Direct support
Adolescent fertility				
Level of concern	..	..	..	Minor concern
Policies and programmes	..	..	..	Yes
Health and mortality				
View				
Life expectancy at birth	..	..	..	Acceptable
Under-five mortality	..	..	..	Unacceptable
Maternal mortality	..	..	..	Acceptable
Level of concern about HIV/AIDS	..	..	..	Major concern
Measures to respond to HIV/AIDS*	..	..	..	1,2,3,5
Grounds on which abortion is permitted**	..	..	..	1,2,3,4,5,6,7
Spatial distribution and internal migration				
View on spatial distribution	..	..	..	Major change desired
Policies on internal migration				
From rural to urban areas	..	..	..	Lower
From rural to rural areas	..	..	..	..
From urban to rural areas	..	..	..	..
From urban to urban areas	..	..	..	..
Into urban agglomerations	..	..	..	..
International migration				
Immigration				
View	..	..	..	Satisfactory
Policy	..	..	..	Maintain
Permanent settlement	..	..	..	Maintain
Temporary workers	..	..	..	Maintain
Highly skilled workers	..	..	..	Maintain
Family reunification	..	..	..	..
Integration of non-citizens	..	..	..	..
Emigration				
View	..	..	..	Satisfactory
Policy	..	..	..	No intervention
Encouraging the return of citizens	..	..	..	..

* Measures implemented to respond to HIV/AIDS: (1) blood screening; (2) information/education campaigns; (3) antiretroviral treatment; (4) non-discriminatory policies; (5) distribution of condoms.
** Grounds on which abortion is permitted: (1) to save the woman's life; (2) to preserve physical health; (3) to preserve mental health; (4) rape or incest; (5) foetal impairment; (6) economic or social reasons; (7) on request.

Population indicators

Indicator	1975	1985	1995	2009
Population size and growth				
Population size (thousands)	549	576	624	624
Annual growth rate (percentage)*	1.1	0.0	1.2	0.0
Population age structure				
Percentage of population under age 15	30	27	24	19
Percentage of population aged 60 or over	11	11	14	18
Fertility and family planning				
Total fertility (children per woman)*	2.4	2.2	1.8	1.6
Adolescent fertility rate (per 1,000 women, aged 15 - 19)*	..	..	25.0	15.0
Percentage of births to women under age 20*	..	..	7	5
Percentage of births to women aged 35 or over*	..	..	11	12
Percentage of married women using contraception				
Modern methods	..	..	30[a]	17[b]
All methods	..	..	53[a]	39[b]
Health and mortality				
Life expectancy at birth (years)*				
Males	68	72	73	72
Females	73	77	79	76
Both sexes combined	71	74	76	74
Infant mortality rate (per 1,000 live births)*	30	23	14	9
Under-five mortality (per 1,000 live births)*	..	25	16	10
Maternal mortality ratio (per 100,000 live births) (2005)	..	..	..	..
HIV/AIDS				
People living with HIV/AIDS (thousands)	..	..	..	..
Adult prevalence (percentage)	..	..	..	..
Spatial distribution				
Population density (per sq. km)	40	42	45	45
Urban population (percentage)	32	42	53	60
Annual urban population growth rate (percentage)	4.3	2.7	3.8	-0.3
Annual rural population growth rate (percentage)	-0.3	-1.9	-0.4	0.8
International migration				
Migrant stock				
Number of migrants (thousands)	..	..	..	43**
As percentage of total population	0.0	0.0	..	6.8**

* For the periods 1970-1975, 1980-1985, 1990-1995 and 2005-2010.
** For 2010.
[a] For 2000.
[b] For 2005/2006.

Government views and policies

Population policy variable	1976	1986	1996	2009
Population size and growth				
View on growth	Too high	Too high	Too high	Too high
Policy on growth	Lower	Lower	Lower	Lower
Population age structure				
Level of concern about				
Size of the working-age population	..	..	..	Major concern
Ageing of the population	..	..	..	Minor concern
Fertility and family planning				
View on fertility level	Too high	Too high	Too high	Satisfactory
Policy	Lower	Lower	Lower	Lower
Access to contraceptive methods	Direct support	Direct support	Direct support	Direct support
Adolescent fertility				
Level of concern	..	..	Minor concern	Minor concern
Policies and programmes	..	..	..	Yes
Health and mortality				
View				
Life expectancy at birth	Unacceptable	Unacceptable	Unacceptable	Acceptable
Under-five mortality	..	..	Unacceptable	Unacceptable
Maternal mortality	..	..	..	Unacceptable
Level of concern about HIV/AIDS	..	..	Minor concern	Major concern
Measures to respond to HIV/AIDS*	..	..	..	1,2,3,4,5
Grounds on which abortion is permitted**	..	..	1,2	1,2,3
Spatial distribution and internal migration				
View on spatial distribution	Major change desired	Major change desired	Minor change desired	Minor change desired
Policies on internal migration				
From rural to urban areas	..	..	..	Lower
From rural to rural areas	..	..	..	..
From urban to rural areas	..	..	..	..
From urban to urban areas	..	..	..	..
Into urban agglomerations	..	Lower	Lower	Lower
International migration				
Immigration				
View	Satisfactory	Satisfactory	Satisfactory	Too high
Policy	Maintain	Maintain	No intervention	Lower
Permanent settlement	..	..	No intervention	Maintain
Temporary workers	..	..	No intervention	Lower
Highly skilled workers	..	..	..	Maintain
Family reunification	..	..	No intervention	Maintain
Integration of non-citizens	..	..	No	Yes
Emigration				
View	Satisfactory	Too low	Satisfactory	Too low
Policy	Maintain	Raise	No intervention	Maintain
Encouraging the return of citizens	..	..	..	Yes

* Measures implemented to respond to HIV/AIDS: (1) blood screening; (2) information/education campaigns; (3) antiretroviral treatment; (4) non-discriminatory policies; (5) distribution of condoms.
** Grounds on which abortion is permitted: (1) to save the woman's life; (2) to preserve physical health; (3) to preserve mental health; (4) rape or incest; (5) foetal impairment; (6) economic or social reasons; (7) on request.

Population indicators

Indicator	1975	1985	1995	2009
Population size and growth				
Population size (thousands)	17 305	22 299	26 951	31 993
Annual growth rate (percentage)*	2.5	2.6	1.7	1.2
Population age structure				
Percentage of population under age 15	47	42	37	28
Percentage of population aged 60 or over	5	6	7	8
Fertility and family planning				
Total fertility (children per woman)*	6.9	5.4	3.7	2.4
Adolescent fertility rate (per 1,000 women, aged 15 - 19)*	..	..	38.0	19.0
Percentage of births to women under age 20*	..	..	5	4
Percentage of births to women aged 35 or over*	..	..	31	23
Percentage of married women using contraception				
Modern methods	..	21[a]	42	52[b]
All methods	..	26[a]	50	63[b]
Health and mortality				
Life expectancy at birth (years)*				
Males	51	58	64	69
Females	55	62	68	73
Both sexes combined	53	60	65	71
Infant mortality rate (per 1,000 live births)*	123	88	58	31
Under-five mortality (per 1,000 live births)*	..	130	77	36
Maternal mortality ratio (per 100,000 live births) (2005)	..	..	..	240
HIV/AIDS				
People living with HIV/AIDS (thousands)	..	..	5.1	21[c]
Adult prevalence (percentage)	..	..	<0.1	0.1[c]
Spatial distribution				
Population density (per sq. km)	39	50	60	72
Urban population (percentage)	38	45	52	56
Annual urban population growth rate (percentage)	4.2	3.9	2.1	1.9
Annual rural population growth rate (percentage)	1.3	1.0	0.8	0.3
International migration				
Migrant stock				
Number of migrants (thousands)	90	60	55	49**
As percentage of total population	0.5	0.3	0.2	0.2**

* For the periods 1970-1975, 1980-1985, 1990-1995 and 2005-2010.
** For 2010.
[a] For 1984.
[b] For 2003/2004.
[c] For 2007.

Government views and policies

Population policy variable	1976	1986	1996	2009
Population size and growth				
View on growth	Too low	Satisfactory	Too high	Too high
Policy on growth	Raise	No intervention	No intervention	No intervention
Population age structure				
Level of concern about				
Size of the working-age population	..	..	..	..
Ageing of the population	..	..	..	Major concern
Fertility and family planning				
View on fertility level	Satisfactory	Satisfactory	Too high	Too high
Policy	Maintain	No intervention	Lower	Lower
Access to contraceptive methods	Direct support	Direct support	Direct support	Direct support
Adolescent fertility				
Level of concern	..	..	Major concern	Major concern
Policies and programmes	..	..	No	Yes
Health and mortality				
View				
Life expectancy at birth	Unacceptable	Unacceptable	Unacceptable	Unacceptable
Under-five mortality	..	..	Unacceptable	Unacceptable
Maternal mortality	..	..	..	Unacceptable
Level of concern about HIV/AIDS	..	..	Major concern	Major concern
Measures to respond to HIV/AIDS*	..	..	..	1,2,3,4,5
Grounds on which abortion is permitted**	..	..	1	1,2,3
Spatial distribution and internal migration				
View on spatial distribution	Major change desired	Major change desired	Major change desired	Major change desired
Policies on internal migration				
From rural to urban areas	..	..	..	Lower
From rural to rural areas	..	..	..	No intervention
From urban to rural areas	..	..	..	No intervention
From urban to urban areas	..	..	..	No intervention
Into urban agglomerations	No intervention	No intervention	No intervention	Lower
International migration				
Immigration				
View	Satisfactory	Satisfactory	Satisfactory	Satisfactory
Policy	Maintain	Maintain	No intervention	Maintain
Permanent settlement	..	..	No intervention	..
Temporary workers	..	..	No intervention	Maintain
Highly skilled workers	..	..	..	..
Family reunification	..	..	No intervention	..
Integration of non-citizens	..	..	..	..
Emigration				
View	Satisfactory	Satisfactory	Satisfactory	Satisfactory
Policy	Maintain	Lower	No intervention	No intervention
Encouraging the return of citizens	No	..	Yes	..

* Measures implemented to respond to HIV/AIDS: (1) blood screening; (2) information/education campaigns; (3) antiretroviral treatment; (4) non-discriminatory policies; (5) distribution of condoms.
** Grounds on which abortion is permitted: (1) to save the woman's life; (2) to preserve physical health; (3) to preserve mental health; (4) rape or incest; (5) foetal impairment; (6) economic or social reasons; (7) on request.

Population indicators

Indicator	1975	1985	1995	2009
Population size and growth				
Population size (thousands)	10 614	13 324	15 945	22 894
Annual growth rate (percentage)*	2.3	1.9	3.3	2.3
Population age structure				
Percentage of population under age 15	44	45	44	44
Percentage of population aged 60 or over	5	5	5	5
Fertility and family planning				
Total fertility (children per woman)*	6.6	6.4	6.1	5.1
Adolescent fertility rate (per 1,000 women, aged 15 - 19)*	..	..	113.0	149.0
Percentage of births to women under age 20*	..	..	9	15
Percentage of births to women aged 35 or over*	..	..	31	21
Percentage of married women using contraception				
Modern methods	..	..	5[a]	12[b]
All methods	..	..	6[a]	17[b]
Health and mortality				
Life expectancy at birth (years)*				
Males	39	41	43	47
Females	42	44	46	49
Both sexes combined	40	43	44	48
Infant mortality rate (per 1,000 live births)*	158	143	135	90
Under-five mortality (per 1,000 live births)*	..	249	233	153
Maternal mortality ratio (per 100,000 live births) (2005)	..	..	..	520
HIV/AIDS				
People living with HIV/AIDS (thousands)	..	..	370	1 500[c]
Adult prevalence (percentage)	..	..	4.5	12.5[c]
Spatial distribution				
Population density (per sq. km)	13	17	20	29
Urban population (percentage)	9	17	26	38
Annual urban population growth rate (percentage)	11.1	5.1	7.2	3.9
Annual rural population growth rate (percentage)	1.8	-0.6	1.5	0.6
International migration				
Migrant stock				
Number of migrants (thousands)	37	61	246	450**
As percentage of total population	0.3	0.5	1.5	1.9**

* For the periods 1970-1975, 1980-1985, 1990-1995 and 2005-2010.
** For 2010.
[a] For 1997.
[b] For 2003/2004.
[c] For 2007.

Government views and policies

Population policy variable	1976	1986	1996	2009
Population size and growth				
View on growth	Satisfactory	Satisfactory	Satisfactory	Satisfactory
Policy on growth	No intervention	No intervention	No intervention	No intervention
Population age structure				
Level of concern about				
Size of the working-age population	..	..	..	Major concern
Ageing of the population	..	..	..	Minor concern
Fertility and family planning				
View on fertility level	Satisfactory	Satisfactory	Too high	Satisfactory
Policy	No intervention	No intervention	No intervention	Maintain
Access to contraceptive methods	No support	Indirect support	Direct support	Direct support
Adolescent fertility				
Level of concern	..	..	Not a concern	Major concern
Policies and programmes	..	..	No	Yes
Health and mortality				
View				
Life expectancy at birth	Unacceptable	Unacceptable	Unacceptable	Unacceptable
Under-five mortality	..	..	Unacceptable	Unacceptable
Maternal mortality	..	..	..	Unacceptable
Level of concern about HIV/AIDS	..	..	Major concern	Major concern
Measures to respond to HIV/AIDS*	..	..	..	1,2,3,5
Grounds on which abortion is permitted**	..	..	1	1
Spatial distribution and internal migration				
View on spatial distribution	Minor change desired	Minor change desired	Satisfactory	Minor change desired
Policies on internal migration				
From rural to urban areas	..	..	..	Lower
From rural to rural areas	..	..	..	..
From urban to rural areas	..	..	..	..
From urban to urban areas	..	..	..	Maintain
Into urban agglomerations	..	..	No intervention	Lower
International migration				
Immigration				
View	Satisfactory	Satisfactory	Satisfactory	Satisfactory
Policy	Maintain	Maintain	Maintain	Lower
Permanent settlement	..	..	Maintain	Lower
Temporary workers	..	..	No intervention	Maintain
Highly skilled workers	..	..	..	Maintain
Family reunification	..	..	No intervention	No intervention
Integration of non-citizens	..	..	No	No
Emigration				
View	Satisfactory	Satisfactory	Satisfactory	Satisfactory
Policy	Maintain	Maintain	Maintain	Maintain
Encouraging the return of citizens	..	..	Yes	Yes

* Measures implemented to respond to HIV/AIDS: (1) blood screening; (2) information/education campaigns; (3) antiretroviral treatment; (4) non−discriminatory policies; (5) distribution of condoms.
** Grounds on which abortion is permitted: (1) to save the woman's life; (2) to preserve physical health; (3) to preserve mental health; (4) rape or incest; (5) foetal impairment; (6) economic or social reasons; (7) on request.

Population indicators

Indicator	1975	1985	1995	2009
Population size and growth				
Population size (thousands)	29 886	37 443	43 864	50 020
Annual growth rate (percentage)*	2.5	2.2	1.4	0.9
Population age structure				
Percentage of population under age 15	41	39	34	27
Percentage of population aged 60 or over	7	7	8	8
Fertility and family planning				
Total fertility (children per woman)*	5.9	4.6	3.1	2.3
Adolescent fertility rate (per 1,000 women, aged 15 - 19)*	..	..	34.0	18.0
Percentage of births to women under age 20*	..	..	6	4
Percentage of births to women aged 35 or over*	..	..	23	17
Percentage of married women using contraception				
Modern methods	..	..	28[a]	33[b]
All methods	..	..	33[a]	37[b]
Health and mortality				
Life expectancy at birth (years)*				
Males	51	56	57	59
Females	55	60	61	63
Both sexes combined	53	58	59	61
Infant mortality rate (per 1,000 live births)*	106	86	83	75
Under-five mortality (per 1,000 live births)*	..	131	124	111
Maternal mortality ratio (per 100,000 live births) (2005)	..	..	..	380
HIV/AIDS				
People living with HIV/AIDS (thousands)	..	..	230	240[c]
Adult prevalence (percentage)	..	..	0.8	0.7[c]
Spatial distribution				
Population density (per sq. km)	44	55	65	74
Urban population (percentage)	24	24	26	33
Annual urban population growth rate (percentage)	2.4	2.2	2.6	2.8
Annual rural population growth rate (percentage)	2.3	1.7	0.9	-0.2
International migration				
Migrant stock				
Number of migrants (thousands)	266	133	114	89**
As percentage of total population	0.9	0.4	0.3	0.2**

* For the periods 1970-1975, 1980-1985, 1990-1995 and 2005-2010.
** For 2010.
[a] For 1997.
[b] For 2001.
[c] For 2007.

Government views and policies

Population policy variable	1976	1986	1996	2009
Population size and growth				
View on growth	..	..	Too high	Satisfactory
Policy on growth	..	..	Lower	Lower
Population age structure				
Level of concern about				
Size of the working-age population	..	..	..	Major concern
Ageing of the population	..	..	..	Minor concern
Fertility and family planning				
View on fertility level	..	..	Too high	Satisfactory
Policy	..	..	No intervention	Lower
Access to contraceptive methods	..	..	Direct support	Direct support
Adolescent fertility				
Level of concern	..	..	Major concern	Major concern
Policies and programmes	..	..	Yes	Yes
Health and mortality				
View				
Life expectancy at birth	..	..	Unacceptable	Unacceptable
Under-five mortality	..	..	Unacceptable	Unacceptable
Maternal mortality	..	..	..	Unacceptable
Level of concern about HIV/AIDS	..	..	Major concern	Major concern
Measures to respond to HIV/AIDS*	..	..	..	1,2,3,4,5
Grounds on which abortion is permitted**	..	..	1,2,3,4,5	1,2,3,4,5
Spatial distribution and internal migration				
View on spatial distribution	..	..	Satisfactory	Major change desired
Policies on internal migration				
From rural to urban areas	..	..	..	Lower
From rural to rural areas	..	..	..	No intervention
From urban to rural areas	..	..	..	Raise
From urban to urban areas	..	..	..	No intervention
Into urban agglomerations	..	..	Maintain	Lower
International migration				
Immigration				
View	..	..	Satisfactory	Satisfactory
Policy	..	..	Raise	Maintain
Permanent settlement	..	..	Raise	Maintain
Temporary workers	..	..	Lower	Maintain
Highly skilled workers	..	..	..	Raise
Family reunification	..	..	Lower	Maintain
Integration of non-citizens	..	..	No	Yes
Emigration				
View	..	..	Satisfactory	Satisfactory
Policy	..	..	Maintain	No intervention
Encouraging the return of citizens	..	..	No	No

* Measures implemented to respond to HIV/AIDS: (1) blood screening; (2) information/education campaigns; (3) antiretroviral treatment;
(4) non-discriminatory policies; (5) distribution of condoms.
** Grounds on which abortion is permitted: (1) to save the woman's life; (2) to preserve physical health; (3) to preserve mental health; (4) rape or incest;
(5) foetal impairment; (6) economic or social reasons; (7) on request.

Population indicators

Indicator	1975	1985	1995	2009
Population size and growth				
Population size (thousands)	906	1 151	1 620	2 171
Annual growth rate (percentage)*	3.0	2.6	2.7	1.9
Population age structure				
Percentage of population under age 15	44	47	43	37
Percentage of population aged 60 or over	5	5	5	6
Fertility and family planning				
Total fertility (children per woman)*	6.6	6.2	4.9	3.4
Adolescent fertility rate (per 1,000 women, aged 15 - 19)*	..	..	103.0	74.0
Percentage of births to women under age 20*	..	..	11	11
Percentage of births to women aged 35 or over*	..	..	29	23
Percentage of married women using contraception				
Modern methods	..	..	26[a]	54[b]
All methods	..	..	29[a]	55[b]
Health and mortality				
Life expectancy at birth (years)*				
Males	52	57	61	60
Females	56	61	65	62
Both sexes combined	54	59	63	61
Infant mortality rate (per 1,000 live births)*	101	75	57	35
Under-five mortality (per 1,000 live births)*	..	104	80	52
Maternal mortality ratio (per 100,000 live births) (2005)	..	..	..	210
HIV/AIDS				
People living with HIV/AIDS (thousands)	..	..	56	200[c]
Adult prevalence (percentage)	..	..	6.8	15.3[c]
Spatial distribution				
Population density (per sq. km)	1	1	2	3
Urban population (percentage)	24	26	30	37
Annual urban population growth rate (percentage)	3.5	5.2	4.5	2.9
Annual rural population growth rate (percentage)	2.0	3.9	2.1	0.3
International migration				
Migrant stock				
Number of migrants (thousands)	55	89	118	139**
As percentage of total population	6.1	7.7	7.3	6.3**

* For the periods 1970-1975, 1980-1985, 1990-1995 and 2005-2010.
** For 2010.
[a] For 1992.
[b] For 2006/2007.
[c] For 2007.

Government views and policies

Population policy variable	1976	1986	1996	2009
Population size and growth				
View on growth	Too low	Too low	Too low	Too high
Policy on growth	Raise	Raise	Raise	No intervention
Population age structure				
Level of concern about				
Size of the working-age population	..	..	..	..
Ageing of the population	..	..	..	..
Fertility and family planning				
View on fertility level	Satisfactory	Satisfactory	Satisfactory	Satisfactory
Policy	Maintain	Maintain	Maintain	Maintain
Access to contraceptive methods	Direct support	Direct support	Direct support	Direct support
Adolescent fertility				
Level of concern	..	..	..	..
Policies and programmes	..	..	..	..
Health and mortality				
View				
Life expectancy at birth	Acceptable	Acceptable	Acceptable	Acceptable
Under-five mortality	..	..	..	Unacceptable
Maternal mortality	..	..	..	Unacceptable
Level of concern about HIV/AIDS	..	..	..	Major concern
Measures to respond to HIV/AIDS*	..	..	..	2
Grounds on which abortion is permitted**	..	..	1,2,3	1,2,3
Spatial distribution and internal migration				
View on spatial distribution	Satisfactory	Satisfactory	Satisfactory	Satisfactory
Policies on internal migration				
From rural to urban areas	..	..	..	No intervention
From rural to rural areas	..	..	..	No intervention
From urban to rural areas	..	..	..	No intervention
From urban to urban areas	..	..	..	No intervention
Into urban agglomerations	..	..	..	No intervention
International migration				
Immigration				
View	Satisfactory	Satisfactory	Satisfactory	Satisfactory
Policy	Maintain	Maintain	Maintain	Maintain
Permanent settlement	..	..	Maintain	Maintain
Temporary workers	..	..	..	Lower
Highly skilled workers	..	..	..	..
Family reunification	..	..	..	..
Integration of non-citizens	..	..	..	..
Emigration				
View	Satisfactory	Satisfactory	Satisfactory	Satisfactory
Policy	Maintain	Maintain	Maintain	Maintain
Encouraging the return of citizens	..	..	..	..

* Measures implemented to respond to HIV/AIDS: (1) blood screening; (2) information/education campaigns; (3) antiretroviral treatment; (4) non-discriminatory policies; (5) distribution of condoms.
** Grounds on which abortion is permitted: (1) to save the woman's life; (2) to preserve physical health; (3) to preserve mental health; (4) rape or incest; (5) foetal impairment; (6) economic or social reasons; (7) on request.

Population indicators

Indicator	1975	1985	1995	2009
Population size and growth				
Population size (thousands)	7	8	10	10
Annual growth rate (percentage)*	1.7	1.8	1.7	0.3
Population age structure				
Percentage of population under age 15	..	..	..	..
Percentage of population aged 60 or over	..	..	..	..
Fertility and family planning				
Total fertility (children per woman)*	..	..	..	..
Adolescent fertility rate (per 1,000 women, aged 15 - 19)*	..	..	..	..
Percentage of births to women under age 20*	..	..	..	..
Percentage of births to women aged 35 or over*	..	..	..	..
Percentage of married women using contraception				
Modern methods	..	..	..	23[a]
All methods	..	..	..	36[a]
Health and mortality				
Life expectancy at birth (years)*				
Males	..	..	..	..
Females	..	..	..	..
Both sexes combined	..	..	..	..
Infant mortality rate (per 1,000 live births)*	..	..	..	..
Under-five mortality (per 1,000 live births)*	..	..	..	..
Maternal mortality ratio (per 100,000 live births) (2005)	..	..	..	..
HIV/AIDS				
People living with HIV/AIDS (thousands)	..	..	..	..
Adult prevalence (percentage)	..	..	..	..
Spatial distribution				
Population density (per sq. km)	336	389	475	486
Urban population (percentage)	100	100	100	100
Annual urban population growth rate (percentage)	1.2	2.2	0.6	0.4
Annual rural population growth rate (percentage)	0.0	0.0	0.0	0.0
International migration				
Migrant stock				
Number of migrants (thousands)	3	4	4	5**
As percentage of total population	37.3	44.6	42.5	51.8**

* For the periods 1970-1975, 1980-1985, 1990-1995 and 2005-2010.
** For 2010.
[a] For 2007.

Government views and policies

Population policy variable	1976	1986	1996	2009
Population size and growth				
View on growth	Too high	Too high	Too high	Too high
Policy on growth	Lower	Lower	Lower	Lower
Population age structure				
Level of concern about				
Size of the working-age population	..	..	..	Major concern
Ageing of the population	..	..	..	Minor concern
Fertility and family planning				
View on fertility level	Too high	Too high	Too high	Too high
Policy	Lower	Lower	Lower	Lower
Access to contraceptive methods	Direct support	Direct support	Direct support	Direct support
Adolescent fertility				
Level of concern	..	..	Minor concern	Major concern
Policies and programmes	..	..	No	Yes
Health and mortality				
View				
Life expectancy at birth	Unacceptable	Unacceptable	Unacceptable	Unacceptable
Under-five mortality	..	..	Unacceptable	Unacceptable
Maternal mortality	..	..	..	Unacceptable
Level of concern about HIV/AIDS	..	..	Minor concern	Major concern
Measures to respond to HIV/AIDS*	..	..	..	1,2,3,4,5
Grounds on which abortion is permitted**	..	..	1	1,2,3,4,5,6,7
Spatial distribution and internal migration				
View on spatial distribution	Major change desired	Major change desired	Major change desired	Major change desired
Policies on internal migration				
From rural to urban areas	..	..	..	Maintain
From rural to rural areas	..	..	..	No intervention
From urban to rural areas	..	..	..	No intervention
From urban to urban areas	..	..	..	Maintain
Into urban agglomerations	..	No intervention	Lower	Maintain
International migration				
Immigration				
View	Too high	Too high	Too high	Too high
Policy	Lower	Lower	Lower	Maintain
Permanent settlement	..	..	Lower	Maintain
Temporary workers	..	..	No intervention	Lower
Highly skilled workers	..	..	..	Maintain
Family reunification	..	..	No intervention	Maintain
Integration of non-citizens	..	..	No	No
Emigration				
View	Satisfactory	Satisfactory	Satisfactory	Satisfactory
Policy	Maintain	Lower	No intervention	Raise
Encouraging the return of citizens	..	..	No	Yes

* Measures implemented to respond to HIV/AIDS: (1) blood screening; (2) information/education campaigns; (3) antiretroviral treatment; (4) non-discriminatory policies; (5) distribution of condoms.
** Grounds on which abortion is permitted: (1) to save the woman's life; (2) to preserve physical health; (3) to preserve mental health; (4) rape or incest; (5) foetal impairment; (6) economic or social reasons; (7) on request.

Population indicators

Indicator	1975	1985	1995	2009
Population size and growth				
Population size (thousands)	13 356	16 962	21 624	29 331
Annual growth rate (percentage)*	2.3	2.4	2.5	1.8
Population age structure				
Percentage of population under age 15	42	43	42	37
Percentage of population aged 60 or over	5	5	5	6
Fertility and family planning				
Total fertility (children per woman)*	6.1	5.7	4.9	2.9
Adolescent fertility rate (per 1,000 women, aged 15 - 19)*	..	..	132.0	101.0
Percentage of births to women under age 20*	..	..	13	17
Percentage of births to women aged 35 or over*	..	..	17	10
Percentage of married women using contraception				
Modern methods	3[a]	14[b]	26[c]	44[d]
All methods	3[a]	14[b]	29[c]	48[d]
Health and mortality				
Life expectancy at birth (years)*				
Males	44	50	56	66
Females	44	49	55	67
Both sexes combined	44	50	55	67
Infant mortality rate (per 1,000 live births)*	156	123	92	42
Under-five mortality (per 1,000 live births)*	..	182	131	54
Maternal mortality ratio (per 100,000 live births) (2005)	..	..	..	830
HIV/AIDS				
People living with HIV/AIDS (thousands)	..	..	25	70[e]
Adult prevalence (percentage)	..	..	0.3	0.5[e]
Spatial distribution				
Population density (per sq. km)	91	115	147	199
Urban population (percentage)	5	7	11	18
Annual urban population growth rate (percentage)	6.9	6.0	6.7	4.8
Annual rural population growth rate (percentage)	2.0	2.0	1.9	1.3
International migration				
Migrant stock				
Number of migrants (thousands)	299	314	625	946**
As percentage of total population	2.2	1.9	2.9	3.2**

* For the periods 1970-1975, 1980-1985, 1990-1995 and 2005-2010.
** For 2010.
[a] For 1976.
[b] For 1986.
[c] For 1996.
[d] For 2006.
[e] For 2007.

Government views and policies

Population policy variable	1976	1986	1996	2009
Population size and growth				
View on growth	Satisfactory	Satisfactory	Satisfactory	Satisfactory
Policy on growth	No intervention	No intervention	No intervention	No intervention
Population age structure				
Level of concern about				
Size of the working-age population	..	..	..	Major concern
Ageing of the population	..	..	..	Major concern
Fertility and family planning				
View on fertility level	Satisfactory	Satisfactory	Satisfactory	Satisfactory
Policy	No intervention	No intervention	No intervention	No intervention
Access to contraceptive methods	Indirect support	Indirect support	Indirect support	Indirect support
Adolescent fertility				
Level of concern	..	..	Major concern	Major concern
Policies and programmes	..	..	Yes	Yes
Health and mortality				
View				
Life expectancy at birth	Acceptable	Acceptable	Acceptable	Unacceptable
Under-five mortality	..	..	Acceptable	Unacceptable
Maternal mortality	..	..	..	Acceptable
Level of concern about HIV/AIDS	..	..	Major concern	Major concern
Measures to respond to HIV/AIDS*	..	..	..	1,2,3
Grounds on which abortion is permitted**	..	..	1,2,3,4,5,6,7	1,2,3,4,5,6,7
Spatial distribution and internal migration				
View on spatial distribution	Major change desired	Satisfactory	Satisfactory	Minor change desired
Policies on internal migration				
From rural to urban areas	..	..	..	No intervention
From rural to rural areas	..	..	..	No intervention
From urban to rural areas	..	..	..	No intervention
From urban to urban areas	..	..	..	No intervention
Into urban agglomerations	..	Raise	Maintain	Maintain
International migration				
Immigration				
View	Too high	Too high	Too high	Too high
Policy	Lower	Lower	Lower	Lower
Permanent settlement	..	..	Lower	Maintain
Temporary workers	..	..	No intervention	Raise
Highly skilled workers	..	..	..	Raise
Family reunification	..	..	Maintain	Lower
Integration of non-citizens	..	..	Yes	Yes
Emigration				
View	Satisfactory	Too low	Satisfactory	Satisfactory
Policy	Maintain	Raise	No intervention	No intervention
Encouraging the return of citizens	No	..	No	No

* Measures implemented to respond to HIV/AIDS: (1) blood screening; (2) information/education campaigns; (3) antiretroviral treatment; (4) non-discriminatory policies; (5) distribution of condoms.

** Grounds on which abortion is permitted: (1) to save the woman's life; (2) to preserve physical health; (3) to preserve mental health; (4) rape or incest; (5) foetal impairment; (6) economic or social reasons; (7) on request.

Population indicators

Indicator	1975	1985	1995	2009
Population size and growth				
Population size (thousands)	13 666	14 488	15 448	16 592
Annual growth rate (percentage)*	0.9	0.5	0.7	0.4
Population age structure				
Percentage of population under age 15	25	19	18	18
Percentage of population aged 60 or over	15	17	18	21
Fertility and family planning				
Total fertility (children per woman)*	2.1	1.5	1.6	1.7
Adolescent fertility rate (per 1,000 women, aged 15 - 19)*	..	..	6.0	4.0
Percentage of births to women under age 20*	..	..	2	1
Percentage of births to women aged 35 or over*	..	..	15	21
Percentage of married women using contraception				
Modern methods	69	72	76[a]	65[b]
All methods	75	76	79[a]	67[b]
Health and mortality				
Life expectancy at birth (years)*				
Males	71	73	74	78
Females	77	79	80	82
Both sexes combined	74	76	77	80
Infant mortality rate (per 1,000 live births)*	12	8	6	4
Under-five mortality (per 1,000 live births)*	..	10	8	6
Maternal mortality ratio (per 100,000 live births) (2005)	..	..	..	6
HIV/AIDS				
People living with HIV/AIDS (thousands)	..	..	13	18[c]
Adult prevalence (percentage)	..	..	0.2	0.2[c]
Spatial distribution				
Population density (per sq. km)	329	349	372	400
Urban population (percentage)	63	67	73	82
Annual urban population growth rate (percentage)	1.3	1.2	1.8	0.7
Annual rural population growth rate (percentage)	-0.1	-0.6	-2.5	-2.6
International migration				
Migrant stock				
Number of migrants (thousands)	344	761	1 387	1 753**
As percentage of total population	2.5	5.3	9.0	10.5**

* For the periods 1970-1975, 1980-1985, 1990-1995 and 2005-2010.
** For 2010.
[a] For 1993.
[b] For 2003.
[c] For 2007.

Government views and policies

Population policy variable	1976	1986	1996	2009
Population size and growth				
View on growth	Too high	Satisfactory	Satisfactory	Satisfactory
Policy on growth	No intervention	No intervention	No intervention	No intervention
Population age structure				
Level of concern about				
Size of the working-age population	..	..	..	Not a concern
Ageing of the population	..	..	..	Minor concern
Fertility and family planning				
View on fertility level	Satisfactory	Satisfactory	Satisfactory	Satisfactory
Policy	No intervention	No intervention	No intervention	Maintain
Access to contraceptive methods	Direct support	Indirect support	Direct support	Direct support
Adolescent fertility				
Level of concern	..	..	Major concern	Major concern
Policies and programmes	..	..	Yes	Yes
Health and mortality				
View				
Life expectancy at birth	Acceptable	Acceptable	Unacceptable	Acceptable
Under-five mortality	..	..	Unacceptable	Unacceptable
Maternal mortality	..	..	..	Acceptable
Level of concern about HIV/AIDS	..	..	Minor concern	Major concern
Measures to respond to HIV/AIDS*	..	..	..	1,2,3,4,5
Grounds on which abortion is permitted**	..	..	1,2,3,4,5	1,2,3,4,5
Spatial distribution and internal migration				
View on spatial distribution	Minor change desired	Minor change desired	Minor change desired	Minor change desired
Policies on internal migration				
From rural to urban areas	..	..	..	No intervention
From rural to rural areas	..	..	..	No intervention
From urban to rural areas	..	..	..	No intervention
From urban to urban areas	..	..	..	No intervention
Into urban agglomerations	..	No intervention	No intervention	No intervention
International migration				
Immigration				
View	Too high	Satisfactory	Too low	Too low
Policy	Lower	Maintain	Raise	Raise
Permanent settlement	..	..	Raise	Raise
Temporary workers	..	..	Maintain	Raise
Highly skilled workers	..	..	..	Raise
Family reunification	..	..	Maintain	Raise
Integration of non-citizens	..	..	Yes	Yes
Emigration				
View	Satisfactory	Too high	Too high	Satisfactory
Policy	Maintain	Maintain	No intervention	No intervention
Encouraging the return of citizens	..	..	No	Yes

* Measures implemented to respond to HIV/AIDS: (1) blood screening; (2) information/education campaigns; (3) antiretroviral treatment;
(4) non−discriminatory policies; (5) distribution of condoms.
** Grounds on which abortion is permitted: (1) to save the woman's life; (2) to preserve physical health; (3) to preserve mental health; (4) rape or incest;
(5) foetal impairment; (6) economic or social reasons; (7) on request.

Population indicators

Indicator	1975	1985	1995	2009
Population size and growth				
Population size (thousands)	3 083	3 274	3 685	4 266
Annual growth rate (percentage)*	1.8	0.8	1.7	0.9
Population age structure				
Percentage of population under age 15	30	25	23	20
Percentage of population aged 60 or over	13	14	15	18
Fertility and family planning				
Total fertility (children per woman)*	2.8	2.0	2.1	2.0
Adolescent fertility rate (per 1,000 women, aged 15 - 19)*	..	..	33.0	23.0
Percentage of births to women under age 20*	..	..	8	6
Percentage of births to women aged 35 or over*	..	..	11	18
Percentage of married women using contraception				
Modern methods	62[a]	..	72	..
All methods	70[a]	..	75	..
Health and mortality				
Life expectancy at birth (years)*				
Males	69	71	73	78
Females	75	77	79	82
Both sexes combined	72	74	76	80
Infant mortality rate (per 1,000 live births)*	16	12	8	5
Under-five mortality (per 1,000 live births)*	..	14	9	6
Maternal mortality ratio (per 100,000 live births) (2005)	..	..	..	9
HIV/AIDS				
People living with HIV/AIDS (thousands)	..	..	1.2	1.4[b]
Adult prevalence (percentage)	..	..	0.1	0.1[b]
Spatial distribution				
Population density (per sq. km)	11	12	14	16
Urban population (percentage)	83	84	85	87
Annual urban population growth rate (percentage)	1.0	1.0	1.2	1.0
Annual rural population growth rate (percentage)	-0.8	0.2	0.5	-0.1
International migration				
Migrant stock				
Number of migrants (thousands)	493	480	594	962**
As percentage of total population	16.0	14.7	16.1	22.4**

* For the periods 1970-1975, 1980-1985, 1990-1995 and 2005-2010.
** For 2010.
[a] For 1976.
[b] For 2007.

Government views and policies

Population policy variable	1976	1986	1996	2009
Population size and growth				
View on growth	Too high	Satisfactory	Too high	Too high
Policy on growth	No intervention	No intervention	Lower	Lower
Population age structure				
Level of concern about				
Size of the working-age population	..	..	..	Major concern
Ageing of the population	..	..	..	Minor concern
Fertility and family planning				
View on fertility level	Too high	Satisfactory	Too high	Too high
Policy	No intervention	No intervention	Lower	Lower
Access to contraceptive methods	Direct support	Indirect support	Direct support	Direct support
Adolescent fertility				
Level of concern	..	..	Major concern	Major concern
Policies and programmes	..	..	Yes	Yes
Health and mortality				
View				
Life expectancy at birth	Unacceptable	Unacceptable	Unacceptable	Unacceptable
Under-five mortality	..	..	Unacceptable	Unacceptable
Maternal mortality	..	..	..	Unacceptable
Level of concern about HIV/AIDS	..	..	Minor concern	Major concern
Measures to respond to HIV/AIDS*	..	..	..	1,2,3,4,5
Grounds on which abortion is permitted**	..	..	1	Not permitted
Spatial distribution and internal migration				
View on spatial distribution	Minor change desired	Major change desired	Major change desired	Minor change desired
Policies on internal migration				
From rural to urban areas	..	..	..	No intervention
From rural to rural areas	..	..	..	No intervention
From urban to rural areas	..	..	..	No intervention
From urban to urban areas	..	..	..	No intervention
Into urban agglomerations	Lower	Lower	Lower	No intervention
International migration				
Immigration				
View	Satisfactory	Satisfactory	Satisfactory	Satisfactory
Policy	Maintain	Maintain	No intervention	Maintain
Permanent settlement	..	..	No intervention	Maintain
Temporary workers	..	..	No intervention	Maintain
Highly skilled workers	..	..	..	Maintain
Family reunification	..	..	No intervention	Maintain
Integration of non-citizens	..	..	Yes	No
Emigration				
View	Satisfactory	Too high	Satisfactory	Too high
Policy	Maintain	Lower	No intervention	Maintain
Encouraging the return of citizens	No	..	Yes	No

* Measures implemented to respond to HIV/AIDS: (1) blood screening; (2) information/education campaigns; (3) antiretroviral treatment; (4) non-discriminatory policies; (5) distribution of condoms.
** Grounds on which abortion is permitted: (1) to save the woman's life; (2) to preserve physical health; (3) to preserve mental health; (4) rape or incest; (5) foetal impairment; (6) economic or social reasons; (7) on request.

Population indicators

Indicator	1975	1985	1995	2009
Population size and growth				
Population size (thousands)	2 798	3 710	4 659	5 743
Annual growth rate (percentage)[*]	3.1	2.6	2.4	1.3
Population age structure				
Percentage of population under age 15	47	47	44	35
Percentage of population aged 60 or over	4	5	5	6
Fertility and family planning				
Total fertility (children per woman)[*]	6.8	5.9	4.5	2.8
Adolescent fertility rate (per 1,000 women, aged 15 - 19)[*]	..	..	157.0	113.0
Percentage of births to women under age 20[*]	..	..	17	20
Percentage of births to women aged 35 or over[*]	..	..	18	14
Percentage of married women using contraception				
Modern methods	..	23[a]	50[b]	69[c]
All methods	..	27[a]	55[b]	72[c]
Health and mortality				
Life expectancy at birth (years)[*]				
Males	54	56	64	70
Females	57	63	69	76
Both sexes combined	55	59	66	73
Infant mortality rate (per 1,000 live births)[*]	98	80	48	21
Under-five mortality (per 1,000 live births)[*]	..	117	62	26
Maternal mortality ratio (per 100,000 live births) (2005)	..	..	..	170
HIV/AIDS				
People living with HIV/AIDS (thousands)	..	..	1.5	7.7[d]
Adult prevalence (percentage)	..	..	0.1	0.2[d]
Spatial distribution				
Population density (per sq. km)	22	29	36	44
Urban population (percentage)	49	51	54	57
Annual urban population growth rate (percentage)	3.6	2.7	2.5	1.9
Annual rural population growth rate (percentage)	2.6	1.8	1.6	0.7
International migration				
Migrant stock				
Number of migrants (thousands)	23	42	27	40[**]
As percentage of total population	0.8	1.1	0.6	0.7[**]

[*] For the periods 1970-1975, 1980-1985, 1990-1995 and 2005-2010.
[**] For 2010.
[a] For 1981.
[b] For 1992/1993.
[c] For 2006/2007.
[d] For 2007.

Government views and policies

Population policy variable	1976	1986	1996	2009
Population size and growth				
View on growth	Satisfactory	Too high	Too high	Too high
Policy on growth	No intervention	Lower	No intervention	Lower
Population age structure				
Level of concern about				
Size of the working-age population	..	..	..	Major concern
Ageing of the population	..	..	..	Minor concern
Fertility and family planning				
View on fertility level	Satisfactory	Too high	Too high	Too high
Policy	No intervention	Lower	Lower	Lower
Access to contraceptive methods	No support	Direct support	Direct support	Direct support
Adolescent fertility				
Level of concern	..	..	Not a concern	Major concern
Policies and programmes	..	..	No	Yes
Health and mortality				
View				
Life expectancy at birth	Unacceptable	Unacceptable	Unacceptable	Unacceptable
Under-five mortality	..	..	Unacceptable	Unacceptable
Maternal mortality	..	..	..	Unacceptable
Level of concern about HIV/AIDS	..	..	Major concern	Major concern
Measures to respond to HIV/AIDS*	..	..	..	1,2,3,4,5
Grounds on which abortion is permitted**	..	..	1	1
Spatial distribution and internal migration				
View on spatial distribution	Major change desired	Major change desired	Major change desired	Minor change desired
Policies on internal migration				
From rural to urban areas	..	..	..	No intervention
From rural to rural areas	..	..	..	No intervention
From urban to rural areas	..	..	..	No intervention
From urban to urban areas	..	..	..	No intervention
Into urban agglomerations	No intervention	..	No intervention	No intervention
International migration				
Immigration				
View	Satisfactory	Satisfactory	Satisfactory	Satisfactory
Policy	Maintain	Maintain	No intervention	No intervention
Permanent settlement	..	..	No intervention	No intervention
Temporary workers	..	..	No intervention	No intervention
Highly skilled workers	..	..	..	..
Family reunification	..	..	No intervention	No intervention
Integration of non-citizens	..	..	No	No
Emigration				
View	Satisfactory	Satisfactory	Satisfactory	Satisfactory
Policy	Maintain	Maintain	No intervention	No intervention
Encouraging the return of citizens	No	..	No	Yes

* Measures implemented to respond to HIV/AIDS: (1) blood screening; (2) information/education campaigns; (3) antiretroviral treatment; (4) non-discriminatory policies; (5) distribution of condoms.
** Grounds on which abortion is permitted: (1) to save the woman's life; (2) to preserve physical health; (3) to preserve mental health; (4) rape or incest; (5) foetal impairment; (6) economic or social reasons; (7) on request.

Population indicators

Indicator	1975	1985	1995	2009
Population size and growth				
Population size (thousands)	5 090	6 827	9 302	15 290
Annual growth rate (percentage)*	3.0	2.8	3.3	3.9
Population age structure				
Percentage of population under age 15	48	49	49	50
Percentage of population aged 60 or over	3	3	3	4
Fertility and family planning				
Total fertility (children per woman)*	7.7	8.1	7.8	7.1
Adolescent fertility rate (per 1,000 women, aged 15 - 19)*	..	..	228.0	157.0
Percentage of births to women under age 20*	..	..	15	11
Percentage of births to women aged 35 or over*	..	..	25	9
Percentage of married women using contraception				
Modern methods	..	..	2[a]	5[b]
All methods	..	..	4[a]	11[b]
Health and mortality				
Life expectancy at birth (years)*				
Males	38	40	42	50
Females	38	40	43	52
Both sexes combined	38	40	43	51
Infant mortality rate (per 1,000 live births)*	162	161	148	88
Under-five mortality (per 1,000 live births)*	..	308	281	172
Maternal mortality ratio (per 100,000 live births) (2005)	..	..	..	1 800
HIV/AIDS				
People living with HIV/AIDS (thousands)	..	..	14	60[c]
Adult prevalence (percentage)	..	..	0.3	0.8[c]
Spatial distribution				
Population density (per sq. km)	4	5	7	12
Urban population (percentage)	11	15	16	17
Annual urban population growth rate (percentage)	8.3	4.5	4.1	4.2
Annual rural population growth rate (percentage)	2.5	2.7	3.5	3.3
International migration				
Migrant stock				
Number of migrants (thousands)	86	116	171	202**
As percentage of total population	1.7	1.7	1.8	1.3**

* For the periods 1970-1975, 1980-1985, 1990-1995 and 2005-2010.
** For 2010.
[a] For 1992.
[b] For 2006.
[c] For 2007.

Government views and policies

Population policy variable	1976	1986	1996	2009
Population size and growth				
View on growth	Satisfactory	Too high	Too high	Too high
Policy on growth	No intervention	Lower	Lower	Lower
Population age structure				
Level of concern about				
Size of the working-age population	..	..	..	Major concern
Ageing of the population	..	..	..	Minor concern
Fertility and family planning				
View on fertility level	Satisfactory	Too high	Too high	Too high
Policy	No intervention	Lower	Lower	Lower
Access to contraceptive methods	Direct support	Direct support	Direct support	Direct support
Adolescent fertility				
Level of concern	..	..	..	Major concern
Policies and programmes	..	..	..	Yes
Health and mortality				
View				
Life expectancy at birth	Unacceptable	Unacceptable	Unacceptable	Unacceptable
Under-five mortality	..	..	..	Unacceptable
Maternal mortality	..	..	..	Unacceptable
Level of concern about HIV/AIDS	..	..	..	Major concern
Measures to respond to HIV/AIDS*	..	..	..	1,2,3,4,5
Grounds on which abortion is permitted**	..	..	1	1,2,3
Spatial distribution and internal migration				
View on spatial distribution	Major change desired	Major change desired	Major change desired	Major change desired
Policies on internal migration				
From rural to urban areas	..	..	..	Lower
From rural to rural areas	..	..	..	..
From urban to rural areas	..	..	..	..
From urban to urban areas	..	..	..	..
Into urban agglomerations	..	..	..	Lower
International migration				
Immigration				
View	Satisfactory	Satisfactory	Satisfactory	Satisfactory
Policy	Maintain	Maintain	Maintain	Maintain
Permanent settlement	..	..	Maintain	Maintain
Temporary workers	..	..	..	Maintain
Highly skilled workers	..	..	..	Maintain
Family reunification	..	..	..	Maintain
Integration of non-citizens	..	..	..	..
Emigration				
View	Satisfactory	Satisfactory	Satisfactory	Satisfactory
Policy	Maintain	Maintain	No intervention	No intervention
Encouraging the return of citizens	No	..	..	Yes

* Measures implemented to respond to HIV/AIDS: (1) blood screening; (2) information/education campaigns; (3) antiretroviral treatment; (4) non-discriminatory policies; (5) distribution of condoms.
** Grounds on which abortion is permitted: (1) to save the woman's life; (2) to preserve physical health; (3) to preserve mental health; (4) rape or incest; (5) foetal impairment; (6) economic or social reasons; (7) on request.

Population indicators

Indicator	1975	1985	1995	2009
Population size and growth				
Population size (thousands)	63 948	85 151	110 449	154 729
Annual growth rate (percentage)*	2.5	2.7	2.5	2.3
Population age structure				
Percentage of population under age 15	44	46	45	43
Percentage of population aged 60 or over	5	5	5	5
Fertility and family planning				
Total fertility (children per woman)*	6.7	6.9	6.4	5.3
Adolescent fertility rate (per 1,000 women, aged 15 - 19)*	..	..	153.0	127.0
Percentage of births to women under age 20*	..	..	12	12
Percentage of births to women aged 35 or over*	..	..	24	22
Percentage of married women using contraception				
Modern methods	..	1[a]	11[b]	9[c]
All methods	..	5[a]	13[b]	15[c]
Health and mortality				
Life expectancy at birth (years)*				
Males	40	44	44	47
Females	43	46	45	48
Both sexes combined	41	45	45	48
Infant mortality rate (per 1,000 live births)*	153	131	133	109
Under-five mortality (per 1,000 live births)*	..	229	230	187
Maternal mortality ratio (per 100,000 live births) (2005)	..	..	..	1 100
HIV/AIDS				
People living with HIV/AIDS (thousands)	..	..	1 200	2 600[c]
Adult prevalence (percentage)	..	..	2.2	3.1[c]
Spatial distribution				
Population density (per sq. km)	69	92	120	167
Urban population (percentage)	26	32	39	49
Annual urban population growth rate (percentage)	5.2	5.0	4.6	3.6
Annual rural population growth rate (percentage)	2.1	1.9	1.6	0.8
International migration				
Migrant stock				
Number of migrants (thousands)	704	348	582	1 128**
As percentage of total population	1.1	0.4	0.5	0.7**

* For the periods 1970-1975, 1980-1985, 1990-1995 and 2005-2010.
** For 2010.
[a] For 1982.
[b] For 1994.
[c] For 2007.

Government views and policies

Population policy variable	1976	1986	1996	2009
Population size and growth				
View on growth	..	..	Too low	Too low
Policy on growth	..	..	Raise	Raise
Population age structure				
Level of concern about				
Size of the working-age population	..	..	..	..
Ageing of the population	..	..	..	..
Fertility and family planning				
View on fertility level	..	..	Too low	Too low
Policy	..	..	Raise	Raise
Access to contraceptive methods	..	..	..	Indirect support
Adolescent fertility				
Level of concern	..	..	..	Major concern
Policies and programmes	..	..	No	Yes
Health and mortality				
View				
Life expectancy at birth	..	..	Acceptable	Acceptable
Under-five mortality	..	..	..	Acceptable
Maternal mortality	..	..	..	Acceptable
Level of concern about HIV/AIDS	..	..	..	Major concern
Measures to respond to HIV/AIDS*	..	..	..	2
Grounds on which abortion is permitted**	..	..	1,2,3	1,2,3
Spatial distribution and internal migration				
View on spatial distribution	..	..	Satisfactory	Satisfactory
Policies on internal migration				
From rural to urban areas	..	..	..	..
From rural to rural areas	..	..	..	..
From urban to rural areas	..	..	..	..
From urban to urban areas	..	..	..	..
Into urban agglomerations	..	..	..	..
International migration				
Immigration				
View	..	..	Satisfactory	Too low
Policy	..	..	No intervention	Raise
Permanent settlement	..	..	..	Raise
Temporary workers	..	..	..	Raise
Highly skilled workers	..	..	..	..
Family reunification	..	..	..	..
Integration of non-citizens	..	..	..	..
Emigration				
View	..	..	Too high	Too high
Policy	..	..	Lower	Lower
Encouraging the return of citizens	..	..	Yes	Yes

* Measures implemented to respond to HIV/AIDS: (1) blood screening; (2) information/education campaigns; (3) antiretroviral treatment; (4) non-discriminatory policies; (5) distribution of condoms.
** Grounds on which abortion is permitted: (1) to save the woman's life; (2) to preserve physical health; (3) to preserve mental health; (4) rape or incest; (5) foetal impairment; (6) economic or social reasons; (7) on request.

Population indicators

Indicator	1975	1985	1995	2009
Population size and growth				
Population size (thousands)	4	3	2	1
Annual growth rate (percentage)*	-3.8	-4.9	-1.6	-2.7
Population age structure				
Percentage of population under age 15	..	..	..	..
Percentage of population aged 60 or over	..	..	..	..
Fertility and family planning				
Total fertility (children per woman)*	..	..	..	..
Adolescent fertility rate (per 1,000 women, aged 15 - 19)*	..	..	..	..
Percentage of births to women under age 20*	..	..	..	..
Percentage of births to women aged 35 or over*	..	..	..	..
Percentage of married women using contraception				
Modern methods	..	..	..	..
All methods	..	..	..	..
Health and mortality				
Life expectancy at birth (years)*				
Males	..	..	..	..
Females	..	..	..	..
Both sexes combined	..	..	..	..
Infant mortality rate (per 1,000 live births)*	..	..	..	..
Under-five mortality (per 1,000 live births)*	..	..	..	..
Maternal mortality ratio (per 100,000 live births) (2005)	..	..	..	..
HIV/AIDS				
People living with HIV/AIDS (thousands)	..	..	..	..
Adult prevalence (percentage)	..	..	..	..
Spatial distribution				
Population density (per sq. km)	16	10	8	6
Urban population (percentage)	23	31	31	39
Annual urban population growth rate (percentage)	-1.0	-2.0	-1.3	0.0
Annual rural population growth rate (percentage)	-5.1	-5.8	-2.5	-2.6
International migration				
Migrant stock				
Number of migrants (thousands)	0	0	0	0**
As percentage of total population	10.3	17.5	20.6	25.6**

* For the periods 1970-1975, 1980-1985, 1990-1995 and 2005-2010.
** For 2010.

Government views and policies

Population policy variable	1976	1986	1996	2009
Population size and growth				
View on growth	Satisfactory	Satisfactory	Satisfactory	Satisfactory
Policy on growth	No intervention	No intervention	No intervention	No intervention
Population age structure				
Level of concern about				
Size of the working-age population	..	..	..	Minor concern
Ageing of the population	..	..	..	Major concern
Fertility and family planning				
View on fertility level	Satisfactory	Satisfactory	Satisfactory	Satisfactory
Policy	No intervention	No intervention	No intervention	Maintain
Access to contraceptive methods	Direct support	Direct support	Direct support	Direct support
Adolescent fertility				
Level of concern	..	..	Minor concern	Minor concern
Policies and programmes	..	..	Yes	Yes
Health and mortality				
View				
Life expectancy at birth	Acceptable	Acceptable	Unacceptable	Acceptable
Under-five mortality	..	..	Unacceptable	Acceptable
Maternal mortality	..	..	..	Acceptable
Level of concern about HIV/AIDS	..	..	Minor concern	Major concern
Measures to respond to HIV/AIDS*	..	..	..	1,2,3,5
Grounds on which abortion is permitted**	..	..	1,2,3,4,5,6,7	1,2,3,4,5,6,7
Spatial distribution and internal migration				
View on spatial distribution	Minor change desired	Satisfactory	Minor change desired	Major change desired
Policies on internal migration				
From rural to urban areas	..	..	..	Lower
From rural to rural areas	..	..	..	No intervention
From urban to rural areas	..	..	..	No intervention
From urban to urban areas	..	..	..	Raise
Into urban agglomerations	Lower	Maintain	Lower	Lower
International migration				
Immigration				
View	Too high	Satisfactory	Satisfactory	Satisfactory
Policy	Lower	Maintain	Lower	Maintain
Permanent settlement	..	..	Lower	Maintain
Temporary workers	..	..	Lower	Maintain
Highly skilled workers	..	..	..	Raise
Family reunification	..	..	Maintain	Maintain
Integration of non-citizens	..	..	Yes	Yes
Emigration				
View	Satisfactory	Satisfactory	Satisfactory	Satisfactory
Policy	Maintain	Maintain	No intervention	No intervention
Encouraging the return of citizens	No	..	No	No

* Measures implemented to respond to HIV/AIDS: (1) blood screening; (2) information/education campaigns; (3) antiretroviral treatment; (4) non-discriminatory policies; (5) distribution of condoms.
** Grounds on which abortion is permitted: (1) to save the woman's life; (2) to preserve physical health; (3) to preserve mental health; (4) rape or incest; (5) foetal impairment; (6) economic or social reasons; (7) on request.

Population indicators

Indicator	1975	1985	1995	2009
Population size and growth				
Population size (thousands)	4 007	4 153	4 359	4 812
Annual growth rate (percentage)*	0.7	0.3	0.5	0.9
Population age structure				
Percentage of population under age 15	24	20	19	19
Percentage of population aged 60 or over	19	21	20	21
Fertility and family planning				
Total fertility (children per woman)*	2.2	1.7	1.9	1.9
Adolescent fertility rate (per 1,000 women, aged 15 - 19)*	..	..	13.0	9.0
Percentage of births to women under age 20*	..	..	3	2
Percentage of births to women aged 35 or over*	..	..	13	16
Percentage of married women using contraception				
Modern methods	65[a]	69[b]	78[c]	82[d]
All methods	71[a]	74[b]	87[c]	88[d]
Health and mortality				
Life expectancy at birth (years)*				
Males	71	73	74	78
Females	78	80	80	83
Both sexes combined	74	76	77	81
Infant mortality rate (per 1,000 live births)*	12	8	6	3
Under-five mortality (per 1,000 live births)*	..	10	7	5
Maternal mortality ratio (per 100,000 live births) (2005)	..	..	..	7
HIV/AIDS				
People living with HIV/AIDS (thousands)	..	..	1.7	3[e]
Adult prevalence (percentage)	..	..	0.1	0.1[e]
Spatial distribution				
Population density (per sq. km)	10	11	11	12
Urban population (percentage)	68	71	74	78
Annual urban population growth rate (percentage)	1.2	0.6	0.9	0.7
Annual rural population growth rate (percentage)	-1.0	-0.1	-0.5	0.2
International migration				
Migrant stock				
Number of migrants (thousands)	99	148	237	485**
As percentage of total population	2.5	3.6	5.4	10.0**

* For the periods 1970-1975, 1980-1985, 1990-1995 and 2005-2010.
** For 2010.
[a] For 1977.
[b] For 1988/1989.
[c] For 1998.
[d] For 2005.
[e] For 2007.

Government views and policies

Population policy variable	1976	1986	1996	2009
Population size and growth				
View on growth	Too low	Too low	Too low	Satisfactory
Policy on growth	Raise	Raise	Raise	Maintain
Population age structure				
Level of concern about				
Size of the working-age population	..	..	..	Major concern
Ageing of the population	..	..	..	Not a concern
Fertility and family planning				
View on fertility level	Satisfactory	Satisfactory	Satisfactory	Satisfactory
Policy	Maintain	Maintain	Maintain	Lower
Access to contraceptive methods	No support	No support	No support	Direct support
Adolescent fertility				
Level of concern	..	..	..	Minor concern
Policies and programmes	..	..	..	No
Health and mortality				
View				
Life expectancy at birth	Unacceptable	Unacceptable	Unacceptable	Acceptable
Under-five mortality	..	..	..	Acceptable
Maternal mortality	..	..	..	Acceptable
Level of concern about HIV/AIDS	..	..	..	Major concern
Measures to respond to HIV/AIDS*	..	..	..	1,2,3,5
Grounds on which abortion is permitted**	..	..	1	1,5
Spatial distribution and internal migration				
View on spatial distribution	Minor change desired	Minor change desired	Minor change desired	Satisfactory
Policies on internal migration				
From rural to urban areas	..	..	..	Lower
From rural to rural areas	..	..	..	Raise
From urban to rural areas	..	..	..	No intervention
From urban to urban areas	..	..	..	No intervention
Into urban agglomerations	..	..	..	No intervention
International migration				
Immigration				
View	Satisfactory	Satisfactory	Too high	Satisfactory
Policy	Maintain	Maintain	Lower	Maintain
Permanent settlement	..	..	..	No intervention
Temporary workers	..	..	..	Lower
Highly skilled workers	..	..	..	Maintain
Family reunification	..	..	..	Raise
Integration of non-citizens	..	..	..	No
Emigration				
View	Satisfactory	Satisfactory	Satisfactory	Satisfactory
Policy	Maintain	Maintain	Maintain	No intervention
Encouraging the return of citizens	..	..	..	No

* Measures implemented to respond to HIV/AIDS: (1) blood screening; (2) information/education campaigns; (3) antiretroviral treatment; (4) non-discriminatory policies; (5) distribution of condoms.
** Grounds on which abortion is permitted: (1) to save the woman's life; (2) to preserve physical health; (3) to preserve mental health; (4) rape or incest; (5) foetal impairment; (6) economic or social reasons; (7) on request.

Population indicators

Indicator	1975	1985	1995	2009
Population size and growth				
Population size (thousands)	917	1 527	2 172	2 845
Annual growth rate (percentage)*	4.1	5.0	3.3	2.1
Population age structure				
Percentage of population under age 15	47	45	40	31
Percentage of population aged 60 or over	4	3	3	5
Fertility and family planning				
Total fertility (children per woman)*	7.2	7.2	6.3	3.1
Adolescent fertility rate (per 1,000 women, aged 15 - 19)*	..	..	77.0	10.0
Percentage of births to women under age 20*	..	..	6	2
Percentage of births to women aged 35 or over*	..	..	30	26
Percentage of married women using contraception				
Modern methods	..	8[a]	18	..
All methods	..	9[a]	24	..
Health and mortality				
Life expectancy at birth (years)*				
Males	51	61	70	74
Females	53	64	73	77
Both sexes combined	52	63	71	76
Infant mortality rate (per 1,000 live births)*	110	58	24	12
Under-five mortality (per 1,000 live births)*	..	78	28	14
Maternal mortality ratio (per 100,000 live births) (2005)	..	..	..	64
HIV/AIDS				
People living with HIV/AIDS (thousands)	..	..	..	..
Adult prevalence (percentage)	..	..	..	..
Spatial distribution				
Population density (per sq. km)	3	5	7	9
Urban population (percentage)	38	57	72	72
Annual urban population growth rate (percentage)	9.6	7.4	2.5	2.2
Annual rural population growth rate (percentage)	1.9	-0.3	2.6	1.8
International migration				
Migrant stock				
Number of migrants (thousands)	75	282	582	826**
As percentage of total population	8.2	18.5	26.8	28.4**

* For the periods 1970-1975, 1980-1985, 1990-1995 and 2005-2010.
** For 2010.
[a] For 1988/1989.

Government views and policies

Population policy variable	1976	1986	1996	2009
Population size and growth				
View on growth	Too high	Too high	Too high	Too high
Policy on growth	Lower	Lower	Lower	Lower
Population age structure				
Level of concern about				
Size of the working-age population	..	..	..	Major concern
Ageing of the population	..	..	..	Minor concern
Fertility and family planning				
View on fertility level	Too high	Too high	Too high	Too high
Policy	Lower	Lower	Lower	Lower
Access to contraceptive methods	Direct support	Direct support	Direct support	Direct support
Adolescent fertility				
Level of concern	..	..	Not a concern	Major concern
Policies and programmes	..	..	No	Yes
Health and mortality				
View				
Life expectancy at birth	Unacceptable	Unacceptable	Acceptable	Unacceptable
Under-five mortality	..	..	Unacceptable	Unacceptable
Maternal mortality	..	..	..	Unacceptable
Level of concern about HIV/AIDS	..	..	Major concern	Major concern
Measures to respond to HIV/AIDS*	..	..	..	1,2,3,4,5
Grounds on which abortion is permitted**	..	..	1,2,3	1,2,3
Spatial distribution and internal migration				
View on spatial distribution	Major change desired	Major change desired	Satisfactory	Major change desired
Policies on internal migration				
From rural to urban areas	..	..	..	Lower
From rural to rural areas	..	..	..	No intervention
From urban to rural areas	..	..	..	Raise
From urban to urban areas	..	..	..	Maintain
Into urban agglomerations	..	Lower	Lower	Lower
International migration				
Immigration				
View	Satisfactory	Too high	Satisfactory	Too high
Policy	Maintain	Lower	No intervention	Lower
Permanent settlement	..	..	No intervention	Lower
Temporary workers	..	..	No intervention	Maintain
Highly skilled workers	..	..	..	Maintain
Family reunification	..	..	No intervention	Lower
Integration of non-citizens	..	..	No	No
Emigration				
View	Satisfactory	Satisfactory	Too low	Satisfactory
Policy	Maintain	Raise	Raise	Raise
Encouraging the return of citizens	..	..	Yes	Yes

* Measures implemented to respond to HIV/AIDS: (1) blood screening; (2) information/education campaigns; (3) antiretroviral treatment; (4) non-discriminatory policies; (5) distribution of condoms.
** Grounds on which abortion is permitted: (1) to save the woman's life; (2) to preserve physical health; (3) to preserve mental health; (4) rape or incest; (5) foetal impairment; (6) economic or social reasons; (7) on request.

Population indicators

Indicator	1975	1985	1995	2009
Population size and growth				
Population size (thousands)	71 238	98 309	130 397	180 808
Annual growth rate (percentage)*	2.9	3.5	2.4	2.2
Population age structure				
Percentage of population under age 15	43	43	43	37
Percentage of population aged 60 or over	7	6	6	6
Fertility and family planning				
Total fertility (children per woman)*	7.0	6.6	5.7	4.0
Adolescent fertility rate (per 1,000 women, aged 15 - 19)*	..	..	73.0	46.0
Percentage of births to women under age 20*	..	..	6	6
Percentage of births to women aged 35 or over*	..	..	25	20
Percentage of married women using contraception				
Modern methods	4	6	13	22[a]
All methods	5	8	18	30[a]
Health and mortality				
Life expectancy at birth (years)*				
Males	55	58	61	66
Females	55	58	62	67
Both sexes combined	55	58	61	66
Infant mortality rate (per 1,000 live births)*	113	98	85	64
Under-five mortality (per 1,000 live births)*	..	148	125	89
Maternal mortality ratio (per 100,000 live births) (2005)	..	..	..	320
HIV/AIDS				
People living with HIV/AIDS (thousands)	..	..	16	96[b]
Adult prevalence (percentage)	..	..	<0.1	0.1[b]
Spatial distribution				
Population density (per sq. km)	89	123	164	227
Urban population (percentage)	26	29	32	37
Annual urban population growth rate (percentage)	4.1	4.5	3.3	3.2
Annual rural population growth rate (percentage)	2.3	3.4	2.1	1.1
International migration				
Migrant stock				
Number of migrants (thousands)	4 574	6 288	4 077	4 234**
As percentage of total population	6.4	6.4	3.1	2.3**

* For the periods 1970-1975, 1980-1985, 1990-1995 and 2005-2010.
** For 2010.
[a] For 2006/2007.
[b] For 2007.

Government views and policies

Population policy variable	1976	1986	1996	2009
Population size and growth				
View on growth	..	..	Satisfactory	Too low
Policy on growth	..	..	No intervention	No intervention
Population age structure				
Level of concern about				
Size of the working-age population	..	..	..	..
Ageing of the population	..	..	..	Minor concern
Fertility and family planning				
View on fertility level	..	..	Satisfactory	Too low
Policy	..	..	No intervention	No intervention
Access to contraceptive methods	..	..	..	Indirect support
Adolescent fertility				
Level of concern	..	..	..	Minor concern
Policies and programmes	..	..	No	No
Health and mortality				
View				
Life expectancy at birth	..	..	Acceptable	Acceptable
Under-five mortality	..	..	..	Unacceptable
Maternal mortality	..	..	..	Acceptable
Level of concern about HIV/AIDS	..	..	..	Major concern
Measures to respond to HIV/AIDS*	..	..	..	1,2,3,4,5
Grounds on which abortion is permitted**	..	..	1	1
Spatial distribution and internal migration				
View on spatial distribution	..	..	Minor change desired	Minor change desired
Policies on internal migration				
From rural to urban areas	..	..	..	..
From rural to rural areas	..	..	..	..
From urban to rural areas	..	..	..	..
From urban to urban areas	..	..	..	..
Into urban agglomerations	..	..	..	..
International migration				
Immigration				
View	..	..	Too high	Too high
Policy	..	..	No intervention	No intervention
Permanent settlement	..	..	..	..
Temporary workers	..	..	..	Lower
Highly skilled workers	..	..	..	..
Family reunification	..	..	..	..
Integration of non-citizens	..	..	..	..
Emigration				
View	..	..	Too high	Too high
Policy	..	..	No intervention	Lower
Encouraging the return of citizens	..	..	Yes	Yes

* Measures implemented to respond to HIV/AIDS: (1) blood screening; (2) information/education campaigns; (3) antiretroviral treatment; (4) non-discriminatory policies; (5) distribution of condoms.
** Grounds on which abortion is permitted: (1) to save the woman's life; (2) to preserve physical health; (3) to preserve mental health; (4) rape or incest; (5) foetal impairment; (6) economic or social reasons; (7) on request.

Population indicators

Indicator	1975	1985	1995	2009
Population size and growth				
Population size (thousands)	12	14	17	20
Annual growth rate (percentage)[*]	1.3	2.2	2.7	0.4
Population age structure				
Percentage of population under age 15	..	..	..	..
Percentage of population aged 60 or over	..	..	..	..
Fertility and family planning				
Total fertility (children per woman)[*]	..	..	..	..
Adolescent fertility rate (per 1,000 women, aged 15 - 19)[*]	..	..	..	..
Percentage of births to women under age 20[*]	..	..	..	..
Percentage of births to women aged 35 or over[*]	..	..	..	..
Percentage of married women using contraception				
Modern methods	..	..	..	30[a]
All methods	..	..	..	33[a]
Health and mortality				
Life expectancy at birth (years)[*]				
Males	..	..	..	..
Females	..	..	..	..
Both sexes combined	..	..	..	..
Infant mortality rate (per 1,000 live births)[*]	..	..	..	..
Under-five mortality (per 1,000 live births)[*]	..	..	..	..
Maternal mortality ratio (per 100,000 live births) (2005)	..	..	..	..
HIV/AIDS				
People living with HIV/AIDS (thousands)	..	..	..	..
Adult prevalence (percentage)	..	..	..	..
Spatial distribution				
Population density (per sq. km)	26	30	37	45
Urban population (percentage)	61	67	71	82
Annual urban population growth rate (percentage)	0.9	3.1	2.4	1.5
Annual rural population growth rate (percentage)	-0.3	-0.6	3.7	-5.0
International migration				
Migrant stock				
Number of migrants (thousands)	1	1	5	6[**]
As percentage of total population	4.2	9.6	27.3	28.1[**]

[*] For the periods 1970-1975, 1980-1985, 1990-1995 and 2005-2010.
[**] For 2010.
[a] For 2003.

Government views and policies

Population policy variable	1976	1986	1996	2009
Population size and growth				
View on growth	Satisfactory	Satisfactory	Satisfactory	Satisfactory
Policy on growth	No intervention	No intervention	No intervention	Maintain
Population age structure				
Level of concern about				
Size of the working-age population	..	..	..	Minor concern
Ageing of the population	..	..	..	Major concern
Fertility and family planning				
View on fertility level	Too high	Satisfactory	Satisfactory	Satisfactory
Policy	No intervention	No intervention	No intervention	Maintain
Access to contraceptive methods	Direct support	Direct support	Direct support	Direct support
Adolescent fertility				
Level of concern	..	..	Major concern	Major concern
Policies and programmes	..	..	Yes	Yes
Health and mortality				
View				
Life expectancy at birth	Acceptable	Acceptable	Acceptable	Acceptable
Under-five mortality	..	..	Unacceptable	Unacceptable
Maternal mortality	..	..	..	Unacceptable
Level of concern about HIV/AIDS	..	..	Major concern	Major concern
Measures to respond to HIV/AIDS*	..	..	..	1,2,3,5
Grounds on which abortion is permitted**	..	..	1,4,5	1,2,4
Spatial distribution and internal migration				
View on spatial distribution	Major change desired	Major change desired	Major change desired	Minor change desired
Policies on internal migration				
From rural to urban areas	..	..	..	Lower
From rural to rural areas	..	..	..	..
From urban to rural areas	..	..	..	..
From urban to urban areas	..	..	..	Raise
Into urban agglomerations	No intervention	Lower	No intervention	Lower
International migration				
Immigration				
View	Satisfactory	Satisfactory	Satisfactory	Satisfactory
Policy	Maintain	Maintain	Maintain	Lower
Permanent settlement	..	..	Maintain	Lower
Temporary workers	..	..	No intervention	Lower
Highly skilled workers	..	..	..	Maintain
Family reunification	..	..	No intervention	Lower
Integration of non-citizens	..	..	Yes	..
Emigration				
View	Satisfactory	Satisfactory	Satisfactory	Too high
Policy	Maintain	Maintain	No intervention	No intervention
Encouraging the return of citizens	No	..	No	Yes

* Measures implemented to respond to HIV/AIDS: (1) blood screening; (2) information/education campaigns; (3) antiretroviral treatment; (4) non-discriminatory policies; (5) distribution of condoms.
** Grounds on which abortion is permitted: (1) to save the woman's life; (2) to preserve physical health; (3) to preserve mental health; (4) rape or incest; (5) foetal impairment; (6) economic or social reasons; (7) on request.

Population indicators

Indicator	1975	1985	1995	2009
Population size and growth				
Population size (thousands)	1 724	2 177	2 673	3 454
Annual growth rate (percentage)*	2.7	2.2	2.0	1.6
Population age structure				
Percentage of population under age 15	43	38	33	29
Percentage of population aged 60 or over	7	7	8	10
Fertility and family planning				
Total fertility (children per woman)*	4.9	3.5	2.9	2.6
Adolescent fertility rate (per 1,000 women, aged 15 - 19)*	..	..	91.0	83.0
Percentage of births to women under age 20*	..	..	16	16
Percentage of births to women aged 35 or over*	..	..	12	10
Percentage of married women using contraception				
Modern methods	46[a]	54[b]	..	..
All methods	54[a]	58[b]	..	..
Health and mortality				
Life expectancy at birth (years)*				
Males	65	68	70	73
Females	68	73	76	78
Both sexes combined	66	71	72	76
Infant mortality rate (per 1,000 live births)*	44	32	27	18
Under-five mortality (per 1,000 live births)*	..	43	34	24
Maternal mortality ratio (per 100,000 live births) (2005)	..	..	..	130
HIV/AIDS				
People living with HIV/AIDS (thousands)	..	..	12	20[c]
Adult prevalence (percentage)	..	..	0.8	1.0[c]
Spatial distribution				
Population density (per sq. km)	23	29	35	46
Urban population (percentage)	49	52	60	74
Annual urban population growth rate (percentage)	3.1	2.7	4.0	2.5
Annual rural population growth rate (percentage)	2.0	1.4	-1.0	-1.3
International migration				
Migrant stock				
Number of migrants (thousands)	53	54	73	121**
As percentage of total population	3.1	2.5	2.7	3.4**

* For the periods 1970-1975, 1980-1985, 1990-1995 and 2005-2010.
** For 2010.
[a] For 1976.
[b] For 1984.
[c] For 2007.

Government views and policies

Population policy variable	1976	1986	1996	2009
Population size and growth				
View on growth	Too high	Too high	Too high	Too high
Policy on growth	Lower	Lower	Lower	Lower
Population age structure				
Level of concern about				
Size of the working-age population	..	..	..	Major concern
Ageing of the population	..	..	..	..
Fertility and family planning				
View on fertility level	Too high	Too high	Too high	Too high
Policy	Lower	No intervention	Lower	Lower
Access to contraceptive methods	Direct support	Direct support	Direct support	Direct support
Adolescent fertility				
Level of concern	..	..	..	Major concern
Policies and programmes	..	..	..	Yes
Health and mortality				
View				
Life expectancy at birth	Unacceptable	Unacceptable	Unacceptable	Unacceptable
Under-five mortality	..	..	..	Unacceptable
Maternal mortality	..	..	..	Unacceptable
Level of concern about HIV/AIDS	..	..	..	Major concern
Measures to respond to HIV/AIDS*	..	..	..	1,2,3,4,5
Grounds on which abortion is permitted**	..	..	1,2,3	1,2,3
Spatial distribution and internal migration				
View on spatial distribution	Major change desired	Minor change desired	Minor change desired	Major change desired
Policies on internal migration				
From rural to urban areas	..	..	..	Lower
From rural to rural areas	..	..	..	..
From urban to rural areas	..	..	..	..
From urban to urban areas	..	..	..	..
Into urban agglomerations	..	No intervention	..	Lower
International migration				
Immigration				
View	Satisfactory	Satisfactory	Satisfactory	Satisfactory
Policy	Maintain	Maintain	Maintain	Maintain
Permanent settlement	..	..	..	No intervention
Temporary workers	..	..	..	Maintain
Highly skilled workers	..	..	..	Raise
Family reunification	..	..	..	Maintain
Integration of non-citizens	..	..	..	Yes
Emigration				
View	Satisfactory	Satisfactory	Satisfactory	Satisfactory
Policy	Maintain	Maintain	Maintain	No intervention
Encouraging the return of citizens	..	..	..	Yes

* Measures implemented to respond to HIV/AIDS: (1) blood screening; (2) information/education campaigns; (3) antiretroviral treatment; (4) non−discriminatory policies; (5) distribution of condoms.
** Grounds on which abortion is permitted: (1) to save the woman's life; (2) to preserve physical health; (3) to preserve mental health; (4) rape or incest; (5) foetal impairment; (6) economic or social reasons; (7) on request.

Population indicators

Indicator	1975	1985	1995	2009
Population size and growth				
Population size (thousands)	2 866	3 637	4 709	6 732
Annual growth rate (percentage)*	2.3	2.6	2.6	2.4
Population age structure				
Percentage of population under age 15	44	43	41	40
Percentage of population aged 60 or over	4	4	4	4
Fertility and family planning				
Total fertility (children per woman)*	6.1	5.5	4.7	4.1
Adolescent fertility rate (per 1,000 women, aged 15 - 19)*	..	..	82.0	55.0
Percentage of births to women under age 20*	..	..	9	7
Percentage of births to women aged 35 or over*	..	..	25	17
Percentage of married women using contraception				
Modern methods	..	..	20[a]	..
All methods	..	..	26[a]	..
Health and mortality				
Life expectancy at birth (years)*				
Males	44	51	53	59
Females	46	55	59	63
Both sexes combined	45	52	55	61
Infant mortality rate (per 1,000 live births)*	112	79	69	51
Under-five mortality (per 1,000 live births)*	..	112	99	69
Maternal mortality ratio (per 100,000 live births) (2005)	..	..	..	470
HIV/AIDS				
People living with HIV/AIDS (thousands)	..	..	1.7	54[b]
Adult prevalence (percentage)	..	..	0.1	1.5[b]
Spatial distribution				
Population density (per sq. km)	6	8	10	15
Urban population (percentage)	12	14	14	12
Annual urban population growth rate (percentage)	4.0	3.9	1.4	2.1
Annual rural population growth rate (percentage)	1.9	2.3	2.9	1.8
International migration				
Migrant stock				
Number of migrants (thousands)	44	40	31	25**
As percentage of total population	1.5	1.1	0.7	0.4**

* For the periods 1970-1975, 1980-1985, 1990-1995 and 2005-2010.
** For 2010.
[a] For 1996.
[b] For 2007.

Government views and policies

Population policy variable	1976	1986	1996	2009
Population size and growth				
View on growth	Too low	Satisfactory	Satisfactory	Too high
Policy on growth	No intervention	No intervention	No intervention	No intervention
Population age structure				
Level of concern about				
Size of the working-age population	..	..	..	Minor concern
Ageing of the population	..	..	..	Major concern
Fertility and family planning				
View on fertility level	Satisfactory	Satisfactory	Satisfactory	Too high
Policy	No intervention	No intervention	No intervention	No intervention
Access to contraceptive methods	Direct support	Indirect support	Direct support	Direct support
Adolescent fertility				
Level of concern	..	..	Major concern	Major concern
Policies and programmes	..	..	No	Yes
Health and mortality				
View				
Life expectancy at birth	Unacceptable	Acceptable	Acceptable	Acceptable
Under-five mortality	..	..	Unacceptable	Unacceptable
Maternal mortality	..	..	..	Unacceptable
Level of concern about HIV/AIDS	..	..	Major concern	Major concern
Measures to respond to HIV/AIDS*	..	..	..	1,2,3,5
Grounds on which abortion is permitted**	..	..	1	1
Spatial distribution and internal migration				
View on spatial distribution	Major change desired	Major change desired	Satisfactory	Minor change desired
Policies on internal migration				
From rural to urban areas	..	..	..	Lower
From rural to rural areas	..	..	..	..
From urban to rural areas	..	..	..	..
From urban to urban areas	..	..	..	..
Into urban agglomerations	..	Lower	No intervention	Lower
International migration				
Immigration				
View	Satisfactory	Too low	Too low	Satisfactory
Policy	Maintain	Raise	Raise	Maintain
Permanent settlement	..	..	..	Maintain
Temporary workers	..	..	..	Maintain
Highly skilled workers	..	..	..	Maintain
Family reunification	..	..	..	Maintain
Integration of non-citizens	..	..	Yes	Yes
Emigration				
View	Too high	Satisfactory	Satisfactory	Satisfactory
Policy	Lower	Lower	No intervention	No intervention
Encouraging the return of citizens	..	..	Yes	Yes

* Measures implemented to respond to HIV/AIDS: (1) blood screening; (2) information/education campaigns; (3) antiretroviral treatment; (4) non-discriminatory policies; (5) distribution of condoms.
** Grounds on which abortion is permitted: (1) to save the woman's life; (2) to preserve physical health; (3) to preserve mental health; (4) rape or incest; (5) foetal impairment; (6) economic or social reasons; (7) on request.

Population indicators

Indicator	1975	1985	1995	2009
Population size and growth				
Population size (thousands)	2 805	3 704	4 802	6 349
Annual growth rate (percentage)*	2.4	2.9	2.4	1.8
Population age structure				
Percentage of population under age 15	44	42	40	34
Percentage of population aged 60 or over	6	6	6	7
Fertility and family planning				
Total fertility (children per woman)*	5.4	5.2	4.3	3.1
Adolescent fertility rate (per 1,000 women, aged 15 - 19)*	..	..	92.0	72.0
Percentage of births to women under age 20*	..	..	11	12
Percentage of births to women aged 35 or over*	..	..	22	19
Percentage of married women using contraception				
Modern methods	23[a]	29[b]	41	70[c]
All methods	29[a]	45[b]	56	79[c]
Health and mortality				
Life expectancy at birth (years)*				
Males	64	65	66	70
Females	68	69	71	74
Both sexes combined	66	67	69	72
Infant mortality rate (per 1,000 live births)*	53	49	43	32
Under-five mortality (per 1,000 live births)*	..	65	55	38
Maternal mortality ratio (per 100,000 live births) (2005)	..	..	..	150
HIV/AIDS				
People living with HIV/AIDS (thousands)	..	..	3.1	21[d]
Adult prevalence (percentage)	..	..	0.1	0.6[d]
Spatial distribution				
Population density (per sq. km)	7	9	12	16
Urban population (percentage)	39	45	52	61
Annual urban population growth rate (percentage)	3.9	4.5	3.5	2.7
Annual rural population growth rate (percentage)	1.6	1.5	0.9	0.2
International migration				
Migrant stock				
Number of migrants (thousands)	101	174	183	161**
As percentage of total population	3.6	4.7	3.8	2.5**

* For the periods 1970-1975, 1980-1985, 1990-1995 and 2005-2010.
** For 2010.
[a] For 1977.
[b] For 1987.
[c] For 2008.
[d] For 2007.

Government views and policies

Population policy variable	1976	1986	1996	2009
Population size and growth				
View on growth	Satisfactory	Too high	Too high	Satisfactory
Policy on growth	No intervention	Lower	Lower	Lower
Population age structure				
Level of concern about				
Size of the working-age population	..	..	..	Major concern
Ageing of the population	..	..	..	Major concern
Fertility and family planning				
View on fertility level	Satisfactory	Too high	Too high	Too high
Policy	No intervention	Lower	Lower	Lower
Access to contraceptive methods	Direct support	Direct support	Direct support	Direct support
Adolescent fertility				
Level of concern	..	..	Major concern	Major concern
Policies and programmes	..	..	Yes	Yes
Health and mortality				
View				
Life expectancy at birth	Unacceptable	Unacceptable	Unacceptable	Unacceptable
Under-five mortality	..	..	..	Unacceptable
Maternal mortality	..	..	..	Unacceptable
Level of concern about HIV/AIDS	..	..	Minor concern	Major concern
Measures to respond to HIV/AIDS*	..	..	..	1,2,3,4,5
Grounds on which abortion is permitted**	..	..	1,2	1,2,3
Spatial distribution and internal migration				
View on spatial distribution	Major change desired	Major change desired	Major change desired	Minor change desired
Policies on internal migration				
From rural to urban areas	..	..	..	Lower
From rural to rural areas	..	..	..	..
From urban to rural areas	..	..	..	..
From urban to urban areas	..	..	..	Raise
Into urban agglomerations	..	Lower	Lower	Lower
International migration				
Immigration				
View	Satisfactory	Satisfactory	Satisfactory	Satisfactory
Policy	Maintain	Maintain	No intervention	Maintain
Permanent settlement	..	..	No intervention	Maintain
Temporary workers	..	..	No intervention	Maintain
Highly skilled workers	..	..	..	Maintain
Family reunification	..	..	No intervention	Maintain
Integration of non-citizens	..	..	Yes	No
Emigration				
View	Satisfactory	Satisfactory	Too high	Satisfactory
Policy	Maintain	Maintain	No intervention	No intervention
Encouraging the return of citizens	..	..	Yes	Yes

* Measures implemented to respond to HIV/AIDS: (1) blood screening; (2) information/education campaigns; (3) antiretroviral treatment; (4) non-discriminatory policies; (5) distribution of condoms.
** Grounds on which abortion is permitted: (1) to save the woman's life; (2) to preserve physical health; (3) to preserve mental health; (4) rape or incest; (5) foetal impairment; (6) economic or social reasons; (7) on request.

Population indicators

Indicator	1975	1985	1995	2009
Population size and growth				
Population size (thousands)	15 164	19 525	23 943	29 165
Annual growth rate (percentage)*	2.8	2.4	1.9	1.2
Population age structure				
Percentage of population under age 15	43	40	36	30
Percentage of population aged 60 or over	6	6	7	9
Fertility and family planning				
Total fertility (children per woman)*	6.0	4.7	3.6	2.6
Adolescent fertility rate (per 1,000 women, aged 15 - 19)*	..	..	70.0	55.0
Percentage of births to women under age 20*	..	..	10	11
Percentage of births to women aged 35 or over*	..	..	22	21
Percentage of married women using contraception				
Modern methods	11[a]	23[b]	41[c]	47[d]
All methods	31[a]	46[b]	64[c]	71[d]
Health and mortality				
Life expectancy at birth (years)*				
Males	54	59	64	71
Females	57	64	69	76
Both sexes combined	56	62	67	73
Infant mortality rate (per 1,000 live births)*	110	82	48	21
Under-five mortality (per 1,000 live births)*	..	117	77	33
Maternal mortality ratio (per 100,000 live births) (2005)	..	..	..	240
HIV/AIDS				
People living with HIV/AIDS (thousands)	..	..	30	76[e]
Adult prevalence (percentage)	..	..	0.2	0.5[e]
Spatial distribution				
Population density (per sq. km)	12	15	19	23
Urban population (percentage)	61	67	70	72
Annual urban population growth rate (percentage)	3.8	2.9	1.7	1.4
Annual rural population growth rate (percentage)	1.1	1.0	1.3	0.7
International migration				
Migrant stock				
Number of migrants (thousands)	67	62	51	38**
As percentage of total population	0.4	0.3	0.2	0.1**

* For the periods 1970-1975, 1980-1985, 1990-1995 and 2005-2010.
** For 2010.
[a] For 1977.
[b] For 1986.
[c] For 1996.
[d] For 2004/2006.
[e] For 2007.

Government views and policies

Population policy variable	1976	1986	1996	2009
Population size and growth				
View on growth	Too high	Too high	Too high	Satisfactory
Policy on growth	Lower	Lower	Lower	Lower
Population age structure				
Level of concern about				
Size of the working-age population	..	..	..	Major concern
Ageing of the population	..	..	..	Minor concern
Fertility and family planning				
View on fertility level	Too high	Too high	Too high	Satisfactory
Policy	Lower	Lower	Lower	Lower
Access to contraceptive methods	Direct support	Direct support	Direct support	Direct support
Adolescent fertility				
Level of concern	..	..	Major concern	Major concern
Policies and programmes	..	..	Yes	Yes
Health and mortality				
View				
Life expectancy at birth	Acceptable	Acceptable	Unacceptable	Acceptable
Under-five mortality	..	..	Unacceptable	Acceptable
Maternal mortality	..	..	..	Unacceptable
Level of concern about HIV/AIDS	..	..	Minor concern	Major concern
Measures to respond to HIV/AIDS*	..	..	..	1,2,3,4,5
Grounds on which abortion is permitted**	..	..	1	1
Spatial distribution and internal migration				
View on spatial distribution	Major change desired	Major change desired	Major change desired	Minor change desired
Policies on internal migration				
From rural to urban areas	..	..	..	Lower
From rural to rural areas	..	..	..	No intervention
From urban to rural areas	..	..	..	No intervention
From urban to urban areas	..	..	..	No intervention
Into urban agglomerations	Lower	Lower	Lower	Lower
International migration				
Immigration				
View	Satisfactory	Satisfactory	Satisfactory	Satisfactory
Policy	Maintain	Maintain	Lower	Maintain
Permanent settlement	..	..	Lower	Maintain
Temporary workers	..	..	No intervention	Raise
Highly skilled workers	..	..	..	Lower
Family reunification	..	..	No intervention	Raise
Integration of non-citizens	..	..	No	Yes
Emigration				
View	Satisfactory	Satisfactory	Satisfactory	Satisfactory
Policy	Maintain	Maintain	No intervention	Maintain
Encouraging the return of citizens	Yes	..	No	Yes

* Measures implemented to respond to HIV/AIDS: (1) blood screening; (2) information/education campaigns; (3) antiretroviral treatment; (4) non-discriminatory policies; (5) distribution of condoms.

** Grounds on which abortion is permitted: (1) to save the woman's life; (2) to preserve physical health; (3) to preserve mental health; (4) rape or incest; (5) foetal impairment; (6) economic or social reasons; (7) on request.

Population indicators

Indicator	1975	1985	1995	2009
Population size and growth				
Population size (thousands)	42 038	55 032	69 965	91 983
Annual growth rate (percentage)*	2.8	2.7	2.3	1.8
Population age structure				
Percentage of population under age 15	44	42	39	34
Percentage of population aged 60 or over	5	5	5	7
Fertility and family planning				
Total fertility (children per woman)*	6.0	5.0	4.1	3.1
Adolescent fertility rate (per 1,000 women, aged 15 - 19)*	..	..	51.0	45.0
Percentage of births to women under age 20*	..	..	6	7
Percentage of births to women aged 35 or over*	..	..	22	19
Percentage of married women using contraception				
Modern methods	11[a]	21[b]	26	36[c]
All methods	18[a]	46[b]	51	51[c]
Health and mortality				
Life expectancy at birth (years)*				
Males	56	60	65	70
Females	60	64	69	74
Both sexes combined	58	62	67	72
Infant mortality rate (per 1,000 live births)*	80	61	43	23
Under-five mortality (per 1,000 live births)*	..	83	54	27
Maternal mortality ratio (per 100,000 live births) (2005)	..	..	..	230
HIV/AIDS				
People living with HIV/AIDS (thousands)	..	..	..	8.3[d]
Adult prevalence (percentage)	..	..	..	..
Spatial distribution				
Population density (per sq. km)	140	183	233	307
Urban population (percentage)	36	43	54	66
Annual urban population growth rate (percentage)	3.8	5.0	3.9	2.9
Annual rural population growth rate (percentage)	2.2	0.4	0.1	-0.2
International migration				
Migrant stock				
Number of migrants (thousands)	162	146	210	435**
As percentage of total population	0.4	0.3	0.3	0.5**

* For the periods 1970-1975, 1980-1985, 1990-1995 and 2005-2010.
** For 2010.
[a] For 1973.
[b] For 1986.
[c] For 2005/2006.
[d] For 2007.

Government views and policies

Population policy variable	1976	1986	1996	2009
Population size and growth				
View on growth	Satisfactory	Satisfactory	Satisfactory	Too low
Policy on growth	No intervention	No intervention	No intervention	Raise
Population age structure				
Level of concern about				
Size of the working-age population	..	..	..	Major concern
Ageing of the population	..	..	..	Major concern
Fertility and family planning				
View on fertility level	Satisfactory	Satisfactory	Satisfactory	Too low
Policy	Maintain	Maintain	No intervention	Raise
Access to contraceptive methods	Direct support	Direct support	Direct support	No support
Adolescent fertility				
Level of concern	..	..	Minor concern	Major concern
Policies and programmes	..	..	No	No
Health and mortality				
View				
Life expectancy at birth	Acceptable	Unacceptable	Unacceptable	Acceptable
Under-five mortality	..	..	Unacceptable	Unacceptable
Maternal mortality	..	..	..	Acceptable
Level of concern about HIV/AIDS	..	..	Major concern	Major concern
Measures to respond to HIV/AIDS*	..	..	..	1,2,3,4,5
Grounds on which abortion is permitted**	..	..	1,2,4,5	1,2,3,4,5
Spatial distribution and internal migration				
View on spatial distribution	Minor change desired	Minor change desired	Minor change desired	Satisfactory
Policies on internal migration				
From rural to urban areas	..	..	..	Raise
From rural to rural areas	..	..	..	Maintain
From urban to rural areas	..	..	..	Maintain
From urban to urban areas	..	..	..	Raise
Into urban agglomerations	Raise	Lower	Lower	Raise
International migration				
Immigration				
View	Satisfactory	Satisfactory	Satisfactory	Satisfactory
Policy	Maintain	Maintain	Maintain	Raise
Permanent settlement	..	..	Maintain	Maintain
Temporary workers	..	..	Maintain	Raise
Highly skilled workers	..	..	..	Raise
Family reunification	..	..	No intervention	No intervention
Integration of non-citizens	..	..	Yes	Yes
Emigration				
View	Satisfactory	Satisfactory	Too high	Too high
Policy	Maintain	Maintain	No intervention	Lower
Encouraging the return of citizens	No	..	No	No

* Measures implemented to respond to HIV/AIDS: (1) blood screening; (2) information/education campaigns; (3) antiretroviral treatment;
(4) non-discriminatory policies; (5) distribution of condoms.
** Grounds on which abortion is permitted: (1) to save the woman's life; (2) to preserve physical health; (3) to preserve mental health; (4) rape or incest;
(5) foetal impairment; (6) economic or social reasons; (7) on request.

Population indicators

Indicator	1975	1985	1995	2009
Population size and growth				
Population size (thousands)	34 015	37 202	38 595	38 074
Annual growth rate (percentage)*	0.8	0.9	0.3	-0.1
Population age structure				
Percentage of population under age 15	24	26	23	15
Percentage of population aged 60 or over	14	14	16	19
Fertility and family planning				
Total fertility (children per woman)*	2.3	2.3	1.9	1.3
Adolescent fertility rate (per 1,000 women, aged 15 - 19)*	..	..	25.0	14.0
Percentage of births to women under age 20*	..	..	7	6
Percentage of births to women aged 35 or over*	..	..	9	11
Percentage of married women using contraception				
Modern methods	26[a]	..	28[b]	..
All methods	75[a]	..	73[b]	..
Health and mortality				
Life expectancy at birth (years)*				
Males	67	67	67	71
Females	74	75	76	80
Both sexes combined	70	71	72	76
Infant mortality rate (per 1,000 live births)*	27	20	15	7
Under-five mortality (per 1,000 live births)*	..	21	16	8
Maternal mortality ratio (per 100,000 live births) (2005)	..	..	..	8
HIV/AIDS				
People living with HIV/AIDS (thousands)	..	..	4.1	20[c]
Adult prevalence (percentage)	..	..	..	0.1[c]
Spatial distribution				
Population density (per sq. km)	105	115	119	118
Urban population (percentage)	55	60	61	61
Annual urban population growth rate (percentage)	2.0	1.3	0.1	-0.2
Annual rural population growth rate (percentage)	-0.6	-0.3	-0.1	-0.1
International migration				
Migrant stock				
Number of migrants (thousands)	1 808	1 320	964	827**
As percentage of total population	5.3	3.5	2.5	2.2**

* For the periods 1970-1975, 1980-1985, 1990-1995 and 2005-2010.
** For 2010.
[a] For 1977.
[b] For 1991.
[c] For 2007.

Government views and policies

Population policy variable	1976	1986	1996	2009
Population size and growth				
View on growth	Satisfactory	Satisfactory	Too low	Too low
Policy on growth	No intervention	No intervention	No intervention	Raise
Population age structure				
Level of concern about				
Size of the working-age population	..	..	..	Not a concern
Ageing of the population	..	..	..	Major concern
Fertility and family planning				
View on fertility level	Satisfactory	Satisfactory	Too low	Too low
Policy	No intervention	No intervention	No intervention	Raise
Access to contraceptive methods	Direct support	Direct support	Direct support	Direct support
Adolescent fertility				
Level of concern	..	..	Major concern	Major concern
Policies and programmes	..	..	Yes	Yes
Health and mortality				
View				
Life expectancy at birth	Acceptable	Unacceptable	Acceptable	Acceptable
Under-five mortality	..	..	Acceptable	Acceptable
Maternal mortality	..	..	..	Acceptable
Level of concern about HIV/AIDS	..	..	Minor concern	Major concern
Measures to respond to HIV/AIDS*	..	..	..	1,2,3,4,5
Grounds on which abortion is permitted**	..	..	1,2,3,4,5	1,2,3,4,5,6,7
Spatial distribution and internal migration				
View on spatial distribution	Minor change desired	Major change desired	Major change desired	Minor change desired
Policies on internal migration				
From rural to urban areas	..	..	..	Lower
From rural to rural areas	..	..	..	Maintain
From urban to rural areas	..	..	..	No intervention
From urban to urban areas	..	..	..	No intervention
Into urban agglomerations	No intervention	..	No intervention	Lower
International migration				
Immigration				
View	Satisfactory	Satisfactory	Satisfactory	Satisfactory
Policy	Maintain	Maintain	Lower	Maintain
Permanent settlement	..	..	Lower	Maintain
Temporary workers	..	..	Maintain	Maintain
Highly skilled workers	..	..	..	Maintain
Family reunification	..	..	Maintain	Maintain
Integration of non-citizens	..	..	Yes	Yes
Emigration				
View	Too low	Satisfactory	Satisfactory	Satisfactory
Policy	Raise	Maintain	No intervention	Maintain
Encouraging the return of citizens	No	..	No	No

* Measures implemented to respond to HIV/AIDS: (1) blood screening; (2) information/education campaigns; (3) antiretroviral treatment; (4) non-discriminatory policies; (5) distribution of condoms.
** Grounds on which abortion is permitted: (1) to save the woman's life; (2) to preserve physical health; (3) to preserve mental health; (4) rape or incest; (5) foetal impairment; (6) economic or social reasons; (7) on request.

Population indicators

Indicator	1975	1985	1995	2009
Population size and growth				
Population size (thousands)	9 093	10 029	10 038	10 707
Annual growth rate (percentage)*	0.9	0.5	0.1	0.3
Population age structure				
Percentage of population under age 15	28	24	18	15
Percentage of population aged 60 or over	15	17	20	23
Fertility and family planning				
Total fertility (children per woman)*	2.7	2.0	1.5	1.4
Adolescent fertility rate (per 1,000 women, aged 15 - 19)*	..	..	22.0	16.0
Percentage of births to women under age 20*	..	..	7	6
Percentage of births to women aged 35 or over*	..	..	10	17
Percentage of married women using contraception				
Modern methods	33[a]	..	..	63[b]
All methods	66[a]	..	..	67[b]
Health and mortality				
Life expectancy at birth (years)*				
Males	65	69	71	75
Females	71	76	78	82
Both sexes combined	68	72	75	79
Infant mortality rate (per 1,000 live births)*	45	20	9	4
Under-five mortality (per 1,000 live births)*	..	24	12	5
Maternal mortality ratio (per 100,000 live births) (2005)	..	..	..	11
HIV/AIDS				
People living with HIV/AIDS (thousands)	..	..	21	34[c]
Adult prevalence (percentage)	..	..	0.4	0.5[c]
Spatial distribution				
Population density (per sq. km)	99	109	109	116
Urban population (percentage)	41	45	51	60
Annual urban population growth rate (percentage)	2.5	1.2	1.6	1.3
Annual rural population growth rate (percentage)	0.8	-0.9	-1.1	-1.3
International migration				
Migrant stock				
Number of migrants (thousands)	164	346	528	919**
As percentage of total population	1.8	3.5	5.3	8.6**

* For the periods 1970-1975, 1980-1985, 1990-1995 and 2005-2010.
** For 2010.
[a] For 1979/1980.
[b] For 2005/2006.
[c] For 2007.

Government views and policies

Population policy variable	1976	1986	1996	2009
Population size and growth				
View on growth	Too low	Too low	Too low	Satisfactory
Policy on growth	Raise	Raise	Raise	Maintain
Population age structure				
Level of concern about				
Size of the working-age population	..	..	..	Minor concern
Ageing of the population	..	..	..	Major concern
Fertility and family planning				
View on fertility level	Satisfactory	Satisfactory	Satisfactory	Satisfactory
Policy	Maintain	Maintain	Maintain	Raise
Access to contraceptive methods	No support	No support	No support	Direct support
Adolescent fertility				
Level of concern	..	..	..	Not a concern
Policies and programmes	..	..	..	No
Health and mortality				
View				
Life expectancy at birth	Acceptable	Acceptable	Acceptable	Acceptable
Under-five mortality	..	..	..	Acceptable
Maternal mortality	..	..	..	Acceptable
Level of concern about HIV/AIDS	..	..	..	Major concern
Measures to respond to HIV/AIDS*	..	..	..	1,2,3
Grounds on which abortion is permitted**	..	..	1,2,5	1
Spatial distribution and internal migration				
View on spatial distribution	Satisfactory	Satisfactory	Satisfactory	Satisfactory
Policies on internal migration				
From rural to urban areas	..	..	..	Lower
From rural to rural areas	..	..	..	No intervention
From urban to rural areas	..	..	..	Maintain
From urban to urban areas	..	..	..	Lower
Into urban agglomerations	..	Lower	..	Lower
International migration				
Immigration				
View	Satisfactory	Satisfactory	Satisfactory	Too high
Policy	Maintain	Maintain	Maintain	Lower
Permanent settlement	..	..	..	No intervention
Temporary workers	..	..	..	Lower
Highly skilled workers	..	..	..	Maintain
Family reunification	..	..	..	Maintain
Integration of non-citizens	..	..	..	Yes
Emigration				
View	Satisfactory	Satisfactory	Satisfactory	Satisfactory
Policy	Maintain	Maintain	Maintain	No intervention
Encouraging the return of citizens	..	..	..	No

* Measures implemented to respond to HIV/AIDS: (1) blood screening; (2) information/education campaigns; (3) antiretroviral treatment; (4) non-discriminatory policies; (5) distribution of condoms.
** Grounds on which abortion is permitted: (1) to save the woman's life; (2) to preserve physical health; (3) to preserve mental health; (4) rape or incest; (5) foetal impairment; (6) economic or social reasons; (7) on request.

Population indicators

Indicator	1975	1985	1995	2009
Population size and growth				
Population size (thousands)	171	361	526	1 409
Annual growth rate (percentage)*	8.6	9.0	2.4	10.7
Population age structure				
Percentage of population under age 15	33	28	27	16
Percentage of population aged 60 or over	3	2	2	2
Fertility and family planning				
Total fertility (children per woman)*	6.8	5.5	4.1	2.4
Adolescent fertility rate (per 1,000 women, aged 15 - 19)*	..	..	28.0	16.0
Percentage of births to women under age 20*	..	..	3	3
Percentage of births to women aged 35 or over*	..	..	19	21
Percentage of married women using contraception				
Modern methods	..	29[a]	32[b]	..
All methods	..	32[a]	43[b]	..
Health and mortality				
Life expectancy at birth (years)*				
Males	61	65	68	75
Females	64	70	73	77
Both sexes combined	62	67	70	76
Infant mortality rate (per 1,000 live births)*	57	33	17	8
Under-five mortality (per 1,000 live births)*	..	38	20	10
Maternal mortality ratio (per 100,000 live births) (2005)	..	..	..	12
HIV/AIDS				
People living with HIV/AIDS (thousands)	..	..	..	..
Adult prevalence (percentage)	..	..	..	..
Spatial distribution				
Population density (per sq. km)	16	33	48	128
Urban population (percentage)	89	90	94	96
Annual urban population growth rate (percentage)	5.8	7.0	2.8	1.8
Annual rural population growth rate (percentage)	5.0	4.2	-3.1	-0.1
International migration				
Migrant stock				
Number of migrants (thousands)	119	282	406	1 305**
As percentage of total population	69.6	78.2	77.2	86.5**

* For the periods 1970-1975, 1980-1985, 1990-1995 and 2005-2010.
** For 2010.
[a] For 1987.
[b] For 1998.

Government views and policies

Population policy variable	1976	1986	1996	2009
Population size and growth				
View on growth	Too high	Too high	Satisfactory	Too low
Policy on growth	Lower	Lower	No intervention	Raise
Population age structure				
Level of concern about				
Size of the working-age population	..	..	..	Minor concern
Ageing of the population	..	..	..	Major concern
Fertility and family planning				
View on fertility level	Too high	Too high	Satisfactory	Too low
Policy	Lower	Lower	No intervention	Raise
Access to contraceptive methods	Direct support	Direct support	Direct support	Direct support
Adolescent fertility				
Level of concern	..	..	Minor concern	Major concern
Policies and programmes	..	..	Yes	Yes
Health and mortality				
View				
Life expectancy at birth	Unacceptable	Unacceptable	Unacceptable	Acceptable
Under-five mortality	..	..	..	Unacceptable
Maternal mortality	..	..	..	Unacceptable
Level of concern about HIV/AIDS	..	..	Major concern	Major concern
Measures to respond to HIV/AIDS*	..	..	..	1,2,3,4,5
Grounds on which abortion is permitted**	..	..	1,2,3,4,5	1,2,3,4,5
Spatial distribution and internal migration				
View on spatial distribution	Minor change desired	Major change desired	Major change desired	Major change desired
Policies on internal migration				
From rural to urban areas	..	..	..	..
From rural to rural areas	..	..	..	..
From urban to rural areas	..	..	..	..
From urban to urban areas	..	..	..	Maintain
Into urban agglomerations	..	Lower	Lower	Lower
International migration				
Immigration				
View	Satisfactory	Satisfactory	Satisfactory	Satisfactory
Policy	Maintain	Maintain	Lower	Raise
Permanent settlement	..	..	Lower	Raise
Temporary workers	..	..	Lower	Raise
Highly skilled workers	..	..	Lower	Maintain
Family reunification	..	..	..	Raise
Integration of non-citizens	..	..	Lower	Maintain
			Yes	Yes
Emigration				
View	Too low	Too low	Too low	Too high
Policy	Raise	Raise	Raise	No intervention
Encouraging the return of citizens	..	..	No	Yes

* Measures implemented to respond to HIV/AIDS: (1) blood screening; (2) information/education campaigns; (3) antiretroviral treatment; (4) non-discriminatory policies; (5) distribution of condoms.

** Grounds on which abortion is permitted: (1) to save the woman's life; (2) to preserve physical health; (3) to preserve mental health; (4) rape or incest; (5) foetal impairment; (6) economic or social reasons; (7) on request.

Population indicators

Indicator	1975	1985	1995	2009
Population size and growth				
Population size (thousands)	34 721	40 505	44 651	48 333
Annual growth rate (percentage)[*]	2.0	1.6	0.8	0.4
Population age structure				
Percentage of population under age 15	38	30	23	17
Percentage of population aged 60 or over	6	7	9	15
Fertility and family planning				
Total fertility (children per woman)[*]	4.3	2.2	1.7	1.2
Adolescent fertility rate (per 1,000 women, aged 15 - 19)[*]	..	..	4.0	5.0
Percentage of births to women under age 20[*]	..	..	1	2
Percentage of births to women aged 35 or over[*]	..	..	4	22
Percentage of married women using contraception				
Modern methods	27[a]	59	70[b]	..
All methods	35[a]	70	81[b]	80[c]
Health and mortality				
Life expectancy at birth (years)[*]				
Males	58	63	69	76
Females	64	71	77	83
Both sexes combined	61	67	73	79
Infant mortality rate (per 1,000 live births)[*]	58	27	9	4
Under-five mortality (per 1,000 live births)[*]	..	34	12	6
Maternal mortality ratio (per 100,000 live births) (2005)	..	..	..	14
HIV/AIDS				
People living with HIV/AIDS (thousands)	..	..	1.7	13[d]
Adult prevalence (percentage)	..	..	..	<0.1[d]
Spatial distribution				
Population density (per sq. km)	349	407	449	486
Urban population (percentage)	48	65	78	82
Annual urban population growth rate (percentage)	5.2	3.8	1.4	0.6
Annual rural population growth rate (percentage)	-1.6	-4.2	-1.1	-1.0
International migration				
Migrant stock				
Number of migrants (thousands)	305	560	584	535[**]
As percentage of total population	0.9	1.4	1.3	1.1[**]

[*] For the periods 1970-1975, 1980-1985, 1990-1995 and 2005-2010.
[**] For 2010.
[a] For 1974.
[b] For 1997.
[c] For 2005.
[d] For 2007.

Government views and policies

Population policy variable	1976	1986	1996	2009
Population size and growth				
View on growth	..	..	Too low	Too low
Policy on growth	..	..	Raise	Raise
Population age structure				
Level of concern about				
Size of the working-age population	..	..	..	..
Ageing of the population	..	..	..	Minor concern
Fertility and family planning				
View on fertility level	..	..	Satisfactory	Too low
Policy	..	..	No intervention	Raise
Access to contraceptive methods	..	..	Direct support	Direct support
Adolescent fertility				
Level of concern	..	..	..	Not a concern
Policies and programmes	..	..	..	Yes
Health and mortality				
View				
Life expectancy at birth	..	..	Unacceptable	Unacceptable
Under-five mortality	..	..	..	Unacceptable
Maternal mortality	..	..	..	Unacceptable
Level of concern about HIV/AIDS	..	..	..	Major concern
Measures to respond to HIV/AIDS*	..	..	..	1,2,3,4,5
Grounds on which abortion is permitted**	..	..	1,2,3,4,5,6,7	1,2,3,4,5,6,7
Spatial distribution and internal migration				
View on spatial distribution	..	..	Major change desired	Satisfactory
Policies on internal migration				
From rural to urban areas	..	..	..	..
From rural to rural areas	..	..	..	..
From urban to rural areas	..	..	..	..
From urban to urban areas	..	..	..	..
Into urban agglomerations	..	..	..	..
International migration				
Immigration				
View	..	..	Satisfactory	Satisfactory
Policy	..	..	No intervention	Maintain
Permanent settlement	..	..	..	Maintain
Temporary workers	..	..	..	Lower
Highly skilled workers	..	..	..	..
Family reunification	..	..	..	Maintain
Integration of non-citizens	..	..	..	..
Emigration				
View	..	..	Too high	Too high
Policy	..	..	Lower	No intervention
Encouraging the return of citizens	..	..	..	Yes

* Measures implemented to respond to HIV/AIDS: (1) blood screening; (2) information/education campaigns; (3) antiretroviral treatment; (4) non-discriminatory policies; (5) distribution of condoms.

** Grounds on which abortion is permitted: (1) to save the woman's life; (2) to preserve physical health; (3) to preserve mental health; (4) rape or incest; (5) foetal impairment; (6) economic or social reasons; (7) on request.

Population indicators

Indicator	1975	1985	1995	2009
Population size and growth				
Population size (thousands)	3 839	4 215	4 339	3 604
Annual growth rate (percentage)*	1.3	1.0	-0.1	-1.0
Population age structure				
Percentage of population under age 15	29	27	27	17
Percentage of population aged 60 or over	11	12	13	16
Fertility and family planning				
Total fertility (children per woman)*	2.6	2.6	2.1	1.5
Adolescent fertility rate (per 1,000 women, aged 15 - 19)*	..	..	72.0	34.0
Percentage of births to women under age 20*	..	..	17	11
Percentage of births to women aged 35 or over*	..	..	6	7
Percentage of married women using contraception				
Modern methods	..	..	50[a]	43[b]
All methods	..	..	74[a]	68[b]
Health and mortality				
Life expectancy at birth (years)*				
Males	62	62	64	65
Females	69	68	71	72
Both sexes combined	65	65	67	68
Infant mortality rate (per 1,000 live births)*	46	35	29	18
Under-five mortality (per 1,000 live births)*	..	43	36	23
Maternal mortality ratio (per 100,000 live births) (2005)	..	..	..	22
HIV/AIDS				
People living with HIV/AIDS (thousands)	..	..	<0.1	8.9[c]
Adult prevalence (percentage)	..	..	..	0.4[c]
Spatial distribution				
Population density (per sq. km)	113	125	128	106
Urban population (percentage)	36	44	46	41
Annual urban population growth rate (percentage)	3.3	2.7	-0.9	-1.1
Annual rural population growth rate (percentage)	-0.4	-0.4	-0.6	-0.3
International migration				
Migrant stock				
Number of migrants (thousands)	..	..	473	408**
As percentage of total population	0.0	0.0	10.9	11.4**

* For the periods 1970-1975, 1980-1985, 1990-1995 and 2005-2010.
** For 2010.
[a] For 1997.
[b] For 2005.
[c] For 2007.

Government views and policies

Population policy variable	1976	1986	1996	2009
Population size and growth				
View on growth	Satisfactory	Satisfactory	Too low	Too low
Policy on growth	No intervention	Raise	No intervention	Raise
Population age structure				
Level of concern about				
Size of the working-age population	..	..	..	Minor concern
Ageing of the population	..	..	..	Major concern
Fertility and family planning				
View on fertility level	Satisfactory	Too low	Too low	Too low
Policy	Maintain	Raise	Raise	Raise
Access to contraceptive methods	Direct support	Limits	Direct support	Direct support
Adolescent fertility				
Level of concern	..	..	Not a concern	Minor concern
Policies and programmes	..	..	Yes	Yes
Health and mortality				
View				
Life expectancy at birth	Acceptable	Acceptable	Unacceptable	Unacceptable
Under-five mortality	..	..	Unacceptable	Unacceptable
Maternal mortality	..	..	..	Unacceptable
Level of concern about HIV/AIDS	..	..	Major concern	Major concern
Measures to respond to HIV/AIDS*	..	..	..	1,2,3,4,5
Grounds on which abortion is permitted**	..	..	1,2,3,4,5,6,7	1,2,3,4,5,6,7
Spatial distribution and internal migration				
View on spatial distribution	Minor change desired	Satisfactory	Satisfactory	Minor change desired
Policies on internal migration				
From rural to urban areas	..	..	..	Lower
From rural to rural areas	..	..	..	..
From urban to rural areas	..	..	..	..
From urban to urban areas	..	..	..	..
Into urban agglomerations	Lower	Lower	No intervention	No intervention
International migration				
Immigration				
View	Satisfactory	Satisfactory	Satisfactory	Satisfactory
Policy	Maintain	Maintain	Lower	Maintain
Permanent settlement	..	..	Lower	Maintain
Temporary workers	..	..	Lower	Maintain
Highly skilled workers	..	..	Lower	Maintain
Family reunification	..	..	..	No intervention
Integration of non-citizens	..	..	Lower	Maintain
			No	Yes
Emigration				
View	Satisfactory	Satisfactory	Too high	Satisfactory
Policy	Maintain	Maintain	No intervention	Maintain
Encouraging the return of citizens	No	..	Yes	Yes

* Measures implemented to respond to HIV/AIDS: (1) blood screening; (2) information/education campaigns; (3) antiretroviral treatment; (4) non-discriminatory policies; (5) distribution of condoms.
** Grounds on which abortion is permitted: (1) to save the woman's life; (2) to preserve physical health; (3) to preserve mental health; (4) rape or incest; (5) foetal impairment; (6) economic or social reasons; (7) on request.

Population indicators

Indicator	1975	1985	1995	2009
Population size and growth				
Population size (thousands)	21 245	22 725	22 681	21 275
Annual growth rate (percentage)*	1.0	0.5	-0.5	-0.4
Population age structure				
Percentage of population under age 15	25	25	20	15
Percentage of population aged 60 or over	14	14	17	20
Fertility and family planning				
Total fertility (children per woman)*	2.6	2.3	1.5	1.3
Adolescent fertility rate (per 1,000 women, aged 15 - 19)*	..	..	47.0	31.0
Percentage of births to women under age 20*	..	..	16	12
Percentage of births to women aged 35 or over*	..	..	5	9
Percentage of married women using contraception				
Modern methods	5[a]	..	30[b]	38[c]
All methods	58[a]	..	64[b]	70[c]
Health and mortality				
Life expectancy at birth (years)*				
Males	67	67	66	69
Females	71	73	73	76
Both sexes combined	69	70	69	73
Infant mortality rate (per 1,000 live births)*	40	26	23	15
Under-five mortality (per 1,000 live births)*	..	32	28	18
Maternal mortality ratio (per 100,000 live births) (2005)	..	..	..	24
HIV/AIDS				
People living with HIV/AIDS (thousands)	..	..	10	15[d]
Adult prevalence (percentage)	..	..	0.1	0.1[d]
Spatial distribution				
Population density (per sq. km)	89	95	95	89
Urban population (percentage)	43	50	54	54
Annual urban population growth rate (percentage)	2.1	2.0	-0.7	0.0
Annual rural population growth rate (percentage)	0.1	-0.9	-0.3	-1.0
International migration				
Migrant stock				
Number of migrants (thousands)	239	170	135	133**
As percentage of total population	1.1	0.7	0.6	0.6**

* For the periods 1970-1975, 1980-1985, 1990-1995 and 2005-2010.
** For 2010.
[a] For 1978.
[b] For 1999.
[c] For 2004.
[d] For 2007.

Government views and policies

Population policy variable	1976	1986	1996	2009
Population size and growth				
View on growth	..	..	Satisfactory	Too low
Policy on growth	..	..	No intervention	Raise
Population age structure				
Level of concern about				
Size of the working-age population	..	..	..	Major concern
Ageing of the population	..	..	..	Major concern
Fertility and family planning				
View on fertility level	..	..	Too low	Too low
Policy	..	..	No intervention	Raise
Access to contraceptive methods	..	..	Direct support	Indirect support
Adolescent fertility				
Level of concern	..	..	Minor concern	Major concern
Policies and programmes	..	..	Yes	No
Health and mortality				
View				
Life expectancy at birth	..	..	Unacceptable	Unacceptable
Under-five mortality	..	..	Unacceptable	Unacceptable
Maternal mortality	..	..	..	Unacceptable
Level of concern about HIV/AIDS	..	..	Minor concern	Major concern
Measures to respond to HIV/AIDS*	..	..	..	1,2,3,4,5
Grounds on which abortion is permitted**	..	..	1,2,3,4,5,6,7	1,2,3,4,5,6,7
Spatial distribution and internal migration				
View on spatial distribution	..	..	Major change desired	Major change desired
Policies on internal migration				
From rural to urban areas	..	..	..	Lower
From rural to rural areas	..	..	..	Raise
From urban to rural areas	..	..	..	Raise
From urban to urban areas	..	..	..	..
Into urban agglomerations	..	..	No intervention	..
International migration				
Immigration				
View	..	..	Too high	Too high
Policy	..	..	Lower	Lower
Permanent settlement	..	..	Lower	Lower
Temporary workers	..	..	Maintain	Lower
Highly skilled workers	..	..	..	Raise
Family reunification	..	..	No intervention	No intervention
Integration of non-citizens	..	..	Yes	Yes
Emigration				
View	..	..	Too high	Too high
Policy	..	..	Lower	No intervention
Encouraging the return of citizens	..	..	Yes	Yes

* Measures implemented to respond to HIV/AIDS: (1) blood screening; (2) information/education campaigns; (3) antiretroviral treatment; (4) non-discriminatory policies; (5) distribution of condoms.

** Grounds on which abortion is permitted: (1) to save the woman's life; (2) to preserve physical health; (3) to preserve mental health; (4) rape or incest; (5) foetal impairment; (6) economic or social reasons; (7) on request.

Population indicators

Indicator	1975	1985	1995	2009
Population size and growth				
Population size (thousands)	134 233	143 541	148 497	140 874
Annual growth rate (percentage)*	0.6	0.7	0.1	-0.4
Population age structure				
Percentage of population under age 15	23	23	21	15
Percentage of population aged 60 or over	14	14	17	18
Fertility and family planning				
Total fertility (children per woman)*	2.0	2.0	1.5	1.4
Adolescent fertility rate (per 1,000 women, aged 15 - 19)*	..	..	52.0	25.0
Percentage of births to women under age 20*	..	..	17	9
Percentage of births to women aged 35 or over*	..	..	5	8
Percentage of married women using contraception				
Modern methods	..	..	48	..
All methods	..	..	63	..
Health and mortality				
Life expectancy at birth (years)*				
Males	63	61	60	60
Females	74	73	73	73
Both sexes combined	69	67	66	66
Infant mortality rate (per 1,000 live births)*	28	26	22	12
Under-five mortality (per 1,000 live births)*	..	31	26	16
Maternal mortality ratio (per 100,000 live births) (2005)	..	..	..	28
HIV/AIDS				
People living with HIV/AIDS (thousands)	..	..	3.7	940[a]
Adult prevalence (percentage)	..	..	..	1.1[a]
Spatial distribution				
Population density (per sq. km)	8	8	9	8
Urban population (percentage)	67	72	73	73
Annual urban population growth rate (percentage)	1.5	1.3	-0.1	-0.5
Annual rural population growth rate (percentage)	-1.3	-0.7	-0.1	-0.6
International migration				
Migrant stock				
Number of migrants (thousands)	..	..	11 707	12 270**
As percentage of total population	0.0	0.0	7.9	8.7**

* For the periods 1970-1975, 1980-1985, 1990-1995 and 2005-2010.
** For 2010.
[a] For 2007.

Government views and policies

Population policy variable	1976	1986	1996	2009
Population size and growth				
View on growth	Satisfactory	Too high	Too high	Too high
Policy on growth	No intervention	Lower	Lower	Lower
Population age structure				
Level of concern about				
Size of the working-age population	..	..	..	Major concern
Ageing of the population	..	..	..	Major concern
Fertility and family planning				
View on fertility level	Too high	Too high	Too high	Too high
Policy	No intervention	Lower	Lower	Lower
Access to contraceptive methods	No support	Direct support	Direct support	Direct support
Adolescent fertility				
Level of concern	..	..	Minor concern	Major concern
Policies and programmes	..	..	Yes	Yes
Health and mortality				
View				
Life expectancy at birth	Acceptable	Acceptable	Unacceptable	Unacceptable
Under-five mortality	..	..	Unacceptable	Unacceptable
Maternal mortality	..	..	..	Unacceptable
Level of concern about HIV/AIDS	..	..	Major concern	Major concern
Measures to respond to HIV/AIDS[*]	..	..	..	1,2,3,4,5
Grounds on which abortion is permitted[**]	..	..	1,2	1,2,3
Spatial distribution and internal migration				
View on spatial distribution	Major change desired	Major change desired	Major change desired	Major change desired
Policies on internal migration				
From rural to urban areas	..	..	..	Lower
From rural to rural areas	..	..	..	Raise
From urban to rural areas	..	..	..	No intervention
From urban to urban areas	..	..	..	Raise
Into urban agglomerations	No intervention	No intervention	No intervention	Lower
International migration				
Immigration				
View	Satisfactory	Satisfactory	Satisfactory	Satisfactory
Policy	Maintain	Maintain	No intervention	Maintain
Permanent settlement	..	..	No intervention	Maintain
Temporary workers	..	..	No intervention	Maintain
Highly skilled workers	..	..	..	Raise
Family reunification	..	..	No intervention	Raise
Integration of non-citizens	..	..	No	Yes
Emigration				
View	Satisfactory	Too low	Too high	Satisfactory
Policy	Maintain	Maintain	Lower	Maintain
Encouraging the return of citizens	No	..	Yes	Yes

[*] Measures implemented to respond to HIV/AIDS: (1) blood screening; (2) information/education campaigns; (3) antiretroviral treatment; (4) non-discriminatory policies; (5) distribution of condoms.
[**] Grounds on which abortion is permitted: (1) to save the woman's life; (2) to preserve physical health; (3) to preserve mental health; (4) rape or incest; (5) foetal impairment; (6) economic or social reasons; (7) on request.

Population indicators

Indicator	1975	1985	1995	2009
Population size and growth				
Population size (thousands)	4 410	6 111	5 440	9 998
Annual growth rate (percentage)*	3.1	3.2	-5.5	2.7
Population age structure				
Percentage of population under age 15	48	48	49	42
Percentage of population aged 60 or over	4	4	4	4
Fertility and family planning				
Total fertility (children per woman)*	8.2	8.3	6.2	5.4
Adolescent fertility rate (per 1,000 women, aged 15 - 19)*	..	..	67.0	37.0
Percentage of births to women under age 20*	..	..	5	3
Percentage of births to women aged 35 or over*	..	..	35	29
Percentage of married women using contraception				
Modern methods	..	1[a]	7[b]	26[c]
All methods	..	10[a]	14[b]	36[c]
Health and mortality				
Life expectancy at birth (years)*				
Males	43	44	22	48
Females	46	48	26	52
Both sexes combined	45	46	24	50
Infant mortality rate (per 1,000 live births)*	134	124	132	100
Under-five mortality (per 1,000 live births)*	..	199	224	155
Maternal mortality ratio (per 100,000 live births) (2005)	..	..	..	1 300
HIV/AIDS				
People living with HIV/AIDS (thousands)	..	..	240	150[d]
Adult prevalence (percentage)	..	..	7.0	2.8[d]
Spatial distribution				
Population density (per sq. km)	167	232	207	380
Urban population (percentage)	4	5	8	19
Annual urban population growth rate (percentage)	7.7	6.2	14.3	4.4
Annual rural population growth rate (percentage)	3.0	4.7	2.9	2.5
International migration				
Migrant stock				
Number of migrants (thousands)	47	81	337	465**
As percentage of total population	1.1	1.3	6.2	4.5**

* For the periods 1970-1975, 1980-1985, 1990-1995 and 2005-2010.
** For 2010.
[a] For 1983.
[b] For 1996.
[c] For 2007/2008.
[d] For 2007.

Government views and policies

Population policy variable	1976	1986	1996	2009
Population size and growth				
View on growth	..	Too high	Too high	Satisfactory
Policy on growth	..	Lower	Lower	No intervention
Population age structure				
Level of concern about				
Size of the working-age population	..	..	..	Minor concern
Ageing of the population	..	..	..	Minor concern
Fertility and family planning				
View on fertility level	..	Too high	Too high	Satisfactory
Policy	..	Lower	Lower	No intervention
Access to contraceptive methods	..	Direct support	Direct support	Direct support
Adolescent fertility				
Level of concern	..	..	..	Minor concern
Policies and programmes	..	..	..	Yes
Health and mortality				
View				
Life expectancy at birth	..	Unacceptable	Unacceptable	Acceptable
Under-five mortality	..	..	..	Acceptable
Maternal mortality	..	..	..	Acceptable
Level of concern about HIV/AIDS	..	..	..	Major concern
Measures to respond to HIV/AIDS*	..	..	..	1,2,3,5
Grounds on which abortion is permitted**	..	..	1,2,3	1,2,3,4
Spatial distribution and internal migration				
View on spatial distribution	..	Minor change desired	Minor change desired	Minor change desired
Policies on internal migration				
From rural to urban areas	..	..	..	..
From rural to rural areas	..	..	..	..
From urban to rural areas	..	..	..	..
From urban to urban areas	..	..	..	Raise
Into urban agglomerations	..	..	..	Lower
International migration				
Immigration				
View	..	Satisfactory	Satisfactory	Satisfactory
Policy	..	Maintain	Maintain	Maintain
Permanent settlement	..	..	..	Maintain
Temporary workers	..	..	..	Maintain
Highly skilled workers	..	..	..	Maintain
Family reunification	..	..	..	..
Integration of non-citizens	..	..	..	..
Emigration				
View	..	Satisfactory	Satisfactory	Too high
Policy	..	Maintain	Maintain	No intervention
Encouraging the return of citizens	..	..	..	Yes

* Measures implemented to respond to HIV/AIDS: (1) blood screening; (2) information/education campaigns; (3) antiretroviral treatment; (4) non-discriminatory policies; (5) distribution of condoms.
** Grounds on which abortion is permitted: (1) to save the woman's life; (2) to preserve physical health; (3) to preserve mental health; (4) rape or incest; (5) foetal impairment; (6) economic or social reasons; (7) on request.

Population indicators

Indicator	1975	1985	1995	2009
Population size and growth				
Population size (thousands)	44	42	43	52
Annual growth rate (percentage)*	-0.3	-0.5	1.1	1.3
Population age structure				
Percentage of population under age 15	..	..	..	..
Percentage of population aged 60 or over	..	..	..	..
Fertility and family planning				
Total fertility (children per woman)*	..	..	..	..
Adolescent fertility rate (per 1,000 women, aged 15 - 19)*	..	..	..	..
Percentage of births to women under age 20*	..	..	..	..
Percentage of births to women aged 35 or over*	..	..	..	..
Percentage of married women using contraception				
Modern methods	..	37a	..	..
All methods	..	41a	..	..
Health and mortality				
Life expectancy at birth (years)*				
Males	..	..	..	..
Females	..	..	..	..
Both sexes combined	..	..	..	..
Infant mortality rate (per 1,000 live births)*	..	..	..	..
Under-five mortality (per 1,000 live births)*	..	..	..	..
Maternal mortality ratio (per 100,000 live births) (2005)	..	..		..
HIV/AIDS				
People living with HIV/AIDS (thousands)	..	..	..	..
Adult prevalence (percentage)	..	..	..	..
Spatial distribution				
Population density (per sq. km)	170	161	165	198
Urban population (percentage)	35	35	34	32
Annual urban population growth rate (percentage)	0.2	-1.2	0.8	1.6
Annual rural population growth rate (percentage)	-0.6	-0.6	1.6	1.1
International migration				
Migrant stock				
Number of migrants (thousands)	3	3	4	5**
As percentage of total population	6.0	6.9	8.4	9.6**

* For the periods 1970-1975, 1980-1985, 1990-1995 and 2005-2010.
** For 2010.
a For 1984.

Government views and policies

Population policy variable	1976	1986	1996	2009
Population size and growth				
View on growth	..	Too high	Too high	Satisfactory
Policy on growth	..	Lower	Lower	Lower
Population age structure				
Level of concern about				
Size of the working-age population	..	..	..	Minor concern
Ageing of the population	..	..	..	Major concern
Fertility and family planning				
View on fertility level	..	Too high	Too high	Satisfactory
Policy	..	Lower	Lower	Maintain
Access to contraceptive methods	..	Direct support	Direct support	Direct support
Adolescent fertility				
Level of concern	..	..	Major concern	Major concern
Policies and programmes	..	..	Yes	Yes
Health and mortality				
View				
Life expectancy at birth	..	Unacceptable	Unacceptable	Acceptable
Under-five mortality	..	..	Unacceptable	Unacceptable
Maternal mortality	..	..	..	Unacceptable
Level of concern about HIV/AIDS	..	..	Major concern	Major concern
Measures to respond to HIV/AIDS*	..	..	..	1,2,3,5
Grounds on which abortion is permitted**	..	..	1,2,3	1,2,3,4
Spatial distribution and internal migration				
View on spatial distribution	..	Minor change desired	Satisfactory	Minor change desired
Policies on internal migration				
From rural to urban areas	..	..	..	..
From rural to rural areas	..	..	..	..
From urban to rural areas	..	..	..	..
From urban to urban areas	..	..	..	..
Into urban agglomerations	..	..	No intervention	..
International migration				
Immigration				
View	..	Satisfactory	Satisfactory	Satisfactory
Policy	..	Maintain	Lower	Maintain
Permanent settlement	..	..	Lower	Maintain
Temporary workers	..	..	Lower	Maintain
Highly skilled workers	..	..	..	Maintain
Family reunification	..	..	Lower	Maintain
Integration of non-citizens	..	..	No	..
Emigration				
View	..	Satisfactory	Satisfactory	Too high
Policy	..	Maintain	No intervention	No intervention
Encouraging the return of citizens	..	..	No	..

* Measures implemented to respond to HIV/AIDS: (1) blood screening; (2) information/education campaigns; (3) antiretroviral treatment; (4) non-discriminatory policies; (5) distribution of condoms.
** Grounds on which abortion is permitted: (1) to save the woman's life; (2) to preserve physical health; (3) to preserve mental health; (4) rape or incest; (5) foetal impairment; (6) economic or social reasons; (7) on request.

Population indicators

Indicator	1975	1985	1995	2009
Population size and growth				
Population size (thousands)	110	127	147	172
Annual growth rate (percentage)*	1.0	1.4	1.2	1.0
Population age structure				
Percentage of population under age 15	47	41	35	26
Percentage of population aged 60 or over	7	8	10	9
Fertility and family planning				
Total fertility (children per woman)*	5.7	4.2	3.2	2.0
Adolescent fertility rate (per 1,000 women, aged 15 - 19)*	..	..	91.0	62.0
Percentage of births to women under age 20*	..	..	14	15
Percentage of births to women aged 35 or over*	..	..	22	17
Percentage of married women using contraception				
Modern methods	..	46ᵃ	..	..
All methods	..	47ᵃ	..	..
Health and mortality				
Life expectancy at birth (years)*				
Males	62	67	69	72
Females	68	74	74	76
Both sexes combined	65	71	71	74
Infant mortality rate (per 1,000 live births)*	39	23	17	13
Under-five mortality (per 1,000 live births)*	..	31	22	16
Maternal mortality ratio (per 100,000 live births) (2005)	..	..	..	..
HIV/AIDS				
People living with HIV/AIDS (thousands)	..	..	..	..
Adult prevalence (percentage)	..	..	..	..
Spatial distribution				
Population density (per sq. km)	204	235	273	319
Urban population (percentage)	25	28	30	28
Annual urban population growth rate (percentage)	2.4	2.7	0.9	1.5
Annual rural population growth rate (percentage)	1.0	1.3	0.9	0.9
International migration				
Migrant stock				
Number of migrants (thousands)	3	4	6	10**
As percentage of total population	2.9	3.4	4.3	5.9**

* For the periods 1970-1975, 1980-1985, 1990-1995 and 2005-2010.
** For 2010.
ᵃ For 1988.

Government views and policies

Population policy variable	1976	1986	1996	2009
Population size and growth				
View on growth	..	Too high	Too high	Satisfactory
Policy on growth	..	Lower	Lower	Maintain
Population age structure				
Level of concern about				
Size of the working-age population	..	..	..	Major concern
Ageing of the population	..	..	..	Minor concern
Fertility and family planning				
View on fertility level	..	Too high	Too high	Satisfactory
Policy	..	Lower	Lower	Maintain
Access to contraceptive methods	..	Direct support	Direct support	Direct support
Adolescent fertility				
Level of concern	..	..	Major concern	Major concern
Policies and programmes	..	..	Yes	Yes
Health and mortality				
View				
Life expectancy at birth	..	Unacceptable	Acceptable	Acceptable
Under-five mortality	..	..	Unacceptable	Acceptable
Maternal mortality	..	..	..	Acceptable
Level of concern about HIV/AIDS	..	..	Major concern	Major concern
Measures to respond to HIV/AIDS*	..	..	..	1,2,3,5
Grounds on which abortion is permitted**	..	..	1,2,3,4,5	1,2,3,4,5,6
Spatial distribution and internal migration				
View on spatial distribution	..	Minor change desired	Satisfactory	Minor change desired
Policies on internal migration				
From rural to urban areas	..	..	..	Lower
From rural to rural areas	..	..	..	..
From urban to rural areas	..	..	..	..
From urban to urban areas	..	..	..	..
Into urban agglomerations	..	..	No intervention	Lower
International migration				
Immigration				
View	..	Satisfactory	Satisfactory	Satisfactory
Policy	..	Maintain	No intervention	Maintain
Permanent settlement	..	..	No intervention	Maintain
Temporary workers	..	..	No intervention	Maintain
Highly skilled workers	..	..	..	Maintain
Family reunification	..	..	No intervention	No intervention
Integration of non-citizens	..	..	No	..
Emigration				
View	..	Satisfactory	Satisfactory	Satisfactory
Policy	..	Maintain	No intervention	No intervention
Encouraging the return of citizens	..	..	No	..

* Measures implemented to respond to HIV/AIDS: (1) blood screening; (2) information/education campaigns; (3) antiretroviral treatment; (4) non-discriminatory policies; (5) distribution of condoms.
** Grounds on which abortion is permitted: (1) to save the woman's life; (2) to preserve physical health; (3) to preserve mental health; (4) rape or incest; (5) foetal impairment; (6) economic or social reasons; (7) on request.

Population indicators

Indicator	1975	1985	1995	2009
Population size and growth				
Population size (thousands)	96	104	108	109
Annual growth rate (percentage)*	1.1	0.8	0.1	0.1
Population age structure				
Percentage of population under age 15	47	40	34	27
Percentage of population aged 60 or over	8	8	9	9
Fertility and family planning				
Total fertility (children per woman)*	5.5	3.6	2.9	2.1
Adolescent fertility rate (per 1,000 women, aged 15 - 19)*	..	..	88.0	59.0
Percentage of births to women under age 20*	..	..	15	14
Percentage of births to women aged 35 or over*	..	..	15	12
Percentage of married women using contraception				
Modern methods	..	56[a]	..	..
All methods	..	58[a]	..	..
Health and mortality				
Life expectancy at birth (years)*				
Males	60	65	67	69
Females	63	69	72	74
Both sexes combined	62	67	70	72
Infant mortality rate (per 1,000 live births)*	64	42	30	23
Under-five mortality (per 1,000 live births)*	..	53	36	28
Maternal mortality ratio (per 100,000 live births) (2005)	..	..	..	..
HIV/AIDS				
People living with HIV/AIDS (thousands)	..	..	..	..
Adult prevalence (percentage)	..	..	..	..
Spatial distribution				
Population density (per sq. km)	246	269	279	281
Urban population (percentage)	27	34	43	47
Annual urban population growth rate (percentage)	1.1	4.9	1.2	1.3
Annual rural population growth rate (percentage)	1.0	-1.2	0.1	-0.3
International migration				
Migrant stock				
Number of migrants (thousands)	2	3	5	9**
As percentage of total population	2.3	2.8	5.1	7.9**

* For the periods 1970-1975, 1980-1985, 1990-1995 and 2005-2010.
** For 2010.
[a] For 1988.

Government views and policies

Population policy variable	1976	1986	1996	2009
Population size and growth				
View on growth	Too high	Too high	Too high	Too high
Policy on growth	Lower	Lower	Lower	Lower
Population age structure				
Level of concern about				
Size of the working-age population	..	..	..	Major concern
Ageing of the population	..	..	..	Minor concern
Fertility and family planning				
View on fertility level	Too high	Too high	Too high	Too high
Policy	Lower	Lower	Lower	Lower
Access to contraceptive methods	Direct support	Direct support	Direct support	Direct support
Adolescent fertility				
Level of concern	..	..	..	Major concern
Policies and programmes	..	..	..	Yes
Health and mortality				
View				
Life expectancy at birth	Acceptable	Unacceptable	Unacceptable	Unacceptable
Under-five mortality	..	..	..	Unacceptable
Maternal mortality	..	..	..	Acceptable
Level of concern about HIV/AIDS	..	..	..	Major concern
Measures to respond to HIV/AIDS*	..	..	..	1,2,3,5
Grounds on which abortion is permitted**	..	..	1,2,3	1,2,3
Spatial distribution and internal migration				
View on spatial distribution	Major change desired	Major change desired	Major change desired	Major change desired
Policies on internal migration				
From rural to urban areas	..	..	..	..
From rural to rural areas	..	..	..	..
From urban to rural areas	..	..	..	..
From urban to urban areas	..	..	..	..
Into urban agglomerations	..	..	..	..
International migration				
Immigration				
View	Satisfactory	Too high	Too high	Satisfactory
Policy	Maintain	Maintain	Maintain	Maintain
Permanent settlement	..	..	..	Maintain
Temporary workers	..	..	..	Maintain
Highly skilled workers	..	..	..	Maintain
Family reunification	..	..	..	Maintain
Integration of non-citizens	..	..	..	..
Emigration				
View	Satisfactory	Satisfactory	Satisfactory	Satisfactory
Policy	Maintain	Maintain	Maintain	Maintain
Encouraging the return of citizens	..	..	..	..

* Measures implemented to respond to HIV/AIDS: (1) blood screening; (2) information/education campaigns; (3) antiretroviral treatment; (4) non−discriminatory policies; (5) distribution of condoms.

** Grounds on which abortion is permitted: (1) to save the woman's life; (2) to preserve physical health; (3) to preserve mental health; (4) rape or incest; (5) foetal impairment; (6) economic or social reasons; (7) on request.

Population indicators

Indicator	1975	1985	1995	2009
Population size and growth				
Population size (thousands)	150	157	168	179
Annual growth rate (percentage)*	1.1	0.2	0.8	0.0
Population age structure				
Percentage of population under age 15	45	40	39	39
Percentage of population aged 60 or over	3	4	6	7
Fertility and family planning				
Total fertility (children per woman)*	5.7	4.9	4.7	4.0
Adolescent fertility rate (per 1,000 women, aged 15 - 19)*	..	..	32.0	28.0
Percentage of births to women under age 20*	..	..	3	3
Percentage of births to women aged 35 or over*	..	..	31	23
Percentage of married women using contraception				
Modern methods	..	..	23[a]	..
All methods	..	..	25[a]	..
Health and mortality				
Life expectancy at birth (years)*				
Males	53	58	63	69
Females	60	65	70	75
Both sexes combined	56	61	66	72
Infant mortality rate (per 1,000 live births)*	69	52	36	22
Under-five mortality (per 1,000 live births)*	..	66	45	27
Maternal mortality ratio (per 100,000 live births) (2005)	..	..	..	..
HIV/AIDS				
People living with HIV/AIDS (thousands)	..	..	..	..
Adult prevalence (percentage)	..	..	..	..
Spatial distribution				
Population density (per sq. km)	53	55	59	63
Urban population (percentage)	21	21	21	23
Annual urban population growth rate (percentage)	1.1	0.4	1.4	1.8
Annual rural population growth rate (percentage)	0.7	0.4	1.0	0.5
International migration				
Migrant stock				
Number of migrants (thousands)	4	2	5	9**
As percentage of total population	2.5	1.5	2.7	5.0**

* For the periods 1970-1975, 1980-1985, 1990-1995 and 2005-2010.
** For 2010.
[a] For 1998.

Government views and policies

Population policy variable	1976	1986	1996	2009
Population size and growth				
View on growth	Satisfactory	Satisfactory	Satisfactory	Satisfactory
Policy on growth	No intervention	Maintain	Maintain	No intervention
Population age structure				
Level of concern about				
Size of the working-age population	..	..	..	Not a concern
Ageing of the population	..	..	..	Minor concern
Fertility and family planning				
View on fertility level	Satisfactory	Satisfactory	Satisfactory	Satisfactory
Policy	No intervention	No intervention	No intervention	No intervention
Access to contraceptive methods	No support	No support	No support	No support
Adolescent fertility				
Level of concern	..	..	..	Not a concern
Policies and programmes	..	..	..	No
Health and mortality				
View				
Life expectancy at birth	Acceptable	Acceptable	Acceptable	Acceptable
Under-five mortality	..	..	..	Acceptable
Maternal mortality	..	..	..	Acceptable
Level of concern about HIV/AIDS	..	..	..	Major concern
Measures to respond to HIV/AIDS*	..	..	..	1,2,3,5
Grounds on which abortion is permitted**	..	..	1	1
Spatial distribution and internal migration				
View on spatial distribution	Satisfactory	Satisfactory	Satisfactory	Satisfactory
Policies on internal migration				
From rural to urban areas	..	..	..	..
From rural to rural areas	..	..	..	..
From urban to rural areas	..	..	..	..
From urban to urban areas	..	..	..	..
Into urban agglomerations	No intervention	..	..	No intervention
International migration				
Immigration				
View	Too high	Too high	Too high	Satisfactory
Policy	Lower	Lower	Lower	No intervention
Permanent settlement	..	..	..	No intervention
Temporary workers	..	..	..	No intervention
Highly skilled workers	..	..	..	No intervention
Family reunification	..	..	..	No intervention
Integration of non-citizens	..	..	..	Yes
Emigration				
View	Satisfactory	Satisfactory	Satisfactory	Satisfactory
Policy	Maintain	Maintain	Maintain	No intervention
Encouraging the return of citizens	No	..	..	No

* Measures implemented to respond to HIV/AIDS: (1) blood screening; (2) information/education campaigns; (3) antiretroviral treatment; (4) non-discriminatory policies; (5) distribution of condoms.
** Grounds on which abortion is permitted: (1) to save the woman's life; (2) to preserve physical health; (3) to preserve mental health; (4) rape or incest; (5) foetal impairment; (6) economic or social reasons; (7) on request.

Population indicators

Indicator	1975	1985	1995	2009
Population size and growth				
Population size (thousands)	20	23	26	31
Annual growth rate (percentage)*	0.6	1.3	1.2	0.8
Population age structure				
Percentage of population under age 15	..	..	..	..
Percentage of population aged 60 or over	..	..	..	..
Fertility and family planning				
Total fertility (children per woman)*	..	..	..	..
Adolescent fertility rate (per 1,000 women, aged 15 - 19)*	..	..	..	..
Percentage of births to women under age 20*	..	..	..	..
Percentage of births to women aged 35 or over*	..	..	..	..
Percentage of married women using contraception				
Modern methods	..	..	..	..
All methods	..	..	..	..
Health and mortality				
Life expectancy at birth (years)*				
Males	..	..	..	..
Females	..	..	..	..
Both sexes combined	..	..	..	..
Infant mortality rate (per 1,000 live births)*	..	..	..	..
Under-five mortality (per 1,000 live births)*	..	..	..	..
Maternal mortality ratio (per 100,000 live births) (2005)	..	..	..	..
HIV/AIDS				
People living with HIV/AIDS (thousands)	..	..	..	..
Adult prevalence (percentage)	..	..	..	..
Spatial distribution				
Population density (per sq. km)	324	374	421	514
Urban population (percentage)	71	88	92	94
Annual urban population growth rate (percentage)	4.1	2.4	1.3	0.6
Annual rural population growth rate (percentage)	-6.3	-8.7	-4.0	-0.4
International migration				
Migrant stock				
Number of migrants (thousands)	8	9	9	12**
As percentage of total population	41.1	37.4	34.9	37.0**

* For the periods 1970-1975, 1980-1985, 1990-1995 and 2005-2010.
** For 2010.

Government views and policies

Population policy variable	1976	1986	1996	2009
Population size and growth				
View on growth	Satisfactory	Satisfactory	Satisfactory	Satisfactory
Policy on growth	No intervention	Maintain	No intervention	No intervention
Population age structure				
Level of concern about				
Size of the working-age population	..	..	..	Major concern
Ageing of the population	..	..	..	..
Fertility and family planning				
View on fertility level	Satisfactory	Satisfactory	Too high	Too high
Policy	No intervention	Maintain	No intervention	No intervention
Access to contraceptive methods	No support	Direct support	Direct support	Direct support
Adolescent fertility				
Level of concern	..	..	Not a concern	Minor concern
Policies and programmes	..	..	..	Yes
Health and mortality				
View				
Life expectancy at birth	Unacceptable	Unacceptable	Acceptable	Unacceptable
Under-five mortality	..	..	Unacceptable	Unacceptable
Maternal mortality	..	..	..	Unacceptable
Level of concern about HIV/AIDS	..	..	Major concern	Major concern
Measures to respond to HIV/AIDS*	..	..	..	1,2,3,5
Grounds on which abortion is permitted**	..	..	1	1
Spatial distribution and internal migration				
View on spatial distribution	Major change desired	Major change desired	Satisfactory	Minor change desired
Policies on internal migration				
From rural to urban areas	..	..	..	Lower
From rural to rural areas	..	..	..	..
From urban to rural areas	..	..	..	..
From urban to urban areas	..	..	..	..
Into urban agglomerations	..	..	No intervention	..
International migration				
Immigration				
View	Satisfactory	Satisfactory	Satisfactory	Satisfactory
Policy	Maintain	Maintain	No intervention	No intervention
Permanent settlement	..	..	No intervention	..
Temporary workers	..	..	No intervention	..
Highly skilled workers	..	..	..	..
Family reunification	..	..	No intervention	..
Integration of non-citizens	..	..	No	..
Emigration				
View	Satisfactory	Satisfactory	Satisfactory	Satisfactory
Policy	Maintain	Maintain	No intervention	No intervention
Encouraging the return of citizens	..	..	No	..

* Measures implemented to respond to HIV/AIDS: (1) blood screening; (2) information/education campaigns; (3) antiretroviral treatment;
(4) non−discriminatory policies; (5) distribution of condoms.
** Grounds on which abortion is permitted: (1) to save the woman's life; (2) to preserve physical health; (3) to preserve mental health; (4) rape or incest;
(5) foetal impairment; (6) economic or social reasons; (7) on request.

Population indicators

Indicator	1975	1985	1995	2009
Population size and growth				
Population size (thousands)	82	104	128	163
Annual growth rate (percentage)*	2.2	1.8	1.9	1.6
Population age structure				
Percentage of population under age 15	47	47	45	41
Percentage of population aged 60 or over	6	7	7	5
Fertility and family planning				
Total fertility (children per woman)*	6.5	6.2	5.2	3.9
Adolescent fertility rate (per 1,000 women, aged 15 - 19)*	..	..	108.0	66.0
Percentage of births to women under age 20*	..	..	11	9
Percentage of births to women aged 35 or over*	..	..	18	15
Percentage of married women using contraception				
Modern methods	..	..	27[a]	..
All methods	..	..	29[a]	..
Health and mortality				
Life expectancy at birth (years)*				
Males	55	59	61	64
Females	58	62	64	67
Both sexes combined	56	60	63	66
Infant mortality rate (per 1,000 live births)*	75	74	83	72
Under-five mortality (per 1,000 live births)*	..	98	114	95
Maternal mortality ratio (per 100,000 live births) (2005)	..	..	..	..
HIV/AIDS				
People living with HIV/AIDS (thousands)	..	..	..	..
Adult prevalence (percentage)	..	..	..	..
Spatial distribution				
Population density (per sq. km)	85	108	133	169
Urban population (percentage)	32	38	49	61
Annual urban population growth rate (percentage)	3.9	5.0	3.8	2.9
Annual rural population growth rate (percentage)	2.3	0.3	0.0	-0.5
International migration				
Migrant stock				
Number of migrants (thousands)	7	6	6	5**
As percentage of total population	8.4	6.0	4.4	3.2**

* For the periods 1970-1975, 1980-1985, 1990-1995 and 2005-2010.
** For 2010.
[a] For 2000.

Government views and policies

Population policy variable	1976	1986	1996	2009
Population size and growth				
View on growth	Too low	Too low	Too low	Satisfactory
Policy on growth	Raise	Raise	Raise	Maintain
Population age structure				
Level of concern about				
Size of the working-age population	..	..	..	Minor concern
Ageing of the population	..	..	..	Minor concern
Fertility and family planning				
View on fertility level	Satisfactory	Satisfactory	Satisfactory	Satisfactory
Policy	Maintain	Maintain	Maintain	No intervention
Access to contraceptive methods	Limits	Limits	Limits	No support
Adolescent fertility				
Level of concern	..	..	..	Not a concern
Policies and programmes	..	..	..	No
Health and mortality				
View				
Life expectancy at birth	Unacceptable	Unacceptable	Unacceptable	Unacceptable
Under-five mortality	..	..	..	Unacceptable
Maternal mortality	..	..	..	Unacceptable
Level of concern about HIV/AIDS	..	..	..	Major concern
Measures to respond to HIV/AIDS*	..	..	..	1,2,3,4
Grounds on which abortion is permitted**	..	..	1,2	1,2,3
Spatial distribution and internal migration				
View on spatial distribution	Minor change desired	Minor change desired	Minor change desired	Minor change desired
Policies on internal migration				
From rural to urban areas	..	..	..	Lower
From rural to rural areas	..	..	..	No intervention
From urban to rural areas	..	..	..	Raise
From urban to urban areas	..	..	..	Raise
Into urban agglomerations	..	..	..	Lower
International migration				
Immigration				
View	Too low	Satisfactory	Too high	Too high
Policy	Raise	Maintain	Lower	Lower
Permanent settlement	..	..	..	No intervention
Temporary workers	..	..	..	Lower
Highly skilled workers	..	..	..	Maintain
Family reunification	..	..	..	Maintain
Integration of non-citizens	..	..	..	Yes
Emigration				
View	Satisfactory	Satisfactory	Satisfactory	Satisfactory
Policy	Maintain	Maintain	Maintain	Lower
Encouraging the return of citizens	..	..	..	Yes

* Measures implemented to respond to HIV/AIDS: (1) blood screening; (2) information/education campaigns; (3) antiretroviral treatment; (4) non−discriminatory policies; (5) distribution of condoms.
** Grounds on which abortion is permitted: (1) to save the woman's life; (2) to preserve physical health; (3) to preserve mental health; (4) rape or incest; (5) foetal impairment; (6) economic or social reasons; (7) on request.

Population indicators

Indicator	1975	1985	1995	2009
Population size and growth				
Population size (thousands)	7 251	12 867	18 255	25 721
Annual growth rate (percentage)*	4.7	5.8	2.3	2.1
Population age structure				
Percentage of population under age 15	44	42	42	32
Percentage of population aged 60 or over	5	4	4	4
Fertility and family planning				
Total fertility (children per woman)*	7.3	7.0	5.4	3.2
Adolescent fertility rate (per 1,000 women, aged 15 - 19)*	..	..	47.0	26.0
Percentage of births to women under age 20*	..	..	4	4
Percentage of births to women aged 35 or over*	..	..	34	29
Percentage of married women using contraception				
Modern methods	..	..	29[a]	..
All methods	..	..	32[a]	24[b]
Health and mortality				
Life expectancy at birth (years)*				
Males	52	62	67	71
Females	56	65	71	75
Both sexes combined	54	63	69	73
Infant mortality rate (per 1,000 live births)*	105	56	32	19
Under-five mortality (per 1,000 live births)*	..	75	39	22
Maternal mortality ratio (per 100,000 live births) (2005)	..	..	..	18
HIV/AIDS				
People living with HIV/AIDS (thousands)	..	..	..	..
Adult prevalence (percentage)	..	..	..	..
Spatial distribution				
Population density (per sq. km)	3	6	8	12
Urban population (percentage)	58	73	79	82
Annual urban population growth rate (percentage)	7.9	7.1	2.7	2.4
Annual rural population growth rate (percentage)	1.5	0.7	1.3	0.9
International migration				
Migrant stock				
Number of migrants (thousands)	929	3 401	4 611	7 289**
As percentage of total population	12.8	26.4	25.3	27.8**

* For the periods 1970-1975, 1980-1985, 1990-1995 and 2005-2010.
** For 2010.
[a] For 1996.
[b] For 2007.

Government views and policies

Population policy variable	1976	1986	1996	2009
Population size and growth				
View on growth	Too high	Too high	Too high	Too high
Policy on growth	No intervention	Lower	Lower	Lower
Population age structure				
Level of concern about				
Size of the working-age population	..	..	..	..
Ageing of the population	..	..	..	Major concern
Fertility and family planning				
View on fertility level	Too high	Too high	Too high	Too high
Policy	No intervention	Lower	Lower	Lower
Access to contraceptive methods	No support	Direct support	Direct support	Direct support
Adolescent fertility				
Level of concern	..	..	Major concern	Major concern
Policies and programmes	..	..	Yes	Yes
Health and mortality				
View				
Life expectancy at birth	Unacceptable	Unacceptable	Unacceptable	Unacceptable
Under-five mortality	..	..	Unacceptable	Unacceptable
Maternal mortality	..	..	..	Unacceptable
Level of concern about HIV/AIDS	..	..	Major concern	Major concern
Measures to respond to HIV/AIDS*	..	..	..	1,2,3,5
Grounds on which abortion is permitted**	..	..	1	1
Spatial distribution and internal migration				
View on spatial distribution	Major change desired	Minor change desired	Major change desired	Major change desired
Policies on internal migration				
From rural to urban areas	..	..	..	Lower
From rural to rural areas	..	..	..	..
From urban to rural areas	..	..	..	..
From urban to urban areas	..	..	..	Raise
Into urban agglomerations	Lower	No intervention	Lower	Lower
International migration				
Immigration				
View	Satisfactory	Satisfactory	Satisfactory	Satisfactory
Policy	Maintain	Maintain	No intervention	No intervention
Permanent settlement	..	..	No intervention	No intervention
Temporary workers	..	..	No intervention	No intervention
Highly skilled workers	..	..	..	No intervention
Family reunification	..	..	No intervention	No intervention
Integration of non-citizens	..	..	Yes	..
Emigration				
View	Satisfactory	Satisfactory	Satisfactory	Satisfactory
Policy	Maintain	Maintain	No intervention	Maintain
Encouraging the return of citizens	..	..	Yes	Yes

* Measures implemented to respond to HIV/AIDS: (1) blood screening; (2) information/education campaigns; (3) antiretroviral treatment;
(4) non−discriminatory policies; (5) distribution of condoms.
** Grounds on which abortion is permitted: (1) to save the woman's life; (2) to preserve physical health; (3) to preserve mental health; (4) rape or incest;
(5) foetal impairment; (6) economic or social reasons; (7) on request.

Population indicators

Indicator	1975	1985	1995	2009
Population size and growth				
Population size (thousands)	4 888	6 514	8 660	12 534
Annual growth rate (percentage)[*]	3.2	2.9	2.8	2.6
Population age structure				
Percentage of population under age 15	45	47	46	44
Percentage of population aged 60 or over	4	4	4	4
Fertility and family planning				
Total fertility (children per woman)[*]	7.5	7.3	6.5	5.0
Adolescent fertility rate (per 1,000 women, aged 15 - 19)[*]	..	..	129.0	104.0
Percentage of births to women under age 20[*]	..	..	10	10
Percentage of births to women aged 35 or over[*]	..	..	29	24
Percentage of married women using contraception				
Modern methods	1[a]	2[b]	8[c]	10[d]
All methods	4[a]	11[b]	13[c]	12[d]
Health and mortality				
Life expectancy at birth (years)[*]				
Males	43	48	51	54
Females	45	50	54	57
Both sexes combined	44	49	53	55
Infant mortality rate (per 1,000 live births)[*]	108	88	72	58
Under-five mortality (per 1,000 live births)[*]	..	196	149	120
Maternal mortality ratio (per 100,000 live births) (2005)	..	..	..	980
HIV/AIDS				
People living with HIV/AIDS (thousands)	..	..	7.1	67[e]
Adult prevalence (percentage)	..	..	0.2	1.0[e]
Spatial distribution				
Population density (per sq. km)	25	33	44	64
Urban population (percentage)	34	38	40	43
Annual urban population growth rate (percentage)	4.8	4.0	3.1	3.1
Annual rural population growth rate (percentage)	1.8	2.4	2.4	1.8
International migration				
Migrant stock				
Number of migrants (thousands)	155	170	291	210[**]
As percentage of total population	3.2	2.6	3.4	1.6[**]

[*] For the periods 1970-1975, 1980-1985, 1990-1995 and 2005-2010.
[**] For 2010.
[a] For 1978.
[b] For 1986.
[c] For 1997.
[d] For 2005.
[e] For 2007.

Government views and policies

Population policy variable	1976	1986	1996	2009
Population size and growth				
View on growth	..	..	..	Too low
Policy on growth	..	..	..	Raise
Population age structure				
Level of concern about				
Size of the working-age population	..	..	..	Major concern
Ageing of the population	..	..	..	Major concern
Fertility and family planning				
View on fertility level	..	..	..	Too low
Policy	..	..	..	Raise
Access to contraceptive methods	..	..	..	Direct support
Adolescent fertility				
Level of concern	..	..	..	Minor concern
Policies and programmes	..	..	..	Yes
Health and mortality				
View				
Life expectancy at birth	..	..	..	Acceptable
Under-five mortality	..	..	..	Acceptable
Maternal mortality	..	..	..	Acceptable
Level of concern about HIV/AIDS	..	..	..	Major concern
Measures to respond to HIV/AIDS*	..	..	..	1,2,3,5
Grounds on which abortion is permitted**	..	..	..	1,2,3,4,5,6,7
Spatial distribution and internal migration				
View on spatial distribution	..	..	..	Major change desired
Policies on internal migration				
From rural to urban areas	..	..	..	Lower
From rural to rural areas	..	..	..	No intervention
From urban to rural areas	..	..	..	Raise
From urban to urban areas	..	..	..	No intervention
Into urban agglomerations	..	..	..	Maintain
International migration				
Immigration				
View	..	..	..	Satisfactory
Policy	..	..	..	Maintain
Permanent settlement	..	..	..	Maintain
Temporary workers	..	..	..	Maintain
Highly skilled workers	..	..	..	Lower
Family reunification	..	..	..	Raise
Integration of non-citizens	..	..	..	Yes
Emigration				
View	..	..	..	Too high
Policy	..	..	..	Lower
Encouraging the return of citizens	..	..	..	Yes

* Measures implemented to respond to HIV/AIDS: (1) blood screening; (2) information/education campaigns; (3) antiretroviral treatment; (4) non-discriminatory policies; (5) distribution of condoms.
** Grounds on which abortion is permitted: (1) to save the woman's life; (2) to preserve physical health; (3) to preserve mental health; (4) rape or incest; (5) foetal impairment; (6) economic or social reasons; (7) on request.

Population indicators

Indicator	1975	1985	1995	2009
Population size and growth				
Population size (thousands)	8 536	9 272	10 204	9 850
Annual growth rate (percentage)*	0.9	0.7	1.3	0.0
Population age structure				
Percentage of population under age 15	24	24	22	18
Percentage of population aged 60 or over	13	14	18	19
Fertility and family planning				
Total fertility (children per woman)*	2.4	2.3	2.0	1.6
Adolescent fertility rate (per 1,000 women, aged 15 - 19)*	..	..	37.0	22.0
Percentage of births to women under age 20*	..	..	9	7
Percentage of births to women aged 35 or over*	..	..	7	10
Percentage of married women using contraception				
Modern methods	..	..	32[a]	19[b]
All methods	..	..	59[a]	41[b]
Health and mortality				
Life expectancy at birth (years)*				
Males	67	68	69	72
Females	71	73	74	76
Both sexes combined	69	70	72	74
Infant mortality rate (per 1,000 live births)*	47	34	17	12
Under-five mortality (per 1,000 live births)*	..	39	20	14
Maternal mortality ratio (per 100,000 live births) (2005)	..	..	..	..
HIV/AIDS				
People living with HIV/AIDS (thousands)	..	..	3.1	6.4[c]
Adult prevalence (percentage)	..	..	0.1	0.1[c]
Spatial distribution				
Population density (per sq. km)	97	105	115	111
Urban population (percentage)	43	48	51	52
Annual urban population growth rate (percentage)	2.3	1.4	0.5	0.6
Annual rural population growth rate (percentage)	-0.1	-0.3	0.3	-0.3
International migration				
Migrant stock				
Number of migrants (thousands)	..	..	874	525**
As percentage of total population	0.0	0.0	8.1	5.3**

* For the periods 1970-1975, 1980-1985, 1990-1995 and 2005-2010.
** For 2010.
[a] For 2000.
[b] For 2005.
[c] For 2007.

Government views and policies

Population policy variable	1976	1986	1996	2009
Population size and growth				
View on growth	Too high	Too high	Too high	Satisfactory
Policy on growth	Lower	Lower	Lower	No intervention
Population age structure				
Level of concern about				
Size of the working-age population	..	..	..	Major concern
Ageing of the population	..	..	..	Minor concern
Fertility and family planning				
View on fertility level	Too high	Too high	Too high	Satisfactory
Policy	Lower	Lower	Lower	No intervention
Access to contraceptive methods	Direct support	Direct support	Direct support	Direct support
Adolescent fertility				
Level of concern	..	..	..	Major concern
Policies and programmes	..	..	..	Yes
Health and mortality				
View				
Life expectancy at birth	Unacceptable	Acceptable	Acceptable	Acceptable
Under-five mortality	..	..	..	Acceptable
Maternal mortality	..	..	..	Acceptable
Level of concern about HIV/AIDS	..	..	..	Major concern
Measures to respond to HIV/AIDS*	..	..	..	1,2,3,5
Grounds on which abortion is permitted**	..	..	1,2,3,4,5	1,2,3,4,5
Spatial distribution and internal migration				
View on spatial distribution	Major change desired	Major change desired	Major change desired	Minor change desired
Policies on internal migration				
From rural to urban areas	..	..	..	No intervention
From rural to rural areas	..	..	..	No intervention
From urban to rural areas	..	..	..	No intervention
From urban to urban areas	..	..	..	No intervention
Into urban agglomerations	..	..	..	No intervention
International migration				
Immigration				
View	Satisfactory	Satisfactory	Satisfactory	Satisfactory
Policy	Maintain	Maintain	Maintain	Maintain
Permanent settlement	..	..	..	Maintain
Temporary workers	..	..	..	Maintain
Highly skilled workers	..	..	..	..
Family reunification	..	..	..	Maintain
Integration of non-citizens	..	..	..	..
Emigration				
View	Satisfactory	Too high	Too high	Satisfactory
Policy	Maintain	Maintain	Maintain	Maintain
Encouraging the return of citizens	..	..	..	..

* Measures implemented to respond to HIV/AIDS: (1) blood screening; (2) information/education campaigns; (3) antiretroviral treatment; (4) non-discriminatory policies; (5) distribution of condoms.
** Grounds on which abortion is permitted: (1) to save the woman's life; (2) to preserve physical health; (3) to preserve mental health; (4) rape or incest; (5) foetal impairment; (6) economic or social reasons; (7) on request.

Population indicators

Indicator	1975	1985	1995	2009
Population size and growth				
Population size (thousands)	61	67	76	84
Annual growth rate (percentage)*	2.9	0.3	1.0	0.5
Population age structure				
Percentage of population under age 15	..	..	..	..
Percentage of population aged 60 or over	..	..	..	..
Fertility and family planning				
Total fertility (children per woman)*	..	..	..	..
Adolescent fertility rate (per 1,000 women, aged 15 - 19)*	..	..	..	..
Percentage of births to women under age 20*	..	..	..	..
Percentage of births to women aged 35 or over*	..	..	..	..
Percentage of married women using contraception				
Modern methods	..	..	..	..
All methods	..	..	..	..
Health and mortality				
Life expectancy at birth (years)*				
Males	..	..	..	..
Females	..	..	..	..
Both sexes combined	..	..	..	..
Infant mortality rate (per 1,000 live births)*	..	..	..	..
Under-five mortality (per 1,000 live births)*	..	..	..	..
Maternal mortality ratio (per 100,000 live births) (2005)	..	..	..	..
HIV/AIDS				
People living with HIV/AIDS (thousands)	..	..	..	..
Adult prevalence (percentage)	..	..	..	..
Spatial distribution				
Population density (per sq. km)	133	147	166	185
Urban population (percentage)	46	49	50	55
Annual urban population growth rate (percentage)	5.6	1.0	1.7	1.3
Annual rural population growth rate (percentage)	-0.5	1.1	0.9	-0.9
International migration				
Migrant stock				
Number of migrants (thousands)	3	3	4	11**
As percentage of total population	4.8	5.1	5.6	12.8**

* For the periods 1970-1975, 1980-1985, 1990-1995 and 2005-2010.
** For 2010.

Government views and policies

Population policy variable	1976	1986	1996	2009
Population size and growth				
View on growth	Too high	Too high	Too high	Too high
Policy on growth	No intervention	No intervention	No intervention	No intervention
Population age structure				
Level of concern about				
Size of the working-age population	..	..	..	Minor concern
Ageing of the population	..	..	..	..
Fertility and family planning				
View on fertility level	Too high	Too high	Too high	Too high
Policy	No intervention	No intervention	Lower	Lower
Access to contraceptive methods	Direct support	Indirect support	Indirect support	Direct support
Adolescent fertility				
Level of concern	..	..	Major concern	Major concern
Policies and programmes	..	..	Yes	Yes
Health and mortality				
View				
Life expectancy at birth	Unacceptable	Unacceptable	Unacceptable	Unacceptable
Under-five mortality	..	..	Unacceptable	Unacceptable
Maternal mortality	..	..	..	Unacceptable
Level of concern about HIV/AIDS	..	..	Major concern	Major concern
Measures to respond to HIV/AIDS*	..	..	..	1,2,3,5
Grounds on which abortion is permitted**	..	..	1,2,3	1,2,3
Spatial distribution and internal migration				
View on spatial distribution	Minor change desired	Major change desired	Minor change desired	Major change desired
Policies on internal migration				
From rural to urban areas	..	..	..	Lower
From rural to rural areas	..	..	..	..
From urban to rural areas	..	..	..	..
From urban to urban areas	..	..	..	Raise
Into urban agglomerations	No intervention	No intervention	No intervention	Lower
International migration				
Immigration				
View	Satisfactory	Satisfactory	Satisfactory	Satisfactory
Policy	Maintain	Maintain	Lower	No intervention
Permanent settlement	..	..	No intervention	No intervention
Temporary workers	..	..	..	No intervention
Highly skilled workers	..	..	..	No intervention
Family reunification	..	..	..	No intervention
Integration of non-citizens	..	..	No	..
Emigration				
View	Satisfactory	Satisfactory	Satisfactory	Satisfactory
Policy	Maintain	Maintain	No intervention	No intervention
Encouraging the return of citizens	No	..	No	Yes

* Measures implemented to respond to HIV/AIDS: (1) blood screening; (2) information/education campaigns; (3) antiretroviral treatment; (4) non-discriminatory policies; (5) distribution of condoms.
** Grounds on which abortion is permitted: (1) to save the woman's life; (2) to preserve physical health; (3) to preserve mental health; (4) rape or incest; (5) foetal impairment; (6) economic or social reasons; (7) on request.

Population indicators

Indicator	1975	1985	1995	2009
Population size and growth				
Population size (thousands)	2 931	3 631	3 989	5 696
Annual growth rate (percentage)*	1.9	2.2	-0.5	2.7
Population age structure				
Percentage of population under age 15	40	42	42	43
Percentage of population aged 60 or over	6	5	4	4
Fertility and family planning				
Total fertility (children per woman)*	5.8	5.7	5.5	5.2
Adolescent fertility rate (per 1,000 women, aged 15 - 19)*	..	..	156.0	126.0
Percentage of births to women under age 20*	..	..	14	12
Percentage of births to women aged 35 or over*	..	..	24	28
Percentage of married women using contraception				
Modern methods	..	..	2[a]	6[b]
All methods	..	..	3[a]	8[b]
Health and mortality				
Life expectancy at birth (years)*				
Males	36	41	37	46
Females	39	44	40	49
Both sexes combined	37	42	38	47
Infant mortality rate (per 1,000 live births)*	195	154	160	104
Under-five mortality (per 1,000 live births)*	..	261	271	148
Maternal mortality ratio (per 100,000 live births) (2005)	..	..	..	2 100
HIV/AIDS				
People living with HIV/AIDS (thousands)	..	..	21	55[c]
Adult prevalence (percentage)	..	..	1.0	1.7[c]
Spatial distribution				
Population density (per sq. km)	41	51	56	79
Urban population (percentage)	27	32	34	38
Annual urban population growth rate (percentage)	3.5	4.0	1.5	2.8
Annual rural population growth rate (percentage)	1.2	2.3	0.3	1.3
International migration				
Migrant stock				
Number of migrants (thousands)	94	92	101	107**
As percentage of total population	3.2	2.5	2.5	1.8**

* For the periods 1970-1975, 1980-1985, 1990-1995 and 2005-2010.
** For 2010.
[a] For 1992.
[b] For 2008.
[c] For 2007.

Government views and policies

Population policy variable	1976	1986	1996	2009
Population size and growth				
View on growth	Satisfactory	Too low	Satisfactory	Too low
Policy on growth	No intervention	Raise	Maintain	Raise
Population age structure				
Level of concern about				
Size of the working-age population	..	..	..	Major concern
Ageing of the population	..	..	..	Major concern
Fertility and family planning				
View on fertility level	Satisfactory	Too low	Too low	Too low
Policy	No intervention	Raise	Raise	Raise
Access to contraceptive methods	Direct support	Direct support	Direct support	Direct support
Adolescent fertility				
Level of concern	..	..	Minor concern	Minor concern
Policies and programmes	..	..	Yes	Yes
Health and mortality				
View				
Life expectancy at birth	Acceptable	Acceptable	Acceptable	Acceptable
Under-five mortality	..	..	Acceptable	Acceptable
Maternal mortality	..	..	..	Acceptable
Level of concern about HIV/AIDS	..	..	Minor concern	Major concern
Measures to respond to HIV/AIDS*	..	..	..	1,2,5
Grounds on which abortion is permitted**	..	..	1,2,3,4,5,6,7	1,2,3,4,5,6,7
Spatial distribution and internal migration				
View on spatial distribution	Satisfactory	Satisfactory	Satisfactory	Satisfactory
Policies on internal migration				
From rural to urban areas	..	..	..	No intervention
From rural to rural areas	..	..	..	No intervention
From urban to rural areas	..	..	..	No intervention
From urban to urban areas	..	..	..	No intervention
Into urban agglomerations	..	..	No intervention	No intervention
International migration				
Immigration				
View	Satisfactory	Satisfactory	Satisfactory	Too low
Policy	Maintain	Maintain	Raise	Raise
Permanent settlement	..	..	Raise	Raise
Temporary workers	..	..	No intervention	Maintain
Highly skilled workers	..	..	..	Raise
Family reunification	..	..	No intervention	Maintain
Integration of non-citizens	..	..	No	Yes
Emigration				
View	Satisfactory	Satisfactory	Satisfactory	Too high
Policy	Maintain	Maintain	No intervention	Lower
Encouraging the return of citizens	..	..	No	Yes

* Measures implemented to respond to HIV/AIDS: (1) blood screening; (2) information/education campaigns; (3) antiretroviral treatment; (4) non-discriminatory policies; (5) distribution of condoms.

** Grounds on which abortion is permitted: (1) to save the woman's life; (2) to preserve physical health; (3) to preserve mental health; (4) rape or incest; (5) foetal impairment; (6) economic or social reasons; (7) on request.

Population indicators

Indicator	1975	1985	1995	2009
Population size and growth				
Population size (thousands)	2 263	2 709	3 480	4 737
Annual growth rate (percentage)*	1.7	2.3	2.9	2.5
Population age structure				
Percentage of population under age 15	33	24	22	16
Percentage of population aged 60 or over	7	8	9	15
Fertility and family planning				
Total fertility (children per woman)*	2.6	1.7	1.8	1.3
Adolescent fertility rate (per 1,000 women, aged 15 - 19)*	..	..	8.0	5.0
Percentage of births to women under age 20*	..	..	2	2
Percentage of births to women aged 35 or over*	..	..	15	17
Percentage of married women using contraception				
Modern methods	53[a]	51[b]	53[c]	..
All methods	60[a]	67[b]	62[c]	..
Health and mortality				
Life expectancy at birth (years)*				
Males	67	69	74	78
Females	72	75	78	83
Both sexes combined	70	72	76	80
Infant mortality rate (per 1,000 live births)*	19	8	6	3
Under-five mortality (per 1,000 live births)*	..	10	7	4
Maternal mortality ratio (per 100,000 live births) (2005)	..	..	..	14
HIV/AIDS				
People living with HIV/AIDS (thousands)	..	..	<1	4.2[d]
Adult prevalence (percentage)	..	..	..	0.2[d]
Spatial distribution				
Population density (per sq. km)	3 313	3 966	5 095	6 935
Urban population (percentage)	100	100	100	100
Annual urban population growth rate (percentage)	1.3	2.1	3.1	1.1
Annual rural population growth rate (percentage)	0.0	0.0	0.0	0.0
International migration				
Migrant stock				
Number of migrants (thousands)	529	619	992	1 967**
As percentage of total population	23.4	22.9	28.5	40.7**

* For the periods 1970-1975, 1980-1985, 1990-1995 and 2005-2010.
** For 2010.
[a] For 1973.
[b] For 1987.
[c] For 1997.
[d] For 2007.

Government views and policies

Population policy variable	1976	1986	1996	2009
Population size and growth				
View on growth	..	..	Too low	Satisfactory
Policy on growth	..	..	Raise	Maintain
Population age structure				
Level of concern about				
Size of the working-age population	..	..	..	Minor concern
Ageing of the population	..	..	..	Major concern
Fertility and family planning				
View on fertility level	..	..	Too low	Too low
Policy	..	..	Raise	Raise
Access to contraceptive methods	..	..	No support	No support
Adolescent fertility				
Level of concern	..	..	Not a concern	Not a concern
Policies and programmes	..	..	No	No
Health and mortality				
View				
Life expectancy at birth	..	..	Unacceptable	Acceptable
Under-five mortality	..	..	..	Acceptable
Maternal mortality	..	..	..	Acceptable
Level of concern about HIV/AIDS	..	..	..	Major concern
Measures to respond to HIV/AIDS*	..	..	..	1,2,3,5
Grounds on which abortion is permitted**	..	..	1,2,3,4,5,6,7	1,2,3,4,5,6,7
Spatial distribution and internal migration				
View on spatial distribution	..	..	Satisfactory	Major change desired
Policies on internal migration				
From rural to urban areas	..	..	..	No intervention
From rural to rural areas	..	..	..	No intervention
From urban to rural areas	..	..	..	No intervention
From urban to urban areas	..	..	..	No intervention
Into urban agglomerations	..	..	..	No intervention
International migration				
Immigration				
View	..	..	Satisfactory	Satisfactory
Policy	..	..	Lower	Maintain
Permanent settlement	..	..	Lower	Maintain
Temporary workers	..	..	Lower	Maintain
Highly skilled workers	..	..	Lower	Maintain
Family reunification	..	..	..	Maintain
Integration of non-citizens	..	..	Lower	Maintain
			Yes	Yes
Emigration				
View	..	..	Satisfactory	Satisfactory
Policy	..	..	No intervention	No intervention
Encouraging the return of citizens	..	..	No	No

* Measures implemented to respond to HIV/AIDS: (1) blood screening; (2) information/education campaigns; (3) antiretroviral treatment; (4) non-discriminatory policies; (5) distribution of condoms.
** Grounds on which abortion is permitted: (1) to save the woman's life; (2) to preserve physical health; (3) to preserve mental health; (4) rape or incest; (5) foetal impairment; (6) economic or social reasons; (7) on request.

Population indicators

Indicator	1975	1985	1995	2009
Population size and growth				
Population size (thousands)	4 735	5 140	5 352	5 406
Annual growth rate (percentage)*	0.9	0.6	0.4	0.1
Population age structure				
Percentage of population under age 15	26	27	23	15
Percentage of population aged 60 or over	14	14	15	17
Fertility and family planning				
Total fertility (children per woman)*	2.5	2.3	1.9	1.3
Adolescent fertility rate (per 1,000 women, aged 15 - 19)*	..	..	38.0	21.0
Percentage of births to women under age 20*	..	..	10	8
Percentage of births to women aged 35 or over*	..	..	6	10
Percentage of married women using contraception				
Modern methods	..	..	66[a]	..
All methods	..	..	80[a]	..
Health and mortality				
Life expectancy at birth (years)*				
Males	67	67	68	71
Females	73	75	76	79
Both sexes combined	70	71	72	75
Infant mortality rate (per 1,000 live births)*	24	18	12	7
Under-five mortality (per 1,000 live births)*	..	20	14	8
Maternal mortality ratio (per 100,000 live births) (2005)	..	..	..	6
HIV/AIDS				
People living with HIV/AIDS (thousands)	..	..	..	<0.5[b]
Adult prevalence (percentage)	..	..	..	<0.1[b]
Spatial distribution				
Population density (per sq. km)	97	105	109	110
Urban population (percentage)	46	54	57	57
Annual urban population growth rate (percentage)	3.3	1.4	0.1	0.3
Annual rural population growth rate (percentage)	-1.0	-0.5	0.3	-0.4
International migration				
Migrant stock				
Number of migrants (thousands)	..	..	114	131**
As percentage of total population	0.0	0.0	2.1	2.4**

* For the periods 1970-1975, 1980-1985, 1990-1995 and 2005-2010.
** For 2010.
[a] For 1997.
[b] For 2007.

Government views and policies

Population policy variable	1976	1986	1996	2009
Population size and growth				
View on growth	..	..	Too low	Too low
Policy on growth	..	..	Raise	Raise
Population age structure				
Level of concern about				
Size of the working-age population	..	..	..	Major concern
Ageing of the population	..	..	..	Major concern
Fertility and family planning				
View on fertility level	..	..	Too low	Too low
Policy	..	..	Raise	Raise
Access to contraceptive methods	..	..	Direct support	Direct support
Adolescent fertility				
Level of concern	..	..	..	Minor concern
Policies and programmes	..	..	No	Yes
Health and mortality				
View				
Life expectancy at birth	..	..	Acceptable	Unacceptable
Under-five mortality	..	..	..	Acceptable
Maternal mortality	..	..	..	Unacceptable
Level of concern about HIV/AIDS	..	..	..	Minor concern
Measures to respond to HIV/AIDS*	..	..		1,2,3,4,5
Grounds on which abortion is permitted**	..	..	1,2,3,4,5,6,7	1,2,3,4,5,6,7
Spatial distribution and internal migration				
View on spatial distribution	..	..	Minor change desired	Minor change desired
Policies on internal migration				
From rural to urban areas	..	..	..	Lower
From rural to rural areas	..	..	..	..
From urban to rural areas	..	..	..	..
From urban to urban areas	..	..	..	..
Into urban agglomerations	..	..	..	Lower
International migration				
Immigration				
View	..	..	Satisfactory	Satisfactory
Policy	..	..	Lower	Maintain
Permanent settlement	..	..	..	Maintain
Temporary workers	..	..	..	Lower
Highly skilled workers	..	..	..	Maintain
Family reunification	..	..	..	Maintain
Integration of non-citizens	..	..	..	Yes
Emigration				
View	..	..	Satisfactory	Satisfactory
Policy	..	..	No intervention	No intervention
Encouraging the return of citizens	..	..	Yes	Yes

* Measures implemented to respond to HIV/AIDS: (1) blood screening; (2) information/education campaigns; (3) antiretroviral treatment; (4) non-discriminatory policies; (5) distribution of condoms.
** Grounds on which abortion is permitted: (1) to save the woman's life; (2) to preserve physical health; (3) to preserve mental health; (4) rape or incest; (5) foetal impairment; (6) economic or social reasons; (7) on request.

Population indicators

Indicator	1975	1985	1995	2009
Population size and growth				
Population size (thousands)	1 742	1 883	1 966	2 020
Annual growth rate (percentage)*	0.8	0.6	0.4	0.2
Population age structure				
Percentage of population under age 15	24	22	18	14
Percentage of population aged 60 or over	15	15	18	22
Fertility and family planning				
Total fertility (children per woman)*	2.2	1.9	1.4	1.4
Adolescent fertility rate (per 1,000 women, aged 15 - 19)*	..	..	18.0	5.0
Percentage of births to women under age 20*	..	..	7	2
Percentage of births to women aged 35 or over*	..	..	7	13
Percentage of married women using contraception				
Modern methods	..	..	63	..
All methods	..	..	79	..
Health and mortality				
Life expectancy at birth (years)*				
Males	66	67	70	75
Females	74	75	78	82
Both sexes combined	70	71	74	78
Infant mortality rate (per 1,000 live births)*	22	13	8	4
Under-five mortality (per 1,000 live births)*	..	16	9	5
Maternal mortality ratio (per 100,000 live births) (2005)	..	..	..	6
HIV/AIDS				
People living with HIV/AIDS (thousands)	..	..	..	<0.5[a]
Adult prevalence (percentage)	..	..	..	<0.1[a]
Spatial distribution				
Population density (per sq. km)	86	93	97	100
Urban population (percentage)	42	50	51	48
Annual urban population growth rate (percentage)	3.7	0.8	0.3	-0.5
Annual rural population growth rate (percentage)	-0.9	0.1	0.2	0.4
International migration				
Migrant stock				
Number of migrants (thousands)	..	..	200	164**
As percentage of total population	0.0	0.0	10.2	8.1**

* For the periods 1970-1975, 1980-1985, 1990-1995 and 2005-2010.
** For 2010.
[a] For 2007.

Government views and policies

Population policy variable	1976	1986	1996	2009
Population size and growth				
View on growth	..	Too high	Too high	Too high
Policy on growth	..	No intervention	Lower	Lower
Population age structure				
Level of concern about				
Size of the working-age population	..	..	..	Major concern
Ageing of the population	..	..	..	Minor concern
Fertility and family planning				
View on fertility level	..	Too high	Too high	Too high
Policy	..	No intervention	Lower	Lower
Access to contraceptive methods	..	Direct support	Direct support	Indirect support
Adolescent fertility				
Level of concern	..	..	..	Minor concern
Policies and programmes	..	..	..	Yes
Health and mortality				
View				
Life expectancy at birth	..	Unacceptable	Unacceptable	Unacceptable
Under-five mortality	..	..	..	Unacceptable
Maternal mortality	..	..	..	Unacceptable
Level of concern about HIV/AIDS	..	..	..	Major concern
Measures to respond to HIV/AIDS*	..	..	..	1,2,3,5
Grounds on which abortion is permitted**	..	..	1	1
Spatial distribution and internal migration				
View on spatial distribution	..	Minor change desired	Minor change desired	Minor change desired
Policies on internal migration				
From rural to urban areas	..	..	..	Lower
From rural to rural areas	..	..	..	..
From urban to rural areas	..	..	..	..
From urban to urban areas	..	..	..	..
Into urban agglomerations	..	..	..	Lower
International migration				
Immigration				
View	..	Satisfactory	Satisfactory	Satisfactory
Policy	..	Maintain	Maintain	Maintain
Permanent settlement	..	..	..	..
Temporary workers	..	..	..	Maintain
Highly skilled workers	..	..	..	Maintain
Family reunification	..	..	..	..
Integration of non-citizens	..	..	..	..
Emigration				
View	..	Satisfactory	Satisfactory	Satisfactory
Policy	..	Maintain	Maintain	Maintain
Encouraging the return of citizens	..	..	..	..

* Measures implemented to respond to HIV/AIDS: (1) blood screening; (2) information/education campaigns; (3) antiretroviral treatment; (4) non-discriminatory policies; (5) distribution of condoms.
** Grounds on which abortion is permitted: (1) to save the woman's life; (2) to preserve physical health; (3) to preserve mental health; (4) rape or incest; (5) foetal impairment; (6) economic or social reasons; (7) on request.

Population indicators

Indicator	1975	1985	1995	2009
Population size and growth				
Population size (thousands)	193	272	362	523
Annual growth rate (percentage)*	3.6	3.4	2.9	2.5
Population age structure				
Percentage of population under age 15	48	47	44	39
Percentage of population aged 60 or over	5	5	5	5
Fertility and family planning				
Total fertility (children per woman)*	7.2	6.4	5.5	3.9
Adolescent fertility rate (per 1,000 women, aged 15 - 19)*	..	..	77.0	42.0
Percentage of births to women under age 20*	..	..	7	5
Percentage of births to women aged 35 or over*	..	..	24	17
Percentage of married women using contraception				
Modern methods	..	..	..	..
All methods	..	..	..	..
Health and mortality				
Life expectancy at birth (years)*				
Males	55	58	58	65
Females	56	60	59	67
Both sexes combined	56	59	58	66
Infant mortality rate (per 1,000 live births)*	91	76	78	44
Under-five mortality (per 1,000 live births)*	..	105	109	57
Maternal mortality ratio (per 100,000 live births) (2005)	..	..	..	220
HIV/AIDS				
People living with HIV/AIDS (thousands)	..	..	..	..
Adult prevalence (percentage)	..	..	..	..
Spatial distribution				
Population density (per sq. km)	7	9	13	18
Urban population (percentage)	9	12	15	18
Annual urban population growth rate (percentage)	5.1	6.2	4.2	4.1
Annual rural population growth rate (percentage)	3.3	2.6	2.6	1.8
International migration				
Migrant stock				
Number of migrants (thousands)	4	4	5	7**
As percentage of total population	2.2	1.6	1.5	1.3**

* For the periods 1970-1975, 1980-1985, 1990-1995 and 2005-2010.
** For 2010.

Government views and policies

Population policy variable	1976	1986	1996	2009
Population size and growth				
View on growth	Satisfactory	Satisfactory	Satisfactory	Satisfactory
Policy on growth	No intervention	No intervention	No intervention	No intervention
Population age structure				
Level of concern about				
Size of the working-age population	..	..	..	..
Ageing of the population	..	..	..	..
Fertility and family planning				
View on fertility level	Satisfactory	Satisfactory	Satisfactory	Satisfactory
Policy	No intervention	No intervention	No intervention	No intervention
Access to contraceptive methods	No support	Indirect support	Indirect support	Indirect support
Adolescent fertility				
Level of concern	..	..	..	..
Policies and programmes	..	..	..	..
Health and mortality				
View				
Life expectancy at birth	Unacceptable	Unacceptable	Unacceptable	Unacceptable
Under-five mortality	..	..	..	Unacceptable
Maternal mortality	..	..	..	Unacceptable
Level of concern about HIV/AIDS	..	..	..	Major concern
Measures to respond to HIV/AIDS*	..	..	..	1,2
Grounds on which abortion is permitted**	..	..	1	1
Spatial distribution and internal migration				
View on spatial distribution	Major change desired	Major change desired	Minor change desired	Minor change desired
Policies on internal migration				
From rural to urban areas	..	..	..	..
From rural to rural areas	..	..	..	..
From urban to rural areas	..	..	..	..
From urban to urban areas	..	..	..	..
Into urban agglomerations	No intervention	No intervention	..	..
International migration				
Immigration				
View	Satisfactory	Too high	Satisfactory	Satisfactory
Policy	Maintain	Lower	No intervention	No intervention
Permanent settlement	..	..	..	..
Temporary workers	..	..	..	..
Highly skilled workers	..	..	..	..
Family reunification	..	..	..	..
Integration of non-citizens	..	..	..	..
Emigration				
View	Satisfactory	Too high	Satisfactory	Satisfactory
Policy	Maintain	Lower	No intervention	No intervention
Encouraging the return of citizens	No	..	..	..

* Measures implemented to respond to HIV/AIDS: (1) blood screening; (2) information/education campaigns; (3) antiretroviral treatment; (4) non-discriminatory policies; (5) distribution of condoms.
** Grounds on which abortion is permitted: (1) to save the woman's life; (2) to preserve physical health; (3) to preserve mental health; (4) rape or incest; (5) foetal impairment; (6) economic or social reasons; (7) on request.

Population indicators

Indicator	1975	1985	1995	2009
Population size and growth				
Population size (thousands)	4 116	6 361	6 521	9 133
Annual growth rate (percentage)*	2.7	-0.2	-0.2	2.3
Population age structure				
Percentage of population under age 15	46	45	43	45
Percentage of population aged 60 or over	5	5	4	4
Fertility and family planning				
Total fertility (children per woman)*	7.1	6.7	6.5	6.4
Adolescent fertility rate (per 1,000 women, aged 15 - 19)*	..	..	71.0	70.0
Percentage of births to women under age 20*	..	..	5	5
Percentage of births to women aged 35 or over*	..	..	30	28
Percentage of married women using contraception				
Modern methods	..	..	1[a]	1[b]
All methods	..	..	8[a]	15[b]
Health and mortality				
Life expectancy at birth (years)*				
Males	39	42	42	48
Females	43	46	45	51
Both sexes combined	41	44	43	50
Infant mortality rate (per 1,000 live births)*	155	138	141	110
Under-five mortality (per 1,000 live births)*	..	230	236	180
Maternal mortality ratio (per 100,000 live births) (2005)	..	..	..	1 400
HIV/AIDS				
People living with HIV/AIDS (thousands)	..	..	5.4	24[c]
Adult prevalence (percentage)	..	..	0.2	0.5[c]
Spatial distribution				
Population density (per sq. km)	6	10	10	14
Urban population (percentage)	25	28	31	37
Annual urban population growth rate (percentage)	10.4	1.3	2.1	4.2
Annual rural population growth rate (percentage)	9.1	0.0	0.4	2.1
International migration				
Migrant stock				
Number of migrants (thousands)	14	775	19	23**
As percentage of total population	0.3	12.2	0.3	0.2**

* For the periods 1970-1975, 1980-1985, 1990-1995 and 2005-2010.
** For 2010.
[a] For 1999.
[b] For 2005/2006.
[c] For 2007.

Government views and policies

Population policy variable	1976	1986	1996	2009
Population size and growth				
View on growth	Too high	Too high	Too high	Satisfactory
Policy on growth	Lower	Lower	Lower	Maintain
Population age structure				
Level of concern about				
Size of the working-age population	..	..	..	Major concern
Ageing of the population	..	..	..	Major concern
Fertility and family planning				
View on fertility level	Too high	Too high	Too high	Satisfactory
Policy	Lower	Lower	Lower	Maintain
Access to contraceptive methods	Direct support	Direct support	Direct support	Direct support
Adolescent fertility				
Level of concern	..	..	Major concern	Major concern
Policies and programmes	..	..	Yes	Yes
Health and mortality				
View				
Life expectancy at birth	Unacceptable	Unacceptable	Unacceptable	Unacceptable
Under-five mortality	..	..	Unacceptable	Unacceptable
Maternal mortality	..	..	..	Unacceptable
Level of concern about HIV/AIDS	..	..	Major concern	Major concern
Measures to respond to HIV/AIDS*	..	..	..	1,2,3,4,5
Grounds on which abortion is permitted**	..	..	1,2,3,4,5,6,7	1,2,3,4,5,6,7
Spatial distribution and internal migration				
View on spatial distribution	Minor change desired	Minor change desired	Major change desired	Major change desired
Policies on internal migration				
From rural to urban areas	..	..	..	Lower
From rural to rural areas	..	..	..	No intervention
From urban to rural areas	..	..	..	Raise
From urban to urban areas	..	..	..	Maintain
Into urban agglomerations	Lower	..	..	Lower
International migration				
Immigration				
View	Too low	Too high	Satisfactory	Too high
Policy	Raise	Lower	Maintain	Lower
Permanent settlement	..	..	..	Lower
Temporary workers	..	..	..	Maintain
Highly skilled workers	..	..	..	Raise
Family reunification	..	..	..	Maintain
Integration of non-citizens	..	..	..	Yes
Emigration				
View	Satisfactory	Too high	Satisfactory	Too high
Policy	Maintain	Lower	No intervention	Lower
Encouraging the return of citizens	No	..	..	Yes

* Measures implemented to respond to HIV/AIDS: (1) blood screening; (2) information/education campaigns; (3) antiretroviral treatment; (4) non-discriminatory policies; (5) distribution of condoms.

** Grounds on which abortion is permitted: (1) to save the woman's life; (2) to preserve physical health; (3) to preserve mental health; (4) rape or incest; (5) foetal impairment; (6) economic or social reasons; (7) on request.

Population indicators

Indicator	1975	1985	1995	2009
Population size and growth				
Population size (thousands)	25 698	32 959	41 375	50 110
Annual growth rate (percentage)*	2.7	2.5	2.4	1.0
Population age structure				
Percentage of population under age 15	42	40	36	31
Percentage of population aged 60 or over	5	5	5	7
Fertility and family planning				
Total fertility (children per woman)*	5.5	4.6	3.3	2.6
Adolescent fertility rate (per 1,000 women, aged 15 - 19)*	..	..	91.0	59.0
Percentage of births to women under age 20*	..	..	14	12
Percentage of births to women aged 35 or over*	..	..	21	17
Percentage of married women using contraception				
Modern methods	35[a]	48[b]	55[c]	60[d]
All methods	37[a]	50[b]	56[c]	60[d]
Health and mortality				
Life expectancy at birth (years)*				
Males	51	55	58	50
Females	57	62	65	53
Both sexes combined	54	58	61	52
Infant mortality rate (per 1,000 live births)*	77	61	50	49
Under-five mortality (per 1,000 live births)*	..	85	68	72
Maternal mortality ratio (per 100,000 live births) (2005)	..	..	..	400
HIV/AIDS				
People living with HIV/AIDS (thousands)	..	..	1 500	5 700[e]
Adult prevalence (percentage)	..	..	6.2	18.1[e]
Spatial distribution				
Population density (per sq. km)	21	27	34	41
Urban population (percentage)	48	49	54	61
Annual urban population growth rate (percentage)	2.6	3.2	3.0	1.2
Annual rural population growth rate (percentage)	2.4	1.1	1.1	-0.8
International migration				
Migrant stock				
Number of migrants (thousands)	962	1 808	1 098	1 863**
As percentage of total population	3.7	5.5	2.7	3.7**

* For the periods 1970-1975, 1980-1985, 1990-1995 and 2005-2010.
** For 2010.
[a] For 1976.
[b] For 1988.
[c] For 1998.
[d] For 2003.
[e] For 2007.

Government views and policies

Population policy variable	1976	1986	1996	2009
Population size and growth				
View on growth	Satisfactory	Satisfactory	Satisfactory	Satisfactory
Policy on growth	No intervention	No intervention	No intervention	No intervention
Population age structure				
Level of concern about				
Size of the working-age population	..	..	..	Minor concern
Ageing of the population	..	..	..	Major concern
Fertility and family planning				
View on fertility level	Satisfactory	Satisfactory	Satisfactory	Too low
Policy	No intervention	No intervention	No intervention	Raise
Access to contraceptive methods	Limits	Direct support	Direct support	Indirect support
Adolescent fertility				
Level of concern	..	..	..	Minor concern
Policies and programmes	..	..	..	Yes
Health and mortality				
View				
Life expectancy at birth	Acceptable	Acceptable	Acceptable	Acceptable
Under-five mortality	..	..	..	Acceptable
Maternal mortality	..	..	..	Acceptable
Level of concern about HIV/AIDS	..	..	..	Major concern
Measures to respond to HIV/AIDS*	..	..	..	1,2,3,4,5
Grounds on which abortion is permitted**	..	..	1,2,3,4,5	1,2,3,4,5
Spatial distribution and internal migration				
View on spatial distribution	Minor change desired	Minor change desired	Satisfactory	Minor change desired
Policies on internal migration				
From rural to urban areas	..	..	..	No intervention
From rural to rural areas	..	..	..	No intervention
From urban to rural areas	..	..	..	No intervention
From urban to urban areas	..	..	..	No intervention
Into urban agglomerations	..	No intervention	..	No intervention
International migration				
Immigration				
View	Satisfactory	Satisfactory	Satisfactory	Satisfactory
Policy	Maintain	Lower	Lower	Maintain
Permanent settlement	..	..	..	Lower
Temporary workers	..	..	..	Maintain
Highly skilled workers	..	..	..	Raise
Family reunification	..	..	..	Maintain
Integration of non-citizens	..	..	Yes	Yes
Emigration				
View	Too high	Too high	Satisfactory	Too high
Policy	Lower	Lower	Lower	Lower
Encouraging the return of citizens	..	..	Yes	Yes

* Measures implemented to respond to HIV/AIDS: (1) blood screening; (2) information/education campaigns; (3) antiretroviral treatment; (4) non-discriminatory policies; (5) distribution of condoms.
** Grounds on which abortion is permitted: (1) to save the woman's life; (2) to preserve physical health; (3) to preserve mental health; (4) rape or incest; (5) foetal impairment; (6) economic or social reasons; (7) on request.

Population indicators

Indicator	1975	1985	1995	2009
Population size and growth				
Population size (thousands)	35 688	38 425	39 391	44 904
Annual growth rate (percentage)[*]	1.1	0.5	0.3	1.0
Population age structure				
Percentage of population under age 15	27	23	17	15
Percentage of population aged 60 or over	15	17	21	22
Fertility and family planning				
Total fertility (children per woman)[*]	2.9	1.9	1.3	1.4
Adolescent fertility rate (per 1,000 women, aged 15 - 19)[*]	..	..	10.0	12.0
Percentage of births to women under age 20[*]	..	..	4	4
Percentage of births to women aged 35 or over[*]	..	..	14	24
Percentage of married women using contraception				
Modern methods	20[a]	38	66[b]	62[c]
All methods	51[a]	59	72[b]	66[c]
Health and mortality				
Life expectancy at birth (years)[*]				
Males	70	73	74	78
Females	76	79	81	84
Both sexes combined	73	76	77	81
Infant mortality rate (per 1,000 live births)[*]	21	11	7	4
Under-five mortality (per 1,000 live births)[*]	..	13	8	5
Maternal mortality ratio (per 100,000 live births) (2005)	..	..	..	4
HIV/AIDS				
People living with HIV/AIDS (thousands)	..	..	110	140[d]
Adult prevalence (percentage)	..	..	0.5	0.5[d]
Spatial distribution				
Population density (per sq. km)	71	76	78	89
Urban population (percentage)	70	74	76	77
Annual urban population growth rate (percentage)	2.1	0.6	0.3	0.7
Annual rural population growth rate (percentage)	-1.1	-0.6	-0.1	-0.1
International migration				
Migrant stock				
Number of migrants (thousands)	466	717	1 041	6 378[**]
As percentage of total population	1.3	1.9	2.6	14.1[**]

[*] For the periods 1970-1975, 1980-1985, 1990-1995 and 2005-2010.
[**] For 2010.
[a] For 1977.
[b] For 1999.
[c] For 2006.
[d] For 2007.

Government views and policies

Population policy variable	1976	1986	1996	2009
Population size and growth				
View on growth	Too high	Too high	Too high	Satisfactory
Policy on growth	Lower	Lower	Lower	Maintain
Population age structure				
Level of concern about				
Size of the working-age population	..	..	..	Not a concern
Ageing of the population	..	..	..	Minor concern
Fertility and family planning				
View on fertility level	Too high	Too high	Too high	Satisfactory
Policy	Lower	Lower	Lower	Maintain
Access to contraceptive methods	Direct support	Direct support	Direct support	Direct support
Adolescent fertility				
Level of concern	..	..	Minor concern	Minor concern
Policies and programmes	..	..	Yes	Yes
Health and mortality				
View				
Life expectancy at birth	Acceptable	Unacceptable	Unacceptable	Acceptable
Under-five mortality	..	..	Unacceptable	Acceptable
Maternal mortality	..	..	..	Acceptable
Level of concern about HIV/AIDS	..	..	Major concern	Minor concern
Measures to respond to HIV/AIDS*	..	..	..	1,2,3,5
Grounds on which abortion is permitted**	..	..	1	1
Spatial distribution and internal migration				
View on spatial distribution	Major change desired	Major change desired	Minor change desired	Minor change desired
Policies on internal migration				
From rural to urban areas	..	..	..	Raise
From rural to rural areas	..	..	..	..
From urban to rural areas	..	..	..	..
From urban to urban areas	..	..	..	Maintain
Into urban agglomerations	..	Lower	No intervention	Raise
International migration				
Immigration				
View	Satisfactory	Satisfactory	Satisfactory	Satisfactory
Policy	Maintain	Maintain	Maintain	Maintain
Permanent settlement	..	..	Maintain	Maintain
Temporary workers	..	..	Maintain	..
Highly skilled workers	..	..	..	Maintain
Family reunification	..	..	Maintain	..
Integration of non-citizens	..	..	Yes	..
Emigration				
View	Satisfactory	Satisfactory	Satisfactory	Satisfactory
Policy	Maintain	Maintain	No intervention	Maintain
Encouraging the return of citizens	..	..	Yes	Yes

* Measures implemented to respond to HIV/AIDS: (1) blood screening; (2) information/education campaigns; (3) antiretroviral treatment; (4) non-discriminatory policies; (5) distribution of condoms.

** Grounds on which abortion is permitted: (1) to save the woman's life; (2) to preserve physical health; (3) to preserve mental health; (4) rape or incest; (5) foetal impairment; (6) economic or social reasons; (7) on request.

Population indicators

Indicator	1975	1985	1995	2009
Population size and growth				
Population size (thousands)	13 790	16 168	18 233	20 238
Annual growth rate (percentage)*	1.9	1.4	1.1	0.9
Population age structure				
Percentage of population under age 15	37	34	29	24
Percentage of population aged 60 or over	6	8	9	12
Fertility and family planning				
Total fertility (children per woman)*	4.0	3.2	2.5	2.3
Adolescent fertility rate (per 1,000 women, aged 15 - 19)*	..	..	31.0	30.0
Percentage of births to women under age 20*	..	..	6	6
Percentage of births to women aged 35 or over*	..	..	19	16
Percentage of married women using contraception				
Modern methods	20	41[a]	44[b]	53[c]
All methods	43	62[a]	66[b]	68[c]
Health and mortality				
Life expectancy at birth (years)*				
Males	62	66	67	70
Females	66	72	73	78
Both sexes combined	64	69	70	74
Infant mortality rate (per 1,000 live births)*	55	33	23	16
Under-five mortality (per 1,000 live births)*	..	43	28	20
Maternal mortality ratio (per 100,000 live births) (2005)	..	..	..	58
HIV/AIDS				
People living with HIV/AIDS (thousands)	..	..	1.9	3.8[d]
Adult prevalence (percentage)	..	..	..	..
Spatial distribution				
Population density (per sq. km)	210	246	278	308
Urban population (percentage)	19	18	16	15
Annual urban population growth rate (percentage)	1.2	0.5	-0.1	0.7
Annual rural population growth rate (percentage)	2.1	1.5	1.0	0.4
International migration				
Migrant stock				
Number of migrants (thousands)	886	495	426	340**
As percentage of total population	6.4	3.1	2.3	1.7**

* For the periods 1970-1975, 1980-1985, 1990-1995 and 2005-2010.
** For 2010.
[a] For 1987.
[b] For 1993.
[c] For 2006/2007.
[d] For 2007.

Government views and policies

Population policy variable	1976	1986	1996	2009
Population size and growth				
View on growth	Satisfactory	Satisfactory	Too high	Too high
Policy on growth	No intervention	No intervention	Lower	Lower
Population age structure				
Level of concern about				
Size of the working-age population	..	..	..	..
Ageing of the population	..	..	..	Minor concern
Fertility and family planning				
View on fertility level	Satisfactory	Satisfactory	Too high	Too high
Policy	No intervention	No intervention	Lower	Lower
Access to contraceptive methods	Direct support	Direct support	Direct support	Direct support
Adolescent fertility				
Level of concern	..	..	Not a concern	Not a concern
Policies and programmes	..	..	No	No
Health and mortality				
View				
Life expectancy at birth	Unacceptable	Unacceptable	Unacceptable	Unacceptable
Under-five mortality	..	..	Unacceptable	Unacceptable
Maternal mortality	..	..	..	Unacceptable
Level of concern about HIV/AIDS	..	..	Major concern	Major concern
Measures to respond to HIV/AIDS*	..	..	..	1,2,3,5
Grounds on which abortion is permitted**	..	..	1,4	1,4
Spatial distribution and internal migration				
View on spatial distribution	Major change desired	Major change desired	Major change desired	Major change desired
Policies on internal migration				
From rural to urban areas	..	..	..	..
From rural to rural areas	..	..	..	..
From urban to rural areas	..	..	..	..
From urban to urban areas	..	..	..	..
Into urban agglomerations	Lower	..	Lower	..
International migration				
Immigration				
View	Too low	Too high	Satisfactory	Satisfactory
Policy	Raise	Lower	Raise	Maintain
Permanent settlement	..	..	Raise	..
Temporary workers	..	..	Raise	Maintain
Highly skilled workers	..	..	..	..
Family reunification	..	..	Raise	..
Integration of non-citizens	..	..	No	..
Emigration				
View	Satisfactory	Satisfactory	Too high	Too high
Policy	Maintain	Maintain	Lower	Lower
Encouraging the return of citizens	Yes	..	Yes	..

* Measures implemented to respond to HIV/AIDS: (1) blood screening; (2) information/education campaigns; (3) antiretroviral treatment; (4) non-discriminatory policies; (5) distribution of condoms.
** Grounds on which abortion is permitted: (1) to save the woman's life; (2) to preserve physical health; (3) to preserve mental health; (4) rape or incest; (5) foetal impairment; (6) economic or social reasons; (7) on request.

Population indicators

Indicator	1975	1985	1995	2009
Population size and growth				
Population size (thousands)	17 493	24 052	30 841	42 272
Annual growth rate (percentage)*	3.0	3.2	2.6	2.2
Population age structure				
Percentage of population under age 15	45	45	43	39
Percentage of population aged 60 or over	5	5	5	6
Fertility and family planning				
Total fertility (children per woman)*	6.6	6.3	5.8	4.2
Adolescent fertility rate (per 1,000 women, aged 15 - 19)*	..	..	97.0	57.0
Percentage of births to women under age 20*	..	..	8	7
Percentage of births to women aged 35 or over*	..	..	28	23
Percentage of married women using contraception				
Modern methods	4[a]	6[b]	5[c]	6[d]
All methods	5[a]	9[b]	7[c]	8[d]
Health and mortality				
Life expectancy at birth (years)*				
Males	46	49	52	56
Females	49	52	55	60
Both sexes combined	47	50	53	58
Infant mortality rate (per 1,000 live births)*	121	106	91	69
Under-five mortality (per 1,000 live births)*	..	174	153	111
Maternal mortality ratio (per 100,000 live births) (2005)	..	..	..	450
HIV/AIDS				
People living with HIV/AIDS (thousands)	..	..	210	320[e]
Adult prevalence (percentage)	..	..	1.3	1.4[e]
Spatial distribution				
Population density (per sq. km)	7	10	12	17
Urban population (percentage)	19	22	31	44
Annual urban population growth rate (percentage)	4.1	6.1	5.6	4.1
Annual rural population growth rate (percentage)	2.8	1.5	1.2	0.6
International migration				
Migrant stock				
Number of migrants (thousands)	322	1 408	1 111	753**
As percentage of total population	1.8	5.9	3.6	1.7**

* For the periods 1970-1975, 1980-1985, 1990-1995 and 2005-2010.
** For 2010.
[a] For 1979.
[b] For 1989/1990.
[c] For 1999.
[d] For 2006.
[e] For 2007.

Government views and policies

Population policy variable	1976	1986	1996	2009
Population size and growth				
View on growth	Satisfactory	Satisfactory	Satisfactory	Satisfactory
Policy on growth	No intervention	No intervention	No intervention	Maintain
Population age structure				
Level of concern about				
Size of the working-age population	..	..	..	Not a concern
Ageing of the population	..	..	..	Minor concern
Fertility and family planning				
View on fertility level	Satisfactory	Satisfactory	Satisfactory	Satisfactory
Policy	No intervention	No intervention	No intervention	Maintain
Access to contraceptive methods	No support	Direct support	Direct support	Indirect support
Adolescent fertility				
Level of concern	..	..	Major concern	Major concern
Policies and programmes	..	..	No	Yes
Health and mortality				
View				
Life expectancy at birth	Unacceptable	Unacceptable	Acceptable	Acceptable
Under-five mortality	..	..	..	Unacceptable
Maternal mortality	..	..	..	Unacceptable
Level of concern about HIV/AIDS	..	..	Major concern	Major concern
Measures to respond to HIV/AIDS*	..	..	..	1,2,3,5
Grounds on which abortion is permitted**	..	..	1	1
Spatial distribution and internal migration				
View on spatial distribution	Major change desired	Major change desired	Major change desired	Major change desired
Policies on internal migration				
From rural to urban areas	..	..	..	Lower
From rural to rural areas	..	..	..	Raise
From urban to rural areas	..	..	..	Maintain
From urban to urban areas	..	..	..	No intervention
Into urban agglomerations	..	..	No intervention	Lower
International migration				
Immigration				
View	Satisfactory	Satisfactory	Too high	Too low
Policy	Maintain	Maintain	Lower	Raise
Permanent settlement	..	..	No intervention	Raise
Temporary workers	..	..	Lower	No intervention
Highly skilled workers	..	..	..	Raise
Family reunification	..	..	Maintain	No intervention
Integration of non-citizens	..	..	No	Yes
Emigration				
View	Too high	Too high	Too high	Too high
Policy	Lower	Lower	Lower	Lower
Encouraging the return of citizens	..	..	Yes	No

* Measures implemented to respond to HIV/AIDS: (1) blood screening; (2) information/education campaigns; (3) antiretroviral treatment;
(4) non-discriminatory policies; (5) distribution of condoms.
** Grounds on which abortion is permitted: (1) to save the woman's life; (2) to preserve physical health; (3) to preserve mental health; (4) rape or incest;
(5) foetal impairment; (6) economic or social reasons; (7) on request.

Population indicators

Indicator	1975	1985	1995	2009
Population size and growth				
Population size (thousands)	364	376	436	520
Annual growth rate (percentage)*	-0.4	0.6	1.4	1.0
Population age structure				
Percentage of population under age 15	48	36	32	29
Percentage of population aged 60 or over	6	7	8	9
Fertility and family planning				
Total fertility (children per woman)*	5.3	3.7	2.6	2.4
Adolescent fertility rate (per 1,000 women, aged 15 - 19)*	..	..	50.0	39.0
Percentage of births to women under age 20*	..	..	10	8
Percentage of births to women aged 35 or over*	..	..	13	12
Percentage of married women using contraception				
Modern methods	..	..	47[a]	41[b]
All methods	..	..	48[a]	42[b]
Health and mortality				
Life expectancy at birth (years)*				
Males	62	64	64	65
Females	67	70	71	73
Both sexes combined	64	66	68	69
Infant mortality rate (per 1,000 live births)*	49	42	34	22
Under-five mortality (per 1,000 live births)*	..	58	47	31
Maternal mortality ratio (per 100,000 live births) (2005)	..	..	..	72
HIV/AIDS				
People living with HIV/AIDS (thousands)	..	..	1	6.8[c]
Adult prevalence (percentage)	..	..	0.4	2.4[c]
Spatial distribution				
Population density (per sq. km)	2	2	3	3
Urban population (percentage)	49	64	70	75
Annual urban population growth rate (percentage)	1.4	3.9	1.4	1.0
Annual rural population growth rate (percentage)	-3.1	-3.5	-0.4	-0.9
International migration				
Migrant stock				
Number of migrants (thousands)	14	15	22	39**
As percentage of total population	3.8	3.9	5.1	7.5**

* For the periods 1970-1975, 1980-1985, 1990-1995 and 2005-2010.
** For 2010.
[a] For 1992.
[b] For 2000.
[c] For 2007.

Government views and policies

Population policy variable	1976	1986	1996	2009
Population size and growth				
View on growth	Too high	Too high	Too high	Too high
Policy on growth	Lower	No intervention	Lower	Lower
Population age structure				
Level of concern about				
Size of the working-age population	..	..	..	Minor concern
Ageing of the population	..	..	..	Minor concern
Fertility and family planning				
View on fertility level	Too high	Too high	Too high	Too high
Policy	Lower	Lower	Lower	Lower
Access to contraceptive methods	Direct support	Direct support	Direct support	Direct support
Adolescent fertility				
Level of concern	..	..	..	Minor concern
Policies and programmes	..	..	..	Yes
Health and mortality				
View				
Life expectancy at birth	Unacceptable	Unacceptable	Unacceptable	Unacceptable
Under-five mortality	..	..	..	Unacceptable
Maternal mortality	..	..	..	Unacceptable
Level of concern about HIV/AIDS	..	..	..	Major concern
Measures to respond to HIV/AIDS*	..	..	..	1,2,3,5
Grounds on which abortion is permitted**	..	..	1	1,2,3,5
Spatial distribution and internal migration				
View on spatial distribution	Major change desired	Major change desired	Minor change desired	Major change desired
Policies on internal migration				
From rural to urban areas	..	..	..	Lower
From rural to rural areas	..	..	..	Raise
From urban to rural areas	..	..	..	..
From urban to urban areas	..	..	..	Lower
Into urban agglomerations	No intervention	No intervention	..	Lower
International migration				
Immigration				
View	Satisfactory	Satisfactory	Satisfactory	Satisfactory
Policy	Maintain	Maintain	Maintain	Maintain
Permanent settlement	..	..	..	..
Temporary workers	..	..	..	..
Highly skilled workers	..	..	..	..
Family reunification	..	..	..	..
Integration of non-citizens	..	..	..	..
Emigration				
View	Satisfactory	Satisfactory	Satisfactory	Too high
Policy	Maintain	Maintain	No intervention	Lower
Encouraging the return of citizens	No	..	..	..

* Measures implemented to respond to HIV/AIDS: (1) blood screening; (2) information/education campaigns; (3) antiretroviral treatment; (4) non-discriminatory policies; (5) distribution of condoms.
** Grounds on which abortion is permitted: (1) to save the woman's life; (2) to preserve physical health; (3) to preserve mental health; (4) rape or incest; (5) foetal impairment; (6) economic or social reasons; (7) on request.

Population indicators

Indicator	1975	1985	1995	2009
Population size and growth				
Population size (thousands)	517	706	969	1 185
Annual growth rate (percentage)*	3.0	3.1	2.3	1.3
Population age structure				
Percentage of population under age 15	48	49	48	39
Percentage of population aged 60 or over	4	4	4	5
Fertility and family planning				
Total fertility (children per woman)*	6.9	6.5	5.3	3.6
Adolescent fertility rate (per 1,000 women, aged 15 - 19)*	..	..	125.0	84.0
Percentage of births to women under age 20*	..	..	12	12
Percentage of births to women aged 35 or over*	..	..	23	19
Percentage of married women using contraception				
Modern methods	..	17[a]	..	47[b]
All methods	..	20[a]	..	51[b]
Health and mortality				
Life expectancy at birth (years)*				
Males	48	54	58	46
Females	51	58	63	45
Both sexes combined	50	56	61	46
Infant mortality rate (per 1,000 live births)*	124	90	67	66
Under-five mortality (per 1,000 live births)*	..	127	96	102
Maternal mortality ratio (per 100,000 live births) (2005)	..	..	..	390
HIV/AIDS				
People living with HIV/AIDS (thousands)	..	..	58	190[c]
Adult prevalence (percentage)	..	..	11.9	26.1[c]
Spatial distribution				
Population density (per sq. km)	30	41	56	68
Urban population (percentage)	14	22	23	25
Annual urban population growth rate (percentage)	10.2	7.7	2.2	1.8
Annual rural population growth rate (percentage)	1.9	2.7	2.0	0.1
International migration				
Migrant stock				
Number of migrants (thousands)	28	41	35	40**
As percentage of total population	5.4	5.8	3.6	3.4**

* For the periods 1970-1975, 1980-1985, 1990-1995 and 2005-2010.
** For 2010.
[a] For 1988.
[b] For 2006/2007.
[c] For 2007.

Government views and policies

Population policy variable	1976	1986	1996	2009
Population size and growth				
View on growth	Satisfactory	Satisfactory	Satisfactory	Satisfactory
Policy on growth	No intervention	No intervention	No intervention	No intervention
Population age structure				
Level of concern about				
Size of the working-age population	..	..	..	Major concern
Ageing of the population	..	..	..	Major concern
Fertility and family planning				
View on fertility level	Satisfactory	Too low	Satisfactory	Satisfactory
Policy	No intervention	No intervention	No intervention	No intervention
Access to contraceptive methods	Direct support	Direct support	Direct support	Direct support
Adolescent fertility				
Level of concern	..	..	Minor concern	Minor concern
Policies and programmes	..	..	Yes	Yes
Health and mortality				
View				
Life expectancy at birth	Acceptable	Acceptable	Acceptable	Acceptable
Under-five mortality	..	..	Acceptable	Acceptable
Maternal mortality	..	..	..	Acceptable
Level of concern about HIV/AIDS	..	..	Major concern	Major concern
Measures to respond to HIV/AIDS*	..	..	..	1,2,3,4,5
Grounds on which abortion is permitted**	..	..	1,2,3,4,5,6,7	1,2,3,4,5,6,7
Spatial distribution and internal migration				
View on spatial distribution	Satisfactory	Minor change desired	Minor change desired	Satisfactory
Policies on internal migration				
From rural to urban areas	..	..	..	No intervention
From rural to rural areas	..	..	..	No intervention
From urban to rural areas	..	..	..	No intervention
From urban to urban areas	..	..	..	No intervention
Into urban agglomerations	Lower	Lower	No intervention	No intervention
International migration				
Immigration				
View	Too high	Satisfactory	Satisfactory	Too low
Policy	Lower	Lower	Lower	Raise
Permanent settlement	..	..	Lower	Raise
Temporary workers	..	..	Maintain	Raise
Highly skilled workers	..	..	..	Raise
Family reunification	..	..	Maintain	Maintain
Integration of non-citizens	..	..	Yes	Yes
Emigration				
View	Satisfactory	Satisfactory	Satisfactory	Satisfactory
Policy	Maintain	Maintain	No intervention	No intervention
Encouraging the return of citizens	No	..	No	No

* Measures implemented to respond to HIV/AIDS: (1) blood screening; (2) information/education campaigns; (3) antiretroviral treatment; (4) non-discriminatory policies; (5) distribution of condoms.

** Grounds on which abortion is permitted: (1) to save the woman's life; (2) to preserve physical health; (3) to preserve mental health; (4) rape or incest; (5) foetal impairment; (6) economic or social reasons; (7) on request.

Population indicators

Indicator	1975	1985	1995	2009
Population size and growth				
Population size (thousands)	8 193	8 350	8 827	9 249
Annual growth rate (percentage)*	0.4	0.1	0.6	0.5
Population age structure				
Percentage of population under age 15	21	18	19	17
Percentage of population aged 60 or over	21	24	22	25
Fertility and family planning				
Total fertility (children per woman)*	1.9	1.6	2.0	1.9
Adolescent fertility rate (per 1,000 women, aged 15 - 19)*	..	..	12.0	8.0
Percentage of births to women under age 20*	..	..	3	2
Percentage of births to women aged 35 or over*	..	..	15	18
Percentage of married women using contraception				
Modern methods	..	72[a]	65[b]	..
All methods	..	78[a]	75[b]	..
Health and mortality				
Life expectancy at birth (years)*				
Males	72	73	75	79
Females	78	79	81	83
Both sexes combined	75	76	78	81
Infant mortality rate (per 1,000 live births)*	10	7	5	3
Under-five mortality (per 1,000 live births)*	..	9	7	4
Maternal mortality ratio (per 100,000 live births) (2005)	..	..	..	3
HIV/AIDS				
People living with HIV/AIDS (thousands)	..	..	4.5	6.2[c]
Adult prevalence (percentage)	..	..	0.1	0.1[c]
Spatial distribution				
Population density (per sq. km)	18	19	20	21
Urban population (percentage)	83	83	84	85
Annual urban population growth rate (percentage)	0.4	0.3	0.3	0.5
Annual rural population growth rate (percentage)	-0.1	0.3	-0.3	-0.1
International migration				
Migrant stock				
Number of migrants (thousands)	578	654	906	1 306**
As percentage of total population	7.1	7.8	10.3	14.1**

* For the periods 1970-1975, 1980-1985, 1990-1995 and 2005-2010.
** For 2010.
[a] For 1981.
[b] For 1996.
[c] For 2007.

Government views and policies

Population policy variable	1976	1986	1996	2009
Population size and growth				
View on growth	Satisfactory	Satisfactory	Satisfactory	Satisfactory
Policy on growth	No intervention	No intervention	No intervention	No intervention
Population age structure				
Level of concern about				
Size of the working-age population	..	..	..	Major concern
Ageing of the population	..	..	..	Major concern
Fertility and family planning				
View on fertility level	Satisfactory	Satisfactory	Too low	Satisfactory
Policy	No intervention	No intervention	No intervention	No intervention
Access to contraceptive methods	Indirect support	Indirect support	No support	No support
Adolescent fertility				
Level of concern	..	..	Not a concern	Not a concern
Policies and programmes	..	..	No	No
Health and mortality				
View				
Life expectancy at birth	Acceptable	Acceptable	Acceptable	Acceptable
Under-five mortality	..	..	Acceptable	Acceptable
Maternal mortality	..	..	..	Acceptable
Level of concern about HIV/AIDS	..	..	Major concern	Minor concern
Measures to respond to HIV/AIDS*	..	..	..	1,2,3
Grounds on which abortion is permitted**	..	..	1,2,3	1,2,3,4,5,6,7
Spatial distribution and internal migration				
View on spatial distribution	Minor change desired	Minor change desired	Minor change desired	Satisfactory
Policies on internal migration				
From rural to urban areas	..	..	..	No intervention
From rural to rural areas	..	..	..	No intervention
From urban to rural areas	..	..	..	No intervention
From urban to urban areas	..	..	..	No intervention
Into urban agglomerations	..	No intervention	Raise	No intervention
International migration				
Immigration				
View	Satisfactory	Satisfactory	Too high	Satisfactory
Policy	Maintain	Lower	Lower	Maintain
Permanent settlement	..	..	Lower	Maintain
Temporary workers	..	..	Lower	Maintain
Highly skilled workers	..	..	..	Maintain
Family reunification	..	..	Maintain	Maintain
Integration of non-citizens	..	..	Yes	Yes
Emigration				
View	Satisfactory	Satisfactory	Satisfactory	Satisfactory
Policy	Maintain	Maintain	No intervention	No intervention
Encouraging the return of citizens	..	..	No	No

* Measures implemented to respond to HIV/AIDS: (1) blood screening; (2) information/education campaigns; (3) antiretroviral treatment; (4) non−discriminatory policies; (5) distribution of condoms.
** Grounds on which abortion is permitted: (1) to save the woman's life; (2) to preserve physical health; (3) to preserve mental health; (4) rape or incest; (5) foetal impairment; (6) economic or social reasons; (7) on request.

Population indicators

Indicator	1975	1985	1995	2009
Population size and growth				
Population size (thousands)	6 338	6 470	7 038	7 568
Annual growth rate (percentage)*	0.5	0.5	0.9	0.4
Population age structure				
Percentage of population under age 15	22	18	18	15
Percentage of population aged 60 or over	17	19	20	23
Fertility and family planning				
Total fertility (children per woman)*	1.8	1.5	1.5	1.5
Adolescent fertility rate (per 1,000 women, aged 15 - 19)*	..	..	6.0	6.0
Percentage of births to women under age 20*	..	..	2	2
Percentage of births to women aged 35 or over*	..	..	14	20
Percentage of married women using contraception				
Modern methods	..	65[a]	78	..
All methods	..	71[a]	82	..
Health and mortality				
Life expectancy at birth (years)*				
Males	71	73	75	79
Females	77	80	81	84
Both sexes combined	74	76	78	82
Infant mortality rate (per 1,000 live births)*	13	8	6	4
Under-five mortality (per 1,000 live births)*	..	9	7	5
Maternal mortality ratio (per 100,000 live births) (2005)	..	..	..	5
HIV/AIDS				
People living with HIV/AIDS (thousands)	..	..	20	25[b]
Adult prevalence (percentage)	..	..	0.5	0.6[b]
Spatial distribution				
Population density (per sq. km)	154	157	170	183
Urban population (percentage)	57	65	74	74
Annual urban population growth rate (percentage)	-0.1	3.4	0.4	0.5
Annual rural population growth rate (percentage)	0.1	-4.1	0.7	0.0
International migration				
Migrant stock				
Number of migrants (thousands)	1 089	1 203	1 471	1 763**
As percentage of total population	17.2	18.6	20.9	23.2**

* For the periods 1970-1975, 1980-1985, 1990-1995 and 2005-2010.
** For 2010.
[a] For 1980.
[b] For 2007.

Government views and policies

Population policy variable	1976	1986	1996	2009
Population size and growth				
View on growth	Satisfactory	Satisfactory	Satisfactory	Too high
Policy on growth	No intervention	No intervention	No intervention	Lower
Population age structure				
Level of concern about				
Size of the working-age population	..	..	..	Major concern
Ageing of the population	..	..	..	Major concern
Fertility and family planning				
View on fertility level	Satisfactory	Satisfactory	Satisfactory	Satisfactory
Policy	No intervention	No intervention	No intervention	Lower
Access to contraceptive methods	Direct support	Direct support	Direct support	Direct support
Adolescent fertility				
Level of concern	..	..	..	Major concern
Policies and programmes	..	..	..	No
Health and mortality				
View				
Life expectancy at birth	Unacceptable	Acceptable	Acceptable	Acceptable
Under-five mortality	..	..	..	Acceptable
Maternal mortality	..	..	..	Acceptable
Level of concern about HIV/AIDS	..	..	..	Major concern
Measures to respond to HIV/AIDS*	..	..	..	1,2,3,4,5
Grounds on which abortion is permitted**	..	..	1	1
Spatial distribution and internal migration				
View on spatial distribution	Minor change desired	Minor change desired	Minor change desired	Satisfactory
Policies on internal migration				
From rural to urban areas	..	..	..	Raise
From rural to rural areas	..	..	..	No intervention
From urban to rural areas	..	..	..	Lower
From urban to urban areas	..	..	..	Lower
Into urban agglomerations	..	Lower	..	Raise
International migration				
Immigration				
View	Satisfactory	Satisfactory	Satisfactory	Satisfactory
Policy	Maintain	Maintain	Maintain	Lower
Permanent settlement	..	..	..	Maintain
Temporary workers	..	..	..	Maintain
Highly skilled workers	..	..	..	Maintain
Family reunification	..	..	..	Maintain
Integration of non-citizens	..	..	..	Yes
Emigration				
View	Too low	Too high	Too high	Too high
Policy	Raise	Lower	Lower	No intervention
Encouraging the return of citizens	..	..	..	Yes

* Measures implemented to respond to HIV/AIDS: (1) blood screening; (2) information/education campaigns; (3) antiretroviral treatment; (4) non-discriminatory policies; (5) distribution of condoms.

** Grounds on which abortion is permitted: (1) to save the woman's life; (2) to preserve physical health; (3) to preserve mental health; (4) rape or incest; (5) foetal impairment; (6) economic or social reasons; (7) on request.

Population indicators

Indicator	*1975*	*1985*	*1995*	*2009*
Population size and growth				
Population size (thousands)	7 537	10 815	14 610	21 906
Annual growth rate (percentage)*	3.4	3.7	2.8	3.3
Population age structure				
Percentage of population under age 15	48	49	45	35
Percentage of population aged 60 or over	4	4	4	5
Fertility and family planning				
Total fertility (children per woman)*	7.5	7.2	4.9	3.3
Adolescent fertility rate (per 1,000 women, aged 15 - 19)*	..	..	78.0	61.0
Percentage of births to women under age 20*	..	..	8	9
Percentage of births to women aged 35 or over*	..	..	27	23
Percentage of married women using contraception				
Modern methods	15[a]	..	28[b]	43[c]
All methods	20[a]	..	40[b]	58[c]
Health and mortality				
Life expectancy at birth (years)*				
Males	56	63	68	72
Females	59	67	71	76
Both sexes combined	57	65	69	74
Infant mortality rate (per 1,000 live births)*	83	50	31	16
Under-five mortality (per 1,000 live births)*	..	66	38	18
Maternal mortality ratio (per 100,000 live births) (2005)	..	..	..	130
HIV/AIDS				
People living with HIV/AIDS (thousands)	..	..	..	..
Adult prevalence (percentage)	..	..	..	..
Spatial distribution				
Population density (per sq. km)	41	58	79	118
Urban population (percentage)	45	48	50	55
Annual urban population growth rate (percentage)	4.1	3.9	3.1	2.9
Annual rural population growth rate (percentage)	2.8	3.1	1.9	1.5
International migration				
Migrant stock				
Number of migrants (thousands)	429	628	817	2 206**
As percentage of total population	5.7	5.8	5.6	9.8**

* For the periods 1970-1975, 1980-1985, 1990-1995 and 2005-2010.
** For 2010.
[a] For 1978.
[b] For 1993.
[c] For 2006.

Government views and policies

Population policy variable	1976	1986	1996	2009
Population size and growth				
View on growth	..	..	Satisfactory	Too high
Policy on growth	..	..	No intervention	Lower
Population age structure				
Level of concern about				
Size of the working-age population	..	..	..	Major concern
Ageing of the population	..	..	..	Minor concern
Fertility and family planning				
View on fertility level	..	..	Too high	Too high
Policy	..	..	Lower	Lower
Access to contraceptive methods	..	..	Direct support	Direct support
Adolescent fertility				
Level of concern	..	..	Not a concern	Minor concern
Policies and programmes	..	..	No	Yes
Health and mortality				
View				
Life expectancy at birth	..	..	Acceptable	Unacceptable
Under-five mortality	..	..	Unacceptable	Unacceptable
Maternal mortality	..	..	..	Unacceptable
Level of concern about HIV/AIDS	..	..	Not a concern	Major concern
Measures to respond to HIV/AIDS*	..	..	..	1,2,3,4,5
Grounds on which abortion is permitted**	..	..	1,2,3,4,5,6,7	1,2,3,4,5,6,7
Spatial distribution and internal migration				
View on spatial distribution	..	..	Minor change desired	Major change desired
Policies on internal migration				
From rural to urban areas	..	..	..	Raise
From rural to rural areas	..	..	..	Raise
From urban to rural areas	..	..	..	..
From urban to urban areas	..	..	..	..
Into urban agglomerations	..	..	No intervention	No intervention
International migration				
Immigration				
View	..	..	Satisfactory	Satisfactory
Policy	..	..	No intervention	Maintain
Permanent settlement	..	..	No intervention	Maintain
Temporary workers	..	..	No intervention	Maintain
Highly skilled workers	..	..	..	..
Family reunification	..	..	No intervention	..
Integration of non-citizens	..	..	Yes	..
Emigration				
View	..	..	Too high	Satisfactory
Policy	..	..	No intervention	Maintain
Encouraging the return of citizens	..	..	Yes	Yes

* Measures implemented to respond to HIV/AIDS: (1) blood screening; (2) information/education campaigns; (3) antiretroviral treatment; (4) non−discriminatory policies; (5) distribution of condoms.
** Grounds on which abortion is permitted: (1) to save the woman's life; (2) to preserve physical health; (3) to preserve mental health; (4) rape or incest; (5) foetal impairment; (6) economic or social reasons; (7) on request.

Population indicators

Indicator	1975	1985	1995	2009
Population size and growth				
Population size (thousands)	3 442	4 567	5 775	6 952
Annual growth rate (percentage)*	3.1	2.9	1.7	1.6
Population age structure				
Percentage of population under age 15	45	43	44	37
Percentage of population aged 60 or over	7	6	6	5
Fertility and family planning				
Total fertility (children per woman)*	6.8	5.5	4.9	3.5
Adolescent fertility rate (per 1,000 women, aged 15 - 19)*	..	..	41.0	28.0
Percentage of births to women under age 20*	..	..	4	4
Percentage of births to women aged 35 or over*	..	..	18	14
Percentage of married women using contraception				
Modern methods	..	..	..	33[a]
All methods	..	..	..	38[a]
Health and mortality				
Life expectancy at birth (years)*				
Males	58	60	59	64
Females	63	65	66	69
Both sexes combined	61	63	62	67
Infant mortality rate (per 1,000 live births)*	125	107	88	60
Under-five mortality (per 1,000 live births)*	..	142	114	78
Maternal mortality ratio (per 100,000 live births) (2005)	..	..	..	170
HIV/AIDS				
People living with HIV/AIDS (thousands)	..	..	<0.5	10[b]
Adult prevalence (percentage)	..	..	..	0.3[b]
Spatial distribution				
Population density (per sq. km)	24	32	40	49
Urban population (percentage)	36	33	29	26
Annual urban population growth rate (percentage)	2.1	2.5	-0.5	1.9
Annual rural population growth rate (percentage)	3.3	3.5	2.2	1.5
International migration				
Migrant stock				
Number of migrants (thousands)	..	..	305	284**
As percentage of total population	0.0	0.0	5.3	4.0**

* For the periods 1970-1975, 1980-1985, 1990-1995 and 2005-2010.
** For 2010.
[a] For 2005.
[b] For 2007.

Government views and policies

Population policy variable	1976	1986	1996	2009
Population size and growth				
View on growth	Too high	Satisfactory	Too high	Too low
Policy on growth	Lower	Lower	Lower	Maintain
Population age structure				
Level of concern about				
Size of the working-age population	..	..	..	Major concern
Ageing of the population	..	..	..	Major concern
Fertility and family planning				
View on fertility level	Too high	Too high	Too high	Satisfactory
Policy	Lower	Lower	Lower	Maintain
Access to contraceptive methods	Direct support	Direct support	Direct support	Direct support
Adolescent fertility				
Level of concern	..	..	Major concern	Major concern
Policies and programmes	..	..	Yes	Yes
Health and mortality				
View				
Life expectancy at birth	Acceptable	Acceptable	Unacceptable	Acceptable
Under-five mortality	..	..	Unacceptable	Unacceptable
Maternal mortality	..	..	..	Unacceptable
Level of concern about HIV/AIDS	..	..	Major concern	Major concern
Measures to respond to HIV/AIDS[*]	..	..	..	1,2,3,5
Grounds on which abortion is permitted[**]	..	..	1,2,4,5	1,2,3,4,5
Spatial distribution and internal migration				
View on spatial distribution	Major change desired	Minor change desired	Major change desired	Major change desired
Policies on internal migration				
From rural to urban areas	..	..	..	Lower
From rural to rural areas	..	..	..	Maintain
From urban to rural areas	..	..	..	Raise
From urban to urban areas	..	..	..	No intervention
Into urban agglomerations	..	Lower	Lower	Lower
International migration				
Immigration				
View	Satisfactory	Too high	Satisfactory	Satisfactory
Policy	Maintain	Lower	Lower	Raise
Permanent settlement	..	..	..	Maintain
Temporary workers	..	..	..	Lower
Highly skilled workers	..	..	..	Maintain
Family reunification	..	..	..	Maintain
Integration of non-citizens	..	..	..	No
Emigration				
View	Satisfactory	Satisfactory	Satisfactory	Satisfactory
Policy	Maintain	Raise	Maintain	No intervention
Encouraging the return of citizens	..	..	..	No

[*] Measures implemented to respond to HIV/AIDS: (1) blood screening; (2) information/education campaigns; (3) antiretroviral treatment; (4) non-discriminatory policies; (5) distribution of condoms.

[**] Grounds on which abortion is permitted: (1) to save the woman's life; (2) to preserve physical health; (3) to preserve mental health; (4) rape or incest; (5) foetal impairment; (6) economic or social reasons; (7) on request.

Population indicators

Indicator	1975	1985	1995	2009
Population size and growth				
Population size (thousands)	42 236	52 545	60 140	67 764
Annual growth rate (percentage)*	2.5	2.1	1.2	0.7
Population age structure				
Percentage of population under age 15	43	34	27	22
Percentage of population aged 60 or over	6	6	9	11
Fertility and family planning				
Total fertility (children per woman)*	5.1	2.9	2.1	1.8
Adolescent fertility rate (per 1,000 women, aged 15 - 19)*	..	..	55.0	37.0
Percentage of births to women under age 20*	..	..	13	10
Percentage of births to women aged 35 or over*	..	..	13	13
Percentage of married women using contraception				
Modern methods	30	59[a]	70[b]	80[c]
All methods	33	59[a]	72[b]	81[c]
Health and mortality				
Life expectancy at birth (years)*				
Males	58	65	65	66
Females	63	71	73	72
Both sexes combined	61	68	69	69
Infant mortality rate (per 1,000 live births)*	58	35	19	7
Under-five mortality (per 1,000 live births)*	..	47	26	10
Maternal mortality ratio (per 100,000 live births) (2005)	..	..	..	110
HIV/AIDS				
People living with HIV/AIDS (thousands)	..	..	750	610[d]
Adult prevalence (percentage)	..	..	2.1	1.4[d]
Spatial distribution				
Population density (per sq. km)	82	102	117	132
Urban population (percentage)	24	28	30	34
Annual urban population growth rate (percentage)	4.8	2.4	1.7	1.7
Annual rural population growth rate (percentage)	1.5	1.1	0.9	0.0
International migration				
Migrant stock				
Number of migrants (thousands)	345	407	549	1 157**
As percentage of total population	0.8	0.8	0.9	1.7**

* For the periods 1970-1975, 1980-1985, 1990-1995 and 2005-2010.
** For 2010.
[a] For 1984.
[b] For 1996/1997.
[c] For 2006.
[d] For 2007.

Government views and policies

Population policy variable	1976	1986	1996	2009
Population size and growth				
View on growth	..	..	Too high	Too low
Policy on growth	..	..	Lower	Raise
Population age structure				
Level of concern about				
Size of the working-age population	..	..	..	Major concern
Ageing of the population	..	..	..	Major concern
Fertility and family planning				
View on fertility level	..	..	Too high	Too low
Policy	..	..	Lower	Raise
Access to contraceptive methods	..	..	Direct support	Direct support
Adolescent fertility				
Level of concern	..	..	Major concern	Major concern
Policies and programmes	..	..	Yes	Yes
Health and mortality				
View				
Life expectancy at birth	..	..	Unacceptable	Unacceptable
Under-five mortality	..	..	Unacceptable	Unacceptable
Maternal mortality	..	..	..	Unacceptable
Level of concern about HIV/AIDS	..	..	Minor concern	Major concern
Measures to respond to HIV/AIDS*	..	..	..	1,2,3,5
Grounds on which abortion is permitted**	..	..	1,2,3,4,5,6,7	1,2,3,4,5,6,7
Spatial distribution and internal migration				
View on spatial distribution	..	..	Minor change desired	Major change desired
Policies on internal migration				
From rural to urban areas	..	..	..	Lower
From rural to rural areas	..	..	..	No intervention
From urban to rural areas	..	..	..	No intervention
From urban to urban areas	..	..	..	No intervention
Into urban agglomerations	..	..	Lower	Lower
International migration				
Immigration				
View	..	..	Too high	Satisfactory
Policy	..	..	Lower	Maintain
Permanent settlement	..	..	Lower	Maintain
Temporary workers	..	..	Lower	Maintain
Highly skilled workers	..	..	..	Maintain
Family reunification	..	..	Lower	Maintain
Integration of non-citizens	..	..	Yes	No
Emigration				
View	..	..	Too high	Too high
Policy	..	..	Lower	Lower
Encouraging the return of citizens	..	..	Yes	Yes

* Measures implemented to respond to HIV/AIDS: (1) blood screening; (2) information/education campaigns; (3) antiretroviral treatment; (4) non–discriminatory policies; (5) distribution of condoms.

** Grounds on which abortion is permitted: (1) to save the woman's life; (2) to preserve physical health; (3) to preserve mental health; (4) rape or incest; (5) foetal impairment; (6) economic or social reasons; (7) on request.

Population indicators

Indicator	1975	1985	1995	2009
Population size and growth				
Population size (thousands)	1 676	1 828	1 963	2 042
Annual growth rate (percentage)*	1.3	0.4	0.6	0.1
Population age structure				
Percentage of population under age 15	31	27	25	18
Percentage of population aged 60 or over	9	10	13	17
Fertility and family planning				
Total fertility (children per woman)*	2.8	2.3	2.1	1.4
Adolescent fertility rate (per 1,000 women, aged 15 - 19)*	..	..	38.0	22.0
Percentage of births to women under age 20*	..	..	9	8
Percentage of births to women aged 35 or over*	..	..	6	8
Percentage of married women using contraception				
Modern methods	..	..	..	10[a]
All methods	..	..	..	14[a]
Health and mortality				
Life expectancy at birth (years)*				
Males	66	68	69	72
Females	69	72	74	77
Both sexes combined	67	70	72	74
Infant mortality rate (per 1,000 live births)*	74	45	27	15
Under-five mortality (per 1,000 live births)*	..	52	30	17
Maternal mortality ratio (per 100,000 live births) (2005)	..	..	..	10
HIV/AIDS				
People living with HIV/AIDS (thousands)	..	..	..	<0.5[b]
Adult prevalence (percentage)	..	..	..	<0.1[b]
Spatial distribution				
Population density (per sq. km)	65	71	76	79
Urban population (percentage)	51	56	60	67
Annual urban population growth rate (percentage)	2.7	1.4	1.4	0.7
Annual rural population growth rate (percentage)	0.3	-0.3	-0.8	-1.5
International migration				
Migrant stock				
Number of migrants (thousands)	..	..	115	130**
As percentage of total population	0.0	0.0	5.8	6.3**

* For the periods 1970-1975, 1980-1985, 1990-1995 and 2005-2010.
** For 2010.
[a] For 2005/2006.
[b] For 2007.

Government views and policies

Population policy variable	1976	1986	1996	2009
Population size and growth				
View on growth	..	..	..	Too high
Policy on growth	..	..	..	No intervention
Population age structure				
Level of concern about				
Size of the working-age population	..	..	..	Major concern
Ageing of the population	..	..	..	Minor concern
Fertility and family planning				
View on fertility level	..	..	..	Too high
Policy	..	..	..	No intervention
Access to contraceptive methods	..	..	..	Direct support
Adolescent fertility				
Level of concern	..	..	..	..
Policies and programmes	..	..	..	..
Health and mortality				
View				
Life expectancy at birth	..	..	..	Unacceptable
Under-five mortality	..	..	..	Unacceptable
Maternal mortality	..	..	..	Unacceptable
Level of concern about HIV/AIDS	..	..	..	Major concern
Measures to respond to HIV/AIDS*	..	..	..	1,2,3,5
Grounds on which abortion is permitted**	..	..	..	1
Spatial distribution and internal migration				
View on spatial distribution	..	..	..	Major change desired
Policies on internal migration				
From rural to urban areas	..	..	..	Raise
From rural to rural areas	..	..	..	..
From urban to rural areas	..	..	..	..
From urban to urban areas	..	..	..	..
Into urban agglomerations	..	..	..	Lower
International migration				
Immigration				
View	..	..	..	Satisfactory
Policy	..	..	..	Maintain
Permanent settlement	..	..	..	Maintain
Temporary workers	..	..	..	Maintain
Highly skilled workers	..	..	..	Maintain
Family reunification	..	..	..	Maintain
Integration of non-citizens	..	..	..	..
Emigration				
View	..	..	..	Satisfactory
Policy	..	..	..	No intervention
Encouraging the return of citizens	..	..	..	..

* Measures implemented to respond to HIV/AIDS: (1) blood screening; (2) information/education campaigns; (3) antiretroviral treatment; (4) non-discriminatory policies; (5) distribution of condoms.
** Grounds on which abortion is permitted: (1) to save the woman's life; (2) to preserve physical health; (3) to preserve mental health; (4) rape or incest; (5) foetal impairment; (6) economic or social reasons; (7) on request.

Population indicators

Indicator	1975	1985	1995	2009
Population size and growth				
Population size (thousands)	672	659	849	1 134
Annual growth rate (percentage)*	2.1	2.5	2.7	3.3
Population age structure				
Percentage of population under age 15	42	40	42	45
Percentage of population aged 60 or over	5	4	4	5
Fertility and family planning				
Total fertility (children per woman)*	6.2	5.4	5.7	6.5
Adolescent fertility rate (per 1,000 women, aged 15 - 19)*	..	..	93.0	54.0
Percentage of births to women under age 20*	..	..	8	4
Percentage of births to women aged 35 or over*	..	..	30	26
Percentage of married women using contraception				
Modern methods	..	..	21[a]	7[b]
All methods	..	..	23[a]	10[b]
Health and mortality				
Life expectancy at birth (years)*				
Males	39	39	48	60
Females	41	41	49	62
Both sexes combined	40	40	49	61
Infant mortality rate (per 1,000 live births)*	183	183	129	67
Under-five mortality (per 1,000 live births)*	..	273	191	92
Maternal mortality ratio (per 100,000 live births) (2005)	..	..	..	380
HIV/AIDS				
People living with HIV/AIDS (thousands)	..	..	..	..
Adult prevalence (percentage)	..	..	..	..
Spatial distribution				
Population density (per sq. km)	45	44	57	76
Urban population (percentage)	15	19	23	28
Annual urban population growth rate (percentage)	0.7	4.9	1.1	4.8
Annual rural population growth rate (percentage)	-2.1	2.0	-0.9	2.7
International migration				
Migrant stock				
Number of migrants (thousands)	9	8	10	14**
As percentage of total population	1.3	1.3	1.1	1.2**

* For the periods 1970-1975, 1980-1985, 1990-1995 and 2005-2010.
** For 2010.
[a] For 1994.
[b] For 2003.

Government views and policies

Population policy variable	1976	1986	1996	2009
Population size and growth				
View on growth	Satisfactory	Satisfactory	Too high	Too high
Policy on growth	No intervention	Maintain	No intervention	Lower
Population age structure				
Level of concern about				
Size of the working-age population	..	..	..	..
Ageing of the population	..	..	..	Minor concern
Fertility and family planning				
View on fertility level	Satisfactory	Satisfactory	Satisfactory	Too high
Policy	No intervention	Maintain	Maintain	Lower
Access to contraceptive methods	Indirect support	Direct support	Direct support	Direct support
Adolescent fertility				
Level of concern	..	..	Major concern	Minor concern
Policies and programmes	..	..	No	Yes
Health and mortality				
View				
Life expectancy at birth	Unacceptable	Unacceptable	Unacceptable	Unacceptable
Under-five mortality	..	..	Unacceptable	Unacceptable
Maternal mortality	..	..	..	Unacceptable
Level of concern about HIV/AIDS	..	..	Major concern	Major concern
Measures to respond to HIV/AIDS*	..	..	..	1,2,3,4,5
Grounds on which abortion is permitted**	..	..	1	1,2,4,5
Spatial distribution and internal migration				
View on spatial distribution	Major change desired	Major change desired	Major change desired	Satisfactory
Policies on internal migration				
From rural to urban areas	..	..	..	No intervention
From rural to rural areas	..	..	..	No intervention
From urban to rural areas	..	..	..	No intervention
From urban to urban areas	..	..	..	No intervention
Into urban agglomerations	No intervention	..	No intervention	No intervention
International migration				
Immigration				
View	Satisfactory	Satisfactory	Satisfactory	Satisfactory
Policy	Maintain	Maintain	No intervention	No intervention
Permanent settlement	..	..	No intervention	No intervention
Temporary workers	..	..	No intervention	No intervention
Highly skilled workers	..	..	..	No intervention
Family reunification	..	..	No intervention	No intervention
Integration of non-citizens	..	..	No	Yes
Emigration				
View	Satisfactory	Satisfactory	Satisfactory	Satisfactory
Policy	Maintain	Maintain	No intervention	No intervention
Encouraging the return of citizens	No	..	No	..

* Measures implemented to respond to HIV/AIDS: (1) blood screening; (2) information/education campaigns; (3) antiretroviral treatment;
(4) non−discriminatory policies; (5) distribution of condoms.
** Grounds on which abortion is permitted: (1) to save the woman's life; (2) to preserve physical health; (3) to preserve mental health; (4) rape or incest;
(5) foetal impairment; (6) economic or social reasons; (7) on request.

Population indicators

Indicator	1975	1985	1995	2009
Population size and growth				
Population size (thousands)	2 448	3 345	4 432	6 619
Annual growth rate (percentage)*	2.8	3.7	2.4	2.5
Population age structure				
Percentage of population under age 15	45	47	45	40
Percentage of population aged 60 or over	5	5	5	5
Fertility and family planning				
Total fertility (children per woman)*	7.2	7.1	6.0	4.3
Adolescent fertility rate (per 1,000 women, aged 15 - 19)*	..	..	110.0	65.0
Percentage of births to women under age 20*	..	..	9	8
Percentage of births to women aged 35 or over*	..	..	29	25
Percentage of married women using contraception				
Modern methods	..	3[a]	7[b]	11[c]
All methods	..	34[a]	24[b]	17[c]
Health and mortality				
Life expectancy at birth (years)*				
Males	49	54	56	61
Females	52	58	60	64
Both sexes combined	51	56	58	62
Infant mortality rate (per 1,000 live births)*	130	107	99	71
Under-five mortality (per 1,000 live births)*	..	166	145	98
Maternal mortality ratio (per 100,000 live births) (2005)	..	..	..	510
HIV/AIDS				
People living with HIV/AIDS (thousands)	..	..	69	130[d]
Adult prevalence (percentage)	..	..	3.0	3.3[d]
Spatial distribution				
Population density (per sq. km)	43	59	78	117
Urban population (percentage)	23	27	33	43
Annual urban population growth rate (percentage)	3.8	5.7	5.3	4.2
Annual rural population growth rate (percentage)	1.9	2.8	2.4	1.3
International migration				
Migrant stock				
Number of migrants (thousands)	149	156	169	185**
As percentage of total population	6.1	4.7	3.8	2.7**

* For the periods 1970-1975, 1980-1985, 1990-1995 and 2005-2010.
** For 2010.
[a] For 1988.
[b] For 1998.
[c] For 2006.
[d] For 2007.

Government views and policies

Population policy variable	1976	1986	1996	2009
Population size and growth				
View on growth	Too high	Too high	Too low	Too low
Policy on growth	Lower	Lower	No intervention	No intervention
Population age structure				
Level of concern about				
Size of the working-age population	..	..	..	Minor concern
Ageing of the population	..	..	..	Minor concern
Fertility and family planning				
View on fertility level	Too high	Too high	Satisfactory	Satisfactory
Policy	Lower	Lower	Maintain	Maintain
Access to contraceptive methods	Direct support	Direct support	Direct support	Direct support
Adolescent fertility				
Level of concern	..	..	Minor concern	Minor concern
Policies and programmes	..	..	No	No
Health and mortality				
View				
Life expectancy at birth	Unacceptable	Unacceptable	Unacceptable	Unacceptable
Under-five mortality	..	..	..	Unacceptable
Maternal mortality	..	..	..	Unacceptable
Level of concern about HIV/AIDS	..	..	Major concern	Major concern
Measures to respond to HIV/AIDS*	..	..	..	1
Grounds on which abortion is permitted**	..	..	1	1
Spatial distribution and internal migration				
View on spatial distribution	Minor change desired	Minor change desired	Satisfactory	Minor change desired
Policies on internal migration				
From rural to urban areas	..	..	..	Lower
From rural to rural areas	..	..	..	..
From urban to rural areas	..	..	..	..
From urban to urban areas	..	..	..	..
Into urban agglomerations	..	..	Maintain	Lower
International migration				
Immigration				
View	Satisfactory	Satisfactory	Satisfactory	Satisfactory
Policy	Maintain	Maintain	Maintain	Maintain
Permanent settlement	..	..	Maintain	..
Temporary workers	..	..	Maintain	Lower
Highly skilled workers	..	..	..	Maintain
Family reunification	..	..	Maintain	..
Integration of non-citizens	..	..	No	..
Emigration				
View	Satisfactory	Satisfactory	Satisfactory	Satisfactory
Policy	Maintain	Maintain	Maintain	Maintain
Encouraging the return of citizens	..	..	No	..

* Measures implemented to respond to HIV/AIDS: (1) blood screening; (2) information/education campaigns; (3) antiretroviral treatment; (4) non-discriminatory policies; (5) distribution of condoms.
** Grounds on which abortion is permitted: (1) to save the woman's life; (2) to preserve physical health; (3) to preserve mental health; (4) rape or incest; (5) foetal impairment; (6) economic or social reasons; (7) on request.

Population indicators

Indicator	1975	1985	1995	2009
Population size and growth				
Population size (thousands)	94	93	97	104
Annual growth rate (percentage)*	-1.0	-0.9	0.6	0.5
Population age structure				
Percentage of population under age 15	47	41	40	37
Percentage of population aged 60 or over	4	6	8	8
Fertility and family planning				
Total fertility (children per woman)*	5.5	5.5	4.5	4.0
Adolescent fertility rate (per 1,000 women, aged 15 - 19)*	..	..	20.0	23.0
Percentage of births to women under age 20*	..	..	2	3
Percentage of births to women aged 35 or over*	..	..	32	26
Percentage of married women using contraception				
Modern methods	..	..	..	..
All methods	..	..	..	..
Health and mortality				
Life expectancy at birth (years)*				
Males	65	67	68	69
Females	67	70	71	75
Both sexes combined	66	68	70	72
Infant mortality rate (per 1,000 live births)*	37	31	26	22
Under-five mortality (per 1,000 live births)*	..	38	32	26
Maternal mortality ratio (per 100,000 live births) (2005)	..	..	..	..
HIV/AIDS				
People living with HIV/AIDS (thousands)	..	..	..	..
Adult prevalence (percentage)	..	..	..	..
Spatial distribution				
Population density (per sq. km)	144	143	150	160
Urban population (percentage)	20	22	23	25
Annual urban population growth rate (percentage)	0.2	0.8	0.4	1.7
Annual rural population growth rate (percentage)	0.1	-0.5	0.2	0.0
International migration				
Migrant stock				
Number of migrants (thousands)	1	3	2	1**
As percentage of total population	1.0	3.7	2.3	0.8**

* For the periods 1970-1975, 1980-1985, 1990-1995 and 2005-2010.
** For 2010.

Government views and policies

Population policy variable	1976	1986	1996	2009
Population size and growth				
View on growth	Too high	Too high	Too high	Satisfactory
Policy on growth	Lower	Lower	Lower	Maintain
Population age structure				
Level of concern about				
Size of the working-age population	..	..	..	Major concern
Ageing of the population	..	..	..	Major concern
Fertility and family planning				
View on fertility level	Too high	Too high	Too high	Satisfactory
Policy	Lower	Lower	Lower	Maintain
Access to contraceptive methods	Direct support	Direct support	Direct support	Direct support
Adolescent fertility				
Level of concern	..	..	..	Major concern
Policies and programmes	..	..	..	Yes
Health and mortality				
View				
Life expectancy at birth	Acceptable	Acceptable	Acceptable	Unacceptable
Under-five mortality	..	..	Acceptable	Unacceptable
Maternal mortality	..	..		Unacceptable
Level of concern about HIV/AIDS	..	..	Major concern	Major concern
Measures to respond to HIV/AIDS*	..	..	..	1,2,3,5
Grounds on which abortion is permitted**	..	..	1,2,3	1,2,3
Spatial distribution and internal migration				
View on spatial distribution	Major change desired	Major change desired	Major change desired	Minor change desired
Policies on internal migration				
From rural to urban areas	..	..	..	Lower
From rural to rural areas	..	..	..	..
From urban to rural areas	..	..	..	..
From urban to urban areas	..	..	..	..
Into urban agglomerations	No intervention	..	..	Lower
International migration				
Immigration				
View	Satisfactory	Satisfactory	Satisfactory	Satisfactory
Policy	Maintain	Maintain	Maintain	Maintain
Permanent settlement	..	..	..	Maintain
Temporary workers	..	..	..	Maintain
Highly skilled workers	..	..	..	Maintain
Family reunification	..	..	..	Maintain
Integration of non-citizens	..	..	..	Yes
Emigration				
View	Too high	Too high	Too high	Too high
Policy	Lower	Lower	Lower	No intervention
Encouraging the return of citizens	Yes	..	..	No

* Measures implemented to respond to HIV/AIDS: (1) blood screening; (2) information/education campaigns; (3) antiretroviral treatment; (4) non-discriminatory policies; (5) distribution of condoms.
** Grounds on which abortion is permitted: (1) to save the woman's life; (2) to preserve physical health; (3) to preserve mental health; (4) rape or incest; (5) foetal impairment; (6) economic or social reasons; (7) on request.

Population indicators

Indicator	1975	1985	1995	2009
Population size and growth				
Population size (thousands)	1 012	1 176	1 265	1 339
Annual growth rate (percentage)*	0.8	1.7	0.7	0.4
Population age structure				
Percentage of population under age 15	38	34	31	21
Percentage of population aged 60 or over	8	8	8	10
Fertility and family planning				
Total fertility (children per woman)*	3.5	3.2	2.1	1.6
Adolescent fertility rate (per 1,000 women, aged 15 - 19)*	..	..	54.0	35.0
Percentage of births to women under age 20*	..	..	13	11
Percentage of births to women aged 35 or over*	..	..	13	14
Percentage of married women using contraception				
Modern methods	46[a]	44[b]	..	38[c]
All methods	52[a]	53[b]	..	43[c]
Health and mortality				
Life expectancy at birth (years)*				
Males	64	65	65	66
Females	68	71	73	73
Both sexes combined	66	68	69	69
Infant mortality rate (per 1,000 live births)*	41	31	28	26
Under-five mortality (per 1,000 live births)*	..	40	34	33
Maternal mortality ratio (per 100,000 live births) (2005)	..	..	..	45
HIV/AIDS				
People living with HIV/AIDS (thousands)	..	..	7.3	14[d]
Adult prevalence (percentage)	..	..	1.0	1.5[d]
Spatial distribution				
Population density (per sq. km)	197	229	247	261
Urban population (percentage)	11	10	10	14
Annual urban population growth rate (percentage)	0.2	-1.4	3.0	2.9
Annual rural population growth rate (percentage)	1.2	1.3	0.3	0.0
International migration				
Migrant stock				
Number of migrants (thousands)	61	56	46	34**
As percentage of total population	6.0	4.7	3.6	2.6**

* For the periods 1970-1975, 1980-1985, 1990-1995 and 2005-2010.
** For 2010.
[a] For 1977.
[b] For 1987.
[c] For 2006.
[d] For 2007.

Government views and policies

Population policy variable	1976	1986	1996	2009
Population size and growth				
View on growth	Too high	Too high	Satisfactory	Satisfactory
Policy on growth	Lower	Lower	Lower	Lower
Population age structure				
Level of concern about				
Size of the working-age population	..	..	..	Major concern
Ageing of the population	..	..	..	Minor concern
Fertility and family planning				
View on fertility level	Too high	Too high	Too high	Satisfactory
Policy	Lower	Lower	Lower	Lower
Access to contraceptive methods	Direct support	Direct support	Direct support	Direct support
Adolescent fertility				
Level of concern	..	..	Not a concern	Not a concern
Policies and programmes	..	..	No	No
Health and mortality				
View				
Life expectancy at birth	Unacceptable	Unacceptable	Acceptable	Acceptable
Under-five mortality	..	..	..	Acceptable
Maternal mortality	..	..	..	Unacceptable
Level of concern about HIV/AIDS	..	..	..	Minor concern
Measures to respond to HIV/AIDS*	..	..	..	1,2,3,4,5
Grounds on which abortion is permitted**	..	..	1,2,3,4,5,6,7	1,2,3,4,5,6,7
Spatial distribution and internal migration				
View on spatial distribution	Minor change desired	Major change desired	Major change desired	Minor change desired
Policies on internal migration				
From rural to urban areas	..	..	..	Lower
From rural to rural areas	..	..	..	No intervention
From urban to rural areas	..	..	..	No intervention
From urban to urban areas	..	..	..	No intervention
Into urban agglomerations	Lower	Lower	Lower	Lower
International migration				
Immigration				
View	Satisfactory	Satisfactory	Satisfactory	Satisfactory
Policy	Maintain	Maintain	Maintain	No intervention
Permanent settlement	..	..	..	No intervention
Temporary workers	..	..	..	No intervention
Highly skilled workers	..	..	..	No intervention
Family reunification	..	..	..	No intervention
Integration of non-citizens	..	..	..	No
Emigration				
View	Satisfactory	Satisfactory	Satisfactory	Satisfactory
Policy	Maintain	Maintain	Raise	Raise
Encouraging the return of citizens	Yes	..	No	No

* Measures implemented to respond to HIV/AIDS: (1) blood screening; (2) information/education campaigns; (3) antiretroviral treatment; (4) non-discriminatory policies; (5) distribution of condoms.
** Grounds on which abortion is permitted: (1) to save the woman's life; (2) to preserve physical health; (3) to preserve mental health; (4) rape or incest; (5) foetal impairment; (6) economic or social reasons; (7) on request.

Population indicators

Indicator	1975	1985	1995	2009
Population size and growth				
Population size (thousands)	5 668	7 330	8 935	10 272
Annual growth rate (percentage)*	2.0	2.5	1.7	1.0
Population age structure				
Percentage of population under age 15	44	40	34	23
Percentage of population aged 60 or over	6	6	9	10
Fertility and family planning				
Total fertility (children per woman)*	6.2	4.9	3.1	1.9
Adolescent fertility rate (per 1,000 women, aged 15 - 19)*	..	..	18.0	7.0
Percentage of births to women under age 20*	..	..	3	2
Percentage of births to women aged 35 or over*	..	..	24	23
Percentage of married women using contraception				
Modern methods	25[a]	34[b]	51[c]	52[d]
All methods	31[a]	41[b]	60[c]	60[d]
Health and mortality				
Life expectancy at birth (years)*				
Males	55	63	68	72
Females	56	66	72	76
Both sexes combined	56	64	70	74
Infant mortality rate (per 1,000 live births)*	119	64	34	20
Under-five mortality (per 1,000 live births)*	..	80	40	22
Maternal mortality ratio (per 100,000 live births) (2005)	..	..	..	100
HIV/AIDS				
People living with HIV/AIDS (thousands)	..	..	<1	3.7[e]
Adult prevalence (percentage)	..	..	..	0.1[e]
Spatial distribution				
Population density (per sq. km)	35	45	55	63
Urban population (percentage)	48	54	61	67
Annual urban population growth rate (percentage)	3.7	4.0	2.1	1.6
Annual rural population growth rate (percentage)	1.3	0.6	0.4	-0.1
International migration				
Migrant stock				
Number of migrants (thousands)	38	38	38	34**
As percentage of total population	0.7	0.5	0.4	0.3**

* For the periods 1970-1975, 1980-1985, 1990-1995 and 2005-2010.
** For 2010.
[a] For 1978.
[b] For 1983.
[c] For 1994/1995.
[d] For 2006.
[e] For 2007.

Government views and policies

Population policy variable	1976	1986	1996	2009
Population size and growth				
View on growth	Too high	Too high	Too high	Satisfactory
Policy on growth	Lower	Lower	Lower	Maintain
Population age structure				
Level of concern about				
Size of the working-age population	..	..	..	Major concern
Ageing of the population	..	..	..	Minor concern
Fertility and family planning				
View on fertility level	Too high	Too high	Too high	Satisfactory
Policy	Lower	Lower	Lower	Maintain
Access to contraceptive methods	Direct support	Direct support	Direct support	Direct support
Adolescent fertility				
Level of concern	..	..	Not a concern	Minor concern
Policies and programmes	..	..	No	Yes
Health and mortality				
View				
Life expectancy at birth	Unacceptable	Unacceptable	Unacceptable	Acceptable
Under-five mortality	..	..	Unacceptable	Acceptable
Maternal mortality	..	..	..	Unacceptable
Level of concern about HIV/AIDS	..	..	Minor concern	Minor concern
Measures to respond to HIV/AIDS*	..	..	..	1,2,3,4,5
Grounds on which abortion is permitted**	..	..	1,2,3,4,5,6,7	1,2,3,4,5,6,7
Spatial distribution and internal migration				
View on spatial distribution	Major change desired	Minor change desired	Minor change desired	Minor change desired
Policies on internal migration				
From rural to urban areas	..	..	..	Lower
From rural to rural areas	..	..	..	No intervention
From urban to rural areas	..	..	..	Raise
From urban to urban areas	..	..	..	No intervention
Into urban agglomerations	Lower	Lower	Lower	Lower
International migration				
Immigration				
View	Satisfactory	Satisfactory	Satisfactory	Satisfactory
Policy	Maintain	Maintain	Lower	No intervention
Permanent settlement	..	..	Lower	No intervention
Temporary workers	..	..	Maintain	No intervention
Highly skilled workers	..	..	..	No intervention
Family reunification	..	..	Maintain	No intervention
Integration of non-citizens	..	..	No	Yes
Emigration				
View	Too low	Too low	Satisfactory	Satisfactory
Policy	Raise	Raise	Maintain	Maintain
Encouraging the return of citizens	No	..	No	No

* Measures implemented to respond to HIV/AIDS: (1) blood screening; (2) information/education campaigns; (3) antiretroviral treatment; (4) non-discriminatory policies; (5) distribution of condoms.
** Grounds on which abortion is permitted: (1) to save the woman's life; (2) to preserve physical health; (3) to preserve mental health; (4) rape or incest; (5) foetal impairment; (6) economic or social reasons; (7) on request.

Population indicators

Indicator	1975	1985	1995	2009
Population size and growth				
Population size (thousands)	41 211	51 289	61 206	74 816
Annual growth rate (percentage)*	2.6	2.1	1.7	1.2
Population age structure				
Percentage of population under age 15	41	39	33	27
Percentage of population aged 60 or over	7	6	7	9
Fertility and family planning				
Total fertility (children per woman)*	5.5	4.0	2.9	2.1
Adolescent fertility rate (per 1,000 women, aged 15 - 19)*	..	..	62.0	39.0
Percentage of births to women under age 20*	..	..	11	9
Percentage of births to women aged 35 or over*	..	..	10	13
Percentage of married women using contraception				
Modern methods	14[a]	31[b]	38[c]	43[d]
All methods	38[a]	63[b]	64[c]	71[d]
Health and mortality				
Life expectancy at birth (years)*				
Males	55	59	64	69
Females	59	63	69	74
Both sexes combined	57	61	66	72
Infant mortality rate (per 1,000 live births)*	138	93	54	28
Under-five mortality (per 1,000 live births)*	..	116	65	32
Maternal mortality ratio (per 100,000 live births) (2005)	..	..	..	44
HIV/AIDS				
People living with HIV/AIDS (thousands)	..	..	..	<2[e]
Adult prevalence (percentage)	..	..	..	..
Spatial distribution				
Population density (per sq. km)	53	65	78	95
Urban population (percentage)	42	52	62	69
Annual urban population growth rate (percentage)	3.6	4.8	2.6	1.9
Annual rural population growth rate (percentage)	1.5	-1.1	0.3	-0.3
International migration				
Migrant stock				
Number of migrants (thousands)	145	933	1 212	1 411**
As percentage of total population	0.4	1.8	2.0	1.9**

* For the periods 1970-1975, 1980-1985, 1990-1995 and 2005-2010.
** For 2010.
[a] For 1978.
[b] For 1988.
[c] For 1998.
[d] For 2003.
[e] For 2007.

Government views and policies

Population policy variable	1976	1986	1996	2009
Population size and growth				
View on growth	..	..	Satisfactory	Too low
Policy on growth	..	..	No intervention	Raise
Population age structure				
Level of concern about				
Size of the working-age population	..	..	..	..
Ageing of the population	..	..	..	Minor concern
Fertility and family planning				
View on fertility level	..	..	Satisfactory	Too low
Policy	..	..	No intervention	Raise
Access to contraceptive methods	..	..	No support	Indirect support
Adolescent fertility				
Level of concern	..	..	..	Minor concern
Policies and programmes	..	..	Yes	Yes
Health and mortality				
View				
Life expectancy at birth	..	..	Unacceptable	Unacceptable
Under-five mortality	..	..	..	Unacceptable
Maternal mortality	..	..	..	Unacceptable
Level of concern about HIV/AIDS	..	..	..	Major concern
Measures to respond to HIV/AIDS*	..	..	..	1,2,4
Grounds on which abortion is permitted**	..	..	1,2,3,4,5,6,7	1,2,3,4,5,6,7
Spatial distribution and internal migration				
View on spatial distribution	..	..	Minor change desired	Minor change desired
Policies on internal migration				
From rural to urban areas	..	..	..	..
From rural to rural areas	..	..	..	..
From urban to rural areas	..	..	..	..
From urban to urban areas	..	..	..	..
Into urban agglomerations	..	..	..	..
International migration				
Immigration				
View	..	..	Satisfactory	Satisfactory
Policy	..	..	No intervention	Lower
Permanent settlement	..	..	..	Lower
Temporary workers	..	..	..	Lower
Highly skilled workers	..	..	..	..
Family reunification	..	..	..	..
Integration of non-citizens	..	..	..	No
Emigration				
View	..	..	Too high	Too high
Policy	..	..	No intervention	Lower
Encouraging the return of citizens	..	..	..	..

* Measures implemented to respond to HIV/AIDS: (1) blood screening; (2) information/education campaigns; (3) antiretroviral treatment; (4) non-discriminatory policies; (5) distribution of condoms.
** Grounds on which abortion is permitted: (1) to save the woman's life; (2) to preserve physical health; (3) to preserve mental health; (4) rape or incest; (5) foetal impairment; (6) economic or social reasons; (7) on request.

Population indicators

Indicator	1975	1985	1995	2009
Population size and growth				
Population size (thousands)	2 520	3 229	4 187	5 110
Annual growth rate (percentage)*	2.8	2.4	2.6	1.3
Population age structure				
Percentage of population under age 15	43	41	39	29
Percentage of population aged 60 or over	7	6	6	6
Fertility and family planning				
Total fertility (children per woman)*	6.2	4.8	4.0	2.5
Adolescent fertility rate (per 1,000 women, aged 15 - 19)*	..	..	23.0	20.0
Percentage of births to women under age 20*	..	..	3	4
Percentage of births to women aged 35 or over*	..	..	16	10
Percentage of married women using contraception				
Modern methods	..	..	..	45[a]
All methods	..	..	..	62[a]
Health and mortality				
Life expectancy at birth (years)*				
Males	56	58	59	61
Females	63	65	67	69
Both sexes combined	59	62	63	65
Infant mortality rate (per 1,000 live births)*	111	91	75	50
Under-five mortality (per 1,000 live births)*	..	117	96	64
Maternal mortality ratio (per 100,000 live births) (2005)	..	..	..	130
HIV/AIDS				
People living with HIV/AIDS (thousands)	..	..	..	<0.5[b]
Adult prevalence (percentage)	..	..	..	<0.1[b]
Spatial distribution				
Population density (per sq. km)	5	7	9	10
Urban population (percentage)	48	46	45	49
Annual urban population growth rate (percentage)	2.5	2.0	2.1	2.2
Annual rural population growth rate (percentage)	2.7	2.9	1.6	0.4
International migration				
Migrant stock				
Number of migrants (thousands)	..	..	260	208**
As percentage of total population	0.0	0.0	6.2	4.0**

* For the periods 1970-1975, 1980-1985, 1990-1995 and 2005-2010.
** For 2010.
[a] For 2000.
[b] For 2007.

Government views and policies

Population policy variable	1976	1986	1996	2009
Population size and growth				
View on growth	..	Too high	Too high	Too high
Policy on growth	..	Lower	Lower	Lower
Population age structure				
Level of concern about				
Size of the working-age population	..	..	..	..
Ageing of the population	..	..	..	..
Fertility and family planning				
View on fertility level	..	Too high	Too high	Too high
Policy	..	Lower	Lower	Lower
Access to contraceptive methods	..	Direct support	Direct support	Direct support
Adolescent fertility				
Level of concern	..	..	..	Major concern
Policies and programmes	..	..	..	Yes
Health and mortality				
View				
Life expectancy at birth	..	Unacceptable	Unacceptable	Unacceptable
Under-five mortality	..	..	..	Unacceptable
Maternal mortality	..	..	..	Acceptable
Level of concern about HIV/AIDS	..	..	..	Major concern
Measures to respond to HIV/AIDS*	..	..	..	1,2,3,5
Grounds on which abortion is permitted**	..	..	1	1
Spatial distribution and internal migration				
View on spatial distribution	..	Minor change desired	Major change desired	Major change desired
Policies on internal migration				
From rural to urban areas	..	..	..	Lower
From rural to rural areas	..	..	..	..
From urban to rural areas	..	..	..	..
From urban to urban areas	..	..	..	..
Into urban agglomerations	..	..	..	Lower
International migration				
Immigration				
View	..	Satisfactory	Satisfactory	Satisfactory
Policy	..	Maintain	Maintain	Maintain
Permanent settlement	..	..	..	..
Temporary workers	..	..	..	..
Highly skilled workers	..	..	..	..
Family reunification	..	..	..	..
Integration of non-citizens	..	..	..	..
Emigration				
View	..	Satisfactory	Satisfactory	Too low
Policy	..	Maintain	Maintain	Raise
Encouraging the return of citizens	..	..	..	..

* Measures implemented to respond to HIV/AIDS: (1) blood screening; (2) information/education campaigns; (3) antiretroviral treatment;
(4) non-discriminatory policies; (5) distribution of condoms.
** Grounds on which abortion is permitted: (1) to save the woman's life; (2) to preserve physical health; (3) to preserve mental health; (4) rape or incest;
(5) foetal impairment; (6) economic or social reasons; (7) on request.

Population indicators

Indicator	1975	1985	1995	2009
Population size and growth				
Population size (thousands)	8	9	9	10
Annual growth rate (percentage)*	1.0	1.4	0.7	0.4
Population age structure				
Percentage of population under age 15	..	..	..	..
Percentage of population aged 60 or over	..	..	..	..
Fertility and family planning				
Total fertility (children per woman)*	..	..	..	..
Adolescent fertility rate (per 1,000 women, aged 15 - 19)*	..	..	..	..
Percentage of births to women under age 20*	..	..	..	..
Percentage of births to women aged 35 or over*	..	..	..	..
Percentage of married women using contraception				
Modern methods	..	..	..	..
All methods	..	..	..	..
Health and mortality				
Life expectancy at birth (years)*				
Males	..	..	..	..
Females	..	..	..	..
Both sexes combined	..	..	..	..
Infant mortality rate (per 1,000 live births)*	..	..	..	..
Under-five mortality (per 1,000 live births)*	..	..	..	..
Maternal mortality ratio (per 100,000 live births) (2005)	..	..	..	..
HIV/AIDS				
People living with HIV/AIDS (thousands)	..	..	..	..
Adult prevalence (percentage)	..	..	..	..
Spatial distribution				
Population density (per sq. km)	296	333	355	382
Urban population (percentage)	26	34	44	50
Annual urban population growth rate (percentage)	3.9	5.4	1.7	1.3
Annual rural population growth rate (percentage)	-0.2	-0.1	0.0	-0.5
International migration				
Migrant stock				
Number of migrants (thousands)	0	0	0	0**
As percentage of total population	4,5	3.8	2.9	1.5**

* For the periods 1970-1975, 1980-1985, 1990-1995 and 2005-2010.
** For 2010.

Government views and policies

Population policy variable	1976	1986	1996	2009
Population size and growth				
View on growth	Too high	Too high	Too high	Too high
Policy on growth	Lower	Lower	Lower	Lower
Population age structure				
Level of concern about				
Size of the working-age population	..	..	..	Major concern
Ageing of the population	..	..	..	Major concern
Fertility and family planning				
View on fertility level	Too high	Too high	Too high	Too high
Policy	Lower	Lower	Lower	Lower
Access to contraceptive methods	Direct support	Direct support	Direct support	Direct support
Adolescent fertility				
Level of concern	..	..	Major concern	Major concern
Policies and programmes	..	..	Yes	Yes
Health and mortality				
View				
Life expectancy at birth	Unacceptable	Unacceptable	Unacceptable	Unacceptable
Under-five mortality	..	..	Unacceptable	Unacceptable
Maternal mortality	..	..	..	Unacceptable
Level of concern about HIV/AIDS	..	..	Major concern	Major concern
Measures to respond to HIV/AIDS*	..	..	..	1,2,3,4,5
Grounds on which abortion is permitted**	..	..	1,2,3	1,2,3
Spatial distribution and internal migration				
View on spatial distribution	Minor change desired	Minor change desired	Minor change desired	Minor change desired
Policies on internal migration				
From rural to urban areas	..	..	..	Lower
From rural to rural areas	..	..	..	..
From urban to rural areas	..	..	..	..
From urban to urban areas	..	..	..	..
Into urban agglomerations	Lower	No intervention	Lower	Lower
International migration				
Immigration				
View	Satisfactory	Satisfactory	Satisfactory	Satisfactory
Policy	Maintain	Maintain	Maintain	Maintain
Permanent settlement	..	..	No intervention	Maintain
Temporary workers	..	..	Maintain	..
Highly skilled workers	..	..	..	..
Family reunification	..	..	No intervention	..
Integration of non-citizens	..	..	Yes	No
Emigration				
View	Satisfactory	Satisfactory	Satisfactory	Satisfactory
Policy	Maintain	Maintain	No intervention	No intervention
Encouraging the return of citizens	No	..	Yes	..

* Measures implemented to respond to HIV/AIDS: (1) blood screening; (2) information/education campaigns; (3) antiretroviral treatment;
(4) non−discriminatory policies; (5) distribution of condoms.
** Grounds on which abortion is permitted: (1) to save the woman's life; (2) to preserve physical health; (3) to preserve mental health; (4) rape or incest;
(5) foetal impairment; (6) economic or social reasons; (7) on request.

Population indicators

Indicator	1975	1985	1995	2009
Population size and growth				
Population size (thousands)	10 893	14 795	20 954	32 710
Annual growth rate (percentage)*	2.9	3.1	3.3	3.3
Population age structure				
Percentage of population under age 15	47	48	49	49
Percentage of population aged 60 or over	4	4	4	4
Fertility and family planning				
Total fertility (children per woman)*	7.1	7.1	7.1	6.4
Adolescent fertility rate (per 1,000 women, aged 15 - 19)*	..	..	201.0	150.0
Percentage of births to women under age 20*	..	..	14	12
Percentage of births to women aged 35 or over*	..	..	22	20
Percentage of married women using contraception				
Modern methods	..	3[a]	8	18[b]
All methods	..	5[a]	15	24[b]
Health and mortality				
Life expectancy at birth (years)*				
Males	50	48	45	52
Females	53	51	48	53
Both sexes combined	51	50	46	52
Infant mortality rate (per 1,000 live births)*	103	108	95	74
Under-five mortality (per 1,000 live births)*	..	182	163	122
Maternal mortality ratio (per 100,000 live births) (2005)	..	..	..	550
HIV/AIDS				
People living with HIV/AIDS (thousands)	..	..	1 300	940[c]
Adult prevalence (percentage)	..	..	11.8	5.4[c]
Spatial distribution				
Population density (per sq. km)	45	61	87	136
Urban population (percentage)	7	9	12	13
Annual urban population growth rate (percentage)	4.0	7.4	3.8	4.6
Annual rural population growth rate (percentage)	2.9	3.2	3.0	3.0
International migration				
Migrant stock				
Number of migrants (thousands)	775	633	661	647**
As percentage of total population	7.1	4.3	3.2	1.9**

* For the periods 1970-1975, 1980-1985, 1990-1995 and 2005-2010.
** For 2010.
[a] For 1988/1989.
[b] For 2006.
[c] For 2007.

Government views and policies

Population policy variable	1976	1986	1996	2009
Population size and growth				
View on growth	Too low	Satisfactory	Too low	Too low
Policy on growth	Raise	Maintain	Raise	Raise
Population age structure				
Level of concern about				
Size of the working-age population	..	..	..	Major concern
Ageing of the population	..	..	..	Major concern
Fertility and family planning				
View on fertility level	Satisfactory	Satisfactory	Too low	Too low
Policy	Maintain	Maintain	Raise	Raise
Access to contraceptive methods	Direct support	Direct support	Direct support	Indirect support
Adolescent fertility				
Level of concern	..	..	Major concern	Not a concern
Policies and programmes	..	..	Yes	Yes
Health and mortality				
View				
Life expectancy at birth	Unacceptable	Acceptable	Unacceptable	Unacceptable
Under-five mortality	..	..	Unacceptable	Unacceptable
Maternal mortality	..	..	..	Unacceptable
Level of concern about HIV/AIDS	..	..	Major concern	Major concern
Measures to respond to HIV/AIDS*	..	..	..	1,2,3,4,5
Grounds on which abortion is permitted**	..	..	1,2,3,4,5,6,7	1,2,3,4,5,6,7
Spatial distribution and internal migration				
View on spatial distribution	Minor change desired	Minor change desired	Minor change desired	Satisfactory
Policies on internal migration				
From rural to urban areas	..	..	..	No intervention
From rural to rural areas	..	..	..	No intervention
From urban to rural areas	..	..	..	No intervention
From urban to urban areas	..	..	..	No intervention
Into urban agglomerations	..	Lower	Lower	No intervention
International migration				
Immigration				
View	Satisfactory	Satisfactory	Satisfactory	Satisfactory
Policy	Maintain	Maintain	No intervention	Maintain
Permanent settlement	..	..	No intervention	Maintain
Temporary workers	..	..	No intervention	Maintain
Highly skilled workers	..	..	..	Maintain
Family reunification	..	..	No intervention	Maintain
Integration of non-citizens	..	..	No	No
Emigration				
View	Satisfactory	Satisfactory	Too high	Satisfactory
Policy	Maintain	Maintain	Lower	Lower
Encouraging the return of citizens	...	..	Yes	Yes

* Measures implemented to respond to HIV/AIDS: (1) blood screening; (2) information/education campaigns; (3) antiretroviral treatment; (4) non−discriminatory policies; (5) distribution of condoms.
** Grounds on which abortion is permitted: (1) to save the woman's life; (2) to preserve physical health; (3) to preserve mental health; (4) rape or incest; (5) foetal impairment; (6) economic or social reasons; (7) on request.

Population indicators

Indicator	1975	1985	1995	2009
Population size and growth				
Population size (thousands)	49 016	50 915	51 063	45 708
Annual growth rate (percentage)*	0.7	0.3	-0.2	-0.7
Population age structure				
Percentage of population under age 15	23	22	20	14
Percentage of population aged 60 or over	16	16	18	21
Fertility and family planning				
Total fertility (children per woman)*	2.2	2.0	1.6	1.3
Adolescent fertility rate (per 1,000 women, aged 15 - 19)*	..	..	59.0	28.0
Percentage of births to women under age 20*	..	..	18	11
Percentage of births to women aged 35 or over*	..	..	5	7
Percentage of married women using contraception				
Modern methods	..	..	38[a]	48[b]
All methods	..	..	68[a]	67[b]
Health and mortality				
Life expectancy at birth (years)*				
Males	65	64	64	63
Females	74	74	74	74
Both sexes combined	70	69	69	68
Infant mortality rate (per 1,000 live births)*	22	20	17	12
Under-five mortality (per 1,000 live births)*	..	25	21	15
Maternal mortality ratio (per 100,000 live births) (2005)	..	..	..	18
HIV/AIDS				
People living with HIV/AIDS (thousands)	..	..	7.9	440[b]
Adult prevalence (percentage)	..	..	..	1.6[b]
Spatial distribution				
Population density (per sq. km)	81	84	85	76
Urban population (percentage)	58	65	67	68
Annual urban population growth rate (percentage)	1.7	1.2	-0.6	-0.6
Annual rural population growth rate (percentage)	-1.1	-1.3	-0.8	-1.0
International migration				
Migrant stock				
Number of migrants (thousands)	..	..	6 172	5 258**
As percentage of total population	0.0	0.0	12.1	11.6**

* For the periods 1970-1975, 1980-1985, 1990-1995 and 2005-2010.
** For 2010.
[a] For 1999.
[b] For 2007.

Government views and policies

Population policy variable	1976	1986	1996	2009
Population size and growth				
View on growth	Too low	Satisfactory	Too high	Satisfactory
Policy on growth	Raise	Raise	No intervention	Lower
Population age structure				
Level of concern about				
Size of the working-age population	..	..	..	Major concern
Ageing of the population	..	..	..	Major concern
Fertility and family planning				
View on fertility level	Satisfactory	Satisfactory	Satisfactory	Satisfactory
Policy	Maintain	Raise	No intervention	Maintain
Access to contraceptive methods	No support	No support	No support	No support
Adolescent fertility				
Level of concern	..	..	..	Not a concern
Policies and programmes	..	..	..	No
Health and mortality				
View				
Life expectancy at birth	Acceptable	Acceptable	Acceptable	Acceptable
Under-five mortality	..	..	..	Acceptable
Maternal mortality	..	..	..	Acceptable
Level of concern about HIV/AIDS	..	..	..	Minor concern
Measures to respond to HIV/AIDS*	..	..	..	1,2,3,4
Grounds on which abortion is permitted**	..	..	1	1
Spatial distribution and internal migration				
View on spatial distribution	Minor change desired	Minor change desired	Satisfactory	Satisfactory
Policies on internal migration				
From rural to urban areas	..	..	..	No intervention
From rural to rural areas	..	..	..	No intervention
From urban to rural areas	..	..	..	No intervention
From urban to urban areas	..	..	..	No intervention
Into urban agglomerations	..	No intervention	..	No intervention
International migration				
Immigration				
View	Satisfactory	Too high	Too high	Too high
Policy	Maintain	Lower	Lower	Lower
Permanent settlement	..	..	..	Lower
Temporary workers	..	..	..	Maintain
Highly skilled workers	..	..	..	Maintain
Family reunification	..	..	..	Lower
Integration of non-citizens	..	..	..	..
Emigration				
View	Satisfactory	Satisfactory	Satisfactory	Satisfactory
Policy	Maintain	Maintain	No intervention	No intervention
Encouraging the return of citizens	..	..	..	Yes

* Measures implemented to respond to HIV/AIDS: (1) blood screening; (2) information/education campaigns; (3) antiretroviral treatment; (4) non-discriminatory policies; (5) distribution of condoms.
** Grounds on which abortion is permitted: (1) to save the woman's life; (2) to preserve physical health; (3) to preserve mental health; (4) rape or incest; (5) foetal impairment; (6) economic or social reasons; (7) on request.

Population indicators

Indicator	1975	1985	1995	2009
Population size and growth				
Population size (thousands)	530	1 410	2 432	4 599
Annual growth rate (percentage)*	17.2	6.6	5.3	2.8
Population age structure				
Percentage of population under age 15	28	30	28	19
Percentage of population aged 60 or over	3	2	2	2
Fertility and family planning				
Total fertility (children per woman)*	6.4	5.2	3.9	1.9
Adolescent fertility rate (per 1,000 women, aged 15 - 19)*	..	..	51.0	16.0
Percentage of births to women under age 20*	..	..	7	4
Percentage of births to women aged 35 or over*	..	..	25	24
Percentage of married women using contraception				
Modern methods	..	..	24	..
All methods	..	..	28	..
Health and mortality				
Life expectancy at birth (years)*				
Males	61	67	72	77
Females	64	71	76	79
Both sexes combined	62	69	74	77
Infant mortality rate (per 1,000 live births)*	57	32	16	10
Under-five mortality (per 1,000 live births)*	..	37	18	11
Maternal mortality ratio (per 100,000 live births) (2005)	..	..	..	37
HIV/AIDS				
People living with HIV/AIDS (thousands)	..	..	..	..
Adult prevalence (percentage)	..	..	..	..
Spatial distribution				
Population density (per sq. km)	6	17	29	55
Urban population (percentage)	80	80	78	78
Annual urban population growth rate (percentage)	16.0	5.6	5.6	2.6
Annual rural population growth rate (percentage)	14.2	6.7	6.5	2.0
International migration				
Migrant stock				
Number of migrants (thousands)	312	1 008	1 716	3 293**
As percentage of total population	58.9	71.5	70.6	70.0**

* For the periods 1970-1975, 1980-1985, 1990-1995 and 2005-2010.
** For 2010.

Government views and policies

Population policy variable	1976	1986	1996	2009
Population size and growth				
View on growth	Satisfactory	Satisfactory	Satisfactory	Satisfactory
Policy on growth	No intervention	No intervention	No intervention	No intervention
Population age structure				
Level of concern about				
Size of the working-age population	..	..	..	Major concern
Ageing of the population	..	..	..	Major concern
Fertility and family planning				
View on fertility level	Satisfactory	Satisfactory	Satisfactory	Satisfactory
Policy	No intervention	No intervention	No intervention	No intervention
Access to contraceptive methods	Direct support	Indirect support	Direct support	Direct support
Adolescent fertility				
Level of concern	..	..	Major concern	Major concern
Policies and programmes	..	..	Yes	Yes
Health and mortality				
View				
Life expectancy at birth	Unacceptable	Unacceptable	Unacceptable	Unacceptable
Under-five mortality	..	..	Unacceptable	Unacceptable
Maternal mortality	..	..	..	Acceptable
Level of concern about HIV/AIDS	..	..	Major concern	Major concern
Measures to respond to HIV/AIDS*	..	..	..	1,2,3,4,5
Grounds on which abortion is permitted**	..	..	1,2,3,5,6	1,2,3,5,6
Spatial distribution and internal migration				
View on spatial distribution	Minor change desired	Minor change desired	Satisfactory	Major change desired
Policies on internal migration				
From rural to urban areas	..	..	..	Raise
From rural to rural areas	..	..	..	..
From urban to rural areas	..	..	..	Lower
From urban to urban areas	..	..	..	..
Into urban agglomerations	Lower	No intervention	Raise	Raise
International migration				
Immigration				
View	Too high	Too high	Too high	Satisfactory
Policy	Lower	Lower	Lower	Maintain
Permanent settlement	..	..	Lower	Maintain
Temporary workers	..	..	Lower	Maintain
Highly skilled workers	..	..	..	Raise
Family reunification	..	..	Lower	Maintain
Integration of non-citizens	..	..	Yes	Yes
Emigration				
View	Satisfactory	Satisfactory	Satisfactory	Satisfactory
Policy	Maintain	Maintain	No intervention	No intervention
Encouraging the return of citizens	No	..	No	No

* Measures implemented to respond to HIV/AIDS: (1) blood screening; (2) information/education campaigns; (3) antiretroviral treatment; (4) non-discriminatory policies; (5) distribution of condoms.
** Grounds on which abortion is permitted: (1) to save the woman's life; (2) to preserve physical health; (3) to preserve mental health; (4) rape or incest; (5) foetal impairment; (6) economic or social reasons; (7) on request.

Population indicators

Indicator	1975	1985	1995	2009
Population size and growth				
Population size (thousands)	56 226	56 554	58 042	61 565
Annual growth rate (percentage)*	0.2	0.1	0.3	0.5
Population age structure				
Percentage of population under age 15	23	19	19	17
Percentage of population aged 60 or over	20	21	21	22
Fertility and family planning				
Total fertility (children per woman)*	2.0	1.8	1.8	1.8
Adolescent fertility rate (per 1,000 women, aged 15 - 19)*	..	..	31.0	24.0
Percentage of births to women under age 20*	..	..	9	7
Percentage of births to women aged 35 or over*	..	..	14	17
Percentage of married women using contraception				
Modern methods	69	78[a]	80	82[b]
All methods	76	81[a]	82	82[b]
Health and mortality				
Life expectancy at birth (years)*				
Males	69	71	74	77
Females	75	77	79	82
Both sexes combined	72	74	76	79
Infant mortality rate (per 1,000 live births)*	17	11	8	5
Under-five mortality (per 1,000 live births)*	..	12	10	6
Maternal mortality ratio (per 100,000 live births) (2005)	..	..	..	8
HIV/AIDS				
People living with HIV/AIDS (thousands)	..	..	22	77[c]
Adult prevalence (percentage)	..	..	0.1	0.2[c]
Spatial distribution				
Population density (per sq. km)	231	233	239	253
Urban population (percentage)	83	89	89	90
Annual urban population growth rate (percentage)	1.5	0.2	0.4	0.5
Annual rural population growth rate (percentage)	-7.0	0.1	-0.4	-0.5
International migration				
Migrant stock				
Number of migrants (thousands)	3 148	3 536	4 191	6 452**
As percentage of total population	5.6	6.3	7.2	10.4**

* For the periods 1970-1975, 1980-1985, 1990-1995 and 2005-2010.
** For 2010.
[a] For 1986.
[b] For 2007/2008.
[c] For 2007.

Government views and policies

Population policy variable	1976	1986	1996	2009
Population size and growth				
View on growth	Satisfactory	Too high	Too high	Too high
Policy on growth	No intervention	No intervention	Lower	Lower
Population age structure				
Level of concern about				
Size of the working-age population	..	..	..	Major concern
Ageing of the population	..	..	..	Major concern
Fertility and family planning				
View on fertility level	Satisfactory	Too high	Too high	Too high
Policy	No intervention	No intervention	Lower	Lower
Access to contraceptive methods	Direct support	Direct support	Direct support	Direct support
Adolescent fertility				
Level of concern	..	..	Minor concern	Major concern
Policies and programmes	..	..	Yes	Yes
Health and mortality				
View				
Life expectancy at birth	Unacceptable	Unacceptable	Unacceptable	Unacceptable
Under-five mortality	..	..	Unacceptable	Unacceptable
Maternal mortality	..	..	..	Unacceptable
Level of concern about HIV/AIDS	..	..	Major concern	Major concern
Measures to respond to HIV/AIDS*	..	..	..	1,2,3,4,5
Grounds on which abortion is permitted**	..	..	1,2,3	1,2,3
Spatial distribution and internal migration				
View on spatial distribution	Major change desired	Major change desired	Major change desired	Major change desired
Policies on internal migration				
From rural to urban areas	..	..	..	Lower
From rural to rural areas	..	..	..	..
From urban to rural areas	..	..	..	..
From urban to urban areas	..	..	..	..
Into urban agglomerations	No intervention	Lower	Lower	Lower
International migration				
Immigration				
View	Satisfactory	Satisfactory	Satisfactory	Satisfactory
Policy	Maintain	Maintain	Lower	No intervention
Permanent settlement	..	..	No intervention	No intervention
Temporary workers	..	..	Lower	No intervention
Highly skilled workers	..	..	..	..
Family reunification	..	..	No intervention	No intervention
Integration of non-citizens	..	..	Yes	No
Emigration				
View	Satisfactory	Satisfactory	Too high	Satisfactory
Policy	Maintain	Maintain	Lower	No intervention
Encouraging the return of citizens	No	..	Yes	No

* Measures implemented to respond to HIV/AIDS: (1) blood screening; (2) information/education campaigns; (3) antiretroviral treatment; (4) non-discriminatory policies; (5) distribution of condoms.
** Grounds on which abortion is permitted: (1) to save the woman's life; (2) to preserve physical health; (3) to preserve mental health; (4) rape or incest; (5) foetal impairment; (6) economic or social reasons; (7) on request.

Population indicators

Indicator	1975	1985	1995	2009
Population size and growth				
Population size (thousands)	15 972	21 811	29 972	43 739
Annual growth rate (percentage)*	3.2	3.1	3.3	2.9
Population age structure				
Percentage of population under age 15	46	46	45	45
Percentage of population aged 60 or over	4	4	4	5
Fertility and family planning				
Total fertility (children per woman)*	6.8	6.6	6.1	5.6
Adolescent fertility rate (per 1,000 women, aged 15 - 19)*	..	..	140.0	130.0
Percentage of births to women under age 20*	..	..	12	12
Percentage of births to women aged 35 or over*	..	..	25	21
Percentage of married women using contraception				
Modern methods	..	..	13[a]	20[b]
All methods	..	..	18[a]	26[b]
Health and mortality				
Life expectancy at birth (years)*				
Males	46	49	48	55
Females	49	52	52	56
Both sexes combined	48	51	50	55
Infant mortality rate (per 1,000 live births)*	119	104	100	65
Under-five mortality (per 1,000 live births)*	..	177	167	106
Maternal mortality ratio (per 100,000 live births) (2005)	...	..	..	950
HIV/AIDS				
People living with HIV/AIDS (thousands)	..	..	1 200	1 400[c]
Adult prevalence (percentage)	..	..	7.4	6.2[c]
Spatial distribution				
Population density (per sq. km)	17	23	32	46
Urban population (percentage)	11	17	21	26
Annual urban population growth rate (percentage)	10.0	5.9	4.3	4.2
Annual rural population growth rate (percentage)	2.3	2.5	2.2	1.8
International migration				
Migrant stock				
Number of migrants (thousands)	608	548	1 134	659**
As percentage of total population	3.8	2.5	3.8	1.5**

* For the periods 1970-1975, 1980-1985, 1990-1995 and 2005-2010.
** For 2010.
[a] For 1996.
[b] For 2004/2005.
[c] For 2007.

Government views and policies

Population policy variable	1976	1986	1996	2009
Population size and growth				
View on growth	Satisfactory	Satisfactory	Satisfactory	Satisfactory
Policy on growth	No intervention	No intervention	No intervention	No intervention
Population age structure				
Level of concern about				
Size of the working-age population	..	..	..	Major concern
Ageing of the population	..	..	..	Major concern
Fertility and family planning				
View on fertility level	Satisfactory	Satisfactory	Satisfactory	Satisfactory
Policy	No intervention	No intervention	No intervention	No intervention
Access to contraceptive methods	Direct support	Direct support	Direct support	Direct support
Adolescent fertility				
Level of concern	..	..	Major concern	Major concern
Policies and programmes	..	..	Yes	Yes
Health and mortality				
View				
Life expectancy at birth	Acceptable	Acceptable	Unacceptable	Unacceptable
Under-five mortality	..	..	Unacceptable	Unacceptable
Maternal mortality	..	..	..	Unacceptable
Level of concern about HIV/AIDS	..	..	Major concern	Major concern
Measures to respond to HIV/AIDS[*]	..	..	..	1,2,3,4,5
Grounds on which abortion is permitted[**]	..	..	1,2,3,4,5,6,7	1,2,3,4,5,6,7
Spatial distribution and internal migration				
View on spatial distribution	Satisfactory	Satisfactory	Satisfactory	Satisfactory
Policies on internal migration				
From rural to urban areas	..	..	..	No intervention
From rural to rural areas	..	..	..	No intervention
From urban to rural areas	..	..	..	No intervention
From urban to urban areas	..	..	..	No intervention
Into urban agglomerations	..	No intervention	No intervention	No intervention
International migration				
Immigration				
View	Satisfactory	Too high	Satisfactory	Satisfactory
Policy	Maintain	Maintain	Maintain	Maintain
Permanent settlement	..	..	Maintain	Maintain
Temporary workers	..	..	Maintain	Maintain
Highly skilled workers	..	..	..	Raise
Family reunification	..	..	Maintain	Maintain
Integration of non-citizens	..	..	Yes	Yes
Emigration				
View	Satisfactory	Satisfactory	Satisfactory	Satisfactory
Policy	Maintain	Maintain	No intervention	No intervention
Encouraging the return of citizens	..	..	No	No

[*] Measures implemented to respond to HIV/AIDS: (1) blood screening; (2) information/education campaigns; (3) antiretroviral treatment; (4) non−discriminatory policies; (5) distribution of condoms.

[**] Grounds on which abortion is permitted: (1) to save the woman's life; (2) to preserve physical health; (3) to preserve mental health; (4) rape or incest; (5) foetal impairment; (6) economic or social reasons; (7) on request.

United Nations Department of Economic and Social Affairs/Population Division

Population indicators

Indicator	1975	1985	1995	2009
Population size and growth				
Population size (thousands)	219 108	240 612	270 648	314 659
Annual growth rate (percentage)*	0.9	0.9	1.2	1.0
Population age structure				
Percentage of population under age 15	25	22	22	20
Percentage of population aged 60 or over	15	16	16	18
Fertility and family planning				
Total fertility (children per woman)*	2.0	1.8	2.0	2.1
Adolescent fertility rate (per 1,000 women, aged 15 - 19)*	..	..	54.0	36.0
Percentage of births to women under age 20*	..	..	13	9
Percentage of births to women aged 35 or over*	..	..	11	14
Percentage of married women using contraception				
Modern methods	61[a]	69[b]	71	68[c]
All methods	68[a]	74[b]	76	73[c]
Health and mortality				
Life expectancy at birth (years)*				
Males	68	71	72	77
Females	75	78	79	81
Both sexes combined	72	74	76	79
Infant mortality rate (per 1,000 live births)*	18	10	8	6
Under-five mortality (per 1,000 live births)*	..	13	10	7
Maternal mortality ratio (per 100,000 live births) (2005)	..	..	..	11
HIV/AIDS				
People living with HIV/AIDS (thousands)	..	..	890	1 200[d]
Adult prevalence (percentage)	..	..	0.6	0.6[d]
Spatial distribution				
Population density (per sq. km)	23	25	28	33
Urban population (percentage)	74	74	77	82
Annual urban population growth rate (percentage)	0.9	1.2	1.6	1.3
Annual rural population growth rate (percentage)	0.9	0.4	-0.6	-0.7
International migration				
Migrant stock				
Number of migrants (thousands)	13 991	19 492	28 522	42 813**
As percentage of total population	6.4	8.1	10.5	13.5**

* For the periods 1970-1975, 1980-1985, 1990-1995 and 2005-2010.
** For 2010.
[a] For 1976.
[b] For 1988.
[c] For 2002.
[d] For 2007.

Government views and policies

Population policy variable	1976	1986	1996	2009
Population size and growth				
View on growth	Too low	Too low	Too low	Too low
Policy on growth	Raise	No intervention	Raise	No intervention
Population age structure				
Level of concern about				
Size of the working-age population	..	..	..	Major concern
Ageing of the population	..	..	..	Major concern
Fertility and family planning				
View on fertility level	Too low	Too low	Too low	Satisfactory
Policy	Raise	No intervention	Raise	No intervention
Access to contraceptive methods	No support	Direct support	Direct support	Direct support
Adolescent fertility				
Level of concern	..	..	..	Major concern
Policies and programmes	..	..	..	Yes
Health and mortality				
View				
Life expectancy at birth	Acceptable	Acceptable	Acceptable	Acceptable
Under-five mortality	..	..	..	Unacceptable
Maternal mortality	..	..	..	Acceptable
Level of concern about HIV/AIDS	..	..	..	Major concern
Measures to respond to HIV/AIDS*	..	..	..	1,2,3,4,5
Grounds on which abortion is permitted**	..	..	1,2	1,2,3,4
Spatial distribution and internal migration				
View on spatial distribution	Major change desired	Major change desired	Major change desired	Minor change desired
Policies on internal migration				
From rural to urban areas	..	..	..	Lower
From rural to rural areas	..	..	..	..
From urban to rural areas	..	..	..	Raise
From urban to urban areas	..	..	..	No intervention
Into urban agglomerations	No intervention	No intervention	..	Lower
International migration				
Immigration				
View	Satisfactory	Too low	Too low	Satisfactory
Policy	Maintain	Raise	Raise	Maintain
Permanent settlement	..	..	..	Maintain
Temporary workers	..	..	..	Maintain
Highly skilled workers	..	..	..	Maintain
Family reunification	..	..	..	Maintain
Integration of non-citizens	..	..	..	No
Emigration				
View	Too high	Too high	Too high	Too high
Policy	Lower	Lower	Lower	No intervention
Encouraging the return of citizens	No	..	Yes	No

* Measures implemented to respond to HIV/AIDS: (1) blood screening; (2) information/education campaigns; (3) antiretroviral treatment; (4) non-discriminatory policies; (5) distribution of condoms.
** Grounds on which abortion is permitted: (1) to save the woman's life; (2) to preserve physical health; (3) to preserve mental health; (4) rape or incest; (5) foetal impairment; (6) economic or social reasons; (7) on request.

Population indicators

Indicator	1975	1985	1995	2009
Population size and growth				
Population size (thousands)	2 830	3 012	3 224	3 361
Annual growth rate (percentage)*	0.1	0.6	0.7	0.3
Population age structure				
Percentage of population under age 15	28	27	25	23
Percentage of population aged 60 or over	14	16	17	18
Fertility and family planning				
Total fertility (children per woman)*	3.0	2.6	2.5	2.1
Adolescent fertility rate (per 1,000 women, aged 15 - 19)*	..	..	71.0	61.0
Percentage of births to women under age 20*	..	..	14	14
Percentage of births to women aged 35 or over*	..	..	14	15
Percentage of married women using contraception				
Modern methods	..	72[a]	..	75[b]
All methods	..	83[a]	..	77[b]
Health and mortality				
Life expectancy at birth (years)*				
Males	66	68	69	73
Females	72	75	77	80
Both sexes combined	69	71	73	76
Infant mortality rate (per 1,000 live births)*	46	33	20	13
Under-five mortality (per 1,000 live births)*	..	37	23	16
Maternal mortality ratio (per 100,000 live births) (2005)	..	..	..	20
HIV/AIDS				
People living with HIV/AIDS (thousands)	..	..	2.7	10[c]
Adult prevalence (percentage)	..	..	0.2	0.6[c]
Spatial distribution				
Population density (per sq. km)	16	17	18	19
Urban population (percentage)	83	87	91	92
Annual urban population growth rate (percentage)	0.9	1.0	1.0	0.5
Annual rural population growth rate (percentage)	-2.2	-2.3	-2.2	-1.1
International migration				
Migrant stock				
Number of migrants (thousands)	131	104	93	80**
As percentage of total population	4.6	3.4	2.9	2.4**

* For the periods 1970-1975, 1980-1985, 1990-1995 and 2005-2010.
** For 2010.
[a] For 1986.
[b] For 2004.
[c] For 2007.

Government views and policies

Population policy variable	1976	1986	1996	2009
Population size and growth				
View on growth	..	..	Too high	Satisfactory
Policy on growth	..	..	Lower	Maintain
Population age structure				
Level of concern about				
Size of the working-age population	..	..	..	Major concern
Ageing of the population	..	..	..	Major concern
Fertility and family planning				
View on fertility level	..	..	Satisfactory	Satisfactory
Policy	..	..	Maintain	Maintain
Access to contraceptive methods	..	..	Direct support	Direct support
Adolescent fertility				
Level of concern	..	..	..	Minor concern
Policies and programmes	..	..	Yes	Yes
Health and mortality				
View				
Life expectancy at birth	..	..	Unacceptable	Acceptable
Under-five mortality	..	..	..	Unacceptable
Maternal mortality	..	..	..	Unacceptable
Level of concern about HIV/AIDS	..	..	..	Major concern
Measures to respond to HIV/AIDS*	..	..	..	1,2,4,5
Grounds on which abortion is permitted**	..	..	1,2,3,4,5,6,7	1,2,3,4,5,6,7
Spatial distribution and internal migration				
View on spatial distribution	..	..	Satisfactory	Minor change desired
Policies on internal migration				
From rural to urban areas	..	..	..	No intervention
From rural to rural areas	..	..	..	..
From urban to rural areas	..	..	..	..
From urban to urban areas	..	..	..	..
Into urban agglomerations	..	..	..	No intervention
International migration				
Immigration				
View	..	..	Satisfactory	Satisfactory
Policy	..	..	No intervention	Maintain
Permanent settlement	..	..	..	Maintain
Temporary workers	..	..	..	Maintain
Highly skilled workers	..	..	..	Maintain
Family reunification	..	..	..	..
Integration of non-citizens	..	..	..	..
Emigration				
View	..	..	Too high	Satisfactory
Policy	..	..	No intervention	Maintain
Encouraging the return of citizens	..	..	..	No

* Measures implemented to respond to HIV/AIDS: (1) blood screening; (2) information/education campaigns; (3) antiretroviral treatment; (4) non-discriminatory policies; (5) distribution of condoms.
** Grounds on which abortion is permitted: (1) to save the woman's life; (2) to preserve physical health; (3) to preserve mental health; (4) rape or incest; (5) foetal impairment; (6) economic or social reasons; (7) on request.

Population indicators

Indicator	1975	1985	1995	2009
Population size and growth				
Population size (thousands)	13 981	18 174	22 919	27 488
Annual growth rate (percentage)*	3.1	2.6	2.2	1.1
Population age structure				
Percentage of population under age 15	43	40	40	29
Percentage of population aged 60 or over	8	6	6	6
Fertility and family planning				
Total fertility (children per woman)*	6.3	4.7	3.9	2.3
Adolescent fertility rate (per 1,000 women, aged 15 - 19)*	..	..	71.0	13.0
Percentage of births to women under age 20*	..	..	9	3
Percentage of births to women aged 35 or over*	..	..	8	9
Percentage of married women using contraception				
Modern methods	..	..	51[a]	59[b]
All methods	..	..	56[a]	65[b]
Health and mortality				
Life expectancy at birth (years)*				
Males	60	63	63	65
Females	67	70	69	71
Both sexes combined	64	66	66	68
Infant mortality rate (per 1,000 live births)*	84	71	59	48
Under-five mortality (per 1,000 live births)*	..	86	71	58
Maternal mortality ratio (per 100,000 live births) (2005)	..	..	..	24
HIV/AIDS				
People living with HIV/AIDS (thousands)	..	..	..	16[c]
Adult prevalence (percentage)	..	..	..	0.1[c]
Spatial distribution				
Population density (per sq. km)	31	41	51	61
Urban population (percentage)	39	41	38	37
Annual urban population growth rate (percentage)	4.0	2.4	0.8	1.8
Annual rural population growth rate (percentage)	2.0	2.5	2.3	1.3
International migration				
Migrant stock				
Number of migrants (thousands)	..	..	1 474	1 176**
As percentage of total population	0.0	0.0	6.4	4.2**

* For the periods 1970-1975, 1980-1985, 1990-1995 and 2005-2010.
** For 2010.
[a] For 1996.
[b] For 2006.
[c] For 2007.

Government views and policies

Population policy variable	1976	1986	1996	2009
Population size and growth				
View on growth	..	Satisfactory	Satisfactory	Too high
Policy on growth	..	No intervention	No intervention	Lower
Population age structure				
Level of concern about				
Size of the working-age population	..	..	..	..
Ageing of the population	..	..	..	..
Fertility and family planning				
View on fertility level	..	Satisfactory	Satisfactory	Too high
Policy	..	No intervention	No intervention	Lower
Access to contraceptive methods	..	Direct support	Direct support	Direct support
Adolescent fertility				
Level of concern	..	..	..	Major concern
Policies and programmes	..	..	..	Yes
Health and mortality				
View				
Life expectancy at birth	..	Unacceptable	Unacceptable	Unacceptable
Under-five mortality	..	..	..	Unacceptable
Maternal mortality	..	..	..	Unacceptable
Level of concern about HIV/AIDS	..	..	..	Major concern
Measures to respond to HIV/AIDS*	..	..	..	2,5
Grounds on which abortion is permitted**	..	..	1,2	1,2,3
Spatial distribution and internal migration				
View on spatial distribution	..	Minor change desired	Satisfactory	Minor change desired
Policies on internal migration				
From rural to urban areas	..	..	..	Lower
From rural to rural areas	..	..	..	..
From urban to rural areas	..	..	..	..
From urban to urban areas	..	..	..	..
Into urban agglomerations	..	No intervention	..	Lower
International migration				
Immigration				
View	..	Satisfactory	Satisfactory	Satisfactory
Policy	..	Maintain	No intervention	No intervention
Permanent settlement	..	..	..	..
Temporary workers	..	..	..	Maintain
Highly skilled workers	..	..	..	..
Family reunification	..	..	..	..
Integration of non-citizens	..	..	..	..
Emigration				
View	..	Satisfactory	Satisfactory	Satisfactory
Policy	..	Maintain	No intervention	No intervention
Encouraging the return of citizens	..	..	..	..

* Measures implemented to respond to HIV/AIDS: (1) blood screening; (2) information/education campaigns; (3) antiretroviral treatment; (4) non-discriminatory policies; (5) distribution of condoms.
** Grounds on which abortion is permitted: (1) to save the woman's life; (2) to preserve physical health; (3) to preserve mental health; (4) rape or incest; (5) foetal impairment; (6) economic or social reasons; (7) on request.

Population indicators

Indicator	1975	1985	1995	2009
Population size and growth				
Population size (thousands)	101	132	172	240
Annual growth rate (percentage)*	3.2	2.4	2.8	2.5
Population age structure				
Percentage of population under age 15	45	45	43	39
Percentage of population aged 60 or over	4	5	5	5
Fertility and family planning				
Total fertility (children per woman)*	6.1	5.4	4.8	4.0
Adolescent fertility rate (per 1,000 women, aged 15 - 19)*	..	..	65.0	47.0
Percentage of births to women under age 20*	..	..	7	6
Percentage of births to women aged 35 or over*	..	..	23	20
Percentage of married women using contraception				
Modern methods	..	..	32	..
All methods	..	..	39	..
Health and mortality				
Life expectancy at birth (years)*				
Males	52	58	63	68
Females	56	62	66	72
Both sexes combined	54	60	65	70
Infant mortality rate (per 1,000 live births)*	99	70	38	28
Under-five mortality (per 1,000 live births)*	..	90	47	34
Maternal mortality ratio (per 100,000 live births) (2005)	..	..	..	..
HIV/AIDS				
People living with HIV/AIDS (thousands)	..	..	..	..
Adult prevalence (percentage)	..	..	..	..
Spatial distribution				
Population density (per sq. km)	8	11	14	20
Urban population (percentage)	13	17	20	25
Annual urban population growth rate (percentage)	4.8	4.8	3.6	4.1
Annual rural population growth rate (percentage)	2.9	1.8	1.8	1.7
International migration				
Migrant stock				
Number of migrants (thousands)	4	3	2	1**
As percentage of total population	3.5	2.1	1.0	0.3**

* For the periods 1970-1975, 1980-1985, 1990-1995 and 2005-2010.
** For 2010.

Government views and policies

Population policy variable	1976	1986	1996	2009
Population size and growth				
View on growth	Satisfactory	Satisfactory	Satisfactory	Satisfactory
Policy on growth	No intervention	No intervention	No intervention	No intervention
Population age structure				
Level of concern about				
Size of the working-age population	..	..	..	Major concern
Ageing of the population	..	..	..	Major concern
Fertility and family planning				
View on fertility level	Satisfactory	Satisfactory	Satisfactory	Satisfactory
Policy	No intervention	No intervention	Lower	No intervention
Access to contraceptive methods	Direct support	Direct support	Direct support	Direct support
Adolescent fertility				
Level of concern	..	..	Major concern	Major concern
Policies and programmes	..	..	Yes	Yes
Health and mortality				
View				
Life expectancy at birth	Unacceptable	Unacceptable	Acceptable	Acceptable
Under-five mortality	..	..	..	Unacceptable
Maternal mortality	..	..	..	Unacceptable
Level of concern about HIV/AIDS	..	..	Minor concern	Major concern
Measures to respond to HIV/AIDS*	..	..	..	1,2,3,4,5
Grounds on which abortion is permitted**	..	..	1	1
Spatial distribution and internal migration				
View on spatial distribution	Major change desired	Major change desired	Major change desired	Major change desired
Policies on internal migration				
From rural to urban areas	..	..	..	Lower
From rural to rural areas	..	..	..	..
From urban to rural areas	..	..	..	..
From urban to urban areas	..	..	..	..
Into urban agglomerations	..	..	No intervention	Lower
International migration				
Immigration				
View	Too high	Too high	Satisfactory	Satisfactory
Policy	Lower	Lower	No intervention	Maintain
Permanent settlement	..	..	No intervention	Maintain
Temporary workers	..	..	No intervention	Maintain
Highly skilled workers	..	..	..	Maintain
Family reunification	..	..	No intervention	Maintain
Integration of non-citizens	..	..	No	..
Emigration				
View	Satisfactory	Satisfactory	Satisfactory	Satisfactory
Policy	Maintain	Maintain	No intervention	No intervention
Encouraging the return of citizens	..	..	No	No

* Measures implemented to respond to HIV/AIDS: (1) blood screening; (2) information/education campaigns; (3) antiretroviral treatment; (4) non−discriminatory policies; (5) distribution of condoms.
** Grounds on which abortion is permitted: (1) to save the woman's life; (2) to preserve physical health; (3) to preserve mental health; (4) rape or incest; (5) foetal impairment; (6) economic or social reasons; (7) on request.

Population indicators

Indicator	1975	1985	1995	2009
Population size and growth				
Population size (thousands)	12 740	17 323	22 092	28 583
Annual growth rate (percentage)*	3.4	2.8	2.3	1.7
Population age structure				
Percentage of population under age 15	43	39	36	30
Percentage of population aged 60 or over	5	5	6	8
Fertility and family planning				
Total fertility (children per woman)*	4.9	4.0	3.3	2.5
Adolescent fertility rate (per 1,000 women, aged 15 - 19)*	..	..	98.0	90.0
Percentage of births to women under age 20*	..	..	15	18
Percentage of births to women aged 35 or over*	..	..	16	13
Percentage of married women using contraception				
Modern methods	38[a]	..	62[b]	..
All methods	49[a]	..	70[b]	..
Health and mortality				
Life expectancy at birth (years)*				
Males	63	66	69	71
Females	69	72	75	77
Both sexes combined	66	69	72	74
Infant mortality rate (per 1,000 live births)*	49	34	23	17
Under-five mortality (per 1,000 live births)*	..	42	29	22
Maternal mortality ratio (per 100,000 live births) (2005)	..	..	..	57
HIV/AIDS				
People living with HIV/AIDS (thousands)	..	..	..	..
Adult prevalence (percentage)	..	..	..	..
Spatial distribution				
Population density (per sq. km)	14	19	24	31
Urban population (percentage)	76	82	87	94
Annual urban population growth rate (percentage)	4.5	3.3	2.6	1.9
Annual rural population growth rate (percentage)	0.5	-0.1	-1.5	-3.1
International migration				
Migrant stock				
Number of migrants (thousands)	731	1 033	1 019	1 007**
As percentage of total population	5.7	6.0	4.6	3.5**

* For the periods 1970-1975, 1980-1985, 1990-1995 and 2005-2010.
** For 2010.
[a] For 1977.
[b] For 1998.

Government views and policies

Population policy variable	1976	1986	1996	2009
Population size and growth				
View on growth	Too high	Too high	Too high	Too high
Policy on growth	Lower	Lower	Lower	Lower
Population age structure				
Level of concern about				
Size of the working-age population	..	..	..	Major concern
Ageing of the population	..	..	..	Major concern
Fertility and family planning				
View on fertility level	Too high	Too high	Too high	Too high
Policy	Lower	Lower	Lower	Lower
Access to contraceptive methods	Direct support	Direct support	Direct support	Direct support
Adolescent fertility				
Level of concern	..	..	Minor concern	Major concern
Policies and programmes	..	..	Yes	Yes
Health and mortality				
View				
Life expectancy at birth	Unacceptable	Unacceptable	Acceptable	Acceptable
Under-five mortality	..	..	Acceptable	Unacceptable
Maternal mortality	..	..	..	Unacceptable
Level of concern about HIV/AIDS	..	..	Major concern	Major concern
Measures to respond to HIV/AIDS*	..	..	..	1,2,3,4,5
Grounds on which abortion is permitted**	..	..	1,2,3,4,5,6,7	1,2,3,4,5,6,7
Spatial distribution and internal migration				
View on spatial distribution	Major change desired	Major change desired	Minor change desired	Major change desired
Policies on internal migration				
From rural to urban areas	..	..	..	No intervention
From rural to rural areas	..	..	..	Maintain
From urban to rural areas	..	..	..	No intervention
From urban to urban areas	..	..	..	No intervention
Into urban agglomerations	..	..	Lower	Maintain
International migration				
Immigration				
View	Satisfactory	Satisfactory	Satisfactory	Satisfactory
Policy	Maintain	Maintain	Lower	Maintain
Permanent settlement	..	..	No intervention	Maintain
Temporary workers	..	..	Lower	Lower
Highly skilled workers	..	..	..	Raise
Family reunification	..	..	Lower	Maintain
Integration of non-citizens	..	..	No	Yes
Emigration				
View	Satisfactory	Satisfactory	Satisfactory	Too low
Policy	Maintain	Maintain	No intervention	Raise
Encouraging the return of citizens	..	..	No	Yes

* Measures implemented to respond to HIV/AIDS: (1) blood screening; (2) information/education campaigns; (3) antiretroviral treatment; (4) non-discriminatory policies; (5) distribution of condoms.

** Grounds on which abortion is permitted: (1) to save the woman's life; (2) to preserve physical health; (3) to preserve mental health; (4) rape or incest; (5) foetal impairment; (6) economic or social reasons; (7) on request.

Population indicators

Indicator	1975	1985	1995	2009
Population size and growth				
Population size (thousands)	47 974	59 789	72 957	88 069
Annual growth rate (percentage)[*]	2.2	2.3	1.9	1.1
Population age structure				
Percentage of population under age 15	43	41	37	26
Percentage of population aged 60 or over	7	7	8	9
Fertility and family planning				
Total fertility (children per woman)[*]	6.7	4.5	3.3	2.1
Adolescent fertility rate (per 1,000 women, aged 15 - 19)[*]	..	..	46.0	17.0
Percentage of births to women under age 20[*]	..	..	7	4
Percentage of births to women aged 35 or over[*]	..	..	12	12
Percentage of married women using contraception				
Modern methods	..	38[a]	44[b]	68[c]
All methods	..	53[a]	65[b]	79[c]
Health and mortality				
Life expectancy at birth (years)[*]				
Males	48	57	66	72
Females	53	61	70	76
Both sexes combined	50	59	68	74
Infant mortality rate (per 1,000 live births)[*]	107	70	38	20
Under-five mortality (per 1,000 live births)[*]	..	108	52	23
Maternal mortality ratio (per 100,000 live births) (2005)	..	..	..	150
HIV/AIDS				
People living with HIV/AIDS (thousands)	..	..	18	290[c]
Adult prevalence (percentage)	..	..	0.1	0.5[c]
Spatial distribution				
Population density (per sq. km)	145	180	220	266
Urban population (percentage)	19	20	22	28
Annual urban population growth rate (percentage)	2.6	2.6	3.5	3.1
Annual rural population growth rate (percentage)	1.9	2.2	1.2	0.6
International migration				
Migrant stock				
Number of migrants (thousands)	5	28	39	69[**]
As percentage of total population	0.0	0.0	0.1	0.1[**]

[*] For the periods 1970-1975, 1980-1985, 1990-1995 and 2005-2010.
[**] For 2010.
[a] For 1988.
[b] For 1994.
[c] For 2007.

Government views and policies

Population policy variable	1976	1986	1996	2009
Population size and growth				
View on growth	Satisfactory	Satisfactory	Too high	Too high
Policy on growth	No intervention	No intervention	Lower	Lower
Population age structure				
Level of concern about				
Size of the working-age population	..	..	..	Major concern
Ageing of the population	..	..	..	Not a concern
Fertility and family planning				
View on fertility level	Satisfactory	Too high	Too high	Too high
Policy	No intervention	Lower	Lower	Lower
Access to contraceptive methods	Direct support	Direct support	Direct support	Direct support
Adolescent fertility				
Level of concern	..	..	Major concern	Major concern
Policies and programmes	..	..	..	Yes
Health and mortality				
View				
Life expectancy at birth	Unacceptable	Acceptable	Unacceptable	Unacceptable
Under-five mortality	..	..	Unacceptable	Unacceptable
Maternal mortality	..	..	..	Unacceptable
Level of concern about HIV/AIDS	..	..	Minor concern	Major concern
Measures to respond to HIV/AIDS*	..	..	..	1,2
Grounds on which abortion is permitted**	..	..	1	1
Spatial distribution and internal migration				
View on spatial distribution	Minor change desired	Minor change desired	Major change desired	Major change desired
Policies on internal migration				
From rural to urban areas	..	..	..	Lower
From rural to rural areas	..	..	..	..
From urban to rural areas	..	..	..	..
From urban to urban areas	..	..	..	..
Into urban agglomerations	..	..	Lower	Lower
International migration				
Immigration				
View	Satisfactory	Satisfactory	Too high	Too high
Policy	Maintain	Maintain	Lower	Lower
Permanent settlement	..	..	Lower	..
Temporary workers	..	..	Lower	Lower
Highly skilled workers	..	..	..	Maintain
Family reunification	..	..	Maintain	..
Integration of non-citizens	..	..	No	..
Emigration				
View	Satisfactory	Too high	Satisfactory	Satisfactory
Policy	Maintain	Lower	Raise	Raise
Encouraging the return of citizens	..	..	No	No

Note: Views and policies for 1976 and 1986 are those of the former Yemen Arab Republic. The views and policies of the former People's Democratic Republic of Yemen may have been different.

* Measures implemented to respond to HIV/AIDS: (1) blood screening; (2) information/education campaigns; (3) antiretroviral treatment; (4) non−discriminatory policies; (5) distribution of condoms.

** Grounds on which abortion is permitted: (1) to save the woman's life; (2) to preserve physical health; (3) to preserve mental health; (4) rape or incest; (5) foetal impairment; (6) economic or social reasons; (7) on request.

Population indicators

Indicator	1975	1985	1995	2009
Population size and growth				
Population size (thousands)	7 093	10 137	15 523	23 580
Annual growth rate (percentage)*	2.1	3.8	4.6	2.9
Population age structure				
Percentage of population under age 15	50	51	50	44
Percentage of population aged 60 or over	4	3	4	4
Fertility and family planning				
Total fertility (children per woman)*	8.7	8.7	7.7	5.3
Adolescent fertility rate (per 1,000 women, aged 15 - 19)*	..	..	126.0	68.0
Percentage of births to women under age 20*	..	..	8	6
Percentage of births to women aged 35 or over*	..	..	28	27
Percentage of married women using contraception				
Modern methods	1[a]	..	10[b]	19[c]
All methods	1[a]	..	21[b]	28[c]
Health and mortality				
Life expectancy at birth (years)*				
Males	40	49	55	61
Females	40	49	56	64
Both sexes combined	40	49	56	63
Infant mortality rate (per 1,000 live births)*	184	126	92	59
Under-five mortality (per 1,000 live births)*	..	186	131	79
Maternal mortality ratio (per 100,000 live births) (2005)	..	..	..	430
HIV/AIDS				
People living with HIV/AIDS (thousands)	..	..	..	..
Adult prevalence (percentage)	..	..	..	..
Spatial distribution				
Population density (per sq. km)	13	19	29	45
Urban population (percentage)	15	18	24	31
Annual urban population growth rate (percentage)	5.1	6.1	5.7	4.8
Annual rural population growth rate (percentage)	2.5	3.2	3.0	2.1
International migration				
Migrant stock				
Number of migrants (thousands)	219	276	378	518**
As percentage of total population	3.1	2.7	2.4	2.1**

* For the periods 1970-1975, 1980-1985, 1990-1995 and 2005-2010.
** For 2010.
[a] For 1979.
[b] For 1997.
[c] For 2006.

Government views and policies

Population policy variable	1976	1986	1996	2009
Population size and growth				
View on growth	Satisfactory	Too high	Too high	Too high
Policy on growth	No intervention	No intervention	Lower	Maintain
Population age structure				
Level of concern about				
Size of the working-age population	..	..	..	Major concern
Ageing of the population	..	..	..	Minor concern
Fertility and family planning				
View on fertility level	Satisfactory	Too high	Too high	Too high
Policy	No intervention	No intervention	Lower	Lower
Access to contraceptive methods	Direct support	Direct support	Direct support	Direct support
Adolescent fertility				
Level of concern	..	..	..	Major concern
Policies and programmes	..	..	..	Yes
Health and mortality				
View				
Life expectancy at birth	Unacceptable	Unacceptable	Unacceptable	Unacceptable
Under-five mortality	..	..	..	Unacceptable
Maternal mortality	..	..	..	Unacceptable
Level of concern about HIV/AIDS	..	..	..	Major concern
Measures to respond to HIV/AIDS*	..	..	..	1,2,3,4,5
Grounds on which abortion is permitted**	..	..	1,2,3,5,6	1,2,3,5,6
Spatial distribution and internal migration				
View on spatial distribution	Major change desired	Major change desired	Major change desired	Major change desired
Policies on internal migration				
From rural to urban areas	..	..	..	Lower
From rural to rural areas	..	..	..	No intervention
From urban to rural areas	..	..	..	Raise
From urban to urban areas	..	..	..	No intervention
Into urban agglomerations	Lower	Lower	..	No intervention
International migration				
Immigration				
View	Satisfactory	Satisfactory	Too high	Satisfactory
Policy	Maintain	Maintain	Lower	Maintain
Permanent settlement	..	..	..	Maintain
Temporary workers	..	..	..	Maintain
Highly skilled workers	..	..	..	Maintain
Family reunification	..	..	..	Maintain
Integration of non-citizens	..	..	..	Yes
Emigration				
View	Satisfactory	Satisfactory	Satisfactory	Too high
Policy	Maintain	Maintain	No intervention	Lower
Encouraging the return of citizens	No	..	..	Yes

* Measures implemented to respond to HIV/AIDS: (1) blood screening; (2) information/education campaigns; (3) antiretroviral treatment; (4) non-discriminatory policies; (5) distribution of condoms.

** Grounds on which abortion is permitted: (1) to save the woman's life; (2) to preserve physical health; (3) to preserve mental health; (4) rape or incest; (5) foetal impairment; (6) economic or social reasons; (7) on request.

Population indicators

Indicator	1975	1985	1995	2009
Population size and growth				
Population size (thousands)	4 899	6 785	9 108	12 935
Annual growth rate (percentage)[*]	3.4	3.2	2.8	2.4
Population age structure				
Percentage of population under age 15	47	47	45	46
Percentage of population aged 60 or over	4	4	4	5
Fertility and family planning				
Total fertility (children per woman)[*]	7.4	7.0	6.3	5.9
Adolescent fertility rate (per 1,000 women, aged 15 - 19)[*]	..	..	116.0	142.0
Percentage of births to women under age 20[*]	..	..	9	12
Percentage of births to women aged 35 or over[*]	..	..	28	22
Percentage of married women using contraception				
Modern methods	..	..	14[a]	27[b]
All methods	..	..	26[a]	41[b]
Health and mortality				
Life expectancy at birth (years)[*]				
Males	49	50	48	45
Females	52	54	51	46
Both sexes combined	50	52	50	45
Infant mortality rate (per 1,000 live births)[*]	107	98	106	95
Under-five mortality (per 1,000 live births)[*]	..	165	177	160
Maternal mortality ratio (per 100,000 live births) (2005)	..	..	..	830
HIV/AIDS				
People living with HIV/AIDS (thousands)	..	..	800	1 100[b]
Adult prevalence (percentage)	..	..	16.3	15.2[b]
Spatial distribution				
Population density (per sq. km)	7	9	12	17
Urban population (percentage)	35	40	37	36
Annual urban population growth rate (percentage)	6.0	3.0	1.3	2.4
Annual rural population growth rate (percentage)	1.8	3.2	3.3	1.6
International migration				
Migrant stock				
Number of migrants (thousands)	297	282	271	233[**]
As percentage of total population	6.1	4.2	3.0	1.8[**]

[*] For the periods 1970-1975, 1980-1985, 1990-1995 and 2005-2010.
[**] For 2010.
[a] For 1996.
[b] For 2007.

Government views and policies

Population policy variable	1976	1986	1996	2009
Population size and growth				
View on growth	..	Too high	Too high	Too high
Policy on growth	..	Lower	Lower	Lower
Population age structure				
Level of concern about				
Size of the working-age population	..	..	..	Major concern
Ageing of the population	..	..	..	Major concern
Fertility and family planning				
View on fertility level	..	Too high	Too high	Too high
Policy	..	Lower	Lower	Lower
Access to contraceptive methods	..	Direct support	Direct support	Direct support
Adolescent fertility				
Level of concern	..	..	Minor concern	Minor concern
Policies and programmes	..	..	Yes	No
Health and mortality				
View				
Life expectancy at birth	..	Unacceptable	Unacceptable	Unacceptable
Under-five mortality	..	..	Unacceptable	Unacceptable
Maternal mortality	..	..	..	Unacceptable
Level of concern about HIV/AIDS	..	..	Major concern	Major concern
Measures to respond to HIV/AIDS*	..	..	..	1,2,3,4,5
Grounds on which abortion is permitted**	..	..	1,2,4,5	1,2,4,5
Spatial distribution and internal migration				
View on spatial distribution	..	Minor change desired	Major change desired	Major change desired
Policies on internal migration				
From rural to urban areas	..	..	..	Lower
From rural to rural areas	..	..	..	..
From urban to rural areas	..	..	..	..
From urban to urban areas	..	..	..	..
Into urban agglomerations	..	Lower	No intervention	Lower
International migration				
Immigration				
View	..	Too high	Satisfactory	Satisfactory
Policy	..	Lower	Lower	No intervention
Permanent settlement	..	..	Lower	..
Temporary workers	..	..	Lower	..
Highly skilled workers	..	..	..	Raise
Family reunification	..	..	Lower	..
Integration of non-citizens	..	..	Yes	..
Emigration				
View	..	Satisfactory	Too high	Too high
Policy	..	Maintain	Lower	Lower
Encouraging the return of citizens	..	..	No	..

* Measures implemented to respond to HIV/AIDS: (1) blood screening; (2) information/education campaigns; (3) antiretroviral treatment; (4) non-discriminatory policies; (5) distribution of condoms.
** Grounds on which abortion is permitted: (1) to save the woman's life; (2) to preserve physical health; (3) to preserve mental health; (4) rape or incest; (5) foetal impairment; (6) economic or social reasons; (7) on request.

Population indicators

Indicator	1975	1985	1995	2009
Population size and growth				
Population size (thousands)	6 168	8 845	11 713	12 523
Annual growth rate (percentage)*	3.4	3.9	2.3	0.3
Population age structure				
Percentage of population under age 15	48	48	44	40
Percentage of population aged 60 or over	5	5	5	6
Fertility and family planning				
Total fertility (children per woman)*	7.4	6.7	4.8	3.5
Adolescent fertility rate (per 1,000 women, aged 15 - 19)*	..	..	111.0	65.0
Percentage of births to women under age 20*	..	..	12	9
Percentage of births to women aged 35 or over*	..	..	24	21
Percentage of married women using contraception				
Modern methods	..	27[a]	42[b]	58[c]
All methods	..	38[a]	48[b]	60[c]
Health and mortality				
Life expectancy at birth (years)*				
Males	54	58	54	43
Females	57	62	63	44
Both sexes combined	56	60	58	44
Infant mortality rate (per 1,000 live births)*	83	63	53	58
Under-five mortality (per 1,000 live births)*	..	102	84	94
Maternal mortality ratio (per 100,000 live births) (2005)	..	..	..	880
HIV/AIDS				
People living with HIV/AIDS (thousands)	..	..	1 600	1 300[d]
Adult prevalence (percentage)	..	..	27.3	15.3[d]
Spatial distribution				
Population density (per sq. km)	16	23	30	32
Urban population (percentage)	20	25	32	38
Annual urban population growth rate (percentage)	5.7	6.4	3.0	2.3
Annual rural population growth rate (percentage)	2.6	2.8	1.2	0.2
International migration				
Migrant stock				
Number of migrants (thousands)	485	514	433	372**
As percentage of total population	7.9	5.8	3.7	2.9**

* For the periods 1970-1975, 1980-1985, 1990-1995 and 2005-2010.
** For 2010.
[a] For 1984.
[b] For 1994.
[c] For 2005/2006.
[d] For 2007.